# BUSINESS ORGANIZATION AND FINANCE

## LEGAL

### AND

## ECONOMIC PRINCIPLES

### ELEVENTH EDITION

By

**WILLIAM A. KLEIN**

Maxwell Professor of Law Emeritus

University of California, Los Angeles

**JOHN C. COFFEE, JR.**

Adolf A. Berle Professor of Law

Columbia University

**FRANK PARTNOY**

George E. Barrette Professor in Law and Finance

University of San Diego

**CONCEPTS AND INSIGHTS SERIES®**

FOUNDATION PRESS

2010

THOMSON REUTERS™

© 1980, 1986, 1988, 1990, 1993, 1996, 2000, 2002, 2004 FOUNDATION PRESS

© 2007 THOMSON REUTERS/FOUNDATION PRESS

© 2010 By THOMSON REUTERS/FOUNDATION PRESS

      195 Broadway, 9th Floor

      New York, NY 10007

      Phone Toll Free 1–877–888–1330

      Fax (212) 367–6799

      foundation–press.com

Printed in the United States of America

**ISBN** 978–1–59941–449–2

Mat #40700668

# PREFACE

The principal objective of this book is to explain, in simple terms but not simplistically, (a) the basic economic elements and legal principles, as well as the language, of business organization and finance; (b) the interrelationships between and among the economic elements and legal principles; and (c) the practical importance of a basic understanding of those elements, principles, and interrelationships. While we like to think that the book contains some sophisticated ideas, we have tried to make it understandable for a person with no background whatsoever in business, in accounting, in economics, or in law. As our audience, we have tried to keep in mind a bright young woman or man from a family of musicians, with a college major in English, now entering a law school or a graduate school of business—on the brink of discovering, with great surprise, that the study of business can be interesting and enjoyable, as well as profitable, and that it need not be intimidating. Another important goal was to humanize big business; to overcome a natural tendency to think of corporations, especially those big enough to have become household names, as bloodless entities; to show that the word "corporation" or a name such as "General Motors" is nothing more than a shorthand device for describing a complex set of relationships among people—people with all the human characteristics of the readers and their friends; and to demonstrate that an awareness of this reality is essential to understanding and learning how to deal with this kind of complex socioeconomic organization.

Because the book is intended for a bright but untutored audience, the order in which topics are considered reflects our intuitive sense of the order in which questions might occur to, and need to be answered for, such a reader. To that extent, we have abandoned a potentially more sophisticated logic that would have focused on such fundamental structural issues as control, risk and return, duration (including termination and withdrawal), conflicts of interest, and additional capital needs. We have also followed the traditional format of separating the law of proprietorship (agency), partnership, and corporations, resisting the temptation to demonstrate how each of these can best be seen as a set of legal rules resolving in different ways the underlying structural issues. We assume, however, that a thoughtful reader will ultimately be unable to avoid recognition and appreciation of that basic theme and its importance to an understanding of business organization.

The final three chapters are concerned with the field known as "corporate finance." At a superficial level, there is a break between these chapters and the three that precede them. Yet there is continuity as well. The various corporate securities (common stock, bonds, etc.) and market instruments (options, margin loans, etc.) that are discussed in Chapter 4 can perhaps best be understood as devices for allocating control, risk, and return and for resolving other issues that are the underlying focal points of the first three chapters. Thus, Chapter 4 represents an effort to provide an understanding not just of the formal characteristics of financial instruments but of their economic function as well. In Chapter 5 the inquiry turns to valuation and considers the question of what difference it might make in the valuation of an enterprise whether control, risk, etc., are allocated one way rather than another. Chapter 5 also reviews some of the recent literature on relationships between managers and shareholders and on financial theory and contains a description of the markets in which securities are issued and traded. Finally, Chapter 6 analyzes the complexities of modern financial markets, and how they affect both the allocation of control, risk, and return, as well as the tensions and conflicts that arise in business relationships. Chapter 6 includes an assessment of the recent financial crisis, as well as the challenges presented by new technologies, structured finance, and derivatives.

This edition of the book—its eleventh over the span of nearly three decades—will be the last to list William A. Klein as an author. Although Professor Klein will be retiring from the book as co-author with this edition, his indelible imprint will remain. This book was his brainchild and will remain committed to his goal that an introduction to finance could be presented in a simple, direct style that minimized jargon and maximized lucidity. The remaining authors will try and live up to the standard of cogency that he set.

JOHN C. COFFEE, JR.

FRANK PARTNOY

June 2010

# SUMMARY OF CONTENTS

## CHAPTER 4   BASIC CORPORATE INVESTMENT DEVICES: ECONOMIC ATTRIBUTES AND FORMAL CHARACTERISTICS

## CHAPTER 5   VALUATION, FINANCIAL STRATEGIES, AND CAPITAL MARKETS

## CHAPTER 6   FINANCIAL MARKETS

# TABLE OF CONTENTS

## IX.  DURATION AND TRANSFERABILITY

## X.  VARIATIONS

## CHAPTER 3  CORPORATIONS

### I.  A BRIEF OVERVIEW

### II.  THE DEVELOPMENT OF THE AMERICAN BUSINESS CORPORATION: A HISTORICAL OVERVIEW

### III.  THE REIFICATION ILLUSION

### IV.  THE BASIC STRUCTURE FOR CONTROL AND OPERATION

### V.  FORMATION

### VI.  OBLIGATIONS OF OFFICERS AND DIRECTORS

FINANCIAL ALTERNATIVES INSIDE AND OUTSIDE
THE FIRM

## CHAPTER 5 VALUATION, FINANCIAL STRATEGIES, AND CAPITAL MARKETS

### I. VALUATION

### II. LEVERAGE AND CHOICE OF CAPITAL STRUCTURE

### III. CAPITAL STRUCTURE

### IV. DIVIDEND POLICY

## CHAPTER 6   FINANCIAL MARKETS

### I.   INTRODUCTION

### II.   RETHINKING BUSINESS ORGANIZATIONS USING DERIVATIVES

### III.   THE EVOLVING NATURE OF FINANCIAL MARKETS

### IV.   MARKET EFFICIENCY AND BEHAVIORAL FINANCE

### V.   NEW REGULATORY APPROACHES

# BUSINESS ORGANIZATION AND FINANCE

## LEGAL

### AND

## ECONOMIC PRINCIPLES

# INTRODUCTION

We begin with an overview describing briefly (a) the *people,* or *participants,* involved in business ventures, categorized according to their economic roles, (b) the business *issues* with which they should be concerned (the economic *elements* of their relationship) and the constraints on their ability to achieve their goals, and (c) the *legal rules and devices* that are used to achieve their organizational or contractual objectives.

## I. PARTICIPANTS

The central figures in business organization are the owners and managerial employees, but lenders may also play an important role (for example, by imposing limitations on an owner's freedom to hire or fire a manager or to expand the business), and often it is important to consider relationships with suppliers, customers, franchisees, and other people who may affect the way the business operates.

An *owner* has what is called an *equity* or *residual* interest in the business. Consider, by analogy, a person, Pamela, who buys a house, for use as her personal residence, using $25,000 of her own money, plus $75,000 borrowed from a bank, to pay the total purchase price of $100,000. The bank has a *fixed claim* for periodic interest payments and for ultimate repayment of the $75,000. The bank is sometimes said to hold the debt interest or debt claim in the house and Pamela the equity. Pamela's equity gives her a residual claim because when the house is sold and the debt must be paid (or assumed by the new buyer), Pamela receives whatever is left of the total sale price. For example, if the house is sold for $90,000, then, assuming none of the $75,000 debt has previously been paid off, Pamela will wind up with $15,000; if the house is sold for $120,000, she will wind up with $45,000. If Pamela were to rent the house to a tenant, she would receive the rent payments (barring misfortune) and would retain whatever is left of these amounts after paying the loan interest, taxes, and other expenses; that is, she would retain the residual. The holder of a residual claim is subject to greater risk of gain or loss than is the holder of a fixed claim. (These ideas are examined more fully in Chapter 1, Sec. II(F).)

Like the owner of a house, the owner of a business has a residual claim in the cash flows that it generates. The owner of a business will also have *control*—that is, the right to decide how the business is operated. The control of an owner may, however, be limited by agreement with a lender or other participant or by the practical necessity of delegating decision-making power to managerial employees.

1

There may, of course, be more than one owner of a business. Indeed, much of what is interesting and important about business organization is the set of relationships among owners.

The categories of owner, employee, and lender are useful ideal types, but one of the goals of this book is to show how they may merge with one another—how they form the ends of a spectrum along which one can move by varying the terms of the agreements among them. Thus, an ideal-type owner has the full residual claim and full control. An ideal-type employee has a fixed claim, to a salary, and is obligated to follow the directions (accede to the control) of the owner. But part or all of the employee's compensation may be a bonus based on profits, which is a residual-type claim that moves the employee along the spectrum in the direction of ownership. An employee with this kind of residual claim may bargain for the right to hire and fire all subordinate employees, thereby gaining a degree of control that moves her or him even closer to the status of an owner. Similarly, a lender may bargain for the right not only to fixed interest payments but also to some portion of any gain on the sale of the business and may have the right to veto the selection of key managerial employees. Moreover, the greater the amount of the debt in relationship to the total value of the business, the greater the risk to the lender and the further the lender moves along the spectrum from lender to owner.

## II. BARGAIN ELEMENTS AND CONSTRAINTS

### A. Bargain Elements

In business relationships, the fundamental bargain elements, which people in business may refer to as the basic "deal points," can be described by four general concepts or terms: (a) risk of loss, (b) return, (c) control, and (d) duration. These elements are interrelated, so the person with the greatest risk of loss generally will have control, the importance of control increases as duration increases, etc. (See Chapter 1, Sec. XII.)

*Risk of loss* refers to the allocation among the participants of losses from the investment in or operation of the business. If the business fails, who pays, or bears the burden of, debts, who is entitled to what portion of any remaining assets, etc.?

*Return* refers to salaries, interest, and other fixed claims, and to shares of the residual (the profit). Division of the residual presents some of the most interesting possibilities. For example, partners A and B might agree to split profits equally or they might agree that A will receive the first $10,000, that they will split the next $30,000 equally, and that B will receive 75 percent and A will receive 25 percent of all profits above $40,000. They might agree to pay some share of profits to a manager. They might grant to a lender an option to convert its fixed claim into some share of the residual (with, perhaps, a corresponding share of control). And so forth. Allocations of return have important effects on incentives, as do allocations of loss.

Allocation of *control* determines who has the right to make the various decisions affecting the business. Generally, control goes with the residual claim, but, as has already been suggested, aspects of control may be allocated to lenders, employees, or other participants.

*Duration* determines how long the relationships among participants will last and is intended to include the conditions on which the relationship can be *terminated* and on which a claim may be *transferred*. One of the most important issues that owners of a business should consider, at the outset of the venture, is what happens if one of them wants to withdraw. Should the other owners be required to buy out the person who wants out, and, if so, on what terms? The answer to this question will have vital implications for risk of loss, return, and control.

## B. Constraints

Participants in business arrangements will bargain over the elements of risk of loss, return, control, and duration subject to three major constraints: (a) conflict of interest, (b) government regulation, and (c) limits on the feasibility of specifying in complete detail all the terms of the relationship.

*Conflict of interest* arises from the fact that people tend to pursue their own self interest; that, consequently, they may cheat, steal, and shirk; and that such self-serving behavior may be difficult to detect or control. The presence of conflict of interest will have important implications for the shaping of the bargain elements. For example, an owner may attempt to deal with the possibility of shirking by a manager by making the manager's compensation dependent to some degree on the profits of the business. Conflict may also be controlled by protective rules, such as prohibitions or limitations on certain transactions between corporations and their officers and directors.

*Government regulation* may limit the freedom of participants in a business venture to adopt rules that they might have chosen. For example, the bankruptcy laws limit the ability of a borrower to agree to an expeditious foreclosure in the event of default on the loan. (See Chapter 4, Sec. III(A)(4).)

Complete *specificity* of all outcomes in all possible situations is not possible and even to the degree it is possible may not be worth the cost. To the degree that specificity is not feasible, people must rely on other devices such as sharing provisions that align their interests, vague general rules, and the good faith and honesty of the other participants.

## III. LEGAL RULES AND DEVICES

This book examines three basic sets of legal rules or doctrines, and legal devices, used in the creation of business arrangements or organizations: those relating to the employment relationship, to partnerships, and to corporations.

Chapter 1 focuses on the employment relationship, for which the relevant legal doctrine is mostly agency law and contract law, with individualized agreements (written or oral, express or implied) playing an important role.

Chapter 2 is concerned with partnerships. Here the basic rules are found in state statutes, mostly following the Uniform Partnership Act (UPA) but with some important variations from state to state. Some of the variations are derived from the recently promulgated Revised Uniform Partnership Act (RUPA). The rules of agency and contract are also important for partnerships. The statutory and common-law rules of partnership, agency, and contract govern the rights and responsibilities of partners, but most of them may be modified by agreement among the partners. In other words, the UPA rules, like the common-law (that is, judge-made) rules of agency and contract law, are mostly "default" provisions (provisions that apply in the absence of agreement to the contrary).

Chapter 3 examines the organization of business in corporate form. Here the basic organizational structure is prescribed in the corporations code (set of statutory rules) of the state in which people choose to incorporate. To a considerable extent, people using the corporate form are not permitted to deviate from the basic formal structure prescribed by the corporations codes, but important substantive organizational rules (e.g., rules relating to sale of an equity interest in the firm and to control) can be tailored to individual needs either in the articles of incorporation or by-laws (which are formal documents of the corporation) or in so-called "ancillary" agreements ("side" agreements among people with interests in the corporation, such as an agreement on how voting rights will be exercised or an agreement by one investor to buy the interest of another on certain conditions). The federal and state securities laws have an important bearing on the nature of the organization of sizable businesses, most of which are incorporated. Agency law is also relevant to corporations (for example, in determining the obligations of officers and directors to the corporation).

Other legal instruments or devices playing important roles in business organization are loan agreements, leases, and franchise agreements.

The purpose of presenting this list of legal rules and devices is not to bore you into a gentle slumber. It is in part to give you some idea of what you can expect to find later in the book, but, more importantly, to suggest that the legal rules and devices on which law-school study tends to focus are nothing more, nor less, than the tools by which *people* entering into business relationships seek to resolve the issues described by the *bargain elements*. A competent lawyer must know the tools and how to use them, but a lawyer who uses the tools without an appreciation of the business setting and the goals of the client will be unable to respond effectively to the client's needs. This proposition helps explain how this book was conceived and written, and why.

# Chapter 1

# THE SOLE PROPRIETOR

## I.  OWNERSHIP ATTRIBUTES

### A.  PROPRIETORSHIPS AS ORGANIZATIONS

Our objective is to understand the nature and functions of business organizations or entities.  It is useful, however, to begin with an examination of the *sole proprietorship,* which is a business owned directly by one individual, called a *sole proprietor.*  Since a sole proprietorship has no formal elements of co-ownership,[1] it is usually not thought of as "business organization" in the legal sense.  The fact is, however, that a business owned by a sole proprietor may be large and complex, involving many people other than the owner, and can plainly be an "organization" in the nonlegal sense of the term.

### B.  OWNERSHIP AND MANAGEMENT

Suppose that a grocery store is owned by a person, Pamela, who devotes her full time to the management of the store.  That is, she owns and operates the store.  The two functions, ownership and management (operation), need not be combined in the same person.  If Pamela hires a person to serve as manager in her place and delegates broad decision-making powers to that person, she is still the owner and is still called a sole proprietor.  The possibility of specialization, or separation of functions, is an attribute of a sophisticated (and efficient) economic system; it also produces the kinds of problems that require the application of lawyer skills.  But that gets ahead of our story.

### C.  NATURE OF OWNERSHIP INTEREST

As sole proprietor of the store, Pamela will acquire an inventory of goods to be sold.  She will become the owner of each individual item in that inventory.  (Conceivably, however, some items might be held by Pamela, in the store, on consignment—that is, under an agreement whereby she will sell on behalf of another person, who retains legal title and certain risks associated with that retention of ownership.)  In the eyes of the law, she owns the food and other goods in the store in the same sense that she owns the food in her refrigerator at home or the shoes on her feet.  She will, of course, keep separate records or accounts

---

[1] We will disregard the element of co-ownership created by the laws of community property.  For our purposes it is best to think of husband and wife in a community property state as if they were a single person or economic unit.

5

of the assets devoted to the business—for the purposes, among others, of filing tax returns and of determining for her own purposes how well, or how badly, the business is doing. But the existence of such records does not diminish our legal system's concept of a sole proprietor's direct ownership of the assets used in the business. It is important to understand this point in order to be able later to appreciate the significance of incorporating the business and thereby interposing a corporate "veil" between individuals and the assets that they devote to a business.

## II.  OWNERS AND CREDITORS

### A.  LIABILITY FOR DEBTS; OPEN ACCOUNTS

Many of the goods in Pamela's store will have been acquired on *open account*. For example, suppose that Shirley, a soft-drink supplier with whom Pamela does business, delivers soft drinks twice a week but mails bills monthly and allows 20 days for payment. The amount owed by Pamela to Shirley will depend on the amount of soft drinks that Shirley delivers to the store, which can vary. Any indebtedness to Shirley on this open account (sometimes called a *trade account*) is a personal obligation of Pamela to Shirley. Pamela must pay the amount owed even if her business becomes worthless. Regardless how much she owes, she personally owns any soft drinks that have not been sold to her customers. If she becomes bankrupt, they are an asset that is available to settle the claims of all of her creditors.

### B.  LIABILITY FOR DEBTS;  UNLIMITED LIABILITY

Shirley is a *general creditor*—as distinguished from a *secured creditor*. A secured creditor is one whose claim is secured by specific property, and who has first claim to the proceeds of the sale of such property. All other creditors are general creditors. Suppose that Pamela owes a total of $10,000 on open accounts with suppliers such as Shirley. Suppose further that she has borrowed $15,000 from a bank for use in the business, on a promissory note without security. (That is, she has borrowed $15,000 and has simply signed a piece of paper evidencing her obligation to repay.) This, again, is a personal obligation; Pamela is bound to repay the $15,000 regardless what happens to the business. This would also be true if the debt were secured by business or other property—for example, if the debt were secured by a mortgage on the land and building used in the business. If the business fails, Pamela can lose more than the amount that she initially decided to invest in the business. This is the frightening prospect that is associated with the notion of personal liability.

## C. NONRECOURSE LOANS

It is possible to avoid personal liability for business debts by executing a *nonrecourse loan*. Such a loan would ordinarily be secured by specific property; the lender would agree that in the event of nonpayment its sole recourse would be to sell the property and apply the proceeds to the debt. Such an arrangement would be unusual in the kind of situation that we are examining. It would be especially unusual and difficult to arrange for accounts with trade creditors such as the soft-drink distributor. But it is a potential device for avoiding personal liability—that is, for limiting loss to the amounts initially invested in the business. A more convenient way to avoid personal liability may be to incorporate the business; we come back to that in Chapter 3.

## D. BUSINESS AND PERSONAL DEBT

Suppose that in addition to the $10,000 owed to trade creditors on open account, and the $15,000 owed to the bank, Pamela owes $1,000 to another bank for expenses that she charged to her credit card on a recent vacation. Obviously this amount is also a personal obligation of Pamela's. If she fails to pay any of the debts, any creditor can go after any asset. Her business creditors can seek recovery from her personal as well as her business assets and her personal creditor can seek recovery from her business as well as her personal assets. In the event of bankruptcy, no distinction is drawn between business and personal debts or between business and personal assets, except that there are modest exemptions for certain personal assets. All non-exempt assets, business and personal, are in the same pot and all creditors take a share from that pot based on the amount owed to them. (Compare Sec. I(C) above.)

## E. DEBT AND EQUITY

This brief reference to personal assets and obligations is intended to emphasize the personal nature of the obligations that Pamela incurs in connection with her business. That point having been made, let us put aside those obligations not connected with the business. At this point it is convenient to introduce the terms *"debt"* and *"equity."* Pamela's business debt, in our example, amounts to a total of $25,000. The difference between the value of the business and the amount of the debt is her equity in the business. Confusion can easily arise over the quantity of debt and equity. For some purposes we may measure the amounts of debt and equity in terms of market values and for other purposes in terms of less realistic but more readily accessible figures. Suppose, for example, that after the bank made its $15,000 loan to Pamela, she experienced a series of reversals in her business that reduced considerably her capacity to repay. The loan is now subject to a far higher risk of default (nonpayment). If a similarly risky loan were made currently, the bank would demand a higher interest rate, to compensate for the greater risk. Let's assume, however, that repayment is not due for another five years so the bank cannot raise the interest rate to reflect the increased riskiness. In these circumstances, the bank's claim will have a market value of less than $15,000. No one would pay $15,000 for the note (that is, for the right to receive from Pamela interest for five years plus $15,000 at the end of the five years) because new loans at the same level of risk would produce a higher interest payment. (Or loans at the same interest rate would produce a lesser risk of default.) While the *market value* of the debt (evidenced by the promissory note) will be less than $15,000, the $15,000 figure may still be used for various purposes on the books of the bank as well as on Pamela's books. Thus, there will be a difference between *book value* and market value. In that situation, book "value" is not really a value figure; it is a historical record.

The same distinction can arise even more obviously with respect to Pamela's equity interest. Suppose, for example, that she initially bought the store (empty) for $75,000; that she acquired an inventory for $10,000 on open account; and that she used the $15,000 borrowed from the bank to remodel the store. She has invested $75,000 of her own money and $25,000 of borrowed funds or a total of $100,000. The book value of her equity is $75,000. But suppose that no sooner had she acquired her inventory and remodeled her store than the community's leading employer announced that it was moving its plant to another state. Obviously, such an event would diminish the market value of Pamela's business and thus reduce the value of her equity in the business. It is unlikely, however, that this misfortune would be reflected on the books that are kept for various purposes, so there would be a disparity between book value of equity and market value of equity.

## F.  LEVERAGE

The word *"leverage"* is used to describe the financial consequences of the use of debt and equity. The use of debt ("other people's money") creates financial leverage for the equity. The greater the debt the greater the leverage. The greater the leverage the greater the potential gains and losses for the equity and the greater the risk of loss for the debt. The effects of leverage result from the facts that (a) the debt holder (the lender) has a *fixed claim* (that is, a claim for a fixed amount of interest and for repayment of the amount of the loan); (b) the return on the investment or business financed by the debt is uncertain; and (c) the equity holder (the borrower) has a *residual claim* (that is, the right to whatever is left after the debt holder's claim is satisfied).

To illustrate, assume that Pamela invests in her business a total of $100,000, half of which is from her own funds and half of which she borrows, at an interest rate of 10 percent per year. Thus, she invests $50,000 of her own money and $50,000 of borrowed funds and is obligated to make an annual interest payment of $5,000. The ratio of debt to equity is 1:1. Assume that Pamela expects to earn $12,000 per year from the $100,000 investment in the business, net after all expenses and allowances, including a reasonable amount for her own services, but before the interest payment. In other words, she expects to earn, before interest, at the rate of 12 percent on the entire investment (a $12,000 return on a $100,000 investment). If this outcome eventuates, leverage will work in her favor: she will have borrowed at 10 percent and invested at 12 percent. Her net return after the interest payment will be $7,000 ($12,000 less the interest payment of $5,000), which will be 14 percent of her $50,000 equity investment. The total investment, with a rate of return of 12 percent, will produce a rate of return on equity of 14 percent.

On the other hand, if the rate of return on the total investment (before interest) turns out to be less than the rate of interest, leverage will work against Pamela. If, for example, the rate of return on the total investment is 8 percent, the net amount earned before interest will be $8,000; the interest payment will still be $5,000; and the return on the equity will be $3,000 (6 percent of the $50,000 equity investment). The "breakeven" point occurs where the return on total investment is 10 percent, the same rate as that paid on debt. At this point, there is no gain or loss from the use of the borrowed funds; the rate of return on total investment, debt, and equity are all 10 percent.

These numbers and relationships, expanded to include the outcomes with returns on total investment at the rates of 6 percent and 14 percent, are displayed in Table 1–1. For those who like graphs, the same information is displayed in Graph 1–1.

## TABLE 1–1

### Effects of Leverage With Debt to Equity Ratio 1:1

| Investment | $100,000 |
|---|---|
| Debt | $50,000 |
| Equity | $50,000 |
| Interest Rate on Debt | 10% |

| | | | | | |
|---|---|---|---|---|---|
| Return on Investment (%) | 6% | 8% | 10% | 12% | 14% |
| Return on Investment ($) | $6,000 | $8,000 | $10,000 | $12,000 | $14,000 |
| Interest Payment ($) | $5,000 | $5,000 | $5,000 | $5,000 | $5,000 |
| Return on Equity ($) | $1,000 | $3,000 | $5,000 | $7,000 | $9,000 |
| Return on Equity (%) | 2% | 6% | 10% | 14% | 18% |

**GRAPH 1-1.**

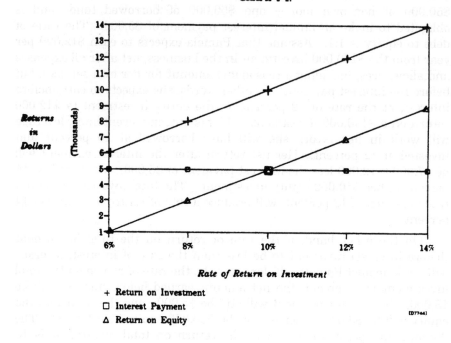

*Rate of Return on Investment*

+ **Return on Investment**
□ **Interest Payment**
△ **Return on Equity**

[D7744]

If the ratio of debt to equity is increased, the effects of leverage are magnified. Table 1–2 displays these effects where the ratio is 3:1 (debt $75,000 and equity $25,000). Note that again there is a "breakeven" point, at 10 percent, where the return on the total investment is equal to the rate of interest on the debt and where, consequently, the rate of return on equity is the same as the rate of return on the total investment. But with the 3:1 ratio, when return on total investment is 12 percent, return on equity is 18 percent; and when return on total investment is 6 percent, the rate of return on equity is a minus 6 percent. Thus, leverage creates risk and the greater the leverage, the greater the risk.

### TABLE 1–2

Effects of Leverage With Debt to Equity Ratio 3:1

| | |
|---|---|
| Investment | $100,000 |
| Debt | $75,000 |
| Equity | $25,000 |
| Interest Rate on Debt | 10% |

| | | | | | |
|---|---|---|---|---|---|
| Return on Investment (%) | 6% | 8% | 10% | 12% | 14% |
| Return on Investment ($) | $6,000 | $8,000 | $10,000 | $12,000 | $14,000 |
| Interest Payment ($) | $7,500 | $7,500 | $ 7,500 | $ 7,500 | $ 7,500 |
| Return on Equity ($) | ($1,500) | $ 500 | $ 2,500 | $ 4,500 | $ 6,500 |
| Return on Equity (%) | -6% | 2% | 10% | 18% | 26% |

Similar effects are observed if one focuses on wealth rather than income. Suppose that we return to the original debt and equity numbers of $50,000 each (ratio 1:1) and that Pamela sells the business for $110,000. This represents a gain of 10 percent on the total amount initially invested. After repaying the $50,000 loan, Pamela will retain the residue of $60,000, so she will have a gain of $10,000, or 20 percent, on her equity investment of $50,000. If she sells the business for $90,000, the loss on the total investment will be 10 percent and the loss on equity will be 20 percent. If the business is sold for $50,000 the loss on the equity is 100 percent and Pamela's investment is wiped out. The numbers are displayed in Table 1–3.

### TABLE 1–3
#### Effects of Leverage on Wealth

| Sale price | $50,000 | $75,000 | $100,000 | $125,000 |
|---|---|---|---|---|
| **1:1 ratio (equity $50,000)** | | | | |
| Debt repayment | $50,000 | $50,000 | $50,000 | $50,000 |
| Residue for equity | 0 | $25,000 | $50,000 | $75,000 |
| Percentage gain or loss | -100% | -50% | 0% | 50% |
| **3:1 ratio (equity $25,000)** | | | | |
| Debt repayment | $50,000 | $75,000 | $75,000 | $75,000 |
| Residue for equity | 0 | 0 | $25,000 | $50,000 |
| Percentage gain or loss | -100% | -100% | 0% | 100% |

### G.  POTENTIAL EQUITY ATTRIBUTES OF DEBT

The foregoing discussion, sharply distinguishing between debt and equity and between owners and creditors, follows a traditional mode of analysis. That mode of analysis may be quite satisfactory for purposes of examining legal doctrine. For purposes of economic analysis, however, we must take a more careful look at the relationship between Pamela and her creditors—especially her general creditors (the only creditors thus far mentioned). Those creditors may well be vitally concerned with how well Pamela is performing her task as manager of the business. If she performs badly and cannot pay her debts, they will lose money; indeed, if the total amount of the debts exceed the amount invested by Pamela (by no means a far-fetched possibility), the general creditors could lose more money than she would. The point is that creditors are subject to varying degrees of *risk* of default. The degree of risk will, of course, depend on the total value of the business as compared to the amount of the debt. As the debt rises in relation to the value of the business, the risk to the general creditors rises. As the risk rises, the general creditors will become more and more concerned with how the business is run and are likely to want increasing degrees of *control*, especially if their funds are committed for more than a few months. The bank, in particular, may condition its loan on Pamela's acceptance of certain constraints on her power to manage (that is, it may insist on negative controls). As risk rises, the bank is also likely to demand a higher interest rate—that is, a higher *return* on its investment in the business. These attributes—risk and control, plus returns that are dependent on the success of the business—are associated with ownership. We can see, then, that the position of lender and that of owner are not clearly distinct categories but rather segments of a spectrum. (Further discussion of the relationships among risk, return, control, and various other elements of economic arrangements is found in Sec. XII of this chapter.)

## III.  OWNERS AND ORDINARY EMPLOYEES

### A.  INTRODUCTION: JOINT ENTERPRISE VERSUS PURCHASED INPUTS

We have examined two kinds of people involved in a simple economic enterprise—owners and creditors. Now we are ready to consider another set of people with a stake in the enterprise—employees. Before proceeding, however, it is important to note a subtle but important perspective that has been introduced into this descriptive account. To some considerable degree, the relationships among creditors, suppliers, employees, and owners are viewed here as ones involving contributors to a *joint economic enterprise.* A more customary approach would depict the owner as the core of the enterprise and the other elements as inputs hired by the owner and having only a very narrow interest in the enterprise. On this latter view, there is less jointness, less communality of interest. Either view is permissible and both are useful. The joint-enterprise perspective seems to offer more fresh insights and a better understanding of economic functions. If we were concerned solely with traditional, established legal doctrine, the perspective in which the owner establishes the business and then hires capital, employees, and other inputs would probably be more appropriate, though some legal institutions may be evolving in the direction of the joint-undertaking model.

### B.  IMPLIED STANDARD CONTRACTS AND THEIR APPEAL

Suppose that Pamela hires Chuck, whose duties will be primarily to stock the shelves and keep the store clean. In a small business it is unlikely that there will be a written contract spelling out the mutual rights and obligations of Chuck and Pamela. Even though not spelled out in writing, however, a set of rights and obligations does exist. The terms of this implicit agreement can be found in part in common-law *doctrines of agency and contract,* and in part in modern legislation affecting the employment relationship (for example, in workers' compensation laws, which provide compensation for certain injuries but which also limit actions that employees might otherwise have against employers). In some settings union rules or contracts may be of considerable relevance. But an individualized written agreement would be unusual. A number of considerations may help to explain the absence of such an agreement here (and, by implication, the need for a written agreement elsewhere). For the ordinary run-of-the-mill employment relationship the rules implied by law—the "default" rules—may be satisfactory. Negotiation of an individualized agreement would take time and might call for the services of a lawyer. The time that might be spent by Chuck and Pamela, and the potential fees for legal services, are what economists call *transaction costs*. Here, those costs are not likely to be trivial. Chuck and Pamela may be unaware of the opportunities for written agreements that vary the contractual terms implied by law and it may not be worth their trouble to explore those opportunities. In other words, the *information costs* (another term familiar to economists) may be too high. The benefits of a negotiated agreement may be low, partly because the terms of the implied agreement may be pretty nearly satisfactory, partly because the employment may not be expected to last for long, and partly because the economic environment may be such that if Chuck becomes dissatisfied with his job, he can fairly readily find another job and if Pamela becomes dissatisfied with Chuck's services, she can find another worker without significant cost. One can begin to see, however, that as these various circumstances change, the usefulness of negotiated agreements (and of legal services) may increase. Part of the contribution of lawyers lies in their knowledge of the common-law or statutory rules—of the bargain implied by law in the absence of express agreement—and their appreciation of when and how it is appropriate to try to modify the "standard-form" bargain implied by law.

## C. COOPERATION, TRUST, FAIRNESS, AND REPUTATION

Much of what follows in this book focuses on divergent interests and confrontation. Confrontation is, of course, second nature to litigators and is the background to most of the case-method study of law in law schools. Lawyers who specialize in helping to shape business transactions must, of course, be aware of divergent interests, but they must also be sensitive to mutual interests and to the importance of cooperation, trust, reputation, and fairness. Many people want to do a good job not only for the financial compensation but also because they take pride in their work. Many people prefer cooperation to confrontation and most people recognize that cooperation and teamwork are often essential to a successful venture. And many people have an internalized commitment to fairness, honesty, and integrity, informed and shaped in part by business and social norms and customs. Even people who are not fully committed internally to these values may recognize the importance of one's reputation for fairness, honesty, and integrity—particularly in repeat relationships.

These intangibles may lead people in business to a disdain for negotiation of detailed contractual relationships—a disdain to which a business lawyer must be sensitive. Indeed, a demand for a detailed contract may send the wrong signal—a signal that one is not committed to cooperation, flexibility guided by fairness, and honesty. At the same time, the lawyer must be aware of the fragility of such intangibles. One's willingness to treat others honestly and fairly depends heavily on reciprocity, and misunderstanding can easily undercut one's sense of being treated honestly and fairly. In light of this reality, a lawyer's effort to recognize divergences in interests, and to anticipate and resolve potential problems, may be thought of as mitigating the risk of misunderstanding and its toxic effect of relationships.

Consider, by way of example, a real estate developer who wants to hire a general contractor to build an apartment building. The developer will be concerned about the contractor's reputation for doing good work, for doing it on time, for reasonableness in dealing with unanticipated problems, and for conformity with generally accepted norms and customs in the industry. That reputation is likely to depend heavily on the contractor's internalized values and on a concern for his or her reputation. The contractor, in turn, will be concerned about the developer's reputation for prompt payment and for reasonable and fair reactions to problems that arise in the construction process. There will, of course, be a set of plans for the apartment building, probably based on the work of an architect and engineer. The plans will be drawn with full recognition that it will be impossible to specify all the details and to anticipate all the problems; at some point greater specificity is not cost effective. To this extent, trust, reputation, and fair dealing play a useful, even a vital, role. But the greater the detail in the plans and the greater the anticipation of problems, the less the possibility of misunderstanding and the less the strain placed on trust and fairness. At the same time, the stronger the commitment to fair dealing and the stronger the concern for reputation, the less the need for specificity.

## IV. OWNERS AND ORDINARY EMPLOYEES: CONTROL

### A. THE SERVANT–TYPE AGENT AND THE LEGAL RIGHT TO CONTROL

In the common parlance, Chuck is an *"employee."* In legal terminology, Pamela is the *"principal"* and Chuck is an *"agent."* Within this category of principal and agent, the law of agency defines a subcategory that covers the Pamela–Chuck relationship, namely, *"master"* and *"servant."* Pamela is the "master" and Chuck is the "servant." These terms are used to describe a relationship in which one person (the master) "controls or has the right to control the *physical conduct* of the other" (the servant). (Quotation from Restatement of the Law, Agency (2d), Sec. 2.) This means that Pamela has the right not only to expect Chuck to perform particular tasks but also to tell him how to perform them. The term "servant" is somewhat confusing. In law, it does not imply servility. The employees of large corporations, working as electricians, carpenters, truck drivers, and the like, as well as the white-collar workers and the executives all the way up to the top person, are "servants" in the legal sense. Similarly, the term "agent" has a broader scope in law than in common parlance; it includes any person who has agreed with another person (the "principal") to "act on his behalf and subject to his control." Restatement, Agency (2d), Sec. 1.

A nonservant agent is one who agrees to act on behalf of the principal but is not subject to the principal's control over how the task is performed. For example, suppose Pamela says to Shirley, "I want you to go to Sam, the soft drink distributor, and buy ten cases of root beer for me." If Shirley agrees to do as Pamela has asked, she becomes Pamela's agent; when she goes to Sam she does so on behalf of Pamela. If Shirley orders the ten cases of root beer from Sam, Pamela becomes contractually bound to Sam.

Apart from the agent's power to bind the principal, there is another important characteristic of the principal-agent relationship. Agents are held to owe a duty of loyalty, or "fiduciary obligation," to their principals. Thus, as an agent of Pamela, Shirley cannot act in a self-serving way. For example, if it happened that Shirley had ten cases of root beer in her garage, she could not sell that root beer to Pamela at a profit without informing Pamela of the source. If she did, Pamela could recover Shirley's profit, even if the price charged by Shirley were the same as the price that would have been charged by Sam.

A principal may be bound by the acts of an agent under any one of three separate principles. First, the principal is bound if the agent's act was authorized, either explicitly or implicitly. Thus, in the example of Pamela and Shirley and the root beer, Shirley has explicit authority to buy the ten cases of root beer from Sam. Shirley would also have implicit authority to incur any customary expenses for delivery. Second, a principal is bound by an agent's acts if the agent had apparent (or ostensible) authority—that is, if the principal engages in conduct that leads a third person reasonably to believe that the agent had authority. For example, suppose Pamela says to Sam, "Shirley is authorized to buy root beer from you for me." Later, Pamela says to Shirley, "Don't ever buy root beer from Sam again," but does not communicate this revocation of authority to Sam. Suppose Shirley then goes to Sam and buys ten cases of root beer purportedly for Pamela. On the way to Pamela's store, Shirley's truck catches fire and the root beer is destroyed. Pamela must pay Sam for the root beer, on the legal theory that Shirley had apparent authority to buy it for her and that she, Pamela, is bound by virtue of that apparent authority.

The third basis for liability is called inherent agency power and operates where there is neither authority nor apparent authority. Suppose Pamela not only owns but manages her grocery store and that the store is called, "Pamela's Grocery." Then she secretly sells the store to

Miguel, who tells her that he wants her to continue to run the store and to keep the fact of his ownership a secret. He also tells her never to buy soft drinks from Sam. Pamela does in fact buy soft drinks from Sam, and runs up a large bill with him. Sam continues to believe that Pamela is the owner of the store; he has never heard of Miguel. Suppose Pamela loses interest in the store and badly mismanages it and that by the time Miguel figures out what is going on, all is lost: the debts far exceed the assets, the customers are shopping elsewhere, and Miguel is forced to go out of business. He is liable for the debts to suppliers other than Sam because Pamela had authority to deal with them. He will also be held liable for the debt to Sam, under the legal doctrine of inherent agency power, which in this case means that a general agent (Pamela) binds an undisclosed principal (Miguel) to contracts that are within the usual scope of authority of agents of the same type (here, store managers), even where the agent had neither authority nor apparent authority.

## B.  THE ECONOMIC SIGNIFICANCE OF THE LEGAL RIGHT TO CONTROL

**1.  Relation to Power to Terminate.** The economic significance of Pamela's legal right to control the manner in which Chuck does his job should not be exaggerated. If Pamela did not have that legal right as a matter of law, what difference would it make? Suppose that the right did not exist and that Pamela did not like the way Chuck was going about the job of stocking shelves. She could still let him know how she thought the job should be done and could indicate that if he did not begin to do it that way, she would fire him. That is precisely the same option that she has in dealing with an independent contractor such as the soft-drink supplier, Shirley. Suppose that Pamela dislikes something about the manner in which Shirley is running her business. Pamela has no legal right to order Shirley to do things differently. But she can certainly suggest that she would like to see a change and that she is prepared to "fire" (that is, stop doing business with) Shirley if no changes are made.

There is, of course, a major economic difference between Shirley and Chuck that relates to control. Chuck works only for Pamela and his performance affects only her. Shirley presumably supplies soft drinks to many customers other than Pamela. If Pamela wants Shirley to change her method of operation in ways that will affect those other customers of Shirley, then Shirley must take account of the effects on the other customers. This may be the vital economic distinction between servant-type agents like Chuck, who work only for one person and are subject to the legal right of control of that person, and people like Shirley, who are not subject to such control (and who may or may not be classified as agents with respect to some of their activities). The point about Pamela's ability to "fire" Shirley, and thereby affect Shirley's conduct, is nonetheless a useful and interesting one.

**2. Relation to Duration of Contract.** On the other side of the coin, even though Pamela has the legal right to tell Chuck how to do his job, if he doesn't want to do it her way he can quit, just as Shirley can quit supplying soft drinks rather than go along with Pamela's demands. The legal right to control physical conduct will affect contract damages in case there is such a dispute. Suppose that Pamela has a week-to-week contract both with Chuck and with Shirley. If on the first day of the week Chuck refuses to follow orders, Pamela can fire him without paying damages for breach of the employment contract. If, on the other hand, Shirley refuses to take Pamela's advice about how to run her business and Pamela "fires" Shirley at the same time, Pamela will be liable for damages for breach of contract. Since the contracts with Chuck and Shirley are of short *duration,* as such contracts are likely to be, the damages will probably be trivial. Thus, the economic importance of the right to control is in part a function of the duration of the contract. Generally, as duration increases the importance of control increases. (Compare Sec. XII(D) of this chapter.)

**3. Relation to Incentives.** This is not to say that control is unimportant or that Pamela will have the same concern about control of Shirley as she does about control of Chuck. It is clear that the manner in which Chuck performs his job will directly affect Pamela's business. If he is slow, she will need more help and that will cost her money. If he is indifferent to customers, that too may cost her money. If Pamela were to reflect on the importance of control, she might ask herself three interrelated questions. First, is it feasible to provide financial *incentives* that will induce Chuck or Shirley (or others) to perform in ways that will promote my interests? Chuck is likely to be paid a fixed hourly, daily, or weekly wage. There may be some financial incentive for him to perform well (the possibility of promotion, for example), but such incentive is likely to be attenuated at best. Since Pamela cannot count on the effect of financial incentive, she may need to rely on the power to control Chuck's performance directly. Shirley, on the other hand, does have an incentive to sell as many soft drinks as possible and in this respect her interests coincide with those of Pamela. Pamela may consider this incentive (combined with other factors) sufficient to protect her own interests. It seems plausible to generalize, then, that there is an important relationship between incentives and power to control. For some employees, particularly those in higher-level management positions, incentives can be provided that tend to align the interests of an employee with those of the employer and to the extent that this happens the importance of control to the employer diminishes. (Compare Sec. VI(E) below.)

**4. Relation to Feasible Degree of Specificity.** The second question that Pamela might ask herself is, to what extent is it possible to specify in advance precisely what it is that I want? To the extent that *specificity* can be achieved, the importance of control diminishes. Pamela can tell Shirley how many cans of each kind of soft drink she wants, when she wants them, and where they are to be placed. That is sufficient. With Chuck, specificity is more difficult. She can tell him that she wants a clean store and well-stocked shelves, but some discretion must be exercised (by Chuck or Pamela) over such matters as when to put aside the mop and start stocking the shelves, whether to interrupt these activities to help a customer, and so on. These are matters that may require judgment and experience that cannot readily be imparted to Chuck. Consequently, Pamela may value the power to direct his efforts, the power to control how he does his job. The need for *judgment* or *discretion* which is the other side of the coin of the difficulty of specifying desired results, is also related to incentives. If it is difficult to specify the desired output or performance, or to observe or measure it, incentive compensation may not be feasible and control may be important. Thus, we see the interrelatedness of control, incentives, and specificity. If it were feasible for Pamela to specify in advance, in a contract with Chuck, exactly what he should do from minute to minute, and if it were easy to observe his level of compliance with the requirements of the contract, it might not be important for her to have the right to tell him what to do and there might be little if any need for incentives (other than the incentive to avoid being fired). If Pamela assumes that Shirley has a strong incentive to do a good job stocking the shelves with soft drinks, Pamela may be unconcerned about specifying how Shirley performs her task or about not having control over Shirley. These principles hold as well for top executives of large corporations: because control and specificity are difficult at best (it is a practical reality that executives must have broad discretion), incentives (such as bonuses based on profits) become important. One of the tasks of a business lawyer is to draft employment contracts, which may include provisions specifying the employee's duties (e.g., the grocery-store manager hires and supervises other employees and is required to be at the store 40 hours a week), the scope of the employer's control (e.g., the owner retains the right to override the manager's decisions on hiring but not on firing), and the terms of incentive compensation (e.g., the manager is eligible for a bonus based on profits, with profits having a special definition designed to encourage the manager to invest in the future).[2] A good lawyer will be aware of the relationships among these elements of the contract (and their relationship in turn with other elements such as duration).

**5.  Relation to Availability of Replacements.**  The third question that Pamela may ask in relation to control is the extent to which she can find *replacements* for either Shirley or Chuck. If Chuck can easily be replaced by more effective workers, Pamela may decide that that alternative is more attractive than trying to tell him how to perform.  By the same token, Chuck's knowledge that he can be replaced

---

[2] For example, profits might be defined, for the purpose of calculating the manager's bonus, as net earnings before any deduction for certain outlays for maintenance of equipment or for support of community-betterment projects.

should have a significant effect on his conduct. The availability of replacements or substitutes will depend on Chuck's uniqueness. This will in turn depend on a variety of factors such as the general labor market in the relevant area. For purposes of examining problems of business organization, however, probably the most important variable is the unique knowledge of the particular job that Chuck may (or may not) have acquired. In any event, competition for jobs is an important element in shaping economic relationships and will affect reliance on other devices such as specificity, incentives, and the power to control.

## C.  VICARIOUS LIABILITY

The question of control, in the context of owners and ordinary employees, has been examined at some length because of its instructive value regarding relationships between owners and managers and, in turn, among co-owners. There is one other element of the master-servant relationship that deserves brief attention in the present context—namely, *vicarious liability*. If Chuck, while performing his duties, negligently injures a customer, the customer can recover damages not only from Chuck but also from Pamela. This is true no matter how many times Pamela has told Chuck to be careful and no matter how careful he has been in the past. In other words, Pamela is liable regardless that she was personally without fault. This is a matter of obvious importance to Pamela. The reason why it is not as important as one might think is simply that Pamela can protect herself by buying liability insurance. As we shall see, however, Pamela may also be exposed to contract liability—for example, liability for the cost of merchandise. Insurance is not available to protect against this kind of liability. It is better examined later, however, in the context of the owner-manager relationship.

## V.  ORGANIZATION WITHIN FIRMS AND ACROSS MARKETS

It is useful at this point to digress somewhat in order to offer a brief sketch of an important theoretical aspect of the issues that have been and will be discussed. This digression should enrich one's understanding of what follows.

In the parlance of economics, the relationship between Pamela and Shirley is referred to as organization of economic activity across *markets* or in the marketplace. The relationship between Pamela and Chuck is said to be organization of economic activity within a *firm*. Chuck is thought to be part of the firm for this purpose (that is, for the purpose of comparing the Pamela–Shirley and the Pamela–Chuck relationships). Economists then worry about the question of why activities are sometimes organized across markets and sometimes within the firm, about what seem to be the most important characteristics of the firm, and about how firms operate. These issues have proved to be surprisingly intractable. It is worth noting that lawyers would view the Pamela–Shirley relationship as that of buyer and seller, of a businessperson dealing at arm's length with another businessperson (called, in law, an independent contractor); and that this perspective is closely parallel to that of economists, who would describe the relationship in terms of independent economic entities engaged in a marketplace transaction (or series of transactions). The legal and economic perspectives are not so neatly parallel with respect to the employer-employee (Pamela–Chuck) relationship. Economic theory, by viewing employer and employee as members of a firm, though in different roles, places greater stress on the communality or jointness of the endeavor than does the hierarchical legal concept of master and servant, of boss and fungible hireling.

However useful economists may find the distinction between organization within firms and organization across markets, the distinction may not be of much value to lawyers concerned with the legal and economic aspects of shaping particular business arrangements. Lawyers who focus on "business organization" are concerned with relationships among co-owners and between owners and managers while economists, when they study and theorize about "firms," are more concerned with the entire enterprise and its relationship to other enterprises. For lawyers, there is little need for manageable theories and much need for unscientific but sensible solutions to problems arising from complex relationships among a large number of relevant variables. Those variables include risk, control, duration, incentives, availability of objective tests of success, opportunities for stealing and for cheating and shirking and other forms of self-dealing, and ability to predict the future. It does seem plain, in any event, that it may be useful for some purposes to think in terms of degrees of conformance to the concept of the firm or the market, rather than in all-or-nothing terms. Thus, for example, within a firm, certain employees may be paid on a piece-work basis, which is a market-type arrangement. They might nonetheless be members of the firm to the extent that their conduct in various respects is subject to the control of the person who pays them. Perhaps the economic concept of firm v. market could usefully be replaced with that of firmishness.

There may be times, nonetheless, when a lawyer may find it useful to think consciously about the polar cases of organization across markets and organization within a firm, in order to generate ideas about how best to tailor an intermediate relationship to meet a client's needs. For example, suppose that Pamela believes her grocery store must have a meat department, but the butcher who has worked for her has quit and she knows little about buying and selling meat. One option available to her might be to rent space in her store to an independent meat-business operator. That would be organization across a market. Among the advantages would be that Pamela would not be exposed to the risk of losing money from the meat operation and would be relieved of concern with the management of that part of the store. Among the problems (for Pamela and her lawyer) would be the need to ensure that the meat department contributed to, rather than detracted from, the attractiveness of the store to its customers. Another option for Pamela might be to hire a butcher on straight salary. That would be organization within the firm. One advantage of such an arrangement would be that Pamela would have control over the style of operation; there would be little need to negotiate about that and little danger of conflict (because as long as the butcher receives the salary, he or she probably will be content to let Pamela make operating decisions). If one were to start with the idea of organization within the firm (that is, hiring a butcher on straight salary) and think about moving in the direction of organization across markets, one might think about compensation based on the meat department's sales or profits. That would create incentives tending to reduce the need for Pamela to exercise control, supervision, and review. Some consideration might be given to requiring the butcher to supply all equipment or to making the butcher responsible for paying other meat-department employees. Any of these provisions moving the agreement in the direction of organization across markets would tend to require reconsideration of the issue of control: a butcher assuming more of the risk of the business would want more control over it. A good lawyer should be aware of the various organizational possibilities and their implications for all aspects of the contract. The dichotomy used by economists— markets v. firms—can be a useful device for stimulating and enhancing that awareness. (For further discussion of incentive compensation, risk, and control, see Sec. VI(E) below.)

## VI.  OWNERS AND MANAGERIAL EMPLOYEES: CONTROL, RISK, AND DURATION OF RELATIONSHIP

### A.  MANAGERS' RESEMBLANCE TO CO–OWNERS

Many of the elements of the relationship between Pamela and Chuck will be present in similar form in Pamela's relationship with higher-level, managerial employees. But as we begin to think of *owner-manager* relationships, we begin to see that the issues of control, reward, risk, and so forth will begin to resemble more closely those that arise among co-owners. That is, the issues will begin to resemble more closely those within the realm of "business organization" rather than "labor-management."

### B. DELEGATION OF BROAD DECISION–MAKING AUTHORITY

Suppose that Pamela decides to withdraw from the active management of the business and to hire a general manager, Morris, to run the business. To some significant degree, Pamela will need to rely on

Morris's judgment about how to manage the store—about such matters as prices, subordinate personnel, merchandise quality, and so on. These decisions will be much broader in scope and greater in impact on the success or failure of the business than the decisions made by lower-level employees such as Chuck. The delegation of decision-making authority is largely unavoidable; the purpose of hiring a general manager is to shift to that person the burden of making important decisions as problems arise. Many of those problems cannot be anticipated and, even if they could, the correct solution could not be specified in advance. Pamela must of necessity rely on Morris's competence and on his good faith. It is true, to be sure, that not all managerial roles call for the same degree of power to make important decisions. The manager of an apartment building, for example, may perform mostly routine functions. In such situations, problems relating to delegation of authority tend to diminish in significance. But all that implies is that some "managers" do not in fact perform managerial functions in the ordinary economic sense of the term, regardless of their title. From an economic perspective, they resemble Chuck more closely than they resemble Morris.

## C. MAJOR VERSUS MINOR DECISIONS

As an employee of Pamela, Morris will, like Chuck, be subject to her legal right to *control*. If all goes well, Pamela will not need to exercise control, but she may consider it very important to have the right to do so. It is, after all, her money (or assets) that will be at risk. Ordinarily, a person with money invested at substantial risk will want to have the right to review and control decisions that can materially affect the value of that investment. This kind of need for control is, of course, limited. Pamela's concern will be mostly with basic policy decisions and she need not be much concerned with minor, day-to-day decisions and routine operating decisions.

## D. DURATION OF RELATIONSHIP, EASE OF REPLACEMENT, AND SYMBIOSIS

Pamela's relationship with Morris, like her relationship with Chuck, will be affected significantly by the ease with which Morris can be *replaced*. This will depend in part on general economic circumstances such as the number of grocery stores in the area and the number of trained managers. It will also depend, however, on the *specific training or knowledge* that Morris acquires in managing Pamela's store. As that specific training or knowledge increases, Morris becomes more and more valuable to Pamela and more and more difficult for her to replace. To that extent, Pamela will become dependent on Morris and will find it costly to replace him. But this is a two-way street. Morris will have acquired training that is valuable to Pamela, and to Pamela alone, and to this extent he is dependent on her. This kind of symbiotic relationship can obviously lead to discord over division of the gains from the joint endeavor. Part of the job of a lawyer is to anticipate such problems and to help provide, in advance, formulas for their resolution. For example, Morris might be protected by providing that if he is discharged without cause he is entitled to a substantial payment (severance pay or liquidated damages). Pamela might be protected by making part of Morris's salary or bonus payable in the future and forfeitable if he quits without cause. Unfortunately, the drafting of such provisions is by no means an easy task. The parties may be unwilling to pay for the lawyer's services. They may be unwilling to spend their own time on the issue. And they may prefer to avoid what they hope is an unnecessary confrontation on what may be a highly charged and possibly irreconcilable matter. Many lawyers consider it unwise to raise such issues, fearing that if they do, they may spoil the deal. (See Chapter 2, Sec. IV(E).)

### E. MODE OF COMPENSATION, INCENTIVE, RISK, AND THE EMPLOYEE'S INTEREST IN CONTROL

Pamela's relationship with Morris will also be affected by how he is compensated. In order to provide Morris with proper incentives, Pamela may insist that part of his reward be contingent on the success of the business. Morris might, in fact, demand such an arrangement. At the same time, there is likely to be a limit to the risk Morris is willing to take and he will probably insist on some assured minimal level of compensation. Thus, the compensation "package" may consist of a salary (a fixed claim) plus a bonus based on profits (a residual claim). The presence of an element of incentive compensation like a bonus based on profits shifts some of the risk of the business to Morris; that is an attribute of any residual, as opposed to fixed, claim. It aligns Morris's objectives and interests with those of Pamela, and thereby allows her to be less concerned with the need for supervision, review, and control. But as Morris's rewards become increasingly dependent on the success of the business, he will become more concerned about control. If he is paid nothing but a fixed wage, he may be willing to follow any orders that Pamela wants to give him (though he may object because of concern for his future). If, on the other hand, his rewards are heavily dependent on the profits of the business, he may want some assurance of freedom from interference by Pamela in his operation of the business. At the same time, if Morris's compensation is heavily dependent on profit, Morris may be tempted to take excessive risks, figuring that he will share in any gains but the losses will fall entirely on Pamela. This becomes particularly a problem if the business is at some risk of failure and Morris is near retirement age and thus not concerned about how his reputation will affect his future employment (the "end game" situation). Thus, Pamela may think it essential to preserve control (as well as to think carefully about the compensation package).

Thus, there are potential conflicts over compensation and its relation to risk and control. The conflict can be addressed in negotiation, but may be difficult to resolve to the satisfaction of both Morris and Pamela, even where each is fully committed to cooperation and reciprocal fairness. Moreover, it should be noted that the formulation of an incentive compensation formula can be a formidable task. For example, Pamela and Morris may decide that Morris is to receive some portion of the net profits of the business. But the concept of "net profits" is not self-defining; it requires a determination, for example, of the appropriate rate of depreciation of assets used in the business. Beyond that, there is the very real possibility that profits will be affected by circumstances such as the behavior of competitors or a widespread improvement in the economy, which may not be related to Morris's performance. There may be good reasons for making the incentive compensation contingent on profits over a fairly long period of time—for example, five years—but then what happens if Pamela wants to sell out after three years? Problems like these, again, can be difficult to resolve in advance, and are fraught with potential antagonism. One can easily appreciate why Morris and Pamela may at the outset choose to pretend that they don't exist or why they may want to assume that mutually acceptable solutions will appear as concrete issues arise.

In connection with the issue of control, it is worth noting that under basic principles of contract law, even where an employee has expressly bargained for control, the employer may resume control, subject only to liability for damages. A court will not grant "specific performance" of a contract provision relating to control; that is, it will not issue an order compelling the employer to allow the employee to exercise control in accordance with the contract. For example, suppose that Pamela agrees that Morris is to make all decisions relating to the hiring and firing of other employees. Now suppose that Pamela fires Chuck and Morris objects. Morris is not entitled to reverse Pamela's decision and rehire Chuck. Morris cannot go to court and get an order compelling Pamela to abide by her contract with him. He can continue to work for Pamela and sue her for damages—which would be difficult to establish. Or he can quit (since Pamela's action is likely to be a "material breach" of his contract of employment) and sue for damages—which again might be difficult to prove. (He would be required to seek another comparable job and his damages would be the difference between what he would have earned working for Pamela over the term of his employment contract and what he in fact earned at the other job.) One frequently stated rationale for this legal result (no specific performance of the agreement giving Morris the right to hire and fire) is that money damages are an adequate remedy for the breach of the contract. If one grants that assumption as to the adequacy of the damages remedy, then the rule can be defended on grounds of economic efficiency. Morris will have his damages and this is an adequate substitute for his right to exercise control; he is made whole. Pamela pays damages, and presumably she was willing to do so as the price of reneging on the contract; she should be at least as well off as she would have been if she had been stuck with her promise, and possibly better off. All is for the best in this best of all possible worlds. Maybe.

## F. RISK, CONTROL, AND DURATION OF CONTRACT

The problems of contingent reward (risk) and control, whose interrelationship we have just seen, are in turn related to the problem of the *duration* of the relationship—in other words, to the problem of termination. Like any other employee, Morris will want as much security of employment as he can get. He will want the option of keeping his job as long as he wants it, though he will have to accept the fact that in most private employment he cannot expect too much in this regard. Pamela may want to tie up Morris's services for as long as possible, without committing herself, though again she will not have much expectation of being able to do so. Where Morris's compensation is contingent to some significant degree on the success of the business, the issue of duration of the contract will take on added importance. At the outset Morris may consider that he will need a substantial period of time to achieve his profit-making expectations. Moreover, if he is to receive a portion of the yearly profits he may want to be able to remain in command in order to protect what he has been able to create. As the length of the contract period increases, however, it becomes increasingly difficult to anticipate and deal with the problems arising from changing circumstances. To a considerable extent it will be necessary to leave problems for resolution as they arise, relying on the proposition that by and large the outcomes prescribed by law, in the absence of explicit agreement, will be consistent with what the parties would have provided had they tried to anticipate and resolve all conceivable issues. But in some circumstances, the failure to resolve issues in some detail in advance will lead to acrimony and costly litigation. That is a risk that perhaps the parties should try to take into account, however vaguely, at the beginning of their association; it is questionable whether many people do so.

A common problem relating to the duration aspect of the owner-employee bargain arises from the difficulty of enforcing the employee's obligations. To take the simplest kind of case, imagine that an employer agrees to pay an employee a fixed salary for five years. An obvious danger is that the employee will become lazy and do a bad job—though just good enough to avoid giving cause for dismissal. A less obvious danger arises where the employee is extremely successful. When that happens, the employee may demand a higher salary or may ask to be released from the contract in order to take a better-paying job elsewhere. If the employer insists on enforcing the contract, the employee may threaten, subtly, to start a "slowdown." There may be little that the employer can do in response to this kind of threat, except accede to the employee's demands. The situation suggested here is perhaps most easily explained by reference to the world of sports and entertainment. Suppose an unsensational college football player signs a long-term contract with a professional team at a generous salary. If he turns out worse than expected he still gets paid. But suppose he turns out to be rookie of the year. Now he demands a higher salary and says that if he doesn't get it he won't have a good attitude toward the game—or he may just decide to quit and live off berries in the woods. He is likely to get a raise. The contract will turn out to be something of a one-way street in favor of the athlete. While this kind of phenomenon is perhaps most common, and most dramatic, in contracts with potential superstar performers in sports and entertainment, it can also occur in the more mundane world of business. It is one element explaining why employers in ordinary businesses may be reluctant to enter into long-term contracts with executives. The executive whose performance turns out to be barely adequate will receive the full benefit of such a contract; the executive whose performance is exceptionally good may be able to extract more than the contract provides. This is not to say that employment contracts have no efficacy in tying up the employee; they do substantially constrain the employee's freedom to bargain for better terms. It is only to say that, because of problems of proof (and of ethics?), the benefits of the bargain may be less than they seem.

One other aspect of the durational element deserves brief mention. Special problems may arise from the difference in time horizons of the employer and employee (or of other participants in an economic venture). Again, the point can be made most forcefully by analogy to the entertainment business. A film star (or director) may be concerned about his or her reputation over the long haul; such a person may have a long time horizon. The producer or investor, on the other hand, may be interested only in the profits on the film currently in production; such a person may have a short-term, "fast buck" attitude. This potential conflict may (and often does) lead to hard bargaining over the issue of control of the quality of the film. (And if the star can command sufficient resources, he or she may resolve the conflict by becoming the producer.) In an ordinary business such as a grocery store the same kind of conflict can arise. The manager may be seeking a fast profit in order to enhance his or her bonus or improve opportunities for employment with competitors. The owner may have the opposite perspective. Or the roles may be reversed, with the owner seeking the fast profit to enhance the potential sales price of the business and the manager concerned about the longer term. Similar divergencies can lead to conflict among co-workers. It scarcely needs to be said that this kind of potential conflict may be very difficult to cope with in advance; and in the absence of advance agreement, it may be extremely difficult to resolve if it arises. In many cases, participants in a venture may simply have to rely on the reasonableness, fairness, and integrity of the other participants, or hope for the best.

## VII. OWNERS AND MANAGERIAL EMPLOYEES: DUTY OF CARE

### A. FOUR TYPES OF LACK OF DUE CARE

We have just examined some of the economic aspects of the relationship between Pamela and Morris. Now we turn to what may be called the legal aspects (which are intertwined with economic considerations and implications). We can begin with Morris's *duty of care.* Let's consider four situations.

**1. Negligent Injury to Third Person.** Case 1. Suppose that Morris, while driving to the bank to deposit the day's receipts, negligently hits and injures an innocent pedestrian. Assume that there is no insurance to cover this event. The injured person can recover damages either from Morris or from Pamela. Morris is personally liable because he was personally negligent and his negligence caused harm. The fact that he was acting on behalf of Pamela in her business does not shield him from liability as a matter of law (though as a practical matter the injured person is likely to seek recovery from Pamela rather than from Morris). Pamela is liable because of the legal doctrine of *respondeat superior.* The Pamela–Morris relationship is in legal conception like the Pamela–Chuck relationship, one of master and servant. Pamela, the master, is liable for personal injuries to third persons caused by her servant, Morris, in the scope of his employment. Suppose that the injured person sues Morris instead of Pamela and recovers a judgment of $10,000 from him. Morris is not entitled to reimbursement from Pamela. He is stuck. Beyond that, and perhaps surprisingly to a person not familiar with the law, if the victim sues Pamela and recovers $10,000 from her, Pamela has the right (at least under the rules of traditional agency law) to recover that amount from Morris. The theory is that the primary liability is that of Morris for his own negligence and that the ultimate burden of the loss should rest on him. Pamela is only vicariously and secondarily liable. That is the law. There is no reason to suppose, however, that that is the practice. Actual recovery by an employer from a negligent employee for damages paid by the employer to a third party would seem harsh, perhaps even unjust. One does not hear of such recoveries and presumably they are rare. But the possibility exists.

**2. Negligent Injury to Employer.** Case 2. Suppose that Morris carelessly drops his lighted cigarette in a wastebasket and the ensuing fire causes $10,000 damage to the store. Again, assume that there is no insurance. Pamela is entitled to recover the $10,000 from Morris because of his *carelessness.* Again, in practice the liability is not likely to be enforced. Imagine, for example, that an employee on the assembly line at a General Motors plant negligently drops a wrench into moving parts and causes $10,000 worth of damage. It is extremely unlikely that

General Motors would seek to recover from the employee, even if we assume that there is no provision in the union-negotiated contract on the matter, or, for that matter, even if the employee were not represented by a union. The employee might well be fired or subjected to some lesser form of discipline, but the suggestion that General Motors might seek money damages seems unrealistic. And this is true even if we imagine an employee who has sufficient assets to pay any judgment without going bankrupt. As we shall see, however, the possibility of a corporation seeking recovery from officers and directors for injuries caused by their lack of care has not seemed to most people to be unrealistic. Far from it. (See Chapter 3, Sec. IV(A).) And this is true regardless that such liability can be sufficient to bankrupt the officer or director. Indeed, legislation in some states imposes significant barriers to efforts by corporations to provide protection against such liability for officers and directors. But that again gets ahead of our story.

**3. Incompetent Business Decision.** Case 3. Suppose that Morris causes a $10,000 loss by the exercise of extremely *bad judgment* in the operation of the business. Suppose, for example, that he stupidly orders far too much of a perishable commodity and it rots in the storeroom. Assuming that Morris had general authority to order such commodities in such quantities (or reasonably appeared to the supplier to have such authority), Pamela must pay for what was ordered and delivered. Again, she is entitled to recover from Morris, unless he had made a reasonable decision that simply turned out badly. No doubt the scope of the concept of a reasonable decision would be broad; Morris must have considerable leeway, as a matter of business necessity. But there are limits that Morris can transcend and beyond those limits he is said to have failed to exercise due care and becomes liable for his dereliction. In this situation, however, there is an added practical element that makes the problem far more serious than those depicted in the first two examples. Insurance will not be available. (Note that we are not concerned here with theft by Morris, for which insurance may be available.)

**4. Inaccurate Information.** Case 4. Consider problems associated with Morris's duty to supply Pamela with *information*. Suppose that Morris is responsible for sending to Pamela monthly reports on the operations of the business and that, by virtue of his carelessness, these reports seriously understate earnings. Now suppose that Pamela, relying on these reports, sells the business to a third person for an amount substantially below what she would have insisted upon had she known the true facts. Again, Pamela may have a right to recover from Morris. Recovery would be based on a theory of negligence or lack of due care. To change the facts, however, let's suppose that Pamela sells the business to Morris. Here, Morris would benefit from his error and the legal standards are understandably far more favorable to Pamela than they are when there is no such element of potentially self-serving behavior on the part of Morris.

## B. CONTRACTS REGARDING DUTY OF CARE

We have seen four possible instances of a failure on the part of Morris to do his job properly—instances of what the law refers to as a failure to exercise due care. Let us now suppose that before Morris and Pamela enter into their employment contract, they try to minimize their potential liabilities and negotiate with each other over who will bear the burden of unavoidable losses.

**1. Insurance for Negligent Injury to Third Person.** In Case 1, involving tort liability to a third person, damages are likely to be covered by insurance. The insurance policy is likely to be taken out by Pamela. Such a policy would not necessarily protect Morris but may be drafted to do so. If the parties think about the issue in advance it seems likely that Morris will insist that Pamela buy protection for him, or will insist on added compensation so that he can buy his own policy. Not all potential problems of tort liability can be resolved by the purchase of insurance, however. Adequate insurance may not be available, for example, for defamation of an employee or a customer. The chance that such behavior will occur may be exceedingly remote, but if the parties want to resolve the matter by agreement in advance, they will be confronted with difficult problems of definition. These problems of definition can, perhaps, be appreciated more fully as they arise in a context not involving insurance.

**2. Self Insurance by Employer.** Suppose that Pamela is a wealthy person who is willing to accept the risk of tort liability to third persons both for herself and for Morris. In other words, suppose that she wants to be a *self-insurer* as to injuries arising from the business. Morris may be willing to accept the protection afforded by her promise to him to assume all liability (that is, by an *indemnity* agreement, under which Pamela agrees to indemnify Morris for liabilities that he may incur). The question then arises, will the law uphold such an agreement relieving Morris of his common-law duty to Pamela? In this context, the answer undoubtedly is "yes." (Note that such an agreement would not affect the right of the injured person to collect from either Morris or Pamela.) As suggested above, however, when Pamela and Morris try to draft the terms of the agreement, they may experience considerable difficulty. While Pamela may be willing to assume the burden of Morris's "ordinary" negligence, she may not be willing to assume the burden of injuries caused by "gross" negligence, or willful behavior, or behavior stemming from Morris's personal activities or self-serving schemes. It may be extremely difficult for Morris and Pamela to agree on a verbal formulation of the limits of Pamela's assumption of liability.

**3. Waiver of Liability for Negligent Injury to Employer.**
Pamela may also want to be a self-insurer with respect to the kinds of
injuries involved in Case 2. Again, she and Morris may be prepared to
agree on the matter. Here, however, the contemplated injury is one
directly to Pamela and it may not be quite so clear that the agreement
will be enforceable. Courts have shown some reluctance to enforce
bargains in which one party is relieved of liability for negligent harm
directly to another (though not so much in the case of arm's-length
bargains affecting people like Pamela, who presumably can take of
themselves). Again, the scope of Pamela's waiver of her rights against
Morris may be difficult to define.

**4. Waiver of Liability for Incompetent Business Decisions;
Effects on Behavior of Employee.** Similar problems of definition
will also arise in connection with any effort to relieve Morris of liability
for the kinds of harm inflicted on Pamela in situations like Case 3 (lack
of due care in making business decisions). In these kinds of situations,
however, we can begin to see another aspect of the problem—one that is
present in the first two situations but is more readily understandable in
the third. Suppose that the agreement between Pamela and Morris
generally relieves Morris of liability for even seriously defective business
decisions, but leaves open some possibility that Morris will be liable for
what Pamela may regard as an outrageously stupid or careless action.
The question is, how will such a possibility affect Morris's behavior? To
some extent, no doubt, the effects will be desirable from almost any
reasonable perspective. If the possibility of outrageous action can be
reduced by the threat of liability, both Pamela and Morris may be better
off: Pamela can expect to earn more and can afford to pay more to
Morris. On the other hand, there is a real danger that Morris will
overreact and will adopt conservative, costly, *self-protective strategies*
that will reduce the returns from the business for both Pamela and
Morris. Viewing the matter from Pamela's perspective, extreme care
must be exercised in arrangements that expose her employees to liability
for their mistakes. On the one hand, if Morris has too little reason to
worry about his potential liability he may be too careless. On the other
hand, if he has too much reason to worry (or thinks he has), he may
become too conservative and may incur too many costs in trying to avoid
liability.

## C. LIMITING SCOPE OF AUTHORITY

**1. Problems of Internal Business Practice.** Pamela may seek
to limit her exposure to loss resulting from Morris's weak business
decisions by limiting the *scope of* his *authority* to act for her. There are,
however, a number of circumstances that constrain her freedom to do
this. Suppose, for example, that Pamela has doubts about Morris's
judgment in ordering fresh vegetables and wants to limit his purchasing

authority. Suppose further that she has in the past ordered as much as $20,000 worth of fresh vegetables in a week and that this is not extraordinary, but she wants to limit Morris to ordering $10,000 worth a week. The first problem is that such a limitation may simply be a bad business strategy. There may be occasions when it will be extremely useful for Morris to have the authority to act as Pamela herself would have acted. In general, people who manage businesses must have considerable decision-making authority if they are to make a success of the business. It may be counterproductive to try too hard to limit their freedom of action.

**2. Problems of Notification of Others.** A second problem in attempting to limit Morris's authority is that such a limit will not bind the supplier unless the supplier knows about it and knows that it has been reached. If Pamela simply tells Morris not to order more than $10,000 worth of fresh vegetables a week and does not so advise the supplier or suppliers, then as long as larger orders are customary in the trade, Pamela will be liable for the full amount of such larger orders. And this is true, under the law of agency, even if the suppliers are unaware of Pamela's existence and believe that Morris is the owner of the store. See Restatement, Agency (2d), Sec. 8A and 194. If a supplier is in fact aware of the limitation on Morris's authority then that supplier will be bound by that limitation, and if the supplier then provides more than $10,000 worth of fresh vegetables Pamela is not obligated to pay for the excess. But it may be difficult to formulate the precise limits of each of a number of potential suppliers, in terms acceptable to them, and to find devices for keeping each of them informed about whether aggregate limits have been reached. Moreover, if the limits are ambiguous Morris may become unduly concerned about his own exposure to risk of liability (to the supplier or to Pamela) for exceeding his authority. In situations where limitations are of necessity to some degree ambiguous, managers (and other employees) will seek to obtain protection against liability for exceeding their authority—or will demand greater compensation, to take account of the risk. But to the degree that the employee is protected from the risk, the employer will not be. Finally, Morris's bad judgment may not be reflected in any single decision upon which limits can be placed, but rather in a series of interrelated decisions or in some failure to take affirmative action to prevent loss. Because of these various circumstances, Pamela cannot avoid exposure to significant loss, even beyond her investment in the business, for Morris's errors in judgment.

**3. Liabilities of Creditors.** In certain circumstances a creditor that exercises control over the operation of another firm to which it has extended credit may become liable for the debtor firm's obligations to other creditors.[3] Suppose, for example, that Pamela has not paid her bills as they have become due and has fallen deeply in debt to a number of

---

[3] See, e.g., A. Gay Jenson Farms Co. v. Cargill, Inc., 309 N.W.2d 285 (Minn.1981). But see Buck v. Nash–Finch Co., 78 S.D. 334, 102 N.W.2d 84 (1960).

creditors including the wholesale grocery company from which she buys most of her goods. The wholesaler may want to help Pamela stay in business because that is the only way it can hope to recover the money it is owed and because it hopes to keep Pamela as a customer. The wholesaler may think that Pamela needs better management, however, and may insist (as a condition of continuing to extend credit to Pamela and not forcing her into bankruptcy) that she hire as manager a person selected by it or that she take various other actions designed to protect the wholesaler's interests. Pamela's equity may well be negative, so all the financial risk is on the wholesaler and it may consider that this amount of control is the least it is entitled to. But as this scenario unfolds, there may come a time when it seems that the business is being run more by, and for the benefit of, the wholesaler than Pamela and the possibility arises that a court may treat the wholesaler as a proprietor, with liability for the debts previously incurred by Pamela in operating the business. This kind of outcome may reflect legalistic myopia rather than common sense. The other creditors may wind up with a windfall (a claim, against the wholesaler, that they had no reason to anticipate or rely on) and other firms in the future in positions like that of the wholesaler may be deterred from preventing a wasteful termination of a business. On the other hand, a creditor that does want to take control of a debtor's business can bargain with the other creditors or can invoke the bankruptcy laws in a manner designed to keep the debtor operating. See Chapter 4, Sec. III(A)(4).

## VIII.  OWNERS AND MANAGERIAL EMPLOYEES: LOYALTY

### A.  CONFLICT CONCERNING INFORMATION PROVIDED TO OWNER

**1.  In Connection With Purchase of Ownership Interests by Employee.** Morris's carelessness can also produce losses for Pamela in situations like those illustrated in Case 4, involving information supplied by Morris. Here, however, we have the element of potential *conflict of interest* in a clearer setting. (In the earlier cases there is also a form of conflict of interest—for example, the conflict between Pamela's interest in profits and Morris's interest in protecting himself from liability—but the conflict was not so apparent and, perhaps, not so serious.) In Case 4, we can also conveniently introduce the possibility of a review by an outsider. In the initial statement of the Case 4 hypothetical, Morris carelessly understated the profits of the business and Pamela relied on this information in selling to an outsider. Morris's negligence caused harm to Pamela, but there was nothing that would typically be called "conflict of interest" on Morris's part since he was not benefited by the understatement; there was no economic incentive to err. (There may have been a conflict between Pamela's desire for maximum effort by Morris and Morris's interest in taking life easy, but this divergence is not usually referred to as a "conflict of interest.")

Where Morris is the buyer, the incentive to err in the direction of understatement is obvious. In this two-person situation, of course, Pamela would be aware of the potential for deliberate error and would be on her guard. Difficult issues of legal doctrine revolve around how far courts should go in situations such as this in protecting people like Pamela from unwise bargains based on less-than-adequate information. These issues are associated with the fact that Morris is both an employee who, in the eyes of the law, owes a *duty of loyalty* (see Sec. VIII(E) below) to Pamela, and a buyer who, in reality, will be looking out for his own interests. It might be tempting, especially in slightly different contexts, to adopt a flat rule prohibiting dealings between Morris and Pamela that raise conflicts between Morris's duty of loyalty and his self-interest. But the potential advantage to both Morris and Pamela of being able to deal with each other is too great to be stifled by rigid legal prohibitions. In the corporate context, courts have in the past adopted rules tending to force the parties to watch out for their own interests, but the more recent trend seems to be toward judicial scrutiny to ensure full disclosure by the corporate counterparts of Morris (managers and other "insiders") and protection of the counterparts of Pamela (shareholders). (See Chapter 3, Sec. IV(B).)

**2. Regarding Performance by Manager.** Purchases of the business (or an interest in it) by employees are, of course, relatively infrequent events in the life of a particular business. A far more common divergence of interest in the supplying of information by managers to owners relates to the manager's success in running the business. Pamela will want to have an accurate and honest appraisal of Morris's operation of the business and to a considerable extent will need to rely on Morris to supply the needed information. No matter how honest and faithful Morris may be, however, his response to this need of Pamela will be affected by his own interest in making himself look as good as possible. Thus, he is likely to emphasize good news and to downplay or explain away bad news. Beyond this, Morris may be a crook and may want to hide the fact that he is stealing.

**3. Role of Auditors.** A common device for dealing with both these problems is for Pamela to hire an outsider to examine the books and the operations of the business. The person who performs this function is likely to be an accountant who performs a function called "auditing." The degree of care that the auditor takes in reviewing books and records will be a major determinant of the likelihood of uncovering theft, innocent exaggeration, or inaccuracy. While there are certain standard procedures used in typical audits, where the accountant is hired to serve the private interests of a person like Pamela, the degree of care presumably is negotiable. One must remember, however, that audits cost money and the more careful the audit, the more expensive it will become. In selecting an auditing firm and in defining the scope of its review, Pamela inevitably becomes involved, consciously or not, in a decision-making process involving the comparison of costs and benefits. Information cannot be obtained without cost, and recognition of that reality is essential to an understanding of much of economic organization, including business relationships.

**4. Loyalty of Auditors.** Another aspect of the auditing function is perhaps less obvious, at least in the context of the large, publicly held firm. This aspect has to do with the question of whose interests the auditor is obligated to serve. If Pamela hires an auditor to help her to watch out over her private interests in the business then it seems plain that the auditor's loyalty should be to Pamela (notwithstanding auditors' image of themselves as independent professionals). But what about Morris's interests (bearing in mind that in some circumstances it may be Morris who actually selects the auditor)? Understandably, Morris will want to present a favorable picture of his conduct of the business. A person unfamiliar with accounting and auditing procedures might assume that these conflicting orientations present no problem since all the auditor needs to do is present an objective picture of the business. The fact is, however, that accountants, especially as the business becomes complex, are faced with "judgment calls" on all sorts of issues (e.g., whether a contested liability should be treated as a current cost; or when profit should be reported on a contract on which performance has not been completed). If the auditor calls too many of the close ones against Morris, he may want to have some way of presenting his view of events in a manner more favorable to himself. If he has the power, he may fire the existing auditor and hire one who is more sympathetic to his own interests. The likely effect of such a prospect on the behavior of an auditor should be obvious. If Morris cannot fire an unsympathetic auditor, he might conceivably insist on an additional auditor to represent him and promote his cause. This would mean two sets of outside reports to Pamela, but that is likely to be excessively costly. The most likely outcome of the conflict between Pamela and Morris over audits will be an effort by the auditor to walk the fine line, trying to serve the interests of both Pamela and Morris as well as possible. We need not pursue this matter of the conflict between Pamela and Morris over control of the auditor. It is sufficient for present purposes to note the interests on both sides and the fact that information cannot be supplied without cost.

## B.　LOYALTY AND CONFLICT PROBLEMS AND THEIR COSTS

We have examined the problems associated with what the law refers to as the duty of care and have begun to see some problems having to do with the duty of loyalty in supplying information. The duty of loyalty is, of course, a more general obligation of employees (and other agents and fiduciaries). Problems of Morris's faithfulness, loyalty, and devotion to

duty are especially troublesome because they are difficult to define and
even more difficult to monitor. Viewing the matter negatively, Pamela
will be concerned about the possibilities of stealing, cheating, and
shirking and how to prevent or limit them. For convenience, we can
refer to stealing, cheating, shirking and other such volitional or control-
lable conduct as *self-dealing*. By a variety of techniques, an employer
can control the incidence of self-dealing by employees, but not without
costs in time or money. There is likely, therefore, to be a residual loss to
the employer from the employee's self-dealing that it is not worthwhile
to try to prevent. For example, to detect stealing by Morris (and others)
Pamela probably will rely on such negative sanctions as the threat of
dismissal, bad references, and even criminal action. To detect criminal
behavior she will need to spend her own time in reviewing operations or
hire others to do so. This is part of the cost of hiring managers. It is a
cost that does not occur when Pamela manages the business herself.
And no matter how great the expenditure on prevention and detection,
there will remain some possibility of undetected theft.

## C. SELF–DEALING AND THE USE OF INCENTIVES

Stealing by managers is not likely to be a central concern of many
business firms. Shirking, and other forms of self-serving behavior such
as lavish use of expense accounts, are more pervasive and significant
problems. Control of shirking may take the form of observation (with
varying degrees of care) of performance or results, followed by reward
(e.g., bonus or promotion) or punishment (e.g., demotion or discharge).
But observation is costly and often inaccurate and rewards and punish-
ments are imperfect, though useful, tools for controlling self-dealing. To
illustrate and expand on this observation, suppose that Pamela moves to
a distant place and must, of necessity, give Morris broad discretion in the
operation of the business. Now consider the question of how many
hours a week he is to work. Suppose that when Pamela managed the
business herself she worked 60 hours a week. Further, let's suppose
that if Morris owned the business himself he would work 60 hours a
week. It does not follow that Morris will work 60 hours a week as
manager of Pamela's business, since the benefit to him from doing so
may not be sufficient to induce that level of effort. Pamela may
recognize that there is no point in trying to specify that Morris will work
a set number of hours per week at some specified level of effort. Even if
it were possible to prescribe unambiguously an appropriate number of
hours and level of effort, it might be too difficult for Pamela to determine the number of hours actually put in by Morris, much less the level
of his effort. Pamela may be better off to rely on the threat of discharge
for inadequate performance (which means that she will incur costs in
observing performance and in gathering information about other managers with whom she might replace Morris) and on the use of rewards
based on results that tend to flow from effort. As we have seen before,

Morris's compensation might, for example, be partly in the form of a percentage of profits and this will tend to make his and Pamela's interests more similar. The guaranteed term of his employment may be kept short, so that he will know that if he doesn't produce he will be out on the street. Even so, he may wind up working less than 60 hours a week and the total financial returns from the business may be less than they would be if either Pamela or Morris were an owner-manager.

Some aspects of the general problem can be dramatized by imagining a dialogue between Morris and Pamela:

| | |
|---|---|
| Morris: | I would like to give you 100 percent effort and be compensated accordingly. |
| Pamela: | That sounds good, but how am I to be sure that you are delivering the kind of effort you promise? |
| Morris: | I'm sorry that you don't have more faith in my honesty and integrity. Be that as it may, if I don't perform, you can fire me or cut back my compensation. |
| Pamela: | I have no doubt about your honesty and integrity, and your pride in doing a good job, otherwise I would not want to hire you. But you are, like all of us, subject to human frailties, and I don't know how I could determine whether you are in fact performing as promised. And I hate to think how you might react if I were to tell you that I think you're not giving me 100 percent. |
| Morris: | Well, if you don't trust me, you can hire someone to check up on me—the kind of person economists so quaintly refer to as a "monitor." |
| Pamela: | You seem to have more faith in monitors than I do. In any case, would you be willing to have your compensation reduced by the amount that I would have to pay the monitor? |
| Morris: | Come now! (Pause.) Maybe we're on the wrong track. Let's start from scratch. The problem is that you would like to have me work my butt off, but the profit goes to you—or at least most of it does. Why don't you just take a fair return on your investment—indeed, a generous return—and let me keep the profit in excess of that return? |
| Pamela: | I suspect that we would have trouble agreeing on what is a "fair return." And what about losses, pal? |
| Morris: | I give up. Let's just stick to the old tried and true salary plus a bonus based on profits. |
| Pamela: | Fair enough, but now you have me worried. I still expect 100 percent effort from you and if I don't get it I'll see to it that you'll never get another job in this town. |

*Exeunt.*

## D.   SELF–DEALING, JOINT VENTURES, "WASTE," AND THE MYTHICAL IDEAL

In the Pamela–Morris kind of situation there is a form of economic specialization, with Pamela supplying risk-bearing capital and Morris supplying managerial skill.   If, in the customary mode, we think of Pamela as the owner, there is a separation of ownership and control. Morris must have considerable decision-making freedom.   Specification of how he should react to all possible issues is not feasible.   Given the need to vest in Morris the power to exercise business judgment or discretion, self-dealing by Morris becomes possible.   The duty of loyalty prescribes—in some situations with clarity and in others only with considerable ambiguity—how Morris is supposed to behave, but this code of conduct is not self-executing.   Moreover, it is impossible to design a system of sharing of rewards that will make Morris's interests identical to those of Pamela.   Pamela will of necessity spend some of her time or her money, or both, trying to determine how faithfully Morris is serving her interests.

Economists (and others) often seem to think of the costs of defining, detecting, and preventing self-dealing as a sort of waste.   Similarly, they find waste to the extent that a benefit that Morris takes for himself, such as leisure, is worth less to him than its cost to Pamela (for example, in lost profits).   (The residual loss to Pamela from self-dealing that cannot feasibly be prevented is not an economic waste since Pamela's loss is Morris's gain.)   That concept of waste is, however, a peculiar one when examined closely.   The possibility of self-dealing is an inevitable product of the decision to hire a manager to run a business.   One can cope with this possibility in a variety of ways, like hiring monitors such as detectives or outside auditors.   The cost of doing so is certainly a departure from what Pamela might hope for and from what she could achieve if she ran the business herself.   But this cost is an inevitable outcome of the facts that she has chosen to retire from active management and that in our imperfect world the people on whom she must rely may not be entirely trustworthy and loyal.   It is unfortunate that people are not all perfectly trustworthy and loyal;   it is unfortunate that people are not all perfect in all respects.   But we must learn to live with the fact of imperfection and the costs thereby imposed.   A violation of the duty of loyalty may be more galling than a violation of other obligations because the violation is likely to involve a sneaky act—an act that the employee knows is wrong but expects to be able to get away with because of problems of detection.   Violation of the duty of loyalty may, therefore, be seen as unethical or immoral (as contrasted, for example, with a violation of the duty of care).   This might justify the imposition of punitive damages or other special remedies (though by and large the law has not proceeded in that direction) or the incurring of extraordinary costs for detection.   Still, there is no more sense in bemoaning the costs of disloyalty than there is in bemoaning the costs of friction in an engine. We lubricate engines to reduce friction, but we are willing to accept some residual level of friction. We continue to use engines, despite the cost of lubrication, and despite the residual friction, because we conclude we are better off by doing so than we would be otherwise. People with capital, like Pamela, hire managers, despite the monitoring costs, because they feel they are better off than they would be with any alternative investment or venture. This observation is, of course, a tautology. It is a useful tautology in that it reminds us of the silliness of worrying about unavoidable departures from unattainable ideals. While the point may seem obvious in the present context, it is often ignored in the context of large, complex economic organizations such as publicly held corporations.

In other words, we must be careful about comparing the actual situation, with division of ownership and management, to the *mythical ideal of the owner-managed firm*. Once Pamela decides, for whatever reason, that she does not want to manage the business, the standard of an owner-managed firm is unattainable. Morris simply cannot be expected to act as he would if he were the owner. He is not an owner; and he is a human being. Pamela is not a manager any longer; she is an investor. Both think that they are better off with the other than without. If that were not so, they would not have made the deal they made. It seems more useful to compare their actual position to what they would have if they could not combine their resources (services and capital) than to what they would have in the unattainable combined-owner-manager situation. In the actual position, with separation of management from ownership of capital, both can be expected to try to bargain for as much as possible in the way of contributions by the other and returns to themselves. It is fatuous to expect that Morris will behave selflessly, as if all the returns to his efforts were his. Pamela might hope for something close to that result, but she would be silly to expect to achieve it. All of this may, again, seem obvious in the small-firm context. For large firms it is also valid but frequently ignored both by lawyers and economists.

## E.  THE LEGAL DUTY OF LOYALTY

Suppose, however, that when Pamela hires Morris, she says, either explicitly or implicitly, that she expects him, as manager, to behave just as she would behave, or as he would behave if he were the owner. And suppose that Morris accepts the job on those terms. To a considerable extent the legal system seems to infer, and even to impose, such bargains. This is what is contemplated by the law when it refers to a duty of loyalty or a *fiduciary obligation*. That duty or obligation is like a golden rule, a broad, vague constraint applied to employment relationships (a one-way rule in favor of the employer). It is the kind of duty associated not only with employees but with trustees, brokers, and a whole host of other kinds of people (fiduciaries) who undertake to accomplish some objective for another person. The need to rely on a vague concept such as the duty of loyalty stems from the difficulty of specifying precisely what it is that the employer expects of the employee (on the need, that is, for discretion in the employee). The rule of law that embodies the duty of loyalty is a useful one. Without it, mutually advantageous economic relationships might not be feasible. As we have seen, however, violations of the duty of loyalty may be extremely difficult to detect. To that extent, and given the infirmities of human nature, the duty of loyalty may to a significant extent embody an unattainable ideal. It is wholly unrealistic to expect that all employees will as a matter of conscience consistently act as faithful retainers, selflessly pursuing the interests of their employers even at their own expense, or that we can be fully effective in efforts to force them to do so. We can publicly deplore the departures from the ideal. It may be useful to do so—to establish ethical standards and use deprivation of respect as a tool for enforcing the loyalty aspect of the business agreement. But we must be careful not to refuse to recognize the reality and cope with it.

## F. LOYALTY AND PROBLEMS OF AMBIGUITY

Enforcement of the duty of loyalty may be difficult not only by virtue of obvious problems of detection of violations, but also, as suggested, because its requirements may be ambiguous. For example, suppose that Morris hears of an *opportunity* to buy another grocery store. Can he seize that opportunity for his own benefit or must he first determine whether Pamela wants to do so? That may be a difficult question to answer, with the outcome depending on how Morris got the information, what assets Pamela has available, how Pamela has reacted to similar opportunities in the past, and so forth. If Morris does decide to buy the other store, and to manage it, he may want to take some of Pamela's employees (his subordinate fellow workers) with him—again raising a difficult problem of defining the scope of his duty of loyalty to Pamela. Some of these kinds of issues may be foreseen and may be the subject of negotiation and resolution at the outset of the Pamela–Morris relationship, but for the most part such solutions will not be feasible and vague common-law standards will apply.

## G. ABSOLUTE BARRIERS TO DISLOYALTY

One approach to the loyalty problem is, as suggested earlier, to erect some sort of *absolute barrier* to acts by Morris that might be in derogation of the interests of Pamela. Suppose, for example, that Morris has a substantial investment interest in a wholesale produce company and that he is also responsible for buying produce for Pamela's store. Since other suppliers are likely to be available, perhaps the best course would be to foreclose any possibility of purchases from the firm in which Morris has an interest.  Pamela is, of course, free to insist on that outcome.  On the other hand, she may believe that she will be better off to allow Morris to make the best deal possible for her, even if that involves him in a conflict of interest.  If so, she is likely to want to make some special arrangement to ensure that her interests are adequately protected.  Creative legal skill may be called for in devising such protections.  But the point is that it may be unwise to try to rule out all possibility of dealings involving conflict of interest on the part of people subject to a duty of loyalty.

## IX.  IRREDUCIBLE DIVERGENCIES OF INTEREST

There may be other aspects of cooperative economic activity that may be thought to create special kinds of "costs"—costs that in the final analysis are purely fictional.  To illustrate, consider a medical team consisting of a surgeon, Sam, and an anesthesiologist, Ann.  Assume that neither can work without the other and that no other partners are available to either of them.  Working together, Sam and Ann can earn a total of $200 per hour, with no limit on the number of hours of work available at that price.  Each of them is physically capable of working 40 hours a week without undue strain or impairment of ability.  Sam wants to work 40 hours a week and Ann want to work 20.  They compromise and work 30 hours a week.  Sam is working 10 hours a week less than he wants to and Ann is working 10 hours more.  That is the price that each pays for the benefits of joint effort.  Plainly the benefits to each must outweigh the "costs."  In some sort of abstract sense perhaps the result is not optimal.  But the point is that the imaginary optimum that is the reference point for such a conclusion (with Sam working 40 hours and Ann 20) does not and cannot exist.  It is no more sensible to talk in terms of a "loss" to Sam or Ann, or a "cost" to them of joint endeavor, than it is to talk about a loss to them associated with the fact that they are not movie stars.  The difference between the possibility of being movie stars and the possibility of being able to work their desired number of hours is a matter of degree.  One might assume that the chance of either of them finding a partner with tastes for work similar to their own is greater than the chance that either of them will become a movie star.  But once we have determined that they have made the best deal possible for their joint activity in their medical specialties, thoughts about what each has "lost" or about the "cost" of joint endeavor seems at best like barren utopianism.

The fact remains, however, that there is a divergency or conflict between the interests and goals of Sam and those of Ann.  The resolution of that divergency or conflict can produce an interesting exercise in game theory or bargaining strategy.  A brief examination of such an exercise will be useful for our purposes because of its relevance to more complex problems associated with creation of other economic enterprises.

Consider three issues: (1) division of rewards, (2) number of hours of work, and (3) level of skill and care. Let's imagine a dialogue over the first of these issues.

Sam: Let's work out the terms of our agreement. First let's talk about how we are going to split the $200 per hour that we are going to charge. I suggest that I get $150 per hour and that you get $50 per hour. I am, after all, the leader of the team, and my job is the more glamorous and more important.

Ann: You always did have a fine sense of humor, Sam. I could play that kind of game too, but let's get serious. Shall we agree to split 50–50?

Sam: Why 50–50? Apart from the fact that I feel my services are worth more than yours, there is the fact that I have four children and you have none so I need the money worse than you do.

Ann: O.K., wise guy. If you want to play guts ball, here's how it's going to be. You and I both recognize that there is no logical solution—it's all a matter of bargaining within the limits set by the most attractive alternative available to each of us. I know that the most you could earn without me is $50 per hour. I'll let you take $75 per hour and that is my final offer. You just told me that you need the money and I believe you. So you'd better take my offer or I'm walking out and you're out of luck.

Sam: That's mighty tough talk, but I don't believe you. Still, this is getting us nowhere and I'm afraid that you're beginning to get nasty, so I'll let you have $70.

Ann: I should insist on more, you greedy devil, but I'll accept $85, provided you are willing to be reasonable about the number of hours we will work.

Sam: I'm glad you mentioned that. You know, when I agreed to 30 hours, I assumed that I would be earning $150 per hour. If I'm only going to get, say, $125 per hour, I'm going to have to work more hours in order to be able to earn a decent living.

Ann: But we already agreed on 30 hours per week.

Sam: Sure, but that was before we talked about division of fees, and now it is clear that we can't really separate the number of hours issue from the hourly rate issue.

Ann: As a matter of fact, now that it is clear to me that I'm going to be getting only, say, $90 per hour, rather than $100, I would like to work fewer hours. My leisure time is very valuable to me and I don't have the same commitment to consumption that you seem to have.

And so on.

It can readily be seen that the essence of this negotiation could be repeated with respect to other issues such as the level of skill and care that they are to devote to their work, the extent to which they do charity work, and so forth. Two principles should be clear. First, there is no patently correct or proper outcome to the bargain over any of these issues. It is by no means true, for example, that a 50–50 split of income is the only proper or imaginable outcome, though to many people it will seem somehow correct. Second, even though there may be an imaginary, abstract sense in which both Sam and Ann have failed to reach their optimal position on an issue such as number of hours of work, both of them are better off than they would be in any other available alternative. Otherwise they would not have agreed to work as a team. The same principles are applicable to other joint economic endeavors. Sometimes the conflicts will be recognized at the outset and will be resolved by explicit bargain. Sometimes conflicts will only become apparent after the activity has been carried on for some time. At that point, of course, there is likely to be at least one additional factor that affects the outcome—the possible loss of the value of a going concern. Conflicts arising in a going concern may be resolved by bargaining among the parties, with, perhaps, one party having an upper hand by virtue of possessing a credible threat of terminating the enterprise. Or the conflict may wind up in the courts. The courts are likely to seek a result that is fair in terms of what the parties probably would have decided had they thought of the issue at the outset. This approach may, in turn, be transformed into a golden-rule criterion. Such a criterion may have the desirable economic consequences of facilitating initial economic cooperation, in that some people may be more willing to make deals if they know that unanticipated eventualities will be resolved fairly. These principles are relevant to the Pamela–Morris relationship and to other, far more complex arrangements involving larger numbers of people.

It may be worth emphasizing that the problems suggested here are not fanciful; they have important real-world analogs. For example, two or more people pooling their capital or services, or both, to start a business must decide how to split the profits. It is not always clear that the split should be in the ratio of the value of their contributions. Two or more people agreeing to work together in a restaurant that they are about to buy must agree on how many hours a day to stay open. Two or more people about to acquire an automobile agency must agree on the types of sales techniques to be used and on the kinds of controls to be adopted to insure honesty in their repair shop. And so on. In all these situations, the complexity of the real world may obscure the underlying economic and psychological forces at work, but those forces are essentially the same as those at work in the possibly simplistic Sam–Ann hypothetical relationship.

## X.  AVOIDANCE OF CONFLICT

We have seen that as long as Pamela owns the capital invested in the business and Morris is the manager, there will be unavoidable problems of self-dealing and divergency of interests and the attendant costs of monitoring.  A solution that may suggest itself is for Morris to acquire Pamela's capital interest in the firm—in other words, for Pamela to sell out to Morris.  Often this will occur, especially in very small businesses, where the amount of capital that Morris will need is relatively small and the monitoring costs may be high in relation to the value of the activity.  Often a purchase will be the only acceptable way to resolve problems of divergency of interest.  The purchase by Morris might be in installments over a number of years from the profits of the business. There are, however, significant obstacles in the way of this solution, particularly as the business grows in size.  In the first place, if Pamela takes her money out of this business, she will have to find some other place to invest it and may then be confronted with the same problem of separation of ownership and management that she had to begin with. More significantly, Morris simply may not be able or willing to come up with the money, even in installments.  He may not have the money and may be unable to raise it.  It may not be economically feasible to finance his purchase out of his share of the profits of the business, especially if the value of the business is large in relation to the value of his services. Even if a purchase might be financially feasible, Morris may be unwilling to take the risk.  He may not want to put all his eggs in one basket. This will be especially likely in a venture with high risks.  Yet any effort by Morris to buy the business is likely to require heavy borrowing and thus the high leverage that creates high risk.  (See discussion of leverage and risk, Chapter 5, Sec. II.)

If Morris is unwilling or unable to bear the risks of the business, Pamela must continue to do so.  If she is going to do so, she will demand either a high interest rate on her investment or the lion's share of the profits.  The high interest rate will probably be regarded as intolerable, so she will be left with an interest in the profits, and an exposure to the losses, of the business.  A person with this kind of stake in a business is likely to expect to have the power to control the business to some significant degree.  So we are right back where we started, with a separation of ownership and management (or, in the context of the large, publicly held business, "separation of ownership and control").

## XI.  RECAPITULATION

The business firm evolves from a process of bargaining between managers and investors (among others).  The bargain may be implicit and the parties may adopt models developed by others.  But regardless of the nature of the process, the people involved in it can be expected to seek to advance their own interests as much as possible.  In the language of economics, managers, like owners, can be expected to seek to maximize their own utilities. It may seem surprising, but this idea is relatively new to economics. In earlier economic thinking, a business firm was thought of as maximizing "its" profits—as if the abstract concept (a firm or a corporation) were an individual acting as an owner-manager. That is, economists until recently (and to this day to some extent) talked as if the behavior of large corporations were the same as that of individual owner-managers. Much the same kind of thinking continues to dominate the legal concept of the firm. Managers (officers, directors, and others) are supposed to behave like faithful retainers, serving only the best interests of their masters (the shareholders or other owners). This is the legal standard. It may serve useful functions in facilitating mutually advantageous bargains, but if taken too seriously it can produce a dangerous myopia about how the business world does and should operate.

The problem of separation of ownership and management (control) cannot be avoided. It is a function not only of division of function (specialization) but also of allocation of risk. Managers of firms, especially large ones, frequently will not be willing or able to have ownership interests that are large in relation to the total value of the firm. Significant risks will therefore of necessity be borne by non-managers. The people bearing such risks will want some control, but will find it costly to exercise control. Managers are hired for their expertise in management; if they are to earn their pay they must be allowed to exercise discretion, to have freedom of action. Owners will rely on some reasonable level of review and supervision of managerial efficiency and loyalty and on other devices, such as incentive pay, whose function is to align the goals of managers with those of owners.

There are certain inevitable consequences of joint economic enterprise that result in departures from an imaginary, unattainable world in which there are no benefits of joint effort and division of economic function. For a gloomy, misanthropic perspective we can observe how far we are from a world of self-employed people, a world of owner-managers, or a world of masters and faithful retainers. For a more cheerful, tolerant, and forgiving perspective, we can observe how far we are from a world in which there is no division of economic function, no joint, mutually beneficial economic endeavor.

One final word of comfort can be added. We have seen that joint economic activity creates problems of inadequate incentive and of self-dealing. The literature of economics, management, and investment tends to focus (at least in our essentially capitalistic society) on these problems and one can scarcely deny their importance. At the same time, one should not forget that joint activity may produce countervailing economically and socially desirable effects of a similar sort (that is, effects other than those associated with economies of scale and specialization). Most of us have felt at times that the sharing of a task with others can make it more bearable or enjoyable and, beyond that, may help us to overcome an inability to get started on a project or to force ourselves to keep at it. Far from creating opportunities for shortchanging others, joint activity may provide a setting that enables us to avoid shortchanging ourselves.

## XII. SPECULATION ON RELATIONSHIPS AMONG RISK, RETURN, CONTROL, DURATION, AND SPECIFICITY

In this chapter we have examined elements of the bargain among participants in a business venture and some of the relationships among those elements. We can now examine those relationships in a more systematic way. What follows is speculative and unscientific; it is intended to be suggestive and provocative, not definitive.

### A. RISK AND RETURN

Most people are risk averse in their major economic decisions. (The phenomenon is called *risk aversion* and is explored more fully in Chapter 4, Sec. II(E).) They like safety and security and are willing to pay to achieve it. They buy insurance, seek protection against discharge from their jobs, put their money in insured savings accounts, etc. They are willing to accept risk only if they are paid to do so. For example, if the *expected rate of return* (for elaboration, see Chapter 4, Sec. II(A)) on a first mortgage investment in a piece of property, or a business, is 10 percent, the expected rate of return on the underlying equity in that enterprise will be several points higher. More generally, as risk rises, expected rate of return or required payment will rise; thus, the residual claim in any enterprise will have a higher expected rate of return than a fixed claim in the same enterprise.

### B. RISK AND CONTROL

Who pays the fiddler calls the tune. In the business world, who bears the risks calls the shots. The holders of the equity, or residual, claim in a firm are more likely to be interested in and to have control of the firm than are the holders of the debt, or fixed claim. This is not to say that the equity investors will necessarily want to manage the business; they may well be incapable of that (for example, if they are the many common shareholders of a large corporation). They are likely, however, to want to have the power to select the managers and to make certain fundamental decisions; that is what is meant here by "control." Or at least it may be said that equity investors are more likely to be concerned about control than are otherwise similarly situated investors, such as lenders, who are subject to less risk.

## C. DURATION AND SPECIFICITY

In a short-term relationship there may be relatively little need for elaborate rules specifying rights and obligations and the cost of supplying such rules may seem high in relation to their expected value. The rules established by common law and statute, though perhaps simple and basic, may seem adequate. As the expected duration of the relationship increases, the likelihood of changes in circumstances seriously affecting the relationship increases and the need for spelling out the consequences of those changes in circumstances may increase. At the same time, the value of the transaction is likely to increase and the cost of negotiation of tailor-made provisions will therefore decline in relation to that value. Thus, for example, where a firm borrows money for a short period of time, it can be expected that relatively little effort will be devoted to anticipation, discussion, and resolution of all sorts of "what if" issues. As the term of the loan changes to one of moderately long duration, it may seem increasingly worthwhile to expend that kind of effort.

## D. DURATION AND CONTROL

Starting with relatively short-term relationships, there may then be reason to expect specificity (that is, private rule elaboration) to increase with duration. At some point, however, that process may end. Predicting the future may be too intimidating a task; the fear of subjecting future generations to outmoded patterns may overwhelm the perceived need for clearly specified rights and obligations. In these circumstances the only viable alternative to specific constraints may be direct, generalized participation in control of the enterprise. This observation may contribute to an explanation of why the duration of business debt is not likely to be more than 30 or 40 years. If a longer relationship were contemplated, the lenders might become excessively concerned about the general nature of the firm's business. They might feel the need to protect themselves by sharing broadly in control. And generally speaking, lenders do not wish to and are not expected to do that.

## E. DURATION AND RISK

As the duration of an investment or relationship increases, certain risks associated with that investment or relationship may increase—though other risks may decrease. A short-term loan is not likely to be as risky as a long-term loan to the same borrower. On the other hand, a person who lends short-term and who expects to reinvest upon the termination of the loan period runs the risk that when the loan is repaid the opportunities for reinvestment may not be as attractive as they had been at the time the initial short-term loan was made. A long-term employment contract may reduce the employee's risk of unemployment; at the same time, to the extent that the employee's skills become specific to the firm, or to the extent that there are other barriers to relocation, such a contract may make the employee's fortunes dependent to some significant degree on the success or failure of the firm. While no strong correlations seem evident, a guarded, limited generalization may prove helpful: one should be alert to the possible relationship between risk and duration and to the opportunities for altering risk by altering duration.

### F.  RISK AND CONTROL—OWNERS AND EMPLOYEES

In the world envisioned by Adam Smith and his disciples, managers and (even more so) lower-level employees are inputs hired from a fungible set of similar inputs and plugged into the production process. Such inputs can easily be replaced. On the other side of the coin, the people supplying those inputs can easily sell their services to other firms. They are not subject to the risks of the firm—to the risks, that is, associated with ownership interests in the firm. If the owners of the firm exercise control unwisely and the firm is forced out of business, or if the owners decide, in their own interests, to alter the production process in a way that results in firing some employees, the employees simply fit themselves into the production process of another firm. They lose little by doing so. There is nothing unique about their relationship with the firm that makes them more valuable in one firm than in another. There is no danger of unemployment. Dislocation is not an issue; either it does not occur or the employee has been compensated for the risk that it might occur. In this world (which, to be sure, is a caricature of the neoclassical model) employees have no need for or interest in control. Control is associated with risk, which is in turn associated with owner-ship and ownership alone. By the same token, however, as we modify our view of reality we must modify our theory of control. As we begin to accept the notion that risks of the firm are at least to some degree risks for its employees, we must reexamine the question of the degree to which employees can be expected to insist on a share in control—or upon some guarantee of freedom from risk (a guarantee that the firm may be unwilling or unable to offer).

### XIII.  TRANSFER OF OWNERSHIP—PURCHASE SUBJECT TO DEBT AND OPTION TO PURCHASE

Suppose that Pamela does decide to sell the business (that is, the building or lease, equipment, inventory, good will, etc.) to Morris. As we have seen (Sec. X), this will probably require that Morris be willing and able to invest some money in the business—to make a downpayment. It will be useful at this point to consider two possible mechanisms by which ownership might be transferred—a purchase and sale subject to an indebtedness and an option to purchase.

## A.  PURCHASE SUBJECT TO DEBT

Suppose that Pamela and Morris agree that the price of the business is to be $100,000.  (Note that the value to Morris may be higher than the value to anyone else and that this differential, this value that is specific to Morris, will lead to the kind of bargaining situation illustrated in Section IX.)  Suppose further that Morris is to pay $30,000 at the outset and is to pay the remaining $70,000 at the end of one year.  This kind of arrangement would be unusual, in requiring payment of the full $70,000 at the end of a year, but it is not inconceivable.  Morris might well consider that if all goes well during the first year he will be able to borrow from a bank on a long-term basis and pay Pamela off.  That is, he might contemplate refinancing the debt.  Pamela might be willing to accept the deal on these terms and only on these terms.  She might, for example, feel that if Morris cannot do well enough to get outside financing and pay her off at the end of the year she will want to be in a position to enforce her debt and take back the business (or what's left of it).  (Let's assume that Pamela is willing to lend nonrecourse (Sec. II(C))—in other words, that Pamela will be content, in the event of default, to take back the business and let Morris off the hook for the remaining $70,000, regardless that the business may then be worth less than that amount.)  If Pamela and Morris enter into this deal, Morris's equity (Sec. II(E)) is $30,000 and his debt is $70,000.  The ratio of debt to equity is 7 to 3.  That is a relatively high ratio for this kind of venture.  Morris is subject to a high degree of risk of loss of his entire investment.  Pamela's position as creditor is also risky.  She is likely to want certain protections that she might not want if the equity "cushion" were larger and her position were consequently more secure.

## B.  OPTION TO PURCHASE

One of the problems that Pamela might contemplate at the outset of negotiations for the transfer of ownership is the difficulty of ousting Morris from possession of the business in the event of default.  It is one thing for Pamela and Morris to agree that if, at the end of one year, he fails, for any reason, to pay the $70,000, then Pamela is entitled to take over the business again.  It is quite another thing for Pamela to compel Morris to return control of the business to her if he resists.  Repossession of property, where there is any resistance, is not instantaneous, painless, or costless, by any means.  The law has erected a variety of barriers to such enforcement of a security interest in property; it has created various kinds of protections (mostly "procedural") for debtors.  Many of these protections cannot be waived by debtors.  The result may be that Pamela and Morris may not be able to enter into the deal that they want.  It might then be worthwhile for them to consider the possibilities for restructuring the legal aspects of the deal so as to avoid these debt-enforcement problems.  One possibility is to cast the deal in the form of an option to purchase. (An option to purchase—sometimes known as a call option—is one type of a broader category of options, which are increasingly common in business deals. We will address options of various kinds in greater detail in Chapter 6.) Morris might pay Pamela $30,000 at the outset in return for an option to buy the business at the end of one year for $70,000, plus her agreement to give him complete control over the business, plus the profits from it, for the one-year period. Assuming that such an agreement would be legally enforceable (one might be a bit concerned about the enforceability of the control aspect, since it divests the nominal owner of all control), it is functionally identical to the arrangement in the form of a purchase subject to debt, except possibly for the question of what happens at end of the year if Morris fails to come up with the $70,000. If the form of the arrangement is respected—that is, if the deal is treated as an option—then at the end of the year, if Morris does not pay, he simply does not become the owner. Pamela remains the owner and should encounter relatively little difficulty in taking over possession and control again. In other words, she takes over with little if any of the delay and expense involved in enforcing a debt. This might seem harsh for Morris, but remember that the potential avoidance of debt-enforcement expense would probably make Pamela willing at the outset to offer Morris a lower price or other more favorable terms than she would otherwise be willing to offer. The question remains, however, whether a court would disregard the form of the option arrangement and, looking to its sub-stance, treat it as a sale subject to a debt (with the creditor having a security interest in the business). That question is well beyond the scope of this book, but it can be said that there is at least a strong likelihood that this view of the substance would prevail over form. (The same question may arise where there is a dispute between Pamela and other creditors. That aspect is specifically covered by a provision of the Uniform Commercial Code defining the term "security interest." There are many cases in which courts have held that particular transactions taking the form of leases are, in substance, sales subject to a security interest. If the de facto security interest has not been "perfected" (generally, by complying with formal notice requirements), the purported lessor's claim to the property may not be superior to that of other creditors.)

One attribute of the deal structured as an option that makes it look like a purchase subject to debt is that the initial payment ($30,000) is relatively high and the second and final payment ($70,000) is likely to be substantially below market price, so there is a high probability that at the end of the year Morris will pay the $70,000 and become the owner in legal form. Suppose we change those financial relationships. Suppose, for example, that Morris pays $5,000 initially for the right to acquire the business one year later by making a second and final payment of $95,000. That looks more like a true option, since the probability of the payment of the $95,000 at the end of the year is much lower (because the purchase price is $25,000 higher). But note that that deal could be structured as a purchase subject to debt. That is, Morris could purport to "buy" the business for $5,000 subject to a "debt" of $95,000, nonrecourse, secured only by the business, and payable one year later. Disregarding questions of control and problems of enforcement, that would be functionally equivalent to an arrangement cast in terms of an option. The true option arrangement can perhaps then be thought of as a purchase subject to a very high ratio of debt to equity (here, 20 to 1) and with low costs of debt enforcement.[4]

## C.  LEASE WITH OPTION TO PURCHASE

Another alternative, related in form more closely to the option than to the sale with debt, is a lease with an option to purchase. Morris would lease the assets of the business from Pamela for one year for $30,000, payable in advance, with an option to purchase at the end of the year for (nominally) $100,000, with the $30,000 rental payment credited against the purchase price. This approach would avoid the need for special agreements regarding profits and control. At the same time, a lease seems to be an awkward device for transferring the use of inventory. (Remember, however, that we are only talking about differences in form. The substantive problems associated with inventory exist no matter what the form.) One conceivable advantage of the lease-with-option-to-purchase form is that some people may think that it looks less like a disguised purchase subject to debt than does the straight option; it may have the "feel" of a "true" lease because leases with options to purchase, with the rent applied toward the purchase price, are commonplace and (rightly or not) are not thought of as disguised sales subject to debt. A disadvantage of the lease approach is that a lessor may have as much difficulty regaining possession as does a person who sells subject to a debt obligation.

The significance of these speculations and observations can only be adumbrated in the present context. The basic principles suggested here are developed more fully in later chapters. (See, especially, Chapter 4, Sec. IV.)

---

[4] The depiction below may help. If not, ignore it.

|  | **Fixed Claim**<br>**Pamela** | **Residual Claim**<br>**Morris** |
|---|---|---|
|  | **Total Investment** |  |
|  | .....................$100,000..................... |  |
|  | **Debt Disguised as Option** |  |
|  | ..........$70,000 ................. $30,000 .......... |  |
|  | Debt | Equity |
|  | **True Option** |  |
|  | ................$95,000 ..................... $5,000 |  |
|  | Ownership | Option |

# Chapter 2

# PARTNERSHIPS AND LIMITED LIABILITY COMPANIES

## I. INTRODUCTION

### A. JOINT OWNERSHIP

We have seen in Chapter 1 that there are business firms that normally are, and sensibly may be, thought of as "owned" by a single individual, the sole proprietor. As we examine such firms more closely, however, we may find a complex set of relationships between and among that owner and other contributors of economic inputs such as suppliers, lenders, and managerial and other employees. We then can see that the nonowner contributors to the economic venture may to various degrees share in ownership attributes such as risk of loss, an interest in profits, and control. Certain of the significant attributes of ownership may also be shared by customers—particularly those who buy much of what they need from the firm and have few, if any, alternative sources of supply. Thus, we can see that since the concept of ownership is not as simple and clearcut as one might have thought, neither are the distinctions among various forms of organization. Indeed, one important objective of this book is to encourage a perspective that emphasizes the functional elements, such as risk and control, that are the common threads in the various forms of business organization that our legal system has developed, and, by the same token, to restrain a natural tendency to think of categories such as proprietorship, partnership, and corporation as airtight compartments.

In recent years the Limited Liability Company (LLC) has become the dominant form of legal organization for small businesses. For the present, however, the basic attributes of LLCs can best be understood by beginning with the more widely understood and more analytically developed legal and economic attributes of partnerships. The legal attributes of LLCs are described in Section X(B) of this Chapter.

Still, even in the most smoothly continuous spectrum, lines can usefully be drawn. Accordingly, at this point in our examination of business organization, while recognizing that the basic elements of one form of organization can gradually be modified to the point where it fades into the next, we can observe that as we turn from proprietorship to partnership we enter the realm of economic arrangements exhibiting clearly the characteristic of straightforward joint ownership. As we examine the law and custom of partnership organization, we will try to give definition to the notion of joint ownership of a firm and try to gain an appreciation of both the problems encountered in such a relationship and the solutions that may be available for coping with those problems.

## B.  RULES DESIGNED FOR SMALL FIRMS

As we proceed from proprietorship to partnership, we move from firms that tend to be very small, to somewhat larger ones.  As one might logically expect, when firm size increases joint ownership becomes more common.  Even so, partnerships[1] themselves ordinarily are engaged in economic ventures of relatively small scope.[2]  This means that partnerships are encountered most frequently in those sectors of the economy (such as legal services and retailing) where the optimal firm size is relatively small.  By the same token, partnerships are not found in those sectors (such as automobile manufacture) where the optimal firm size is large.  This observation is consistent with the observation that the law of partnership, whose major function is to prescribe the economic relationship among the partners, is geared to the needs and circumstances of small firms.  Partnership law is addressed primarily to the firm with a few partners, all of whom involved in the operation of the business and all of whom look to their share of the profits of the business as the return for their contributions of capital or services or both.  While the basic law leaves ample leeway for express agreements designed to alter the rules that it supplies for this kind of firm, one begins, at least, with rules designed for people who have decided that they want to enter actively into business with other people whom they know and with whom they think they can work.  The personal relationship typically is an essential element of the bargain that is manifested in the formation of a partnership.  This is not to say that partners usually like each other—only that ordinarily they know each other, that each has sized up the others, and that they have relied on their judgments about the people with whom they have embarked on the enterprise.  It is likely, moreover, that the partners will, at least to some significant extent, trust one another.  Not always, but usually.  In fact, it is a commonplace among people who have been in business that one is ill-advised to enter into business ventures with others unless one can trust and rely on them.  The attribute of reliance on the personal characteristics of one's partners seems to be present even in firms with a large number of partners, as, for example, in law and accounting.

---

[1] The term "partnership" is used here to refer to what lawyers sometimes call a "general partnership," the word "general" being attached to distinguish what may be thought of as the normal partnership from special forms such as the limited partnership (described in Sec. X(A) of this Chapter).

[2] The partnership form has, however, been used for some large firms, such as the major national and international accounting firms and law firms. In such firms, the basic partnership model tends to be modified by, for example, delegation of control to an executive committee and the use of various levels of partnership status, including "non-equity" partners.

One should not infer from these observations that basic partnership law is in all respects ideally suited to the needs and circumstances of all, or even most, small firms.  We will see that the basic partnership rules concerning the power of partners to bind the partnership (Sec. VIII(C)), personal liability (Sec. VII (D)), and duration and continuity (Sec. IX), do create problems for at least some small firms.  What is suggested, rather, is that partnership rules can best be understood if it is recognized that they seem to have been developed with small firms in mind.

The reader should also be warned that many small firms (sole proprietorships as well as partnerships) are organized as corporations or as limited liability companies (which are a recent development and reflect something of a hybrid of partnership and corporate law). In this Chapter and in Chapter 3 we will see some of the organizational considerations that might be thought to argue for use of the corporate form for a small firm.  In recent years, however, the choice of form has been affected most significantly by tax considerations.  We live in an Alice-in-Wonderland world in which, for example, an entertainer can achieve certain tax benefits only by engaging in the economically meaningless process of forming a fictional entity (a corporation) of which he or she becomes the sole owner (shareholder) and at the same time the sole "employee" (as well as Chair of the Board of Directors, President, etc.).

It is also worth noting that while partnership law is generally associated with small ventures, some large ventures may use the partnership form. For example, two or more large corporations may engage in a joint venture to manufacture and sell a new automobile or airplane. They might decide to set up a new corporation, in which they share ownership, to carry on the joint activity. It is also conceivable, however, that they might operate simply as a "joint venture" (which is a type of partnership). In such situations, the parties are likely to adopt a detailed agreement concerning their relationship with one another. To the extent they do so, the general rules of partnership law, which are mostly "default" rules (that is, rules that apply in default of express agreement), decline in importance. There will, however, inevitably be gaps in the express agreement. If these gaps become significant, they will be filled from the rules of partnership law.

## II.  REASONS FOR JOINT OWNERSHIP

### A.  JOINT OWNERSHIP VERSUS PURCHASED INPUTS

Much of the material in this chapter discusses problems that arise from division among two or more people of the ownership of a business enterprise—problems that are largely avoided when the entire ownership interest is held by one person.  To some extent these are problems of specifying with some precision (but not too much) the rights and obligations of joint owners.  But those problems are manifestations of more fundamental problems that arise from conflicts in goals as well as from dangers of shirking and cheating. Since many of these problems can be avoided or mitigated by concentrating ownership in one person, the question arises, why do we observe joint ownership? At first blush, this question may seem inane; the reasons for joint ownership may seem excessively obvious: we observe joint ownership when the efficient scale of an enterprise is large enough to require resources beyond those available to any single individual who might otherwise be able and willing to engage in it. A moment's reflection should reveal, however, that that kind of response is not sufficient. Physical resources can be bought with borrowed funds and human resources can be hired by paying salaries. Why is it, then, that one individual, with an interest in engaging in an economic activity, sometimes puts together the needed resources by taking on partners rather than by borrowing money or hiring providers of services? What determines the extent to which resources are accumulated by taking on partners and the extent to which they are accumulated by other means?

A full answer to these questions is well beyond the scope of this book. The brief sketch that follows is neither complete, definitive, nor rigorous. It is intended to be provocative, speculative, and suggestive. It is offered with the hope that, however tentative, an effort to explore the reasons why partnerships (and other such joint-ownership arrangements) arise will contribute to the reader's understanding of the nature of such arrangements and of their goals and problems. At the same time this discussion will reemphasize that there is no clear-cut line between sole and joint ownership; that consequently the question of why we observe joint ownership, though meaningful, may be misleading; and, in turn, that the person who seeks to understand, or to shape, a business organization should be wary of thinking of rigidly circumscribed organizational compartments.

## B. THE NEED TO ASSEMBLE AT–RISK CAPITAL

Let's begin with the kind of situation in which the co-owners will contribute capital [3] rather than services. Imagine, for example, that a person, Pamela, has spotted what she regards as an attractive opportunity to buy an existing grocery store. Pamela is familiar with the retail grocery business but does not want to manage the store and is content to continue to employ the present manager, Morris. The total purchase price for the store is $200,000. The maximum amount of her own funds that Pamela is willing or able to invest is $20,000. She can raise

---

[3] The word "capital" is used here to refer to productive capacity—to assets, both tangible (like buildings and machinery) and intangible (like patents), and to the money that may be part of the productive capacity or may be used to acquire it. The same word is used in other contexts to refer to a financial concept. (See Chapter 5, Sec. III(A).)

$150,000 by borrowing nonrecourse [4] (see Chapter 1, Sec. II(C)) from Walter, a wealthy individual, at an interest rate of 10 percent, if she gives Walter first claim on all assets in case of default. Walter is not willing to lend more because any additional investment would involve greater risk than he is willing to accept. Where and how will Pamela raise the additional $30,000?

Obviously, there will be a variety of institutional and individual sources for the kind of "venture capital" that Pamela seeks to raise. For simplicity, let's assume that Pamela has found two individuals, Abe and Bill, who have indicated that they might be interested in investing $15,000 each in the enterprise if the terms are attractive enough to them. Imagine what might happen if Pamela sought simply to borrow the $30,000 (nonrecourse) from Abe and Bill. If it is assumed that Walter will have first claim on all assets in case of default (that is, that Walter's claim is "*senior*"), Abe and Bill would be subject to a higher risk of loss than Walter. If Abe and Bill were willing to take this risk, but if their expected gain were limited to interest on the $30,000, the rate of interest that they would demand would be significantly higher than that paid to Walter. Suppose (arbitrarily, but not unrealistically) that the required rate would be 20 percent, or $6,000, per year—that is, that they would be willing to lend at that rate but not at any lower rate. That $6,000 per year would be a *fixed obligation,* payable without regard to the success of the business. It would constitute a heavy burden for Pamela and would subject her own investment to a level of risk that she might find unacceptable. (The phenomenon at work here is *leverage,* discussed in Chapter 1, Sec. II(F).) Besides, even if Abe and Bill were willing to accept a high risk of loss in return for the high rate of interest, and even if usury laws do not prohibit such a loan, Walter might object. The fixed obligation to Abe and Bill would create a significant additional risk of bankruptcy or of other legal proceedings associated with default. Such proceedings are costly and might adversely affect Walter's interests despite the seniority of his claim. Moreover, with a relatively small investment in the business, Pamela would have an incentive to engage in activities or adopt operating strategies involving high risks, with the thought that the gains would be hers and the losses would be borne mostly by the lenders. (See Chapter 4, Sec. III(A)(9) for a formal statement and proof of this proposition in a related context.) Clearly, this possibility would be of concern to Abe and Bill. Yet they might

---

[4] Though convenient for purposes of exposition, it is somewhat unrealistic to assume the availability of a nonrecourse loan in the small-business context contemplated by the hypothetical used here. If, however, Pamela has no significant assets beyond her $20,000 investment, recourse (that is, personal liability) would be of no value to the lender. Thus, a nonrecourse loan can be thought of as functionally equivalent to a loan with recourse to a person with no significant assets other than those invested in the business. Moreover, the analysis in text is relevant to larger-scale ventures, where the equity investment is likely to take the form of common stock in a corporation. That form of investment provides the same kind of protection against liability as does a nonrecourse loan. (See Chapter 3, Sec. III(D).)

consider that there is no feasible device for controlling Pamela's business decisions.

## C.  CONTROL FOLLOWS RISK

Assuming that some or all of these, and possibly other, considerations rule out the possibility of a loan from Abe and Bill, the alternative is some sort of arrangement in which Abe and Bill share in the risks of the business.  Instead of a fixed return of 20 percent, Pamela might offer them a share of profits with a possible rate of return far greater than 20 percent but no guaranteed annual payment.  There would be no fixed obligation and, therefore, no possibility of default.  There could be a requirement of repayment of the $30,000 at the end of some specified time period, but suppose that the deal settled upon by the parties does not include any such guarantee.  Suppose, that is, that the agreement reached is that Abe and Bill receive a share of the current earnings of the business, if any, and a share of any proceeds of its sale.  Abe and Bill will be subject to the same risks of loss and will have the same prospects for return as Pamela.  All three will have a *residual,* or *equity,* interest in the business.  The interests of Abe and Bill would then be aligned with those of Pamela.  But since Abe and Bill would be sharing in risks and returns, it would be natural for them to ask to share in control as well, and hard for Pamela to refuse.

Neither profit shares nor control, by the way, would of necessity be divided pro rata according to dollar contribution.  That is, even though Abe and Bill contributed, together, $30,000, or 60 percent of a total equity of $50,000, they would not necessarily receive 60 percent of the profits or 60 percent control.  Pamela might, for example, be able to insist on half the profits in return for her $20,000 contribution; or she might be required to settle for 30 percent.  She might receive the right to cast 3 votes on any business decision, with Abe and Bill limited to one vote apiece; or she might receive one vote, with each of them receiving one.  The division of gain (and loss) and control, in other words, would be subject to negotiation, with the outcome dependent not so much on any identifiable notion of fairness or custom as on the relative bargaining positions of the parties.  But whatever the allocation (within reason), once the parties agreed to share in gains and losses and in control, they would become joint or co-owners.  In fact, as we shall see (Sec. IV), whether they realized it or not, they would become "partners."

## D.  RESTATEMENT—AN EXTREME CASE

The point just made can perhaps be seen more clearly in the context of a more extreme (and therefore an unrealistic) example.  Suppose that Pamela wants to buy the grocery store for $200,000 but that she is willing or able to invest only $1,000.  She approaches Abe and Bill, seeking to borrow $199,000, nonrecourse.  Look at the situation from

the perspective of Abe and Bill. Suppose that the loan is to be repaid at
the end of one year. At that time, disregarding for the moment any
obligation to pay interest, if the business can be sold for more than
$199,000, Pamela will be entitled to retain the excess. If, on the other
hand, it is worth less than $199,000, Pamela can walk away from it and
the loss is Abe's and Bill's. Pamela stands to lose, at most, $1,000. Abe
and Bill can lose as much as $199,000 (plus the use of that sum for one
year). The chance of some loss to them is substantial. Assuming that
they continue to think in terms of a loan arrangement, the interest rate
that they will demand will be extremely high. Suppose that they
demand a rate of 50 percent (almost $100,000) for the one-year term of
the loan. At the end of the year Pamela in effect will have the option to
repay the $199,000 loan, plus the interest, a total of almost $300,000. If
it turns out that the business is worth less than that amount, however,
she can abandon it and Abe and Bill will become the owners. Given the
initial value, and the nature of the business, that outcome, with Abe and
Bill winding up as owners and Pamela losing only her initial contribution of $1,000, seems highly probable. In other words, it is highly
probable that all the gains up to almost $100,000 and all the losses
except for $1,000 will be Abe's and Bill's. Now, is it reasonable to
suppose that they will allow Pamela to have full control of the business?
Certainly not. For one thing, they may simply disagree with her about
how to maximize the value of the business; their perceptions and
Pamela's may be, as economists might put it, "asymmetric." In addition,
Pamela's position creates what is called a "moral hazard." This term
refers to the rational indifference that a person who is insured against
loss may have to a risk whose costs fall on others and the effect of that
indifference on the person's conduct. For example, a person fully insured
against loss from a fire may take less precautions against a fire than one
who is not. Here, because Pamela will receive the gains, but the losses
will be suffered by Abe and Bill, she would have an incentive to gamble.
That is a bad deal for Abe and Bill. (This idea is developed further in
Chapter 4, especially at Sec. III(A)(13).) Consequently, Abe and Bill are
likely to insist on at least some share of control in addition to almost all
of the prospective gain and loss. What will Pamela have? She will have
any gains in the value of the business above $299,000. Her position can
perhaps best be thought as of that of the holder of an option. She will
have the option to acquire the business at the end of the one-year term
of the loan by paying Abe and Bill $299,000. Functionally, Abe and Bill
are the "owners," not Pamela—even if the arrangement is cast in the
form of a loan. (See Chapter 1, Sec. XIII and Chapter 4, Sec. IV.) In
fact, a payment of $1,000 for the option is probably unrealistically low.
There is a more realistic treatment of the numbers near the end of
Chapter 5, following the development of some needed analytic tools. See
Chapter 5, Sec. III(O).

The example may also be unrealistic, and perhaps for that reason
misleading, in another respect. In the kind of setting evoked by the

example, it may well be that Pamela would be expected to contribute valuable services without being paid or at a low rate of pay. She may also have found an undervalued opportunity. Thus, the true value of the investment (including the value of her services) might be more than $200,000 and the equity might correspondingly be greater than $1,000. In that case, however, leverage that appears at first blush to be extreme is not in fact so, and the problem that is intended to be raised here disappears.

## E.  OTHER EQUITY–TYPE FORMS OF INVESTMENT

Let's return to the situation in which Pamela invests $20,000 and Abe and Bill each invest $15,000. It was argued that the arrangement that the three people are likely to settle upon will be the classic equity participation, with all three sharing, as joint owners, in risks, returns, and control. It may be helpful to describe very briefly some variations on that classic mode—variations that could provide Abe and Bill with an acceptable combination of return and risk without saddling Pamela with an unduly burdensome fixed obligation. One possibility would be a loan to Pamela from Abe and Bill with an option on their part to convert the loan into an equity interest. Abe and Bill might, for example, accept an interest rate of 10 percent if, in addition, they were given an option to buy (by cancelling the loan) some portion of the equity interest in the business within some finite period of time. This would give them a moderate assured return (a fixed periodic payment), plus some possibility of an additional gain if the business were successful (a residual return), plus a right to be repaid their initial contribution at some point in time if the business were not sufficiently successful to induce them to exercise the option (a contingent fixed payment). The option, giving them a share in the increase in the value of the business if such an increase should occur, would be accepted as a substitute for the additional interest that would be demanded on a straight loan. Abe and Bill would share with Pamela in the gains, but would be in a preferred position (compared with her) in the event of loss.

Another alternative would be for Abe and Bill to receive initially an equity interest combined with a right to demand that Pamela repurchase that interest at some fixed price. For example, in return for $30,000, Abe and Bill might acquire a 50 percent equity interest in the business with a right, at their option, to require that Pamela repurchase their interest at some price (either a fixed sum or an amount determined by a formula) at some specified time in the future. (This kind of arrangement is called a "put," since Abe and Bill would have the right to "put" their interest to Pamela.) Somewhat more concretely, Pamela might, for example, agree that upon demand by Abe and Bill at the end of five years, or upon termination or disposition of the business, if sooner, she would be required to repurchase their equity interest for the amount of the initial contribution, $30,000, plus some additional amount to take account of any profits that had been earned and not paid out (which would require some agreement on how to measure profits). The effect of this provision would be to reduce the risk of loss for Abe and Bill and to give them a convenient device for withdrawing their investment in the business if it did not increase in value. Presumably, they would, in return for the put, accept a lesser share in gains (that is, a lesser equity interest) or in control, or both. (The reader might, at this point, begin to think about what happens, if, at the end of the five years, Abe and Bill disagree on what they should do.) Puts are rarely encountered in the simple kind of situation evoked by the Abe–Bill–Pamela hypothetical, but their use is not uncommon in the larger and more complex ventures for which that hypothetical is intended to serve as a paradigm.

## F.  SUMMARY

This discussion of the reasons for joint or divided ownership can now be summarized, in terms more familiar in the business world. Capital can be contributed to firms in the form of equity (by owners) or debt (by lenders). (See Chapter 1, Sec. II(E).) Equity is the residual claim. It captures the big gains, if any, and is subject to a higher risk of loss than debt. As the amount of debt increases in relation to equity, the fixed obligation of the firm to pay interest increases, both because of the increase in the size of the debt and because of the increase in the rate of return demanded by the lenders. If the relative amount of debt were allowed to rise indefinitely, at some point the lenders would be subject to virtually all the significant risks of gain and loss of the business. They would, in effect, become owners, but without the control that goes with ownership. People (often acting through institutions such as banks) who wish to occupy the role of true lenders will insist that the business be financed with enough equity capital—with a large enough *"equity cushion"*—so that they can feel reasonably secure against risk of default and, possibly, so that they need not concern themselves with problems of control. Given the optimal size of any particular business, no one individual may be willing or able to provide the full amount of this required equity cushion. Two or more such equity investors will then be required to pool their resources. They will become joint owners or co-owners; that is, ownership will be divided between or among them. There are problems, or costs, of co-ownership, but if we assume that the optimal scale requires co-ownership then, by hypothesis, the benefits of increased scale outweigh these costs—otherwise the optimal scale, taking account of the costs of joint ownership would, by hypothesis, be smaller. (See Chapter 1, Sec. XI.)

## G.  THE ELEMENT OF PERSONAL SERVICES

We have seen that joint or divided ownership arises where one person is unwilling or unable to contribute the needed amount of equity capital.  The example that was used is, in fact, not as pure a case of capital contribution as one might like.  It was assumed that Pamela was familiar with the grocery business;  presumably that was a significant element of the entire arrangement.  Even though she was not to be the manager, presumably she was expected to contribute valuable services, at the very least in the form of advice and consent on important decisions.  Abe and Bill might have been expected to do the same, and, in fact, Pamela, Abe and Bill all might have been attracted to the idea of joint ownership because each valued the potential advice and the scrutiny that the others might have been expected to offer (out of their own personal interest in enhancing their own investment).

## H.  COMBINING CAPITAL AND SERVICES

There remains, however, another kind of situation, frequently encountered in small businesses, in which the element of services to the firm is not just part of the explanation of joint ownership but is, instead, the key element.  Often the person who actively manages the business is a partner and in many cases such manager-partners make little or no initial contribution to the partnership, other than the promise to perform services.  For instance, in the grocery store example that we have been using, there may be persuasive reasons why Pamela, Abe, and Bill would want Morris, the manager, to have a partnership interest, despite his inability or unwillingness to contribute any money or other tangible assets.  For one thing, as a partner Morris would share in the gains of the business.  The contributors of capital might well think that it is important for Morris to have some such share in profits as an incentive to devote to the business the kind of energy, imagination, and care that will maximize their own returns.  At the same time, they might be unwilling to pay Morris a fixed salary that is high enough to meet the competition for his services;  they might wish to reduce their own risks by minimizing the fixed salary obligations of the firm (especially if Morris is to have a long-term employment contract).  In other words, in order to have Morris bear part of the risks of the business, they might want to offer him a modest salary plus an additional payment contingent on success (measured by profit), instead of a higher fixed salary.  The objectives of providing an incentive and of having Morris share in the risks of the firm could be achieved without making him a partner;  a simple bonus provision would do the job.  But if Morris's compensation is to turn on the fortunes of the business, if he is thus to be subject to risks similar to those of the capital contributors, he is likely to want to share in control as well.  (Compare Chapter 1, Sec. VI(E).)  The combination of profit share and participation in control amounts to partnership status.  (See Sec. IV below.)  Such status may also provide Morris with a sense of belonging, of acceptance by the other participants in the venture, and of added prestige in the community—all of which may be of value to him and may lead to improved performance on his part.

Finally, it may be convenient for Morris to have the visible authority to act for the firm that is a legal concomitant of partnership status. Such authority can, to be sure, be granted to an agent, but communication to outsiders of the scope of an agent's authority may be a nuisance.

The other partners might be anxious to have Morris make at least a modest capital contribution, in order to be sure that he is sufficiently concerned not only about profits but also losses. On the other hand, he might not have the money (though they could lend it to him) and, even if he did, such an investment might make him more conservative than they would like. Assuming that Morris is not to make any capital contribution, the partnership agreement might provide that in the event of sale or liquidation of the firm, the capital-contributing partners would be entitled to recover their initial contributions first, with the excess then to be divided among all the partners according to their interests in profits.

Even if the capital contributors have no desire to make Morris a partner, he may insist on it. For example, suppose that it was Morris who spotted the opportunity to buy the store, and suppose that he is extremely optimistic about the possibilities of success. He is likely to think of the opportunity as belonging to him. If the opportunity is a good one, its value can be thought of as a capital contribution by him. Indeed, his initial instincts may be those of an entrepreneur who is seeking to "hire capital" from a group of passive investors (Pamela, Abe, and Bill). While recognizing the need for an equity "cushion" that is beyond his own capability, his attitude may be more like that of a borrower than that of a co-owner. Not only will he want to participate in control, he will be reluctant to relinquish any of it, though he may have little choice but to do so. Moreover, because of his optimism, he may attach a far higher monetary value to the profit-sharing element of the partnership interest than do the others. Suppose, for example, that he has been earning $25,000 per year and that he could earn the same amount (and no more) managing any of a number of other stores in the area. Now suppose that he estimates that the profits of the firm will be $40,000 per year, but Pamela, Abe, and Bill estimate that the profits will be $20,000 per year. Finally, suppose that the agreement ultimately reached is that Morris will receive an annual salary of $20,000 plus a 20 percent partnership interest. Morris will think that he has a compensation package worth $28,000 ($20,000 in salary plus 20 percent of the $40,000 profits that he expects); he is likely to think that he has a good deal. The others will think that the compensation package is worth only $24,000 ($20,000 salary plus 20 percent of $20,000 profits) and they too will think that they have a good deal. Everyone is happy—at the outset.

If it turns out that the profits are only $20,000, Morris will be disappointed. If he is a reasonable, mature person, free from neurosis and insecurity, he might accept that outcome as the consequence of a risk that he knowingly accepted and cannot complain about. He might then press on to the greater achievements of the future. If, on the other hand, he is like most of the rest of us ordinary folks, his disappointment might to some extent turn to discontent, even peevishness. He might be inclined to blame others for the unsatisfactory outcome. His attitude might sour and his performance might suffer. This is a real danger that is recognized by people with experience in the use of *performance provisions* (that is, provisions of an economic arrangement under which one's returns are based in part on the performance of the business).

### III.   NATURE AND SIGNIFICANCE OF "PARTNERSHIP"

### A.   NATURE

The remainder of this Chapter is devoted to a discussion of the various legal and economic characteristics of partnerships. It is by those characteristics that the concept of partnership is functionally, and most fully, defined. At this point, however, it may be helpful to offer a brief introductory description, beginning with the terse definition found in the Uniform Partnership Act (1914). The Uniform Partnership Act, or UPA, is a model statute that was drafted at the beginning of this century and approved by the Commissioners on Uniform State Laws, and with modest variations long ago became statutory law in every state except Louisiana. In 1994, the Commissioners adopted a revised Uniform Partnership Act, known as RUPA or, officially, after various revisions, as UPA (1997), which retains most of the core concepts of UPA (1914) but incorporates some significant changes. Even before the adoption of RUPA many states had amended their partnership statutes, in some instances extensively, and a number of others have recently adopted UPA (1997), though often with significant variations. Thus, wholly apart from varying state judicial interpretations, the law of partnership is not uniform. Still, there is a substantial core commonality of structure and rules. Because the elements of commonality are reflected in UPA (1914), and because most of the existing case law arose under UPA (1914), the focus here will be primarily on that older set of provisions.

Section 6(1) of UPA (1914) provides, "A partnership is an association of two or more persons to carry on as co-owners a business for profit." That is obviously not very helpful to a person who is not already familiar with the law. It does reflect the understandable reluctance of the drafters of the Act to offer much of real substance in a brief definition—a reluctance that should serve as a warning about the statements made in the remainder of this paragraph—and it does contain some clues for those who know what they are looking for. A partnership exists when two or more people have agreed ("association" implies a consensual arrangement), expressly or tacitly, to share in the profits and the control ("as co-owners") of a "business." Under the UPA, profit sharing alone is not enough. Thus, for example, a manager who is entitled by contract to a bonus consisting of a share of profits is not, by virtue of that fact alone, a partner. Where two people own real estate as joint tenants, they share in profits and are co-owners, but they are not partners unless the management of the property requires enough activity to constitute a "business." Where people are *engaged in a business,* however, they are partners if they *share in profits and control.* That is the very brief, very rough, imprecise rule-of-thumb definition of partnerships.

## B. SIGNIFICANCE

The significance of the existence of a partnership relationship lies in the fact that once such a relationship is found, that finding determines other, narrower issues. For example, if two or more people are found to be partners, then, as a matter of law, each may have the power to enter into contracts on behalf of the partnership. The obligations incurred under such contracts become the personal obligations of the other partners. Similarly, all partners are subject to liability for damages resulting from the negligent acts of other partners acting in the course of the business. Partners are entitled to share in profits and control. A host of rules relating to rights of creditors and to problems of termination of the business become applicable. Various important tax consequences ensue. And so forth.

## IV. FORMATION

### A. CREATION WITHOUT FORMALITY

A partnership relationship may arise without formality. No meetings need be held, no documents signed, no certificates filed, no fees paid. Indeed, people may become partners without realizing it. As we saw in the preceding section, people become partners when they agree to "carry on as co-owners a business for profit." (UPA (1914), Sec. 6(1).) The agreement may be tacit. A handshake, a nod of the head, or a course of action may make people partners. Despite the consensual nature of the relationship, however, the failure of the associates to label themselves "partners," or to think of themselves as belonging to a partnership, is irrelevant. If they share in the profits and in the control of a business they are partners as a matter of law and are subject to the rights and liabilities that flow from that status, like it or not.

### B. THE "SILENT PARTNER"

It is worth emphasizing that control does not necessarily mean active involvement. One of the most interesting figures in partnership law, in fact, is the "silent" partner—typically a person who has invested in a business in return for a profit share, and who reserves the right to, and to some extent may in fact, participate in major decisions, but who does not expect to participate in routine management decisions, may participate in no decisions at all, and may even be unaware of what is happening in the business for long periods of time. The fact of the person's financial interest in the partnership may be a secret from everyone except the other partners (indeed, such secrecy may be vital). Such a person is nonetheless a partner like any other for purposes, among other things, of personal liability for the debts of the partnership. The law simply does not distinguish between passive and active partners. (But see the discussion below, Sec. X, of a special kind of organization called a "limited partnership.") This may seem surprising, perhaps even unfair, but it is nonetheless a firmly embedded principle of partnership law—a principle found also in the closely related body of law dealing with agency. (See Chapter 1, Sec. VII(C)(2). As we shall see later in this Chapter, much of the law of partnership is a direct application of the law of agency.)

## C.  IMPLIED TERMS

Suppose that two people agree to enter into a business together, as partners, sharing control and gains and losses. Suppose further that they put nothing in writing; they simply shake hands to indicate that they have reached a general agreement. In all probability they will have spent considerable time discussing the nature and operation of the business but will have given little conscious consideration to a variety of conflicts and problems that might arise in their new relationship. There is a body of legal doctrine found in the Uniform Partnership Act (UPA), and in judicial decisions, that addresses itself to many of those conflicts and problems and serves in effect as an implied standard-form agreement of partnership in situations such as these. In many situations the rules supplied by the UPA are entirely adequate; an effort to provide tailor-made rules to fit the needs of the individual firm would not be worth the cost in time and money.

The fact remains, however, that the standard-form rules found in the UPA can produce unfortunate results—results that the partners would have rejected had they thought about the matter. For example, in the absence of an agreement to the contrary, if one partner wants to withdraw, he or she can insist that the other either buy his or her interest or that the business be liquidated (either through sale of the business as a going concern to a third party or through termination of the business with sale of individual assets). In some situations, a business may not be readily salable to a third person at a fair price and may have a considerable value as a going concern that would be lost in the event of a sale of assets. At the same time, the partner who wishes to continue may not be able to raise enough money to buy out the one who wishes to withdraw. Often, in this kind of situation, the parties will be able to reach a mutually satisfactory agreement—for example, spreading the payments to the withdrawing partner over some number of years. But amicable accord is not always possible. Animosity and greed, grudges and self-righteousness, not to mention ordinary differences of perspective, may contribute important elements to the problem. In retrospect it may then seem foolish, or at least unfortunate, that the partners had failed at the outset to work out and agree to a rule different from the one found in the UPA—for example, a rule providing a formula for determining the amount to be paid to the withdrawing partner and specifically permitting the amount to be paid in installments over some reasonable time. As previously suggested, however, the parties may reasonably believe at the outset that efforts to tailor the terms of their agreement to their own special needs and circumstances may not be worth the cost, taking account of the large number of problems that might arise and the remoteness in time or improbability of occurrence of many or most of them. A person might refrain from raising potential problems for fear of revealing a lack of confidence in the venture or of trust in the people participating in it. To the extent that they are deterred by costs or other considerations, partners (and people entering into other business arrangements) must, of course, accept the possibility of results inconsistent with those that they would have decided upon had they been forced to grapple with all significant problems at the outset. At the same time, legislators and judges may need to choose among various types of "default" rules—rules that try to produce the outcomes that the particular disputants would have chosen had they confronted the issue, rules that typical disputants would have chosen, or rules that will tend to force people to confront and resolve potential problems.

## D. TAILOR–MADE PROVISIONS

As the preceding discussion suggests, many of the partnership rules supplied by the UPA can be modified by the private agreement of the partners. For example, the partners might agree that the partnership will last for, say, five years instead of being terminable at the will of any partner, which is the UPA rule in the absence of agreement to the contrary. That may seem to be a simple issue to decide, but once the participants in a venture have started thinking about this seemingly simple issue, they are likely to become aware of a variety of related issues and will quickly perceive the difficulties of formulating a fair and sensible set of rules dealing with those issues. After they agree on a five-year term, for example, they might begin to think about what should happen if one of them dies or becomes incapacitated within the five-year period, about what should be done if they find that they need additional capital, and so on. It may occur to them that there are other problems that they may have ignored. While they well might conclude that such problems should be resolved only if, and as, they arise, quite possibly they will wind up seeking the advice of a lawyer. A competent, experienced lawyer will be painfully aware of a host of potential problems (revealed more fully in later sections of this Chapter) and of the inadequacy of some of the UPA solutions. The lawyer is likely to recommend a tailor-made agreement incorporated in some sort of written document. (That document will itself probably contain many standard provisions taken from a form book or developed by the lawyer over the years, or both.) Depending on the lawyer's own attitudes, on the personalities of the partners, on the size of the firm that is contemplated, and on many other factors, this written partnership agreement may be short and simple or long and complex.

### E.  "SPOILING THE DEAL"

One of the interesting and significant aspects of the process of drafting partnership agreements (and other business agreements as well) has to do with the concern often expressed by experienced lawyers that their efforts might "spoil the deal." One of the most important functions of the lawyer is to look beyond the days of heady optimism and mutual good will that may characterize the initiation of a business venture. The lawyer must bear in mind that as the needs of the parties and the nature of the business change, as the partners encounter issues of business strategy on which they cannot agree, as the firm confronts the often harsh vicissitudes of business existence, the rules that are laid down in the partnership agreement may become critical. There are choices about how these rules should be drafted and many lawyers consider that they should explain those choices to their clients. But this gets tricky, for if the would-be partners start worrying too much about the problems that might arise and become excessively concerned about the difficulty of solving them, they may become overly anxious and walk away from a venture that would have been good for them. Moreover, the parties may reasonably believe that they can trust each other to reach a fair and equitable resolution of any potential conflicts as they arise and that focusing on such problems at the outset may send a bad message about expectations of trust, cooperation, and fairness.

Suppose, for example, that all the partners expect to work in the business and to participate fully in management decisions. At the outset they may be in complete accord on who should do what and how the business should be operated. Given this state of mind, they may have ignored the question of what rules should apply in the event of disagreement. The lawyer might think that it is precisely his or her function to make the client or clients aware of that potential issue (among others). The lawyer might want the parties to choose between, say, a majority voting rule and a unanimity rule for resolving certain kinds of disputes. As the partners begin to focus on the choice, they may, for the first time, begin to be fully aware of the potential difficulties of co-ownership. One issue leads to another. Suppose, for example, that the parties agree on control by majority vote. They might then begin to worry about whether there should be some provision for allowing a dissatisfied dissenter to withdraw and, if so, at what price. (A lawyer may, by the way, represent more than one potential partner, and sometimes may represent all of them—for the obvious reason that hiring a separate lawyer for each partner would be too costly. This kind of role creates special problems for the lawyer in defining his or her obligations to people whose interest may conflict, who may at some future time want his help in seeking an advantage over other partner-clients, etc.)

Some lawyers think it is their responsibility not only to try to raise all the significant issues with which their clients may be confronted in the future but also to be sure that the clients understand those issues. Others will tend to pay less attention to such matters, fearing, as suggested, that it is too easy for the parties, because of their unfamiliarity with the law, or with business, to exaggerate the significance of the problems and, consequently, to forgo a business opportunity that the lawyer thinks they ought not to forgo. This kind of lawyer may express the idea by saying that he did not want to "spoil the deal." Other lawyers will tend more often to think that if raising issues and pointing to problems kills a deal then it deserves to die. Obviously there are no formulas to tell the lawyer how to act with respect to this basic issue of client-handling strategy. No two deals, no two sets of clients, and no two lawyers are alike. There is no widely agreed upon "correct" approach. What does seem plain, however, and what is most significant for our purposes, is that the phenomenon of widespread lawyer concern with the possibility of frustrating worthwhile business ventures reveals, first, the difficulty and complexity of the problems of organization of joint economic activity and, in turn, a belief by some experienced practitioners that excessive anxieties and antagonisms may be aroused by efforts to cope with such difficulties and complexities.

## F. THE PARTNERSHIP AGREEMENT AS A DRAFTING CHALLENGE

A related problem has to do with the uneasiness that some lawyers seem to feel about the task of drafting a partnership agreement, as compared with the task of "forming" a corporation. As has been suggested, the issues that arise in drafting partnership agreements can be quite challenging—for lawyers as well as for the clients. Some lawyers, believe it or not, are lazy or incompetent, or both. They seek to avoid challenges. If a partnership is to be formed, they will recognize that the final product probably will be a typed document that will have the appearance, at least, of having been devised by the lawyer, exercising his or her craft, with the special needs of the particular partnership in mind. This fact alone may make it difficult to avoid confronting the organizational issues. Not impossible, to be sure; some lawyers are quite capable of mindlessly pulling a form partnership agreement out of the drawer, filling in a few blanks, having it typed, and passing it on to the clients for signature as if it were the product of some serious effort to cope with their special problems. But it seems that lawyers are less likely to feel comfortable about taking such an approach with a partnership agreement than they are with the documents required for the formation of a corporation.[5] They are more likely, that is, to feel comfortable about producing an unmodified, standard-form corporation than an unmodified, standard-form partnership. Their attitude is reflected in the thought one sometimes hears expressed that forming a partnership is more difficult than forming a corporation. That expression implies that the issues that arise in the formation of a partnership somehow disappear if the organizational vehicle is, instead, a corporation. That is a delusion. Most lawyers are competent and conscientious and do not suffer from delusions. But it appears that some do. Perhaps the reason has something to do with the phenomenon of reification of the corporation. Partnerships are thought of as associations of human beings engaging jointly in a business venture. If the same human beings elect to form a corporation, rather than a partnership, in order to engage in the same venture, with the same objectives, there is a tendency to think that something significantly different has happened—that a new entity has arisen, with a life all its own. It is to this phenomenon that we will now turn our attention.

## V.  THE ENTITY AND AGGREGATE CONCEPTS

This Section is an inquiry into how people (including the people who have been responsible for developing and shaping the law) think about partnerships. More specifically, do people (and does the law) reify partnerships? Are partnerships endowed with existences of their own, separate from the individual existences of the partners? And what, if anything, is the significance of that question?

## A.  REIFICATION AND THE ENTITY–AGGREGATE DISTINCTION

As most readers will recognize (at least with the benefit of a few moments reflection) there is a very strong tendency in popular thought to reify corporations. This is particularly clear with a large organization such as General Motors. Indeed, it is difficult to think about such a firm without reifying it. It is easy to think in terms of General Motors turning out an automobile and quite a bit more difficult to think about workers, shareholders, executives, and others contributing various inputs that result in the production of the same automobile. Corporations like General Motors are large and complex. With smaller organizations, like most partnerships, reification is a less significant phenomenon.

[5] The reader is warned that this statement would not be accepted by all lawyers and is based solely on the authors' casual empiricism (that is, on conversations with a relatively small number of lawyers over the years).

Correspondingly, the law of partnership exhibits much less tendency to treat partnerships as entities separate and distinct from their owners than does corporate law.  Commentators are prepared to state flatly that corporations are separate entities.  Not so with partnerships; legal commentators have long debated the question whether a partnership is best thought of as a separate entity or, instead, as an aggregation of partners.  In the language of the legal commentary on partnerships, the question becomes, is the partnership an *entity* or an *aggregate*?  The answer is that under the UPA (1914) the issue was left unresolved and sometimes the partnership is treated one way, sometimes the other. The RUPA (Sec. 201), by contrast, expressly adopts the position that a "partnership is an entity," though some of its provisions reflect the aggregate theory (for example, Sec. 801, which provides that a partnership at will dissolves whenever any partner elects to withdraw (that is, to "dissociate")).

## B.  WHO CARES?

At this point a reader untutored in the law of partnership might well ask, who cares?  Is the entity-aggregate distinction of purely metaphysical significance?  The answer is that the distinction can have important legal consequences.  For example, suppose that a firm (note the reification here) organized as a partnership wants to sue another such firm for breach of contract.  Must the individual partners of the plaintiff firm sue the individual partners of the defendant firm, as the aggregate approach would dictate?  Or can the plaintiff partnership in its name sue the defendant partnership in its name, as the entity approach would allow?  The answer to this question might be important in resolving issues relating to matters such as service of process and jurisdiction.

Still, one may wonder why we need be concerned with the entity-aggregate distinction. Why not, for example, simply decide directly the various questions relating to how a lawsuit is to be filed?  The UPA (1914) adopted neither the entity nor the aggregate approach. And, as it happens, the question of suing in the firm name was resolved not in the UPA but, in most states, by other legislation. Most other issues that could be resolved by adopting generally either the entity or the aggregate view were in fact resolved by specific rules under the UPA. The same is true in tax law, where there is no consistent theme and most issues are resolved by express statutory provisions, some consistent with the entity and others with the aggregate approach. Thus, it is clear as a matter of experience as well as logic that one can resolve problems of partnership law without taking a position on the entity-aggregate issue. The fact remains, however, that where issues are not resolved by statute, courts often do rely on one concept or the other in reaching their results. Moreover, it seems fair to say that an awareness of the concepts may help to organize one's thinking about issues.

## C. AN ILLUSTRATION

The following example may provide a sense of how entity-aggregate thinking may offer useful insights into problems of partnership law. Suppose that Pamela and Morris decide to form a partnership to own and operate a grocery store. Pamela is to contribute $50,000 in cash toward the purchase price of the store. Morris will contribute no cash but will agree to provide services as manager of the store, without salary, for three years. Assume that the value of Morris's services for three years is $50,000 and that Morris and Pamela are to be equal partners (that is, that each is to be a 50 percent owner). At the outset the partnership will have two assets—the $50,000 cash contributed by Pamela and the $50,000 worth of services that Morris is obligated to contribute. The total value of the partnership should be $100,000.

Now let's look at the situation from Morris's perspective and ask, just what is it that he has, now that the partnership has been formed? If we were to take an entity approach, we might say that he has a 50 percent interest in a partnership and that that interest is worth $50,000. We might then conclude, for example, that "therefore" he has income of $50,000 for purposes of the income tax laws (having received an asset—the partnership interest—worth $50,000 as an advance payment for his services). The word "therefore" is in quotes to alert the reader to the fact that all we have done is adopt an entity approach. We have given no reason for doing so and thus have provided no reason for the tax result. If we could say that partnership law generally does treat partnerships as entities, then we would have a reason, but that is not the case.

One who is not sensitive to the entity-aggregate issue might unthinkingly adopt the entity result just described. The thought process associated with reification of the business, with treating it as a separate entity, seems to involve two phenomena: (a) the business is treated as something separate from its owners, as having an existence of its own, and (b) the assets are thought of as a bundle rather than as specific separate items. A person who is sensitive to the possibility of conceptualizing business relationships in the more complex aggregate form would at least be aware of an alternative way to look at the situation and will see another possible outcome. Under the aggregate approach, Morris would not be thought to own an interest in a partnership. Instead, he would be thought to own a half interest in each of the assets of the firm (note, again, that by using the word "firm" we are relying on an entity concept). That is, under the aggregate approach, Morris would be seen as owning a half interest in the $50,000 of cash and a half interest in his own obligation to provide services. Under this approach we might then conclude that he has sold half his services for $25,000 and has retained half his services and that he should therefore be taxed on only $25,000.

Issues like the one just described arise repeatedly in the law, especially in tax law. It is possible to resolve such issues without reference to the entity-aggregate distinction, but that distinction often seems helpful.

## VI.   FIDUCIARY OBLIGATION

### A.   FIDUCIARY OBLIGATION—A LEGAL DUTY OF FAIRNESS

A fundamental tenet of the law of partnership is that members of a partnership must treat each other fairly in matters relating to the activities of the partnership. This principle of fairness is referred to in a large body of partnership case law as the "fiduciary obligation" or "fiduciary duty" of partners. The idea that partners must treat each other fairly may seem self-evident or trivial, or both. After all, how can one argue against fairness? But note the far different approach sometimes taken toward the relationship between buyer and seller, reflected in the phrase "buyer beware" (caveat emptor). The attitude of the law of partnership is that people should be able to trust their partners, that they should not have to be on their guard constantly to protect their interests. This is not to say that each partner, in the process of negotiating the terms of the partnership relationship, cannot seek to maximize his or her interests. Private arm's-length agreement—explicit, implicit, or assumed—is at the core of partnership law; the UPA itself can be seen as a set of "default" provisions (that is, provisions applied in default of particularized agreement by the partners). (See Sec. IV(C) above.) Moreover, what is fair depends heavily on what the parties intended or expected, so that to some considerable degree fairness is a function of agreement. But fairness also seems to have a life of its own, establishing what is at least a strong presumption that partners should behave toward one another according to the golden rule, not the law of the jungle. In fact, fiduciaries may in some circumstances be obligated to take affirmative steps to provide advantages to those to whom they owe their fidelity. Fiduciary obligation or duty is also found in the law of agency (see Chapter 1, Sec. VIII(E)) and in corporate law (see Chapter 3, Sec. IV(C)), where the customary descriptive phrase is "duty of loyalty." (Bear in mind that much of the law of partnership and of corporations is a direct application of the law of agency, as must be so since partnerships and corporations are abstractions that can only act through their agents.)

Like the golden rule or any other general guide to fair conduct, the principle of fiduciary obligation is vague and amorphous. While in some instances it may provide clear answers to specific issues, in others it does not. One can, perhaps, usefully go a bit beyond the simple admonition, "be fair." For example, the United States Supreme Court thought it helpful to offer the following list of "shall nots" in partnership dealings:[6]

---

[6] Latta v. Kilbourn, 150 U.S. 524, 541, 14 S.Ct. 201, 207–208, 37 L.Ed. 1169 (1893).

[It is] well settled that one partner cannot, directly or indirectly, use partnership assets for his own benefit; that he cannot, in conducting the business of a partnership, take any profit clandestinely for himself; that he cannot carry on the business of the partnership for his private advantage; that he cannot carry on another business in competition or rivalry with that of the firm, thereby depriving it of the benefit of his time, skill, and fidelity without being accountable to his copartners for any profit that may accrue to him therefrom; that he cannot be permitted to secure for himself that which it is his duty to obtain, if at all, for the firm of which he is a member; nor can he avail himself of knowledge or information which may be properly regarded as the property of the partnership, in the sense that it is available or useful to the firm for any purpose within the scope of the partnership business.

But even this statement, while nicely suggesting some aspects of partnership activity that can lead to problems, seems to add little of substance to the underlying notion expressed by words like "fairness," "honesty," "good faith," and "loyalty." Outcomes in decided cases can be recited to provide examples of conduct that has been found to be on one side of the line or the other. Yet the line remains unclear, the vagueness remains—perhaps unavoidably so, since the principle is designed to cover situations of such wide variety that it would be impractical to try to anticipate and provide clearer rules even for those most likely to occur. Greater specificity may not be worth the cost.[7]

Difficulty is encountered not only in defining precisely the legal content of fiduciary obligation, but also in determining its economic functions and effects. This book is not the right place for anything approaching a comprehensive statement on either the legal or the economic issues. It does seem appropriate, however, to suggest somewhat more concretely the kinds of issues that might arise and some of the paths that a comprehensive study might follow. This will be done here by examining questions relating to the extent to which partners are required to share with one another business opportunities that come to their attention.

[7] UPA (1997) (Sec. 404) attempts to respond to some degree to "the desire to confine broad statements of strict fiduciary standards." (See Comment to Sec. 404.) It divides fiduciary obligations into two categories, duty of loyalty and duty of care. (The discussion in text above focuses exclusively on duty of loyalty.) As to duty of loyalty, Sec. 404(b) lists three types of fiduciary (trustee-like) obligations, including the obligations not to appropriate partnership property or opportunity, not to represent a person with an interest adverse to that of the partnership, and not to compete with the partnership. As to other obligations, Sec. 404(d) requires that a partner act consistently with "good faith and fair dealing," and Sec. 404(e) provides, "A partner does not violate a duty or obligation under this [Act] or under the partnership agreement merely because the partner's conduct furthers the partner's own interest." As to duty of care, UPA (1997) (Sec. 404(c)) imposes liability on a partner only for "gross negligence or willful misconduct" in conducting or winding up the partnership business. Sec. 103(b) imposes modest limitations on the freedom of partners to vary the duty of care and the duty of loyalty by agreement.

## B.  ILLUSTRATION:  THE SCOPE–OF–BUSINESS PROBLEM

Imagine that there is a firm consisting of two people, Matthew and Susan, engaged in the real estate brokerage business (that is, in the business of earning commissions by acting as agents for others in the purchase and sale of real estate).  We can begin with an easy case. Suppose that one day Matthew is sitting alone in the firm's office and a stranger enters, seeking to list for sale a piece of property of great value. Suppose that Matthew knows of a buyer for the property.  Plainly he is not entitled to arrange the sale on his own and keep the commission entirely for himself.  The opportunity belongs to the firm, as does the commission.  This result is one that seems to flow naturally from the fiduciary obligation.  Since the function of that obligation is to effectuate the presumed intent of the parties in the absence of any pertinent express agreement, the result could, to be sure, be altered by such agreement.  One could perhaps conceive of the partners agreeing in advance that any opportunity presented to either one of them, while alone in the office, would be his or hers to exploit for his or her own benefit.  But in the case of a group engaged in the real estate brokerage business it is difficult to see what significant elements of partnership would be left if such a provision were adopted.  The reason for forming a partnership is to achieve the advantages of joint activity.  Once the partnership is formed, it will generally be impossible to associate particular returns with particular contributions of individual partners.  If such separation were feasible, the economic activity could be organized across markets rather than within a firm.  (See Chapter 1, Sec. V.)  All the problems of joint activity could be avoided.  In the Matthew–Susan kind of situation it is conceivable that the two people might have agreed initially simply that they would share the cost of office space and would otherwise act independently.  But when they form a partnership they reflect a mutual decision that it will be to their advantage to contribute jointly to an outcome in which they will share jointly.  Thus, in the situation in which the stranger walks into the office, who is to say whether that customer is there because of Matthew or because of Susan, when it may well be that it was the reputation of the firm established over many years that attracted the customer?  So the benefits of access to the customer belong to the firm, not to Matthew alone.

Now consider a more difficult problem.  Suppose that Matthew learns of an opportunity to invest in a parcel of real estate.  Can he properly buy that parcel solely on his own account or must he at least offer to Susan the opportunity to invest with him?  (This is the basic situation presented in the *Latta* case, quoted above.)  It seems quite plain that we cannot sensibly answer the question without having more facts.  Indeed, one of the common characteristics of judicial decisions resolving problems of fiduciary obligation is that the outcome frequently is said to (and does) require a careful examination of all the facts and circumstances. In the present hypothetical case, one relevant fact might be how Matthew learned of the opportunity. One can readily perceive, for example, why it might be significant that he learned of the opportunity from a stranger who wandered into the firm's office rather than from a cousin while on vacation in another city. Among other potentially relevant facts would be whether Matthew and Susan had previously shared in similar opportunities. In examining such facts, the focus of the inquiry likely would shift from the broad concept of fiduciary obligation to a somewhat narrower one—namely, the scope of the partnership business. The question would become whether the scope of the partnership was broad enough to include the sharing of information about investment opportunities or whether it was limited strictly to brokerage activities. That issue would turn on the intent or expectations of the parties, which, in the absence of express agreement, must be inferred (here we go again) from all the facts and circumstances.

If the inquiry is to take this form, one can properly question whether the principle of fiduciary obligation plays any significant role in the decision-making process. At best, that principle, at least in cases that can be narrowed to an inquiry into the scope of the partnership business, involves an element of circularity. Partners are obligated, as fiduciaries, to behave in ways that are consistent with their expectations or intentions as to the scope of the partnership. But people entering into partnership relationships presumably have a general expectation or intention that they will treat each other fairly, as required by the principle of fiduciary obligation. In other words, it is fair to effectuate expectations or intentions, but part of the set of expectations or intentions is to be fair.

Despite the problem of circularity and the significance of particular facts and circumstances, the principle of fiduciary obligation probably does make some contribution of its own to the decision-making process, even in scope-of-the-business cases. For example, in the famous case of Meinhard v. Salmon, involving the scope of a real estate venture, Judge Benjamin Cardozo began his analysis with the following soul-stirring language:[8]

> [Partners] owe to one another ... the duty of finest loyalty. Many forms of conduct permissible in a workaday world for those acting at arm's length, are forbidden to those bound by fiduciary ties. A trustee is held to something stricter than the morals of the market place. Not honesty alone, but the punctilio of an honor the most sensitive, is then the standard of behavior. As to this there has developed a tradition that is unbending and inveterate. Uncompromising rigidity has been the attitude of courts of equity when petitioned to undermine the rule of undivided loyalty by the "disintegrating erosion" of particular exceptions. ... Only thus has the

---

[8] 249 N.Y. 458, 463–64, 164 N.E. 545, 546 (1928).

level of conduct for fiduciaries been kept at a level higher than that trodden by the crowd. It will not consciously be lowered by any judgment of this court.

This language has been criticized as going too far in stating not only what the law is but what it ought to be. But however excessive the rhetoric may be, one can scarcely doubt its potential capacity to affect the outcome of a particular case, especially where specific evidence of intent is sparse.

## C. ECONOMIC AND OTHER EFFECTS

Judge Cardozo seems to have urged the adoption of a broad concept of the scope of partnership activity. Since such a concept or rule is designed to achieve fairness, by effectuating the presumed intent of the parties, it is the sort of rule that applies only in the absence of express agreement. Even so, it does not follow that the rule has little capacity to promote worthwhile goals or to do mischief. If the rule is inconsistent with what most people would want upon reflection about the matter, then to the extent that such people are aware of the rule they will be forced to go to the trouble (otherwise avoidable) of agreeing upon a different (narrower) one, and to the extent that they are unaware of the rule they may wind up with outcomes that are unfair or disruptive or both.

What the parties are likely to want will depend largely on economic effects. To see what some of these economic effects might be, let's return to the example of the Matthew–Susan real estate brokerage firm. Suppose that Matthew is a serious stamp collector and that he has been able over the years to earn a modest income, in his spare time, by trading in stamps. Is it likely that he and Susan would want to include the stamp-trading activity within the scope of the partnership business? It would by no means be wholly senseless for them to want to do so. If Matthew were forced to share his stamp-trading profits with Susan, he might be inclined to devote less attention to stamps and more to the real estate business. One function of a fiduciary obligation with a broadly defined scope of business is just that—to induce the person subject to the obligation to devote more whole-hearted energy to affairs benefiting the partnership. Without such an impetus for Matthew to devote his efforts to the real estate business, Susan might not be willing to enter into business with him. On the other hand, if the terms of the partnership agreement include stamp trading within the scope of the business, presumably Susan will be required somehow to compensate Matthew for his skill in stamp trading and for gains attributable to the use of what he might think to be his spare time. In other words, Susan will presumably be required to buy a share of his stamp-trading time, energy, and skill. It seems unlikely that she will want to make such an investment. The two activities of real estate brokerage and stamp trading seem quite separate and distinct from one another. Since a person who attaches a high value to membership in a real estate firm may place a low value on membership in a stamp-trading firm with the same partner, a tie-in of the two activities is likely to produce less-than-optimal results. This is probably the strongest reason for the intuitive sense that most people would not want such a tie-in and that it would therefore be improper for a court, in the absence of express agreement, to include stamp-trading activities within the scope of a real estate brokerage business.

The same kinds of considerations will be at work in situations in which one's intuition about the sensible result is not nearly so strong. Suppose again that Matthew and Susan have decided to enter into a real estate brokerage partnership and that Matthew is a man of considerable wealth, with substantial investments in real estate. He and Susan might well be concerned about the extent to which, if at all, they should agree to share information received about real estate investment opportunities. There are, on the one hand, strong reasons for adopting a rule broadly requiring the sharing of all information, no matter how acquired. The principal effect of such a rule would be to shift Matthew's incentives away from the pursuit of his own interests and toward the pursuit of firm business. Moreover, a broad rule would reduce or eliminate problems of distinguishing between information belonging to the firm and information belonging to the individual. On the other hand, Matthew might have valuable sources of information about investments and a valuable skill in exploiting that information. For sharing those sources and that skill with Susan, he might demand a price beyond what she is willing to pay.

In this kind of situation it is not easy to predict what rule the parties would be likely to adopt. Even after serious thought about the issue, they might well be content to rely on the rule of fiduciary obligation supplied by the law in the absence of express agreement, thereby in effect allowing the outcome in case of dispute to turn on all the facts and circumstances and on a vague, general concept of fairness. It may be tempting to suppose that the law should require a high degree of sharing of information and opportunity, on the naive theory that one cannot go too far with openness in dealings among partners. But if the rule supplied by the law is inconsistent with what the parties would have wanted (as the rule stated by Judge Cardozo may be) then, as has previously been suggested, the parties will be forced (needlessly) to engage in possibly costly efforts to shape a rule fitting their true intentions. If they fail through ignorance to do so, then the possibility of unfair outcomes arises.

## D.  PROMOTERS—DRAFTING AROUND THE RULE

Often a partnership may arise as a result of the efforts of a person who finds an investment opportunity and sets up and manages the partnership. Such a person is often referred to as a promoter, a term which, in this context, does not carry negative connotations. The promoter may become a member of a partnership with one or more passive partners who are brought in as investors. The active partner (the promoter) may be involved in many partnerships with different sets of investor partners and may, in addition, have investments not shared with others. In such situations, the active partner is likely to be particularly concerned about the dangers created by the principle of fiduciary obligation. For example, one type of investment activity that presents obvious problems of fiduciary obligation for promoter-partners is exploration and drilling for oil and gas. Just to suggest some of those problems, suppose that a partnership consisting of one active partner and a set of passive investor partners leases a parcel of property and drills for oil. If oil is found, adjacent land may rise in value. What are the obligations of the active partner to the passive investors with respect to opportunities to invest in such land, either before or after discovery of oil on the initial parcel? The promoter may consider that it is not feasible to operate subject to a burden of sharing such opportunities with any existing investment group. Moreover, the promoter may view such opportunities as part of his or her compensation for promotional services. For these and other reasons, the promoter may include in the partnership agreement language like the following (taken from real life):

> The [promoter] and each [investor] may, notwithstanding the existence of this agreement, engage in whatever activities they choose, whether the same be competitive with the partnership or otherwise, without having or incurring any obligation to offer any interest in such to the partnership or any party hereto. Neither this agreement nor any activity undertaken pursuant hereto shall prevent the [promoter] from engaging in the exploration for and production of oil, gas and other minerals individually, jointly with others, or as a party of any other association to which the [promoter] is or may become a party, in any locale and in fields or areas of operation in which the partnership may likewise be active, or require the [promoter] to permit the partnership or any [investor] to participate in any of the foregoing.

Language of this sort is not uncommon in oil and gas ventures. While phrased to apply equally to the promoter and the investors, its practical intent, and effect, is to relieve the promoter of the obligations that might otherwise be imposed by the principle of fiduciary obligation. A note of caution should, however, be added. The quoted provision seems implicitly to say that nothing that the promoter might do in the way of making related investments can be challenged on the basis of unfairness. To the extent that it goes that far, its legal efficacy is doubtful. Courts do not readily accept the notion that parties intend to allow themselves to be treated unfairly.[9] While the agreement surely makes an important

---

[9] See Wartski v. Bedford, 926 F.2d 11, 20
(1st Cir.1991):

contribution to the definition of what is fair, there are limits. For example, it is at least questionable that this language would protect a promoter who deliberately concealed prior ownership of immediately adjacent land that figured to be on top of the pool that the partnership was hoping to find.

We can note several interesting and important aspects of the problem of fiduciary obligation in the kind of situation revealed by the oil and gas venture. First, if we look at the venture from the perspective of the promoter, we can see that there may be compelling, entirely legitimate economic considerations that require a restrictive rule on the obligation to share information or opportunities. Second, the vagueness of the rule of fiduciary obligation may require the adoption of express agreements that seem to go too far in denying any such obligation. The complexities of business life that argue for a broad, vague rule of fiduciary obligation also argue for the kind of sweeping abnegation seen in the above quoted provision. Greater precision may be impractical. And finally, investors confronted with such a provision might be willing to accept it if, and only if, the promoter's reputation is good—only if the promoter has a good record (or, in a misguided metaphor often used in the business world, a good "track record"). By the same token, the promoter has a strong economic incentive to protect and preserve reputation and this incentive may be one of the most important factors bearing on the terms of the agreement that the parties are likely to find acceptable.

## E.  SUMMARY

To recapitulate, the fiduciary obligation is a vague principle designed to achieve fair results by effectuating the presumed intention of members of a partnership as to matters on which they have not reached any express agreement. The vagueness is probably unavoidable because the principle must be applied to a virtually infinite variety of subtly differing situations. Given this variety and the objective of effectuating presumed intentions, application of the principle will usually require a

[E]ven if the partnership agreement can be interpreted as defendant claims, it cannot nullify the fiduciary duty owed ... to the partnership. The fiduciary duty of partners is an integral part of the partnership agreement whether or not expressly set forth therein. It cannot be negated by the words of the partnership agreement....

The court then quotes as follows from a corporate-law case presenting the same issue:

"Exculpatory provisions of corporate articles create no license to steal. They do no more than to validate otherwise invalid agreements if such agreements are shown to be fair." Irwin v. West End Development Co., 342 F.Supp. 687, 701 (D.Colo.1972), affirmed in part and reversed in part on other grounds, 481 F.2d 34 (10th Cir.1973), cert. denied, Vroom v. Irwin, 414 U.S. 1158, 94 S.Ct. 915, 39 L.Ed.2d 110 (1974).

Id.

Section 103(b)(3) of UPA (1997) provides that the duty of loyalty cannot be eliminated by agreement, but "(i) the partnership agreement may identify specific types or categories of activities that do not violate the duty of loyalty, if not manifestly unreasonable."

detailed examination of the peculiar facts and circumstances of particular cases.  Despite the obvious importance of facts and circumstances, it seems fair to suppose that the general principle does set a tone that has a significant impact on the outcome of disputes.  The substantive content of the principle of fiduciary obligation will also have important economic consequences.  For example, a rule that broadly defines the obligation to share the gains from one's activities may significantly affect the allocation of time among various possible activities and may, at the same time, act as a barrier to the formation of partnerships.  The problems encountered in cases in which the principle of fiduciary obligation is invoked often reflect both the underlying conflict in economic goals and constraints and the practical limitations on our ability to anticipate and provide for future events.  A lawyer may be reluctant to draw attention to the underlying conflicts for fear of "spoiling the deal." (See Sec. IV(E) above.)  This is not to deny, however, that it is often feasible and wise to anticipate and resolve in advance some of the concrete problems that are most likely to arise.

## VII.  CONTRIBUTIONS, ACCOUNTS, AND RETURNS

### A.  CAPITAL ACCOUNTS

Suppose that Abe, Bill, Pamela and Morris have formed a partnership for the acquisition and operation of a grocery store.  Abe and Bill each are to contribute $15,000 and Pamela $20,000, in cash or in property to be used in the business.  Morris will contribute neither cash nor property but will agree to manage the store for five years and will receive a salary slightly lower than what he might earn elsewhere.  If the partnership follows customary bookkeeping patterns, its books will show the following information under a heading that is likely to be called "Capital Accounts":

|         |          |
|---------|----------|
| Abe     | $15,000  |
| Bill    | 15,000   |
| Pamela  | 20,000   |
| Morris  | 0        |
| Total   | $50,000  |

Note that, though Morris's obligation to provide services at a below-market rate will presumably be of value to the firm, this value ordinarily will not appear as an asset on the firm's books and, correspondingly, Morris's capital contribution will be zero.  In the absence of an agreement to the contrary, if the business were sold for cash, each partner would be entitled to receive an amount equal to his or her capital account, if available.  Any excess or deficit would be shared in accordance with each partner's share of gain and loss (a point to be illustrated below).

Capital contribution does not necessarily control the sharing of gain and loss, and shares of gain may differ from shares of loss. For example, our four partners could agree that each will be entitled to an equal 25 percent share of any profits, despite the difference in initial contribution. Indeed, this is the result that will be provided by the Uniform Partnership Act (Sec. 18(a)) in the absence of an agreement to the contrary. At the same time, and again in the absence of an agreement to the contrary, no partner will be entitled to interest on his or her capital account. Losses might be allocated equally among the partners (again, the result in the absence of express agreement) or might be allocated first pro rata among the contributors of initial capital, to the extent of such capital, and then, perhaps, equally among all partners. The effect of all of these rules will be illustrated below, but first it is useful to examine how capital accounts might change.

Suppose that all profits and losses are to be shared equally, and suppose that at the end of the first year of operation the profit (after the payment of Morris's salary) is $20,000, or $5,000 per partner. One way of recording this outcome would be to adjust the capital accounts, which would then appear as follows:

|         |          |
|---------|----------|
| Abe     | $20,000* |
| Bill    | 20,000   |
| Pamela  | 25,000   |
| Morris  | 5,000    |
| Total   | $70,000  |

\* $15,000 initial capital plus $5,000 profit share.

If, on the other hand, the firm experienced a loss of $20,000 in its first year of operations, the capital accounts would be:

|         |          |
|---------|----------|
| Abe     | $10,000  |
| Bill    | 10,000   |
| Pamela  | 15,000   |
| Morris  | (5,000)  |
| Total   | $30,000  |

(Parentheses around a number indicate that it is a negative amount.) If, at this point, the business were sold for exactly the amount of the total capital accounts, $30,000, Morris would be required to contribute $5,000 and the resulting total, $35,000, would then be distributed $10,000 each to Abe and Bill and $15,000 to Pamela. This result may seem to be hard on Morris, and there is some legal authority for relieving him of the debt, at least to the extent that he contributed services without adequate compensation. The issue is one that the partners should think about at the outset. They might well agree that losses are to be shared by the partners in accordance with their initial capital contributions. Since Abe and Bill each initially contributed 30 percent and Pamela 40 percent, their shares of the $20,000 loss would then be respectively, $6,000, $6,000 and $8,000 and the capital accounts would be as follows:

| | |
|---|---|
| Abe | $ 9,000 |
| Bill | 9,000 |
| Pamela | 12,000 |
| Morris | 0 |
| Total | $30,000 |

In the presence of such an agreement it might seem appropriate to provide further that any future profits would be allocated first so as to restore the initial capital accounts.

As an alternative to yearly alteration of partner capital accounts, gains and losses could be recorded in a separate set of accounts entitled "Income Accounts" or some such.

## B.  DRAW

Thus far we have referred to profits and losses, which are bookkeeping concepts. It is vital to note that profit does not necessarily generate any spare cash. For example, a new retail store may be highly profitable but may need all its profits to expand its inventory. And even if a firm has had profits and does have spare cash, the partners are not automatically entitled to receive a cash payment. There is a separate term—called "draw"—that is used to describe cash distributions to partners. The amount of the draw of each partner is determined by majority vote of the partners (again, in the absence of some other express agreement) and may be more or less than the profit. For example, in its first year of operations, the firm may show a profit of $20,000 from operations, but may at the same time be building up its inventories or paying off debts so that none of this profit is available for distribution to the partners. On the other hand, the firm might show a loss for accounting purposes and still have cash available for distribution. This situation is common in the initial stages of real estate investments, where there may be large negative bookkeeping allowances for depreciation. The depreciation allowance is designed to account for the fact that an asset such as a building has a limited useful life—that it is slowly wasting away. Depreciation may or may not reflect a true economic decline in the value of assets used in the business but, in any case, it is not a current cash outflow. Thus, a real estate (or other) partnership may be in a position to distribute cash generated by rentals while at the same time showing a loss because of depreciation.

Returning now to the bookkeeping effects of a draw, suppose that our grocery store partnership generates an accounting profit of $20,000 in the first year of its operations. Assume that this is the profit after all deductions, including the deduction for depreciation. (The effect of deducting depreciation from gross revenues at the partnership level will be to allocate depreciation according to profit share—that is, equally among all the partners. Actually, it might make sense, for tax reasons among others, for the partners to agree initially to allocate depreciation in accordance with some other formula, such as pro rata according to initial capital contribution.) We have just seen how this net profit figure can be translated into adjustments to partner capital accounts. Now suppose that there is a draw. Suppose, for example, that the partners agree that each is to be paid $3,000 from partnership funds. The $3,000 would reduce the capital accounts, so they would then be:

| | |
|---|---|
| Abe | $17,000* |
| Bill | 17,000 |
| Pamela | 22,000 |
| Morris | 2,000 |
| Total | $58,000 |

\* $15,000 initial capital account, plus $5,000 profit share, minus $3,000 draw.

Next, assume that there is a loss of $20,000 in the first year, instead of a profit; that the partnership agreement allocates this loss equally among all the partners; and that despite the loss, there is a cash distribution (draw) of $3,000 to each partner. The partnership capital accounts would then be as follows:

| | |
|---|---|
| Abe | $ 7,000* |
| Bill | 7,000 |
| Pamela | 12,000 |
| Morris | (8,000) |
| Total | $18,000 |

\* $15,000 initial capital account, minus $5,000 loss share, minus $3,000 draw.

All of this makes sense if you think about it for a few moments. Bear in mind that the capital accounts are not expected to correspond to values in the firm but instead are merely intended to reflect the relative claims of the partners to the assets of the partnership, which is of importance mostly in the case of withdrawal of a partner or liquidation of the partnership. A partner's share of profit can be thought of as something that he or she has earned and reinvested in the firm. The draw can be thought of as earnings or capital taken out of the firm. The capital account allows us to keep track of relative claims where initial contributions and profit shares differ. The same function is served where, for one reason or another, partners do not draw from the firm amounts strictly in proportion to their profit shares.

## C.   CAPITAL ACCOUNTS AND VALUE OF A PARTNER'S INTEREST

To illustrate the difference between capital account and value, and the role of the capital account, suppose that the partnership capital accounts stand as follows:

| | |
|---|---:|
| Abe | $17,000 |
| Bill | 17,000 |
| Pamela | 22,000 |
| Morris | 2,000 |
| Total | $58,000 |

Suppose that the business has increased in value because of the construction of a large housing development nearby. This is the kind of gain that ordinarily would not be reflected on the partnership books as long as the firm continues to operate with the same owners. Now suppose that the business is sold for $78,000 cash, net of all debts or other obligations. There is a surplus of $20,000 above the amount in the capital accounts (that is, above the amount of the initial contributions increased by profits and decreased by distributions to the partners). This $20,000 can be thought of as previously unrecorded profit; it would be allocated equally among the partners ($5,000 apiece), so that each partner would receive the following amount:

| | |
|---|---:|
| Abe | $22,000* |
| Bill | 22,000 |
| Pamela | 27,000 |
| Morris | 7,000 |
| Total | $78,000 |

\* $17,000 current capital account, plus $5,000 share of profit on sale of business.

Finally, assume that the store is sold for less than the amount in the capital accounts—for example, for $38,000. Here there is a previously unrecognized loss of $20,000. In the absence of an agreement to the contrary, the loss would be borne equally by all the partners (again, $5,000 apiece). The relative claims of the partners would therefore be as follows:

| | |
|---|---|
| Abe | $12,000 |
| Bill | 12,000 |
| Pamela | 17,000 |
| Morris | (3,000) |
| Total | $38,000 |

Morris has a deficit of $3,000. This is his share of a loss suffered by the firm. He would be required to contribute that amount to the total funds available so that the other partners could recover the amounts to which they were entitled.

## D.   ADDITIONAL CAPITAL

One of the most difficult, and potentially one of the most important, issues arising in the organization of small businesses has to do with the possible need for additional capital contributions after the firm has been operating for some time. Such a need can arise from a wide variety of circumstances.   The firm may, for example, find itself in the happy position of having prospered and needing additional capital for expansion. On the other hand, the need may arise from the unhappy circumstance that the firm has suffered setbacks and needs new equity capital in order to be able to continue to operate. Often the partnership agreement will contain a provision dealing with the problem of additional capital contribution. This would be especially true where there is a strong possibility of need—as, for example, in an oil and gas exploration venture, where it can be anticipated that if oil is found, more money may be needed to drill additional wells, or where everyone knows that because of difficulties that may be unusual but not unforeseeable, additional funds may be needed to complete the drilling of a well. Often, however, the partnership agreement will simply ignore the issue—even where the partners are sophisticated in business affairs. It is important to bear in mind in connection with this issue that, in the absence of an agreement to the contrary, a new partner cannot be added, nor can partnership shares be altered, without the unanimous consent of the partners.

To gain some insight into the seriousness and difficulty of the problem of raising additional equity capital, let's return to our grocery store partnership. Suppose that during the first year of operation the firm suffers setbacks attributable to unusual, nonrecurring events; that the prospects for the future still appear to be attractive; that in order to be able to continue to operate, at least an additional $15,000 is needed in order to pay wages and to satisfy the claims of trade creditors who are threatening to discontinue delivery of goods; and that the partnership agreement does not contain any express provision covering this situation. To appreciate the nature of the problem one must have a grasp of the economic framework in which it arises. To set that framework, let's imagine that the partners decide to seek the new capital from an outsider, Nancy, a wealthy investor who is familiar with the grocery business and has a reputation for being tough but fair and honest. Suppose that the partners select Pamela to represent them in bargaining with Nancy. The dialogue between Pamela and Nancy might proceed as follows:

Pamela: As you know, we initially invested $50,000 in the firm, plus the value of Morris's services. We are willing to ignore the advantageous contract with Morris, so we are prepared to offer you a one-third interest in the partnership if you are willing to invest $25,000.

Nancy: I'm sorry, but that is totally unrealistic. Your $50,000 might have been of some relevance if I had been brought in at the outset, but I fail to see its present significance. The fact is that your initial investment has been dissipated to some substantial degree. Otherwise you wouldn't be talking with me.

Pamela: I guess that's right, but I really don't think that there has been all that much decline in the value of our investment. Part of the problem is that our equity contribution was initially quite thin.

Nancy: I recognize that fact and have done some investigating on my own. As I understand it, the reason for that risky start was simply that you and your partners could not personally raise any more money then—and you can't do so now. I'd say that that leaves me in the driver's seat, since I am probably the only person around who knows much about your business; I'm the only one you can find who is in a position to size up the business well enough to be willing to invest in it on any kind of reasonable terms. If I am going to become a partner of yours, I don't want any hard feelings, but I have many other investment opportunities and you must recognize that I am going to drive as hard a bargain as I can. If you cannot accept that, I suggest that we forget about the whole thing.

Pamela: I see your point and I'm prepared to admit that the present value of our equity is only $35,000. But that's a rock bottom figure.

Nancy: I appreciate your candor. $35,000 is exactly the figure that I had come up with and I'm glad that we didn't have to engage in childish haggling to get to it. Moreover, I don't think you really need $25,000. I prefer to invest only $15,000.

Pamela: I think we can get by with $15,000. As I understand it, then, we will be contributing the equivalent of $35,000 and you will be contributing $15,000. That is, we will be contributing 70 percent and you will be contributing 30 percent.

Nancy:      Right.

Pamela:     Well then, I assume that we can agree to share in profits and losses according to those percentages.

Nancy:      Sorry, but I won't buy that. It seems to me that you stand to lose more than I do if we don't reach agreement. As I said, I expect to drive a hard bargain. I'm afraid I must insist on a 40 percent profit share, plus a priority for my $15,000 in the event of liquidation. I'm afraid that that is a take-it-or-leave-it proposition.

Pamela:     Well, I'll present it to my partners. Maybe if we can squeeze out part of Morris's share we can live with it, and Morris may be in no position to resist.

Nancy:      Just one more thing. I never enter into a deal like this as a minority voting member of the partnership. My lawyer has a provision relating to control that gives me veto power with respect to certain kinds of decisions.

Pamela:     We can talk about that if the profit share can be worked out. I'll be in touch with you. So long for now.

. . .

Consider what we can learn from this dialogue. First, it seems plain that any knowledgeable contributor of new money will compare his or her contribution with the current value of the equity in the firm, not with the amount of the initial contribution. Second, in the case of a small business, new money may be hard to find because of the difficulty of learning what one needs to know about the business in order to be willing to invest in it. As an economist would put it, the information costs are high. This phenomenon may limit the sources of funds, which may in turn seriously affect relative bargaining positions. And finally, a supplier of new capital may be able to insist on a share of profits or control, or both, disproportionate to the relative dollar values of contributions.

Now for the moral of the story as it applies to partnership agreements. The position of an existing partner who is asked to contribute more than a pro rata share of any new capital is closely parallel to that of a new partner such as Nancy, except that an effort by an existing partner to drive a hard bargain seems more likely to lead to bad feelings than such an effort by a stranger. To avoid the possibility of bad feelings, or of a mutually destructive impasse, the initial partners may be well advised to reach agreement in advance on a set of rules regarding additional equity capital.

Consider some of the more important issues that such an agreement must cope with and the kinds of rules that might be adopted for some of those issues. First and foremost, to what extent should some or all of the partners be obligated to supply additional capital if needed? Part of the problem in responding to this issue is that one of the partners may not have the money.  If Morris cannot contribute, what happens to his interest?  Perhaps the additional capital should come in as a loan from the wealthier partners.  Beyond that, the partners may be unwilling to make a commitment to add more money to a venture in which they may have lost faith.  One possible response to this kind of concern is to make additional contributions optional but to reduce the interests of the noncontributing partners to reflect not only the fact that new money is being added by less than all the partners, but also the diminution in the value of the initial contributions.  For example, in our hypothetical case, with initial cash and property contributions of $50,000 by Abe, Bill, and Pamela, and with each partner (including Morris) receiving a 25 percent interest in the partnership, suppose the business was initially worth a total of $60,000 (the $50,000 of cash and property plus $10,000 for the value of Morris's agreement to provide services at a below-market rate of compensation).  Suppose further that the partners have agreed to refer to ownership interests as "points," a convenient device often used to reduce the need to translate share interests into percentages.  Suppose the total number of points is 100, initially worth $60,000 (the initial value of the firm), with 25 points, worth $15,000, for each of the four partners.  Next, suppose that after a year of operation the value of the business has fallen to $30,000, that the business needs an additional $15,000 in order to be able to continue to operate, and that Abe is the only partner who might be able to contribute the additional amount. For his initial $15,000, Abe received a 25 percent interest in the profits. Suppose that Bill, Pamela, and Morris have suggested to Abe that for his new $15,000 he should receive 25 additional points (the same number of points received for his initial $15,000).  He would be foolish (or altruistic) to contribute on that basis, since the points are no longer worth what they were when he initially paid $15,000 for 25 points.  The business is by hypothesis now worth only $30,000, there are 100 points, so 25 points are worth $7,500.  For his additional $15,000, Abe should be entitled to insist on 50 points.  If he receives 50 points, the total number of points will be 150.  Abe will have 75 (his initial 25 plus the new 50) and each of the others will have 25.  The business will presumably be worth $45,000 (the $30,000 value before Abe's $15,000 contribution, plus the amount of that contribution).  Abe's 75 points will be half the new total number of points (150) and will be worth $22,500.  This is as it should be.  He started out with an interest worth $7,500, added $15,000, and winds up with an interest worth $22,500.  The other partners started out with interests worth $7,500 each.  They wind up with 25 points each, or one-sixth of the total, which is one-sixth of $45,000, or $7,500.  Everyone should be satisfied.  Thus, a sensible agreement might provide expressly for this kind of result—that is, one in which the increase in the share of the profits and capital of a partner contributing additional capital is determined with reference to the current value of the business (determined perhaps by an outsider or by a formula).  One of the important responsibilities of a business lawyer is to appreciate the usefulness of such agreements and to know how to explain them to clients and tailor them to the needs of particular clients.

The process of adjusting ownership shares to take account of additional capital contributions and changes in the value of the business is often referred to as "dilution" (of the interests of the partners whose percentage of ownership is reduced). The word "dilution" can be misleading. In the example we have just used, before the contribution of the $15,000 by Abe, the business was worth $30,000 and each partner's 25 percent interest was worth $7,500. After the $15,000 additional contribution, the business was worth $45,000 and Abe's share was worth $22,500. His wealth neither increased nor decreased. Similarly, the wealth of the other partners did not change. Each had a one-quarter interest worth $7,500 and wound up with a one-sixth interest worth $7,500. The adjustment of the percentage interests associated with the contribution of the new funds did not dilute the financial value of the investments of any of the partners. It is true that their partnership interests declined in value compared with what they were worth initially. For example, Bill's interest was worth $15,000 at the outset and declined in value to $7,500. But the decline was a result of events preceding and independent of Abe's new contribution and the adjustments required to take account of it. There could be a dilution of the voting power of the partners other than Abe (though voting power could remain one-partner-one-vote despite the change in profit and capital interests). But that seems not to be what people have in mind ordinarily when they speak of dilution in situations such as this one. What they seem to have in mind is a reduction in wealth and they seem to make the mistake of attributing the reduction in wealth to the adjustment in their ownership shares rather than to the earlier events that were the true cause.

It would be possible, of course, to draft an agreement relating to additional capital contributions with an adjustment that would reduce the wealth (that is, truly dilute the financial position) of the noncontributing partners. The partners, at the outset of the venture, might think it would not be feasible to arrive at a fair valuation. They might each expect to be able and willing to provide additional capital if needed, but, at the same time, might be unwilling to commit themselves firmly to making such contributions in unforeseeable circumstances. In the absence of such a commitment, there is a danger of strategic behavior leading to an impasse. This possibility arises because, without prior agreement, it may be impossible to reduce the percentage interest of a partner; a change in partnership share is a fundamental change that requires consent. If the initial contributions have in fact declined in value, each partner may refuse to contribute in the hope all the others will do so and that he or she will, in effect, get a free ride. While the partners are all playing this game of "chicken," the business may go down the drain. One kind of rule that might be adopted to cope with this kind of problem would dilute the interest of a noncontributing partner according to an arbitrary formula that could be expected, in most of the situations about which anyone should be concerned, to penalize the noncontributor (thereby removing any advantage from strategic failure to contribute). For example, the agreement might provide that if additional capital is needed, each new dollar of capital contribution will receive an interest in the partnership four times as great as the interest allocated to each initial dollar. Such a provision would be likely to induce all of the partners to contribute pro rata. It would be likely to prevent the strategic impasse. At the same time, such a provision may be sufficient to allay any fears of being sucked into a bottomless pit, since it does leave an option to refuse to contribute.

The foregoing discussion of required, optional, or encouraged additional contributions assumes that a determination has been made that additional capital is needed. But who is to make that decision and according to what criteria? The answer to this question may depend in part on who will be making the contribution. And then there is the question of what happens if a partner is unable or unwilling to make an additional contribution that is required by the partnership agreement. And so on.

Given all the obvious difficulties of formulating an acceptable solution, might it not be wiser to forget the whole thing and work out any problems as they arise? Or might it not at least be wise to ignore some of the problems, such as refusal to contribute a required amount, as to which the likelihood seems remote or the solution provided by law seems acceptable, or both? The answer to questions such as these may depend heavily on the degree to which the partners trust each other to behave fairly. This observation may in turn help to show why many people say that one should never enter into small-group business ventures except with people one trusts—or, at least, hardly ever. It may be of some comfort to the reader to know that out there in the cold, cruel world of reality, people who don't play fair and square are sometimes punished by exclusion from attractive future ventures.

## E.   DEBT HELD BY, AND SALARIES PAID TO, PARTNERS

Imagine a two-person partnership in which one partner contributes cash or property and the other contributes services. The partners agree that the contribution of cash or property will be treated as a loan to the partnership by the contributing partner, with that contributing partner having a right to a fair return, in the form of interest, on the loan. If need be, the obligation to pay the interest may be deferred. At the same time, the contributor of services can be paid a salary, again with the possibility of some or all of it being deferred. Profits and losses would be calculated, and allocated between the partners, after deducting the interest on the loan and the amount of the salary. This approach may permit the partners to think clearly about their contributions and expectations and may mitigate some of the perplexity that people experience over capital accounts. Special entitlements of partners contributing cash or property, or services, could simply be agreed upon without using labels, or concepts, such as "loan" or "salary," but those are familiar terms and their use may be helpful.

## VIII.  CONTROL, AGENCY, AND LIABILITY

### A.  INTRODUCTION

Each of the three basic rules of partnership organization considered here could be examined separately, and to some significant extent will be. The relationships between and among them are important enough, however, that it seems useful to bring them together under a single major heading. The three rules, stated briefly, are: (1) *Control*. In the absence of an agreement to the contrary, "all partners have equal rights in the management and conduct of the partnership business" (UPA (1914) Sec. 18(e)) and "any difference arising as to ordinary matters connected with the partnership business may be decided by a majority of the partners" (UPA (1914) Sec. 18(h)). (2) *Agency*. "Every partner is an agent of the partnership for the purpose of its business, and the act of every partner ... for apparently carrying on in the usual way the business of the partnership ... binds the partnership." (UPA (1914) Sec. 9(1).) (3) *Liability*.  Under the UPA (1914) each partner may be held personally liable for the full amount of any partnership debt that is not satisfied from partnership property, but recently this rule has been modified in many states.

### B.  CONTROL

**1.  Majority Rule With One Partner, One Vote.** While each member of a partnership has the right to participate in partnership decisions—that is, each partner has the right to be consulted on matters that require a decision—differences are resolved by majority vote, with each partner being entitled to one vote. Both aspects of this rule— majority vote and one partner, one vote—can be altered by agreement among the partners. The rule of majority control is found in UPA Section 18(h), quoted in part above, which further provides, however, that "no act in contravention of any agreement between the partners may be done rightfully without the consent of all the partners."[10] This last phrase protects rights that are part of the bargain reflected in the partnership agreement. For example, in the absence of an agreement to the contrary, the majority does not have the power to decrease the profit share of a partner over his or her objection. Similarly, if the partnership

---

[10] The corresponding language of UPA (1997) Sec. 401(j) reads: "An act outside the ordinary course of business of a part- nership and an amendment to the partner- ship agreement may be undertaken only with the consent of all the partners."

agreement limits the scope of the partnership business and contains no rules for changing those limits, no change in scope is permissible without the consent of all of the partners. If a majority were to violate this kind of rule, any dissenting partner would be entitled to various remedies available under the law (including damages, if provable) for violation of the partnership agreement.

**2. Consequences.** Suppose that the majority of the members of a partnership agree upon a new pattern of doing business. For example, suppose that three of the four members of our grocery-store partnership decide, after full discussion among all four, to buy and install a new, expensive, automated checkout system. Suppose, further, that one of the partners, Abe—the only one with substantial personal assets that are exposed to liability for partnership debts—is strongly opposed to this change and fears that it will result in financial ruin, but is unable to sway his partners. There is legal authority and considerable logic for the proposition that Abe cannot absolve himself of potential liability to creditors by notifying them of his dissent from the policies of the majority. As long as he remains a partner, it would do him no good to notify the seller of the new equipment that he disapproves of its purchase and will not be personally responsible for its cost. Because of the combination of the liability rule and the control rule, Abe may find himself in what he believes to be an untenable position. The only way that he could protect himself would be to withdraw from the partnership. In doing so, however, he might expose himself to liability for damages to the other partners (depending on the agreed-upon duration of the partnership and, of course, on whether his withdrawal did in fact result in harm to the other partners).

**3. Modification of Majority Rule.** This kind of situation suggests the possible appeal of an express agreement altering the standard-form UPA decision-making rule. As a condition to entering into the partnership, a person like Abe might want to insist upon a veto power over some or all partnership decisions. For example, he might insist upon a provision in the partnership agreement to the effect that no capital expenditure of more than $10,000 could be authorized, or no significant change in the manner of conducting the business made, without his consent. In fact, all of the partners might want a veto power of this sort, in which case the decision rule might simply require a unanimous vote on some or all decisions. But the protection thus achieved would not be without its costs. The power to block decisions favors the status quo. It can be used by a dissenter to prevent abandonment of policies or practices that the majority considers unwise, or even potentially disastrous. Indeed, many of the reported cases dealing with partnership control are concerned with problems arising from an impasse in a two-person partnership, where there is no possibility of a majority and where, accordingly, the consent of both partners is required in order to make decisions. When the business is prospering and all the partners are getting along well with one another, the veto power is not likely to have much significance. When the going gets tough, or the partners are at odds with one another, or when their personal relationship begins to deteriorate, the veto power may become important and may give inordinate power to one partner (thereby possibly aggravating disharmony).

If there are five or more votes, a compromise between the majority and the unanimity rule is possible—namely, some percentage vote greater than a majority but less than 100 percent. For example, the partnership agreement might require a two-thirds vote on some or all matters. In the case of a three- or four-person partnership, this rule would have no practical effect; there would be no practical difference between this rule and a simple majority rule. But in a five-person partnership the two-thirds rule would have the effect of requiring the concurrence of four partners instead of just three. That kind of rule might be enough to satisfy legitimate concerns without creating the danger of stifling the firm.

**4. Modification of One Partner, One Vote.** The rule of one person, one vote is perhaps an even better candidate for modification by express agreement of the parties than is the rule of majority control. Where capital contributions are uneven, for example, there is some obvious appeal to a rule that allocates voting power in accordance with capital contribution. Thus, in a three-person partnership in which A contributes $10,000, B contributes $10,000 and C contributes $20,000, A and B might each be given one vote while C is given two. It is interesting to note, by the way, that the effect of a rule that takes this form is that no new decision can be made by A and B without the concurrence of C and no such decision can be made by C without the concurrence of either A or B.

**5. Representative Government.** One other kind of potential control rule deserves mention. Firms with many partners not uncommonly provide by agreement for selection by all the partners of a small group of them to whom decision-making authority is delegated. What is perhaps most interesting about this kind of arrangement is that it shows how a partnership can, by agreement, be modified to take on a characteristic normally associated with corporations—here, centralized decision-making by owner representatives (but the representatives will almost invariably all be partners as opposed to nonpartner professional managers). The delegation and centralization of control in the partnership context can be taken a step further by the use of subpartnerships. By way of illustration, suppose that a partnership consists of Abe, Bill, and Pamela, but that Abe in turn has entered into a partnership with Charles and Dan to share in his interest in the Abe–Bill–Pamela partnership. Diagrammatically we then have this arrangement:

### Abe–Bill–Pamela
↓
### Abe–Charles–Dan

The Abe–Charles–Dan partnership is a subpartner of the Abe–Bill–Pamela partnership.  Charles and Dan are entitled to whatever share of profits and are liable for whatever share of losses that their agreement with Abe provides for.  They are not, however, members of the primary Abe–Bill–Pamela partnership and have no right to participate in control of it, except through Abe.  Bill and Pamela need not be concerned about the personal characteristics of Charles and Dan;  if they are troublesome that is strictly Abe's problem.  It can be seen, then, that subpartnerships are a useful device for coping with practical problems of control in partnerships involving many investors.

**6.  Loan Agreements.** If partners treat their contributions of cash or property as loans to the partnership, they can use the terms of the loan agreement to exercise some degree of control over the partnership.  For example, the loan agreement might prohibit the sale of certain assets or might require that the partnership maintain a sound financial condition. (See discussion of bond "covenants" in Chapter 4, Sec. III(A)(5).) Again, the same constraints could be imposed in the partnership agreement, but certain constraints may be familiar to people in the loan context and therefore more readily understood when placed in that context.

## C.  PARTNERS AS AGENTS OF THE PARTNERSHIP

Under the rule quoted above from Section 9(1) of the UPA, each partner is an agent of the partnership.  The implications and problems of this rule are essentially the same as those relating to employee agents, discussed in Chapter 1, Section VII.  The act of any partner, within the scope of the partnership business, binds the partnership.  Thus, each partner has the power not only to dispose of or dissipate all the partnership assets but also to expose all the other partners to personal liability for obligations in excess of those assets.  This agency authority of partners need not be consciously conferred upon them; it is an incident of their status as partners.  It can be limited or eliminated by the express terms of the partnership agreement (which may be oral or written) but no limitation is effective against a person doing business with the firm unless it has been communicated to that person.[11]  (Compare Chapter 1, Sec. VII.)  To illustrate, consider again our partnership of Abe, Bill, Pamela, and Morris, owning and operating a grocery store.

---

[11] Under UPA (1997) Sec. 303(e) third parties are "deemed to know" of any limitation of a partner's authority to transfer real property if that limitation is contained in a partnership statement filed in the appropriate state office pursuant to Sec. 105.

Even if Abe and Bill are inactive and are unfamiliar with the grocery business, they would have authority to act on behalf of the partnership. If that authority were limited by the partnership agreement (or by a decision of the majority, if authorized by the agreement), they would still have the power to bind the partnership to any agreement made with a person to whom such a limitation had not been communicated. (Note the distinction here between authority and power.) If, for example, Abe happened to find what he thought to be a great bargain for the purchase of meat, he could buy that meat for the firm and the firm would be bound by his agreement of purchase—even though the seller relied on nothing other than Abe's word that he was a partner. If the partnership agreement had been drafted so as to deprive Abe of authority to make such purchases for the partnership, his act would, of course, be in violation of the partnership agreement. As a consequence of that violation Abe would be liable to the other partners for any losses suffered by them as a result of his act. But they would still be bound by the contract with the meat supplier, unless the supplier knew of the restrictive agreement.

One of the critical issues in applying the agency rule presented here is the determination of the scope of the business. If, in the immediately preceding example, Abe had bought an obviously excessive supply of meat, or had bought TV sets, the partnership might not be bound even if he purported to act in its behalf, since his actions would presumably be outside the scope of its business. A determination of the scope of a business is a complex factual matter based, in general, on evidence of the agreement among the partners and on the manner in which the business and similar businesses in the area were conducted.

The partnership agency rule is one of obvious economic significance. On the one hand it creates dangers to the partners—dangers that may impede the formation of such economic organizations, or at least require costly protective planning. On the other hand, the rule might reduce the burden that would otherwise fall on people doing business with a firm in determining whether its partners have authority to act for it; to this extent, the rule will reduce costs of doing business.

### D.  LIABILITY

The general thrust of the traditional UPA rule of liability stated in the introduction to this section is reasonably simple and straightforward. Each partner is potentially liable for the full amount of partnership debts. Application of this general rule requires other rules and concepts that are complex and even confusing. There is one set of rules distinguishing between "joint" liability, on the one hand, and "joint and several" liability on the other. Still other rules govern the rights of one partner to contribution from the others. These rules interact with further rules relating to the jurisdiction of particular courts over particular people and to related matters such as service of process and enforcement of judgments. UPA (1996) substantially simplifies these procedural rules, but what is important is that under either UPA (1914) or UPA (1996) if partnership assets have been exhausted and if a partner has personal assets, sooner or later the creditors are likely to be able to get them.  For many people, and particularly for passive investors in substantial enterprises, this fact of partnership life has created an unacceptable risk, especially in light of the UPA rules on control and agency. Where that is so, the solution may be to organize the firm as a limited partnership (Sec. X(A) below) or as a corporation (see Chapter 3, Sec. III(D)).

Beginning in the early 1990s, however, most states amended their partnership statutes to provide for some degree of limited liability for partners—that is, providing that claims against the partnership may be recovered only from partnership assets, so the partner's exposure to loss is limited to her or his investment in the partnership. The result is a form of organization called the limited liability partnership (LLP). This variation on the general partnership is described in Section X(C) of this Chapter.

## IX.  DURATION AND TRANSFERABILITY

### A.  TERMINOLOGY

The end of the existence of a partnership is more a process than an event.  The process is reflected in three terms that have special meaning in partnership law—"dissolution," "winding up," and "termination" in the 1914 Act and "dissociation," "dissolution," and "winding up" in the 1997 Act.  These terms serve as symbols for some complex and often confusing concepts and ideas.  While the terms will be used in the discussion that follows, no comprehensive definition of them will be offered.  The reader is warned, however, that the terms do have special technical meanings in partnership law and that, unfortunately, these technical meanings are sometimes ignored by courts and practitioners.

### B.  DISSOCIATION AT WILL

In the absence of an agreement to the contrary, a partner's relationship with the other partners (or, if you prefer, with the "firm"), may rightfully be ended at will. To use the language of UPA (1997), the partner may "dissociate" from the partnership at any time. See UPA (1997) Sec. 601. In some cases, however, the partners may have agreed that their relationship shall continue for some definite period of time. Agreement to some term may be tacit and may be inferred from the nature or needs of the undertaking.  To illustrate, consider again our grocery store partnership of Abe, Bill, Pamela, and Morris.  Suppose that at the outset the partners borrow, from a bank, for the business, the sum of $10,000, to be repaid with interest at 15 percent at the end of one year.  Suppose the partners contemplate that the $11,500 due at the end of the year will be paid out of accumulated profits.  In these circumstances a court might find a tacit agreement that the partnership will remain in existence for one year; that is, that the partnership has a one-year term.  Suppose, however, that there is no such loan or other circumstance from which a definite term can be inferred and that Abe wants to end his association with the firm and cash in his interest in the business.  In the absence of an agreement to the contrary, he is legally entitled to do so.  All he needs to do is announce his wish.  But then the question is, what happens?  The answer is that unless some other solution (such as a buy-out by the continuing partners or a sale to a new person who is acceptable to them) is agreed upon, there must be a winding up of the business (in more common parlance, a liquidation), at the end of which the partnership is terminated.  Winding up contemplates a sale that produces a cash fund that is used to pay off all debts, with the surplus, if any, divided among the partners.  Consider four possible ways in which the cash fund might be generated.

**1.  Going-Out-of-Business Sale.**  One possibility is to shut down the store and sell all its assets.  This is a simple, tidy solution, but one that will destroy going concern value, often called "goodwill," which might include the intangible element of a favorable set of attitudes toward the firm on the part of its customers—a tendency on their part to keep coming back; a set of employees who have stood the test of time, who know the business, and who work well together; and a set of physical assets that fit together well.  Obviously, the value of all such intangibles is lost if the business is shut down and the assets sold piecemeal.  And in a prospering business, goodwill is likely to be of substantial value—which explains why shutting down the business and selling the assets often will be a bad way to wind it up.

**2.  Sale of Going Concern to Outsider.**  A second possibility for winding up is a sale of the business as a going concern to an outsider.  Where goodwill is of significant value, this is obviously a more attractive alternative than shutting down and selling assets.  One might imagine that if there is much good will, the partners ought to be able to find an outside buyer willing to pay some reasonable amount for it.  Often, however, it will be difficult, at best, to find such a buyer because of the costs of communicating information about the business to people not familiar with it.  Another problem with sale to an outsider is that some of the values inherent in the business may exist only for its present owners.  For example, the services of an owner like Morris may be uniquely suitable for this particular operation; Pamela and Bill may play minor decision-making roles that give them pleasure; some or all of the partners may have affection for or a sense of obligation to employees; and so forth.  For these and other reasons, some of the partners may consider that sale to an outsider will not sufficiently compensate them for their interest in the firm.

**3. Sale to Majority.** A third possibility is a purchase of the business, as a going concern, from the partnership by those partners (Bill, Pamela, and Morris) who wish to continue their investment. Conceptually this is closely akin to the second alternative, with the obvious exception that the sale is to insiders rather than to an outsider. The purchasing partners will be in a position that puts a heavy strain on the fiduciary obligation that they owe, in their conflicting role as sellers, to the noncontinuing partner (Abe). Courts are sensitive to the conflict and to the consequent strain on the fiduciary obligation and will carefully review the fairness of the sale/purchase price. Apart from the potential problems created by this rule, Bill, Pamela, and Morris may be hard pressed to raise the cash they need to buy off Abe. After all, they needed him at the outset and it may be difficult to find someone to take his place (again, largely because of information barriers). Abe, knowing this, may be in a position to drive a hard bargain (within the limits imposed upon him by fiduciary obligation and other judicial doctrines).

**4. Sale to Minority.** A fourth alternative, a variation on the third, is a purchase by Abe, either alone or with new partners. If Abe's reason for wanting to withdraw from the partnership is his inability to get along with the others, and if he considers the business to be a good investment, he may be willing to buy the interests of the others instead of selling his interest to them. Indeed, one approach sometimes taken to the split-up of a partnership (or any other joint ownership arrangement) is for a partner to set a fixed price at which he or she is willing either to buy or to sell.

**5. Conceptual Aspects.** Note that in the third alternative the concept used was that of a purchase of the partnership business by some of the partners, while in the fourth alternative the concept was a purchase by one partner of the interests of the others. The two concepts are functionally identical. Thus, if there are four equal partners and the concept is that three of them buy the entire business for $100,000, the effect is that the fourth receives $25,000 and that this amount must come from the other three; this is exactly what happens if the concept is that the three who continue with the business buy, not the business as a whole, but rather the interest of the withdrawing partner. The difference in concept may, however, be of more than purely intellectual significance; it could, for example, have important tax consequences.

## C.　PROVIDING FOR CONTINUITY

**1. Usefulness of Agreement.** If there is significant goodwill, the partners are likely to be able to work out some sort of method of preserving it—by a sale either to an outsider or to one or more partners who will continue to operate the business. Because of rancor or miscalculation or other such manifestations of human frailties, however, it is possible that a sensible outcome, one preserving the value of the good will, may not be achieved. And in any event, the process of finding the business-preserving solution may be traumatic and expensive. This being so, one senses the importance of thought and care in setting up the organization at the outset.

**2. Agreement on Duration.** One solution to the problem of easy withdrawal, or lack of continuity, in the standard-form UPA partnership is an agreement by the parties at the outset on a definite term of existence. In our grocery-store hypothetical, for example, the partners might agree that the partnership will continue for ten years, and thereafter from year to year in the absence of 60 days' notice by any partner of an intention to withdraw. While such a provision would provide some protection against early dissolution, under partnership law that protection is not complete. Suppose, for example, that the partnership agreement provides for a ten-year term but that Abe decides after one year that he wants to withdraw—either because he detests the other partners; or because he desperately needs the money; or because he fears that the business is being operated in ways that expose him to too much danger of liability to creditors; or for any of a variety of other reasons. Under partnership law he is entitled to withdraw, even though his act in doing so is in violation of the partnership agreement. (See UPA (1914), Sec. 31(2); UPA (1997), Sec. 602.) The consequences of his withdrawal are described immediately below.

**3. Consequences of Withdrawal in Contravention of Agreement.** If Abe withdraws in contravention of the partnership agreement, the other partners have two alternatives. One alternative is to wind up the business; this means that they sell it as a going concern or they stop doing business and sell the assets in a liquidation sale. They must pay all debts. Any money that is left is distributed to the partners according to their capital accounts and profit shares, except that Abe is liable to the other partners for any damages caused by his wrongful withdrawal. The other alternative available to Bill, Morris, and Pamela upon Abe's wrongful withdrawal is to continue to operate the business. (They may have an agreement that obligates the three of them to do this; otherwise none of the nonwithdrawing partners would be required to continue.) If they follow this route the principal consequences are as follows. First, if the firm's creditors are informed of the withdrawal, Abe is no longer liable for any debts thereafter incurred (which may be Abe's main objective), though he remains liable on debts previously incurred. Second, Abe is entitled to be paid the value of his interest, reduced by any damages for which he may be liable by virtue of his breach of the partnership agreement.[12] Third, the continuing partners may continue

---

[12] Under UPA (1997) Sec. 701, Abe would be entitled to a payment that reflected his share of goodwill, but under UPA (1914) Sec. 38(c)(II) he would not be entitled to his pro rata share of goodwill, which might result in a substantial penalty to him.

to use the partnership property and need not pay Abe the amount to which he is entitled until the end of the agreed-upon term. The continuing partners must, however, post a bond (or, under UPA (1997), "adequate[ ] secur[ity]") to guarantee ultimate payment to Abe and to protect him from the claims of creditors for pre-dissolution obligations.

**4. Unresolved Problems.** For a variety of reasons, these rules may not seem to meet the needs of the parties. The continuing partners may be confronted with litigation over the value of Abe's interest and the amount of damages. Posting a bond or other security may be difficult. In some circumstances the continuing partners may have trouble finding the cash with which to pay Abe at the end of the initial term. From Abe's perspective, the damages may seem far too harsh— especially if his action has stemmed from an uncontrollable and sympathy-provoking circumstance such as a serious illness.

**5. Continuation and Buy–Out Agreements.** What the parties need, beyond an agreement on the initial term of the endeavor, is a set of provisions that amount to what lawyers call *"continuation agreements"* or *"buy-out agreements."* These agreements will list certain events (for example, death, serious illness, or withdrawal for any other reason) and will prescribe a method of disposition of the partner's interest (sale to other partners, offer to outsiders, etc.). The agreement should establish a method of valuation of the interest (for example, book value, appraisal value, or some multiple of average annual earnings over some specified period of years) and a method of payment (for example, installment payments over a specified time period with interest at a specified rate) and should prescribe the obligations of the nonwithdrawing partners. (Under UPA (1997), however, the default rules may provide for continuation, so a tailored continuation agreement may be less important.) This kind of agreement can protect the legitimate interests both of the partners who wish to continue and those who wish to withdraw. It can provide the stability and continuity that is such an important characteristic of the corporate form.

## D.　TRANSFERABILITY

We have seen that the basic rules of partnership organization are suited to the needs of a small group of partners each of whom enters into the relationship in reliance on the personal characteristics of the others. This concept is consistent with the rule (among others) that each partner has the power to act on behalf of the partnership within the scope of its business. The idea that each partner deliberately chooses the particular people with whom he or she agrees to associate in partnership is expressed in the latin phrase, delectus personae (choice of person). The idea of delectus personae is in turn reflected in the rule that partnership interests are not transferable—that a person cannot, without the consent of all the other partners, substitute another person for himself.

In many situations the rule of nontransferability may make some sense—for example, in a small law partnership.  In others it may be entirely inappropriate—for example, in a venture for the development of a shopping center, with many partners, most of whom are passive investors.  The basic rule of nontransferability can be modified by agreement among the partners.  For example, the partners can agree to allow transfer (with substitution) either without restraint or subject to some condition (for example, subject to the approval of the majority of the other partners).[13]  Such an agreement may help to solve the problem of the partner who wants, or needs, to withdraw, but it is not a complete solution in all cases.  Suppose, for example, that Abe wants to withdraw because he feels that the other partners have been treating him unfairly by paying themselves salaries that he believes are too high; but suppose that he doubts that he could make that charge stick in court.  On his view of the facts, he is a victim of the rule that gives control to the majority.  His interest will be of little value, precisely for the reason that leads him to want to sell it; transferability will be of little use because any prospective buyer of Abe's interest will presumably expect to be victimized by the majority to the same extent that he is.  What Abe needs in the way of protection against this danger is some sort of provision that is carefully drafted to require the others to buy his interest from him at a fair price.  If he does have such protection, transferability will be of little, if any, importance; if he doesn't, it may be of little, if any, value.

## X.  VARIATIONS

### A.  LIMITED PARTNERSHIPS

A limited partnership consists of one or more general partners plus one or more limited partners.  The rules for limited partnerships are found in the Uniform Limited Partnership Act (ULPA) and the Revised Uniform Limited Partnership Act (RULPA).  The rules relating to general partners are essentially the same as those relating to members of ordinary partnerships.  Most importantly, general partners are personally liable for the debts of the firm, have the power to act on behalf of the firm, and control it.  Limited partners do not participate in control, do not have the power to act for the firm, and are not personally liable for the debts of the firm.  Limited liability is the most appealing nontax feature of limited partnerships, as compared with general partnerships, especially in ventures such as real estate development, where there may be a large number of relatively passive investors.  Limited liability can, however, be achieved by use of the corporate form without requiring a

---

[13] Technically, under UPA (1914) a transfer of ownership, or any other change in membership, results in a "dissolution" of the original partnership and the formation of a new partnership.  As a practical matter, however, no one is likely to perceive the change in such dramatic terms.

sacrifice of control by investors and for many years limited partnerships were little used. Beginning in the early sixties, however, tax considerations made limited partnerships popular as vehicles for passive investments in real estate, cattle and certain other farming operations, oil and gas, and so forth, as well as for more active investments in "venture capital" firms. For federal income tax purposes, the limited partnership was preferred over the corporation mainly because limited partners, like ordinary partners but unlike shareholders in ordinary corporations, were allowed to take their pro rata share of the losses of the firm as losses on their individual returns, to be offset against income from other activities. For example, suppose that one hundred people invested $10,000 each (a total of $1,000,000) as the equity in a newly constructed office building. Under tax accounting rules the investment might have showed a loss for tax purposes for several years even if it was a sound and successful investment. Suppose the tax loss in the first year was $500,000 (in fact, it could have been substantially greater than that). If the corporate form had been used, the corporation would have reported that loss, but there would have been no tax benefit since the corporation would have had no income to be offset. The loss could have been carried forward by the corporation to offset future income, but that is not what investors wanted. If the investment had been made in the form of a limited partnership, the $500,000 loss would have been allocated pro rata among the one hundred partners, so each partner would have been entitled to report currently a $5,000 loss, which would have offset income from other sources and thereby reduced tax liability (by the amount of the loss deduction multiplied by the investor's marginal tax rate). This tax benefit generated a substantial "tax shelter" industry (that is, a set of promoters of investments whose principal focus was on tax saving) and a proliferation of tax shelter limited partnerships.

The Tax Reform Act of 1986, by adding a new provision affecting "passive activity losses," drastically limited the opportunities for limited partners to take advantage of losses and correspondingly reduced the use of limited partnerships for tax shelter investments. At the same time, the 1986 act increased the attractiveness of limited partnerships for ordinary investments. This increased attractiveness arises from the fact that use of the partnership form allows people to avoid the so-called double tax on corporate income. If a business is operated in corporate form, its income is taxed to the corporation, at the corporate rate, as earned. When the remaining income (after the payment of the corporate tax) is distributed to shareholders (as dividends), it is taxed to them at the appropriate individual rate. If the business is operated in partnership form, the income is taxed to the individual partners, as earned, at their rates; there is only one tax. During most of the history of the federal income tax, the top corporate rate was significantly lower than the top individual rate, so the disadvantage of the double tax was offset by the advantage of the lower corporate rate for income that was not distributed as dividends. In 1981, the gap was narrowed: the top individual rate was reduced to 50 percent and the top corporate rate was 46 percent. There then appeared a few "master limited partnerships"—limited partnerships that were not tax shelters, with limited partnership interests that were widely held and were traded on public exchanges. These early master limited partnerships were mostly for passive investments in oil and gas properties. The 1986 act changed the relationship between the individual and the corporate rate; beginning in 1988 the top individual rate was 28 or 33 percent and the top corporate rate was 34 percent. This change in relationship increased the appeal of master limited partnerships and resulted in a substantial increase in their use. Moreover, they came to be used for investment in active, operating businesses, not just passive investments. In 1987, Congress again changed the rules, this time imposing corporate tax treatment on limited partnerships that are publicly traded and whose income is other than "passive-type income" (such as real property rents).

While the current popularity of limited partnerships is attributable largely to tax considerations, they are also used for nontax reasons, especially in transactions with foreign investors, and they are of interest in our study of business organization because of the pattern of control that they adopt. As stated above, limited partners are not entitled to participate in control except, to some degree under the ULPA and to a greater degree under the RULPA, for certain major decisions such as dissolution; if limited partners do participate in control (e.g., in operating decisions such as producing a new product), they may lose their limited liability (that is, liability limited to their investment in the firm), which is usually a vital attribute for investors. Much of the commentary on limited partnerships seems to assume that the limited partners would prefer to participate in operating or strategic control, but that in a trade-off between control and limited liability, the latter wins out (assuming that the corporate form has been ruled out for tax reasons). In fact, the nonparticipation in such control may be no sacrifice at all; it may be desirable. Control will be vested in the general partner, who will (or at least should) have experience in the business. Each limited partner may actually find comfort in the fact that decisions relating to the management of the business will not be in the hands of people as inexperienced as himself or himself. This observation suggests that in some instances the owners of an enterprise may wish to deny control to themselves in order to ensure that others like them will not have it. In any event, it is interesting to note that many investors are quite willing to enter into ventures in which they lack even the semblance of control associated with the ownership of shares of common stock of public corporations.

## B.  LIMITED LIABILITY COMPANIES

The limited liability company (LLC) is a recent statutory development that reflects the importance in the organization of many business entities of two objectives:  (a) limitation of the liability of investors to the amount invested in the firm and (b) avoidance of the double tax on corporate income. What investors want is a form of organization that has the corporate characteristic of limited liability, but is treated as a partnership for purposes of federal income taxation. For closely held firms (that is, firms with relatively few equity investors), the LLC achieves this objective. (Publicly held firms might be able to organize as LLCs, but under Sec. 7704 of the Internal Revenue Code would continue to be subject to the double tax.)

The first statute authorizing an LLC in this country was adopted by the Wyoming legislature in 1977. That statute is an amalgam of provisions taken from the laws defining partnerships, limited partnerships, and corporations. The Wyoming innovation lay mostly dormant until the issuance of a favorable tax ruling by the Internal Revenue Service in 1988, which ultimately led to the adoption of LLC statutes by all 50 states. The statutes vary in some important respects, but their similarities are greater than their differences and for our purposes it is only the common characteristics that matter. By the beginning of the 21st Century, the LLC had become the dominant form of organization for new closely held businesses.

The formation of an LLC, like the formation of a corporation, requires the drafting and filing of certain documents. Once the LLC is formed, the equity investors, by operation of law, achieve the corporate characteristic of limited liability (see Chapter 3, Sec. III(D)).

A limited term of existence, or duration, generally must be stated— under some statutes not more than thirty years. This is in contrast to a corporation, where the duration is generally unlimited. Moreover, investors (typically referred to as "members") may withdraw at will, generally with six months' notice. Finally, under most statutes dissolution is caused by any member's death, withdrawal, bankruptcy, etc. The other members can continue to operate the business if they agree unanimously to do so or pursuant to any agreement that they may have entered into in advance (though in some circumstances such an agreement may jeopardize the desired tax result of avoidance of classification as a corporation). Because of limited liability, a member of an LLC who withdraws is not confronted with the same risks of liability to existing creditors that are confronted by a withdrawing general partner.

A member who withdraws from an LLC is entitled to be paid off. The amount may be determined under the LLC agreement, which generally is the best approach. If there is no agreement, the amount is determined under the applicable state statute and varies from state to state. The most common rule provides for payment of the fair market value of the withdrawing member's interest (whatever that may mean), reduced by any damages. Under the law of some states the member is entitled to a return of his or her initial contribution and in a few states the amount is determined by the liquidation value of the LLC. In some states, the payment is not due until the LLC's dissolution.

As for transferability, members of LLCs may transfer, or assign, their financial interest in the LLC, but, in the absence of unanimous consent of the other members or a provision or an agreement to the contrary, not their right to participate in management (that is, their voting rights). This characteristic of LLCs is a substantial impediment to their use for sizable ventures with large numbers of investors.

Under most statutes, in the absence of a provision or agreement to the contrary, management of the LLC is vested in the members, who are like general partners in this respect, and who not only participate in decision-making but also may have the power to bind the company. In some states, however, managers must be selected (thus providing centralized management) and in other states this alternative is available to the members.

The LLC offers the advantage over a limited partnership that all investors can participate in management, plus the advantage that there need be no person comparable to the general partner with exposure to unlimited liability. Under federal income tax law, certain corporations, called "S" corporations, are able to escape the double tax on corporate earnings (see Chapter 3, Sec. VII(E)). The LLC has the advantage over the S corporation that it is not subject to limitations as to number and type of interests and that it is permitted to make certain partnership-like allocations of tax attributes.

## C.  LIMITED LIABILITY PARTNERSHIPS

The newest organizational innovation is the limited liability partnership (LLP). LLPs are general partnerships for which the liability of the general partners is restricted. Although the statutes vary, essentially a partner in an LLP is not personally liable for partnership obligations arising from negligence, wrongful acts, or similar misconduct unless the negligence, wrongful act, or misconduct was committed by the individual partner or a person operating under that partner's direct supervision and control. Thus, the partner's loss with respect to the tort liability arising from the conduct of his or her partners is limited to his or her investment in the partnership.  Some states (e.g., Maryland, Minnesota, and New York) provide this protection for contract as well as tort liability. As the price for the restriction on liability, some states require a minimum amount of liability insurance coverage or to segregate liquid assets in a special account in a similar amount.[14]

---

[14] Under § 1546 of the Delaware Limited Liability Partnership Act, a Delaware LLP must maintain $1,000,000 in liability insurance coverage covering the kinds of liabilities "for which liability is limited." Under § 3.08(d) of the Texas Limited Liability Partnership Act there is a similar requirement but the specified amount is only $100,000.

## D. MINING PARTNERSHIPS

The special characteristics and needs of mining ventures (including oil and gas) lead to some significant variations in the law of partnership as it applies to such ventures. These rules developed initially through judicial decision-making (that is, through what lawyers call the common-law process) and now have been embodied in statutes in many states. The most important divergencies between mining partnerships and ordinary partnerships are that in the former, interests are freely transferable (the principle of delectus personae is abandoned); there is no dissolution at death or by bankruptcy; the duration of the venture is defined by its scope (for example, the completion of the process of drilling for oil and pumping it out); and the partners have only narrow powers to bind the partnership. Thus, the mining partnership is interesting in showing us the kinds of deviations from the UPA rules that may be appropriate to the needs of particular kinds of economic ventures, and how the law sometimes responds to such needs.

# Chapter 3

# CORPORATIONS

## I.  A BRIEF OVERVIEW

### A.  PRELIMINARY OBSERVATIONS

From a legal perspective a corporation is a particular set of rules for the organization of economic entities. The core rules are found, for the most part, in the statutes—the corporation codes—of the various states. While the rules vary to some degree from state to state, the basic rules are much the same and are sufficiently complete so that little, if any, modification is required. The equity[1] investors are called shareholders or stockholders; their ownership interests are reflected in shares of the common stock of the firm. The shareholders elect a board of directors, who in turn select the officers who run the business. The rules found in the corporation codes provide for how the elections take place, for the authority of the directors, for the duration of the enterprise, for the distribution of profits, for mergers with other corporations, and so forth. The founders of a corporation create the corporation (they "incorporate") by filing certain documents with the appropriate state agency and may choose to do so in any of the fifty states. Once a firm is incorporated in a particular state, it is the law of that state that is controlling as to the matters covered in the corporations code.

The focus in this chapter is primarily on "public" corporations—that is, large firms with many shareholders and with active trading of shares. The shareholders in such corporations do not expect to participate actively in the operation of the business. They are passive investors. Indeed, an important aspect of the corporation is its facilitation of passive investments and, thus, the aggregation of individual savings, which in turn permits large-scale investment and large-scale operation. For public corporations, federal law has a significant impact on the rights and duties of shareholders, directors, and officers, and to some degree on the structure and operation of the enterprise. The core of federal corporate law is a complex system, enacted originally in 1933 and 1934, requiring disclosure of the important facts relating to operations and financial performance. See Sec. VII(B)(4). Beyond disclosure, federal law includes rules prohibiting "insider trading"—that is, trading by corporate officers, directors, and employees on the basis of material nonpublic information (see Sec. VI(C)); rules relating to shareholder voting by use of mail or electronic "proxies" (see Sec. VII(B)(1)); and rules controlling attempted corporate takeovers by the use of tender offers (see Sec. VII(B)(2)(d)). Class-action suits on behalf of shareholders,

---

[1] "Equity" is described in Chapter 1, Sec. II(E).

based on the federal securities laws and filed in federal courts, claiming violation of federal disclosure obligations, have become an important reality in the relationship between shareholders, on the one hand, and officers and directors on the other hand.[2] Moreover, the two major exchanges on which the shares of public corporations are traded (the New York Stock Exchange and NASDAQ) both impose rules requiring, among other things, a minimum number of independent directors.

At the other end of the corporate spectrum is the closely held corporation. The principal distinguishing feature of the closely held corporation is a small number of shareholders, though in all likelihood the firm will also be one of relatively modest economic scope (whether measured by revenues, by assets, or on any other scale), and generally (though by no means always) the people owning a substantial portion of the total shares will occupy the top managerial positions or will be involved in a meaningful way in the selection and monitoring of the people who do occupy those positions as well as in the formulation of corporate strategies and policies.[3] For such firms, the Limited Liability Company (LLC) has become an attractive alternative organizational device. However, because an LLC blends characteristics of partnerships and corporations, an understanding of corporate law and of partnership law is, at the very least, helpful in understanding the nature of an LLC.

*A caveat.* The strategy of this book has been to develop in the context of the discussion of sole proprietorships (Chapter 1) and partnerships (Chapter 2) most of the important underlying economic principles and many of the legal doctrines that govern all forms of business organization, including corporations. Thus, much of the basic material relevant to an understanding of corporations is found in the two previous chapters. At the same time, much is deferred to the succeeding two chapters. Those chapters cover what is usually called "corporate finance," which can be thought of as the field that explores in detail the nature of the claims in a corporation (common stock, bonds, etc.), the relationships among those claims, and the factors bearing on the choice of the mix of those claims—a choice, roughly speaking, of the amount of capital to be contributed by owners and the amount to be contributed by lenders. These observations should serve as a warning to the reader who

---

[2] See Robert B. Thompson and Hillary A. Sale, Securities Fraud as Corporate Governance: Reflections Upon Federalism, 56 Vanderbilt L. Rev. 859 (2003).

[3] Many states have special "close corporation" statutes; typically, these permit a more informal mode of operation, under which the shareholders (or some designated number or group of them) can directly manage the firm instead of being required to act, formally, through a board of directors. In effect, these statutes do not change the basic structure of the corporation, nor even necessarily modify its prevailing default rules, but they do permit a wider range of private ordering solutions to reflect the more detailed, face to face bargaining that is possible within this context. Most of what can be accomplished under the close corporation provisions can be accomplished by agreements among shareholders of a standard corporation, or by use of the LLC form. Relatively little use has been made of the close corporation statutes.

might think that this chapter is the appropriate starting and ending point for learning about corporations.

## B. THE IMPORTANT CHARACTERISTICS

The public corporation has a number of characteristics that, collectively, account for its success in organizing economic activity on a large scale. These characteristic will be examined in more detail in the remainder of this chapter, but a brief summary will be helpful.

1. *Separate Entity.* A corporation is treated as a "separate entity." This is pure conceptualization—that is, a way of thinking about a complex reality—but it is a powerful conceptualization, which plays an important role in determining various rules of corporate law. As a separate entity, it is the corporation, not the shareholders, that enters into contracts, incurs debt, and files or is the defendant in law suits. The officers and other employees act on behalf of the firm, subject to approval of the board of directors as to major decisions. Shareholders have no power to act on behalf of the corporation.

2. *Divisible Ownership.* Equity ownership is reflected in shares of stock. Generally, corporations issue enough shares so that each one is of relatively modest value (rarely more than $100). This means that corporations can be financed by a large number of investors, each with a relatively small investment (though nowadays most small investors who want to invest in corporate equities turn their money over to professional managers who pool the funds of many such investors, in "mutual funds," and invest in a diversified portfolio of stocks or bonds or both).

3. *Assets Separated from Shareholders.* Consistently with the concept of the corporation as a separate entity, the assets of a corporation are held by the corporation. Shareholders cannot remove from the corporation their pro rata share of the corporation's assets. This protects the stability of the corporation and the interest of the other shareholders in that stability. Perhaps more important, it protects the creditors of the corporation. Personal creditors of a shareholder may be able to gain ownership of the shareholder's shares, but they cannot go after the assets of the corporation and if the corporation is liquidated, the corporate creditors (as holders of debt obligations) will have priority over the personal creditors of shareholders (as holders of equity). This result is reached without the corporate creditors perfecting any security interest in the corporate assets.[4]

---

[4] This has been called "affirmative assets partitioning," while limited liability is called "defensive assets partitioning." See Henry Hansmann & Reinier Kraakman, The Essential Role of Organizational Law, 110 Yale L.J. 387, 393 (2000).

4.  *Limited Liability.* Also consistently with the concept of the corporation as a separate entity, contractual obligations and debts incurred by employees of the corporation are strictly obligations and debts of the corporation, not of the shareholders (or the employees or directors). Simply stated, shareholders are not liable for the debts of the corporation. They risk losing the amount of their investment, but no more. This attribute may be essential to large-scale, dispersed, passive investment.

5.  *Indefinite Duration.* Generally, there is no limit on the duration of a corporation. It is possible to specify such a limit in the corporate documents, but this is rarely done. The corporation's existence may be terminated as a result of insolvency (in a bankruptcy proceeding), by merger into another corporation, by voluntary liquidation upon a recommendation of the board of directors approved by a vote of a majority of the shareholders, or, in extreme circumstances, by judicial decree on a finding of deadlock or oppressive behavior by the controlling shareholders.

6.  *Transferable and Tradable Shares and Debt Obligations.* The shares of stock of public corporations are freely transferable and may be bought or sold on established markets such as the New York Stock Exchange (NYSE). The existence of a public market means that shares are highly "liquid"—they can be turned into cash by a quick phone call or a few keystrokes on the internet.[5] Again, this attribute may be essential to large-scale, dispersed, passive investment. In the case of closely held corporations, limitations may be imposed on transfer, by agreement among the shareholders. In the absence of such agreement, shares are freely transferable but it may be difficult, at best, to find a buyer. Apart from raising capital (money) by issuing shares of stock, public corporations can borrow money by issuing bonds and debentures, which may be widely held and readily traded. They can also borrow from banks and other lenders and may owe money to suppliers and other trade creditors.

7.  *Centralized Control and Separation of Ownership and Control.* Shareholders elect the members of the board of directors, who in turn appoint the Chief Executive Officer (CEO) and other officers. In large corporations with many thousands of shareholders the reality is that the board is essentially self-perpetuating. No shareholder is likely to have enough at stake to be willing to incur the substantial expense required to try to replace members

---

[5] This is an important point that distinguishes "shareholder democracy" from a political democracy. In politics, not only does the state have coercive power over its citizens but citizens have less ability to "exit" (which requires that he or she transfer citizenship) and hence have more incentive to participate in public affairs. This trade-off between the ability to exit and the incentive to participate was first described by Professor Albert O. Hirschman of Harvard. See A.O. Hirschman, Exit, Voice and Loyalty (1970).

of the board. Thus, there is a "separation of share ownership and control." In the traditional analysis reflected in this phrase, the shareholders are "owners" of the corporation. This depends on a strained use of the word "owner"; shareholders can only vote for directors or on major issues, cannot withdraw their share of the firm's assets, cannot tell employees what to do, are limited in their ability to gain access to books and records, etc. What the notion of separation of ownership and control properly claims is that for corporations with large numbers of shareholders, the shareholder power to elect directors may have little practical effect; boards tend to be self-perpetuating, with new members often chosen by the professional managers. Thus, the board and, even more so, the professional managers, have effective control. The professional managers may have their own interests and objectives, which they may pursue at the expense of the shareholders (a reality captured by the phrase "agency costs")—a serious problem that has led to much public discussion, scholarly examination, and general hand-wringing. It is important to keep in mind, however, that the legal and economic structure of the corporation is inherently attractive to those persons who wish to be passive investors. Shareholder passivity may be at least as much attributable to investor preferences as to managerial domination. Individual shareholders may rationally conclude that they would not want important decisions affecting their investment to be made by people like themselves— though they may wish that they had more practical power to discipline or replace weak boards or managers.

Apart from these particular characteristics of corporations, there are certain characteristics of the American legal system that seem to be essential ingredients of successful economic performance. First, private property rights and contractual obligations are enforced by a legal system that is relatively efficient and largely free of corruption. Second, there is a well established accounting profession that, despite its faults and weaknesses, provides investors with reasonably reliable information about the financial performance of the firms in which they invest. Periodic financial reports, generally required by state or federal law, provide the "transparency" that bolsters investor confidence and willingness to invest. Third, federal and state laws, and the agencies for enforcing those laws, provide substantial, though by no means complete, protection against dishonest representations and fraudulent schemes.

## C. VARIATIONS: CLOSELY HELD, INTERMEDIATE, AND START–UP CORPORATIONS

1. *Closely held corporations.* With closely held businesses (which are generally, but not always, small ones), the corporate form has been attractive in part because the strong entity concept in corporate law (as

opposed to the weaker entity concept in partnership law) makes the economic relationships among investors and the accounting for allocation of gains and losses relatively easy to understand. In the eyes of some people, the corporate form may also offer a sense of higher status than the partnership form, since larger businesses are almost invariably organized as corporations. Of considerable importance is the fact that the corporation provides a convenient, effective, and easily understood device for protecting creditors, by separating assets from shareholders, as explained above. Perhaps most important in the minds of many business owners is that the corporate form provides limited liability (now available also for LLCs and, with some limitations, for partnerships). In the case of loans from banks (and debt owed to certain trade creditors), the benefit of limited liability is likely to be largely illusory: personal guarantees by some or all of the shareholders are likely to be required. But limited liability does protect against debts owed to some trade creditors and, more important in many cases, to tort creditors (and other "involuntary" creditors).

As one might expect, the functional role of the board of directors of a closely held corporation is likely to be minimal and purely formalistic. The shareholders (who are likely to be the members of the board) will make the decisions and are unlikely to think much about their roles as shareholders or directors. There will be no separation of ownership and control. Since it will be unfeasible to sell shares to outsiders, the shareholders may enter into an "ancillary" agreement among themselves to provide some mechanism by which they may liquidate their shares—for example, by selling to the other shareholders at some price determined by a formula or by a process such as arbitration. The shareholders may also, by express agreement, impose limitations on the freedom of shareholders to sell their shares (generally taking the form of a "right of first refusal").

2. *Intermediate types.* The preceding discussion relies on a dichotomy between large, public corporations and small, closely held corporations. But the universe of incorporated businesses is not limited to these two ideal types. Although the "closely held-versus-public" distinction can be useful and will be invoked throughout the remainder of this chapter, often it may be more instructive to contrast "owner-controlled" and "management-controlled" firms. This distinction has been used by a number of empirical researchers (see Sec. VII(A)(2) below), who have found that firms in which there is a controlling, or at least powerful, single shareholder (that is, one shareholder owning, for example, 25 percent of the voting stock or more) tend to behave quite differently from those in which no single shareholder is able as easily to restrain management. In short, it may be less the number of shareholders, and more the structure of share ownership, that determines the degree of shareholder control (or the lack thereof) over managerial behavior.

3. *Startup corporations and venture capital.* A particularly interesting and important intermediate type of corporation is the startup financed by a venture capital fund. Suppose that an entrepreneurial computer software engineer and a few associates figure that they can get rich by developing a new software program. Getting started will take some money, which is likely to come out of their own pockets or from friends and relatives. If they are good or lucky, or, even better, both, they will reach a stage of development where they will need to raise some serious money in order to keep growing (with the alternative likely to be failure). This is where the venture capital fund (VC) enters the picture. The money in such funds comes from wealthy individuals or from institutions such as pension funds and University endowments. The fund will be managed by savvy people who invest the money in promising startup ventures such as our software company, hoping for huge gains to make up for the inevitable losers. What makes this interesting is that the VC managers will bargain not only for a share of the gain if the venture is successful but also for participation in control and for various protections. Often, the parties will recognize that the amount of the VC's initial investment will not be enough to keep the firm going until it reaches full viability; additional stages of financing will be required. The additional financing may come from the initial VC or from other such funds, or both. This gives the VC certain de facto power of control over the entrepreneurial group. In addition, the VC is likely to insist on seats on the board of directors, a priority in case of liquidation, and certain rights with respect to creating a public market for the shares and selling its shares in that market. The behavior of the VC representatives is decidedly not like that of passive investors. Generally these representatives (who get rich when their funds do well) have experience and connections that will be of value to the venture and will be appreciated by the entrepreneur. But conflicts may arise—particularly when the going gets tough—and the VC representatives may be able to impose their will. The point is that the VC is not directly involved in running the business but neither is it a passive investor.

## II. THE DEVELOPMENT OF THE AMERICAN BUSINESS CORPORATION: A HISTORICAL OVERVIEW

At the time of the American Revolution, the legal nature and economic functions of corporations were very different from what they are today. The English law in the 18th Century was that only the king in Parliament could grant a corporate charter. Corporate status was then viewed as a special, limited concession of the sovereign, and corporate charters were usually granted to achieve a specific political objective, such as colonizing a territory, developing foreign trade, or exploiting a particular trade opportunity or natural resource.[6] In England, this

---

[6] Think, for example, of the East India Company or the Hudson's Bay Company.      For a short history of this era, see J. Willard Hurst, The Legitimacy of the Business

cautious attitude toward the granting of corporate status appears to have been the product of both a royal desire to maximize its wealth and power by controlling access to economic opportunities as well as a hostile public reaction toward corporations in the wake of the "South Sea Bubble," which was a speculative mania that arose in the trading of the stock of a company that had planned to colonize the South Pacific. The ultimate collapse of this bubble caused a stock market crash, which was followed in turn by an economic depression. In response, English legislation in the early 1700s restricted (and even criminalized) the issuance of corporate securities in the belief that trading produced speculative excesses.

Within the infant American Republic, many shared the English skepticism of the corporate form, but for different reasons. The Jeffersonians feared industrialization and did not want to facilitate the aggregation of large amounts of capital in private enterprises. Most of the enterprises organized in corporate form in the United States by the end of the 18th Century were quasi-public ones: cities, boroughs, churches, canal and turnpike companies, and the first banks and insurance companies. Well into the 19th Century, corporate law in many states remained extremely restrictive.[7] Corporate charters were granted only by the legislature; amendments also required a legislative act. Frequently, the legislature restricted the amount of capital that could be raised, the duration of the corporation's existence, or the corporate activities that could be pursued. Occasionally, the corporation would be required to aid specific charities or other public purposes as a condition of its existence, and in a few cases shareholders were made liable for the corporation's debts. In general, the state saw itself as a partner in the corporate enterprise.

The essential transition in the legal nature of the corporation occurred during the mid–19th Century and was attended with some controversy. In this period the corporation came to be seen, not as an *ad hoc* creation that was vested by the state with exclusive control over a public asset or natural resource, but as an available form by which private parties could conduct any business. When the Supreme Court decided in the famous case of Dartmouth College v. Woodward[8] that the charter granted by the English crown to Dartmouth College could not be amended by the State of New Hampshire, the significance of the case was widely understood to have implications that extended beyond the educational context. Its message was that a corporate charter was a contract whose obligations the Constitution would not permit a subsequent legislature to impair. The decision evoked much contemporary protest, because to many it seemed to imply that once a corporate

Corporation in the Law of the United States, 1780–1970, at 3–9 (1980).

[7] See Lawrence M. Friedman, A History of American Law (1973) at 166–175.

[8] 17 U.S. (4 Wheat.) 518, 4 L.Ed. 629 (1819).

charter was granted, the corporation was beyond legislative control. In fact, its significance was more limited than this because, as Justice Story pointed out in his important concurring opinion, the state could insert a provision in any charter that it granted reserving its right to amend or further condition the charter. This "reserved power" has in fact become standard, and every state's corporation code today contains a section stating that any certificate of incorporation granted pursuant to it will be subject to subsequently enacted changes in the state's corporation law.

Although the *Dartmouth College* case signaled the gradual ascendancy of a new view that corporations should be seen as essentially private arrangements among investors, rather than as state-created concessions, two other developments in the mid–19th century did as much to hasten the end of the restrictive approach to corporate chartering. First, the process of special chartering by which each corporate charter required a legislative act overburdened the legislature and invited corruption. Those able to lobby state legislatures could obtain a corporate charter, while less influential or affluent people could not. In consequence, a reform movement that sought to afford equal access to corporate chartering swept through many states, at roughly the same time that the Jacksonian reform era was seeking to eliminate other special privileges. Second, by the end of the century, a competition developed among the states for the right to issue corporate charters, in part to maximize the franchise taxes that a corporation pays to its state of incorporation. This competition was spurred by a Supreme Court decision in 1868 that ultimately facilitated the ability of a corporation incorporated in one state to do business in another.[9] By the end of the century, New Jersey, and later Delaware and Maine, had enacted permissive enabling laws that made it comparatively simple to incorporate in those jurisdictions and that also abandoned any attempt to regulate substantive corporate behavior through the chartering process. This development in turn invited corporations facing restrictive chartering regulation in their own state of principal residence to re-incorporate in these jurisdictions. Much subsequent debate has focused on the impact of this competition, with many maintaining that it produced a "race to the bottom" and others arguing that it only eliminated archaic regulations as shareholders sought the most favorable jurisdiction in which to incorporate. Indisputably, however, interstate competition spelled the end of any serious

---

[9] Paul v. Virginia, 75 U.S. (8 Wall.) 168, 19 L.Ed. 357 (1868). This decision is a curious and transitional one, because it first held that a corporation was not a citizen entitled to the benefit of the "privileges and immunities" clause of the Constitution. This was consistent with the restrictive and skeptical view of the corporation that courts generally held. However, the Court then indicated that interstate transactions involving corporations fell within the power of Congress to regulate interstate commerce. The implication of this statement was that a state could only preclude a foreign corporation from engaging in transactions within its own borders if these transactions did not amount to interstate commerce (as they did not in *Paul*). Consequently, as the definition of interstate commerce expanded during the 19th Century, so also did the ability of corporations to migrate to other states.

attempt to use state corporation codes to effect substantive regulation of corporate conduct.

Still, even at the end of the 19th Century, industrial businesses were not necessarily organized in corporate form. Andrew Carnegie ran his famous steel company as a limited partnership, in order that he, as a general partner, would not have to share control with his fellow investors (who as shareholders would have had a proportionate right to vote). John D. Rockefeller used the trust device to hold control of the various oil companies that he had assembled into the Standard Oil Trust, because state corporate law at the time typically forbade one corporation from owning stock in another. (Hence, Congress eventually passed "antitrust" laws instead of "anti-corporation" laws.) However, the passage of the Sherman Antitrust Act of 1890, and its subsequent judicial construction to bar, as a *per se* offense, any price-fixing agreement among competitors, set off the greatest merger wave in American history at the end of the century. Lawyers and businessmen recognized that, although price-fixing cartels were illegal, competing businesses could merge into a single entity, and their merger would be subject only to the lesser scrutiny of a "rule of reason" test. When the resulting consolidation was completed, for example, Andrew Carnegie's steel company and many of its competitors had combined into the U.S. Steel Corporation. As a result, by the early 20th Century, the corporate form had become associated with a much greater scale of industrial operations, and the degree of concentration within most industries had significantly increased. The corporate form alone did not cause this transition, but it is doubtful that this sudden growth in the scale of business organization could have occurred as easily if businesses had still operated through the partnership or trust forms.

American businesses also underwent important internal changes in the late 19th and early 20th Century.[10] A transition in internal structure probably began with the growth and expansion of the railroads in the mid–19th Century. Railroads required a higher level of internal administrative coordination than earlier industrial enterprises in order to meet timetables, assemble trains, and ship freight across connecting lines; they also needed substantial infusions of capital to expand. As a result, the general purpose business manager who handled all administrative matters began to give way to functional specialists. Over time, railroad corporations and later telegraph and steel corporations developed internal structures consisting of functionally specialized divisions: production managers, sales managers, financial and accounting experts, engineers— the manager inevitably became a specialist. Business historians, most notably Harvard's Alfred Chandler, have theorized that the rise of the professional manager during this period significantly changed the nature

---

[10] For the path-breaking description of this important transition in the internal organizational structure of firms, see Alfred D. Chandler, Jr., The Visible Hand: The Managerial Revolution in American Business (1977).

of the corporation. From an institution that was externally controlled either by a family group or a group of investment bankers who raised its capital, the industrial business corporation became an internally controlled organization run by professional managers who made the firm's pricing, output, wage and employment decisions with relatively little external supervision or control. This new form of "managerial capitalism" was largely in place, Professor Chandler has found, by the end of World War I.

One further internal development within the American corporation deserves special note. During the 1920s, business historians have concluded, the largest U.S. corporations suffered a crisis in internal control as their senior managers found themselves overburdened by the increasing volume of decisions requiring their attention. The largest corporations in this era (such as General Motors and DuPont) had already become multi-unit enterprises that produced diverse and often unrelated products. Although managers had earlier become functionally specialized, all decisions that required internal coordination between different specialties (for example, finance and production staffs) still flowed to the top. As a result, senior managers found themselves excessively burdened with operational decisions. In response to these "informational overload" crises, the largest corporations began in the 1920s to reorganize their internal structures to achieve greater decentralization. Divisional managers became more autonomous, and the task of senior managers became increasingly that of strategic planning and capital budgeting— that is, their focus of attention shifted to determining the products and services that the corporation would produce and how to finance their production, either from internally generated funds or from the credit and capital markets, or from both. As senior managers became more and more divorced from operational decision-making, their role in the operation of the business became essentially that of "monitoring" middle-level managers. Senior managers would replace those middle-level managers who proved unsuccessful, but generally granted them relative autonomy in day-to-day affairs.

Over time, the structure of many large corporations evolved into that of the modern conglomerate (that is, a firm that managed a wide assortment of divisions that produced largely unrelated products). The first such firms were probably companies such as General Electric or Westinghouse, and their essential outlines were visible before World War II. However, the full flowering of the conglomerate form came in the 1950s and 1960s, as corporations such as IT & T, Textron, and Gulf & Western began to acquire subsidiaries whose operations spanned virtually all sectors of the economy. Structurally, the modern conglomerate began to resemble a holding company that supervised a portfolio of diverse companies in a decentralized fashion. Today, senior management, assisted by a much expanded auditing and planning staff, continually re-shuffles this portfolio of companies, selling off those that they believe have low growth prospects and buying others. Some economists have argued that this structure promotes efficiency, because the senior management team can monitor the performance of this portfolio of companies more efficiently than can the capital market; in particular, it can replace inefficient division level managers and swiftly transfer funds among divisions. In this light, senior managers function much like a miniature capital market, shifting the cash flow from, for example, a steady, but low growth, division to finance a higher growth one. These observations are further examined in Section VII(A) below, but during the 1980s there emerged an apparent counter-trend toward "deconglomeration," as large conglomerate corporations have begun to reduce their size and scope of operations, possibly under the threat of a hostile takeover, which can oust the senior managers of an inefficiently run company. This development suggests that some large conglomerates may have grown to an inefficient size, which conclusion leaves the comparative advantage of the conglomerate form in some doubt. Still, the basic pattern seems clear that senior managers today tend to be functionally engaged in monitoring and planning activities and must of necessity delegate operational management to subordinate levels. Thus, such a senior management stands in relation to its operating levels much as the law has traditionally assumed that the board of directors stands in relation to its officers. Of course, only the board can monitor the corporation's most senior managers, but it is important to understand that monitoring has ceased to be the exclusive responsibility of the board. Indeed, it is today questionable whether the board is even the primary monitoring body in the large public corporation.

## III.  THE REIFICATION ILLUSION

### A.  "DECOMPOSING" THE CORPORATION

Both lawyers and laypersons tend to speak instinctively of the corporation as an "it"—that is, as a thing that has an identity and existence of its own. While this is sometimes a helpful shorthand form of expression, a basic message of this book is that corporations should not be analyzed in this fashion, except when the complexity of the actual relationships becomes so unmanageable as to make it necessary to reify. Generally, to gain a clear understanding of how a firm behaves and why it is structured in a particular fashion, one must decompose the firm into the various categories of participants whose activities are coordinated within the firm: equity investors, creditors, managers, employees, suppliers, etc.[11]

This statement may seem confusing, because it is clear that the law, itself, does not do this. In general, the corporation is reified. (See

---

[11] For a fuller examination of these participants and their respective interests, see William A. Klein, *The Modern Business Or-* *ganization: Bargaining Under Constraints,* 91 Yale L.J. 1521 (1982).

Chapter 2, Sec. V.) That is, the law conceives of the corporation as having an existence separate from that of its employees, customers, suppliers, and so forth—but mainly, from its shareholders. Sometimes, to be sure, the corporation is called a "fictional" entity—in apparent recognition of the abstract and potentially misleading nature of the concept. Still, there is the basic notion of a barrier, a psychological wall, between the shareholders (and other participants in the venture) and the corporation. Thus, for example, as a matter of law a shareholder (even the sole shareholder) of a corporation does not own the assets devoted to the business of the corporation; he or she instead owns only shares of stock of the corporation, and the corporation owns the assets. (Contrast the model of the sole proprietor, described in Chapter 1, Sec. I(C).) Sometimes the process goes a step further. The fictional (conceptual) entity becomes a putative person—capable, for example, of committing a crime or of bearing the burden of a tax. In other words, reification sometimes leads to anthropomorphism—that is, treating the corporation as if it were a human being.

Admittedly, reification may sometimes be a useful device, because it allows us to manage complexity. It is useful to think, for example, of the United States entering into a relationship with China, rather than thinking of the citizens of each of the two countries acting through complex mechanisms to alter their relationships with one another in an infinite variety of ways. On a smaller scale, it is easier to talk about the owner of a hardware store taking in another person as a "partner" in the "store" or the "business" than to talk, or think, about transferring to that person an undivided half interest in each lock, each barrel, each other item in stock, and each account receivable and payable, as well as an equal share in control and liability, etc. In law, the idea of the separate entity serves the further, more mundane, function of symbolizing a set of important legal rules or doctrines, such as the limited liability of shareholders. Entity thinking also encapsulates a set of rules, vital to the economic appeal of the corporate form, that deny individual investors (shareholders), and their creditors, the right to withdraw their share of the firm's assets. These rules in effect cordon off the assets of the firm, giving creditors of the firm a prior claim (over investors and their creditors) to the assets of the firm, and protecting creditors and shareholders from premature diminution of corporate assets. At the same time, when the entity theory leads to bad results, the courts often find ways to avoid or ignore it. Still, reification is a device for making something that is in fact complex seem simple, and that can be dangerous. In reality, only individuals enjoy the benefits, or bear the burdens and the responsibilities, of actions affecting other individuals.

The following illustrations are designed to serve two goals: first, to demonstrate the significance of reification, and, second, to show how important it is for a lawyer or a business person to be able to understand, work with, and make use of, but not be deluded by, this concept.

## B.  ILLUSTRATIONS

**1.  Loan–Out Corporations.** Loan-out corporations are used by entertainers, athletes, and others to achieve certain tax advantages. Suppose, for example, that Sean Starr is an actor and works, on average, in three motion pictures each year. In each of these jobs he is an employee of the independent company that produces the motion picture. Each company is separate from the others. Thus, Sean is engaged in a series of employments. He is not considered to be self-employed. Because of the short duration of his employment, he is not covered by any employer-sponsored plan for health or retirement benefits.

Suppose that in a particular year Starr's income subject to taxation is $400,000, and that he pays $15,000 for health insurance and sets aside $30,000 for retirement. As an employee, he will not be entitled to a tax deduction for the health insurance payments and will be entitled to only a modest deduction for his retirement savings.

Suppose Starr learns from his accountant that he can reduce the amount of his income subject to taxation, without any substantive change in his activities, by setting up a corporation. The corporation might be called "Sean Starr, Inc." All that is required to form the corporation is filing some standard-form documents with a state official and paying a modest fee to the state, and not-quite-so-modest, but still reasonable, fees to his lawyer and accountant. Starr, the individual, will own all the common stock of the corporation. He will be a director and, if the state law requires more than one director, will, as shareholder, elect the other directors. The board of directors will then probably appoint Starr as president of the corporation and fill the other offices to the extent required by law. Now there is a full-fledged corporation—a separate entity. The corporation will be engaged in the business of supplying the services of its employees to motion picture production companies. The corporation then will hire Starr, who will become its only employee, and it will "loan out" his services to the production companies.

The production companies will pay the corporation for Starr's services. For tax purposes, the corporation will be deemed to have earned the $400,000. Starr's employment agreement with Sean Starr, Inc., will provide for a salary to be paid by the corporation to him and will require the corporation to pay for health insurance and retirement benefits for him. The salary will be set at an amount that will soak up all the income after paying the $15,000 health insurance premium and the $30,000 contribution to the retirement fund (and other expenses that we can ignore). That is, the corporation will pay a salary of $355,000 to Starr, who will report this amount—instead of $400,000—as his income subject to taxation. Starr will have the same medical and retirement benefits that he would have had without the incorporation, and the same amount of money in his pocket after the payment of those benefits, but the federal income tax law is such that $45,000 in "fringe benefits" will not be included in his income. The corporation will be a taxable entity, subject to a corporation income tax, and will have gross income of $400,000 from the payments it receives from the production companies. In determining its net income subject to taxation, however, it will be allowed to deduct the salary paid to Starr, plus the $15,000 health insurance payment and the $30,000 retirement payment. After the deductions, the corporation's taxable income should be zero, so it will have no tax liability.

The net effect will be the same as if Starr had not formed the corporation and had been allowed to deduct the amounts of the health insurance premium and the contribution to the retirement fund. It is all done with legal forms that have no substantive importance. It is a matter of—call it what you will—legal magic, smoke and mirrors, form over substance.

After incorporation, nothing will change except the legal documents. Starr will still rely on his agent to find jobs for him. The producer or director of the production companies that want Starr's services will negotiate with him and his agent. When the time comes to sign a contract, however, the nominal parties will be the production company and Sean Starr, Inc. The representatives of the production company will have no problem with this arrangement; everyone knows how the game is played, and why. The production company will make its payments to Sean Starr, Inc., rather than to Sean Starr. (Adjustments will be made to take account of the shifting burden of Social Security taxes.) Starr will behave exactly as he would if he had no corporation, except that he will be required to perform certain minor rituals (such as simulating board meetings and keeping corporate minutes or adopting shareholder resolutions) and otherwise act as though the corporation were truly something separate from himself.

Starr will have done nothing unlawful—or, in his line of business, unusual. Moreover, the tax result may be consistent with sound tax policy. Starr will have achieved a tax position comparable to that of corporate executives and other continuing employees. But any reader of this book who thinks it is sensible to make the tax benefit contingent on the hocus-pocus (and waste of legal and other resources) involved in the process of incorporation needs remedial work.

**2. The Triangular Merger.** Another dramatic illustration of the role of reification and the opportunities it offers is the use of a third corporation to accomplish what is essentially a two-corporation merger. Again, we will consider a typical transaction (many variations are possible) at a very general level, isolating the elements bearing most plainly on reification.

Suppose that General Motors (note the reification here) wants to acquire P Corp., an automobile parts manufacturer. All of the common shares are owned by Jennifer Owner, who is also President and Chair of the Board of P Corp. P Corp. employs 2,000 people and has annual sales of $70 million and profits of $3 million, which makes it tiny compared to General Motors. There are many ways in which General Motors might acquire the P Corp. business. It could acquire P Corp.'s assets directly from it for cash or in exchange for General Motors common stock. It could buy Owner's common stock in P Corp. for cash or exchange General Motors common stock for Owner's P Corp. stock. There are tax, contractual, labor, liability, and corporate law considerations that will bear on the choice of form. The fact that any of these issues turns on the choice of form is, or should be, somewhat puzzling or disturbing, but we will focus on just two issues—shareholder voting procedures and the legal right to an appraisal that arises in a merger.

Suppose that Jennifer Owner and General Motors' representatives (note the partial avoidance of reification here) have agreed that General Motors will transfer some shares of its common stock to Owner in return for all of Owner's shares of P Corp.'s common stock. For a variety of reasons, General Motors' lawyers may decide that the transaction should take the form of what is called a "statutory merger," so called because it involves a procedure expressly contemplated and prescribed by state statutes governing such transactions. The kind of transaction for which the state laws are designed is one involving two corporations of roughly similar size. Since merger in that setting is thought to be a fundamental change in the nature of the investment of each corporation's shareholders, state laws might require not just board of director approval (as in the case of transactions less fundamental in nature), but also the voting approval of the shareholders of both corporations. In addition, state laws give those shareholders who are dissatisfied with the merger the right to seek a judicial determination of the fair value of their shares. This "appraisal remedy" leads ultimately to a judicial order to the corporation to pay these shareholders the amount so determined in return for their shares. (See Sec. VII(B)(5) below.) In the merger of P Corp. and General Motors, it is all well and good to require the vote of the P Corp. shareholder, Owner, who is substantially affected. Furthermore, it is clear that Owner will not opt for appraisal, because the deal would not have been done if she thought the price was too low. Thus, state law imposes no burden of any consequence on this side of the transaction, and that would likely remain true even if there were more than one shareholder. On the other hand, these requirements could block the transaction if they required a vote of the General Motors shareholders. Legal ingenuity has, however, discovered an easy way out. General Motors can form a wholly owned subsidiary corporation. The subsidiary will be treated as a separate entity. The subsidiary can then enter into the transaction on behalf of General Motors, and the merger can take place between P Corp. and the General Motors subsidiary. It will still be possible to transfer common stock of General Motors (the parent) to Owner in return for her P stock, so she is indifferent as to the use of the subsidiary. A vote of the shareholders of both merging corporations will still be required, but, because General Motors will no longer be a direct party to the merger, the only shareholder entitled to vote will be the shareholder of the subsidiary. That shareholder is General Motors, which votes by a vote of its board of directors. The individual shareholders of General Motors need not be consulted, nor need General Motors fear that any of its shareholders will go to court to seek a judicial appraisal of their shares.

In overview, this is an example where sensible lawyering has reduced the transaction costs of the deal by finding the lowest cost means to the desired end. In this light, we can think of the corporate lawyer as a "transaction cost" engineer who seeks to lead the business client through a regulatory maze at the lowest possible cost, both in terms of money and delay. Nor is this a case where we should be ethically troubled by this manipulation of legal forms. The outcome makes sense here. The transaction is so small in relation to the total size of General Motors that a vote of its shareholders does not seem appropriate.[12] But the point is that the desired result is achieved by using magic—by creating a fictional entity.

A word of warning is needed. The kind of transaction described here is a victory of form over substance. The substance of the transaction is a purchase of P Corp. by General Motors for its common stock. This purchase is transformed first into a merger and then, more particularly, into a merger of P Corp. and a General Motors subsidiary. In some situations, especially where the outcome seems to be inconsistent with the policy objectives of the law, courts will ignore the form of a transaction and require compliance with rules that would have been applied if the transaction had followed the more natural form (the substance). This principle is found throughout the law—in tax law, corporate law, securities law, and so forth. One of the toughest jobs of a lawyer is to try to figure out when the form will be respected and when the substance will control—and, sometimes, to figure out what is the substance and what is the form.

## IV. THE BASIC STRUCTURE FOR CONTROL AND OPERATION

### A. INTRODUCTION

The formal structure for control and operation of a corporation can best be described by reference to three basic groups—shareholders,

[12] In fact, the laws of some states now provide that no vote of the shareholders of the surviving corporation is required if the number of new shares of that corporation that are issued in the merger is small enough. See Cal. Corp. Code § 1201(b) (no surviving corporation's shareholder approval required if its shareholders retain more than five-sixths of voting power); Del.Gen. Corp. Law § 251(f) (approval not required if surviving corporation's shareholders retain 80 percent of voting power). Under the Revised Model Business Corporations Act, § 11.03(g), a shareholder vote is not required if the new voting shares issued by the surviving corporation do not exceed 20 percent of its total outstanding voting shares before the merger.

directors, and officers. The interests of individual shareholders are reflected in "shares of common stock" issued by the corporation and held by the shareholders (generally in the form of notations in the electronic files of an intermediary such as a stock broker or, less commonly now, in the form of paper certificates). In the absence of an agreement to the contrary (generally seen only in closely held corporations), the shares are freely tradable and, in the case of public corporations, are in fact actively traded. (The characteristics of shares of common stock are described more fully in Chapter 4, Sec. III(B).)

Shareholders are said to collectively own the residual or equity interest in the corporation; this interest entitles them to all earnings and appreciation in the value of the corporation's assets after the fixed claims of the corporation's senior securityholders (i.e., bondholders and other creditors and preferred shareholders) are satisfied. At the same time, they bear the risk of loss, up to the amount of their investments. The commonly held notion of the shareholders as the sole residual claimants does require some qualification. It is not just shareholders who gain or lose when the firm gains or loses, but often, as well, the firm's employees, its suppliers, its customers, and the entire community of which it is a member.

Shareholders can control the operation of the corporation only by electing directors, who form the board of directors and collectively exercise general supervisory control over the business. The directors are responsible for hiring and monitoring the officers, who perform or supervise the day-to-day managerial functions and who are likely, as well, to prepare and submit to the board for approval plans for long-term investment and operations strategy.

In overview, the most basic structural fact about corporate law is that management authority is vested in the board of directors, not in the shareholders. For public corporations, with many shareholders and complex businesses, such centralization of control is, of course, essential. The broad authority vested in the board is protected by a legal doctrine, known as the "business judgment rule," that largely immunizes managerial decisions from judicial review or shareholder challenge. (See Sec. VI(A) below.) Nonetheless, because managerial and shareholder interests can conflict in some areas, corporate law balances its broad delegation of authority with a system of checks that seeks to maintain the accountability of corporate managers to their shareholders. The tension between the need to delegate wide discretionary authority to managers and the need to maintain accountability generates most of the important issues in corporate law.

In the case of a closely held corporation, the shareholders are likely to be active in the management of the business and to be members of the board. The role of the board is then likely to be trivial and formalistic, except perhaps when there is a schism among the shareholders. In venture capital firms, as previously discussed (see Sec. I(C)(3)), the venture capital representatives (VC) are likely to serve on the board along with the founder/entrepreneurs and the VC may exercise significant managerial influence through its board membership. The VC may also exercise control in other ways. Generally, if all goes as expected, the relationship between the VC and the entrepreneur will be mutually cooperative and respectful. Trust and cooperation are highly valued in business relationships. The VC will often have valuable experience, insights, and contacts—all of which will be appreciated by the entrepreneur. But the VC is also likely to have control that does not depend entirely on good intentions. The VC may, for example, bargain for a veto power over any change in the identity of the top managers or in basic business strategy. Moreover, the VC may have control over future sources of finance. The firm is likely to need additional investment funds as it grows or if the business does not progress as well as initially expected. As a practical matter, the initial VC is likely to be able to determine whether such funds will be made available; if it is not willing to invest, others are not likely to be willing to do so. Given this make-or-break financial power in the hands of the VC, the entrepreneur may feel compelled to accept, however grudgingly, whatever advice the VC offers. More broadly, control is not a matter simply of formal structure but also of trust and cooperation, ancillary agreements, economic power, and various other factors.

## B.  SHAREHOLDERS

**1.  Shareholder Voting.** By statute, common shareholders have the right to vote (at annual or specially called meetings) for the election of directors and on certain "fundamental matters." Under most state statutes, the "fundamental matters" that require a common shareholder vote include: (1) mergers involving the corporation (except, under some statutes, when the corporation acquires a much smaller firm), (2) any amendment to the certificate of incorporation, (3) the sale of substantially all the corporation's assets, and (4) liquidation. Legally, the shareholders are neither agents nor principals of the corporation, and they can neither act on behalf of the corporation nor give orders to officers or other employees of the firm. They vote to elect directors, who are expected to use their own best judgment. In addition, shareholders can generally only vote on a merger or charter amendment if it has been first approved by the board of directors.[13] Some commentators have criticized this statutory pattern on the ground that shareholders, as owners,

---

[13] A few states, including New York, permit shareholders to amend the certificate of incorporation at a shareholders' meeting  without prior board approval of the resolution.

should not need the approval of the board to sell or restructure the firm. Still, the impact of this requirement for prior board approval is probably not very significant, except in special circumstances, such as a takeover battle, where a hostile bidder can acquire a majority of the shares and still may not be able to control the board of directors until the next annual election.[14]

Generally, shareholders vote in proportion to the number of shares they hold. Since the mid–19th Century, shareholder democracy has traditionally meant "one share, one vote." This principle may be modified by specific provisions in the certificate of incorporation, giving different classes of stock either greater or lesser voting rights. At the extreme is a corporation with one class of common shares, with one vote per share, and another class of shares that are identical to those of the first class in all ways (particularly in the claim to dividends and to a pro rata share of the proceeds of liquidation) but have no vote at all. In less extreme cases, the high-vote shares might, for example, carry ten votes each while the low-vote shares carried one vote each. It is important to distinguish, however, between those situations in which a corporation (a) sells newly issued nonvoting or low-vote shares to the public and those in which it (b) engages in a "recapitalization"—that is, beginning with a single class of shares held by the public, it creates a new, lower-vote class and provides the public shareholders with an incentive to exchange existing shares for the new, lower-vote shares. In the former situation, the use of differential voting rights may have benign purposes and effects[15] and, with a willing buyer and seller, it may be difficult to find any sound basis for objection to the difference in voting power. In the latter situation, on the other hand, the purposes and effects are more suspicious (as explained immediately below) and there may be an element of coercion of the public shareholders.

Dual-class recapitalizations became a topic of considerable attention in the 1980s and offer a nice illustration of conflicts between sharehold-

---

[14] In most states (but not Delaware), shareholders may not remove a director between annual meetings except "for cause," meaning for some specific act of disloyalty or incompetence. Determining that such an act occurred requires a formal hearing, and it is infeasible to hold such a hearing before the assembled shareholders of a public corporation. A minority of the states permits removal without cause, but even then the ability of the shareholders to call a special meeting to do so may be limited by by-law or charter provisions that chill this right as a practical matter. Under a few statutes (such as § 228 of the Delaware General Corporation Law), shareholders may act by majority consent in lieu of a shareholders' meeting, unless the certificate of incorporation provides otherwise. Such a statute

would effectively allow a hostile bidder to assume control immediately, unless its effect were cancelled by a provision in the target's certificate of incorporation.

[15] For example, suppose all the shares of the common stock of a corporation are held by a small group of its founders. The corporation has been successful and the time has come to raise new equity capital for expansion. The founders are unwilling to invest any more of their own money because too much of their wealth is already concentrated in this investment. At the same time, they are reluctant to risk losing control. The sale of nonvoting shares may be an effective and inoffensive method for the corporation to raise money.

ers and managers and the types of tactics used by the latter. Essentially, dual-class recapitalizations were a response by incumbent managers (or controlling shareholders with less than a majority of the voting shares) to perceived threats to their control. Dual-class common was seen as a device for concentrating voting power in the hands of the managers and their allies and thereby barring any threat to their incumbency and autonomy. If the management group, owning some shares, could induce other shareholders to trade their voting shares for no-vote or low-vote shares, they would be able, with a small proportion of the equity, to block a takeover.

But why would the other shareholders accept the reduced vote? Two kinds of inducements were offered. One was the promise of an increased cash payout on all the shares. This kind of promise led critics to argue that the shareholders were being "bribed" with their own money—money that should have been distributed to them anyway. Another type of inducement was that the no-vote or low-vote shares would be entitled to a higher dividend than the other shares. Each of the nonmanagement shareholders would be inclined to accept this tradeoff. The choice seen by each would be between (a) shares with no vote and a higher dividend and (b) shares with a vote that wouldn't matter because other shareholders would accept the no-vote or low-vote shares and management's control, through ownership of a majority of the full-vote shares, would be immune from challenge. Thus, there was a problem of collective action. A majority of the nonmanagement shareholders might be opposed to the recapitalization (because they might hope to be bought out at a high price in a takeover), but each of them acting alone would have an incentive to accept the new high-dividend, low-vote share for fear of being stuck with low-dividend, worthless-vote shares after most of the other shareholders had accepted the exchange. Accordingly, the dual-class recapitalization was thought to be coercive and therefore unfair to shareholders.[16]

---

[16] The term "coercive" needs a word of explanation. In its simplest sense, it implies that shareholders will sometimes vote for a charter amendment that makes them worse off because they fear the alternative is being made still worse off. For example, if management could credibly threaten to delist the company and thereby eliminate their access to a secondary trading market if shareholders did not consent, such a threat could produce a distorted choice in which the shareholders compared not the amendment with the present charter, but the amendment with this still worse possibility. See Jeffrey N. Gordon, *Ties that Bond: Dual Class Common Stock and the Problem of Shareholder Choice*, 76 Calif.L.Rev. 3 (1988). A more pervasive problem with charter amendments has been suggested by

Professor Bebchuk: management does not internalize the cost of value-decreasing amendments. At the corporate formation stage, the promoters of the firm have to realize that if a particular charter provision will reduce the value of the firm's stock from, say, $100 to $90, this $10 loss will be borne by them. This is not so at the charter amendment stage, when the loss falls entirely on the shareholders. Thus, managers have an incentive that promoters lack to propose value decreasing charter amendments, because they have little to lose and may anticipate that high information costs and collective action problems will cause shareholders to behave in an apparently passive fashion (i.e., "rational apathy"). Also, because few, if any, shareholders believe that their vote will be decisive, few

This prospect of coercion seemed to have ended in 1988, when the SEC adopted Rule 19c–4, under the Securities Exchange Act of 1934. The new rule prohibited the listing on any stock exchange or on NASDAQ (the principal computerized over-the-counter market) of the common shares of firms that had used recapitalization to reduce the voting power of existing shareholders. The prospect of delisting effectively barred corporations from engaging in dual-class recapitalizations. In the case of original issuance of no-vote or low-vote shares, on the other hand, the element of coercion is missing and the SEC's prohibition did not apply.[17] However, in 1990, the D.C. Circuit ruled that the SEC had exceeded its authority in promulgating Rule 19c–4 and invalidated it.[18] The court reasoned that the SEC's authority under § 19(c) of the 1934 Act extended only to ensuring competition among the exchanges and not to regulating substantive corporate governance or shareholder voting (which are matters of state corporate law). In 1994, however, the three principal exchanges—the New York Stock Exchange, the American Stock Exchange, and NASDAQ—all adopted a rule that substantially restricts the freedom of corporations to reduce the voting power of outstanding shares, but protects dual-class structures that had been accomplished before the rule was adopted.

**2. Voting by Proxy.** Shareholders may vote only at a meeting called for that purpose. Because the shareholders of a publicly held corporation will generally not find it worthwhile to attend a meeting, especially at a distant site, a system known as "proxy voting" has been devised to permit them to vote through designated agents. Under this system, shareholders are permitted to give to another person a *proxy*, which is a document transferring to that person the right to vote the shareholder's shares in the manner indicated on the proxy. Generally, this proxy is revocable at the discretion of the shareholder, who can

shareholders are likely to investigate the impact of the amendment. See Lucian A. Bebchuk, *Limiting Contractual Freedom in Corporate Law: The Desirable Constraints on Charter Amendments,* 102 Harv.L.Rev. 1820 (1989). An empirical study of 178 dual-class recapitalizations reports that when the controlling shareholder managers do not list their high-vote shares on a stock exchange, the value of the stock substantially outperforms the market average during the four years following announcement. Where the high-vote shares are listed, the value is about the same as the market average in the subsequent four years. Valentin Dimitrov and Prem Jain, The Effect of Dual Class Recapitalizations on Long–Run Stock Returns, available on SSRN at http://papers.ssrn.com/sol3/papers.cfm?abstract_id=422080 (2003). This seems to be strong evidence that dual-class recapitalizations increase shareholder value. It might be, how-

ever, that the firms were running scared, because of weak management, that this was why management wanted the dual-class recapitalization, and that, while management did improve, the firms would have been performed even better if they had not recapitalized.

[17] Some have criticized this distinction between the initial charter provisions and charter amendments on the ground that the conditions in the initial public offering ("IPO") market do not at all approximate the conditions of an efficient market. See Louis Lowenstein, *Shareholders Voting Rights: A Response to SEC Rule 19c–4 and to Professor Gilson,* 89 Colum.L.Rev. 979 (1989)(arguing that new issues are "sold, not bought" and underinformed investors systematically lose).

[18] Business Roundtable v. SEC, 905 F.2d 406 (D.C.Cir.1990).

change his or her mind up to the moment of the election. In the case of corporations with many thousands of shareholders, most of the voting is done by proxy, as it must be for practical reasons.

In most public corporations, the managers (officers or directors or both) use the corporate shareholder list and corporate funds to solicit proxies. Thus, management is said to control the *proxy machinery*, but other shareholders who wish to seek election to the board are generally entitled to access to the corporation's shareholder list. The proxies sent out by management to shareholders for signature will seek authority to vote in favor of a list (or "slate") of people to serve on the board of directors. Generally, these will be people selected by management or of whom management approves. (The characteristics of directors are discussed more fully in Sec. IV(C) below.) Management, in its proxy solicitations, may also seek authority to vote on other issues requiring shareholder approval (such as amendments to the certificate of incorporation, approval of stock options for management, appointment of the independent auditors, etc.). Historically, both on the election of directors and on specific issues, shareholders have tended to vote overwhelmingly in support of the management's recommendation. The one exception to this pattern is voting on management-proposed "shark repellents," which are amendments to the certificate of incorporation that are designed to discourage a tender offer or other hostile takeover. Because takeovers typically result in lucrative offers for the shareholders' shares, there have been situations where shareholders have either voted down or only narrowly approved management's proposals.

Proxies can also be sought by people outside of management. For example, a "dissident" shareholder may seek proxies from other shareholders in an effort to unseat incumbent, management-supported directors. Or a shareholder may seek proxies to vote against an amendment to the articles of incorporation proposed by the board. In the case of a publicly held corporation, before proxies may be solicited, the federal securities laws require that dissident shareholders and management provide shareholders with full disclosure by distributing a document known as a "proxy statement." Contests for proxies, pitting outsiders against management and frequently involving litigation over the accuracy of the disclosures provided by both sides, are called "proxy fights"; they can be expensive and, since they are often based, at least implicitly, on a challenge to management's competence or good faith, or both, these battles can lead to bitter exchanges between management and the dissidents. Proxy contests are discussed further in Sec. VII(B)(1) below, but, generally speaking, only a person with a substantial number of shares will find it worthwhile to take on management in a proxy fight.

In addition to seeking proxies, a shareholder of a publicly held corporation is entitled under federal law to place certain specified kinds of proposals on the corporation's own proxy statement. This tactic is frequently used by church groups and other social activists to focus attention on the corporation's conduct or its relationship with broader social issues (such as involvement in countries with objectionable human-rights policies). Although these proposals have almost never been approved by a majority of the corporation's shareholders (and rarely receive 5 percent of the vote), they are employed as a tactic by which to dramatize issues (and possibly embarrass the corporation), and at this they may succeed. Also, where the potential for embarrassment is high, the corporation's board may agree to the proposal, even though the board could defeat the proposal at the shareholders' meeting.

**3. Special Voting Mechanisms.** A number of devices have been used by incorporated firms to modify the most common method of shareholder voting, which is based on the principle of one-share, one-vote with separate balloting for each seat on the board of directors. Some classes of stock may be issued that carry no voting rights; typically, preferred stock of public corporations (see Chapter 4, Sec. III(D)) will not carry voting rights, unless its dividends are in default. Different voting rights may also be given to different classes of stock or two classes may each be given the right, voting separately, to elect one-half of the directors. These devices are typically employed in the closely held firm to allocate control and shares in the firm's earnings (or its assets on liquidation) according to different formulae.

Even when shares are non-voting, some state statutes will provide special voting rights, known as "class voting," when certain amendments to the certificate of incorporation are proposed that would adversely affect a class. "Class voting" essentially permits a majority of one class to veto a proposal, even when they are a minority of all outstanding shares, because under "class voting" each class must separately approve the proposed transaction or amendment. One reason for the legislative adoption of class voting was to avoid the possibility that common shareholders could amend the certificate of incorporation to eliminate any dividend priority or liquidation preference rights given to preferred shareholders.

Another once-popular device for protecting minority shareholders is cumulative voting, which is required under the laws of some states. Cumulative voting applies only to the election of directors and is designed to assure minority shareholders some representation on the board. Under normal voting procedures, each position on the board is in practical effect filled separately by majority vote; consequently, the majority shareholders have the power to elect all the directors. Under cumulative voting, by contrast, all positions on the board are in effect voted upon at once, and each shareholder may concentrate his or her voting rights by casting all his or her votes for one (or more) candidates; consequently, minority shareholders may be able to elect one or more directors by casting all their votes for a few candidates and not voting for the other positions. To illustrate, suppose that a corporation has two shareholders, Amy and Bill; that Amy owns 300 shares and Bill owns

200 shares; and that three directors are to be elected. Under straight voting, Amy would in effect outvote Bill on each position and would thus be able to elect all the directors. Under cumulative voting, Bill would be allowed to cast all his votes for one person and there is no way in which Amy could cast enough votes for more than two people to defeat Bill's candidate. Amy would fill two positions, or seats, and Bill would fill one.[19]

Most corporate managements tend to be hostile to cumulative voting, believing that it produces an adversarial board and results in critical decisions being reached in private meetings held by the majority faction prior to the board meeting. At one time almost half of the states required cumulative voting, but beginning in the 1950s the states began to make cumulative voting optional and by 1992 only six states continued to have mandatory cumulative voting.[20] In those states where cumulative voting has been required, its impact has often been negated by the tactic of reducing the board's size, because mathematically this increases the percentage that a dissident shareholder must own to be assured of board representation.

**4.   Shares with Altered Economic Claims.** The idea that voting control should be vested in the holders of common shares depends, roughly speaking, on the assumption that shareholders have the residual economic interest in the corporation and that since it is their investment that is most at risk they should call the shots. Shareholders presumably have a common interest in maximizing the value of the corporation, though they may differ in their ideas about how to achieve that outcome. But what if legal ownership is separated from economic ownership?

Suppose, for example, that Amy owns 100 shares of X Corp. and that she sells to Betty the option to buy those shares for $100 per share (a total of $10,000) any time within the next year. (For a more detailed discussion of options see Chapter 4, Sec. III(C)(2).) Suppose further that the market price of the shares rises to $160 while the option still has 8 months until it expires. The option is said to be "deep in the money." It is almost certain that Betty will exercise the option before it expires. Betty in effect bears the economic risk associated with the shares, but

---

[19] Technically, under the typical cumulative voting procedure, each shareholder receives a number of votes equal to the number of his or her shares multiplied by the number of the directors to be elected. Thus, Amy would have 900 votes and Bill would have 600. Suppose that Bill uses all his 600 votes for himself. Next, suppose that Amy tries to elect herself and two friends, Dan and Ellen. If she spreads her votes evenly, each of the three will receive 300 votes and Bill will be elected. Amy can assure herself of two positions by casting 450 votes for

herself and 450 for one of her friends. There is no way in which Bill can spread his votes so as to elect anyone other than himself (or a candidate of his choice).

[20] See Jeffrey N. Gordon, Institutions as Relational Investors: A New Look at Cumulative Voting, 94 Colum. L. Rev. 124, 145 (1994). The six states were Arizona, Kentucky, Nebraska, North Dakota, South Dakota, and West Virginia. Id. at fn. 53. Massachusetts did not permit cumulative voting. Id. at 145.

Amy still has legal title and the corresponding right to vote (in the absence of an agreement with Betty).

Or suppose that Carl owns 100 shares of Y Corp. stock. Don owns no Y Corp. shares and is convinced that the market price of the shares will drop significantly within the near future. So Don borrows Carl's shares (probably in a transaction arranged by Carl's stock broker without Carl's awareness), sells those shares to Emily, and pockets the proceeds. Don must ultimately replace Carl's shares, but he figures he will be able to buy the replacement shares at a low price in the future, so he'll be ahead the difference between the price at which he sold and the price at which he buys. This type of transaction is called a "short sale." During the time when Don is "short" on the shares he borrowed from Carl and sold to Emily, who should be entitled to vote?

The voting aspects of transactions like the ones in these two examples, and more complex variations, have only recently begun to attract some attention.[21] It is not clear whether there is a serious problem, but there have been some troubling transactions.[22]

**5. Preferred Shares.** In public corporations, the claim of the preferred shareholders is typically limited to a fixed dividend and a fixed amount on liquidation, but this claim must be satisfied before the common shareholders can receive anything. Thus, preferred shares are a relatively low-risk investment and, correspondingly, generally do not have the right to vote, except when they have not received the dividend to which they are entitled. Viewed from another angle, the rationale for disenfranchising the preferred shareholders is that they can rely on their fixed contractual rights and do not need to participate in corporate governance. Their rights to a prior, but limited, dividend resemble the rights of creditors, who also must rely on their contractual rights and do not vote in the election of directors. In contrast, because the common shareholders are entitled to the firm's residual earnings, after all prior claims are paid, they have a greater need to monitor management in order to ensure that the firm's returns are maximized, so they elect directors as their agents.

## C. DIRECTORS

The directors, collectively called the "board of directors" or "board," have the legal power and duty to manage the affairs of the firm. Traditionally, state corporation laws have provided that the business and affairs of a corporation "shall be managed" by its board of directors. More recently, these statutes have been updated to state that

---

[21] See Shaun Martin and Frank Partnoy, Encumbered Shares, 2005 U. Ill. L. Rev. 775.

[22] See Henry T.C. Hu and Bernard S. Black, Hedge Funds, Insiders, and Empty Voting: Decoupling of Economic and Voting Ownership in Public Companies (March 2006). ECGI—Law Working Paper No. 56/2006 Available at SSRN: http://ssrn.com/abstract=874098.

the business "shall be managed by or under the direction of the board." This reflects the growing recognition that the principal responsibility of the board is to monitor rather than to manage. Directors are not full-time employees of the corporation, although some officers of the corporation will invariably be elected to the board. Directors meet as a board periodically (typically monthly or quarterly, but various committees of the board may meet more frequently or as needed) to review and approve significant investment and operational decisions, such as building a new plant or adding a new product line, to approve or review a budget, to decide financial matters, such as issuance of new securities or payment of dividends, and, of most importance in many situations, to appoint, monitor, and determine the compensation of the person chiefly responsible for the front-line operation of the business—the person who has come to be known as the chief executive officer or "CEO." As with shareholders, individual directors have no inherent authority to bind the corporation; their authority is only collective—as the board, as a delegated committee, or as an agent thereof.

Although the directors are not agents of the shareholders in the legal sense, they are considered to be quasi-trustees who are subject to "fiduciary duties" owed to the corporation; in essence, these duties amount to the same kind of duty of loyalty and duty of care that an agent owes to his or her principal. (See Chapter 1, Sec. VII and VIII and this Chapter, Sec. VI.)

Directors are accorded wide discretion in their conduct of the corporation's business. Courts almost never interfere with a decision reached by the board, or impose liability on board members, unless it appears that there was a background of self-dealing, conflict of interest, or illegality. The principle relied upon by courts in deferring to the board's decision is known as the "business judgment rule" and is discussed in more detail below (at Section VI(A)). However, there are limits to the breadth of the directors' discretion. In a classic statement, those limits were defined in *Dodge v. Ford Motor,* where the court said:

> A business corporation is organized and carried on primarily for the profit of the stockholders. The powers of the directors are to be employed for that end. The discretion of directors is to be exercised in the choice of means to attain that end, and does not extend to a change in the end itself, to the reduction of profits, or to the nondistribution of profits among stockholders in order to devote them to other purposes.[23]

In short, directors have great discretion over how to maximize the return to shareholders, but not whether to. Certain deviations from the goal of shareholder wealth maximization, such as in the case of charitable contributions, are tolerated but are subject to a "rule of reason" standard. Moreover, as a practical matter, because of the protection of

[23] 204 Mich. 459, 507, 170 N.W. 668, 684 (1919).

the business judgment rule, boards may act, to some degree, in the interests of "other constituencies," such as employees, suppliers, or customers—even when doing so may not maximize shareholder wealth. Some commentators approve, others even applaud such actions.

Shareholders can choose not to re-elect directors upon the expiration of their terms of office and can vote to remove them from office (for any reason in some jurisdictions, but only "for cause" in other jurisdictions). If state law or the certificate of incorporation permits directors to be removed without cause, a new majority shareholder may be able to remove an old board quickly by calling a special meeting of shareholders; otherwise, this shareholder must wait until the next annual meeting of shareholders to take action. This point has considerable significance in takeover battles. Still, the shareholders of a publicly held corporation generally lack the legal power to interfere directly in the directors' managerial functions.[24] In practice, of course, directors generally pay heed to shareholders with meaningful voting power.

**1. The Closely Held Corporation.** In closely held corporations, directors are usually controlling shareholders or people selected by, and responsive to the wishes of, these shareholders. Put simply, it is the shareholders, not the directors, who will be calling the shots. There are exceptions to this generalization, usually arising when the shareholders are at odds with one another; then voting rules and procedures may become important. But, for the most part, in a closely held corporation the board of directors acts as a rubber stamp. Indeed, under some modern statutes no directors are required in a closely held corporation, and shareholders may directly manage the corporation if the certificate of incorporation so provides.

Shareholders of closely held corporations often enter into various forms of agreement relating to control. For example, three shareholders holding 60 percent of the voting shares might enter into an agreement to vote all their shares according to the wishes of a majority of them or in some specified manner. Of considerable significance are agreements designed to assure that particular individuals will have jobs in the firm, with designated duties or salaries, or both. These agreements help protect the expectations of the parties and prevent abuse by controlling shareholders, who might otherwise divert dividend income into overly generous salaries for themselves and their associates. Shareholder agreements permit the minority shareholders to be assured of some participation in control of the corporation plus a current return (the salary). In other words, the minority shareholder is protected, to some degree,

---

[24] As noted earlier at note 14, some statutes (such as Delaware Corporation Law § 228) permit shareholders to act by majority consent. This power not only authorizes shareholders to take actions that could have been taken at a shareholders' meeting, but can be used to expand the size of the board and then to elect new directors to fill these vacancies. In this manner, a majority shareholder can achieve its will if such a statute is applicable.

against being left out in the cold, holding shares worth less than their pro rata share of the total value of the firm.

Another common kind of protective agreement relating to control is one that assures a shareholder a seat on the board of directors. Standing alone, this may assure a minority shareholder somewhat better access to information about the operations of the firm than would otherwise be available. Beyond that, board membership, if combined with a requirement in the articles of incorporation or bylaws that certain proposals be unanimously approved by the board, can give a shareholder (as director) veto power over those proposals—for better or worse. (See Chapter 2, Sec. VIII(B)(3).)

The law today will uphold shareholders' agreements, subject to an important exception where these agreements bind a director's discretion in his or her capacity to vote as a director. That is, while shareholders may agree to vote their shares to elect each other to the board, an agreement to vote as a director to elect themselves or a third party to be a corporate officer has traditionally been held to be unenforceable. Why is this distinction drawn? The law in most states continues to see the director as, in effect, a kind of quasi-public servant who must be free to vote according to his or her own best judgment and not as a contract (i.e., the shareholders' agreement) dictates. This principle is understandable (for example, one would not want a member of Congress or a judge to vote or act as a contract dictated), but is possibly misapplied in the context of closely held corporations. In any event, in the case of closely held corporations, the modern trend is to uphold even agreements that marginally affect the director's voting discretion.[25]

To enforce a shareholders' agreement without resort to litigation, shareholders will sometimes agree to deposit their shares in a trust under which a mutually agreed upon trustee will vote these shares. The shareholders will receive certificates of beneficial interest in the trust. Depending upon the trust agreement, the trustee may vote according to his or her own discretion or as a majority of the participants direct. State law regulates these voting trust agreements, usually placing a ten-year limit on their duration to avoid "dead hand" control of the corporation by a permanent trustee. This is similar in intent to the rule against perpetuities in trusts and estates law, which limits the period during which a testator may direct the disposition or control of his or her property. However, the voting trust agreement can be renewed at the end of ten years by those shareholders who then so desire.

**2. The Public Corporation.** In the case of public corporations, the directors may be divided into three categories: (a) insiders (officers

---

[25] In Delaware, a special statute authorizes shareholders' agreements that affect the board's discretion, but only in the case of a "close corporation" (as defined). See Del.Gen.Corp. Law § 350. Elsewhere, some judicial decisions have liberalized this rule, but again only in the case of close corporations. See Galler v. Galler, 32 Ill.2d 16, 203 N.E.2d 577 (1964).

and other employees of the corporation); (b) persons having some other significant relationship with the corporation's management (such as the corporation's outside lawyers or investment bankers); and (c) true outsiders or "independent" directors (those who do not fit into either of the other two categories). Most of the independent directors of large corporations will be people (mostly men) who are top executives of other corporations, although there may also be a sprinkling of university presidents, Nobel Prize winners, ex-generals, ambassadors, and other public figures.

The shares of most sizable public corporations are traded (and "listed") on either the New York Stock Exchange (NYSE) or on NASDAQ (originally National Association of Securities Dealers Automated Quotations). Each of these exchanges has rules on who qualifies as an independent director. For example, the NYSE rule provides that a person is not independent if he or she was an employee within the past three years or for any twelve months in the past three years received from the company more than $100,000 as compensation for services, other than as a director. Under the rules imposed by both the NYSE and NASDAQ, a company seeking to be listed for trading must provide that a majority of its directors will be independent.

The question remains, however, whether a lack of economic affiliation with management makes these directors tough-minded evaluators of management's performance. Some indications do exist that boards have fired the chief executive officer with more frequency in recent years, but such internal coups d'etat still remain the exception rather than the rule and are vastly dwarfed by the number of externally induced changes in corporate control. Those who are skeptical of the ability of independent directors to monitor management point to the limited information and incentives that outside directors possess to question management closely. Because most boards lack any staff to develop information for them, directors are largely dependent on the data that management provides them. Although an outside director may question the chief executive closely for a half-hour or more at a board meeting, it is the rare (and probably inept) chief executive who cannot easily withstand this polite assault. Typically, their dialogue involves a mismatch between a full-time professional (the CEO) and a part-time observer (the director) who, while intelligent, neither wants to be so skeptical as to seem offensive nor has the same depth of knowledge about the specific matter under consideration. Thus, some critics worry that the trend toward independent directors may lead courts to defer excessively to decisions actually reached by corporate managers who may be self-interested.[26]

On the other side of this debate, a persuasive argument can be made that independent directors have significantly improved corporate gover-

---

[26] For expressions of this concern, see Victor Brudney, *The Independent Director— Heavenly City or Potemkin Village?*, 95 Harv.L.Rev. 597 (1982); Note, *The Propriety of Judicial Deference to Corporate Boards of Directors*, 96 Harv.L.Rev. 1894 (1983).

nance, even if they are not informed or motivated enough to resist management on all, or even most, occasions. When independent directors are in the majority, the possibility that ineffective senior managers can be removed presumably increases. Not only is removal itself more likely, but the fear of removal for poor performance may have a salutary effect, because it probably deters shirking and managerial consumption of excessive perquisites. Persistent questioning by informed directors may also have an impact by requiring management to articulate its policies and to seek consistency among them, even if the board seldom actually rebuffs the chief executive officer.

The proponents of the independent director would also point to the considerably revised structure of the modern board of directors to support their thesis that the board makes a significant difference. Today, the work of the board is chiefly done in committees, where independent directors may specialize and focus their attention. Within such a structure, independent directors may be more effective. Over the last decade, there has been a significant movement toward the institution of two important committees of outside directors—the audit committee and the nominating committee.

The audit committee selects and reviews the work of the corporation's outside, independent auditing firm, which examines the corporation's accounting reports and procedures to ensure that they fully and fairly reflect its financial condition. In 2002, in response to misleading accounting reports by, and the ultimate financial collapse of, a few major corporations (most famously Enron), Congress enacted legislation (the Sarbanes–Oxley Act) requiring that all audit committee members be independent directors (with a stringent definition of independence). This legislation also has a number of other provisions designed to ensure the objectivity of the independent auditor. Typically, the audit committee meets regularly with the independent auditors. The importance of the audit committee lies in large part in the fact that it affords a forum at which the independent directors can learn from the independent auditor, outside the presence of senior managers, about any deficiencies in the firm's auditing controls or accounting policies. For example, if the auditor believes that the corporation is pursuing overly aggressive policies in reporting earnings or if there are legal problems or other contingent liabilities of which the directors were not adequately apprised, the audit committee is the place where these problems can be candidly discussed. Because the firm's independent auditor is in effect the "inspector general" of the corporation, this channel of communication through the audit committee to the independent directors can do much to restore the information imbalance between management and the board.

The nominating committee is probably even more important and more controversial than the audit committee. Shareholders seem generally to be indifferent to the composition of the board of directors, and tend to be concerned with its performance chiefly in dramatic circumstances, such as a hostile takeover or a leveraged buyout, where the board's decisions will have an immediate effect on the corporation's stock price. Traditionally, in most public corporations, the chief executive has played a dominant role in selecting the outside directors whom the board, in its proxy statement, will propose to the shareholders for election. When the chief executive officer selects the outside directors, it is at least possible (some would say certain) that these directors will feel a personal loyalty to the CEO. An independent nominating committee may increase the objectivity and change the orientation of the outside directors, even if it produces individuals who are no more qualified or energetic. The rules of the NYSE require that "[l]isted companies must have a nominating committee composed entirely of independent directors."[27] NASDAQ has a rule with much the same practical effect.[28]

Another important committee is the compensation committee, which makes recommendations to the full board on the compensation of the CEO and other senior executives. This committee has become increasingly important since the 1990s, when the salaries of CEOs began to skyrocket. Again, the rules of the NYSE require that "[l]isted companies must have a compensation committee composed entirely of independent directors,"[29] and NASDAQ has a rule with much the same practical effect.[30]

There no longer seems to be much political or legislative interest in requiring that the board of directors include members representing particular non-shareholder constituencies (such as consumers, labor, minority groups, etc.). Proposals for such a constituency-based board were floated by Ralph Nader and others during the 1970s but have subsequently received little discernible support.

## D. OFFICERS

Legally, the officers (and other employees) of the corporation are agents of the corporation whose authority comes from a delegation by the board. Authority may be delegated either pursuant to a by-law (such as one authorizing the president to act as the general manager of the corporation and manage its day-to-day affairs) or by a resolution of the board (such as one instructing a manager to buy or sell a specific asset) or by implication (for example, the foregoing resolution might also grant authority by implication to hire lawyers and brokers to negotiate the purchase). The president will also likely be found by most courts to have some implied or "inherent" authority by virtue of his or her office to conduct day-to-day affairs and enter transactions in the ordinary course

---

[27] NYSE Listed Company Manual § 303A.04 (2004).

[28] NASD Marketplace Rules, Rules 4350(c)(4).

[29] NYSE Listed Company Manual § 303A.05 (2004).

[30] NASD Marketplace Rules, Rules 4350(c)(3).

of business. Still, no officer has the right to bind the corporation in a major transaction, such as borrowing a significant sum of money in the corporation's name, without board approval.

Litigation over employee authority to bind the corporation is recurrent and often involves a fact pattern where the corporation, after a deal has turned sour, seems to be "welshing" on a commitment made by its officer. In these situations, courts often find that the officer had "apparent authority" (or, in some cases, "inherent agency power"). Under the doctrine of apparent authority, when a prior course of conduct on the corporation's part (involving conduct by persons in addition to the unauthorized agent) gives the appearance to reasonable persons that the agent was authorized to act as he or she did, the corporation is held responsible for creating the impression that the agent had actual, delegated authority to so act and may not avoid or invalidate the transaction. Generally, the party seeking to use this doctrine must have been aware of some prior instances in which the corporation permitted its agent to act in such a fashion. In effect, courts decide in these cases who should bear the risk of the unauthorized agent's acts—the corporation or the "innocent" third party. When it would have been possible for the third party to ascertain the agent's authority at low cost to itself, courts have sometimes declined to find that the agent had apparent authority.[31] The case law in this area is far from consistent, and a variety of factors have been given weight by different courts. Still, from an economic perspective, the efficient rule of law would seemingly place the risk of loss on the superior "cost avoider"—that is, the party which at a lower cost could have prevented the loss from occurring. If the corporation is held liable because the agent is found to have had apparent authority, the corporation could in theory hold its agent liable for acting beyond the scope of his or her delegated authority. In practice, however, the agent's pocket will seldom be deep enough to cover the corporation's loss.

State corporation codes typically provide that a corporation shall have four officers: a president, a secretary, a treasurer, and one or more vice-presidents. Generally, the bylaws will spell out the authority of each of these officers. One person can occupy more than one of these positions, subject to a standard limitation that the same person cannot be both president and secretary. This last limitation arises because the corporate secretary's primary function is to certify that the person

---

[31] For example, in South Sacramento Drayage Co. v. Campbell Soup Co., 220 Cal. App.2d 851, 34 Cal.Rptr. 137 (3d Dist. 1963), the court declined to find that a California traffic manager for Campbell Soup, a New Jersey company, had authority to enter into a fifteen year exclusive dealing contract for the intrastate hauling of tomatoes in California. In so doing, the court emphasized that the other party to the contract had not contacted Campbell Soup to ascertain the scope of its agent's authority. In terms of relative costs, it seems clear here that it would have been much cheaper for the other party to inquire of Campbell Soup as to its agent's authority than for Campbell to attempt to broadcast to unknown future contracting parties the same information.

signing as the CEO is in fact that person and has been duly authorized. It would make little sense for the CEO to certify as to his or her own status and authority, because an imposter would happily certify these facts as well.

Federal legislation (the Sarbanes–Oxley Act of 2002) requires that the CEO and the CFO (chief financial officer) certify that they exercised due care to ensure the accuracy of corporation's SEC filings and financial statements.

## V.  FORMATION

### A.  THE FORMAL PROCESS

Persons seeking to do business as a corporation need only follow a simple and quite mechanical process in order to form a corporation. Failure to comply with this process, however, can result in shareholders forfeiting their limited liability on the ground that they are in fact partners in a *de facto* partnership. (See Sec. V(E) below.)

The central step in the incorporation process is the filing with a state official (sometimes called the Secretary of State, the Commissioner of Corporations, or some similar title) of a document usually called the "articles of incorporation" or the "charter." On receipt of these articles plus a usually nominal filing fee, the state official will issue a certificate of incorporation, which is a certificate evidencing that the attached articles have been filed with him or her. The certificate is the only conclusive evidence that a corporation has been formed.

The articles of incorporation are usually a brief and easily comprehensible document, which may take only a page or two. Its contents track closely the requirements of the incorporation statute of the jurisdiction of incorporation, which statute usually sets forth in very specific terms the necessary minimal contents of these articles. Typically, the articles will specify the corporation's name in its first paragraph, then provide in a second paragraph that its duration will be perpetual (or more limited if the shareholders so specify), and then in the following paragraphs set forth the corporation's powers and purposes; these paragraphs will typically be phrased in broad and inclusive "boiler plate" provisions, which generally end up authorizing "any other lawful purpose for which a corporation may be formed."

The articles of incorporation also specify the classes of stock that can be issued and define their rights. Often the articles (especially at the time of the initial formation of the corporation) will authorize only one class of common stock, but preferred stock may also be authorized.[32]

---

[32] Sometimes the power to specify the rights of preferred stock is delegated by the certificate of incorporation to the board of directors in order to preserve the opportunity to respond to market conditions at the time of issuance. This is because preferred stock dividend rates have to be competitive with prevailing interest rates. A preferred

There may be more than one class of common stock; the difference may relate to rights to dividends or to voting power, or both. For example, a corporation may have Class A common shares and Class B common shares, identical in all respects except that the Class A shares have ten votes per share and the Class B only one vote per share. To compensate for the lower voting power the Class B shares might be entitled to a 10 percent greater dividend per share and a 10 percent greater distribution on liquidation. Typically, the articles will also "authorize" the issuance of a maximum number of shares of each class. The fact that shares are "authorized" to be issued does not mean that they will be issued, but only that the board of directors may from time to time issue up to the number specified for each class, without a shareholder vote to amend the articles to authorize a larger number.

Another provision in the articles will specify the corporation's registered office in the jurisdiction of incorporation (or name an agent for service of process if the corporation's offices are outside the state). Under some statutes, the articles will also name the initial directors of the corporation, while in other jurisdictions the articles will only set forth the names of the "incorporators," who are the persons who sign the articles and who serve in effect as directors until the first board can be elected at the first meeting of the shareholders.

Once the articles are filed and the certificate issued, the directors (if they were named in the articles) hold their first meeting. There, they issue shares to the corporation's shareholders, dispose of various housekeeping matters (opening bank accounts, approving the form of stock certificate, appointing officers, etc.), and adopt bylaws. The bylaws typically cover such matters as number and qualification of directors, committees of the board and their responsibilities, quorum and notice requirements for meetings of shareholders and of directors, and titles and duties of the corporation's officers. If the jurisdiction is one that does not name the initial board of directors in the articles, then it is necessary to have a "Meeting of the Incorporators," who will take these same actions.

The important point here is that all this can be accomplished with a minimum of fuss in a single day, and little thought is required in the normal case to draft the articles of incorporation or the bylaws. In many jurisdictions, one person can serve as the sole incorporator, sole shareholder, sole director and chief executive officer of the corporation; the corporate secretary must, however, be someone else—typically, in these one-person corporations, a spouse or an attorney serves in this role. The articles of incorporation will almost invariably be accepted routinely by

stock whose rights are to be determined at issuance by the board is popularly called a "blank check" preferred. Corporate managements have used this power to block or chill a hostile takeover, by designing special securities called "poison pills" that are issued pursuant to this "blank check" authority. See description at Section VII(B)(2)(f) below. It seems highly doubtful that the shareholders actually intended to authorize these securities at the time they delegated this authority.

the state agency with which it is filed, and, if the normal procedures have been followed, the certificate will be issued without delay.

It may well be asked why there is any requirement that the articles of incorporation be filed with the state. The basic answer is historical: the public was once anxious about granting limited liability and wanted some public review. Indeed, limited partnerships, whose limited partners also have limited liability, must make such a filing. In both cases, identifying the directors in the articles of incorporation or the limited partners in a certificate of limited partnership is thought (correctly or otherwise) to help creditors identify who they are actually dealing with (although creditors, if they are concerned, probably can better protect themselves through representations in any contract with the corporation or by a credit check with a credit agency, such as Dun & Bradstreet). Another reason for the filing requirement is that it affords a convenient opportunity for the state to collect fees and taxes. In addition to the initial filing fee, and any income taxes, corporations pay franchise taxes to their state of incorporation; these taxes are usually based on either the corporation's assets or its outstanding stock. The filing requirement may also, in a few cases, protect against some egregious deviation from the usual norms of corporate law (such as a provision exculpating corporate officials from any liability for a breach of their duty of loyalty). To be sure, courts would probably not uphold such provisions in any event, but a filing requirement may reduce uncertainty by providing an earlier opportunity for a review of the validity of the provision. Finally, a public filing requirement gives notice to the world of the corporation's governance structure, and this can be important in some instances (as when, for example, a hostile bidder wishes to make a tender offer and needs to know whether the directors can be removed from office).

## B. AMENDMENT

The corporation's articles of incorporation typically may be amended by a vote of a majority of the shares (unless a higher vote is required in the articles). This presents a potential problem for minority shareholders: can protections they relied upon in the articles be eliminated by subsequent amendment? Originally, courts developed a protective doctrine that certain provisions in the charter created "vested" property rights that could not be modified without unanimous consent. Thus, for example, the courts would invalidate an amendment reducing the dividend rate, or the dividend arrearages, on the preferred stock or to eliminate dividend arrearages.[33] The doctrinal rationale would be that such an amendment deprived the preferred shareholder of a "vested" property right. The scope of this doctrine was always uncertain, and

[33] For an overview, see Herbert Hovenkamp, *The Classical Corporation in American Thought,* 76 Geo.L.J. 1593 (1988); Michael J. Halloran, *Equitable Limitations on the Power to Amend Articles of Incorporation,* 4 Pac.L.J. 47 (1973).

some cases even found amendments that simply expanded the corporate articles' purposes clause to violate vested rights. In any event, modern corporate law has abandoned the "vested rights" doctrine and replaced it with procedural protections. Today, under most statutes, proposed charter provisions that adversely affect the legal rights of a specific class of stock will require "class voting"; that is, the amendment must be adopted both by a majority of all shareholders and by a majority of the adversely affected class. In addition, some states give an appraisal remedy to shareholders in the event of certain adverse charter amendments so that they can in effect "cash in" their shares at a judicially determined fair price.

Nonetheless, even with the protections, the capacity of a majority to amend the articles, possibly to the detriment of the minority, is an important fact of corporate law. In part for this reason, some legal and economic theorists refer to the corporate articles as a "relational contract"[34]—that is, a document creating a long-term relationship in which not contingencies can be provided for in advance so that the contract necessarily contemplates its own modification. Unlike simple contracts for the sale of specific goods, the corporate articles essentially provide a governance mechanism for issues that cannot be fully anticipated at the time of corporate formation.

The articles of incorporation will determine whether power to amend the bylaws is vested in either the board or the shareholders, or in both concurrently. While action to amend the articles typically must be initiated by the board, amendment of the bylaws can be initiated by the shareholders, unless the power of amendment is vested solely in the board.

## C.  NEGOTIATIONS AT THE FORMATION STAGE

Although it is easy to form a corporation, there are important issues that the participants will need to discuss and negotiate among themselves. Assume that two individuals, Amy Inventor and Carl Capitalist, wish to form a corporation to exploit a new form of computer software that Amy Inventor has designed and believes she can make highly profitable. Carl Capitalist has agreed to invest $2,000,000 on this speculative flyer in return for 40 percent of the profits; Inventor has no funds and will, by agreement, purchase her 60 percent interest at a nominal price. This sale of the stock at different prices is generally permissible if done with the consent and knowledge of both sides.

---

[34] The term was coined by Professor Ian R. MacNeil. See MacNeil, *The Many Futures of Contract,* 47 S.Cal.L.Rev. 691 (1974). Economists who focus on the transaction costs of alternative organizational structures have also emphasized the neces- sarily incomplete character of the corporate charter. See Oliver E. Williamson, *Transaction–Cost Economics: The Governance of Contractual Relations,* 22 J.L. & Econ. 233 (1979).

Consider now the issues that should be faced by the parties but that may not have been recognized.

First, is Inventor really to have a 60 percent voting interest? This will give her total control of the board and deny Capitalist much say in how the business is run. In all likelihood, this is the one issue that the parties will have faced. Various solutions are possible so that Capitalist and Inventor can share control equally, even though Inventor is to get 60 percent of the profits. For example, the board can be "classified"— that is, two classes of stock can be issued with each having the right to elect two the directors. Although this approach has the advantage of allowing Inventor to own 60 percent of the shares without giving her total control, it has the disadvantage that, if one director on one side does not show up at a meeting, the other side has an effective majority. Another approach would be to use a shareholders' agreement, though in some jurisdictions there may be difficult legal issues as to when these agreements can bind the discretion of directors. Alternatively, a super-majority provision could be inserted in the articles of incorporation, requiring that the board act unanimously. Effectively, this would give each side a veto power. The problem with this approach is that, while it may work well enough for a two-shareholder corporation, the prospect of minority vetoes and the constant threat of deadlock becomes more troublesome if additional shareholders later join the firm.

Next, consider what happens if the firm is deadlocked and the parties wish to dissolve it. This can happen very quickly if the two parties have the large egos that are common to people in these risky start-up ventures. Is Inventor really to get 60 percent of the firm's assets on liquidation, when the assets consist largely of the $2,000,000 that Capitalist has contributed? If this seems unfair, then in order to insure that Capitalist gets his $2,000,000 back on any dissolution before Inventor gets anything, we have to give Capitalist a liquidation preference. This requires issuing him a senior class of stock, typically called "preferred stock," which will have equal dividend rights, but priority status upon liquidation.

What about salaries? Inventor will be working, while Capitalist will be inactive. If Inventor draws a salary, this may change the 60:40 split of profits that they have written into the articles of incorporation. Perhaps this 60:40 split contemplated that Amy Inventor would also receive a salary, but perhaps not. One solution would be to have Capitalist advance part of his capital contribution as a loan on which he will receive interest. Both the salary paid to Inventor and the interest paid to Capitalist would be deductible for tax purposes and so would reduce the corporation's tax liability (if any). This solution also gives Capitalist a priority in terms of repayment of his loan in the event of a liquidation. Perhaps this is a desirable solution; perhaps not.

Similarly, the parties need to face the Internal Revenue Code's Subchapter S election decision. Subchapter S is discussed further at Sec.

XIII(E), but essentially it treats the firm's profits and losses as if they had been realized directly by the shareholders—as they would be if the firm were a partnership. As a consequence, no taxes are paid at the corporate level, but the shareholders are taxed on their share of the firm's earnings (or may deduct their share of the firm's losses) even though these earnings are not paid out to them. More to the point for startup firms, the early losses that generally can be expected, can be used as deductions by the shareholders. This may appeal to Capitalist, but Inventor, who may have little other income to absorb these losses, may wish to keep them in the corporation to carry forward and apply against future corporate profits.

In all these areas (and many others, including those discussed in the next section), the parties can have quite reasonable conflicts that are best faced and negotiated at the outset. Note, however, that a lawyer engaged to advise both parties is in an exposed and difficult position, since some solutions to a problem may favor one side and some the other. This presents the question whether an attorney should agree to be "counsel to the transaction"? In many cases, there is no attractive alternative if legal costs are to be kept at a reasonable level for a relatively small transaction.

## D.  DURATION AND TRANSFERABILITY

Corporations are often said to have perpetual or unlimited life. That idea is a bit misleading, because a corporation may be dissolved upon a shareholder vote or, in extreme situations, by judicial or other governmental order. The notion of unlimited life does, however, serve the useful purpose of contrasting corporations and partnerships. Under partnership law, it is easy for a partner to terminate his or her involvement in the firm; in drafting a partnership agreement, the lawyer's challenge, as we have seen, is to find ways to override the Uniform Partnership Act's rules in order to insure an appropriate degree of continuity and protection against withdrawal. (See Chapter 2, Sec. IX.) Corporate law creates just the opposite problem (which is sometimes referred to as "lock-in"). The articles of incorporation of most corporations provide for indefinite duration (although limitations are permissible under state corporation codes). In the absence of an agreement to the contrary, or special circumstances justifying judicial intervention (such as fraud or other oppression by the majority, depending on state law), a minority shareholder has no legal power to terminate the existence of the firm or to withdraw his or her capital.

Still, although the shareholders may be unable to withdraw their capital, they may be more readily able than partners to sell their interests. We have earlier seen that in a partnership, in the absence of an agreement to the contrary, a partner cannot transfer his or her partnership interest to another person. By contrast, in a corporation, shares of stock are freely transferable unless there is an express agreement to the contrary set forth in the corporation's articles or bylaws and noted on the stock certificate. Moreover, a transfer of a general partnership interest from one person to another (with the consent of the continuing partners) technically dissolves the original partnership and creates a new one; in short, a change in the identity of any of the partners changes the identity of the partnership. (See Chapter 2, Sec. IX(D).) In contrast, a change in the identity of any of the shareholders is thought to have no effect on the identity of the corporation.

At the formation stage, shareholders in a closely held corporation may very well want to restrict share transferability. If Inventor and Capitalist in our preceding hypothetical think about it, they may not wish to deal with other persons as shareholders (particularly if they have required a unanimous shareholder vote for some decisions). However, because the common law will not tolerate "unreasonable" restraints on alienation, it would not be advisable (at least in a number of jurisdictions) to require that all transfers of shares be approved by the board. (In other jurisdictions, this would be enforceable if the restriction were clearly specified on the stock certificate.) Other means to the same end, however, can be found. Each party can grant a "right of first refusal" to the other. Under this approach, if a person wishes to sell his or her shares to an outsider, the shares must first be offered to the other existing shareholders (or to the corporation) at the price the outsider is willing to pay. This type of provision will make it difficult to find an outsider willing to make an offer, but that is a risk to which all shareholders are presumably, at the outset, equally exposed. Courts will usually enforce such provisions, even if the result is that a person seeking to sell must accept a price below the shares' value in an arm's length transaction between a willing buyer and a willing seller.

Another mechanism for resolving disputes without litigation that merits consideration at this formation stage is a "buy/sell" agreement. Under such an agreement, any shareholder (on the occurrence of specified events or simply at the will of that shareholder if the agreement so provides) can demand to be bought out. Usually, the "buy/sell" agreement will specify a formula for determination of the price of the shares. Typically, the other shareholders can then elect to buy the dissident shareholder's shares at the formula price or to liquidate the corporation. Alternatively, the agreement may provide that the shareholder who wishes to exit can specify a price for his or her shares. The other party then has the option of either buying the first party's shares at that price or selling his or her own shares to the first party at the same price. In effect, this compels dissolution of their relationship without dissolving the corporation. As a practical matter, however, "buy/sell" agreements tend to favor the wealthier party. For example, if Capitalist in our earlier example believed that his shares were worth $10 per share, he could specify a price of only $5 per share if he knew that Inventor, who had few liquid assets and could not withdraw money from the business, could pay no more than $3 per share. As a result, Capitalist could compel a bargain sale to him by Inventor. To meet this problem, a careful lawyer representing Inventor might insist that Inventor be given an opportunity to make installment payments over an extended period.

After the formation of the corporation, it is still possible to restrict share transferability by amending the certificate of incorporation or bylaws, but only with a unanimous shareholder vote. The common law has not permitted the majority to retroactively restrict the transferability of shares, except by consent. Individual shareholders can still enter into first-refusal or buy/sell agreements that bind themselves but not non-signatory shareholders.

If all else fails, minority shareholders in closely held corporations may be able to seek relief under various state statutes that permit a court to order dissolution where the minority shareholder can prove the majority has been guilty of oppression. State statutes differ widely in this regard, with some (including Delaware) authorizing dissolution only when the board is deadlocked and cannot manage the company, while others are more expansive and permit dissolution whenever the minority's "reasonable expectations" have been frustrated.[35] Often, some specified percentage of the shareholders must petition the court before dissolution may be ordered on grounds of oppression,[36] and as an alternative to dissolution the majority may be given an opportunity—or may be required—to buy out the minority at an agreed price, or, if agreement is not reached, at a fair price, as determined by arbitration or by the court.[37]

## E.   LIMITED LIABILITY AND ITS EXCEPTIONS

When Investor and Capitalist form their corporation, they will assume in all likelihood that they have "limited liability." Simply stated, this means that shareholders are not liable for debts incurred in the operation of the firm. Thus, shareholder losses are limited to the amounts invested by them—that is, to the amounts originally contributed to the corporation in return for their shares. This principle is a corollary (though not a necessary corollary) of the concept of the corporation as an entity;[38] it is the corporation that incurs the debts, not the shareholders.

---

[35] Typically, these expectations related to continued employment or a consistent dividend payment. See Robert Thompson, Corporate Dissolution and Shareholders' Reasonable Expectations, 66 Wash. U. L. Q. 193 (1988). See also, e.g., In re Kemp & Beatley, Inc., 64 N.Y.2d 63, 484 N.Y.S.2d 799, 473 N.E.2d 1173 (1984); Meiselman v. Meiselman, 309 N.C. 279, 307 S.E.2d 551 (1983).

[36] See N.Y. Bus. Corp. Law § 1104–(a) (1986) (20 percent of outstanding shares must petition court).

[37] See, e.g., N.Y. Bus. Corp. Law § 1118 (1986); Alaska Plastics, Inc. v. Coppock, 621 P.2d 270 (Alaska 1980).

[38] In the early history of corporate law in this country, shareholders did not enjoy limited liability. See Stephen B. Presser,

In the case of publicly held corporations, limited liability is of vital importance. Without such a rule, dispersed owners would be exposed to risks that many, if not most, investors would consider unacceptable. Under the alternative of joint and several liability, each shareholder would be potentially liable for the corporation's entire debt, which would probably mean, as a practical matter, that the wealthy shareholders would bear the burden. Even under a regime of pro rata liability—which would present severe administrative problems—the risk, and the uncertainty associated with that risk, would be a deterrent to large-scale public investment.

Still, limited liability for public corporations is troubling. Its effect is that losses are borne by creditors rather than by shareholders, who, at least formally, control the corporation. For voluntary creditors such as suppliers and bank lenders, this outcome may be defended simply by noting that such creditors should be aware of the risk of loss when they extend credit and can, if they are concerned, demand various protections. The same cannot be said, however, for involuntary creditors, such as tort victims. On balance, the rule of limited liability resolves the conflicting goals, on the one hand, of protection of involuntary creditors and efficient allocation of risk of damage, and, on the other hand, of encouraging investment, in favor of the latter.

In the case of closely held corporations as well, limited liability may serve the goal of encouraging investment. For such firms, however, the argument that it is not feasible for the shareholders to monitor and control the activities of the firm loses much of its force. Yet, it is hard to imagine a regime in which limited liability would be available to large, widely held firms and not to smaller, closely held ones. At the same time, for closely held firms the significance of limited liability is often overrated. In such corporations, again one must think of both voluntary and involuntary (tort) creditors. Limited liability will not protect a shareholder/manager from personal liability if his or her own personal negligence proximately causes injury. Moreover, in most situations there is an easy, obvious and common solution to the problem of potential liability for personal injuries—namely, insurance. As for voluntary creditors, the limited liability of shareholders often must be sacrificed. Almost invariably, banks and other such lenders will not extend credit to a closely held corporation unless its principal shareholders add their personal guarantees to the obligation of the corporation. A lender that is willing to lend without such guarantees ought also to be willing to lend to an individual or to a partnership without recourse. (See Chapter 1, Sec. II(C) and Chapter 2, Sec. II(B).) Suppliers also often require personal

Piercing the Corporate Veil § 1.03[1] (1991). "Limited liability is a statutory development that represents the rising power of business interests." Phillip I. Blumberg, Limited Liability and Corporate Groups, 11 J. Corp. L. 573, 576 (1986). For a brief summary of policy discussions, see William A. Klein and Eric M. Zolt, Business Forms, Limited Liability, and Tax Regimes: Lurching Toward a Coherent Outcome? 66 U. Colo. L. Rev. 1001, 1029–36 (1995).

guarantees and, when the risk of non-payment is high, may deal only on a cash basis (that is, with payment in advance or c.o.d.). Moreover, when a small business finds itself in financial difficulty, the equity owners very often will feel compelled to add additional funds to keep it going.

In some instances shareholders, including parent corporations, can be held liable for the debts of a corporation even though they have not agreed to accept liability (and even where the creditor had no reason to expect such liability). The phrases most widely used in law to describe this result are "piercing the corporate veil" or, less commonly, the "alter ego" doctrine. The law in this area varies some from state to state, but generally a plaintiff seeking to "pierce the corporate veil" in order to reach the assets of a shareholder must establish (a) the "unity" of the shareholder and the corporation and (b) an unjust or inequitable outcome if the shareholder is not held liable. The doctrine is an equitable one, with considerable scope for judicial discretion for judges to weigh multiple facts with only vague guidelines. The unity prong of the two-part test turns on such factors as a failure to observe corporate formalities, a commingling of individual and corporate assets, the absence of separate offices, and treatment of the corporation as a mere shell without employees or assets. The unjust-result prong is harder to specify; one common example would be a shareholder stripping essential assets from the corporation by dividends or excessive salaries or other payments for services.

A more uncertain basis for "piercing the corporate veil" arises when creditors claim that the shareholders knowingly "undercapitalized" the corporation at its formation so that it could not pay its foreseeable debts. Cases that have relied on this "gross undercapitalization" justification to hold shareholders liable have typically involved fairly simple fact patterns where the shareholders systematically withdrew earnings from a corporation, and thus left it unable to meet its future foreseeable debts, or where a parent corporation controlled and operated a subsidiary in a manner that denied it any opportunity to make an arm's length profit. Although a few opinions have stated that gross undercapitalization alone (in terms of the predictable liabilities that the corporation would incur) may provide an independent basis for piercing the veil, no decision appears yet to have clearly held shareholders liable based solely upon a finding of gross undercapitalization.[39]

A related problem arises when a single business is fragmented among different corporations, all owned by the same shareholder. A classic example arose when the owner of a fleet of taxicabs organized his enterprise in the form of a series of separate corporations, each of which owned two of the taxicabs. The objective of this use of multiple "brother/sister" corporations apparently was to ensure that the negligence of one driver could not result in a judgment that would be enforceable

---

[39] See William P. Hackney and Tracey G. Benson, *Shareholder Liability for Inade-* *quate Capital,* 43 U.Pitt.L.Rev. 837, 885 (1982).

against all of the taxicabs in the fleet. The Court of Appeals of New York held that, upon proof that the business was in fact carried on by a single enterprise (for example, with one corporation entering into transactions with its siblings, without an expectation of profit), a tort victim might be allowed to recover against the assets of the entire enterprise (though the individual owner of the shares of the corporations would not be personally liable).[40] Similarly, but on a much larger scale, this same theory of enterprise liability was used in the much publicized case of the Amoco Cadiz oil spill off the coast of France in order to hold liable a giant oil corporation for damages caused by a tanker that it owned through a corporate subsidiary. Because the tanker was used exclusively by the parent corporation and was specially designed for its use, the court treated it as a fragment of a larger enterprise and held the parent company liable for its tort debts.

No case has ever held individual shareholders of a public, as opposed to a closely held, corporation to be personally liable.[41] While some academics have argued that shareholders (even of public corporations) should be personally liable to tort victims, even if they are not liable to other creditors,[42] the courts have shown no greater inclination to pierce the corporate veil for the benefit of tort victims than for the benefit of other creditors.[43] Nor have the courts shown a greater tendency to pierce where the shareholder is another corporation (that is, the parent corporation in a parent/subsidiary relationship) than when the shareholder is an individual.[44]

A shareholder may also become liable for debts that the shareholder thought were those of the corporation when the shareholder acted as a promoter and entered into contracts on behalf of the corporation before its formation. Unless these contracts were drafted to state clearly that the individual would have no personal liability, the tendency has been for courts to hold the individual liable if the corporation either failed to adopt the contract after its formation or if it subsequently became

---

[40] Walkovszky v. Carlton, 18 N.Y.2d 414, 276 N.Y.S.2d 585, 223 N.E.2d 6 (1966).

[41] See Robert B. Thompson, Piercing the Corporate Veil: An Empirical Study, 76 Cornell L.Rev. 1036, 1047 (1991)(reporting a study of 1600 reported decisions through 1985).

[42] See Henry Hansmann and Reinier Kraakman, *Toward Unlimited Liability for Corporate Torts,* 100 Yale L.J. 1879 (1991). However, in a world of widely dispersed shareholders and complex financial techniques such as futures, swaps, etc., enforcement of shareholder liability might be impractical. See Joseph A. Grundfest, The Limited Future of Unlimited Liability: A Capital Markets Perspective, 102 Yale L.J. 387 (1992).

[43] See Thompson, supra note 35, at 1058. But see Stephen B. Presser, *Thwarting the Killing of the Corporation: Limited Liability, Democracy, and Economics,* 87 Nw. U.L.Rev. 148 (1992).

[44] See Thompson, supra note 35, at 1056. In this situation, the arguments for limited liability are not the same as they are with respect to individual shareholders. The argument would have to be that as long as individual shareholders are not liable, if parent corporations were liable for the debts of their subsidiaries, high risk ventures would wind up being held by individual shareholders as separate entities—a result that generates organizational inefficiency without protecting creditors. See Klein and Zolt, supra note 32, at 1034, n. 100.

insolvent and unable to pay or perform. The doctrinal justification for this result has been borrowed from agency law, under which an agent who acts for a non-existent principal is liable as a principal. By analogy, courts have said that a still unformed corporation is the same as a non-existent principal. This reasoning seems formalistic. Perhaps a better ground for these decisions would be that the agent somehow misrepresented the corporation's still unformed status or otherwise gave the impression that he or she would guarantee the contract. Otherwise, it is difficult to see any policy justification for holding the agent liable, because the creditors have not been misled.

A final circumstance in which the shareholder faces individual liability is when the corporation has been defectively organized. Here, if the defect is trivial, courts will forgive it and treat the corporation as a *de jure* corporation. If the defect is more serious (typically a failure to file the articles of incorporation with the appropriate state official), a common-law doctrine applied by the courts is the other side of the coin of limited liability. Far from ignoring the corporate existence, the courts, in certain circumstances, treated the unincorporated firm as if it had incorporated, calling it a "de facto" corporation, and extending the protection of limited liability. The equitable doctrine allowing de facto corporate status is available to would-be shareholders if, roughly speaking, they had made some effort to incorporate and believed in good faith that they had done so and if the creditor seeking individual recovery also believed that he or she was dealing with a corporation.[45] Moreover, in some situations, the would-be shareholders may be protected, even in the absence of a good faith effort to incorporate, under a theory of estoppel, where a creditor dealt with the firm as if it had been a corporation and had no expectation of recourse to individual assets. These doctrines prevent windfalls to creditors, and thereby promote fairness, while sacrificing a possible tool for enforcing compliance with statutorily imposed filing obligations.

## F.  CHOICE OF LAW

People may freely choose to form their corporations in any of the fifty states. While there is much uniformity in the laws of the various states, significant variations exist. For example, some states require that a merger or sale of all the corporation's assets be approved by a simple majority vote; others require a supermajority (typically, two thirds). The law of dividends is particularly divided, with some states requiring only that the dividend not render the corporation foreseeably insolvent and others that it come out of a carefully defined fund on the corporation's balance sheet. Some of these differences—especially those dealing with

---

[45] An early version of the Model Business Corporation Act attempted to abolish the de facto corporation doctrine, an effort that was resisted by some courts. A 1984 revision of the Act contains language that is consistent with the common-law doctrine. See MBCA § 2.04. But some MBCA states have not adopted § 2.04.

mechanical procedures and housekeeping rules (such as the number of days notice that must be given before a meeting of shareholders may be called)—are probably a product chiefly of the time elapsed since the state's corporation code was last updated. Others, however, reflect important state policies, on issues such as (1) the scope of permissible takeover defensive tactics (including whether a shareholder vote is required before a shareholder may acquire more than defined levels of the corporation's stock without the permission of the board), (2) the events that trigger an appraisal remedy, and (3) the ability of the board to terminate derivative litigation brought in the corporation's name. These differences are discussed later in this Chapter. For present purposes, the most important point is that, regardless of where the corporation operates or where its shareholders or assets are located, it will be the law of the state of incorporation that controls these issues of internal corporate governance. This is known as the "internal affairs" rule,[46] and it obviously presents those forming the corporation with an important choice. Those states that allow participants in the venture the greatest freedom to shape the rules that will govern them sometimes are called "permissive."

For smaller corporations, the advantages of being able to choose the state of incorporation are usually outweighed by the additional costs of incorporating in a state other than where its principal operations are located. If a small corporation is likely to do business principally in one state, it makes little sense to incorporate in another state, because then the corporation will have to pay franchise taxes (that is, taxes on the privilege of doing business in the state) to both states. Also, the corporation will need to hire an agent (and possibly local counsel) to represent its interests in the state of incorporation (assuming that it does not have an office in the state). For the larger corporation, doing business in many states, these costs are relatively less significant.

The ability to select the state of incorporation allows larger corporations to choose the body of law that will govern the important aspects of the relationships among shareholders and between shareholders and management. A corporation that starts out small and incorporates in the state where most of the original shareholders live, and where the principal activities of the business are conducted, may wind up doing business, and having shareholders, in many states. At some point, those in control of the corporation may decide to switch the state of incorporation, usually to obtain greater flexibility or the ability to accomplish specific transactions without a shareholder vote (or with a lower requi-

---

[46] The Supreme Court had justified this doctrine as necessary to promote certainty and avoid jurisdictional conflicts among states, given their potentially overlapping interests and contacts with the same corporation. See Shaffer v. Heitner, 433 U.S. 186, 97 S.Ct. 2569, 53 L.Ed.2d 683 (1977); Van-tagePoint Venture Partners 1996 v. Examen, Inc., 871 A.2d 1108, 1113 (Del. 2005) ("The internal affairs doctrine applies to those matters that pertain to the relationships among or between the corporation and its officers, directors, and shareholders.")

site vote). Another perhaps even more important advantage of incorporation in a state like Delaware is that, because it has had more litigation over corporate-law matters than other states, its law is more settled and more familiar to investors and their lawyers than that of less popular states.[47] This increased certainty facilitates planning. Thus, we observe that the majority of large corporations with publicly traded shares are incorporated in liberal, or "permissive," states, such as Delaware and Nevada.[48] On the other hand, over more recent years a principal reason for switching the state of incorporation may have been to take advantage of laws providing protection against hostile takeovers. These statutes are anything but permissive, because any anti-takeover provision that shareholders wanted could easily have been inserted in their corporation's articles of incorporation (with the enthusiastic cooperation of management). Instead, these statutes mandate legal rules that shareholders may not want, but which managements desire for their own protection. In this light, the decision as to where to incorporate may sometimes involve a conflict between managerial and shareholder interests.[49]

It must be emphasized, however, that even if a permissive state, like Delaware, is chosen as the state of incorporation, a firm can still be made to comply with most of the significant rules and regulations of those states in which it does business. All states require a "foreign" corporation (that is, a corporation incorporated in another state) to "qualify" to do business in their jurisdiction (although usually this is required simply to identify the foreign corporation as a potential taxpayer); in addition, some major states, such as New York and California, have "pseudo-foreign" corporation statutes that require foreign corporations whose activities are principally located within their boundaries to comply with the essential provisions of their incorporation statutes. The constitutional validity of these "pseudo-foreign" corporation statutes, when they conflict with the law of the state of incorporation, has not, however, been resolved.

To some significant extent (increasing in recent years), the governance of corporations is controlled by federal law. Moreover, the Delaware legislators and judges may feel constrained by the possibility that if they go too far in catering to powerful local interests, Congress may enact preemptive federal laws. If so, the legislators and judges, being

---

[47] See Michael Klausner, *Corporations, Corporate Law, and Networks of Contracts,* 81 Va. L. Rev. 757 (1995).

[48] In 1999, of a universe of 6,530 publicly traded nonfinancial firms incorporated in the United States and having their headquarters in the United States, 3,744 (57.57%) were incorporated in Delaware; of these only 27 had their headquarters in Delaware. By contrast, of the 1,254 corporations with their headquarters in California, only 273 (21.77%) were incorporated in the state. For New York, there were 576 firms

with headquarters in the state and only 141 (24.48 %) of these were incorporated in the state. Lucian Bebchuk, Alma Cohen & Allen Ferrell, *Does the Evidence Favor State Competition in Corporate Law?* 90 Calif. L. Rev. 1775 (2002).

[49] See Guhan Subramanian, *The Influence of Antitakeover Statutes on Incorporation Choice: Evidence on the "Race" Debate and Antitakeover Overreaching,* 150 Pa. L. Rev. 1795 (2002)

anxious to maintain Delaware's preeminence in corporate law, must be responsive to some degree to groups that enjoy political power in Washington, though not in Delaware.[50]

A much debated topic among corporate law scholars has been whether the competition among states for corporate charters produces a "race to the bottom" or a "race to the top." Those who argue the former position maintain that the desire of Delaware and similar jurisdictions to maximize their corporate franchise tax revenues (which account for approximately 20 percent of Delaware's tax revenues) inclines these jurisdictions to attract incorporations by offering legal rules that deprive shareholders of the fiduciary and other legal protections that their original home jurisdiction gave them.[51] The premise here is that the choice of incorporation is made by managers, who will act in their own interest. In contrast, those who believe that state competition tends to produce value-maximizing rules that benefit shareholders argue that market forces and the need for shareholder approval of any reincorporation prevent managers from moving to jurisdictions where the legal rules are unfavorable to shareholders.[52] From this perspective, Delaware succeeds by offering more efficient "default" rules in its corporate law, which shareholders are in any event free to modify.[53]

More recently, commentators have argued that the race can be in either direction, depending on the specific legal rule and the particular corporation in question. That is, state competition may sometimes produce efficient legal rules and sometimes inefficient ones. The key variable is likely to be whether the party making the incorporation or reincorporation decision has a conflict of interest with the interests of the other shareholders.[54] For example, where the corporation has a

---

[50] See Mark J. Roe, Delaware's Politics, 118 Harv. L. Rev. 2491 (2005); Renee M. Jones, Rethinking Corporate Federalism in the Era of Corporate Reform, 29 J. Corp. L. 625 (2004).

[51] See William L. Cary, *Federalism & Corporate Law: Reflections Upon Delaware*, 83 Yale L.J. 663 (1974); Bebchuk et al., supra note 42. For the subtler theory that sees Delaware as acting to protect the interest of the corporate bar, which is a major local industry in Delaware, see Jonathan R. Macey and Geoffrey P. Miller, *Toward an Interest Group Theory of Delaware Corporation Law*, 65 Texas L.Rev. 469 (1987); Roberta Romano, *Law As Product: Some Pieces of the Incorporation Puzzle*, 1 J.L. Econ. & Org. 225 (1985).

[52] See Ralph K. Winter, Jr. *State Law, Shareholder Protection and the Theory of the Corporation*, 6 J. Legal Stud. 251 (1977). Professor Roberta Romano examined the effect on share values of reincorporations in Delaware and found small short-term positive returns from such reincorpo-

rations, and "an insignificant positive effect over the longer interval, −3 to +3, as well as over the 71–day period −10 to +60," and states that other studies are "suggestive but not conclusive." The Genius of American Corporate Law 21 (1993). See also Roberta Romano, *The State Competition Debate in Corporate Law*, 8 Cardozo L.Rev. 709 (1987) (adopting an intermediate position, but closer to that of Winter, and emphasizing transaction-cost effects). See also, Marcel Kahan and Ehud Kamar, *The Myth of State Competition in Corporate Law*, 55 Stanford L. Rev. 679 (2002) (arguing that, apart from Delaware, states do not compete for incorporations).

[53] It is striking that Delaware's law relating to hostile takeovers (Del. Gen. Corp. L. § 203) is significantly less protective of incumbency than is the law of many other states. See infra Sec. V(B)(2)(h).

[54] See Lucian A. Bebchuk, *Federalism and the Corporation: The Desirable Limits on State Competition in Corporate Law*, 105 Harv.L.Rev. 1437 (1992).

majority shareholder who can dictate the incorporation decision, the majority shareholder has a logical incentive to prefer a jurisdiction that would enable it to squeeze out the minority shareholders at an unfairly low price. Thus, Delaware could at the same time offer a model set of efficient legal rules relating to all areas where managers or majority shareholders do not have a conflict between their interests and those of the public shareholders, while providing sub-optimal rules that permit wealth transfers in those areas where a conflict exists.

The available empirical evidence has not resolved this debate.[55] Indeed, given the uncertain motivations and effects of incorporation decisions, and their relatively minor consequence for shareholder value, empirical resolution may be impossible. In general, stock price studies have shown little or no change in share prices when a corporation moves from one jurisdiction to another, and the implications of the empirical findings are often unclear.[56] It is often difficult to differentiate those reincorporations that are motivated by a desire to obtain more modern, more efficient, or better developed legal rules and institutions from those that are motivated by the desire of either managers or controlling shareholders to gain the benefit of legal rules that facilitate wealth transfers to them. The studies may reflect many factors whose net effect is uncertain. Moreover, it seems likely that to the extent that there is a competition among the states, the outcome is significantly affected by the prospect that if the states ignore shareholder (or other) interests, the federal government may step in—a prospect that will be recognized by the states (particularly Delaware) and will persistently constrain state lawmaking.[57]

Stock price studies as a measure of whether state law adequately protects shareholders are also subject to another objection: critics argue that existing differences among states are at most marginal because the race to the bottom long ago compelled most states to amend their laws to stay close to those of the principal "permissive" jurisdictions (i.e., Delaware and Nevada). In this view, the contemporary significance of the competition among the states is mainly to chill regulatory innovations by other jurisdictions which are afraid that their innovations will elicit further corporate departures. Of course, another possibility is that shareholders care very little about most legal differences or remedies, except when the potential for a lucrative takeover looms.

---

[55] See Romano, supra notes 44 and 45; Bebchuk, supra note 47, at 1448–1451.

[56] For example, Romano finds a small, statistically significant gain in the share prices of firms that reincorporate in Delaware to take advantage of its anti-takeover rules, but observes that the gain may be attributable to identification of the firm as a takeover target. Romano, supra note 44, 1 J.L. & Econ.Org. at 270–271. A more recent study reports evidence that incorporation in Delaware increases shareholder wealth. Robert Daines, Does Delaware Law Improve Firm Value?, 62 J. Fin. Econ. 525 (2001).

[57] See Mark J. Roe, *Delaware's Competition*, 117 Harvard L. Rev. (forthcoming 2003).

## G.  PURPOSES, POWERS, AND ULTRA VIRES

In earlier times it was common for the articles to state the "purpose" of the corporation. For example, the articles might state that "the purpose of this corporation is to engage in the business of building and operating a railroad." A limiting statement of corporate purpose such as this can serve the useful function of keeping the people in control from straying into unrelated activities, either directly or by acquiring other firms. The shareholders might reasonably prefer to rely on their own individual decisions whether to invest their funds in other businesses. On the other hand, a specific statement of purpose may have the effect of foreclosing potentially profitable investments in related, or unrelated, activities—investments that might be available to the corporation but not to its shareholders. Moreover, a specific statement of purpose tends to create line-drawing problems and the squabbles and litigation that one associates with such problems. For example, a "railroad" company's managers may want to buy trucks to transport containers of the sort that are carried on railroad cars between major cities and then must be delivered to places not accessible by rail. Is the operation of a fleet of trucks (sometimes perhaps rented to others to achieve operating efficiencies) part of the "railroad" business? If not, then the purchase of the trucks would be beyond the purposes or powers of the corporation. The Latin phrase is *ultra vires* (beyond the powers). An *ultra vires* contract is not enforceable, so the question of the scope of the purposes of the corporation could wind up being litigated in a suit to enforce a contract. Originally, the *ultra vires* issue could arise when the corporation, asserting a lack of authority under the charter, sought to renege on a contract entered into by an agent in its name. In that situation, the *ultra vires* doctrine would, among other things, lead to unjust enrichment of the corporation, if benefits had already been received. Moreover, people who dealt with the corporation might be required to take costly precautions to avoid problems arising from the doctrine. As a result, today most corporation statutes preclude the corporation from asserting the *ultra vires* defense.[58] Shareholders, however, can still sue to enjoin a prospective transaction that they claim is unauthorized or to hold corporate management liable to the corporation for damages resulting from any *ultra vires* transaction. To avoid these kinds of problems and burdens, it is now customary to state the corporate purpose in a nonlimiting way (for example, "the purpose of this corporation is to engage in any lawful business") and most modern corporation statutes specifically allow this type of statement.[59]

The *powers* of a corporation are the acts in which the corporation can engage in order to achieve its purposes—for example, a railroad

---

[58] See, e.g., Revised Model Business Corporation Act § 3.04.

[59] Indeed, Revised Model Business Corporation Act § 3.01(a), creates a presumption that the purpose of a corporation is to "engage[e] in any lawful business unless a more limited purpose is set forth in the articles of incorporation."

corporation should have the power to buy and hold land, to borrow money, to execute mortgages, etc.—though the distinction between purposes and powers is sometimes unclear and, in any event, often ignored. Again, the modern practice is to avoid trouble by using broad, nonlimiting language, or to have no provision for powers and to rely on the implied power to do what is necessary to carry out the corporation's purposes.

Most people who know anything about litigation in earlier times over the *ultra vires* problem are relieved that under modern practices and attitudes that litigation has largely dried up. But perhaps we now are too little sensitive to the potentially valuable function of a limiting statement of a corporation's purposes—especially for closely held corporations but perhaps for others as well. Bear in mind that the articles, including the purposes provision, can be amended. All it takes is approval by the shareholders, under whatever voting rule they have agreed to. For a charter specification of purposes to be fully effective in protecting minority shareholders, however, the charter must preclude amendment by majority vote.

## VI.  OBLIGATIONS OF OFFICERS AND DIRECTORS

### A.  DUTY OF CARE

At one time the avowed standard of conduct for corporate officers and directors throughout the United States was that they were expected to perform their duties "with the care, skill, and prudence of like persons in a like position." This principle is, of course, a simple and direct application of the law of agency, which also requires the agent to exercise due care. (See Chapter 1, Sec. VII.) Read literally, this formulation would seem to have imposed liability for what amounts to simple negligence—a liability that could have been enforced in a derivative action. Yet, reported cases in which liability has in fact been imposed are remarkably few and generally have involved instances in which corporate officials were suspiciously inattentive to an impending disaster under circumstances where the court may have believed that the defendants were subject to a conflict of interest. As explained below, this reality is now reflected in far less demanding statements of the standard of conduct and is the product as well of a initial barrier to liability erected by the so-called "business judgment rule."

A critical issue in understanding the duty of care is the extent to which the traditional phrasing of the duty is intended primarily as an aspirational statement, having only a precatory impact, or as a true liability-creating rule. Obviously, it is desirable as an aspirational matter that directors be prudent, careful, and diligent, but for several reasons it is far from obvious that they should be liable for damages for failure to meet these standards. First, it is generally in the shareholders' interest for the directors to accept reasonable risks (which they might be deterred from doing if there were a substantial risk of liability for negligence). Second, courts have little ability to evaluate the risk/return calculus that directors and managers constantly face. Finally, directors are not in the same position as the firm's outside auditors or its investment bankers, who serve many firms and can thus spread their risk of liability. Rather, directors serve at most relatively few firms, and this fact may make them poor "cost avoiders" because they cannot effectively absorb potential liability as a cost of doing business by incorporating it into the price they charge for their services. Given the inevitability that some risky business decisions will result in failure, the prospect of judicial "second guessing" might make corporate officials overly risk averse, to the detriment of shareholders.

For essentially these reasons, American law has always qualified its recognition of the duty of care with a balancing legal doctrine known as the "business judgment rule." Essentially, by directing courts not to examine the substantive merits of business decisions that are not accompanied by a conflict of interest, the business judgment rule (which is actually more a standard of review than a rule) shelters directors from liability for decisions that prove in hindsight to have been ill-advised or simply unlucky. The verbal formulation of the business judgment rule, however, varies from jurisdiction to jurisdiction. In some of the more "conservative" jurisdictions, the rule is said to protect and make non-reviewable any decision made by the board (or an authorized committee thereof) when the directors had no disqualifying conflict of interest and did not behave illegally or "recklessly." In the majority of jurisdictions, however, the relationship between the duty of care and the business judgment rule is requires a further inquiry and thus becomes more complex. Under the majority formulation, any business judgment is immune from judicial review only if the directors first followed adequate procedures in reaching it. In effect, there is a procedural precondition to the rule's application, which immunizes only those decisions with respect to which the directors first exercised due care and adequately informed themselves under the circumstances. As these courts sometimes say, business judgment is protected only if it was in fact exercised—that is, a business decision was deliberately reached. Thus, if a board did not consult experts (such as lawyers or appraisers) on matters beyond their own competence, its judgment would not be protected by the business judgment rule (unless there were other reasons justifying their haste). Thus, the Delaware Supreme Court stated:

> Courts do not measure, weigh or quantify directors' judgments. We do not even decide if they are reasonable in this context. Due care in the decisionmaking context is process due care only. Irrationality is the outer limit of the business judgment rule. Irrationality may be

the functional equivalent of the waste test or it may tend to show that the decision is not made in good faith, which is a key ingredient of the business judgment rule.[60]

Even when the business judgment rule does not protect a decision or action, successful challenges to decisions of boards of directors are rare.[61] The Delaware case law now holds that liability is imposed on officers and directors only for gross negligence and accords the directors a presumption that they acted honestly and in good faith.[62] Moreover, even when the directors breach their duty of care, they can escape liability under Delaware law if they can sustain the burden of proving the "entire fairness" of the transaction they approved.[63]

There are a few well known cases in which courts have shown a willingness to impose liability, but, when closely examined, they usually

[60] Brehm v. Eisner, 746 A.2d 244, 264 (Del. Supr.2000) (footnotes omitted). Some commentators dispute the policy justifications for this procedural precondition to the application of the business judgment rule. They argue that this emphasis on procedure and actual deliberation only creates a Full Employment Act for lawyers, investment bankers, and other highly paid advisers. Regardless, once we understand the procedural foundation of the business judgment rule, we can better understand much of what corporate lawyers actually do. A good deal of their activity consists of trying to obtain the protection of the business judgment rule for the board (and other corporate officials) by making certain that the procedural conditions for its application are satisfied. Often, this consists of building a paper record ("creating a paper trail") evidencing that the board consulted experts, was otherwise well-advised, and deliberated sufficiently.

It is worth noting, however, that on remand of the case, the plaintiffs having produced additional evidence, the trial court concluded that the "directors failed to exercise *any* business judgment and failed to make *any* good faith attempt to fulfill their fiduciary duties to [the corporation] and its stockholders." In re Walt Disney Co. Derivative Litigation, 825 A.2d 275 (Del. Ch. 2003).

[61] See Bernard S. Black, Brian R. Cheffins, and Michael Klausner, Liability Risk for Outside Directors: A Cross–Border Analysis, 11 European Financial Management Journal 153 (2005).

[62] Aronson v. Lewis, 473 A.2d 805, 812 (Del.1984). Delaware law also applies a "gross negligence" test to the determination of whether a business decision was an

"informed" one. See Smith v. Van Gorkom, 488 A.2d 858, 873 (Del.1985).

[63] In Cinerama, Inc. v. Technicolor, Inc., 663 A.2d 1156 (Del.1995), the Delaware Supreme Court upheld a finding that the directors of Technicolor had sustained their burden of proving the "entire fairness" of a merger pursuant to which their company was sold to MacAndrews & Forbes Group, Inc. It did so despite the fact that it had earlier held that the directors had breached their duty of care by failing to conduct an adequate "market check" to determine if a higher price was available from other bidders. To prove "entire fairness," defendants must satisfy two elements: fair price and fair dealing. The first is substantive, the second largely procedural. The court distinguished Smith v. Van Gorkom, 488 A.2d 858 (Del. 1985) (described in text below) chiefly on the ground that in that case there had also been a breach of an independent duty of disclosure and that, given that breach, the "fair dealing" element could not be satisfied. In contrast, in *Technicolor*, full disclosure was made, and there was considerable evidence of a substantial effort (mostly by the CEO) to obtain the highest possible price, and of reliance on the carefully prepared advice of competent professionals. The "fair price" element was satisfied because in an earlier proceeding the Delaware Chancery Court had appraised the fair value of Technicolor and found it to be less than the price paid by MacAndrews & Forbes. The Supreme Court also noted that there was no basis for objection to the timing, initiation, or structure of the transaction, and that more than seventy-five percent of the shareholders had expressed their approval of the transaction by tendering their shares.

involve either (1) a suspected conflict of interest, which the court may not have felt entitled to rely upon as the formal basis for its decision[64] (2) a request for an injunction (usually in a contested takeover battle) where the defendants would not incur personal liability.[65] An exception to this pattern is the 1985 decision of the Delaware Supreme Court in Smith v. Van Gorkom,[66] which imposed liability on the directors of a public corporation for approving the acquisition of their corporation (at a substantial premium over the market price), essentially because they were inattentive to the possibility of better offers from third parties. This decision sent shock waves through the corporate bar, although in fact it did not nominally change the pre-existing law (but only enforced it literally). Nonetheless, in response to the *Van Gorkom* decision, many states amended their corporate statutes to restrict due care liability. The most popular route, initiated by Delaware itself, has been to authorize shareholders to adopt charter provisions under which directors (and in some states officers as well) will be liable only for conduct that involves illegality, a breach of the duty of loyalty, or intentional misconduct.[67] Other states have redefined the duty itself, making it either a wholly subjective standard (i.e., requiring the officer or director only to act in good faith) or specifying that the corporate official will only be liable for damages (as opposed to an injunction) if his conduct constitutes "willful misconduct or recklessness."[68]

[64] In Francis v. United Jersey Bank, 162 N.J.Super. 355, 392 A.2d 1233 (1978), affirmed 87 N.J. 15, 432 A.2d 814 (1981), the defendant was the estate of a deceased director of a corporation that went bankrupt as the result of a major financial fraud perpetrated by its officers. The seemed to rely on the fact that the deceased director was totally passive and inattentive. Yet the more important fact may have been that she was the mother of the principal officers who had perpetrated the fraud. The court may have believed that in holding her estate liable it was simply recouping ill-gotten gains from the family.

[65] For such a case, see Hanson Trust PLC v. ML SCM Acquisition, Inc., 781 F.2d 264 (2d Cir.1986) (enjoining asset lock-up in contested takeover as a violation of the duty of care).

[66] 488 A.2d 858 (Del. Supr.1985). The key to the holding was that, because the directors did not inform themselves or seek expert advice, they could not claim the protection of the business judgment rule for an uninformed judgment. Critics of this case have argued that the merger offer was at a price ($55 per share) that was sufficiently above the prior trading price ($38 per share, which was itself near the five-year high for the stock) to justify immediate acceptance and to make shareholders ecstatic. The board, however, was told by the corporation's own financial staff that the price was near the low end of the fairness range for the corporation, and the Supreme Court appears to have believed that the directors succumbed to pressure from the corporation's CEO, who was about the retire and seemed eager to sell his own shares.

[67] See Del. Gen. Corp. Law § 102(b)(7) (Supp. 1986).

[68] See Ind. Code Ann. § 23–1–35(1)(e)(2) (West Supp. 1986). For the good faith standard, see Va. Code Ann. § 13.1–690 (1985). Under the Model Business Corporation Act (1984), the basic standard, in § 8.30(a) requires only that the director "act: (1) in good faith and (2) in a manner the director reasonably believes to be in the best interests of the corporation." MBCA § 8.30(b), covering the duty to become informed, requires "the care that a person in a like position would reasonably believe appropriate under similar circumstances," but the remainder of § 8.30 protects directors who rely on lawyers, accountants, or other such people, on officers or employees, or on committees of the board.

One important continuing area of potential liability for directors with respect to the duty of care concerns not business decisions actually made, but omissions. Suppose, for example, the members of the board receive information that suggests a corporate official may be perpetrating a fraud against the corporation, but, without deliberating further, they take no action. In this context, the business judgment rule is likely inapplicable because no business decision has been made.[69] The problem for the directors here is that over time they may learn of many "clues" that suggest that something has gone wrong, but they may be so overloaded with information and responsibilities that they cannot respond fully to each such instance. To mitigate this problem, the law has recognized the right of corporate directors to rely upon committees of the board or to delegate monitoring responsibilities to specified corporate officials. This "reliance defense" substantially lessens the risk of liability for negligent omissions, but it is a limited defense that requires that the defendant have a reasonable basis for relying upon the delegated official or committee. Again, the structure of this defense tells us much about what corporate lawyers actually do, because counsel's responsibility here is to make certain that these preconditions to the reliance defense are satisfied. Thus, a cautious corporate counsel will want to structure the board's relationship with its committees so that there are clear lines of delegation to board committees, covering all areas of potential liability. In turn, these subcommittees will receive regular reports from corporate officers on whom they may reasonably rely. Depending on one's perspective, the net result is either (as most probably believe) to create a more effective monitoring structure in which directors specialize or, if one doubts the social utility of the duty of care, to waste funds on costly programs to minimize a liability that arises only because of an ill-considered legal rule.

Another area that has drawn considerable attention in recent years has to do with corporate policies to ensure compliance with various federal laws and regulations, including antitrust laws and environmental protection laws. A Delaware case is illustrative.[70] Caremark International Inc. was in the business of providing health care services. It was prosecuted for violation of the federal Anti–Referral Payments Law for making certain "consulting" and "research" payments to doctors who referred patients to it, and ultimately settled by paying $250 million to various government and private entities. Some Caremark shareholders then filed a derivative action seeking damages from the directors. The decision in this derivative action approved a settlement under which the directors paid nothing, Caremark promised to sin no more, and the

---

[69] Of course, directors could consider the matter and make a decision to take no action because they judged the risks to be reasonable or the possible precautions to be too costly or ineffective. Such an actual decision to take no action presumably would be protected by the business judgment rule.

[70] In re Caremark International Inc. Derivative Litigation, 698 A.2d 959 (Del. Ch. 1996).

plaintiffs' lawyers collected fees of $870,000. Caremark had in fact had in place a compliance program with internal audits, published warnings in its employee manual, and training sessions. As a result of cases such as this,[71] it has become standard practice for lawyers to advise their corporate clients to adopt compliance programs with teeth in them— programs with substantial high-level commitment and review, frequent and meaningful communication to employees, serious monitoring and auditing, appropriate discipline where violations are discovered, etc.[72] Nonetheless, the state-law legal standard as typically formulated would seem to protect directors who rationally adopt a minimalist compliance program after weighing costs against benefits.

There are also certain potential liabilities of officers and directors that are governed by rules other than the general duty of care. These include liability for unauthorized payment of dividends and liability for violation of requirements of the federal securities laws with respect to disclosure in certain formal documents ("due diligence" standard). In addition, as explained below (Sec. VI(C)), there is potential liability for insider trading and for informal disclosures that are untrue (for example, in press releases).

A realistic assessment of the impact of the duty of care must take note of the fact that directors of large corporations typically obtain insurance covering most liabilities that arise under the duty of care. The corporation almost invariably pays the premiums on these policies. In addition, except as noted below, the corporation may indemnify corporate officials for the costs, expenses, and liabilities that they incur as a result of their position. Thus, the actual exposure of directors to a catastrophic loss for a negligent act or omission is considerably less than it initially appears to be. Still, there remain reasons why directors cannot always sleep comfortably. Most state indemnification statutes prohibit indemnification of the judgment or any settlement in a derivative action, which is the principal means by which the duty of care is enforced (expenses can still be indemnified even in such an action, subject to various limitations if the court finds that the defendant breached a duty to the corporation). Hence, the corporate official must rely on insurance to fill the void created by this deliberate statutory restriction on the corporation's ability to indemnify judgments and settlements, in derivative actions. Liability insurance policies for di-

---

[71] The leading Delaware case before *Caremark* was Graham v. Allis–Chalmers Mfg. Co., 188 A.2d 125 (Del.Supr.1963), in which the directors were absolved of liability after the corporation had been convicted of an antitrust violation.

[72] One commentator has pointed out, however, that under a system of strict liability (as under most state laws) the corporation is faced with a dilemma: to the extent that its compliance program is ef-fective, it will increasingly be required to report violations that will subject it to significant penalties. See Jennifer Arlen, The Potential Perverse Effects of Corporate Criminal Liability, 23 J. Leg. Stud. 833 (1994). Under the federal sentencing guidelines this problem is mitigated by provisions that reduce corporate penalties where the corporation has adopted appropriate compliance measures.

rectors and officers have become more difficult to obtain in recent years, and most such policies contain substantial deductibles, co-insurance provisions, and restrictions on coverage that place considerable risk on the insured. Thus, the possibility remains that for some outside directors, particularly those serving financially troubled or higher risk companies, the risks of serving may exceed the relatively modest benefits of directorial office. During the 1980s, there were repeated instances in which outside directors of large public corporations resigned because they were unable to secure liability insurance. It was this development, as much as the shock waves from the *Van Gorkom* decision, that spurred many states to revise their corporation statutes to limit due care liability.

Given the availability of insurance, it is ultimately unclear how effective or important the threat of liability for a lack of due care is in enforcing directorial diligence and prudence. Those who believe that corporate managers are principally motivated by market pressures and the desire to maintain their professional reputations see little need for the use of a litigation remedy in this context (as opposed to the duty of loyalty context, where it is more useful). Those who believe that the duty of care has a socially desirable function maintain that courts have imposed liability on this basis only in instances where officers and directors have behaved egregiously, in a manner that shows they were not disciplined by market or peer pressures.

## B. DUTY OF LOYALTY

As with the duty of care, the duty of loyalty is an extension of the law of agency and the law of trusts. (See Chapter 1, Sec. VIII and Chapter 2, Sec. VI.) Conceptually, the duty of loyalty represents a single obligation that corporate officers and directors owe the corporation, but it is easiest to analyze this duty in terms of several recurring fact patterns.

**1. Self–Dealing Transactions.** Probably the longest standing concern of corporate law has been that corporate officials may cause the corporation to enter into overly generous transactions with themselves. The corporate official might, for example, sell property to the corporation at an inflated price or buy assets from the corporation at a bargain price. To guard against this kind of danger, the 19th Century law made any transaction between the corporation and a director voidable at the option of the corporation.[73] This rule has been steadily relaxed throughout this century,[74] possibly because it proved too strict or possibly

---

[73] See Harold Marsh, Jr., Are Directors Trustees? Conflicts of Interest and Corporate Morality, 22 Bus. Law. 35 (1966).

[74] Ahmed Bulbulia and Arthur R. Pinto, Statutory Responses to Interested Directors

Transactions: A Watering Down of Fiduciary Standard?, 53 Notre Dame Lawyer 201 (1977).

because the competition among states for corporate franchises produced a weakening of fiduciary standards. Those who believe the prophylactic rule of the 19th Century was too strict can argue that often a corporation, in its start-up years, must turn to its directors for financing or specific assets. Also, directors frequently represent the various constituencies with which the corporation does business: customers, suppliers, creditors—each of whom may want a representative on the board to monitor the corporation. These representatives may provide useful advice and expertise for the corporation. Finally, with the emergence in recent decades of independent boards of directors, staffed by outside directors, it may be that the need for judicial monitoring declined. On the other side of the debate, there is the view that all that has happened is that corporate managers were successful as an interest group, aided perhaps by their lawyers, in convincing legislatures to relax fiduciary standards. And, possibly, courts did not want to become ensnared in complicated valuation issues and so preferred a rule under which they could defer to a nominally disinterested board.

Whatever the reason, it is clear that, by early in this century, the rule on self-dealing transactions had changed from a rule that they were voidable at the corporation's election to a rule that the corporate official bore the burden of proving the fairness of the transaction if it were challenged. This rule also created continuing uncertainty over whether a transaction would be upheld, if challenged. The rule did inhibit abuse, and today it still has its strong proponents. Most modern statutes, however, establish a procedure by which to "sanitize" transactions between a director and the corporation. A typical statute creates a "safe harbor" rule under which a director's conflict does not render the transaction voidable if the transaction was (1) approved by disinterested directors after full disclosure as to the conflict (and, in some states, as to all the facts relevant to the transaction), (2) approved by shareholders after similar disclosure, or (3) approved by a court as fair.[75] This statutory structure raises a question about the role of fairness in transactions approved by the board or shareholders: may the court invalidate a transaction that it considers unfair even if it was properly approved? A number of decisions have answered yes (as discussed below), while the current version of the Model Business Corporation Act adopts a much detailed statutory treatment of "interested director" transactions under which the judicial role is substantially curtailed (and probably eliminated) if its requisite procedures are followed.[76]

As suggested above, one of the issues on which state statutes may differ is the type of disclosure that is required in order to protect the

---

[75] See Revised Model Business Corporation Act § 8.61; Del. Gen. Corp. Law § 144; Calif. Corp. Code § 310.

[76] See Model Business Corporation Act, § 8.61. For a critique, see Douglas M. Branson, *Assault on Another Citadel: Attempts to Curtail the Fiduciary Standard of Loyalty Applicable to Corporate Fiduciaries*, 57 Ford. L. Rev. 375 (1988).

transaction from attack. Under the more permissive statutes (such as New York's), the corporate official need only disclose that he or she has an interest in the transaction (i.e., "conflict disclosure"), while under other statutes (such as California's) full disclosure must be made of all material information about the transaction that is known to such corporate official, unless the information is already known by the directors asked to approve it. This difference can be significant. Consider the following example: A director, who is also the controlling shareholder, wishes to sell to the corporation a building for which the corporation has a legitimate use. The director knows, but does not advise the board, that the building has sustained some termite damage, which may render it unsuitable for its intended purpose. Under the former, more permissive statute, the director might only disclose that the building is owned by the director's family, but under the second type of statute, disclosure of any material defect is necessary.

Perhaps the most important difference among courts interpreting these "sanitizing" statutes involves the role of the courts in examining the fairness of challenged transactions. Some courts have treated compliance with the procedures set forth in these statutes as eliminating any role for substantive judicial review,[77] while probably the majority of courts view such compliance as only shifting the burden of proof to the plaintiff to prove that the transaction was clearly unfair.[78] That is, whereas the common law rule placed the burden on the defendant to establish fairness in an interested transaction, these statutes are seen as reversing this burden of proof, not as withdrawing the substantive issue of fairness from judicial consideration. Of course, "fairness" can be an elusive question, and different estimates and standards of valuation are usually available. Thus, where there has been approval by disinterested directors after full disclosure, the modern tendency is to require the plaintiff to prove that the transaction was grossly unfair by showing that no reasonable board of directors would have approved it.[79]

**2. Corporate Opportunity.** Not infrequently, corporate officers and directors may learn of business opportunities that are of potential interest to their corporation. For example, an officer may realize the corporation is seeking to assemble a plot of land in a certain area to build an office building. If the officer discovers an opportunity to buy a piece of land in this same area, which opportunity the officer realizes the

---

[77] See Puma v. Marriott, 283 A.2d 693 (Del.Ch.1971) (business judgment rule applied once disinterested approval given). The Model Business Corporation Act, §§ 8.60–8.63, would seem to eliminate any possibility of judicial review if the statutory requirements have been satisfied. However, comment 2 to § 8.61 states that the board's action must be consistent with the requirements in § 8.30(a) that the board acted in good faith.

[78] See, e.g., Remillard Brick Co. v. Remillard–Dandini Co., 109 Cal.App.2d 405, 241 P.2d 66 (1952); Fliegler v. Lawrence, 361 A.2d 218 (Del.1976).

[79] Sometimes courts will refer to this standard of review as the "waste" standard; essentially, it means that no arguably reasonable method of valuation could justify the transaction.

corporation may have wanted to exploit, the officer may not purchase the land in order to resell it to the corporation at a profit. Instead, corporate law requires that the officer turn the opportunity over to the corporation without profit. Nor may an officer or director personally accept an opportunity that was offered with the expectation that the officer or director would take it to the corporation for its consideration. The unifying principle underlying these cases is that an officer or director may not make use of his or her corporate position or of information learned therefrom to seize opportunities that the corporation might accept if they were presented to it. (Compare Chapter 2, Secs. VI(B), (C) and (D).) However, a corporate official may accept the opportunity if the official first offers it to the corporation with full disclosure and the corporation then rejects it.

There is, however, a more problematic aspect to the corporate opportunity doctrine. Suppose the director is a well-known investor or entrepreneur who learns of an opportunity that would be of interest to the corporation but that was offered to the director in an individual capacity. Must the director sacrifice his or her own interests and turn this opportunity over? Some decisions say that the director must do so if the opportunity is sufficiently closely related to an existing line of business that the corporation is engaged in, while other decisions say that opportunities that come to the director in an individual capacity need never be turned over.[80] To require that the corporate official subordinate his or her own interests to those of the corporation goes beyond the principle that information or opportunities acquired because of one's corporate position may not be diverted and assumes that a disinterested official should always be seeking business opportunities for any corporation that he or she serves. This version of the duty begins from the premise that a disinterested official would violate his or her duty of care by failing to notify the corporation of an opportunity that the official knew would be of interest to the corporation. Therefore, if a disinterested official must notify the corporation of such an opportunity, why should an official who is personally interested owe any lesser duty? Even under this view, problems still arise when a director serves two or more corporations, each of which would be interested in the opportunity. What should the director do here? Perhaps the director could offer the opportunity to both corporations and then let them compete for it. Nonetheless, the law is unsettled regarding opportunities that were offered to an individual (where the actual offeree was not sought out as an agent of the corporation).

   **3.  Competition.** A difficult issue in corporate law involves the degree to which a corporate official may compete with the corporation,

---

[80] For a review of the murky tests used by courts in this area to determine if the corporation had an "expectancy" in the opportunity, see Victor Brudney and Robert C. Clark, *A New Look at Corporate Opportunities,* 94 Harv.L.Rev. 989 (1981). See also Miller v. Miller, 301 Minn. 207, 222 N.W.2d 71 (1974).

either by also serving a rival business or, more typically, by resigning and taking information learned at one corporation to a rival. State law varies considerably in this area, but some general principles can be stated with confidence: First, corporate law does not forbid competition, but only unfair competition (such as where business secrets are transferred to a competitor). Second, unless restricted by an employment contract, a corporate officer or director may always resign and move to a competitor. What he or she may not do is take "proprietary" information (such as customer lists, trade secrets, etc.). Third, if disinterested directors of the corporation approve, an officer or director may compete with the firm even though harm is caused to the corporation.

A particularly troublesome area involves the conduct a corporate officer may engage in while preparing to leave. Often, such an officer may wish to approach customers or fellow employees and ask them to follow him. This is generally considered a violation of the duty of loyalty owed to the corporation so long as the officer remains in the corporation's employ. Once the officer resigns, however, he or she may seek to contact customers and employees or to compete vigorously in other ways. The difficult trade-off here is that the law favors both loyalty to one's employer and vigorous competition. In some industries (such as information technology), new competitors seem to emerge chiefly from former employees of established firms in the industry. A stronger, more prophylactic rule in this area might then inhibit socially desirable competition.

**4. Federal Law.** The federal Public Company Accounting Reform and Investor Protection Act (popularly known as the Sarbanes–Oxley Act), enacted in 2002, prohibits publicly held companies from making loans to or arranging credit for their officers and directors. The Act also requires every public corporation to adopt a code of ethics for its CEO, CFO (chief financial officer), controller, and chief accountant.

**5. Protecting Control: The Basic Conflict.** When a bidder makes an unsolicited tender offer for the stock of a "target" company, the directors and senior management of the target know that they are likely to be replaced if the offer is successful; this is a well-known fact of corporate life in the wake of control changes. At the least, they are likely to lose their autonomy, which may be of considerable importance to them. This knowledge certainly may give the target's management an incentive to resist a takeover, even though the tender offer is at a high premium over the current market price and may be desired by the corporation's shareholders.

On the other hand, if the directors and managers consider an offer to be too low, they have an obligation to the shareholders to tell them so. Moreover, the shareholders may want the board to negotiate on their behalf to secure either a higher price from the bidder or, if the bidder has made only a partial bid, an offer for more shares. An uncertain trade-off thus results because, at least once an initial takeover bid has been made, shareholders may want their management to serve as their collective agent and conduct a value-maximizing auction. Still, they almost certainly do not want management to resort to "scorched earth" tactics that cause the original bid to be withdrawn. In short, some resistance may be good, but too much is definitely bad.

Clearly, then, a potential takeover involves a conflict between the interest of managers in their jobs and the interest of shareholders in maximizing share values. This conflict is one of great importance and is difficult to resolve. By and large, however, the courts have not faced up to the fact of conflict and have not applied the rules and doctrines that govern other conflict situations. Instead, they have clothed management with the protective mantel of the business judgment rule and then have modified that doctrine to take account of the reality of an inherent self-serving bias against takeover. At the same time, lawyers representing incumbent directors and managers have developed, and boards have adopted, a wide array of anti-takeover tactics. These tactics have been augmented by state anti-takeover legislation. The law relating to these defensive devices is described in some detail later in this chapter. (See Sec. VII(B)(2).)

As an alternative to reliance on legal rules and litigation, shareholders can to try to align the interests of managers with their own. One device that may align interests is the compensatory stock option, which is simply an option, granted to managers, to buy common stock of the corporation at a set price. Compensatory stock options have the obvious desirable effect (from the shareholders' perspective) of providing managers an incentive to maximize share values. To put the idea slightly differently, managers with stock options share in the gains realized by shareholders when the common stock rises in value. One important general objection to compensatory stock options is that a rise in the value of the common stock may have little or nothing to do with the efforts of the manager holding an option on the stock. In the takeover context this objection fades: an option has the desirable effect of encouraging management to accept a high bid. Even though the gain to the managers may seem in some sense to be unearned and therefore undeserved, allowing managers to claim some part of the gain to be realized by shareholders does encourage them to act in the best interests of the shareholders. Such financial encouragement is likely to be far more effective than moralizing about fiduciary obligation or rephrasing the rules on that obligation.

But if stock options can be used to align the interests of shareholders and managers by allowing managers to share in the gain from a takeover, why not accomplish the same objective in a more direct and focused manner by cash payments? Why not use a rifle rather than a shotgun? The focused approach consists of a substantial cash payment triggered by termination of employment following a takeover. This approach has come to be known as a "golden parachute." Many people are offended by the idea of making large extra payments to managers to induce them to do what they ought to do anyway.[81] But if, as a shareholder, you are more interested in maximizing your own wealth than in demonstrating your commitment to the principle of fiduciary obligation, you might want to insist that the employment contracts of your top managers include golden parachute provisions. You will want to be careful, however, to ensure that the payment is not structured in such a way as to lead managers to sell the corporation too readily, at too low a price.

In thinking about golden parachutes and stock options, one may do well to consider a disguised substitute. Suppose A Corp. is seeking to acquire B Corp. and is concerned about resistance from B's management. A common reaction by A Corp. to the resistance has been to offer the B managers long-term employment contracts at good salaries. Then, once the acquisition is accomplished and a decent period of time has elapsed, the B managers are fired and paid off (according to the liquidated damages provisions in their long-term contracts). Once again, the need to an inducement to management to support a sale of the corporation may be inconsistent with fiduciary obligation, but may nonetheless be consistent with shareholder wealth maximization.

**6. Shareholder Duties.** Fiduciary duties basically apply to officers and directors, but, to the extent that a shareholder holds the power to control the corporation, courts have shown some willingness to apply these duties to such a shareholder as well. This principle has been most clearly established in the close corporation context,[82] but it has also been

---

[81] This sentiment, combined with some concern for other people adversely affected by takeovers, may explain the rules of federal income taxation that disallow deduction of, and impose an excise tax on, certain golden parachute payments. See Int. Rev. Code §§ 280G and 4999. A study of 245 firms that adopted golden parachutes during 1980–1994 found, however, that fears that golden parachutes would lead executives to run down firms to make them attractive as takeover candidates were unfounded and that, to the contrary, the effect of golden parachutes has been to encourage desirable restructuring of firms. M.P. Narayanan and Anant K. Sundaram, A Safe Landing? Golden Parachutes and Corporate Behavior, U. Mich. Bus. School Working Paper 98–015R (1998).

[82] Various often-cited Massachusetts decisions have applied partnership fiduciary obligations to shareholders of closely held corporations. See, e.g., Donahue v. Rodd Electrotype Co., 367 Mass. 578, 328 N.E.2d 505 (1975); Wilkes v. Springside Nursing Home, Inc., 370 Mass. 842, 353 N.E.2d 657 (1976). Even a minority shareholder has been held liable where, under a provision in the articles that gave each shareholder a

veto power over all corporate actions, he blocked the payment of dividends, which had the effect of subjecting the corporation to a tax penalty. See Smith v. Atlantic Properties, Inc., 12 Mass.App.Ct. 201, 422 N.E.2d 798 (1981).

In Meiselman v. Meiselman, 309 N.C. 279, 307 S.E.2d 551 (1983), a minority shareholder invoked a statute that allowed a court to order dissolution to protect the "rights and interests" of the complaining shareholder, or (as interpreted by the court) to grant alternative relief in the form of a buy-out of the complaining shareholder's shares. The court interpreted "rights and interests" to include "reasonable expectations," including the expectation of participating in the management of the business or of being employed by the corporation. The court reviewed decisions in other states and referred to academic writings in support of the idea that it is often unrealistic to expect minority shareholders in close corporations to bargain for protection of their expectations and that, consequently, judicial intervention on their behalf is appropriate.

applied in one well-known case to the controlling shareholder of a public corporation, where actions were taken that deprived the minority share-holders of their access to the stock market.[83] In this well-known Califor-nia Supreme Court decision, the court asserted that "majority sharehold-ers ... have a fiduciary responsibility to the minority and to the corporation to use their ability to control the corporation in a fair, just, and equitable manner."[84]

One of the most intriguing issues relating to the obligations of controlling shareholders has to do with the sale of a controlling block of shares (sometimes less than a voting majority) for a price per share above the price available to the other shareholders—in other words, a sale of control for a premium above the price that would be paid for those shares without control. While the payment of such premiums seems to be common, and while several commentators have questioned the fairness of a practice that results in some shareholders reaping a benefit not available to others, all modern decisions have affirmed the right of a controlling shareholder to receive a control premium. Only under special circumstances (such as when there is reason to believe that the buyer of the control block will loot the corporation or somehow take unfair advantage of the minority shareholders) is the sale of control for a premium legally impermissible.[85] One rationale for this result is that it is often socially desirable that a new management team be able to "bribe" the controlling shareholder in this fashion to turn over control. After all, their payment of such a premium may signify that the incoming share-holder or management team thinks it can operate the firm more profit-ably and so will pay an above-market price to get that opportunity. If control premiums were barred, the effect might be perpetuation of the existing ownership, with inferior managers who are unwilling to give up the salaries and perquisites of corporate office.

One must be careful, however, to distinguish situations in which a shareholder who is serving as an officer or director of a corporation learns of the willingness of an outsider to buy the assets of the firm, or

---

[83] Jones v. H. F. Ahmanson & Co., 1 Cal.3d 93, 81 Cal.Rptr. 592, 460 P.2d 464 (1969). Here, the defendants held about 85 percent of the common shares of a savings and loan association. They exchanged these shares for the shares of a new corporation that they formed and owned and then be-gan to sell their shares of the new corpora-tion to the public at a great profit. The effect was that the majority created a public market for their shares while the minority (the remaining 15% of the initial sharehold-ers, including the plaintiff) had no market in which they could sell for anywhere near the same price. This was held to be a breach of the majority's fiduciary obligation to the minority, despite the fact that the case involved no exercise of control over the corporation itself (that is, over the opera-tion of the business) and no use of a posi-tion as an officer or director.

[84] Id. at 109, 81 Cal.Rptr. at 598, 460 P.2d at 471.

[85] For a well known case in this area, see Perlman v. Feldmann, 219 F.2d 173 (2d Cir.1955), certiorari denied, 349 U.S. 952, 75 S.Ct. 880, 99 L.Ed. 1277 (1955). Here, the court seems to have found that it was foreseeable to the sellers that the incoming control group intended to divert a corporate advantage to itself. The selling shareholders were therefore required to pay to the corpo-ration the premium they had received for control.

to acquire a controlling interest from the corporation itself, and then seizes that opportunity for himself or herself, rather than offering to share it with other shareholders. Here, there may well be a violation of the corporate opportunity doctrine discussed earlier. The line between these two situations may seem an artificial one because the bidder is generally interested in the corporation's assets and less concerned about whether he purchases them in one transaction or piecemeal in a series of transactions with different shareholders at different prices. At the same time, the controlling shareholders may be unwilling to sell less than all of their shares and may be unwilling as well to accept a price that reflects what the bidder is willing to pay for the entire firm but with all shareholders receiving the same price. Thus, if the bidder expresses a willingness to buy all shares for the same price, the controlling share-holders may be uninterested—and they have no obligation to accept the offer, even if it is one that the noncontrolling shareholders would find attractive.

## C. DUTIES REGARDING INFORMATION: RULE 10b–5

Corporate insiders often have access to material, non-public infor-mation about their corporation that has value and could be used profit-ably in the stock market. At common law, the majority view was that a corporate official could purchase shares from a shareholder based on "inside" information, because the corporate official owed no duty direct-ly to the shareholder and thus had only to observe the same standards regarding fraud that applied to the purchase or sale of any chattel in the marketplace. To be sure, an astute shareholder might in theory demand to know if a purchasing corporate official possessed material, non-public information, and a false denial might amount to fraud, but, because most transactions were faceless ones effected through the medium of a stock exchange, no mechanism for asking such a question existed. Presently, the common law no-duty rule seems still to be the law in some states for faceless transactions, though other state courts have long held that insiders must disclose any material information before they trade. In addition, most of the states that continue to follow the no-duty rule for faceless transactions follow the so-called "special circumstances" rule for face to face transactions, and in cases involving such transactions are likely to hold that the corporate official owed a duty to disclose to the individual shareholder on the other side of the transaction.[86]

---

[86] See Stephen M. Bainbridge, Securities Law: Insider Trading 7–16 (1999); Bailey v. Vaughan, 178 W.Va. 371, 359 S.E.2d 599 (1987) (describing the somewhat confused state of the law). A leading case illustrating the special circumstances rule is Strong v. Repide, 213 U.S. 419, 29 S.Ct. 521, 53 L.Ed. 853 (1909), in which the Supreme Court held that a chief executive who purchased shares through an undisclosed agent was liable to the selling shareholder, where the chief executive had just successfully con-cluded secret negotiations to sell corporate assets to the United States. The defendant was both a director and majority owner of the corporation and personally negotiated the transaction giving rise to the undis-closed information. Thus, the case involved

State cases have seldom examined this issue in recent years, because the topic of insider trading has been largely subsumed by federal law. In 1942, the Securities and Exchange Commission learned that the president of a company was personally visiting its shareholders and offering to repurchase their stock because he knew that the company had received a very valuable war procurement contract. Literally overnight, the SEC adopted a rule to prohibit this conduct, which it called Rule 10b–5, because it was the fifth rule adopted pursuant to Section 10(b) of The Securities Exchange Act of 1934. Rule 10b–5, which was initially adopted to protect the defrauded sellers in the above-described case, also applies today to protect purchasers by making it unlawful for any person in connection with the purchase or sale of a security "to make any untrue statement of a material fact or to omit to state a material fact necessary in order to make the statements made, in the light of the circumstances under which they were made, not misleading. . . ." In 1961, in In re Cady, Roberts & Co.,[87] the SEC interpreted Rule 10b–5 to impose on "corporate 'insiders,' particularly officers, directors, or controlling stockholders" an "affirmative duty of disclosure . . . when dealing in securities." This duty, it said, required the insider who possessed material, non-public information to "disclose or abstain"—that is, to disclose the information or refrain from trading. Basic and important as this rule was, it did not produce much litigation until seven years later in the seminal case of SEC v. Texas Gulf Sulphur Co.[88] There, upon learning of a uniquely valuable ore strike that Texas Gulf Sulphur had made in Canada, various corporate officials purchased substantial amounts of the company's stock. The SEC successfully sued these insiders for disgorgement of their profits, and, in the wake of its victory, a host of private damages actions followed. In the same case, the SEC succeeded in holding the corporation itself liable for violation of Rule 10b–5 for a misleading the public in a press release authorized by the corporation's president, even though the corporation did not trade in its stock. Although *Texas Gulf Sulphur* was an SEC enforcement action, later cases established that Rule 10b–5 could be enforced in private damage actions as well. Private actions became increasingly important with the slow development of the law with respect to the large class action, for which the judicial rules were formalized only in the late 1960s. Gradually, lawyers began to appreciate that they could bring nationwide class actions and recover sometimes large damages plus generous legal fees (and, sometimes, generous legal fees even when damages were modest).

It is important to emphasize that the *Texas Gulf Sulphur* case established two distinct principles: First, it held that insiders violated

"concealment of identity by the defendant and failure to disclose significant facts having a dramatic impact on the stock price." Bainbridge, supra, at 9.

[87] 40 SEC 907 (1961).

[88] 401 F.2d 833 (2d Cir.1968), certiorari denied, 394 U.S. 976, 89 S.Ct. 1454, 22 L.Ed.2d 756 (1969).

Rule 10b–5 when they traded on material non-public information. Second, and probably more importantly, the corporation was also found to have violated Rule 10b–5, on the ground that its misleading press release caused some shareholders to sell their shares at an undervalued price.

**1. False or Misleading Statements.** The potential scope of corporate liability for false or misleading statements was significantly expanded in 1988, when the Supreme Court, in Basic Inc. v. Levinson,[89] adopted the "fraud on the market" theory, under which people who trade on the open market are said to have relied on the "integrity of the market" and the accuracy of the price set by the market. Thus, they can be said to have been legally injured by a misrepresentation even if they were unaware of it at the time they traded. *Basic* involved a commonly occurring fact pattern in which a corporation is asked by the press to comment on rumors that it is involved in merger transactions. The defendant corporation, Basic, Inc., was engaged in such negotiations, and the price of its shares had begun to rise. Nonetheless, Basic issued a press release that conveyed the misleading impression that no such negotiations were in progress. Two issues confronted the Court: (1) Was the misrepresented status of the merger negotiations "material"? (2) Could shareholders who had not learned of the misstatement sue simply because they sold at a price that reflected the market's new doubts (based on the company's denial) that there would be a merger? On the materiality issue, prior cases, beginning with *Texas Gulf Sulphur*, had developed a standard that traded off probability against magnitude so that even a low-probability fact could be material if its impact on the corporation would have been large if it occurred. However, some later courts had taken the view that preliminary merger negotiations were never material as a matter of law. In *Basic*, the Court rejected this latter view, ruling that any omitted or misrepresented information could be material "if there is a substantial likelihood that a reasonable investor would consider it important" in making an investment decision. Then, on the reliance issue, the Court created a rebuttable presumption that an investor had relied on misrepresented or omitted information if it was material. This rule, which is the heart of the fraud-on-the-market theory, effectively removes the issue of reliance from a class action lawsuit. After *Basic*, the harm covered by Rule 10b–5 is not limited to instances of lying to investors in the old-fashioned sense contemplated by doctrines of fraud and deceit; rather, according to the Court, investors are entitled to rely on the "integrity of the market price"[90]—that is, they

---

[89] 485 U.S. 224, 108 S.Ct. 978, 99 L.Ed.2d 194 (1988).

[90] The Court supported its common-sense judgment about market reactions by referring to a financial theory known as the Efficient Capital Market Hypothesis (ECMH) (see Chapter 5, Sec. (V)(B)), but one scarcely needs that financial theory, or the evidence in support of it, for the limited proposition that was required for the decision—namely, that when the price of a corporation's shares has risen on rumors of a merger, a denial that merger negotiations in progress is likely, if believed, to drive down the price of the corporation's shares. The Court left open the possibility of proof

are entitled to assume that the market price has not been contaminated by misleading information, including information informally released in contacts with the press.

Taken together, the decision in Basic Inc. v. Levinson, and the earlier developments, increased the possibility that corporations might be liable for potentially astronomical damages as a result of issuing an informal, hastily drafted document, such as a press release. Although decisions subsequent to *Texas Gulf Sulphur* have narrowed the possibility that mere carelessness could create liability, the potential for substantial liability still explains much about the functional activity of corporate lawyers, who today normally review press releases and other public statements of their corporate clients. The risks have seemed particularly troublesome in situations such as that involving Basic, Inc., where merger discussions are underway and where there are good reasons for trying to keep the fact of those discussions confidential,[91] but rumors are spreading, the price of the shares is rising, and reporters and analysts are clamoring for definitive information. One possible response for the target is to adopt and consistently apply a firm "no comment" policy in response to requests for information. The Supreme Court, in its *Basic Inc.* decision, expressly approved this approach, while making clear that if any statement about the merger discussion is made, that statement must not be misleading. Corporate managers are not permitted to be disingenuous with investors, even though they sincerely believe that disingenuousness is required in order to best serve the interests of most of the shareholders. Some protection of the corporation (and its current shareholders) is afforded by the requirement that the plaintiff prove that the corporation acted with "scienter" (that is, that its agents either knew the information reaching the market was materially inaccurate or were "reckless" about the possibility that this was the case).

by the defendant that the denial was not believed by the people whose trades determined the market price. What might be troubling to some observers is that in so far as the Court purported to place reliance on the ECMH, it may be thought to have accepted a particular version of that theory—namely, the "semi-strong" form—under which the market price accurately reflects all public information, but not undisclosed information. The decision implicitly rejects a "strong form" of the theory, under which the market price would also reflect undisclosed facts—in this case, the fact that there was a serious prospect of merger and that the denial of negotiations was therefore disingenuous.

The efficiency of the market for information is relevant not only to the reliance issue but also, and perhaps more importantly, to the amount of damages. Suppose a

corporation falsely denies that merger talks are in progress. That denial may result in a lower price for the corporation's shares, but how much lower depends on how much credence investors attach to the denial, which in turn may depend on how much nonpublic information they have. The calculation of damages requires the use of modern techniques of financial analysis, but also some largely speculative assumptions about the facts. See Bradford Cornell and R. Gregory Morgan, *Using Finance Theory to Measure Damages in Fraud on the Market Cases,* 37 UCLA L.Rev. 883 (1990).

[91] For example, the potential acquirer may insist on secrecy in order to avoid attracting the attention of rival acquirers, or the target management may fear adverse effects on employee morale during a possibly prolonged period of negotiation, which might lead to nothing.

**2. Insider Trading.** Following years of doctrinal development in the courts of appeal, the Supreme Court, in a 1983 case, Dirks v. SEC,[92] narrowed the law on what amounts to insider trading for purposes of Rule 10b–5. Basically, the Court held that only those corporate persons (officers, employees and directors)who breach a fiduciary duty to the corporation, and those who knowingly aid or abet or benefit from such a breach, violate Rule 10b–5 when they trade based on possession of material non-public information. Thus, persons who simply learn of non-public information (for example, by overhearing it or learning of it through market rumors) are not today liable. However, in an important footnote, the Court added that other persons, such as lawyers and investment bankers, who serve the corporation as agents and advisers, are to be deemed "constructive insiders" and hence also fall within the reach of Rule 10b–5 for insider trading.

The scope of Rule 10b–5 has been extended, under the "misappropriation" theory, to certain people who are not corporate insiders. For example, suppose that Corporation X is engaged in secret negotiations to acquire Corporation Y and that when this information becomes public the price of Corporation Y stock will rise dramatically. If an employee of Corporation Y, the acquisition target, buys its stock, that employee, an insider, has violated Rule 10b–5 under the "traditional" theory. If an employee of Corporation X, the acquiring corporation, violates a rule of policy of Corporation X and buys stock of Corporation Y, that employee is not an "insider" of the corporation whose stock is purchased but nonetheless has violated Rule 10b–5 under the misappropriation theory.[93]

*Should* insider trading be prohibited? A serious academic debate continues over the wisdom of the prohibition. The majority view has long been that management should be required to hold material, non-public information in trust as a fiduciary and thus may use it only for corporate purposes, but critics of the prohibition question whether anyone is injured by insider trading.[94] They argue that the investor who lacks the information possessed by the insider typically has already decided to sell his or her shares and presumably will still do so (at the same price) even if the insider "abstains." Moreover, when the insider trades, these critics

---

[92] 463 U.S. 646, 103 S.Ct. 3255, 77 L.Ed.2d 911 (1983).

[93] After many years of uncertainty in the lower courts the misappropriation theory was approved and applied by the Supreme Court in United States v. O'Hagan, 521 U.S. 642, 117 S.Ct. 2199 (1997). The defendant in the case was a lawyer who learned that a client of his firm was planning a takeover and who bought shares of the target firm based on this confidential information. One of the curiosities of the misappropriation theory arises from a suggestion in

the Supreme Court opinion that the defendant could have avoided liability by simply notifying his law firm that he intended to trade—even if the firm objected. It is likely to be an extremely rare case, however, where the employee is willing to thumb his or her nose at the employer in this way.

[94] For an expression of the view that insider trading should be legalized, see Dennis W. Carlton & Daniel R. Fischel, *The Regulation of Insider Trading*, 35 Stan. L.Rev. 857 (1983). See also H. Manne, Insider Trading and the Stock Market (1966).

argue, this action points the market in the right direction, because management's purchases will drive the share price up and its sales will drive the price down. Some commentators also believe that management should receive a portion of any significant market appreciation in their corporation's stock in order to give them an appropriate entrepreneurial stake in the corporation; insider trading, viewed this way, allows management to share in the value their efforts create. Finally, these commentators claim that if insider trading were harmful, corporations would prohibit it, themselves, but few have done so.

Most commentators remain convinced, however, that insider trading can cause harm, though they tend to divide over how to define both the injury and the victim. Some emphasize the adverse impact on the market's allocational efficiency; others focus on the individual investor whose purchase or sale is preempted; still other critics have stressed the harm to the corporation itself.[95] Essentially, insider trading allows management to earn a secret profit as to which the shareholders have neither knowledge nor control. This can create perverse incentives under which the manager's interests are not aligned with the shareholders. The most obvious example arises if management can "sell short" when the market price falls and thereby make a profit on their firm's decline. "Short selling" involves sale of stock that the seller borrows from another (usually a broker dealer), sells at a high price before the market declines, and then repurchases after the decline at a much lower price in order to restore the stock to the party from whom it was borrowed. The net effect is that a profit can be realized on bad news just as it can on good news. As a result, the insider can profit either when the corporation's prospects are about to improve or to deteriorate drastically. This set of opportunities may give the insider an incentive to cause the corporation to undertake high risk investments or business strategies. Although the shareholders might decline this course of action if they could choose, the insider will know the outcome of the gamble before the market does and can profit whichever way the market is about to move. Not only would this incentive misalign the manager's preferences, so that they would conflict with those of the shareholders, but it also seems an inefficient way of compensating managers. In effect, it compensates managers by giving them the equivalent of a lottery ticket, because they will profit only in the event of a boom or bust. In all likelihood, the typical manager would prefer a form of compensation that had a lower degree of variance associated with it.

[95] See James D. Cox, Insider Trading and Contracting: A Critical Response to the "Chicago School," 1986 Duke L.J. 628 (emphasizing injury to corporation); William K.S. Wang, Trading on Material Nonpublic Information on Impersonal Stock Markets: Who is Harmed, and Who Can Sue Whom Under SEC Rule 10b–5?, 54 S.Cal.L.Rev. 1217 (1981)(emphasizing injury to investor whose purchase or sale is preempted by the insider); Joel Seligman, The Reformation of Federal Securities Law Concerning Nonpublic Information, 73 Georgetown L.J. 1083 (1985) (emphasizing impact on timing of disclosure and market efficiency).

Another corporate injury occurs when the potential for profits from insider trading causes a corporate manager to prematurely release "private" corporation information. For example, in a fact pattern like that in the *Texas Gulf Sulphur* case, an insider who has purchased shares on learning of the ore strike may wish to cause the corporation to disclose the information prematurely, before Texas Gulf Sulphur has been able to exploit its discovery fully (by buying the land surrounding the site). This premature release would enable the insider to profit before other market or general economic events (e.g., interest rate movements, wars, etc.) could erode the gain that should occur on release of the non-public information. Indeed, merely by trading in significant amounts the insider is apt to signal unintentionally to others that some material development has occurred; eventually, non-public information tends to leak out under such circumstances. Alternatively, an insider who has not already purchased may delay corporate disclosures until she or he can arrange to make substantial stock purchases.

The view that insider trading is simply a form of incentive compensation, much like stock options, is also subject to several cogent objections. For example, insider trading may tend to compensate the "wrong" manager: not the individual who perfects a new invention or introduces a new marketing strategy, but rather, the lawyer, public relations specialist, or financial manager who better understands the likely market significance of the undisclosed information, even though he or she did not create it. Also, the view that insider trading is simply analogous to a stock option granted by the shareholders to management ignores that the profits from insider trading are potentially unlimited. That is, although shareholders are often willing to give management an option to purchase a specified number of shares at the current market price for a specified future period (in order to enhance the managers' incentive to maximize the value of the firm's shares), it seems highly unlikely that they would be willing to grant managers an unlimited option to purchase all shares available on the market at the then current price while these managers were in possession of inside information indicating that the stock had a higher value. Such a right would give managers the ability to seize potentially all the gain from any sudden or otherwise hidden development affecting the firm's value, and the cost would be borne disproportionately by those shareholders who sold, rather than evenly by all (as it is in the case of a stock option). Finally, insider trading allows management to profit (by selling short) even when the firm is experiencing material adverse developments—hardly the circumstance under which shareholders would normally wish to reward management. For all these reasons, the claim that insider trading is simply an efficient system of managerial compensation has some seemingly obvious deficiencies, because it interferes with the corporation's ability to relate compensation to executive performance.

The impact of insider trading on the overall efficiency of the securities market has been much debated. Those who defend insider trading believe that it will seldom slow, and may even expedite, the disclosure of material information (because the insider can trade and then cause the corporation to disclose the material development on the same day). On the other hand, it has been argued that investors in the market who see the company's stock rise for no apparent reason, but in fact because insiders are trading based on undisclosed positive information, will incorrectly believe the stock to be overpriced and so will sell, thereby missing the ultimate appreciation in value on disclosure of the information. Legalizing insider trading may also encourage managers to "bunch up" items of information, which, if released as individual items, would not be as likely to have a significant market impact; this tactic would assure those who traded in advance that these packages of information would have a predictable impact (and thus make insider trading an even surer bet). If such a bunching effect did result, it would create a more volatile securities market, characterized by uneven information flows and sharper price fluctuations—in short, investors would face greater uncertainty and should demand a higher return on their investments in response.

The debate over insider trading will continue, but neither Congress, the SEC, nor the courts seem inclined to abandon the "disclose or abstain" rule. Indeed, Congress enacted in 1984 a special treble damages penalty to create a greater deterrent against insider trading.

## VII.  CORPORATE ACCOUNTABILITY: THE ISSUE OF SEPARATION OF OWNERSHIP AND CONTROL

As suggested in the preceding section, shareholders and managers have many potential conflicts. Managers may pay themselves overly generous salaries, consume excessive perquisites, or enter into unfair transactions with the corporation. Conflicts may also arise among shareholders; for example, controlling shareholders may seek to force minority shareholders out at an unfairly low price by effecting a "squeeze-out" merger.[96] No one doubts that instances of abuse can occur, but the much debated topic is how pervasive these problems are and what reforms, if any, they justify. This section will begin by looking at how this problem has been assessed by theorists and then will examine the legal and market mechanisms that protect shareholders from exploitation and the legal devices that circumscribe those mechanisms.

---

[96] Typically, such a merger is accomplished by merging the corporation with a newly formed corporation owned by the controlling shareholders. The shares held by the minority shareholders are cancelled pursuant to the merger agreement and these shareholders receive a cash payment. Although the minority shareholders can contest the adequacy of the price they receive by exercising their appraisal remedy (see Sec. VII(B)(5) below), courts in most jurisdictions will not enjoin such a merger if full disclosure is made.

## A.  IMPLICATIONS OF THE SEPARATION
## OF OWNERSHIP AND CONTROL

To the extent that the shareholders of the typical publicly held corporation are widely dispersed and no single shareholder owns a significant percentage of the firm's shares, it is apparent that they will find it difficult to coordinate their actions so as to monitor management effectively. Sixty years ago, this observation led Adolf Berle and Gardiner Means in a famous book, The Modern Corporation and Private Property, to argue that management in the publicly held corporation had become largely autonomous. As they saw it, management could hire equity capital much as it could hire the other factors of production. Moreover, they observed that most large corporations did not need more equity capital, because management could refrain from paying dividends and could instead re-invest the corporation's own earnings in order to finance projects they wished the firm to undertake. The Berle/Means thesis that the separation of ownership and control in the public corporation made management largely autonomous has been the subject of much debate and controversy. Without doubt, it has remained the point of departure for most modern commentary about the publicly held corporation. To the extent one believes that management is free from constraints, it is easy to expect that the interests of shareholders will not be well served and to question the legitimacy of the exercise of economic power by management. Responses to, and elaboration on, these and related concerns tend to fall into three categories.

**1.  The Neo-classical School.** Economists of the Neo-classical School (sometimes referred to as the "Chicago School") concede that managerial and shareholder interests may diverge, but they argue that managers have a strong incentive to contract with shareholders to reduce their opportunities to depart from the shareholders' interests.[97] This is because the market value of the firm's stock should decline to the extent that shareholders believe the firm's managers will be able to divert the firm's earnings to their own benefit, and the impact of this reduced market value will be borne in part by the managers as the value of their own shares in the firm declines. The key point in this analysis is that incentive compensation arrangements, such as stock options or bonuses based on profits, can be designed so as to give the manager a strong interest in maximizing the market value of the firm's stock; these techniques, it is claimed, should align the manager's self-interest with that of the shareholders.

In addition, managers can agree to install monitoring safeguards (such as independent directors and auditors) in order to convince the stock market that they will not have the ability to exploit shareholders.

---

[97] See Michael C. Jensen & William H. Meckling, *Theory of the Firm: Managerial* *Behavior, Agency Costs and Ownership Structure*, 3 J.Fin.Econ. 305 (1976).

The costs of such safeguards represent part of what are called "agency costs"—namely, the costs that inherently attend the principal/agent relationship. "Agency costs" consist in total of three components: (1) the monitoring costs that the principals (here, the shareholders) pay to supervise their agents (the managers); (2) any "bonding" expenditures that the agent incurs in order to assure the principal of the agent's loyalty (for example, if an agent agrees to place a portion of his or her salary in escrow to assure faithful performance, the cost of doing is a "bonding" cost); and (3) the irreducible minimum of losses attributable to the agent's self-serving performance that are too costly to prevent. For example, it would be uneconomic to expend $10,000 of monitoring costs to prevent $5,000 of "shirking" by lazy or under-motivated agents.

The neo-classical position is that market forces have minimized the firm's agency costs, and further legal interventions are thus unnecessary and wasteful. In other words, the parties to the corporation are seen as having voluntarily installed those monitoring devices that are cost-efficient (i.e., that will prevent greater losses than they, themselves, cost). Legally mandated reforms therefore simply result in inefficient expenditures. Many lawyers disagree, believing that changes in the legal rules governing derivative actions, proxy contests, or takeovers would reduce agency costs even further. Yet, both sides in this debate agree that the shareholders' interests are best served when agency costs are minimized; they disagree only over the empirical issue of whether legal reforms raise or lower those costs.

**2. The Managerialists.** Beginning around 1960, one school of economists argued that, in the case of the publicly held corporation, corporate managers tend not to pursue profit maximization, but rather size or growth maximization.[98] According to this view, managers tend to "profit-satisfice," rather than profit maximize. Their goal is to obtain that level of profits that will sufficiently satisfy shareholders and creditors as to stave off effective opposition, while at the same time they seek to expand the size of the empires that they control.

The managerialists also saw managers as preferring to re-invest earnings in the firm, rather than pay dividends. This bias in favor of earnings retention and "empire-building" may be in the interest of managers (but not shareholders) for several reasons. First, levels of compensation have been positively correlated with firm size;[99] second, larger size gives the manager greater immunity from either a takeover

---

[98] See, e.g., Richard M. Cyert & James G. March, A Behavioral Theory of the Firm (1963); W. Baumol, Business Behavior, Value and Growth (1959); Robin L. Marris, The Economic Theory of "Managerial" Capitalism (1964); Oliver E. Williamson, The Economics of Discretionary Behavior: Managerial Objectives in a Theory of the Firm (1964).

[99] See Kevin J. Murphy, *Executive Compensation*, Ch. 38 in Handbook of Labor Economics (Orley Ashenfelter and David Card, eds.) p. 2485, 2493 (1999). For an excellent review of early studies in these areas, both about managerial compensation and the tendency toward earnings retention, see William A. McEachern, Managerial Control and Performance (1975).

or the risk of bankruptcy; third, there is obvious psychic income associated with being a senior manager of a "Fortune 500" firm or other well known corporation; and finally, growth, particularly through acquisitions, implies greater opportunities for managers to advance within the firm by acquiring new responsibilities and a higher position (and hence higher pay). By financing expansion with retained earnings, managers can avoid the kind of scrutiny, and the constraints, associated with borrowing or with seeking additional equity investment.

There has been considerable debate about how substantial the bias in favor of internally financed growth is. Some empirical studies have found that the rate of return on internally generated funds has been well below that on funds raised in the capital markets from either lenders or shareholders.[100] This finding suggests that managers retain funds that would be better paid out to shareholders, and re-invested by them; it again supports the managerialist position that there is an incentive for inefficient growth, which leads firms to retain funds for internal expansion that might be more profitably paid out to shareholders. The impact of the hostile tender offer may in the past have constrained the ability of corporate managers to pursue growth maximizing policies that are unprofitable to shareholders,[101] and such takeovers, while now more difficult to achieve, are still a possibility. The risk of a takeover may lead downsizing, as firms sell off subsidiaries and divisions that they are unable to operate profitably.

**3. The Transaction Cost School.** Another general theory about corporate behavior builds on the previously discussed historical work of Alfred Chandler (see Sec. II above), which found that large corporations had moved to a more decentralized structure earlier in this century as the result of an informational and decisional overload that was crippling their senior executives' ability to manage. The upshot was the appearance of a new form of internal structure in which senior managers essentially concentrated on monitoring and capital budgeting and delegated operational control to divisional managers, replacing them if they proved ineffective, but seldom intervening. Some economists, most nota-

---

[100] See McEachern, supra note 91, at 39–51. McEachern's own findings were that "management controlled" firms had a rate of return only half that of "owner managed" firms. For similar findings about the low rate of return on retained earnings, see also William J. Baumol, Peggy Heim, Burton G. Malkiel, and Richard E. Quandt, *Efficiency of Corporate Investment: Reply*, 55 Rev. Econ. & Statistics 128 (1973)(using regression equations to differentiate the rate of return on corporate investments financed through "ploughback" earnings— i.e., a term defined to mean earnings plus depreciation minus dividends—these authors found the rate of return to be near zero on "ploughback" earnings of firms

that avoided the capital markets and did not issue new equity, but near average on those firms that did issue new equity). The implication of this research would appear to be that, when managers can escape the discipline of the capital markets, they can pursue their preference for earnings retention, even when it is unprofitable to do so. See also Michael C. Jensen, *Takeovers: Their Causes and Consequences*, 2 J. Economic Perspectives 21 (1988).

[101] For this view, see Michael C. Jensen, *Agency Costs of Free Cash Flow, Corporate Finance, and Takeovers*, 76 Am.Econ.Rev. 323 (1986).

bly Oliver Williamson of Yale,[102] have read this evidence to suggest that this new type of firm (which they call the multi-unit or "M–Form" firm) evolved because it had monitoring capabilities superior to those of the market. After all, they argue, a corporation is simply a means of organizing various inputs (credit, labor, management, supplies, etc.) in order to produce an output. The market can also organize these inputs, but the task is accomplished within the firm because it can be accomplished internally at lower cost. The focus here is on the "transaction costs" associated with organizing economic activity. As these theorists recognize, sometimes the market has lower transaction costs, and sometimes the firm does. (See Chapter 1, Sec. V.) For example, few firms produce all their own inputs. To illustrate, IBM does not own copper or silicon mines to produce the components for its computers' circuits, but rather it buys these products in the market. The boundaries of the firm (i.e., its scope of operations) are thus set by those areas within which it can organize economic activity more cheaply than can the market.

Why was it then that a transition in firm structure began around the 1920s toward a holding company structure? The answer to this question is not obvious, because shareholders could probably themselves own stock in the same portfolio of individual companies that the modern conglomerate has assembled into one investment package. The transaction cost theorists answer this question by claiming that the performance of the divisional managers in these firms could be better monitored within the conglomerate or "M–Form" structure than it could be by the stock market. In effect, placing these individual firms in one corporate basket reduced the transaction costs associated with corporate governance and thereby increased the aggregate value of the components of the M–Form firm. Empirically, this thesis is open to question, in part because there is little evidence that conglomerates have a higher stock value than other firms. In fact, some conglomerates have been the targets of takeover bids made by bidders who believed that their asset value on liquidation exceeded their current stock values. This disparity between stock and asset values hardly seems associated with superior efficiency.

To summarize, the managerialists see the firm as having a tendency to grow toward an inefficient size (in terms of the shareholders' interests), while the transaction cost school would view this same growth more optimistically as often associated with the adoption of the more efficient "M–Form" structure. The debate will no doubt continue, but one should recognize that monitoring is an essential activity that can potentially be accomplished in various ways, either through a conglomerate structure, under an active and independent board of directors, by the

[102] See Oliver E. Williamson, Markets and Hierarchies: Antitrust Implications (1975).

stock market, or through the activities of takeover bidders searching for undervalued firms.

**4. Political Theories of the American Corporation.** Although the Berle/Means model of the public corporation holds that the separation of ownership and control was an inevitable consequence of the growth in the size, scope, and scale of the modern corporation, the newest and most revisionist group of theorists see political forces as having determined the public corporation structure. In their view, dispersed stock ownership was never inevitable. They observe that in other industrialized nations (most notably Germany and Japan) financial intermediaries assumed a monitoring role. Why did not powerful institutional investors evolve in the United States (as they did elsewhere) to hold large equity stakes and play an efficient monitoring role? The answer of these theorists is simple and direct: "Politics never allowed financial institutions to become powerful enough to control operating companies. American politics destroyed the most prominent alternative to the Berle–Means corporation: concentrated institutional ownership."[103] Specifically, these theorists point to political forces and a prevailing ideology within the United States that distrusted financial institutions as corporate monitors. Some of these forces—such as the federal structure of the United States—pre-existed the appearance of an industrial economy, but nonetheless served to keep the size of financial institutions small (in relation to the overall size of the economy) by limiting the ability of banks incorporated in one state from doing business in another. In the case of insurance companies and pension funds, legislation designed to protect policy holders and beneficiaries had the consequence (whether or not intended) of restricting the ability of these institutions to hold large equity stakes in public corporations. In the case of some legislation, however, the intent seems evident. Federal legislation—such as the Glass–Steagall Act, which separated commercial from investment banking, and federal statutes regulating mutual funds—seem expressly designed to preclude financial institutions from playing a powerful role. In part, such legislation may have been the product of the Populist Era's distrust of the Robber Barons of the late 19th Century or of the later Progressive Era's skepticism about J.P. Morgan and the financial cartels of that period. Whatever the source, some public distrust of Wall Street has deep roots in American history, and its contemporary manifestation may be the adverse public reaction to hostile takeovers in the 1980s. Viewed from this perspective, the managements of operating companies appear to have once again found

---

[103] See Mark J. Roe, *A Political Theory of American Corporate Finance,* 91 Colum.L.Rev. 10, 17 (1991). Professor Roe's thesis is developed more fully in his book, Strong Managers, Weak Owners: The Political Roots of American Corporate Finance (1994). For a critique, see the review of Roe's book by Stephen M. Bainbridge, *The Politics of Corporate Governance,* 18 Harv. J.L. & Pub.Pol'y 671 (1995). See also, Joseph A. Grundfest, *Subordination of American Capital,* 27 J.Fin.Econ. 89 (1990).

protection from market forces through the political wave of anti-takeover statutes that swept the majority of the states during the 1980s.

Even the SEC's rules became the target of this criticism. Some commentators argued that, whatever their original purpose, the contemporary impact of the SEC's rules governing proxy contests and tender offers was to chill insurgents and protect incumbents.[104] The impact of the SEC's rules on proxy contests is more specifically examined infra in Section B(1).

Although most recent commentators have acknowledged that there may be some overregulation both of specific mechanisms of corporate accountability (such as tender offers and proxy contests) and of financial institutions generally, it remains a more debatable issue whether American financial institutions in the absence of such regulation would have evolved in a manner even faintly resembling that of the German or Japanese banking institutions. Critics of the new political theory of the corporation point to factors independent of the legal or regulatory context that chill shareholder activism, such as (a) a liquidity/control tradeoff that leads institutional investors in an economy organized around a securities market to prefer to sell than to take costly actions to displace management, and (b) the absence of an adequate payoff to the agents who manage the funds held by institutional investors.[105] Also, as institutional investors have increasingly followed a strategy known as "indexing"—under which they cease to invest in individual stocks, but purchase a portfolio that serves as a proxy for the market as a whole—their logistical ability to monitor individual corporations decreases. Indexing may invite institutional passivity even in the absence of hostile regulation. In particular, those who doubt that shareholder activism would increase dramatically in the wake of SEC deregulation point to the British securities market, where institutions dominate ownership to an even greater degree than in the United States and are relatively unregulated. Yet, institutional investors in Britain seem to engage in only a moderately greater degree of shareholder activism. The implication of this comparison is that the demand to participate in corporate governance is far from unlimited, even in an unregulated environment.

---

[104] For the fullest statement of this view, see Bernard Black, *Shareholder Passivity Reexamined,* 89 Mich.L.Rev. 520 (1989) and Bernard Black, *Agents Watching Agents: The Promise of Institutional Investor Voice,* 39 U.C.L.A.L.Rev. 811 (1992); see also, John Pound, Proxy Voting and the SEC: *Democratic Ideals Versus Market Efficiency,* 29 J.Fin.Econ. 241 (1991); Ronald J. Gilson and Reinier H. Kraakman, *Reinventing the Outside Director: An Agenda for Institutional Investors,* 43 Stan.L.Rev. 863 (1991). The state law rules governing proxy contests have similarly been criticized for their lack of neutrality. See Lucian A. Bebchuk and Marcel Kahan, *A Framework For Analyzing Legal Policy Toward Proxy Contests,* 78 Cal. L.Rev. 1071 (1990).

[105] See John C. Coffee, Jr., *Liquidity Versus Control: The Institutional Investor As Corporate Monitor,* 91 Colum.L.Rev. 127 (1991); Edward B. Rock, *The Logic and (Uncertain) Significance of Institutional Shareholder Activism,* 79 Geo.L.J. 445 (1991).

**5. Recent Experience: Enron and the Sarbanes–Oxley Act.**
In late 2001, Enron Corporation filed for bankruptcy in what was then
the largest corporate bankruptcy in U.S. history. It quickly became
apparent that Enron's financial statements had been seriously distorted,
with major liabilities hidden in off-balance-sheet entities and income
grossly overstated. In early 2002, WorldCom followed Enron with an
even larger bankruptcy, again exposing blatant accounting irregularities.
Nor were these cases unique. Between mid–1997 and mid–2002, some 10
percent of all publicly listed U.S. companies restated their certified
financial statements at least once[106]; the annual rate of financial restatements soared by approximately 500 percent from the beginning of 1990
to 2002. Such a sudden increase in financial irregularity is a characteristic of a bubble, and the era from 1997 to 2001 appears in retrospect to
have been a fairly classic bubble.

Widespread financial irregularity undermines the credibility of corporate financial reporting and the objectivity of the professional "gatekeepers" who serve investors by preparing, verifying, assessing or certify-
ing corporate disclosures to the market. As security prices plummeted in
2002, Congress responded with new legislation, the Sarbanes–Oxley Act
of 2002, which passed Congress with nearly unanimous votes in both the
House and the Senate and whose focus, essentially, is on the conduct of
auditors, securities analysts, and attorneys, subjecting each to tighter
controls. The provisions of Sarbanes–Oxley are briefly examined in
Section VIII(B)(6) below, but the basic point is that the concept of
agency costs applies not only to a corporation's managers and employees,
but also to its outside agents. Although the costs and benefits of
Sarbanes–Oxley cannot yet be accurately assessed, much in the experience of the late 1990s suggests that the performance of corporate
gatekeepers, both inside the firm and outside, cannot be adequately
controlled by a purely private system of contractual controls.

What caused the sudden outburst of financial irregularity at the end
of the 1990s? Any answer is speculative, but the growing consensus
assigns considerable causal responsibility to a fundamental shift in
executive compensation. As executive compensation shifted from being
almost exclusively cash-based (as of 1990) to over 66 percent equity-
based (as of 2001),[107] the incentives of managers changed correspond-
ly. Stock compensation, at least in the absence of other restrictions, gives
managers an interest in maximizing the short-term stock price of their
corporation, by manipulating reported earnings. Even if the resulting
price spike cannot be sustained for long, managers can profit by selling
their shares before reality becomes apparent and the stock price declines.

[106] See United States General Accounting
Office, Report to the Chairman, Committee
on Banking, Housing, and Urban Affairs,
U.S. Senate, FINANCIAL STATEMENT
RESTATEMENTS: TRENDS, MARKET
IMPACTS, REGULATORY RESPONSES
AND REMAINING CHALLENGES (Oct.
2002) at 4.

[107] See Brian J. Hall, "Six Challenges in
Designing Equity–Based Pay," in 15 Accen-
ture Journal of Applied Corporate Finance
21, at 23 (Spring 2003).

Thus, managers can bail out at the top of the market, leaving other shareholders behind. At Enron and other companies, there is evidence that this in fact occurred. Again, there is an underlying conflict here between managers and shareholders, as the former have in effect "excess liquidity."[108] The most logical reforms, suggested by a number of corporate governance reform organizations since Enron, are mandatory holding periods and retention ratios, which limit the ability of executives to sell their option shares while they remain in office (and possibly for some brief period thereafter). Whatever the best reform, the critical point is that rapid change in executive compensation practices, without corresponding change in corporate governance practices, appears to have destabilized American corporate governance at the end of the 1990s by giving executives a perverse incentive to maximize short-term earnings.

## B.  THE MECHANISMS OF CORPORATE ACCOUNTABILITY

A variety of mechanisms operate to induce corporate managers to serve the interests of the shareholders. This section will focus on five: (1) the proxy contest, (2) the takeover bid, (3) the derivative action, (4) public monitoring by the SEC, and (5) the appraisal remedy. Obviously, there are other means as well: a corporate official who engages in an undisclosed and unfair self-dealing transaction may be criminally liable for fraud; state officials have some jurisdiction under their "Blue Sky" statutes (state laws regulating the sale of securities); shareholders also have rights to inspect corporate books and records under state law. Still, the foregoing list consists of the principal means, and this section will examine their comparative effectiveness.

Shareholders are not the only group that wishes to monitor management. Obviously, creditors are concerned that the corporation not accept a higher level of risk or distribute more assets to its shareholders than was bargained for in their loan agreement. Employees may also need to assure themselves that adequate contributions have been made to their pension fund and that its assets have been prudently invested by trustees (who typically are the firm's senior managers). Conflicts of interest are as inevitable as death and taxes, and monitoring mechanisms are a response to this universal problem. This section, however, will focus only on the shareholder/manager relationship.

**1.  The Proxy Contest.** Shareholder democracy differs from political democracy in one initially puzzling aspect: the incumbents seldom lose the election. Given that most managements of publicly held corpora-

---

[108] For a discussion of the misincentives that stock options can create, see Hall, supra note 99. Of course, cash compensation can also produce misincentives that encourage the executive to be more risk adverse than shareholders (who are more diversified than the executive) and to pursue growth-maximizing, rather than profit-maximizing policies, because large corporations typically pay higher salaries. Hence, because perverse incentives exist under many compensation formulas, the optimal compensation policy is clearly not to return to all cash compensation.

tions themselves control only a small portion of the firm's shares (seldom more than 10%), this may seem surprising. Several circumstances probably explain it. First, proxy contests for control of the board are expensive for an insurgent shareholder to wage (while management can utilize corporate funds so long as the contest can be characterized as one over corporate policy, as it almost always can be). Second, because shareholders tend to hold diversified portfolios and thus are shareholders in numerous corporations, most shareholders will not invest the time and attention needed to follow the arguments of the contestants closely. Shareholders may also be risk averse or simply suspicious of the insurgent group's motives (will they "loot" the corporation if they gain control?). Even if they think the incumbents are poor managers, they may fear the unknown evil more than the known evil. This fear is what probably underlies what is known as the "Wall Street Rule": namely, the marked tendency for institutional investors to support management in a proxy fight or to sell their shares. Neither step exposes them to a new risk, and selling shares involves little obvious injury to the investor so long as there is a deep and active stock market in which equivalent investments can be purchased.

Finally, there is an important economic reason why proxy fights tend to be rarities. Suppose you are a dissatisfied shareholder owning 10% of a corporation's stock and you believe that a substitution of new management would create a $10 million gain in the value of the corporation as a whole. How much would you expend on a proxy fight to bring about this change in management? Your answer should be no more than $1,000,000, because you own only 10% of the company and will realize only 10% of any appreciation in value. This is an example of what economists call a "free rider" problem. Your actions in opposing management would gratuitously create value for others, and you will not willingly expend funds just to benefit others. Thus, as a 10% shareholder, you will probably spend less than $1 million, while if all the shareholders could coordinate their actions at low cost they would rationally spend up to—what? It depends on what percentage of the shareholders agreed with you, but in principle, if all did, they would spend up to just below $10 million to realize the $10 million gain.

The free rider problem does not by itself ensure shareholder passivity. Thus, if in the foregoing example it were possible for the 10 percent shareholder to oust the incumbent board for an amount well below $1,000,000, it would certainly have an incentive to do so in order to realize its share of the expected $10,000,000 gain. In this light, the central question becomes how expensive it is to mount a proxy contest. Here, critics of the SEC rules argued that such contests are often disproportionately costly to the insurgent and sometimes logistically infeasible as well. The SEC accepted much of this criticism and in

October 1992 adopted new rules that are intended to reduce the costs and logistical barriers to shareholders seeking to organize.

To understand these reforms, it is useful to start with what prior law simply did not allow. Suppose, for example, you are a 10–percent holder of the stock of a corporation and learn that its managers have just adopted a new stock option plan that will transfer to them an extraordinary percentage of the firm's equity at below-market prices, without any corresponding benefit to the shareholders. The plan must be approved by a shareholder vote, and you know that 50 percent or more of the stock is held by other institutional investors. Ideally, you could simply call them at low cost to yourself and explain why you think they should vote against the plan. Under prior SEC rules, however, you could not do this without first preparing, and filing and clearing with the SEC, a proxy statement. Under SEC Rules 14a–1 and 14a–2, any communication, oral or written, to more than ten shareholders that was reasonably likely to cause them to grant or withhold a proxy had to be preceded by a proxy statement that had been precleared by the SEC. Not only was this process costly, but it might have taken the SEC weeks to respond, so that by the time you distributed your proxy statement, it might have been too late to reach many shareholders.

Problems of this sort caused the California Public Employees Retirement System ("CalPERS") to submit a lengthy memorandum to the SEC in 1990, detailing how the SEC's rules chilled communications among institutional investors. In response, the SEC conducted an extensive examination of its own rules and reached the conclusion (surprising for a bureaucratic agency) that its critics were at least partially correct. As a result, it adopted the following basic changes in its rules:[109]

First, when a person is not seeking to obtain a proxy or voting authority from other shareholders and has no special financial interest in the subject at issue, it is exempted from the requirement that it prepare and file a proxy statement; thus, shareholders can communicate without prior SEC clearance, but subject to the antifraud rules. A person who owns more than $5 million worth of the securities at issue, however, is required to provide to the SEC, and to the national exchange on which the securities are traded, copies of any written materials it uses in communicating with other shareholders.

Second, the SEC eliminated its prior review of preliminary proxy solicitation materials, in order to remove any timing advantage of the incumbent management.

---

[109] SEC Release No. 34–31326 (October 16, 1992). An earlier SEC release proposed more significant reforms, including a federal right for a proxy contestant to receive a full shareholders list from the corporation, but the SEC backed down from aspects of this proposal under pressure from the business community. See SEC Release No. 34–29315 (June 17, 1991).

Third, all proxies are required to "unbundle" proposals so that separate votes would have to be taken on each item up for shareholder approval. In the past, management's ability to manipulate the corporate agenda had enabled it to tie approval of an unpopular proposal to an extraordinary dividend or similar distribution. Although the SEC's proposals do not bar use of such "sweeteners," they require procedurally separate votes.

These reforms do not by themselves create a level playing field. If institutional investors need the votes of public shareholders to secure approval of a proposal (as typically they will), they will still need to prepare and file a proxy statement. This will be costly; the likely costs of a full-scale proxy contest can range from $2 million to $10 million. Management, of course, will have its costs picked up by the corporation, while the institutional investor group can assure itself of reimbursement only if it takes control of the board (which generally it will not seek to do because of the potential liability they could encounter as controlling persons). Thus, some commentators have urged a mandatory partial reimbursement rule, under which the insurgents would have a percentage of their proxy expenses reimbursed equal to the percentage of the vote that they received.

In 2003, following the Enron collapse and the hearing the complaints of many institutional investors, the SEC began a full review of the proxy process and has proposed significant rule changes.[110] The most controversial idea put forward by the SEC is that shareholders should be permitted to directly place the names of one to three nominees on the corporation's own proxy statement, thereby saving insurgents most of the costs that arise in a typical proxy fight.[111] While this proposal would not allow such a shareholder group to obtain more than a minority representation by such a low-cost campaign, its practical impact might be to make boards more receptive and accommodating to shareholder proposals and otherwise more prepared to negotiate with institutional investors (who, if spurned, could seek board representation).

Proponents of such a reform note that relatively few proxy contests over alternative directors occur in the absence of acquisition proposals. The following table shows the recent experience:

---

[110] See SEC Staff Report, REVIEW OF THE PROXY PROCESS REGARDING THE NOMINATION AND ELECTION OF DIRECTORS (July 15, 2003). For the view that then proposed reforms do not go far enough, see Lucian Bebchuk, *The Case for Shareholder Access to the Ballot*, 59 Bus. Law 43 (2003); for the counterview that they go too far, see Martin Lipton and Steven Rosenblum, *Election Contests in the Company's Proxy: An Idea Whose Time Has Not Come*, 42 Bus. Law 67 (2003). See also, Stephen M. Bainbridge, *A Comment on the SEC's Shareholder Access Proposal*, Engage, Fall 2003 (forthcoming).

[111] See Securities Exchange Act Release No. 34–48626 (October 14, 2003) ("Security Holder Director Nominations").

## Contested Proxy Solicitations 1997–2002[112]

| Year | Contested Solicitations | Solicitations Involving Alternative Management Teams Without a Sale or Merger Proposal |
|------|:----:|:----:|
| 2002 | 38 | 14 |
| 2001 | 40 | 16 |
| 2000 | 30 | 7 |
| 1999 | 30 | 13 |
| 1998 | 20 | 13 |
| 1997 | 29 | 5 |

Given that over 10,000 odd companies solicit proxies, this low level of contested solicitations may suggest that costs are a significant barrier. Opponents of the proposal argue, however, that such contests for minority representation will only "balkanize" the board of directors and enable small minority factions of shareholders to demand that their proposals be adopted.

Despite these problems and even before the SEC's revisions, proxy contests seem to have had a positive effect on share values, even when the insurgents have lost. A 1990 study by Georgeson & Co., Inc., a proxy soliciting firm, found that while insurgents achieved complete victory in only 28 percent of proxy contests between 1984 and 1990, even unsuccessful contests produced negotiated settlements or other significant developments (such as a sale of the firm) within one year of the contest.[113] On this basis they estimated that shareholders gained some benefit in 74 percent of proxy contests. Another study finds that, even when management remains in office following a proxy contest, a sale or liquidation of the target, or the resignation of the CEO, follows in about two thirds of the cases within three years of the contest.[114] Apparently, proxy contests are either a catalyst for change or a symptom of deeper corporate ills that in time produce their own crisis, which makes change unavoidable.

### 2. The Takeover Bid.

a. *Beginnings.* Beginning in the 1960s, corporations began to make "tender offers" for the stock of other corporations by inviting shareholders through a general solicitation or advertisement to tender their shares to a representative (typically, a bank) of the bidding corporation; these offers generally were at a substantial premium over the stock market price of the "target" firm (sometimes the premium was 100% or more).

---

[112] See Bebchuk, supra note 102, at 46.

[113] See Georgeson & Co., Inc., Proxy Contest Study, October 1984 to September 1990 (Dec. 14, 1990).

[114] See Harry DeAngelo and Linda DeAngelo, *Proxy Contests and the Governance of* *Publicly Held Corporations,* 23 J.Fin.Econ. 29 (1989). The number of proxy contests, however, remains small: 22 in 1991, but only 16 in 1992. See "Proxy Season Ends Quietly," Institutional Investor, June 15, 1992, at 6.

Typically, these offers were conditioned upon the bidder receiving a specified percentage of the target's shares, sufficient to convey control to the bidder. The tender offer has now become a vital element of the current corporate "takeover" movement.

b. *Developments in the 1980s and 1990s.* While takeover activity has always been highly cyclical, the 1980s witnessed a substantial increase in the magnitude of takeover transactions. The targets were often corporations worth billions of dollars and bore names that are household words. On average, the price paid for a target's shares in a takeover was around 50 percent higher than the price at which the same shares were trading before the emergence of a clear takeover threat.

What explains this increased scale? Much of the answer involved the development of the new financial market for high-yield debt securities (or "junk bonds"). See Chapter 4, Sec. III(A)(4). Until the 1980s, takeovers were almost exclusively financed out of bank borrowings and bidder corporations' own internally generated funds. Few banks would lend more than 50 percent of the combined value of the target and bidder. With the availability of subordinated "junk bond" financing, however, bidders could borrow as much as 85 to 90 percent of the total acquisition cost. Not only did this mean that larger targets could be attacked, but it also helped bring about the appearance of a new type of bidder. Where once takeover bidders were usually large industrial corporations, seeking to capture a company whose divisions they would assimilate and manage, individuals and partnerships increasingly in the early 1980s began to make takeover bids, as financing became available. Typically, these new bidders also had a different motive than the corporate acquirer: they wanted not to run the business, but to liquidate it or financially restructure it in a way that would make possible the payment of a very high cash dividend. Often, these new bidders were motivated by the perceived disparity between the corporation's aggregate value in the stock market and its apparent "break-up" value if its various divisions could be sold to other companies. Typically, such bidders focused on large conglomerate corporations. Eventually, the prices of targets rose, the number of attractive targets was depleted, financing became less available (for a variety of reasons), and, in the early 1990s takeovers—particularly hostile takeovers (see below)—declined dramatically in number. As previously stated, however, takeover activity is cyclical and the mid-and late–1990s witnessed, which continued into the 2000s.

c. *Types of Takeovers.* Takeover bids may be "hostile" or "friendly." A hostile bid is one that is opposed by incumbent management and the board of directors. Friendly bids, on the other hand, are supported by management and the directors. The lines between friendly and hostile bids may be blurred, however, when a hostile bid induces the target to seek out a more appealing acquirer (a "white knight" in the Wall Street metaphor).

Hostile bids were rare before the 1980s; then became a major financial phenomenon; virtually disappeared in the early 1990s; and reappeared at a much-reduced rate in the mid-and late–1990s (when there was a resurgence of friendly takeovers as well). One interesting explanation for the relative decline of hostile bids, compared with friendly (negotiated) bids, in the mid-and late–1990s is that during that time period the compensation of top executives, and directors, increasingly included substantial equity stakes (common stock and options to buy common stock). The effect was to align management's interests with the interests of shareholders in selling out for a premium price (and often with large severance bonuses to target-company executives who stood to lose their jobs). At the same time, the stock market was booming, technology and globalization had changed the economy, and there were huge profits to be taken—even by companies not characterized by outstanding management—companies that were attractive targets precisely for that reason.

Another interesting and important phenomenon of the 1980s—one that virtually disappeared after that decade—is the friendly takeover in the form of a leveraged buyout (LBO) or the closely related management buyout (MBO). An LBO or MBO does not involve the acquisition of one company by another and the combination of the two, but rather the purchase of a company by investors. Generally the purchase was financed by a heavy amount of debt, and a correspondingly small ("thin") amount of equity—thus the term "leveraged." The debt was risky, bore a high interest rate, and came to be referred to as "junk bonds." (See Chapter 4, Sec. III(A)(4); LBOs and MBOs died out but junk bonds— more politely called high-yield debt—have survived.) The debt was secured by the assets of the target and often was relatively short term, which meant that the buyers would have to sell off some of the assets of the target to pay off the debt. Because of the vital role of the debt financing, investment bankers were key figures in planning the transactions. Where the managers of the target were left out of the transaction it was an LBO; where they dominated or were included in the equity-investment group it was an MBO. The terms LBO and MBO do not have precise meanings; they were the products of the patois or jargon of Wall Street and of corporate law and finance.

MBOs present troubling issues of management loyalty to shareholders (as do, to a lesser degree, many friendly takeovers in more recent years). Managers who participate in an MBO expect to make huge profits and often their hopes are realized. They buy the corporation from the shareholders, run it for several years, and sometimes go public again (that is, sell shares to the public), reaping the profits for themselves. Some may ask: Why were they not willing or able to do for the original shareholders what they were willing or able to do for themselves? One answer is that an MBO involves high risks, but many shareholders (particularly those who hold diversified portfolios) presumably would be willing to take those risks.[115] Why is it that the high salaries and bonuses typically paid to managers of public corporations are not sufficient to induce them to maximize share values? At least for the present, these questions must remain largely rhetorical, but it may be helpful to consider the scenario of the leveraged buy-out of RJR Nabisco in 1988— at a total price of $25 billion, at that time the largest takeover in history by a comfortable margin.[116]

RJR's shares had been selling at about $55. A group led by its C.E.O. offered to buy the corporation at a price of $75 per share, in a highly leveraged MBO that held the prospect of a $100 million gain for the C.E.O. Six weeks later, after intense negotiation and spirited bidding, the corporation was sold to another group at a price of $109 per share. The disparity in price between the $55 pre-offer price and the $109 ultimate selling price, and between management's $75 offer and the $109, raises obvious questions about management's fidelity to shareholder interests. One key to maximizing the selling price in this case seems to have been that the board of directors behaved with far more independence, and concern for shareholder welfare, than the C.E.O., and most experienced observers of corporate behavior, might have expected. (The board's behavior may have been in part a reaction to a perception that the C.E.O. had overreached and in part a reaction to a recognition that the story of the transaction would be front page news.) Acting through a special committee, the directors actively promoted the bidding process and encouraged the bidding group that was ultimately successful. One key action taken by the special committee was a directive to members of the management team (for example, the heads of major subsidiaries) to provide confidential business information to serious outside bidders. Without such information, a competing bidder is at a substantial disadvantage compared with the management group. For example, one of the RJR products was Oreo cookies. A bidder might want to know how much it could realize by selling this brand (presumably to a cookie company with a distribution system already in place), and but for the insistence of, and repeated direction from, the board's special committee, such information would have been available to the bidding group led by the C.E.O., but not to competing bidders. (See N.Y. Times, Dec. 2, 1988, page 1, col. 3, and page C16.) The dilemma here is heightened by the fact that the actions contemplated by the bidder for

---

[115] In fact, there have been "public" leveraged buyouts where, instead of a management-led group buying out the public shareholders, the corporation tenders to purchase the majority of its stock, using borrowed funds. This changes the debt-to-equity ratio of the company, but those stockholders so desiring can spurn the takeover premium and remain shareholders. The Kroger Company, a supermarket chain, did this in 1988.

[116] For a more detailed review of this transaction and the legal standards applicable to it, see Deborah A. DeMott, *Introduction—The Biggest Deal Ever,* 1989 Duke L.J. 1. For a valuable, highly readable popular account of this takeover, see the best seller by Bryan Burrough and John Helyar, *Barbarians at the Gate* (1991).

increasing the market value of the firm (i.e., the use of high leverage and the sale of various parts of the firm) could have been accomplished without any change of control. Yet, to radically change the firm's debt/equity ratio in this manner would have imposed risks on management (and other employees) without offering them compensating benefits. Should courts expect management to behave selflessly? If one sought to prohibit MBOs, would the most likely consequence be that shareholders might receive fewer proposals of any kind and thus wind up with less premiums? If so, the cost of "higher" fiduciary standards might be borne by shareholders. It was, after all, the management bid that started the auction for RJR.

d. *The Williams Act.* In 1968, following expressions of concern both about the pace of takeovers and the possibility that shareholders were sometimes coerced into tendering, Congress passed the Williams Act, which is an amendment to the Securities Exchange Act of 1934, to regulate tender offers. Essentially, the Williams Act requires full disclosure by the bidder of its plans, background, and financing. In addition, a purchaser of shares in a publicly held corporation must identify itself and make similar disclosures within ten days after it acquires 5% or more of any class of voting shares, even if it plans no further purchases. This 5% threshold establishes an early warning system that gives both the target and other potential bidders time to prepare; thus its practical effect is to promote auctions and increase the takeover premium that a bidder must offer to secure control. The Williams Act also contains a number of substantive provisions that (1) provide a minimum period for which all tender offers must remain open, (2) specify a maximum period after which shares must be returned if they have not been accepted, (3) permit shareholders to withdraw their shares for a specified period (such a right is important if, for example, a higher bid is made by another bidder), (4) mandate that the highest price paid to any shareholder pursuant to the offer be paid to all, and (5) require that shares be prorated equally if more shares are tendered than the bidder sought (this last proration rule prevents bidders from stampeding shareholders to tender at the outset of the offer through tactics such as making a partial bid on a "first come, first served" basis). Acting pursuant to its rule-making authority under the Act, the SEC has set the minimum period a tender offer must remain open at twenty business days and the withdrawal period at fifteen business days. Collectively, these rules encourage competitive bids (which would be inhibited if a tender offer could be consummated in a brief period before other potential bidders had time to decide whether to compete).

Both the Act and the SEC's rules thereunder also seek to ensure equality of treatment. For example, SEC rules require that tender offers be open to all holders of the class sought and prohibit any purchases made outside the tender offer during its pendency. Absent such rules, bidders could offer different prices to different shareholders, could limit their offer to only institutional shareholders, or could negotiate private purchases at prices above the tender offer price.

It is important to bear in mind, however, that because the substantive provisions of the Williams Act apply only to "tender offers," a term that the Act never defines, bidders can seek to purchase control in the open market or through privately negotiated transactions in order to evade the Act's requirement (this is sometimes called a "creeping control" strategy).

e. *The Problem of Coercion.* The 1980s witnessed the appearance of an interesting strategy for coercing shareholders into accepting a takeover bid. This strategy, called the two-tier coercive tender offer, was rare in the 1980s and virtually disappeared thereafter. Despite its rarity, it is interesting, has had some effect on the shaping of decisional law, and has received much attention. It is, at the very least, part of the basic folklore of corporate law. The way it works is that the bidder tenders for 50% (or a similar level that carries *de facto* control) at one price, but at the outset it announces, or investors strongly suspect, that, once it obtains control, it will use a merger technique to force the sale to it of the remaining minority shares at a lower price. Because the offer is "front loaded," those who hold out will be worse off than those who tender (if the bidder obtains control); effective resistance is thereby crippled, because such an offer creates a competition among shareholders to tender into the "front end" offer. Assume, for example, that the pre-tender price of the stock is $100 per share. If the bidder offers $150 for the first fifty percent and announces that it will pay only $100 in a "squeeze out" merger for the remaining fifty percent, it is in effect offering only a 25% premium on a "blended" or weighted average basis.[117] Even if the bidder does not make an explicitly two-tier bid, the same coercive potential is latent in any partial bid, because shareholders may suspect that the "back end" price will be lower. Indeed, even if the back end price is the same as the front end price, there may be some coercion (that is, an incentive to tender even though one considers the price inadequate), since the front end money is paid immediately and the back end may come much later or, possibly worse, the remaining shares may simply be left outstanding as minority shares of a corporation controlled and dominated by the bidder.

Note that coercion can be either benign or pernicious. Taking the above example, it may be that the blended price of $125 is a good deal for the shareholders—if, for example, there are no other potential bidders and the alternative is continued operation with the present, relatively inefficient, management. If many of the shareholders believe that the target will be worth, say, $150 in the hands of the bidder, they may hold out (that is, refuse to tender), in the hope that enough other shareholders will tender so that the bidder acquires control, and that their

---

[117] The situation could be even more extreme if the "back end" merger price were only $50; now there would be no premium at all, though the appraisal remedy (discussed infra in Section VII(B)(5)) would provide a potential remedy.

minority shares, like the shares of the bidder, will be worth $150. Generally the bidder will have conditioned its offer on the acquisition of a controlling number of shares. If enough shareholders do hold out, the bid will fail, the bidder will go away, and the value of the shares will remain at $100. Thus, coercion may be benign in that it will ensure that the bid succeeds and that the shareholders all wind up with $125 per share.

On the other hand, it may be that the majority of the shareholders reasonably believe that the market has mispriced the shares and that they are truly worth $150 each with the present management. Shareholders may nonetheless be coerced into tendering into the $150 first-tier offer and winding up with a blended price of $125, because the alternative is that the offer will succeed without their support and that they will wind up with the second-tier price of $100 for all their shares. This latter possibility arises only because it is impractical for the shareholders to coordinate and reject the unattractive offer. Shareholders can, however, protect themselves in advance of any pernicious takeover bid by adopting amendments to the corporation's articles of incorporation that discourage partial bids, as discussed below.

f. *Defensive Tactics.* Suppose the shareholders of a target corporation consider a tender offer to be "inadequate" (that is, they would not like to sell at that price or they might, but they believe they can get a higher price if other bidders are solicited). Because each shareholder does not know if the other shareholders also consider the offer inadequate, it is an unsafe strategy not to tender, as one could thereby wind up with a low second-tier price or find oneself holding a minority interest in an illiquid company if the tender offer succeeded. What then can be done? Realistically, defensive tactics break down into two basic categories: (1) measures that the shareholders can approve in advance of any offer; and (2) post-tender-offer defenses, which typically require action by the target's board on behalf of the shareholders.

Prior to a tender offer, shareholders may adopt "shark repellants" in the form of charter provisions that require a supermajority (usually two-thirds or 80 percent) to approve a merger or sale of assets with any person that has purchased more than a specified level (usually 10 percent) of the corporation's shares. Sometimes, there will be an escape clause that permits simple majority approval if the merger or other transaction is at a "fair price" (which is usually defined as the highest of several possible valuation standards, including the highest recent market price). Such provisions discourage a partial bid, but have little impact on an "any and all" tender offer for 100 percent. They are now rarely if ever adopted, largely because they are essentially ineffective and because of the development of the far more effective combination of the poison pill and the staggered board, as described immediately below.

Once a tender offer is made, further shareholder action is usually infeasible within the compressed time period that remains. The target board, however, may adopt, or have in place, a variety of defensive tactics. Perhaps the most intriguing defensive tactic is the "poison pill." This device takes a variety of forms. One form, called the "flip over" pill, generally involves the distribution to existing shareholders of a new security, a "right," that permits them, in the event of a merger that is not approved by the board of directors, to buy the shares of the surviving corporation at a substantial discount.[118] In principle, the formula used to determine the number of shares purchasable at a discount can be adjusted so as to place minority shareholders in the same position as they would be in under a "fair price" charter provision. However, this form of poison pill will deter the bidder only if the bidder is intent on merging the target into itself. It will not work if the bidder is content to acquire control and leave a minority interest outstanding. With a "flip in" pill on the other hand, the right is triggered when the bidder acquires a defined interest (usually 20 percent) in the target; at that time, the target shareholders, other than the bidder, become entitled to buy authorized, but unissued, target shares at a substantial discount (thereby diluting the value of the target shares held by the bidder). A key point is that poison pills are adopted by the board of directors, before or after a hostile bid, without shareholder approval, and the board of directors has the power to eliminate the pill (by paying a small amount to "redeem" the right from the shareholders). The nominal purpose of pills is to require bidders to negotiate with the board, to enable the board to seek competing bids, and to give the board the ability to resist offers that are, in its judgment, inadequate or coercive. The impact of poison pills has clearly been to stretch out the tender offer process (often for six months or more) while the target board seeks other bidders. Still, many observers fear that the actual effect in many cases is to allow incumbent management to resist efforts to oust them, regardless of the interests of the shareholders.[119]

Poison pills have been widely adopted by publicly traded corporations, but their effectiveness as takeover deterrents may be limited, for several reasons. For one thing, the operation of the pill dilutes the value only of the bidder's initial stake (typically not more than 20 percent) and thus does not wipe out the potential gain from a successful tender offer. Moreover, the pill is redeemable by the board of directors, to allow the board to permit a welcome, or negotiated, bid to proceed. The redemption possibility makes the corporation vulnerable in two ways. First, at some point, in some situations, where the hostile offer is good enough and the alternatives sufficiently bleak, the members of the board might be compelled, by virtue of their fiduciary obligation to the shareholders,

---

[118] See Moran v. Household International, Inc., 490 A.2d 1059 (Del.Ch.1985), affirmed, 500 A.2d 1346 (1985)(upholding a "flip over" pill).

[119] It does seem, however, that the power of a poison pill to impede a hostile take-overs has often been exaggerated. See William J. Carney and Leonard A Silverstein, The Illusory Protections of the Poison Pill, 78 Notre Dame L. Rev. (forthcoming 2003), noting the limited dilutive effect of the pill.

to redeem the pill despite themselves. Second, and more realistically and importantly, a hostile bidder could engage in a proxy contest to replace the board with its own nominees, who could be relied upon the redeem the pill. This became a common strategy in the see-saw battles between entrenched managers and their hostile foes and shifted the balance toward the bidders.

The next strategy devised and adopted by the defenders was to combine the poison pill with a staggered, or classified, board. With such a board, typically each director is elected for three years, with one-third of the terms expiring each year (see Del. Gen. Corp. L. § 141(d)), board members cannot be removed without cause (see Del. Gen. Corp. L. § 141(k)(1)), and provisions are adopted to prevent increase in the size of the board. The result is a delay in gaining control of the board that is generally intolerable for the hostile bidder. Thus, the combination of the poison pill and the staggered board has been used by many corporations to restore the board's protective defenses, for better or worse.[120] Many other corporations, however, have been unable to gain the shareholder approval that is required in order to alter the corporate charter to provide for staggered boards. Moreover, beginning roughly in the early 2000s, many corporations, succumbing to shareholder pressure, removed certain takeover defenses (poison pills and staggered boards).[121]

Another line of defense against all tender offers (whether or not coercive) is provided by antitakeover statutes, which the majority of states have now adopted. These statutes, which are described more fully below (Section VII(B)(2)(g)), place barriers of varying degrees of impermeability in the way of tender offers, and in some jurisdictions now provide a complete defense.

Despite these defenses, the success rate of hostile tender offers has not significantly declined.[122] Moreover, hostile tender offers are a small percentage of all tender offers and all tender offers are an even smaller percentage of all acquisitions.[123] Thus, though hostile tender offers, and the defenses against them, may be interesting, particularly to lawyers, it seems that their economic significance is now limited. One plausible explanation for this is that increased executive compensation in the form

---

[120] See Ronald W. Masulis, Cong Wang and Fei Xie, Corporate Governance and Acquirer Returns, November 29, 2005, AFA 2006 Boston Meetings Paper, available at http://ssrn.com/abstract=697501; ("support[ing] the hypothesis that managers at firms protected by more anti-takeover provisions are less subject to discipline from the market for corporate control and thus, are more likely to indulge in empire-building acquisitions that destroy shareholder value") John C. Coates IV, Takeover Defenses in the Shadow of the Pill: A Critique of the Scientific Evidence, 79 Texas L. Rev. 271, 325–28 (2000); Lucian Arye Bebchuk, John C. Coates IV & Guhan Subramanian, *The Powerful Antitakeover Force of Staggered Boards: Theory, Evidence, and Policy*, 54 Stanford L. Rev. 887 (2002).

[121] See Robin Sidel, Where Are All the Poison Pills? Wall St. J., March 2, 2004, C1.

[122] See Carney and Silverstein, supra note 111.

[123] Id.

of stock and stock options has aligned the interests of executives with those of shareholders in accepting value-increasing acquisition offers.

In the past a variety of other techniques have been used to resist hostile takeovers. While perhaps no longer of much practical significance these techniques offer interesting insights into corporate law, structure, and economics. One can begin with the obvious but important observation that a corporation becomes a target when bidders believe that it is undervalued by the market. The obvious defensive response is, of course, to demonstrate a commitment to increased efficiency in operation. Another, less obvious, response is to alter the financial structure by increasing the ratio of debt to equity, which generally will increase the value of the company by (a) producing a better tax result (see Chapter 5, Sec. III(K)) and by (b) limiting the ability of managers to make unwise investments with the company's free cash flow (see Chapter 5, Sec. III(L) and (M)). The increased debt/equity ratio can be accomplished by borrowing heavily and then either paying a large one-time cash dividend to shareholders or by repurchasing much of its stock. Such a restructuring may preclude the bidder from borrowing to finance its own tender offer (or it may simply remove the profit potential the bidder saw).[124] A variety of other, currently less important, defensive measures have also used: (1) the corporation can sell a prize asset or subsidiary (a "crown jewel" in the parlance of takeovers) to a third party or it can grant a third party an option to purchase the asset or subsidiary, which option (called a "lockup" option) may sometimes be made exercisable only if a hostile bidder acquires a specified percentage of the target's shares; (2) it can sell its stock, or an option to purchase its stock, to a third party who will support the incumbent management (a "stock lockup"); (3) it can make a counter-tender offer for its own shares at a higher price than the hostile bidder's offer (a "self tender"); (4) it can make a counter-tender offer for the bidder's stock in the target, at a price above the market price, on the condition that the bidder abandon its takeover effort (a "greenmail payment");[125] (5) it can attempt to create an antitrust barrier to merger by acquiring a competitor of the bidder; (6) it can create an ESOP (Employee Stock Ownership Plan) and assist it to purchase a substantial block of the target's stock on the open market, which stock will be voted by the ESOP's trustees, who are typically corporate officers;[126] or (7) it can seek out, or support, a competing

---

[124] For one of the first cases in which such a tactic was successfully employed to resist a takeover, see GAF Corp. v. Union Carbide Corp., 624 F.Supp. 1016 (S.D.N.Y. 1985).

[125] Greenmail payments are now substantially inhibited by a 1987 amendment to federal income tax law providing for a 50 percent excise tax on gain realized in greenmail transactions. Int. Rev. Code § 5881. The tax applies where the bidder held the

stock for less than two years and made a tender offer and the corporation did not offer to buy out other shareholders at the same price.

[126] To encourage employee ownership, ESOPs receive a variety of tax subsidies, including a partial exclusion from income of the interest they pay to lenders. Thus, they can borrow at a lower cost, and this allows them to pay more in a competitive bidding contest. For a case in which an ESOP was

tender offer by a more palatable bidder (a "white knight").[127] All these techniques can be combined, and the last technique can be used to induce higher bids and an auction. The favored bidder's position can be improved by sharing confidential information with it or, as we have seen, by granting it some form of stock or asset lock-up. Of course, the risk to shareholders of all of these techniques is that they can be used by management in self-serving ways and may cause the original offer to be withdrawn without the shareholders receiving the best possible price for their shares.

    g.  *Motivations and Their Economic Implications.* What motivates the takeover bidder? There are a number of factors or circumstances that may create an opportunity for gain.[128] Some bidders may acquire a competing firm (through a so-called "horizontal" merger) in order to gain increased market power. Another important objective may be to achieve gains through "synergy," resulting in a combined firm worth more than the sum of the original value of its components. The increase in value can occur where the combination produces cost savings as duplicative assets are sold or the number of employees is reduced; or as additional opportunities become available (for example, where a small firm has excellent products but little marketing or research capability); or as capital market efficiencies are achieved (for example, because the combination reduces risk of bankruptcy and thereby permits borrowing

---

used to acquire a critical block of shares to defeat a hostile bid, see Shamrock Holdings, Inc. v. Polaroid Corp., 559 A.2d 278 (Del. Ch.1989).

[127] For a description of the various defensive tactics, see William J. Carney, *Controlling Management Opportunism in the Market for Corporate Control: An Agency Cost Model,* 1988 Wis.L.Rev. 385, 393–402.

[128] There is a substantial body of empirical studies of the various explanations for takeover gains. Description of, and citations to, many of these can be found in Roberta Romano, *A Guide To Takeovers: Theory, Evidence and Regulation,* 9 Yale J. on Regulation (1992). On the broader topic of the value of mergers, see Gregor Andrade, Mark Mitchell, and Eric Stafford, *New Evidence and Perspectives on Mergers,* 15 J. of Econ. Perspectives 103 (2001). See also Bernard Black, *Bidder Overpayment in Takeovers,* 41 Stanford L.Rev. 597 (1989); John C. Coffee, Jr., Louis Lowenstein, and Susan–Ackerman, Knights, Raiders and Targets: The Impact of the Hostile Takeover (1988); Reinier H. Kraakman, *Taking Discounts Seriously: The Implications of "Discounted" Share Prices as an Acquisition Motive,* 88 Columbia L.Rev. 891 (1988); Gregg A. Jarrell, James A. Brickley, and

Jeffrey M. Netter, *The Market for Corporate Control: The Empirical Evidence Since 1980,* 2 J. of Economic Perspectives 49 (1988).

    In the aggregate, most of the gain from takeovers goes to the target shareholders, but a more nuanced study concluded "that bidder shareholders gain when the bidding firm buys a private firm or a subsidiary of a public firm and lose when the bidder buys a public firm." Kathleen Fuller, Jeffrey Netter, & Mike Stegemoller, *What Do Returns to Acquiring Firms Tell Us? Evidence from Firms That Make Many Acquisitions,* 57 J. Finance 1763, 1792 (2002). "After losing $4 billion in the 1980s, acquiring-firm shareholders gained $24 billion from 1991 through 1997 before losing $240 billion from 1998 through 2001." Sara B. Moeller, Frederick P. Schlingemann, and René M. Stulz, Wealth Destruction on a Massive Scale: A Study of Acquiring–Firm Returns in the Recent Merger Wave, 60 J. Finance 757, 758–759 (2005). However, the large aggregate losses were the result of extremely large losses of a relatively small number of firms. Id. at 758. "[E]xcluding just over 2% of the observations [of acquiring firms in the period 1998–2001], shareholder wealth would have increased with acquisition announcements." Id. at 781.

at lower interest rates). Synergy is often the objective of "vertical" combinations, where a firm acquires a supplier in order to assure itself a source of supply and reduce losses associated with the prospect of opportunistic behavior or where a firm acquires a distributor or buyer of its product for similar reasons. Still another reason for acquisition is that the bidder may have superior skills in top-level management, in strategic planning, in research and development, or in capital allocation. This circumstance may lead to a "conglomerate" merger—that is, a merger of unrelated businesses.

Another possible explanation for some mergers is that the bidder simply considers the target to be undervalued. A related explanation is illustrated by an oil company that acquires another oil company with proven oil reserves because it concludes that that method of buying oil is cheaper than drilling for it. Still another important motivation for acquisitions is gain from tax attributes. For example, the target may have tax losses or tax credits that it is unable to exploit.

Not all theories of takeovers stress the efficiency gains that they create. At least two theories as to the source of these gains tend to cast takeovers in an unfavorable light by suggesting that the gains come in part as the result of involuntary wealth transfers from others. One theory is that gains from eliminating jobs, at all levels, top to bottom, may involve not simple introduction of operating efficiency but, instead, violation of implicit understandings. For example, people may have worked hard for a corporation for many years and may have accepted a wage or salary lower than might otherwise have been earned, with the implicit, but not legally enforceable, understanding that they would continue to be employed as long as the corporation made a reasonable, though perhaps not the maximum, profit. In this situation, under the "implicit contract" theory, the takeover, which becomes profitable by virtue of the elimination of jobs, involves an unfair transfer of wealth from employees to shareholders.[129]

The other unfavorable explanation of some takeovers is that they are an excuse for introducing new debt, which has the effect of reducing the value of existing debt and shifting wealth from the existing debtholders to shareholders. To the extent that this happens, the shareholders may be thought to take unfair advantage of the bondholders, which is something shareholders may be able to do for the period of time it takes for bondholders to revise the contracts by which their expectations are protected. Again, the takeover simply generates what many consider to be an unfair wealth transfer to shareholders, in this case from bondhold-

---

[129] See, e.g., Charles R. Knoeber, *Golden Parachutes, Shark Repellents, and Hostile Tender Offers*, 76 Am.Econ.Rev. 155 (1986). For a general review of these wealth-transfer theories, see John C. Coffee, Jr. *Shareholders Versus Managers: The Strain in the Corporate Web*, 85 Mich.L.Rev. (1987). Oth-ers dispute that takeovers have any demonstrable effect on employment. See Charles Brown and James L. Medoff, "The Impact of Firm Acquisitions on Labor," in Corporate Takeovers: Causes and Consequences (Allan J. Auerbach ed. 1988).

ers.[130] As to the long run economic effects, it may be a good thing to spell out the rights of bondholders, but the result is increasingly complex contracts, which may increase negotiation costs and reduce desirable operating flexibility.

Still, even if there are losses to some interest groups, the evidence now seems clear that the gain received by shareholders from takeovers vastly exceeds these collective losses. Much of the gain to shareholders, particularly shareholders of the target corporations, derives from the efficiencies described above. Much of the gain also seems to arise from elimination of wasteful management practices, often referred to a "agency costs." For example, managers may be motivated, in their investment decisions, by the fact, or the perception, that as the size of the firm increases, their financial rewards, prestige, and power also increase. Investment strategies motivated by such considerations may not maximize shareholder wealth, but the managers may be able to delude the shareholders, and themselves, about the true motivation for investments and acquisitions. (See further discussion of this thesis in connection with a description of the managerialist theory, at Sec. VII(A)(2) of this chapter.) Such "empire building" may harm shareholders in either of two ways. First, it may consist of overpaying for acquisitions and other investments. Second, it may lead to the acquisition of investments that management is not able to manage efficiently or to costly, ineffective increase in management personnel—to bloated headquarters staffs, for example.

Empire building may be one aspect of the broader phenomenon of management inefficiency, which is, of course, inconsistent with shareholder wealth maximization. Managerial inefficiency leads to the prospect of gain from replacing the inefficient management and to what many consider to be the most important reason, or justification, for takeovers. The management behavior in question can take a variety of forms other than empire building: incompetence in operating the business; an excessive conservatism about exploring new markets; hoarding cash or liquid assets that shareholders could more profitably invest (if paid out to them as dividends); continuation of capital investment patterns in the face of declining demand; failure to liquidate losing divisions; failure to trim the work force; etc. Investment or operational inefficiency may be reflected in unwise financial policies such as inadequate payment of dividends or unwillingness to incur debt. Regardless of the source or nature of the managerial inefficiency, the bidder may

---

[130] An empirical study reports that only a small part of the gains of target shareholders in takeovers can be attributed to wealth transfers from bondholders. See Paul Asquith and Thierry A. Wizman, *Event Risk, Covenants, and Bondholder Returns in Leveraged Buyouts,* 27 J. Financial Economics 195 (1990). Moreover, bondholder losses in takeovers can be attributed to failure to bargain for adequate protection. Bondholders whose bonds did not include covenants protecting against losses in takeovers on average suffered losses in takeovers, while those with such protection experienced gains. Id.

believe that by displacing incumbent management it can create value. The importance of this motivation for takeovers is that it makes the takeover a mechanism of corporate accountability. Managers know that if they run their companies inefficiently, the share price ultimately will decline sufficiently to attract the attention of bidders, since potential bidders will see the opportunity to profit from acquiring control and replacing the incumbent managers. Thus, the takeover not only operates directly to weed out inefficient managers, it also provides a strong incentive to all managers to maximize shareholder wealth. This disciplinary theory is, however, a controversial one. Some doubt that the stock market is as rational or efficient as the theory holds and believe instead that a volatile market will sooner or later undervalue most firms. The fact that takeovers occur in waves seems inconsistent with the disciplinary hypothesis, since management incompetence or self indulgence would not seem to be a varying phenomenon. Others cite evidence that bidders tend not to pursue inefficiently managed targets, which have considerable risk associated with them, but instead prefer targets within industries that are then in fashion or whose values are underestimated by the stock market. And, of course, management inefficiency may not explain MBOs or other takeovers, in which management is not replaced (though a small group of new controlling shareholders may be able to curb the wasteful habits of otherwise efficient managers and therefore may be willing to retain existing managers even where the takeover is motivated by potential efficiency gains).

All acknowledge that takeovers involve high costs to bidders and for that reason do not serve as a remedy for lesser (or "one-shot") deviations from the goal of shareholder wealth maximization. Nonetheless, the theory that the takeover can check empire building and other inefficient behavior at some point does seem compelling, because if a firm adopts unprofitable strategies or practices, its asset value should exceed its stock value and the disparity should attract bidders committed to changing those strategies or practices.[131] But the change ordinarily will require the replacement of incumbent managers, who can be expected to resist takeovers to save their jobs.

h.  *The Legal System's Response.* In many instances the use of any of the defensive tactics will, as just suggested, raise the suspicion that the directors and managers are trying to save their jobs rather than serve the shareholders, to whom they are said to owe a fiduciary obligation, by maximizing share values. But any defensive tactics ordinarily will have been approved by "independent" directors, who will appear to have little financial interest in retaining their positions. Consequently, the target corporation, if attacked by a dissident share-

---

[131] See Omesh Kini, William Krawac, & Shehzad Mian, The Nature of Discipline by Corporate Takeover, 59 J. Finance 1511, 1550 (2004): "[T]he corporate takeover market acts as a 'court of last resort,' that is, it is an external source of discipline applied when internal control mechanisms are relatively weak or ineffective."

holder, will invoke the business judgment rule, which bestows on the decision of disinterested directors a virtual immunity from judicial review. Until recently, most courts accepted the applicability of the business judgment rule to takeover defense tactics and largely deferred to whatever tactics the independent directors had ratified. The "black letter" law was that management could not use corporate funds to perpetuate itself in office, but in practice defensive tactics were upheld as long as some other motive besides self-perpetuation could plausibly be offered in justification—for example, the belief that the price was too low or that the bidder would exploit the remaining shareholders.

Beginning in the 1980s, however, the Delaware courts moved to a new, "intermediate," standard of judicial review for cases involving takeover defense tactics. This standard is stricter than the business judgment rule used in "due care" cases but more tolerant than the standard imposing a burden of proving "intrinsic fairness," a burden that Delaware requires the defendant to satisfy in cases involving undisclosed self-dealing. Essentially, the Delaware cases, following the standard-setting *Unocal* decision, have asked whether the defensive measure was adopted in good faith, after reasonable investigation and deliberation, and was "reasonable in relation to the threat" posed by the bidder.[132]

Although, under this standard, a target corporation can resist an offer it considers inadequate,[133] or seek to delay the hostile bidder while it searches for better offers, the *Unocal* decision seemed to substantially constrain such action by providing for a two-step review under which a court must first assess the nature of the threat (the "threat" review) and then the reasonableness of the defensive tactics chosen in light thereof (the "proportionality" review).[134] The initial wave of cases after *Unocal* supported this interpretation. For example, when the target corporation simply sought to use a poison pill to block the hostile offer without any strategy for creating greater value, the Delaware Chancery Court ordered the pill's redemption.[135]

Later Delaware cases suggest, however, that the Delaware Supreme Court may have limited the scope of review. More recently, in the

---

[132] See Unocal Corp. v. Mesa Petroleum Co., 493 A.2d 946 (Del.1985); see also AC Acquisitions Corp. v. Anderson, Clayton & Co., 519 A.2d 103 (Del.Ch.1986). *Unocal* upheld a discriminatory self-tender by the target corporation to all its shareholders, other than the bidder, at a premium which effectively gave a dividend to all shareholders, except the bidder, and thus forced the bidder to call off its offer. However, the Delaware Supreme Court upheld this tactic (which is now prohibited by SEC rule) only after finding that the offer was coercive and that the bidder had (in its view) an unsavory reputation as a "greenmailer."

[133] See Moran v. Household International, Inc., 490 A.2d 1059 (Del.Ch.), affirmed, 500 A.2d 1346 (1985)(upholding use of poison pill).

[134] See Ronald J. Gilson & Reinier H. Kraakman, *Delaware's Intermediate Standard for Defensive Tactics: Is There Substance to Proportionality Review?*, 44 Bus. Law. 247 (1989).

[135] See, e.g., Grand Metropolitan PLC v. Pillsbury Companies, 558 A.2d 1049 (Del. Ch.1988); City Capital Associates v. Interco, Inc., 551 A.2d 787 (Del.Ch.1988).

*Unitrin* decision,[136] the court seems to have severely limited the second-step proportionality review. There, the target corporation, Unitrin, Inc., responded to a hostile cash tender offer for all its shares by announcing a repurchase program for 10 million shares (nearly 20 percent of its outstanding voting stock). The effect of this repurchase program would have been to inflate the voting power of the Unitrin board of directors (which already held 23 percent of the outstanding stock). This had special significance because, under Unitrin's certificate of incorporation, a bidder needed to obtain a 75 percent vote to effect a follow-up merger with a greater than 15 percent shareholder. Finding this repurchase program to be a defensive reaction governed by *Unocal*, the Delaware Chancery Court, though acknowledging that there was a "threat" (antitrust problems and a price that might reasonably be considered inadequate), enjoined the repurchase program as a "disproportionate" response to that threat.

On appeal, however, the Delaware Supreme Court reversed. Although it agreed that *Unocal* governed and required enhanced judicial scrutiny, it concluded that the Chancery Court had exaggerated the impact of the repurchase program on the viability of a proxy contest (because institutional investors held at least 42 percent of Unitrin's stock). In any event, it observed, the Chancery Court could not substitute for the business judgment of independent members of the board its own determination that a defensive reaction was "unnecessary." Rather the Chancery Court should only determine whether the board's decision fell within a "range of reasonableness." To invalidate a defensive tactic, a Delaware court must find that "a defensive response was draconian because it was either coercive or preclusive in character."[137] Under this standard the significance of *Unocal*'s proportionality review seemingly shrinks. If a defensive tactic is not "preclusive" or "coercive," it presumptively falls within the "range of reasonableness" in which the board's actions cannot be overturned.

A similar contraction seems to have occurred earlier in a line of Delaware cases holding that once it has become clear that the corporation will be sold or broken up, the board has a duty to conduct an auction or by some other means seek to obtain the highest price for shareholders. Known as the *"Revlon* duty," after the 1985 case in which the doctrine was first enunciated,[138] this line of cases was principally invoked in instances in which the target board tried to prefer one bidder over another, possibly at the cost to shareholders of the highest possible price. At least when it was clear that shareholders were receiving an inferior price because of such a preference, these tactics have been enjoined.[139]

[136] Unitrin, Inc. v. American General Corp., 651 A.2d 1361 (Del.1995).

[137] Id. at 1387.

[138] Revlon v. MacAndrews & Forbes Holdings, Inc., 506 A.2d 173 (Del.1985).

[139] See, e.g., Hanson Trust PLC v. ML SCM Acquisition, Inc., 781 F.2d 264 (2d

Nonetheless, it was often unclear whether a corporation was up for sale so as to trigger the *Revlon* duty. Clearly, if the target accepted a cash merger or tender offer, the outcome would constitute a sale. But what was the status of a statutory merger between two corporations of roughly equal size involving only an exchange of shares? Did such a "marriage of equals" also trigger *Revlon*? This issue arose shortly after Time, Inc. and Warner Communications, Inc. announced a merger in 1989, when Paramount Communications, Inc. made a hostile tender offer for Time at a substantial premium over the merger terms.[140]

Because the merger would have required approval by a shareholder vote and Time shareholders would clearly not vote for a stock merger with Warner when Paramount was offering much more in cash, Time restructured the deal as a "friendly" cash tender offer for Warner. Paramount and some Time shareholders sued, claiming both that the merger meant that Time was up for "sale" (and thus under *Revlon* had to be sold to the highest bidder) and that Time's tender offer was an unreasonable defensive tactic under *Unocal* because the cash offer made by Paramount could not constitute a threat. The Delaware Supreme Court rejected both these arguments, concluding that the board is "not obligated to abandon a deliberately conceived corporate plan for a short-term shareholder profit unless there is clearly no basis to sustain the corporate strategy," and that the action taken was a "reasonable response in relation to a perceived threat." The Court brushed aside the *Revlon* argument with the observation that, on the facts, there was to be no break-up of the corporation. It also approved the lower court finding that control would continue to reside in a "fluid aggregation of unaffiliated shareholders"—that is, that there would in fact be no change in control. Still, some observers expressed dismay that the shareholders had been deprived of the opportunity to accept Paramount's cash offer of $200 a share and wound up instead with shares worth around $138 each.

In the next major Delaware decision,[141] the Supreme Court disapproved of the board's defensive measures and further elaborated the law. Paramount and Viacom had entered into an agreement for a friendly merger—one that would have shifted control of Paramount to Viacom. QVC then sought to acquire Paramount, and the Paramount board resisted. The Court in effect held that *Revlon* duties did apply, since control of Paramount was being sold, and the Paramount shareholders would no longer be able to command a control premium, but that the obligation was to maximize shareholder value, which could be accom-

Cir.1986); Edelman v. Fruehauf Corp., 798 F.2d 882 (6th Cir.1986). See also the somewhat puzzling majority opinion in Omnicare, Inc. v. NCS Healthcare, Inc., 818 A.2d 914 (Del. 2003), discussed in Stephen M. Bainbridge, Mergers and Acquisitions 189–91 (2003).

140 See Paramount Communications, Inc. v. Time Inc., 571 A.2d 1140 (Del.1989). The Delaware Supreme Court emphasized in this case that Time was pursuing a policy that had an independent business purpose and was not simply a defensive ploy.

141 Paramount Communications Inc. v. QVC Network Inc., 637 A.2d 34 (Del.1994).

plished by "an auction, canvassing the market," or some other means. The Court went on to hold that a board may choose from among various defensive measures that are within a "range of reasonableness,"[142] but that the measures adopted by the Paramount board were outside that range. The defensive measures were contained in a contract with Viacom, but the Court declared the relevant provisions of the contract to be "invalid and unenforceable."

State antitakeover statutes, which a majority of the states have now adopted, have strengthened the hand of incumbent management and reduced the effect of these judicial decisions. The statutes take a variety of forms, but follow several basic patterns.[143] One type (the "Control Share Acquisition" statute) provides that when any person acquires "control shares" (usually 20 percent of the voting shares) in the target, those shares cannot be voted without the approval of a majority of the other shareholders.[144] Conceivably, this type of statute may actually work to the advantage of the bidder in that it ultimately requires a shareholder vote. More recently, Delaware and New York have adopted a second type—known as a "moratorium" statute—which prohibits any merger of the target with the bidder (or certain other transactions between them) for some period of time after a defined threshold stake in the target (15 percent under the Delaware statute) is acquired, unless the acquisition was originally approved by the target's board before the purchase of stock that crossed the threshold.[145] Other statutes require approval of a takeover by a supermajority shareholder vote or require that a "fair price" (often quite high) be paid. A few states have adopted "redemption" statutes, designed primarily to deal with partial bids, that require a purchaser of a specified portion of the corporation's shares to buy the remaining shares of those shareholders who decide to seek a statutory right of redemption at a judicially determined fair price. A number of states have also enacted "constituency" statutes that author-

---

[142] This particular phrase is from a later case, Unitrin v. American General Corp., 651 A.2d 1361 (Del.1995).

[143] See E. Norman Veasey, Jesse A. Finkelstein, and Robert J. Shaughnessy, *The Delaware Takeover Law: Some Issues, Strategies and Comparisons*, 43 Bus.Lawyer 865, 876 (1988); Elliott J. Weiss, *A Proposal for a Federal Takeover Law*, 9 Cardozo L.Rev. 1699, 1704 (1988).

[144] Some of these statutes are modeled on an Indiana statute that was challenged as a violation of the commerce clause and on the ground of preemption by the Williams Act and was upheld in CTS Corp. v. Dynamics Corp. of America, 481 U.S. 69 (1987). Other decisions have upheld antitakeover statutes that clearly precluded the bidder from any prospect of making a successful offer. See Amanda Acquisition Corp. v. Universal

Foods Corporation, 877 F.2d 496 (7th Cir. 1989).

[145] This is the pattern followed by the Delaware statute, which bars a merger or similar transactions between a bidder that has acquired 15 percent of the corporation's voting shares and the target for three years thereafter. Del.Gen.Corp.Law § 203. The Delaware statute reflects sensitivity to the interests of shareholders, however, by allowing a merger (cash-out or otherwise) with bidder if (1) the bidder has acquired 85 percent of the voting shares; (2) the merger is approved by the target board and two-thirds of its disinterested shareholders; or (3) the target's board has announced support for a takeover by another bidder. The corporation may opt out of the statutory provision by amendment of its bylaws or articles.

ize the board to consider the interests of other constituencies (such as employees). It is interesting that virtually all of what is accomplished by the foregoing statutes could have been accomplished by individual corporations without legislative action—simply by amending the articles of incorporation (with the requisite shareholder approval). Finally, a few statutes now prevent any acquisition of control without the board's approval.[146] The most broad-ranging set of anti-takeover rules was adopted by Pennsylvania in 1990.[147] Perhaps the most innovative of the Pennsylvania provisions is one that requires disgorgement (that is, payment to the corporation) of any gain from the sale of a corporation's shares by a person within 18 months after that person has sought or expressed an intent to seek control (20 percent of the voting power). Corporations were allowed to opt out of the application of the statute and many did. Still, it has been estimated that the new provisions resulted in losses to shareholders of Pennsylvania corporations of $4 Billion.[148]

By way of contrast it is interesting that Commonwealth countries (where tender offers are as common as in the U.S.) have not allowed target managements to engage in any significant sales of assets or in financial restructurings, at least without shareholder approval, once a tender offer has been launched. The British system in particular restricts both the bidder and the target more than does U.S. law; it effectively prohibits partial bids by the bidder (unless there is a shareholder vote to permit the partial bid) and prohibits virtually all defensive tactics by target management. The net result may be greater certainty and better protection of target shareholders, both from coercive partial bids and from defensive tactics engineered by managements intent on protecting their own positions.

**3. Derivative Litigation.** If a corporate official violates any of the duties he or she owes to the corporation, and the board of directors fails to take appropriate action, American law recognizes the right of a shareholder to sue in the corporation's behalf to redress the injury. The important conceptual point here is that the lawsuit is in the corporation's right (thus it is called a "derivative suit," because the shareholder derives the right to sue from the corporation), and any recovery from the action accrues to the corporation. The corporation is a nominal defendant, but the true defendants are the individuals who have wronged it— usually the corporation's officers or directors or both.

---

[146] See Wis.Stat. § 180.726 (forbidding acquisition of more than 10 percent without board's approval). This statute was upheld in Amanda Acquisition Corp. v. Universal Foods Corp., supra note 134.

[147] See Penn.Consol.Stat., Title 15, §§ 102, 511–512, 1721, 2502, 2561–2567, 2571–2575, 2581–2583, and 2585–2587.

[148] Samuel H. Szewczyk and George P. Tsetsekos, *State Intervention in the Market for Corporate Control: The Case of Pennsylvania Senate Bill 1310,* 31 J. Financial Economics 3 (1992).

If the suit on behalf of the corporation is successful, the corporation is required to pay the plaintiff shareholder's legal expenses, because the shareholder has benefited the other shareholders as a group. This legal rule seemingly solves the "free rider" problem that would otherwise exist (and was earlier discussed with respect to proxy contests) if the individual shareholder who benefited the other shareholders had to bear all the costs of the action. By requiring the corporation to pay the individual plaintiff's legal expenses, the law in effect taxes all shareholders (including the wrongdoer) and thereby equitably apportions the costs of monitoring the defendant's conduct.

The theory and reality of derivative actions tend to diverge. In theory, the action is brought by an aggrieved shareholder; in reality, it is typically brought by a plaintiff's attorney who finds a shareholder, who may own only a few shares, to serve as the nominal plaintiff. If the action is unsuccessful, it will probably be the attorney and not the shareholder who bears the costs.

The folklore of derivative actions has tended to view these lawsuits as disproportionately nuisance actions (or "strike suits" in the popular legal parlance) that, in the absence of the procedural barriers described below, would be brought to extort a small recovery. The accuracy of this accusation is difficult to assess. Sometimes, a suit may be brought essentially for its nuisance value, because it is often more costly for the defendants to defend the action than it is for the plaintiff's attorney (who typically runs a low overhead operation) to bring it. A greater problem may be the tendency for even meritorious actions to result in collusive settlements. The real party in interest tends to be the plaintiff's attorney and this attorney has an economic incentive to strike a deal with the defendants by which they exchange a low recovery for a high award of attorney's fees (paid by the corporation). Although such settlements are improper (because the plaintiff's attorney owes a fiduciary duty to the shareholders, but is here diverting their recovery), there is reason to believe that they sometimes occur, because the economic pressures are strongly in favor of collusion. For example, if the settlement value of the case were $2,000,000, and if the court were to award a typical attorney's fee equal to roughly 25% of the recovery (20% to 25% in fact tends to be the normal fee award range in these actions), then it would be in the interest of the defendants and the plaintiff's attorney to agree instead to a recovery of $1,000,000, in addition to which the corporation would pay an attorney's fee of $750,000 (which is 50% greater than the $500,000 fee that the court would award using a 25 percent fee formula applied to the honest settlement value). Moreover, when the action is settled, the plaintiff's attorney avoids the risk of an adverse verdict (which may even require him to pay all or a portion of the defendants' legal expenses). Finally, the law typically permits the corporation to indemnify the individual defendants' litigation expenses after a settlement, but not if there is an adverse verdict. In short, the scenario for collusive settlements arises because both the defendants and the nominal shareholder plaintiff can pass the real cost of the litigation on to the corporation. Over time, the availability of collusive settlements may encourage the filing of frivolous actions—ones that the plaintiffs would not undertake if they expected the defendants to litigate vigorously.

In part because of these problems, the derivative action has always been surrounded by much procedural complexity. To chill frivolous actions, many states require the plaintiff to post a "security for expenses" bond to cover the defendants' legal expenses if the action is unsuccessful. The plaintiff's standing (that is, his or her eligibility to sue) is limited to those shareholders who owned shares "contemporaneously" at the time of the wrong; the premise of this rule (often inaccurate) is that subsequent holders are not injured by the wrong, because they acquired their shares afterwards at a price that reflected any injury done to the corporation. Special pleading rules also typically apply in derivative actions. Finally, to reduce the possibility of collusive settlements, judicial approval of the settlements reached in class and derivative actions is required in almost all jurisdictions. It is far from clear, however, that there is much that the courts can do (or want to do) to stop parties from settling on a basis that maximizes their own personal interests.[149] The problem with these attempts to chill frivolous actions is that they are overbroad and may chill the filing of meritorious actions as well. In recent years, because of these barriers, plaintiffs' attorneys appear to have become less willing to undertake the often considerable time and expense incident to derivative litigation.

The most substantial present-day barrier to derivative actions, however, is a doctrine under which the corporation's board of directors (or a committee thereof, if some directors have been sued) can successfully move to dismiss the action on the ground that it has reviewed the action and deems it contrary to the corporation's best interests. At first glance, this doctrine may seem an unremarkable application of the business judgment rule. After all, why should the plaintiff, who probably owns very few shares, be able to force the corporation to sue when its chosen representatives wish to resist the suit? One answer may be that such litigation is a necessary monitoring mechanism by which to police the conduct of precisely these representatives and without it fiduciary duties might become meaningless obligations lacking effective enforcement mechanisms. But, what if the directors who make the decision not to sue are clearly disinterested? Should the courts respect their decision the same way they defer to other board decisions under the business judgment rule? Courts have split on this question, and to understand the

---

[149] Courts sometimes do, however, reduce substantially fees to be paid to the plaintiffs' attorneys. See, e.g., In re Abercrombie & Fitch Co. Shareholders Derivative Litigation, 886 A.2d 1271 (2005).

controversy it is useful to begin with a much older procedural rule out of which this current doctrinal controversy emerged.

Procedurally, a plaintiff who wishes to commence a derivative action must either first make a demand on the board of directors to bring the action or demonstrate that demand was excused. In theory, this demand requirement gives the board the opportunity to do one of several things: (1) take corrective actions, or enter into a settlement with the defendant, thereby avoiding the need for the lawsuit; (2) bring the requested action; (3) permit the plaintiff to proceed in its place; or (4) reject the requested action as not in the corporation's best interests. In practice, this last option is almost invariably the one the board exercises (although corrective actions may also be undertaken).[150] If the board rejects demand, the next question becomes whether this rejection was wrongful. Generally, however, plaintiffs seldom make demand, preferring instead to argue that demand was excused. (This is largely because under Delaware law the making of demand concedes that a business judgment test applies to the board's decision to reject demand.[151])

When will demand be excused? Historically, the answer appears to have been that demand was usually excused if the complaint alleged misconduct by any of the board's members.[152] However, the law has clearly shifted, beginning in the mid–1970s, so that in Delaware (and a number of other jurisdictions) the plaintiff must allege that a majority of the board personally benefited from the challenged transaction or was otherwise subject to a legally disabling conflict of interest. For example, suppose that a corporation has seven directors and they vote to award four of their number stock options to purchase a substantial percentage of the corporation's authorized stock at a price well below its current market value. Here, if a plaintiff brought suit, the fact that four directors (a majority) benefited would probably mean that demand on the board would be excused; that is, a court would not expect the board to reverse itself or evaluate the proposed lawsuit impartially simply because one shareholder objected. However, if the numbers are reversed and only three directors benefited, the existing case law suggests that demand might be required, unless the plaintiff could produce specific evidence to show that the decision to grant the options was corrupt or reckless. This may seem to be too fine a distinction upon which to place

---

[150] For an empirical survey of boards' responses in reported cases (which may be a biased sample), see James D. Cox, *Searching for the Corporation's Voice in Derivative Suit Litigation: A Critique of Zapata and the ALI Project*, 1982 Duke L.J. 959.

[151] See Levine v. Smith, 591 A.2d 194 (Del.1991). To make matters worse for the plaintiff, in a demand-refused case a plaintiff is not allowed discovery. Thus, a study of all the derivative actions filed in Delaware in the years 1999 and 2000, "did not find a single case in which demand had been made on the directors." Robert B. Thompson and Randall S. Thomas, The Public and Private Faces of Derivative Suits, 57 Van. L. Rev. 1747, 1782 (2004).

[152] See Richard M. Buxbaum, *Conflict-of-Interest Statutes and the Need for a Demand on Directors in Derivative Actions*, 68 Calif.L.Rev. 1122, 1123 (1980)(demand historically has been "little more than a formal requirement").

great weight, but a leading Delaware case shows that the demand rule will often be strictly enforced, even when there are serious reasons to doubt the board's objectivity. In Aronson v. Lewis,[153] the defendant was the chief executive officer of a company of which he was also the controlling (47 percent) shareholder and founder; in addition, it was alleged that he had personally selected the other directors. The action sought to challenge a self-dealing transaction under which the defendant (who was 75 years old) received (1) a five-year employment agreement, (2) an additional subsequent term as a consultant at a substantial salary, and (3) an annual bonus equal to 5 percent of the company's pre-tax profits each year. Finally, the contract provided that it was to continue regardless of the defendant's inability to perform. Plaintiffs claimed that this contract unfairly diverted a substantial portion of the firm's earnings to the defendant for a period that extended well beyond the point at which he could provide useful services to the company. Still, the court dismissed the lawsuit because the plaintiff had not shown that demand on the directors would have been futile.[154]

Not all jurisdictions follow Delaware's strict demand rule;[155] nor do all accept its "demand required, demand excused" distinction. The North Carolina Supreme Court has held that a derivative action may not be dismissed without a judicial judgment that the action will not benefit the corporation, regardless of whether demand would be required or excused.[156] Similarly, the American Law Institute has recommended that the "demand required, demand excused" distinction be dropped, that demand be required in virtually all cases, but that the court not dismiss any derivative action without first substantively reviewing the board's justifications for dismissal.[157]

---

[153] 473 A.2d 805 (Del.1984).

[154] The approach of Aronson v. Lewis was reaffirmed in Grobow v. Perot, 539 A.2d 180 (Del.1988), which involved a challenge to the repurchase by General Motors, for $745 million, of the stock and certain contingent notes held by H. Ross Perot and his close associates. The repurchase was at an apparent premium over the market price and seemed to be in response to Perot's public criticism of General Motors' management. Because the repurchase agreement included an agreement by Perot to stop the criticism, subject to liquidated damages of $7.5 million, the press labeled these payments "Hushmail." Nonetheless, the court dismissed the suit for failure to make demand on the board. It was not enough, said the court, to argue that Perot's criticism "could cause the directors embarrassment sufficient to lead to their removal from office." 539 A.2d at 188.

[155] New York and other precedents appear to excuse demand on a showing that the board passively acquiesced in a suspicious transaction. See Barr v. Wackman, 36 N.Y.2d 371, 368 N.Y.S.2d 497, 329 N.E.2d 180 (1975); Johnson v. Steel, Inc., 100 Nev. 181, 678 P.2d 676 (1984).

[156] Alford v. Shaw, 320 N.C. 465, 358 S.E.2d 323 (1987). The Iowa Supreme Court has shown a similar skepticism of the board's ability to evaluate an action against its own members and has barred the use of special litigation committees in these instances. See Miller v. Register and Tribune Syndicate, Inc., 336 N.W.2d 709 (Iowa 1983).

[157] See A.L.I., Principles of Corporate Governance, §§ 7.03, 7.08 (1994). The A.L.I. draws a distinction between the duty of care and the duty of loyalty and instructs the court to give greater deference to the board's justifications for dismissal in the former case, in the belief that the historic function of the derivative action has been to monitor duty of loyalty violations.

Even if demand is excused, the plaintiff may still be barred from proceeding. This brings us to the development of the "special litigation committee." As the practice developed in the late 1970s, where a derivative action was filed with the majority of the board properly joined as defendants, and there was adequate evidence to support the allegation of wrongdoing, the board would appoint a "special litigation committee" consisting of directors who were not properly regarded as defendants. Even when all the directors were proper defendants, they could still expand the membership of the board, appoint two or three new directors, who would not have an overt conflict of interest, and then constitute these new directors as the special litigation committee. The special litigation committee would then hire outside counsel and carry out a thorough investigation. The experience has been that special committees almost invariably decide that the derivative action should be dismissed.

Courts have differed as to the standard of review applicable to such a committee's decision when demand is excused. A New York case applied the business judgment rule, under which the substantive basis for the committee's decision could not be examined.[158] Judicial review, it said, is limited to good faith, independence, and adequacy of investigation. At the other extreme, the North Carolina Supreme Court, claiming to follow a recent trend, required review of the merits of the recommendation of the special committee.[159] Under its approach, the trial court may give weight to and "choose to rely" on the special committee's recommendation, but should not do so "blindly." Delaware leaves it in the discretion of the trial court whether or not to engage in substantive review of the special committee's justifications for dismissal in this "demand excused" context.[160]

Obviously, there is a considerable danger that members of special litigation committees, even though nominally independent, will be affected by "structural bias"—that is, by a favorable disposition toward the managers and the other members of the board with whom they work and who may have been instrumental in their appointment to the board. Given this presumed bias, one wonders why courts have been willing to grant any deference at all to their recommendations. One explanation may lie in the fact that some of the early cases, in the 1970s, involved "illegal payments" in foreign countries, where the defendants were charged with allowing payments that looked suspiciously like bribes or illegal domestic political contributions. In these instances, the courts may have believed that even if the conduct was illegal or improper it had not injured the corporation. Yet, once this rule became established in these "due care" cases, it was soon followed in duty of loyalty cases (for example, in Aronson v. Lewis).[161] Another explanation for judicial defer-

---

[158] Auerbach v. Bennett, 47 N.Y.2d 619, 419 N.Y.S.2d 920, 393 N.E.2d 994 (1979).

[159] Alford v. Shaw, supra note 145.

[160] Zapata Corp. v. Maldonado, 430 A.2d 779 (Del.1981); Kaplan v. Wyatt, 499 A.2d 1184, 1192 (Del.1985).

[161] See note 143 supra.

ence is that the justifications frequently given by the special litigation committee for seeking termination of the action are plausible. The most popular justification has been that the expenses of the action, if it were continued, would equal or exceed the expected recovery. Once the corporation pays its own expenses (including the often substantial indirect costs of executive time) and indemnifies the defendant's legal expenses and also pays a court-awarded fee to the plaintiff's lawyer, the total cost may exceed any recovery or benefit. Does this then imply that the derivative action is simply not worthwhile? Here, one must recognize that the general deterrent benefit that such actions may yield could justify their utility, even if they do not typically produce a net recovery. That is, because most shareholders hold a portfolio of stocks, they could benefit because managers, both in the same corporation and in other corporations, might be deterred from future wrongful conduct by a few successful actions. Whether derivative actions in fact generate such a deterrent benefit today (particularly in view of the possibility of collusive settlements) is, however, an open question.

**4. Federal and State Securities Laws.** When a corporation seeks to raise capital in the public securities markets it must comply with the rules and regulations of the federal Securities and Exchange Commission. Under the Securities Act of 1933 (the " '33 Act"), a corporation must file a registration statement with the SEC and have it declared effective by that agency before it can make a public offering to investors. There is, however, an important exemption for offerings to a limited group of sophisticated investors; these are known as "private placements." The registration statement filed by a corporate issuer with the SEC contains a document within it known as a "prospectus," which must be printed in large quantities, distributed to the securities market, and delivered to each investor who purchases shares.

Once a corporation has 500 shareholders in the United States and a minimal level of assets, it becomes a "reporting company" that is required to enter the "continuous disclosure system" established by the Securities Exchange Act of 1934 (the " '34 Act") and file periodic reports on both an annual and quarterly basis. These reports—the Annual Report on Form 10–K (or "10–K" in the parlance of securities law) and the Quarterly Report on Form 10–Q (or "10–Q")—are detailed disclosure documents that are intended to inform a sophisticated, professional audience of securities analysts, institutional investors, stockholders, and investment advisers, who in turn keep the market informed and the security accurately priced to reflect this information. Smaller shareholders typically receive this information only via a filtering process through their brokers or advisers, who are under a duty to familiarize themselves with these disclosures before recommending a purchase of the stock to a customer.

It is sometimes said that the '33 Act registers securities, while the '34 Act registers companies. The distinction underlying this phrase is that the continuous disclosure system focuses on trading in the "second-ary market"—that is, the trading market among investors—while the '33 Act's registration statement informs the "primary market" in which the corporate issuer sells securities directly to the public. Recently, the SEC has begun to integrate these two disclosure systems by allowing the same disclosure documents to suffice for both purposes. This has both lessened the considerable cost of registration with the SEC, and, even more importantly to the issuer, reduced the delay that previously interfered with the issuer's quick access to the securities markets.

"Reporting companies" must also file proxy statements before soliciting proxies for annual or special meetings of shareholders. Here, the required disclosures are intended to inform investors in their voting decisions rather than in their decisions whether to buy, sell, or hold the securities in question. Another set of disclosure requirements applies in tender offers and requires filings by both the bidder and the target (and those acting on their behalf).

Federal law also establishes a series of anti-fraud remedies in the event that full disclosure of all material information is not made in any of the foregoing contexts. The most famous of these remedies is Rule 10b–5, which authorizes a defrauded buyer or seller to sue in a federal court if a material misstatement or non-disclosure is made "in connection with" a purchase or sale of a security. Case law has expanded this Rule's language so that a misleading statement made in a press release by a corporation can result in liability for the corporation, even though it, itself, is neither buying nor selling its securities. (See Sec. IV(B).) Corporations that are listed on a major securities exchange are also required in their listing agreement with the exchange to make timely disclosure of all material developments; this is an important additional requirement, because the federal securities laws do not impose any general requirement of affirmative disclosure on the corporation, but only seek to prohibit misleading or incomplete disclosures.

In administering the federal securities laws, the SEC's staff effectively amounts to a public monitoring body. In theory, corporations are creatures of state, not federal, law. Lawyers familiar with the administration of the federal securities laws, however, understand that the SEC's staff will frequently inquire into the substantive fairness of transactions and seek to appraise the integrity of a firm's management. It is also important to understand that the SEC's role is to protect investors, not shareholders. Not infrequently, the interests of these two overlapping classes can conflict. For example, if the SEC compels the disclosure that a corporation has substantial undisclosed liabilities, this surprise disclosure will protect investors, but may injure existing share-holders by causing the firm's stock price to decline before shareholders can sell. Thus, as a monitoring force, the SEC is not necessarily seeking to protect the specific shareholders of an individual corporation, but rather shareholders generally.

Compliance with the securities laws and regulations is, of course, costly, but those laws and regulations, together with the U.S. court system and other governmental institutions, benefit investors in at least two ways: First, by requiring substantial transparency—that is, by requiring useful, accurate information about the business and finances of the reporting firm; and, second, by protecting investors from dishonest management. These benefits to investors in turn increase the value of the firm's securities. That is one reason why some foreign firms list their shares on the New York Stock Exchange and thereby subject themselves to the U.S. disclosure requirements and other laws and regulations.[162]

On the state level, the securities laws of some states go beyond requiring full disclosure and impose more substantive standards on the sale of shares to the public. These state statutes (known as "Blue Sky" laws) frequently require a state administrator to determine that the transaction is "fair, just and equitable" before the offering may occur. Do you think this is a realistic standard to give a state official? Should investors have the opportunity to accept fully disclosed risks that a state bureaucrat deems ill-advised? As you might guess, the operation of the "fair, just and equitable" standard has produced a continuing controversy over the years, but it exists and represents a form of public monitoring.

**5. The Appraisal Remedy: Protecting the Shareholder's Exit.** Once a corporate shareholder assembles a majority voting block, it frequently seeks today to effect a "cash-out merger" under which it acquires 100% of the corporation and the other shareholders receive cash (or sometimes securities of the majority shareholder). This is now the standard pattern in the aftermath of a tender offer. In some jurisdictions, such as New York, a merger requires approval by a supermajority (e.g., two-thirds) vote of the shareholders, but in Delaware and other "permissive" states the required vote is only 50% (unless a higher percentage requirement is inserted in the articles of incorporation). Can the majority shareholder therefore "cash-out" the minority shareholders at a price that it sets well below the market's price? The answer to this question is "basically no." The shareholders generally have a remedy, known as the "right of appraisal," that entitles them to have a court determine and award the "fair value" of their shares.[163] The appraisal

---

[162] See René M. Stulz, Corporate Governance and Financial Globalization, NBER Reporter, Fall 2005, p. 13, at p. 14 (a short review article, citing various studies by Stulz and others).

[163] Under many statutes, including Delaware's, the appraisal remedy is not available for shareholders of a corporation if they started out with publicly traded shares

and wind up with the same shares or other publicly traded shares. In most situations this is reasonable, since a majority of the shareholders will have approved the transaction and any shareholder who is unhappy with the outcome can sell his or her shares and invest the proceeds in the shares of some other publicly held company.

remedy is a statutory provision, typically triggered by a merger or sale of substantially all the corporation's assets, that authorizes the shareholder to apply to a state court in its jurisdiction of incorporation for a determination of the "fair value" of its shares, which the corporation must then pay.

Historically, appraisal was an ineffective remedy that shareholders seldom used, for two reasons. First, the shareholder would not receive any payment from the corporation until the litigation was resolved years later, and interest was either not paid or paid at an unrealistically low rate over the interval. Second, courts generally would determine fair value using the "Delaware Block" method. This is a weighted averaging approach that balances several different standards of valuation (asset value, market value, dividend history, earnings history, etc.), while corporations tend to be bought and sold in the market on the basis of their highest value. Thus, if one averages this highest value with the other lesser values, one invariably obtains an unrealistically low figure, thereby encouraging cash-out mergers that treat minority shareholders unfavorably.

Possibly as a result, courts during the 1970s began to grant injunctions against these mergers when they felt the offered price was unfairly low. In Singer v. Magnavox Co.,[164] the Delaware Supreme Court established a two-part test that required the majority shareholder both to show a legitimate "business purpose" for expelling the minority shareholders and to prove the "entire fairness" of the transaction. The "business purpose" element soon proved of little consequence and was largely abandoned (although New York and several other states still follow it[165]). It simply required a colorable justification, which good lawyers can always create. The second element—"entire fairness"—was meaningful, but went only to the question of damages (i. e., how much should the minority receive for its stock). The question this raised (as the Delaware Supreme Court eventually clearly saw) was: Why must such a damage determination come before the merger (in the context of an injunction action) rather than after the merger (through the appraisal proceeding)? In consequence, in Weinberger v. UOP, Inc.,[166] the Delaware Supreme Court, only six years after *Singer*, reversed itself. As a result of the decision in *Weinberger*, if the board has not violated its duty of good faith, loyalty, or due care, and has made full disclosure, the sole

---

[164] 380 A.2d 969 (Del.1977).

[165] See Alpert v. 28 Williams Street Corp., 63 N.Y.2d 557, 483 N.Y.S.2d 667, 473 N.E.2d 19 (1984); Coggins v. New England Patriots Football Club, Inc., 397 Mass. 525, 492 N.E.2d 1112 (1986).

[166] 457 A.2d 701 (Del.1983). In subsequent cases, Delaware has also required evidence of arms length bargaining between the committee of directors negotiating for the subsidiary and the parent corporation. See Rabkin v. Philip A. Hunt Chemical Corp., 498 A.2d 1099 (Del.1985). Thus, there remains a substantial emphasis on an independent bargaining process under the Delaware formula, before shareholders are made to rely on appraisal as their exclusive remedy.

remedy is appraisal.[167] At the same time, as part of a careful trade-off, it modernized the appraisal remedy by rejecting the "block averaging" formula and instructing the appraisal court to use those "methods which are generally considered acceptable in the financial community ..." Thus, testimony from financial analysts and investment bankers now constitutes the principal evidence in an appraisal proceeding. New York has amended its statute to adopt a similar approach to valuation.

Does this outcome adequately protect shareholders? One consideration that the Delaware Court did not focus on in *Weinberger* is that its substitution of a post-merger fairness hearing for a pre-merger hearing in the context of an injunctive proceeding forces shareholders to take action on their own initiative in order to protect their rights. To take advantage of the appraisal remedy, each shareholder must follow various procedures to elect that remedy and then be prepared to go to court in what is an individual action (though one that may later be consolidated with other such actions). Holders of small blocks of shares, even if they are prepared to make the decision, and take the initial steps, to perfect their appraisal right, are seldom ready to go to court and cannot easily or cheaply secure counsel, especially in a foreign state (assuming that they do not reside in Delaware). In contrast, in a class action such as the pre-merger hearing in *Weinberger*, the challenge can be initiated by a single shareholder, represented by a single lawyer. All other similarly situated shareholders automatically become plaintiffs and are represented by the same lawyer, unless they opt out. Moreover, and perhaps most importantly, the plaintiffs' attorney in a class action is paid out of the recovery obtained, if any, and thus no payment had to be made up front. As a result, a class action protected small shareholders without their needing to incur significant legal and transaction costs to protect a small investment. In some jurisdictions, the appraisal remedy has been "modernized" to permit individual actions to be consolidated with a single attorney representing all claimants, but, even as so revised, the appraisal remedy lacks the class action's ability to secure automatic representation and a greater recovery for shareholders.

Empirically, only a small minority of the eligible shareholders (generally well under 10%) ever seek appraisal. One reason for this—in addition to the prohibitive transaction costs to the smaller shareholder—is the problem of illiquidity. Few shareholders are willing to hold an illiquid investment (because under most statutes the shares cannot be traded once the remedy is elected) for a year or more simply in the hope of receiving a few dollars more per share. One answer to this problem has now been adopted by the Revised Model Business Corporation Act: it provides that the corporation must pay at the time the shareholder elects

---

[167] If a shareholder can establish that the board violated one or more of these obligations, then the burden shifts to the board to prove the entire fairness of the transaction. If the board fails to do so, the plaintiff is entitled to equitable relief, which could consist of a pre-merger injunction or a post-merger rescissionary remedy. Cf. Cinerama, Inc. v. Technicolor, Inc., described supra note 55.

to seek appraisal its estimate of the shares' fair value. Thus, the action is reduced in scope to one for only the disparity between their two estimates of fair value.

In overview, the key policy issue about the appraisal remedy is the degree to which it should be reformed to resemble the class action and thereby provide some form of collective representation that may be elected at low cost. Absent such a system, the likely valuation to be made by the appraisal court may be of only secondary importance: those planning the merger or other transaction have an incentive to offer an unfairly low price, even if they expect to be required to pay a much higher price to shareholders who seek appraisal, because they anticipate that only a small minority of the shareholders will do so.

**6. Gatekeepers.** Corporate governance has long relied on outside professionals who advise and alert both investors and the corporation's board, typically by providing required verifications or ratings.[168] Obvious examples include: (1) the auditor who certifies the issuer's financial statements as conforming to generally accepted accounting principles; (2) the debt rating agency that rates the issuer's relative creditworthiness; (3) the security analyst who rates and appraises the corporation's prospects for earnings growth; (4) the investment banker who provides a "fairness opinion" in connection with a merger; and (5) the securities attorney who opines in connection with a closing that all material known to the attorney has been disclosed. Although gatekeepers are subject to liability, another and more basic reason motivates them to perform their assigned responsibilities: gatekeepers possess significant reputational capital which they implicitly pledge to investors to make their assurances credible. That is, an auditor may serve thousands of clients and have acquired a reputation for honesty and integrity over a century or more of serving these and other clients. In theory, it would be irrational for an auditor to sacrifice this reputational capital simply to assist one client, intent on maximizing its stock price, in accomplishing a questionable or fraudulent transaction, particularly where that client did not account for even 1 percent of the auditor's annual revenues.[169]

Yet, irrational as it may seem, this is what appears to have happened in the late 1990s, as the rate of financial statement restatements soared, and as auditors, attorneys and securities analysts appear to have acquiesced in dubious financial reporting practices. Why did they did so can be debated, but appears to have involved a conflict within these firms between the interests of the individual partner (who needed to hold onto the client) and the interests of the firm as a whole. In

---

[168] See Reinier Kraakman, *Corporate Liability Strategies and the Costs of Legal Controls*, Yale L.J. 857 (1984).

[169] For exactly this observation by Judge Easterbrook, see DiLeo v. Ernst & Young,

901 F.2d 624 (7th Cir.1990). It is noteworthy that Enron, while a large client, did not account for more than 1 percent of Arthur Andersen's revenues.

response, Congress in the Sarbanes–Oxley Act of 2002 (the "Act") tightened its regulation of all these gatekeepers, as discussed below.

*Auditors.* Like most professions, the accounting profession has been essentially self-regulating. But that has now changed. The Act established the Public Company Accounting Oversight Board ("PCAOB") "to oversee the audit of public companies that are subject to the securities laws, and related matters, in order to protect the interest of investors and further the public interest in the preparation of informative, accurate, and independent audit reports...."[170] All accounting firms that prepare audit reports for public companies must become "registered public accounting firms" by registering with the PCAOB. In addition, the PCAOB was authorized to (i) "establish or adopt ... auditing, quality control, ethics, independence and other standards relating to the preparation of audit reports for issuers"; (ii) conduct regular inspections of registered public accounting firms; and (iii) bring disciplinary proceedings and enforce compliance with the Act.[171]

To further protect the independence and objectivity of the auditor, the Act rewires the internal reporting circuitry within the public corporation. No longer does the auditor report to management; rather, the Act mandates that only the corporation's audit committee can hire, fire, or supervise the auditor; specifically, it must approve in advance the scope of services, including all non-audit services provided by the auditor to a public company. Because Congress believed that some auditors had been bribed into acquiescence with lucrative consulting services contracts, the Act prohibited accounting firms from providing certain specific and highly lucrative non-audit services to audit clients that were public corporations, including computer, EDP, and software systems design and implementation. This prophylactic rule has essentially forced most of the major accounting firms to drop their consulting services and focus on auditing. Finally, the audit committee is also now regulated by federal law. Overriding state law, which empowers the board as a whole to manage the corporation, federal law now provides that the audit committee must have at least one financial or accounting expert, with a level of experience that the SEC has defined, and that the audit committee must "be directly responsible for the appointment, compensation, and oversight of the work" of the independent auditor, meaning that presumably neither the full board nor the shareholders can overrule the audit committee.

*Attorneys.* Section 307 of the Act requires the SEC to prescribe "minimum standards of professional conduct for attorneys" who practice or appear before the SEC. These rules also require attorneys who represent public companies "to report evidence of a material violation of the securities laws or breach of fiduciary duty or similar violation by the

---

[170] See Section 101(a) of the Sarbanes–Oxley Act of 2002 (the "Act").

[171] See Section 101(c) of the Act.

company or any agent thereof" to the company's chief legal officer or CEO. If these officers do not take appropriate corrective action, further "up-the-ladder" reporting is required to the company's audit committee. In 2003, the SEC adopted rules requiring such "up-the-ladder" reporting,[172] but it has deferred action on an even more controversial "noisy withdrawal" proposal under which the attorney would be required to resign and notify the SEC if the audit committee declined to take corrective action and ongoing criminal activity threatened serious injury to the corporation or its securities holders.[173]

*Analysts.* Section 501 of the Act directs the SEC, or, at its discretion, the stock exchanges and the NASD, to adopt rules regulating conflicts of interests affecting securities analysts.[174] This provision was a direct response to the investigation by New York State Attorney General Eliot Spitzer into the stock recommendations made by Merrill Lynch's internet securities analysts, which recommendations appear to have been contradicted or criticized by many of these analysts in contemporaneous internal emails. This and other recent episodes suggested that analysts were under strong pressures to recommend or publish positive research concerning investment banking clients of the firm. In order to improve the objectivity of analyst research, the Act contemplates that these rules will (i) restrict the prepublication clearance or approval of analyst research reports by "persons not directly responsible for investment research"; (ii) limit the supervision and compensatory evaluation of analysts to officials within the broker-dealer not engaged in investment banking activities; (iii) protect analysts from retaliation or threats of retaliation for "adverse, negative or otherwise unfavorable research reports"; (iv) establish blackout periods when analysts working for syndicate members in an underwriting should not publish research reports; and (v) "establish structural and institutional safeguards within registered brokers or dealers to assure that securities analysts are separated by appropriate information partitions within the firm from the review, pressure or oversight of those whose involvement in investment banking activities might potentially bias their judgment or supervision."

The response of the SEC and the self-regulatory organizations ("SROs") to the conflicts of interests surrounding analyst research has gone through several district stages. Initially, even prior to the Act's passage, the SEC approved rule changes proposed by the two leading stock exchanges, NASD and the NYSE, that implemented a variety of structural reforms.[175] First, these rule changes limited the relationships and communications permitted between an investment banking department and its research department, strengthening the previously often

---

[172] See Securities Act Release No. 33–8185 (February 6, 2003).

[173] See Securities Act Release No. 33–8186 (February 6, 2003).

[174] This provision is contained in a new Section 15D of the Securities Exchange Act of 1934.

[175] See Securities Exchange Act Release No. 34–45908 (May 16, 2002).

porous "Chinese Wall" by providing both that no research analyst could be supervised or controlled by investment banking personnel and that pending research reports could not be discussed among them, except in a closely regulated fashion in the presence of compliance personnel. Second, analyst compensation arrangements were revised by rules that prohibited tying such compensation to involvement in investment banking transactions. Third, the analyst was required to disclose in any research report if the analyst's firm had received underwriting or investment banking compensation from the firm over the past 12 months. Fourth, their rules prohibited promises of favorable research in return for, or as an inducement for, the receipt of investment banking business. Fifth, restrictions were placed on an analyst's personal trading, including a prohibition on the receipt of an issuer's securities prior to its IPO (initial public offering). Finally, the rules required disclosure of analysts' ownership of securities and of the firm's rating system (including the percentage of ratings assigned to each category).

Next, in early 2003,the SEC adopted new Regulation Analyst Certification ("Regulation AC"), which requires that a research analyst employed by a broker or dealer certify that the views expressed in the report accurately reflected the analyst's personal views and disclose whether the analyst received compensation or other payments in connection with his or her recommendation or views.[176] Finally, late in 2003, the SEC approved amendments to the NYSE's and NASD's rules intended to achieve full compliance with the Act.[177] Essentially, these rules mandate that the compensation and review of securities analysts be sealed off from investment banking, restrict analyst participation in certain marketing activities by investment brokers, limit when analysts may issue reports concerning IPO companies, and prohibit any attempt by those engaged in investment banking from attempting to retaliate against an analyst for a negative research report or rating.

Will this attempt to cordon off securities analysts from conflicts of interest work over the long-run? Here, some are skeptical, because they view the analyst as essentially involved in a marketing activity in which the analyst is necessarily compensated on the basis of his or her ability to promote stock transactions through the brokerage firm. These critics believe that only a total division between investment banking and securities research would work, but under such a structure, far fewer analysts would be employed. The bottom line then is that it is difficult, and possibly impossible, to convert some professions into gatekeepers, and success probably has to be measured in relative terms. Still, neither boards of directors nor investors can fully inform themselves, and thus gatekeepers are a critical link in corporate governance.

---

[176] See Securities Exchange Act Release No. 34–47384 (February 20, 2003).

[177] See Securities Exchange Act Release No. 34–48252 (August 4, 2003).

## VIII.  FUNDAMENTAL CHANGES: MERGERS AND ACQUISITIONS

Probably the most basic change that the shareholders can make in their corporation is to end its existence—at least its existence as a separate legal entity. Such a termination of corporate existence can occur as the result of either a merger or a sale of the corporation's assets followed by a liquidation. Each of these transactions requires a shareholder vote (and in many jurisdictions a supermajority vote of two thirds the voting shares or more); in addition, a merger or a sale of substantially all the corporation's assets may trigger an appraisal remedy for those shareholders who vote against the transaction and file a formal dissent. Under the appraisal remedy, as previously explained,[178] a shareholder who objects to a merger or sale of assets is entitled to be paid by the corporation in cash an amount equal to the fair market value of his or her shares, determined by agreement or, failing agreement, in a judicial proceeding. The requirement of a shareholder vote reflects the notion that mergers and sales of substantially all of the corporation's assets are sufficiently fundamental as to be beyond the usual discretion of the board of directors (who, however, must still initiate these transactions and then seek shareholder approval).

The term "merger" is sometimes confusing, because it can be used either technically or loosely. Strictly speaking, a merger is a transaction by which one corporation (the acquiring firm) purchases the assets and liabilities of another corporation (the acquired firm) in return for either its own securities or cash, or a combination of both; the acquired firm is deemed to have been absorbed within the acquiring firm. Sometimes, as noted below, it is difficult to distinguish the acquiring and acquired firms, because the transaction can be structured so that either firm is the surviving one (even if this means that the minnow is swallowing the whale).

In reality, one corporation can acquire another by one of three basic techniques: statutory merger, purchase of assets, or purchase of stock. As next discussed, the key differences between these techniques are likely to be (1) whether the acquiring firm must assume the liabilities of the acquired firm; (2) whether shareholders of both, or either, firm must vote to approve the transaction; (3) whether shareholders of the acquired firm receive an appraisal remedy; and (4) the tax treatment of the transaction. Increasingly, however, modern tort law is coming to ignore the differences between these forms and holds the acquiring firm liable for the tort debts of the acquired firm, even in a purchase of assets transaction, if the acquirer purchased substantially all the acquired firm's assets and carried on its business. As a practical matter, this means that the parties may be forced to negotiate as if the acquiring firm would assume the debts of the acquired firm (it also means that the

---

[178] See Sec. V(B)(5).

acquiring firm should insure against contingent liabilities that may arise in the future from the acquired firm's past or present business).

Federal tax law permits an acquirer to choose between these three forms of acquisitions—i.e., merger, purchase of stock or purchase of assets—without major difference in tax treatment necessarily resulting. Lawyers often speak of these three different types of acquisition as A, B, or C type acquisitions, respectively, because of the subsections of the Internal Revenue Code that cover them.[179]

An A-type merger is accomplished pursuant to procedures prescribed in state law and is called a *statutory merger*. By way of illustration, suppose that S is a small corporation and L is a large one and that L is acquiring S. Typically S will merge into L; S will disappear and L will be the survivor. (Sometimes, however, L may be merged into S; either way, L's shareholders wind up in control.) The S shareholders may receive cash or L securities for their S shares (or some cash and some securities). Or some S shareholders can receive cash while others receive securities. One of the virtues of an A-type merger is its flexibility.

A merger is thought to involve fundamental change, at least for the acquired (smaller) corporation. Accordingly, a merger of S and L would require approval by a vote of the S shareholders and often by the L shareholders (depending on the state law that is applicable and the number and type of L securities to be issued). If the merger were approved by the vote of a sufficient number of shareholders (at least a majority and, under the law of some states, a greater percentage), the merger would be accomplished; all of S's assets and liabilities would be absorbed by L. In this sense, the vote of the majority would bind all shareholders. But inasmuch as there would be a fundamental change in the nature of the investment (or so it is thought), shareholders who voted against the merger might have an "appraisal right," which is a statutory right to refuse to accept the terms of the merger and to demand payment in cash for the fair value of one's shares (with the value determined by a court if the dissenting shareholder and the corporation cannot reach agreement). (See Sec. V(B)(5) supra.)

In recent years, most A-type mergers have been accomplished through a wholly owned subsidiary of L (sometimes formed solely for the purpose of accomplishing the acquisition). S could be merged into L's subsidiary or the subsidiary could be merged into S (with L, as share-

---

[179] Shareholders of a corporation who receive common stock or other similar securities in exchange for their common stock in a "reorganization," as defined in the tax law, do not recognize gain or loss on the transaction for tax purposes. The three categories used here, however, correspond only roughly to the A, B, and C reorganizations of the tax law. For example, a corporate purchase of stock for cash will be called a B-type merger here because the buyer gains control, and thereby accomplishes the merger, by buying stock from the shareholders of the corporation that is to be acquired. Such a transaction would not qualify as a B reorganization for tax purposes because of a statutory definition of a B reorganization as one that is solely for the voting stock of the acquiring corporation.

holder of the subsidiary, then receiving $S$ shares). Either way, the $S$ shareholders could be given securities of $L$, even though formally $L$ would not be a party to the merger. Because in this area of the law form often triumphs over substance, the use of the subsidiary as the formal partner in the merger can achieve advantages for $L$ such as insulation from the liabilities of $S$ and avoidance of a vote by, and appraisal rights for, its shareholders.

B-type acquisitions are sometimes called *"informal"* or *"practical"* *mergers*—meaning that they are independent of the processes for amalgamation specified by state law. In the B-type acquisition, $L$ acquires (for cash[180] or for its shares or some of each) enough $S$ shares to give it control of $S$. $S$ thereby becomes an $L$ subsidiary. The amalgamation thus results, formally, from transactions between $L$ and the individual shareholders of $S$; there is no formal involvement of $S$ as a corporation—no action by the board, no shareholder vote, no transfer of title to assets, etc. $S$ remains intact, as does $L$. The B-type acquisition of $S$ by $L$ may be followed by a dissolution of $S$ or by a *"short-form"* A-type merger of $S$ into $L$, pursuant to simplified procedures that are available under the law of some states where one corporation owns a sufficiently high proportion of the shares of another. Typically, "short-form" merger statutes authorize a corporation that owns some specified percentage of the stock of another corporation (usually 90% or 95% of the latter's voting stock) to merge this subsidiary into the parent corporation, without a shareholder vote. Instead, the board of the parent company can alone authorize the transaction, and no action is required of the subsidiary corporation or its shareholders. This saves the time, expense, and possible legal liability associated with proxy solicitation. The rationale for dispensing with a shareholder vote is that a 90% or 95% ownership level makes this a mere formality (and a costly one). In reality, the other shareholders effectively voted "with their feet" when they sold their shares to the party that owns this supermajority level.

A C-type acquisition is also said to be an informal or "practical" merger. $L$ acquires the assets of $S$ for cash or for its securities or some of each.[181] One advantage is that $L$ may be able to avoid succeeding to the liabilities of $S$. $S$ winds up holding the cash or the $L$ securities and then, most often, it liquidates and distributes these assets to its shareholders. In this type of acquisition, formally there is no transaction between $L$ and the $S$ shareholders (though state law may require a shareholder vote by the $S$ shareholders because of the sale of substantially all its assets). Depending on state law, the $S$ shareholders may or may not have an appraisal remedy.

---

[180] If cash is used, the transaction will not qualify as a B reorganization for federal income tax purposes.

[181] Again, the use of cash ordinarily will destroy qualification as a C reorganization for federal income tax purposes. Moreover, even if the transaction qualifies as a basically nontaxable transaction, the cash might be taxable, usually as a dividend.

Once again it is worth noting that in corporate law legal consequences may vary with the form of a transaction. In certain circumstances, however, where a transaction is cast in an unusual form, a court may preserve legal characteristics that would have flowed from the use of a more natural form (which is then called the substance of the transaction). A good example of this phenomenon is the "*de facto* merger doctrine," exemplified in the well-known case of Farris v. Glen Alden Corporation.[182] Glen Alden was to be acquired by the much larger List Industries Corporation. The surviving corporation would have been owned 76.5% by the shareholders of List and 23.5% by the shareholders of Glen Alden. The form of the transaction was an acquisition of List assets by Glen Alden for its shares (followed by a change of name of Glen Alden to List). Thus, formally Glen Alden was the surviving corporation; it was merely acquiring assets. A shareholder of Glen Alden complained that the transaction was in substance equivalent to a merger—that it was a *de facto* merger—and that consequently he was entitled, among other things, to the appraisal right. (See Sec. V(B)(5) above.) The Pennsylvania Supreme Court agreed. The Delaware Supreme Court several years later, however, refused to apply the *de facto* merger doctrine in a case in which the plaintiff argued that a transaction taking the form of a purchase of assets of a smaller corporation by a larger one should be treated as a merger.[183] The court reasoned that where a transaction could be accomplished under either of two different statutory provisions, the parties were free to choose the form, and the substantive provisions, that they wanted.

## IX.  A SLICE OF FINANCIAL HISTORY: "WATERED STOCK" AND ITS LESSONS IN FRAUD

Most state corporation statutes contain some restrictions on the character of the consideration for which stock may be issued. Typically, it is provided that promissory notes and contracts for future services constitute invalid consideration.[184] Thus, a corporation may not issue shares to its president on formation either for his promissory note (even if he is a millionaire) or for his agreement to work for the first year without salary, even if all the other shareholders consent. Shares so issued may be cancelled on a shareholder's suit, or a trustee in bankruptcy may demand full payment in cash for them from the person to whom they were issued. It may well be asked why the law takes this paternalistic stance. Whom is it trying to protect?

The answer is largely historical. The theory of this body of law is that creditors rely on the corporation's balance sheet when they extend

---

[182] 393 Pa. 427, 143 A.2d 25 (1958).

[183] Hariton v. Arco Electronics, Inc., 41 Del.Ch. 74, 188 A.2d 123 (1963).

[184] See, e.g., N.Y. Bus. Corp. Law § 504(b). But see R.M.B.C.A. § 6.21 (permitting contracts for future services to constitute valid consideration for shares).

credit to the corporation. If this theory was ever correct, it is probably irrelevant today when creditors are more likely to examine earnings and assets, seek a credit report from a credit agency, or, in the case of a closely held corporation, demand a personal guarantee.

Still, it is useful to understand the kinds of fraud that the 19th Century faced to see how these restrictions on the permissible consideration for shares evolved. In the 19th Century, upon the formation of a corporation, the founders would assign to its shares of common stock a dollar amount called "par value." For example, the common stock might be assigned a par value of $100 per share. This meant that the corporation was required to receive at least $100 cash or property worth $100 for each share issued. Suppose a corporation is formed to build a railroad and real property is contributed in return for 1,000 shares of $100 par value common stock. The minimum value of the property should be $100,000 and it is the responsibility of the board of directors in authorizing the issuance of the shares to ensure that this minimum value is received. Once the 1,000 shares are issued, the corporate financial statement, known as the corporate "books," will show a "capital" account of 1,000 shares of $100 par value stock for a total of $100,000. The books must balance, meaning that there must be a corresponding entry to show what the corporation got for the common stock, in this case the property. Thus, the books must list the property at a value of $100,000. This set of entries is normally depicted, in a "balance sheet," as shown in Balance Sheet 1 below.

## Balance Sheet 1

| Assets | Capital | |
|---|---|---|
| Property    $100,000 | Capital Stock 1,000 Common Shares ($100 par value) | $100,000 |

Suppose that the property is in fact worth only $40,000. Both sides of the balance sheet are untruthful. The left side, assets, misstates the value of the asset. The right side, capital, reflects this fact in a different way. It purports to show the value of the corporation's equity. Because in reality there are likely to be many entries on the left, all contributing to the capital stock entry on the right, the figure for capital stock is the one on which many people are likely to focus. Thus, people will focus on the fact that the Capital Stock account, or entry, is misrepresented.

The process illustrated by this example is called "watering the stock." The use of this phrase derives from a fraudulent practice used in the cattle business, where cattle drovers would feed salt to their cattle the night before they sold them at market by the pound.[185] The thirsty

---

[185] Interestingly, Mr. Daniel Drew, a 19th Century robber baron, practiced this fraud in the cattle business before becoming a securities financier, where he applied it in a new form to corporations.

cattle would drink gallons of water and would thus temporarily weigh more when they were sold the next day. "Water" is also present in a corporation when it issues shares for overvalued assets and uses the inflated value for its book entries. Here, the injured party may be either a minority shareholder whose percentage interest in the corporation is diluted to the extent of the overvaluation or a creditor who relies on the representation of the value of the corporation's assets and equity.

The process of watering often occurred in more complex settings, where it was more difficult to spot the mischief. For example, suppose an unscrupulous financier—call him, hypothetically, Commodore Vanderbilt—acquires 50 percent of the common stock, and thus control, of a valuable corporation (let's call it the Erie Railroad Corporation), whose common shares have a par value of $10 each. Suppose he also owns all the shares of another corporation, X Corp., which is also in the railroad business but is effectively, though perhaps not technically, insolvent, so its shares are worthless. Vanderbilt contributes the X Corp. shares to Erie in return for the issuance to him by Erie of new shares equal to 50 percent of the shares already outstanding, so he winds up owning two-thirds of the outstanding common stock of Erie, compared with his initial 50 percent.[186] By hypothesis, the corporation has received nothing of value. Nevertheless, the newly issued shares will undoubtedly have a par value of $10 each, so the new asset acquired (X Corp.) will be carried on the Erie books at a figure equal to the total par value of the new shares and the Capital Stock of the corporation will rise by the same amount. As a result, two things will have happened (as suggested above): (1) the existing minority shareholders of Erie will have transferred a percentage of their ownership of Erie (namely, 16⅔ percent—the difference between the 50 percent they formerly owned and the 33⅓ percent they wind up owning) to Vanderbilt in return for nothing and (2) subsequent creditors of Erie may examine the Erie balance sheet and rely to their detriment on the inflated value of the X Corp. stock and of the Capital Stock of Erie.

The injured shareholders could bring a derivative suit to challenge the issuance by the directors of the new shares, but finding and proving the facts would be difficult, at best, as long as the corporation was operating in a satisfactory way. Moreover, the plaintiffs in such a suit would be obliged to overcome the hurdle imposed by the business judgment rule, and, more recently, by state statutory rules giving a presumption of correctness, in the absence of proof of fraud, to determinations by the directors of the value of consideration received for shares.

When the corporation becomes insolvent, however, and its creditors move in to protect their claims, the facts relating to any overvaluation

---

[186] To illustrate, suppose 1,000,000 shares were outstanding, of which Vanderbilt owned 500,000 (or 50 percent). If an additional 50 percent, or 500,000, shares are issued to him, the new total is 1,500,000, of which Vanderbilt owns 1,000,000, or two-thirds of the total.

may become more apparent and easier to prove. In the context of insolvencies, American courts invented the concept of a "trust fund." This concept was designed to give creditors a cause of action, *against shareholders* who received watered stock, for the difference between the par value of the shares they received and the value of the property they contributed. The trust fund theory proved unsatisfactory and in time gave way to other theories, including the "misrepresentation theory" and the "statutory obligation theory," and muddled combinations of these and other theories. Whatever the theory, shareholders who received watered stock were potentially liable to creditors. Thus, in the foregoing example, if the Erie became insolvent, its creditors (and possibly its receiver in bankruptcy)[187] could require Vanderbilt, in his role as shareholder, to pay the full amount of the par value of the shares he received (since the property contributed was worthless). This cause of action is not, however, available to injured shareholders.

Any theory of shareholder liability to creditors for water in their shares is undercut by the reality that sensible creditors, in extending credit, do not rely much, if at all, on book entries; they rely on economic realities. In any event, lawyers long ago figured out how to avoid liability for watered stock. Recall that par value is a dollar amount arbitrarily assigned to stock. In time, lawyers perceived that shares could be issued with low par value, or no par value, so that the amount of the Stated Capital—on which the trust fund, misrepresentation, or statutory obligation theory relied—became trivial. For example, suppose a par value of $1 is assigned to the shares of common stock, but that the original shareholders pay $100 cash for each of 1,000 shares initially issued. The books would then show assets of $100,000 and, on the other side, two entries. One of the right-side entries would be Stated Capital of $1,000 (1,000 shares times the $1 par value). The other entry would be called "Capital Surplus," or something like that, and would display the remaining $99,000. The balance sheet is as shown in Balance Sheet 2.

**Balance Sheet 2**

| Assets | | Capital | |
|---|---|---|---|
| Cash | $100,000 | Capital Stock | |
| | | 1,000 Common Shares | |
| | | ($1 par value) | $ 1,000 |
| | | Capital Surplus | 99,000 |
| | | Total | $100,000 |

One important attribute of the use of low par value would be that dividends could be paid to the extent of the $99,000 Capital Surplus.

---

[187] Under a misrepresentation theory, the creditors are the victims of misrepresentation and only they can recover, while under a statutory obligation theory the receiver can recover. Another consequence of the choice of theories relates to proof of reliance, which is required under the misrepresentation theory but not under the statutory obligation theory.

Only the $1,000 Stated Capital would determine the amount required to be maintained to protect creditors.

But suppose another investor comes along and, through some dishonest connivance with the board of directors, is able to convince them to accept property they know to be worth $5,000 in return for 1,000 new shares issued by the corporation. The result will be that the new shareholder, with a contribution of $5,000, will own half of a corporation with assets of $105,000, and the original shareholders, with a contribution of $100,000, will own the other half. To conceal the fraud, the directors will, of course, claim that the newly contributed property is worth $100,000. Thus, the books will appear as in Balance Sheet 3.

### Balance Sheet 3

| Assets | | Capital | |
|---|---|---|---|
| Cash | $100,000 | Capital Stock | |
| Property | 100,000 | 2,000 Common Shares | |
| Total | $200,000 | ($1 par value) | $    2,000 |
| | | Capital Surplus | 198,000 |
| | | Total | $200,000 |

The original shareholders have a cause of action against the new shareholder and the directors for the fraud, but, as suggested above, as long as the corporation avoids insolvency they may have a difficult time finding and proving the facts. If the corporation becomes insolvent and a creditor can prove that it relied on the balance sheet misrepresentation of the value of the property, it could presumably recover its damages from the directors, and possibly from the second-stage shareholder, also on a simple common-law action for fraud or deceit. But this common-law action would require proof of reliance on a misrepresentation. The cause of action might be particularly difficult to establish against the second-stage shareholder, who may be the person with the deep pocket. The creditor would not have the relative advantage that the courts have accorded creditors, associated with the trust fund or statutory obligation theories and even the misrepresentation theory, if a high par value is used. In that situation, there is a direct action against the shareholder for the amount of water in the stock and proof of reliance is not required.[188]

Watered shares can be distinguished from bonus (or discount) shares, though the latter may present the same issues as the former. A

[188] Under the leading case on the misrepresentation theory, Hospes v. Northwestern Mfg. & Car Co., 48 Minn. 174, 50 N.W. 1117 (1892), the court spins out a theory of misrepresentation in the usual sense but then allows recovery by subsequent creditors (that is, those who extend credit after the issuance of the watered shares), without any allegation of reliance, on the subsidiary theory (now you see it, now you don't) that creditors are presumed to rely on the corporation's financial standing in the community, which is in turn based on the knowledge of others of its stated capital.

common example of bonus (or discount) shares are shares issued to an employee with no cash payment by the employee (or at a discount) in return for services to be rendered in the future. Under the law of most states, services to be rendered in the future are not valid consideration for the issuance of stock in the corporation. Here again the problem generally can be solved by using stock with low par value, selling the shares to the employee at par value and, after full disclosure, selling shares to others at a higher price. Alternatively, the corporation might lend the employee the price of the shares and later forgive the indebtedness. Although the latter technique may seem to elevate form over substance, it does have the virtue of making the transaction visible to all, hence reducing the possibility of confusion.

Acknowledging that "[p]ractitioners and legal scholars have long recognized that the statutory structure embodying 'par value' and 'legal capital' concepts is not only complex and confusing but also fails to serve the original purpose of protecting creditors and senior security holders from payments to junior security holders,"[189] the American Bar Association revised the Model Business Corporation Act in 1980 to eliminate the concepts of par value and stated capital. Today, § 6.21 of the Revised Model Business Corporation Act permits the board of directors to issue stock for any form of "tangible or intangible property or benefit to the corporation, including cash, promissory notes, services performed, contracts for services to be performed, or other securities of the corporation." Thus, even future services can support the issuance of shares. To date, relatively few states have adopted this deregulatory approach to corporate finance, but the tide appears to be running in its direction.

## X.  DIVIDENDS, RETAINED EARNINGS, AND COMPENSATION

### A.  DIVIDENDS

Concepts derived from the old "trust fund" concept also underlie the traditional law of dividends that most states follow. Basically, under the statutory or common-law rules of most states, the maximum dividend that the directors may pay to the shareholders is bounded by two outer limits: First, the dividend may not render the firm insolvent in the sense of being unable to meet its obligations as they become due (this is often called the "equity" definition of bankruptcy). Second, the dividend may not exceed the corporation's Earned Surplus, which is an account on the corporation's balance sheet equal to the sum of all prior earnings minus earlier dividends. Because dividends thus must come out of a fund equal to the sum of prior undistributed earnings, unrealized appreciation on the corporation's assets is normally unavailable to fund dividends. In some jurisdictions, however, it is possible to revalue the assets so as to

---

[189] See A.B.A., Revised Model Business Corporation Act, § 6.21, Official Comment.

place this appreciation in the Capital Surplus account, which account consists basically of all amounts paid into the corporation on the issuance of its shares in excess of each share's "par value." The par value of a share is an amount specified in the corporation's certificate of incorporation (typically, $1.00 or 10per share) for all shares of that class, which amount represents that portion of the consideration received which is permanently committed to the capital of the corporation. The aggregate par value of all issued shares (which amount is in essence the firm's Stated Capital account) may not be invaded to pay dividends. In theory, this capital remains permanently committed to the business as a cushion to protect creditors, but in practice this account is kept small through the use of low par value shares. To illustrate, suppose a corporation issues one thousand shares, each having a $1.00 par value, for $10 each. It will receive $10,000, of which $9,000 will be allocated to Capital Surplus (or Paid–In Capital, as it is sometimes called) and $1,000 to Stated Capital. Assume next that at the end of this corporation's first fiscal year, its income statement shows net earnings of $10,000. This amount will be entered in the Earned Surplus account and will be immediately available for dividends (unless the payment would foreseeably render the corporation unable to pay its debts as they become due). In most jurisdictions, the Capital Surplus account is also available for dividends, at least if the corporation's certificate of incorporation so provides and certain formalities are followed.

The intent of these rules is to protect creditors against the possibility that shareholders will pay large dividends to themselves, thereby stripping the firm of its assets while its debts are still unpaid or at least increasing the level of risk to which its creditors are subject. Of course, creditors could directly contract with the corporation to limit dividends while their loans are outstanding, and frequently they do. Bank loan agreements and bond indentures often contractually restrict the permissible amount of dividends to a level well short of the legally permissible limit. See Chapter 4, Sec. III(A)(5)(b). In most cases, the more restrictive limits imposed by private agreement make the generic restrictions imposed by corporate law irrelevant. Yet, contractual protections may be costly for some, particularly for smaller creditors (such as trade creditors). Possibly then, the legal limit protects these creditors.

A shortcoming of this argument is that a balance sheet test is arbitrary because assets are shown at their historical cost, which may be well below their current market value. For example, suppose a corporation owns a single asset—a building that it rents to others, which it acquired for $1,000,000 and which it could today sell for $20,000,000, but it does not have any earned surplus (that is, its cumulative earnings were earlier distributed as dividends) or Capital Surplus. This corporation could easily borrow $4,000,000 against the building and pay it out as a dividend. Yet, if dividends must be covered by the amounts shown on the corporation's balance sheet in its Earned Surplus and Capital Surplus accounts, it would be improper to pay a dividend here, because the use of historical cost does not reflect unrealized appreciation. Hence, the conservative bias of accounting may unduly restrict the corporation's ability to pay out dividends. For this reason, there has been a movement in "modern" corporation statutes, most notably in California and the Revised Model Business Corporation Act, to drop the balance sheet test and simply require that the directors value the firm's assets and determine that this value exceeds its liabilities (after giving effect to the proposed dividend).[190] In addition, the "equity" test is also retained: the dividend may not render the corporation foreseeably incapable of meeting its liabilities as they mature. This form of statute tends to give creditors somewhat reduced protection, but the underlying judgment may be that most creditors can take care of themselves.

The other major type of legal dispute that recurrently arises regarding dividends is the claim of minority shareholders that a majority faction has suspended the payment of dividends in order to "squeeze out" the minority (i.e., to induce them to sell their shares to the majority at a discount). This could be a realistic concern if the minority faction needed current income from their investment and the majority faction did not (as might be the case where the majority also held jobs with the corporation and thus received salaries). In general, the law gives the board almost complete discretion over whether to pay dividends (within the outer limits of the foregoing tests) or to reinvest earnings in the firm. In the case of the closely held corporation, however, the law of some jurisdictions may provide a remedy if it can be demonstrated to the court's satisfaction that the purpose for withholding dividends was to force some shareholders to sell out cheaply. This "oppression remedy," which is now available under the statutes of many states, entitles the court to order the payment of a dividend or, in an extreme case, to order dissolution of the corporation, if it finds that the majority engaged in "persistent unfairness" or other such oppressive conduct, toward the minority.[191] In the latter case, the majority faction may be given by statute an opportunity to buy out the minority at a judicially approved fair price. This provision in effect converts the liquidation remedy, which is a drastic one that courts are reluctant to utilize, into a buy-out of the dissident faction at a judicially determined price, thereby minimizing the disruption and potential loss of value that may be incident to a judicially ordered liquidation. Generally, the oppression remedy is unavailable in the case of a publicly held corporation, probably on the theory that the availability of a public market provides a superior remedy because other

---

[190] See Revised Model Business Corporation Act, § 6.40. The Official Comment to this section indicates that this revision was part of the statutory movement discussed above to eliminate "par value" and "stated capital" as outmoded.

[191] See, Cal. Corp. Code § 1800(a)(4). See also N.Y. Bus. Corp. Law § 1104–a. The New York statute does not apply to publicly traded corporations and requires that 20% or more of the shareholders join in the petition for judicial dissolution.

potential shareholders are available who do not require current dividend income.

## B.   RETAINED EARNINGS AND CAPITAL GAIN

If a corporation has earned profits in a true economic sense and has paid no dividends, then, all other things equal, the value of its shares should rise by the amount of the retained earnings. (See Chapter 5, Sec. IV.) That increase is called "capital appreciation" or "capital gain." If the shares are not sold, the gain is called unrealized gain or, more popularly, "paper profit." Many people seem to have the notion that paper profit is in some sense unreal. That notion is nonsense. If there is no market for the shares at a price reflecting the supposed gain, then there is simply no gain in any meaningful economic sense. Assuming an available trading market, a gain in the value of the shares of a corporation is just as real as the interest that is credited to a savings account but is not withdrawn. Both are real economic gains readily convertible to cash in hand. The difference between shares of stock and a savings account is that the money value of the shares of stock may decline while the money value of the savings account will not. But the danger that the increase in the value of shares of stock may be lost results from the decision to leave that gain invested instead of cashing in on it. That danger applies equally to the amount initially invested, whose value does not become in any sense less real when it is invested in the shares.

## C.   COMPENSATION FOR SERVICES

Officers and other employees receive returns in the form of salaries, bonuses and other forms of compensation (fringe benefits such as a company car, insurance, etc.) In the small-scale, closely held corporation, such compensation may be used as a substitute for dividends. In fact, there is a large body of tax law dealing with efforts by the Internal Revenue Service to establish that compensation was unreasonably high and that it was therefore a disguised dividend and not a deductible expense of the corporation.

One of the dangers of being a minority shareholder without a guaranteed job with the firm is that the majority shareholders may take their returns in the form of high salaries, leaving little in the way of profits to share with the minority. The courts have shown a singular reluctance to override decisions of boards of directors on matters of compensation, except in the most outrageous cases. Any reasonably competent lawyer, if given the chance by his or her clients, should foresee this potential problem and draft agreements to protect the reasonable expectations of people who may find themselves in the minority position. But clients often are unwilling to pay the cost of drafting, or fail to recognize the need for, such agreements.

Fees may also be paid to directors, but these seem not to have given rise to problems. In public corporations, directors' fees until recently were mostly nominal. People served as directors for the honor, for the contacts, to do a favor for a friend, to pin down a business connection, to gain access to information, and for a variety of other such reasons. Nowadays, fees in public corporations traded on the New York Stock Exchange tend to be more significant (e.g., $30,000 a year for attending, and preparing for, monthly meetings) but for the most part still represent only a small fraction of the director's total income.

## XI.  ADDITIONAL CAPITAL

In the public corporation, needs for additional capital can be met by selling new common stock to the public. Obviously, new shares must be sold at the current market price. This may, of course, be lower or higher than the price at which previously outstanding shares were initially sold. If lower, the new shares will receive a greater percentage interest in the firm per dollar of investment than did the outstanding shares.

In the closely held corporation, the most likely source of additional capital, if it is needed, is the existing shareholders. The problems in raising such capital will be much the same as those encountered in partnerships (see Chapter 2, Sec. VII(D)), except that in the ordinary corporation (that is, in a corporation in which the shareholders have not entered into special agreements) new investors can be brought in without the consent of all the existing investors; if additional shares have been authorized in the certificate of incorporation, all that is needed is a decision by the board of directors to sell new shares, which ordinarily means that the decision is within the control of a majority in interest of the shareholders.

The freedom of a corporation to sell new securities to the public may be limited by "preemptive rights." A preemptive right is a right of a shareholder to buy the same portion of any new issue as he or she holds of the existing stock. State laws vary on whether preemptive rights exist unless the articles of incorporation provide otherwise or whether they exist only if provided for in the articles. In this area, at least, corporate law clearly serves as a model form contract, with the shareholders being entitled to "opt out" of the preemptive right provision if they so choose.

At one time, preemptive rights were thought to be a useful protection against insiders issuing new shares to themselves at a price below their fair value. Nowadays, it is generally thought that the law relating to fiduciary obligations will protect against this danger. In the closely held corporation, a preemptive right may also protect a minority shareholder against the majority shareholders issuing new shares to themselves (at a fair price) in an effort to dilute the minority's voting power (to a point, for example, where the minority no longer has the power to block a transaction requiring a supermajority shareholder vote). Again, fiduciary obligation may provide sufficient protection against this kind of ploy, although the case law in this latter area is not as clearly developed as it is in the case of a below-market bargain-price sale of shares to selected insiders. On the adverse side, preemptive rights can seriously impede the ability of a corporation to engage in legitimate efforts to raise capital from new investors.[192] As a result, most public corporations have eliminated preemptive rights by charter amendments (where state law requires such action). Some modern statutes that create a statutory preemptive right have exempted from their coverage bona fide public offerings of securities and merger and acquisition transactions. This decision reflects a legislative judgment that there is little potential for abuse in such transactions.

## XII.  THE SHAREHOLDER AS LENDER

A person may be both a shareholder and a creditor of a corporation. As a creditor, the person may receive returns in the form of interest payments, while at the same time receiving dividends as a shareholder. Even a person who owns all the common stock of a corporation may also lend it money and become a creditor. This is functionally equivalent to an individual lending money to himself or herself, which most lawyers would find inconceivable, or at least legally meaningless, if done by a sole proprietor. But in the context of the incorporated business the idea seems to be accepted as a matter of course. Such is the power of reification and the wonder of magic. If a corporation becomes insolvent, and if the shareholder/lender has paid attention to all the formalities, then that person is entitled, along with other creditors, to a pro rata share of the assets available to satisfy the claims of all creditors. If the other debt claimants have been at all alert, however, they will have required that the shareholder's debt be subordinated to theirs. A court will sometimes subordinate the shareholder/creditor to other creditors if it finds that the corporation was too "thinly capitalized," which means that it believes more of the shareholder's initial investment in the firm should have been in the form of equity and less in debt, because the corporation had too little chance of paying off all the debt that it had incurred.

## XIII.  FEDERAL INCOME TAX CONSIDERATIONS

### A.  FORMATION

Suppose that Fred owns farmland that he bought several years ago for $100,000 and has used to grow wheat and that he trades this land to

---

[192] In a "subscription offering," the corporation offers shares to its existing shareholders on a *pro rata* basis at a modest discount off the offering price. Typically, it is effected by mailing to shareholders a warrant that entitles them to purchase a specified number of shares at this discount price for a specified period (usually one month). If shareholders do not want to exercise this warrant and make the bargain purchase, they can typically sell the warrant. Such "subscription" or "rights" offerings are common in Great Britain, but less so in the United States, possibly because of the broader participation of public investors in the U.S. securities markets. Such offerings involve delay and cause the corporation to miss short-term "market windows."

another individual for General Motors common stock worth $150,000. That trade would be treated as a taxable exchange, meaning that Fred's gain of $50,000 would be an item required to be reported as income on his individual income tax return.[193]

Now suppose that instead of trading his land for General Motors stock, Fred forms a corporation and contributes the land to the corporation in return for all its common stock. The effect will be that formally Fred will own all the shares of stock of the corporation and the corporation will own the land. Conceptually, there will have been an exchange of the land for the stock in the newly formed corporation, comparable to the exchange of the land for the General Motors stock, and the gain should be taxable. Realistically, however, Fred has merely altered the form of his ownership of the land. This reality has been recognized in the income-tax statute and the gain on the transaction (the transfer of the land to the new corporation) would not be "recognized" (that is, would not be subject to taxation).[194]

## B. SUBSTITUTED ATTRIBUTES

There remains the question of what happens if the property is sold by the corporation. The corporation's "basis" for tax purposes would be the same as Fred's, namely $100,000. The corporation is said to have a substituted basis—substituted from Fred. (Ordinarily, substituted basis is a corollary of a nontaxable exchange.) Thus, if the corporation were to sell the property for $150,000 it would have a gain subject to taxation of $50,000.[195] It can readily be appreciated that the rule providing a substituted basis is needed in order to prevent the use of the corporation as a tax-avoidance device. If the corporation were given a basis of $150,000 for the land (fair market value at the date of transfer), a person like Fred who had decided to sell his land and reinvest the proceeds might first contribute it to a corporation; the corporation could then sell the land without incurring a tax liability and could reinvest the proceeds according to Fred's wishes.

The question that next arises is what happens if Fred sells his stock in the corporation? Fred will have a substituted basis, $100,000, for his

---

[193] Technically, the gain for tax purposes is the "excess of the amount realized ... over the adjusted basis." See Section 1001(a) of the Internal Revenue Code. The amount realized is the value of the GM stock ($150,000). The adjusted basis is the cost of the farmland ($100,000) adjusted for depreciation and other such items. Here the asset is raw land and it is assumed that there have been no adjustments, so the adjusted basis is the same as the initial cost, $100,000.

[194] This result is reached under Section 351(a) of the Code, which provides that "no gain or loss shall be recognized if property is transferred to a corporation by one or more persons ... and immediately after the exchange such person or persons are in control ... of the corporation."

[195] See footnote 152.

stock. That is, his basis in the land will be used as the basis for the stock (for which he exchanged the land in a tax-free transaction). Thus, if Fred were to sell the stock for $150,000 he would have a gain subject to taxation of $50,000. Again, this rule is needed in order to prevent tax avoidance. If Fred were given a basis of $150,000 for the stock, he could avoid a tax on the sale of the land by first contributing the land to a corporation in exchange for its stock and then selling the stock. It should be easy to see, however, that the double substituted basis (corporate and shareholder) has a potential for yielding a double tax on the $50,000 gain, once to the corporation and once to the shareholder.[196]

The rule of substituted basis also applies for purposes of computing the allowance for depreciation. Suppose that the asset is a building instead of land. A building normally has a limited life; it is a wasting asset. Part of its cost can be deducted each year over a number of years specified by the tax law, until the entire cost has been deducted. If, for example, the building had an adjusted basis of $80,000 in Fred's hands, he could deduct a suitable portion each year for some number of years. If the building were contributed to a corporation in return for its common stock in a nontaxable exchange, the corporation's basis would be the same as Fred's, $80,000. If, on the other hand, the building were sold to the corporation for, say, $150,000, in a taxable exchange, Fred would have a gain of $70,000 for tax purposes but the corporation would have a basis of $150,000 for purposes of its depreciation allowance. Needless to say, these competing possibilities create the opportunity for a good deal of imaginative tax planning.

## C.  THE CORPORATION AS A TAXABLE ENTITY

Corporations are treated as separate taxable entities for income-tax purposes. This means that corporations pay a tax on their earnings (at a rate specified for corporations) and that shareholders pay a tax on those earnings when they are distributed as dividends (or dividend equivalents), but not before they are so distributed. Dividend payments are not deductible by the corporation. Thus, to the extent that earnings are distributed to shareholders as dividends, there is a tax on the same earnings at both the individual and the corporate level—though, in partial alleviation of the double tax, dividends are taxed at a rate substantially lower than the rate on other types of income received by individuals.[197] If retained earnings are productively invested, the value of the corporation and, derivatively, the value of the shares of common

---

[196] Of course, if the corporation sold the land before Fred sold the stock, the corporation's value would be diminished by the amount of its tax liability and Fred presumably would not realize $150,000 on the sale of the stock. By the same token, if Fred sold the stock before the corporation sold the land, the buyer of the stock might not be willing to pay $150,000 because of the built-in corporate tax liability. Still, it is not too far off the mark to say that there is a potential double tax.

[197] Code Sec. 1(h)(11), treating dividends as long-term capital gains.

stock of the corporation,[198] should rise. Shareholders can cash in on such gain, without incurring the tax burdens associated with dividend payments, by borrowing against the increased share value (a nontaxable transaction), or by holding their shares until death (when the shares receive a new basis equal to their fair market value at the date of death). To some considerable extent the double tax can be avoided entirely, in small-sized corporations, by making distributions to shareholders in the form of salaries, rents, and interest—which (if reasonable) are deductible by the corporation—rather than in the form of dividends. Certain privately held corporations can also avoid double taxation by electing to be treated as "S" corporations. See discussion of the S election in Subsection E, immediately below. Moreover, closely held firms can now achieve the principal advantage of incorporation—limited liability—without using the corporate form, by organizing as a Limited Liability Company (LLC) (see Chapter 2, Sec. X(B)) or as a Limited Liability Partnership (LLP) (see Chapter 2, Sec. VIII(D)). There are circumstances, however, where small firms may find it advantageous to be taxed as corporations to take advantage of a corporate rate that may be lower than the individual rate.

Thus, the "double tax" of the corporate tax system is, to a considerable extent, extracted only from public corporations and this will be increasingly so as firms take advantage of the new state laws permitting the formation of LLCs and LLPs. As for public corporations, the corporate tax significantly influences financing and investment decisions and dividend policy. These influences are described in Chapter 5, Secs. III(K) and IV(A)(5).

## D. LOSSES

Operating losses suffered by a corporation may be carried back to the preceding two years to offset income of those earlier years and may be carried forward twenty years to offset income in those subsequent years.[199] Such losses may not, however, be used by shareholders in computing their personal tax liability (unless Subchapter S is used). This is the main reason why in recent years certain kinds of investment ventures were organized as partnerships (or limited partnerships) rather than as corporations. For example, one of the important advantages of investments in real estate was that such ventures often generated losses

---

[198] The opportunity to avoid the individual-level tax through corporate retention of earnings is restricted to some degree, for closely held corporations, by a penalty tax on earnings accumulated "beyond the reasonable needs of the business" for the purpose of avoiding shareholder taxation. Sec. 531–533 of the Internal Revenue Code. There is also a penalty tax on the undistributed income of "personal holding companies." Sec. 541 of the Code. Roughly speaking, a personal holding company is a corporation used by one or more individuals to hold passive investments. Personal holding companies have been referred to as "incorporated pocket-books."

[199] Code Sec. 172. Capital losses may be carried back three years and forward five years. Sec. 1212.

for tax purposes (largely because of deductions for depreciation and interest) even though they were profitable from an economic perspective. Before the adoption of the Tax Reform Act of 1986, which contains "passive activity loss" rules that curtail tax shelter investments, investors were able to use the tax losses to offset, or "shelter," income from other sources (such as the practice of medicine or law), but to do so they had to avoid the use of the corporate form of organization.

## E.  "S"  CORPORATIONS

Certain closely held corporations may elect, under Subchapter S of the Code, to be taxed on what amounts to a pass-through or conduit basis. Where the election is in effect, no corporate-level tax is payable and shareholders take into account each year their pro rata share of the corporation's net income or loss (without regard to actual distributions). The Subchapter S election is not available if the corporation has more than 100 shareholders. All shareholders must be individuals or certain simple trusts, and the corporation can have only one class of stock.

# Chapter 4

# BASIC CORPORATE INVESTMENT DEVICES: ECONOMIC ATTRIBUTES AND FORMAL CHARACTERISTICS

## I. INTRODUCTION

In this chapter we will examine terms or concepts that define the basic elements of what is called the *financial structure* of a corporation. The principal focus is on the two classic and most common investment devices, common stock (equity) and bonds or debentures (debt). (Compare Chapter 1, Sec. II(E), discussing debt and equity.) A certificate of common stock is a piece of paper that is tangible evidence of a set of rights, interests, or claims in an incorporated business. It can be thought of as a short-hand expression or symbol for all the rules determining the common shareholder's position in relation to the basic elements that are the bedrock of business organization: risk of loss, return, control, and duration. The same can be said of the piece of paper that we call a bond or debenture. In this chapter we are concerned with the content of financial instruments (common stock and bonds, and certain other instruments such as preferred stock, options, and warrants) and the language and concepts that people use to describe that content. In the next chapter we will begin with an examination of basic principles used in valuation of financial instruments or other assets. Some readers may find it helpful to read that material (in Sec. I of Chapter 5), at least quickly, before starting Sec. III of this chapter. In Chapter 5, following the material on valuation, we will examine the determinants of the relative amounts of debt (bonds and related instruments) and equity (common stock and related instruments) that will be used in financing the business.

Before proceeding, a word of warning and reminder is appropriate. We have already seen (see, especially Chapter 1, Sec. II(G) and Sec. XIII(B)) that simple debt and simple equity are polar cases and that virtually infinite variations are possible as we alter the classic provisions of each type of claim. In this chapter we focus on the classic terms of bonds and common stock, but we must remember that those terms can be varied to suit the needs, tastes, or whims of investors. In fact, a significant number of intelligent, experienced, creative, and highly compensated people spend much of their time in activity that some might think of as fashioning and marketing new financial products. One can also think of their role as finding new ways to define the rights, interests, or claims of the various participants in an economic enterprise—a role much like that of a lawyer who reworks and refines a

240

partnership agreement, a buy-out agreement, or any of the many other agreements defining business relationships.

One final point deserves emphasis. When we examine common stock, bonds, and other securities, particularly in this chapter, we work with abstractions. What is ultimately important, however, is how economic forces and legal rules affect individual human beings. Equity interests in public corporations are held directly by individuals or for their benefit by mutual funds, pension funds, insurance companies, or other intermediaries. Similarly, it is people, not abstractions, who are the source of funds that are lent to corporations. An individual who buys a corporate bond lends directly to the corporation (that is, acquires a debt claim in the corporation, while other individuals, directly or indirectly, acquire equity claims). The individual might lend indirectly to the corporation by investing in a mutual fund, pension fund, or insurance policy. Or the individual can lend money to a bank (that is, make a deposit in or buy a certificate of deposit of the bank), which in turn will lend to the corporation. Especially in thinking about rules that may be thought to protect individuals, and about the emergence of new forms of securities (such as "junk bonds"), it is important to bear in mind the wide variety of institutional intermediaries and mechanisms by which people can and do invest in enterprises. For some purposes, for example, it may be unobjectionable to think simply of a bank lending money to a corporation. For other purposes, however, it may be essential to recognize that the bank is an intermediary through which individuals (depositors and shareholders of the bank) make their funds available to the corporation. Individuals can deposit their money in a bank and earn a modest but secure rate of return, while the bank takes that money, plus the money invested by its shareholders, and lends at a higher rate of return, and with a higher risk, to the corporation. Or the individual can invest in the corporate debt more directly by buying shares in a mutual fund that holds a portfolio of corporate bonds; or invest even more directly by buying the bonds for her or his own personal account. Thus, the terms of investments by individuals are determined not just by the nature of the securities issued by firms seeking funds but also by the relationships between individuals and financial intermediaries. But to avoid delusion, we must keep our eyes on the individuals.

## II. SOME DEFINITIONS

We have previously examined (especially in Chapter 1) concepts of risk, return, control, and duration, and the relationships among them. Compared with the earlier material, the ideas that will be developed here and in subsequent chapters rely less on intuition, experience, and judgment and more on logic and rigorous analysis. That being so, we will require more precise definitions.

## A. EXPECTED RETURN

Expected return is a measure of return that uses rudimentary concepts of probability to take account of risk or uncertainty as to outcome. Technically, expected return is the weighted average (or, if you prefer, arithmetic mean) of all possible outcomes. (The symbol commonly used to denote expected return is $\underline{X}$.)

To illustrate, suppose that you bet $1 on the flip of a coin. If you win, you will have $2, and if you lose, nothing. The expected monetary value of that "investment" is $1, computed as follows:

| Probability | Return | Value |
|:---:|:---:|:---:|
| .5 | $2 | $1 |
| .5 | 0 | 0 |
| 1.0 | | $1 |

Note that here the expected return ignores the amount of the initial investment and thus tells us nothing about profitability. When we are concerned with profit we can use the concept of *expected rate of return,* which is likely to be expressed on an annual basis. Sometimes the term "expected return" is used to refer to rate of return. The meaning should be evident from the context.

Suppose that you buy 100 shares of stock of a corporation that does not pay dividends currently; that you pay $10 per share or $1,000 total; and that you expect to sell at the end of one year. Assume further that your estimate of the prospective sale prices and their probabilities is revealed in the first two columns below, with the corresponding expected return revealed by the third column:

| Probability | Sale Price **Sale Price** (return) | Value |
|:---:|:---:|:---:|
| .20 | $ 900 | $ 180 |
| .50 | 1,000 | 500 |
| .30 | 1,500 | 450 |
| 1.00 | | $1,130 |

The expected return calculation shows that in a statistical or probabilistic sense your investment is expected to yield $1,130, which is the expected return. The expected rate of return is 13 percent ($130 expected end-of-year gain on an investment of $1,000).

Where do these figures come from and how solid are they? The answer to that depends on facts that have not been developed. It is sufficient for our purposes to observe that people do, consciously or unconsciously, make calculations of this sort. Their information may be faulty. They may think in terms of a continuum of probabilities and outcomes or in terms of only two outcomes. The process may to some considerable extent be irrational or nonrational. Still, we need a term to describe the outcome of the process of considering and weighing prospects of various investment possibilities. "Expected return" is such a term.

## B. RISK AND UNCERTAINTY

The word *"risk"* is used in the financial world in two different senses. One should be aware of the confusion that can arise by virtue of the dual meaning.

**1. Volatility Risk.** In much of the professional literature of financial analysis, "risk" refers to the degree of dispersion or variation of possible outcomes. To illustrate, assume that you are confronted with two possible investments whose outcomes, probabilities, and expected returns are as follows:

### INVESTMENT A

| Probability | Outcome Out-come (return) | Value |
|---|---|---|
| .1 | $ 900 | $ 90 |
| .8 | 1,000 | 800 |
| .1 | 1,100 | 110 |
| 1.0 | | $1,000 |

### INVESTMENT B

| Probability | Outcome Out-come (return) | Value |
|---|---|---|
| .3 | $ 0 | $ 0 |
| .4 | 1,000 | 400 |
| .3 | 2,000 | 600 |
| 1.0 | | $1,000 |

The expected return of the two investments is the same but the risk associated with Investment B is much greater than that associated with Investment A. The range or dispersion of possible outcomes for B is greater. It is a potentially more volatile investment. For each investment the expected return or mean (weighted average) ($\underline{X}$) is $1,000. For A, however, the combined chance of a return other than $1,000 is only 20 percent, and the difference between the expected return and extreme outcomes is only $100. For B, on the other hand, the combined chance of a return other than $1,000 is 60 percent and the difference between the expected return and extreme outcomes is $1,000. It can be seen, then, that the concept of volatility, or dispersion, or risk refers to a combination of the probability of deviation from the expected return and the amount of deviation—that is, to the degree of likelihood of receiving more or less than $1,000, and how much more or less. (Note that in the illustrations used above, the distributions of outcomes around the expected return are symmetrical—that is, there is an equal probability of deviation to each side of the expected return and the amount of deviation is the same to each side. This symmetrical kind of distribution has been used only for the sake of simplicity. It is not a necessary feature of the real world or of the analytic model, though it is commonly assumed to be a characteristic of the risks associated with investments in publicly traded common stocks.)

There are several statistical terms that are used to describe relative degrees of volatility (terms such as variance, standard deviation, and coefficient of variation) but we need not be concerned with their definition; they are simply measures of the degree of potential variation of possible outcomes. One investment is said to be more risky than another if the dispersion of potential outcomes is greater. We will refer to this concept of risk as *volatility risk* (recoiling only slightly at the now obvious redundancy of that phrase), though the term more commonly used by financial experts is *variance*.

Some economists have drawn a distinction between risk and uncertainty. "Risk" is then used to refer to variation depending purely on chance (e.g., the outcome of the flip of a coin) or, more broadly, to measurements as to which there is a large body of data or experience so that the probable outcomes can be estimated in a purely mechanical way. "Uncertainty," by contrast, refers to estimates made in situations where there is so little experience that the process of estimation is highly intuitive. It should be apparent from a moment's reflection that the distinction between risk and uncertainty is a fuzzy one and that the two concepts refer to ends of a spectrum. Since the kinds of problems that we will be concerned with are not at either end of that spectrum, we will generally ignore the distinction and treat the two terms as synonymous.

One final point deserves brief mention. In the financial literature, all outcomes are called "probabilities." Thus, for example, a financial analyst would talk about, say, a two percent probability of a certain outcome. In the present discussion, the words "possibility" or "chance" often will be used to refer to such an item of data because those words seem more consistent with common parlance (in which "probable" means more likely than not). They are intended to be synonymous with what a person familiar with statistical concepts and techniques would call a probability.

**2. Default Risk.** In some contexts (especially those outside the realm of formal financial analysis) the term "risk" is used to refer to the possibility of nonpayment of a debt or to the possibility of similar kinds of defaults. Technically, one might argue that the possibility of nonpayment is simply one of a number of possible outcomes, especially when one recognizes the possibility of partial default; that default is in no significant way unique and can fit into the previously developed concepts of risk and expected return; and that accordingly there is no need for a separate concept of *default risk*. The fact is, however, that people in the business and financial world do use a concept that corresponds to default risk and if only for that reason it seems wise that we have a verbal device for easily identifying that concept and distinguishing it from what we have labelled volatility risk.

To illustrate, suppose that a corporation borrows $1,000,000 from a bank for one year at a 10 percent interest rate. Suppose that the lender (the bank) estimates (however uncertainly) that there is a three percent chance that the corporation will become insolvent during the year, in which case the bank will collect nothing; but the bank considers that if that does not happen, it will, at the end of the year, receive the full $1,100,000 to which it is entitled. The expected return (gross) is $1,067,000.[1] The expected rate of return on the initial investment is 6.7 percent. The *promised rate of return* is 10 percent. The difference between the promised rate of return (10 percent) and the expected rate of return (6.7 percent) is 3.3 percent. This is what we will refer to as default risk. Note, however, that in this situation there is more than one possible outcome; there is some volatility risk, albeit a small one, associated with the possibility of default.

Not all calculations of the expected value of a loan will be this simple. The lender may, for example, calculate that there is some chance of complete default and that there are various chances of partial defaults. The concept of default risk as something different from a possible outcome in an expected return calculation then becomes more difficult to maintain. Nonetheless, we have the verbal tools to help us avoid confusion if we are careful.

## C. YIELD

Yield is the rate of return that will be earned by a lender if the full amount of interest and principal that the borrower has agreed to pay are paid on schedule. It is a promised rate of return. The concept is easy to understand where the loan is initially made at par—that is, where the amount that is loaned and the amount that is to be repaid at the end of the loan period are the same. For example, a person may lend money to a corporation by buying a bond from it. Suppose the bond requires the company to pay $1,000 at the end of 10 years and in the meantime to

[1]

| Probability | Return | Value |
|---|---|---|
| .03 | $ 0 | $ 0 |
| .97 | 1,100,000 | 1,067,000 |
| 1.00 | | $1,067,700 |

pay interest of $100 per year at the end of each year. This will be thought of as a $1,000 denomination bond and the certificate will probably feature that number prominently. The original purchaser may actually pay $1,000 for the bond, in which case it is said that the bond is bought by the individual investor (lender) and sold by the company (borrower) at par. In this case, the yield would be 10 percent.

Suppose, however, that the $1,000 denomination, 10 year bond is initially bought (and sold) for $900—that is, for less than par. Now the purchaser will receive an annual interest payment of $100 on an investment of $900. This rate of return is about 11 percent. This 11 percent is referred to as the *current yield*. The current yield is the promised interest payment as a percentage of the initial investment. It is of some significance for tax purposes (for relatively small loans) and for people concerned with cash flow. It does not reveal total yield, since the initial investment is $900 and at maturity the borrower must pay $1,000. This difference of $100 is obviously part of the investor's total return, part of the true yield, which is often called *yield to maturity*. (When the word "yield" is used alone, it means yield to maturity, or total yield.) Calculation of yield is a bit complicated, because of problems of compound interest. Holding everything constant but the passage of time, the bond will become more valuable each year as it comes closer and closer to maturity—closer and closer, that is, to the day when the holder will receive the full $1,000. But the change does not occur at a steady rate of $10 per year; it is lower in the early years and higher in the later years. The yield can be calculated from a complex formula, from special tables, or with an inexpensive pocket calculator. The yield on the bond in the present example happens to be 11.72 percent. It is worth emphasizing that the yield reflects the promised rate of return, not the expected rate of return. One would think that an investor might be more interested in the expected rate than in the promised rate. The fact is, however, that the lingo of the marketplace for bonds does not include the phrase "expected rate of return." Instead, we find a concept called "risk premium" that serves much the same function. Risk premium is described immediately below, but it is worth noting here that knowledge of the risk premium does not permit precise calculation of expected rate of return.

## D.  RISK PREMIUM

In the financial literature relating to bonds, one encounters an essentially empirical concept called "risk premium." Risk premium is defined as the difference between the yield on a particular obligation and the prevailing market rate (yield) on an obligation with identical characteristics but with no risk of default. The most important characteristics that must be held constant (identical) in comparing a risky and a risk-free obligation are duration or maturity date and callability (a term that refers to the circumstances in which the borrower is allowed to pay off the loan before maturity and thus deprive the lender of a favorable investment—see Sec. III(A)(5) below).

For example, suppose that a noncallable corporate bond pays 10 percent annually while a U. S. Treasury bond with the same maturity date (and noncallable by custom) pays 6.5 percent. The risk premium is 3.5 percent. This risk premium compensates both for default risk and for the volatility risk associated with default risk. Since the compensation for the latter risk may be negligible, however, most of the risk premium may represent compensation for default risk. Presumably this is the reason why some of the financial literature seems to assume that risk premium is comprised of nothing but compensation for default risk.

Compensation for volatility risk associated with default risk is discussed in the next section. Before proceeding, however, it will be worthwhile to distinguish this kind of risk from volatility risk associated with changes in the market rate of interest. If the Treasury sells a one-year note with a yield of 6 percent and the next day the market rate on such notes, responding to previously unforeseen factors, rises to 7 percent, the market price of the 6 percent note will decline from its original price. If the market rate of interest falls to 5 percent, the price of the 6 percent note will rise. With any given change in the market rate of interest, the amount of change in the value of existing obligations will depend on the length of time to maturity. The longer the duration of an obligation, the more its market price will change with any change in the market rate of interest. Accordingly, the volatility of the price of long-term obligations is greater than that of short-term obligations. At one time it was widely thought that the rate paid on long-term obligations would therefore necessarily be higher than that on comparable short-term obligations. One way of expressing this thought is to say that there must be a premium to compensate for the greater potential price volatility of long-term obligations. This is sometimes referred to as an illiquidity premium, the thought being that long-term obligations are less liquid (less close to cash) than short-term obligations and that there is an added amount, a premium, in the long-term interest rate, to compensate for this illiquidity. Another expression of the same idea focuses on the price of the obligation rather than the interest rate. If the interest payment is held constant (equal) as between two obligations, and if people prefer the more liquid (shorter-term) obligation, then they will pay a price premium for it compared with the longer-term obligation. Thus, we get the phrase "liquidity premium," referring to price, which corresponds to "illiquidity premium," referring to interest rate. If you think this can get confusing, you're right, but the confusion is trivial and usually can readily be cleared up.

In recent years, considerable doubt has arisen over whether there is in fact any such premium. It has been observed, for example, that illiquidity is a two-way street. The person who is seeking long-term income stability from his or her investments may want to "pin down the interest rate." That kind of investor will actually prefer the long-term obligation, and if such investors are sufficient in numbers they may not only eliminate any illiquidity (rate) premium but drive the short-term rate above the long-term rate.

## E. RISK AVERSION

Suppose that a fairy princess has bestowed upon you a certificate that gives the holder the right to receive $1,000,000 if he or she correctly calls the flip of a coin. Unless you believe in special psychic powers, and if you assume that the coin flip will be done fairly, you will perceive that the outcome of the flip is a random event and that what the certificate provides is precisely a 50 percent chance of receiving $1,000,000. Since there is a 50 percent chance of receiving $1,000,000 and a 50 percent chance of receiving nothing, the expected return on the certificate is $500,000.[2] Suppose that you are free to sell the certificate. Would you be willing to accept less than $500,000 for it? If you are like most other people, the answer will be "Yes." In the financial and economic literature your attitude is called *risk aversion*. You dislike taking risks and will pay some price to avoid them.

Suppose that after you have given the matter considerable thought, you conclude that you would be willing to accept $400,000 for the certificate; but you would not accept a penny less than that. You are willing to accept a certain return of $400,000 in exchange for a risky expected return of $500,000. The $400,000 is said to be the *certainty equivalent* of the risky $500,000. (For further discussion of the use of certainty equivalent, and a comparison with risk-adjusted interest rate, see Ch. 5, Sec. I(E).)

Note carefully that what this illustration is designed to demonstrate is the effect of volatility risk, not default risk. The figure of $500,000 (expected return) fully accounts for the possibility of the zero outcome (which can be analogized to default risk). The difference between the $500,000 and the $400,000 is associated solely with volatility risk. To drive this point home, consider a variation on the facts we have used. Suppose that there has been a lottery in which there are several rounds of picking fewer and fewer potentially winning tickets and suppose there are now only two tickets left, one of which will win the $1,000,000 prize and the other of which will receive nothing. The winning ticket will be selected, purely by chance, in five minutes. Obviously the two tickets together are worth $1,000,000. Suppose you own one of the tickets and cannot communicate with the owner of the other. You might be willing to sell your ticket for $400,000. The owner of the other ticket might

| | Probability | Outcome | Value |
|---|---|---|---|
| [2] Following the approach used earlier in this Chapter, the calculation would be: | .5 | $1,000,000 | $500,000 |
| | .5 | 0 | 0 |
| | 1.0 | | $500,000 |

similarly be willing to sell for $400,000. The total "discount" of $200,000 for risk aversion must be associated solely with volatility risk, since the two tickets together plainly have no default risk. (By the way, note the opportunity here for what might be called "risk arbitrage." A person with cash of $800,000 who could buy both tickets would make a fast profit of $200,000.)

A critical axiom of modern investment analysis is that in their major investment decisions the overwhelming majority of people are risk averse. One corollary is that investors will accept volatility risk only if they are paid to do so. The amount they must be paid to accept volatility risk is sometimes called a risk premium. As suggested earlier (Section II(B) of this Chapter), the use of this term can be confusing since the same term is used to refer to an amount paid to compensate for default risk. Usually one can determine from the context the sense in which the term is being used. Another corollary of the risk aversion axiom is that the higher the risk the higher the return. Another, that as between two investments of equal return, people will prefer the one with the lower risk. Still another, that as between two investments of equal risk, people will prefer the one with the higher return.

The notion of a certainty equivalent is one way of taking account of risk, in an effort to permit comparison of investments with different degrees of risk. The more traditional way of accounting for the difference in risk among investments is to adjust the interest rate upward (or downward) to take account of increased (or decreased) risk—that is, to use a *risk-adjusted interest rate*. This approach was used in Sec. II(D) above. The two methods are further discussed and compared in Chapter 5, Sec. I(E).

## F. COMPENSATION FOR VOLATILITY RISK

It may be useful to digress slightly at this point and discuss briefly the idea of compensating people for volatility risk. Modern theory tells us that investors are compensated only for volatility risk that cannot be avoided by diversification.

Suppose, for example, that we compare two obligations, one issued by the U.S. Treasury and one by X Corporation, providing for payment of $100,000 one year hence, with no interest payment (so that they will be sold at a discount).[3] Assume that the obligations are identical in all respects except that there is a 3 percent chance of total default on the X Corporation obligation. Thus, the expected return on the Treasury obligation is $100,000 (the promised amount) and the expected return on the X Corporation obligation is $97,000 (the promised amount, $100,000,

---

[3] The reason for using noninterest-bearing obligations (usually called "discount notes") in this illustration is to avoid computational complexity that otherwise arises from the fact that default relates to interest as well as to principal. Compare Sec. II(B)(2) (second paragraph), above.

reduced by the 3 percent chance of default). If market rate for one-year risk-free obligations is 6 percent, the Treasury obligation should sell for $94,339.62 ($100,000/1.06). Assume that the X Corporation obligation is also priced to produce an expected yield of 6 percent. On that assumption, it will sell for $91,509.43 ($97,000/1.06). At that price its expected yield will be the same as that of the Treasury obligation—namely, 6 percent. Suppose that these are the only two kinds of debt obligations available on the market. The Treasury obligation has a certain (risk-free) yield of 6 percent. The X Corporation obligation has an expected yield of 6 percent, but with 3 percent chance of paying nothing at the end of the year and a 97 percent chance of paying the promised amount. If you are an ordinary investor, which investment would you prefer at the assumed prices? Your answer should be, the Treasury obligation. (If this was not your answer, review Sec. II(E), immediately above.) Both obligations have the same expected yield, but the X Corporation's obligation has some volatility risk and the Treasury obligation does not. Since most investors are risk averse, they will prefer the Treasury obligation to the X Corporation obligation. Once the Treasury rate is established, if X Corporation expects to sell its obligation, it will be required to lower the price, at least by some small amount, so that the expected yield will be slightly higher than the 6 percent expected yield on the Treasury obligation. In other words, X Corporation must lower the price of its obligation to compensate not only for default risk but for volatility risk as well.

Now let's drop the assumption that only these two obligations are available. Assume that a large number of corporate obligations are available. Assume, further, that each of these obligations has a 3 percent chance of default, but that the corporations have nothing in common that would lead one to predict that if one defaults others will default. In other words, the risk of default is random or uncorrelated as between corporations (a slightly unrealistic assumption). Now suppose that an investor can buy 100 different $1,000 obligations of 100 different companies, each with a 3 percent risk of default, and that the transactions cost of doing so is no greater than the cost of buying a single $100,000 obligation. With 100 different corporate obligations it may be possible to predict with reasonable assurance that 3 of the corporations will default and 97 of them will pay at the promised rate, so that on the entire $100,000 portfolio (that is, on the set of 100 separate $1,000 obligations) the expected return is virtually equivalent to a certain $97,000. In that situation, investors should be willing to accept a 6 percent expected yield on each of the $1,000 obligations. If the expected yield on such obligations were higher than 6 percent (that is, if the price were lower than $91,509.43), investors would bid for them until the price rose to the point ($91,509.43) where the rate fell to 6 percent.

## III.　TYPES OF SECURITIES: FORMAL AND FUNCTIONAL CHARACTERISTICS

### A.　BONDS, DEBENTURES, AND NOTES

**1.　Preface.** The objective of the following discussion of bonds and debentures is twofold: first, to describe the basic elements of these securities and the terms that are used to describe those elements; and second, to examine some of the relationships between investors with different claims in the firm—more particularly, relationships between lenders and equity investors. The second objective accounts for some discussion (especially of callability, sinking funds, and risk-control relationships) that is outside the boundaries of traditional discussions of debt obligations and that would otherwise be excessive in the present work.

The description that follows focuses on traditional obligations, with fixed claims to interest and principal and fixed duration. In recent years there has been considerable innovation with respect to the interest rate (for example, with floating rate obligations) and duration (for example, with puttable and extendible obligations). These innovative obligations are now an important part of the market for newly issued debt, but still account for far less dollar amount than traditional obligations. The innovations will be described briefly at the end of this section (see Section III(A)(20)).

**2.　Some Basic Attributes.** Bonds and debentures are manifestations of commitments of funds to a firm for a relatively long period of time (generally, five years or more). Shorter-term obligations are usually referred to as notes. The commitment reflected in the bonds and debentures is, however, of limited duration: there is a fixed date, called the *maturity date*, at which the firm must pay the principal sum. This will seldom be more than 30 or 40 years in the future and generally will be sooner.

A long-term obligation secured by a mortgage on some property of the issuer is generally referred to as a *bond*, while a long-term unsecured obligation is generally referred to as a *debenture*. In the financial literature and in this book, the distinction is sometimes ignored, or rejected, and the term "bond" is often used to refer to both types of obligation. When we speak of a corporation selling or issuing bonds to the public, what we mean is that the corporation is borrowing money from people and that those people may receive a fancy certificate as tangible evidence of the corporation's obligation to pay interest, to repay principal, and to abide by certain terms and conditions that are spelled out in part on the certificate and more fully elsewhere. Ordinarily a person who owns a bond (that is, a creditor with a set of rights normally associated with bonds) can sell the bond to any other person for any price they agree upon. Corporate bonds and debentures are usually issued in *denominations* of $1,000, though, as we have seen, they will not necessarily be sold at that price. (See Sec. II(C) of this Chapter, discussing yield.) The denomination, *face value,* or *par value,* of a bond may be thought of, then, simply as the amount that must be paid on maturity (that is, at the end of the term of the loan). Regardless of the face value or denomination of the bond, the price quoted in the financial pages will be the price per $100 face value. Thus, if one reads that the price of a bond is 98½, one would normally assume that the bond is in the denomination of $1,000 and that consequently the price is $985.

A bond will manifest the borrower's obligation to pay a *fixed* amount of *interest* at regular intervals (commonly every six months) as well as to pay the face amount at maturity. The total annual interest payment, when expressed as a percentage of the face amount or denomination, is the nominal interest rate (as distinguished from the true interest rate or yield, which will be different if the bond is not bought and sold at par). This nominal interest rate is sometimes called the *coupon rate.* Thus, if a bond obligates a company to pay $85 per year and $1,000 at maturity, the coupon rate would be 8.5 percent; the original sale price and the current market price do not affect the coupon rate. The term coupon rate is a relic of an era when a purchaser of a bond usually received a large, sturdy piece of paper, part of which was divided into small segments called coupons, each of which reflected the obligation of the borrowing company to pay a fixed amount of money (the interest payment) on a particular date, with one coupon for each interest payment date. The owner of the bond collected interest by cashing in the appropriate coupon, usually at a bank. These days, most bonds are registered; the owner's name is registered with the debtor company and the interest payment goes in the mail by check to the registered owner. The term coupon rate is still widely used, however, and reveals the annual dollar amount that the borrower is required to pay. With that information, the current price of the bond, and the length of time to maturity, one can calculate yield.

The *duration* of a bond is a more complex concept than one might imagine. Suppose there are two $1,000 bonds, each with a maturity date ten years hence. Bond *A* pays interest of $100 per year while Bond *B* pays interest of $200 per year. Suppose that because Bond *B* has a much higher risk of default than Bond *A*, the two bonds sell for the same price. At a naive level it may be thought that the two bonds have the same duration, since they are both scheduled for redemption at the end of ten years. A more sophisticated, and more accurate, measure of duration takes account of the difference in promised cash payments. Bond *B*'s cash payments are weighted more heavily toward the early years than Bond *A*'s, and for purposes of comparison of the two bonds, this difference must be taken into account. In sophisticated market analysis of debt obligations, the concept of duration that is used is a weighted average of the time to each cash payment, so Bond $B$'s duration is shorter than Bond $A$'s. This approach is part of a broader perspective on analysis of debt a perspective in which each payment—each interest payment and the principal payment at maturity—is seen as a separate obligation.

**3. Public Versus Private Ownership.** Debt may be issued to, and held by, a large number of people or institutions—that is, it may be "publicly issued" and held. The issuance of debt to the "public" [4] will require, among other things, the filing of a registration statement with the SEC and the use of investment bankers and brokers to sell the securities (or, if you will, to find the lenders). The holders of the debt generally will not know each other or communicate effectively among themselves. The basic terms of the debt, such as duration, interest rate, and the call feature (described below), generally will be worked out by the issuer and the investment banker. Other terms, such as the duties of the indenture trustee (described below), the manner in which the call feature is exercised, and the manner of calculating any limitation on the payment of dividends, will tend to follow standardized forms. Innovations as to details, though perhaps important to particular borrowers (issuers), and potentially acceptable to the well-informed public investors, will be costly to adopt.

Where special circumstances call for the negotiation of nonstandardized terms, the borrower may find it advantageous to use a private placement—that is, to borrow from a single lender or a small number of lenders. The lender may be a wealthy individual or a partnership of wealthy individuals, a mutual fund, an insurance company, or a savings and loan institution. Private placements, which are widely used, not only avoid some of the costs of registration with the SEC, and certain administrative costs, but also allow the issuer and the lender to bargain in ways that benefit both. For example, an issuer seeking a loan that will have a high risk of default may be willing to agree to maintain a certain ratio of assets to liabilities.[5] In return for that agreement, the lender may be willing to accept a lower rate of interest than would otherwise be required. Both the borrower and the lender may consider themselves better off with the combination of the financial-ratio obligation and the lower interest rate than without it. In a public placement it might be impossible to convey to the potential buyers of the debt an adequate

---

[4] The term "public" in the context does not imply individuals. The fact is that most publicly issued corporate bonds (especially high-yield, or "junk," bonds) are held by institutions such as mutual funds, pension funds, savings and loan institutions, and insurance companies. See United States, General Accounting Office, Report, Financial Markets: Issuers, Purchasers, and Purposes of High Yield, Non-Investment Grade Bonds, page 20 (Feb. 29, 1988).

[5] Failure to maintain the ratio would be an act of default, which ordinarily would make the debt due and payable. A borrower that has failed (or is about to fail) to maintain the ratio, might, in order to avoid the consequences of the failure, be forced to raise new equity capital or to grant some new concession to the lender.

understanding of the nature or the importance of the issuer's obligation. Thus, the issuer's willingness to accept a financial-ratio burden might not be met by a sufficient willingness on the part of the buyers to accept a lower interest rate. Moreover, the borrower might be reluctant to agree to a tough obligation without some realistic prospect of negotiation with the lender of some relief (that is, some alternative to default) in the event the obligation is not met, and such negotiation may not be feasible (and possibly not legally permissible [6]) when the debt is publicly held. This observation suggests another general advantage to private placements: the greater ability to negotiate changes in the obligation when circumstances change.

As one might expect, the public-versus-private dichotomy, like most dichotomies, can be misleading: problems of coordination among holders increase gradually as the number of holders increases. Moreover, in many cases, where debt is initially issued to a small number of holders, those holders may contemplate selling some or all of the obligations to larger numbers of investors in the near or distant future. Where that is so, the initial holders, though small in number, may bargain for terms that will be suitable for public offerings.

**4. The Rise of the Original–Issue High–Yield, or "Junk," Bond.** "Junk bond" is a misleading but widely used label for high-yield bonds. The yield on such bonds is high compared with the yield on "investment grade" bonds. An investment grade bond is one that has been "rated" (by a commercial rating service) as having a low credit risk (that is, a low risk of default). Generally, investment grade bonds are issued by the largest corporations. Some high-yield bonds are "fallen angels"—that is, bonds that had been low in risk, and yield, when issued but had become higher in risk and yield as a result of a decline in the fortunes of the issuer. There is also a more substantial market for original-issue high-yield bonds—that is, bonds (and debentures and notes) issued to raise money for a firm for any of a variety of purposes.

In the early years of their use, high-yield bonds were issued primarily by modest-sized, "emerging" corporations—though these were generally well-established companies with substantial assets. Before the development of the original-issue high-yield bond market, the principal source of loans for such firms had been commercial banks or insurance companies, which sometimes imposed on the borrowers restrictions and conditions far more onerous than those commonly found in high-yield bonds and, more important, were generally unwilling to lend long term at fixed rates. Thus, high-yield bonds have been called "securitized commercial loans."

In 2001 the amount raised by high-yield new issues was $83.5 Billion, which was 17 percent of the total of all new issues of debt. The total value of high-yield debt outstanding was about $580 Billion, which

---

[6] See infra Sec. III(A)(6).

was also about 17 percent of the total debt outstanding. Most high-yield debt is held by institutions such as pension funds, insurance companies, and mutual funds. During the period 1985–2001 the average annual return for high-yield debt was 10.54 percent.[7]

**5. Covenants and the Indenture.** *Covenants* are the agreements or obligations of the issuer. They are contained in a document called the *indenture.*

Where bonds are sold to the public, the terms of the indenture must comply with a federal statute called the Trust Indenture Act of 1939. Most of the terms of the indenture will be what lawyers call "boiler-plate"—that is, language that follows an established form—but some terms may be the subject of negotiation. Once bonds have been sold to the public, the job of protecting the interests of the bondholders, of enforcing their rights under the indenture, will fall to an institution called the *indenture trustee,* ordinarily a bank which is appointed at the time of issuance of the bond and which must meet certain requirements of the Trust Indenture Act (where it is applicable).

The general function of the covenants may be thought of as protection or enhancement of the lender's "equity cushion." The equity cushion is simply the amount of the equity, which can be thought of as protecting the lender from loss. For example, if you buy a house for $100,000, with $20,000 of your own money and a loan of $80,000, the lender's equity cushion is your $20,000. If you default on your obligation to make payments on the loan, and the house is sold in a foreclosure, the lender is entitled to satisfy its claim (to the extent of the $80,000 plus unpaid interest) before you get anything. It should be obvious that the bigger the equity cushion, the less the risk of default or of loss if there is a default and, consequently, the better off the lender is. The equity cushion will rise or fall as the value of the house rises or falls and will rise as you pay off the loan bit by bit. If you fail to maintain the house, its value, and the size of the equity cushion, will decline, which will make the lender unhappy. Consequently, the lender may require that you agree (or, to use the quaint language of the law, covenant) to maintain the house. You may be happy to agree to that or you may be unwilling to admit to the lender that you are not.

Among the covenants found in corporate indentures are the following:[8]

---

[7] See Martin S. Fridson, The Year in High Yield—2001, in the Merrill Lynch & Co. publication Extra Credit 3, 20, 37 (January/February 2002).

[8] See Revised Model Simplified Indenture, by the Ad Hoc Committee for Revision of the 1983 Model Simplified Indenture (2000); Model Negotiated Covenants and Related Definitions, by the Committee on Trust Indentures and Indenture Trustees,

ABA Section of Business Law, 61 The Business Lawyer 1439 (2006). A well-known article on bond covenants identifies "four major sources of conflict which arise between bondholders and stockholders" with which covenants are concerned. Clifford T. Smith, Jr. and Jerold B. Warner, *On Financial Contracting: An Analysis of Bond Covenants,* 7 J. Financial Econ. 117, 118–19 (1979). These are "dividend payment,"

a) *Maintenance of property, etc.* A standard provision in the case of debt (including bank loans) secured by property requires that the borrower maintain the property in good condition, repair it, insure it, etc. The borrower will also agree to pay taxes, maintain adequate liability insurance, keep accurate and complete records, and submit reports. These kinds of provisions are "boilerplate"; they are generally accepted as a matter of course and tend to be stated in time-honored language.[9]

b) *Restriction on dividend payments.* Under state corporate law, dividends will not be permitted where the effect would be to render the corporation insolvent and in certain other extreme situations. A common form of indenture restriction will limit dividends to some specified dollar amount, called "the dip" (typically one year's profits), plus profits (or some percentage thereof) after the "peg date" (usually nine months before the date of issuance of the bond), plus any amounts raised by selling new equity. Sometimes the restriction will be tailored more precisely to maintaining an equity cushion—for example, by prohibiting a dividend if, after its payment, debt would exceed 35 percent of net tangible assets or some specified dollar amount. "Dividend" is generally defined to include other transfers from the corporation to the shareholders, such as repurchases of shares. Note that a dividend restriction in connection with currently issued debt may benefit previously issued debt as well, but that any added protection of the old debt continues only as long as the new debt continues to be outstanding.

c) *Restrictions on additional debt.* The issuance of additional debt will generate proceeds that will result in a corresponding increase in the value of the issuing corporation. Still, the additional debt will result in an increase in leverage. As new debt is issued, the size of the equity cushion in relation to the size of the total debt will decline, and the risk of insolvency will increase. Moreover, managers of a firm may use new money to invest in ventures that they cannot operate effectively. Thus, there may be good reasons to impose any of a wide variety of restrictions on the issuance of new debt, subject to any of a wide variety of possible exceptions. The limitation on

---

"claim dilution" (issuance of "additional debt of the same or higher priority"), "asset substitution" (substitution of high-variance for low-variance investments); (see Sec. III(A)(13)), and "underinvestment" (see Sec. III(A)(14)). For a "comprehensive analysis of the pricing and usage of bond covenants," see Sudheer Chava, Praveen Kumar, and Arthur Warga, Agency Costs and the Pricing of Bond Covenants (October 2004), available at SSRN: http://ssrn.com/abstract=611801.

On the use of restrictive covenants in publicly traded bonds, see Morey W. McDaniel, *Bondholders and Corporate Governance*, 41 Bus. Lawyer 413 (1986)(little use of covenants restricting dividends and additional debt); Laurentius Morais, Katherine Schipper, and Abbie Smith, *Wealth Effects of Going Private for Senior Securities*, 23 J. Financial Econ. 155 (1989)(little use of covenants restricting additional debt).

[9] See Richard T. Nassberg, The Lender's Handbook (1986).

new debt also is likely to be applicable to long-term leases, which create obligations similar to those associated with debt. The limitation on the issuance of new debt, combined with a limitation on share redemptions, may be especially important in protecting debtholders from substantial increases in leverage and risk that are often the byproduct of a leveraged buyout. New debt may be prohibited absolutely or unless certain financial conditions are met (e.g., maintenance of the equity cushion or of a ratio of cash flow to interest charges). Alternatively, a covenant may provide that any new debt must be subordinated to the existing debt, just as a second mortgage home loan is subordinated to the first mortgage (in the event of default, the second mortgage lender is not entitled to any payment until the first mortgage lender's claim is fully satisfied). Or there may be a limitation on total debt, so that new debt can be incurred only to the extent that old debt is retired (that is, paid off).

d) *The negative pledge clause.* With unsecured debt, a commonly used provision is the negative pledge clause, which limits the ability of the issuer to issue new debt with a security interest in already-owned property that will result in the new debt ranking above the existing unsecured debt. Typically, the clause provides that the issuer may not mortgage its assets without providing equal security to the debt containing the negative pledge clause, subject to certain exceptions, such as for purchase-money debt (that is, debt incurred in purchasing, and secured by, new property). Negative pledges are widely used, in lieu of mortgages, which may be considered too cumbersome. Use of the negative pledge clause in publicly issued debt has been criticized on the ground that when the corporation is doing well it is unnecessary and when it is doing badly it may harm the debtholders, as well as the equityholders, by limiting flexibility in solving financial problems.[10]

e) *Prohibitions or limitations on mergers and changes in voting control.* The indenture may prohibit mergers, out of concern for possible adverse effects on the safety of the debt. In the presence of such a prohibition, a corporation that is intent on engaging in a merger will be required to pay off (redeem) the debt, subject to the terms of the call provision (described below), which generally will require the payment of some premium. Alternatively, the indenture may permit a merger only if the surviving corporation assumes all the obligations of the issuing corporation, in a manner satisfactory to the indenture trustee, and meets all the financial conditions imposed by the debt. Still another alternative is a right of the bondholders to have the bonds redeemed (at par or a slight premium) in the event of a merger or in the event that the ratings of the

[10] See Morey W. McDaniel, *Are Negative Pledge Clauses in Public Debt Issues Obsolete? 38 Bus. Lawyer 867 (1983).*

bonds are lowered following a merger or in the event of a change in control (e.g., where one person acquires shares with more than 20 percent of the voting power).[11] Such a provision can protect debtholders from the potentially adverse effects of a takeover or leveraged buyout that increases leverage (though there may be better ways to provide such protection), but can also function in a manner similar to a poison pill (see Chapter 3, Sec. IV(C)(4)) [12] or a state's control share acquisition rules (see Chapter 3, Sec. II(B)(1)) to protect incumbent management from hostile takeovers.

f) *Maintenance of financial condition or equity cushion.* The issuer may be required to maintain a specified dollar amount of equity, a specified ratio of cash flow to interest expense, a specified ratio of assets to debt, or some other measure of financial well-being. The failure to meet such conditions can be treated as an act of default, with the debt becoming due and payable.  Another, more recent, variation provides that if a financial condition is not met for, say, two fiscal quarters, the issuer must offer to buy some portion (e.g., 10 percent) of the outstanding obligations at par plus accrued interest. A requirement that the corporation meet a financial condition may force it to issue new equity, at whatever price can be obtained in the market.  The resulting increase in the equity cushion (restoring that cushion to the minimum level contemplated in the covenant) may cause a wealth shift from equityholders to debtholders by "buoying up" the debt (that is, by increasing the value of the debt as a result of increasing the equity cushion and reducing the probability of default)—or, if you prefer, may prevent or remedy a wealth shift from the debtholders to the equityholders. (See Sec. III(A)(14) and (15) below.)

g) *Same business.* At least in small-firm financing, the borrower may agree that it will continue to "engage in business in the same manner and in substantially the same fields of enterprise as conducted by it on the date that the loan agreement took effect." [13] Similarly, the borrower may be subject to other limitations affecting the operation of the business, such as a maximum permissible level of capital expenditure,[14] or a prohibition on the sale of substantially all of the debtor's property, except in the ordinary course of business. The terms of the loan, in some cases, may go so far as to treat as a default "any material adverse change in the business or prospects of the company."

---

[11] This kind of protection may not be effective, however, where, before a merger, the bonds bore a favorable interest rate and sold at a premium.

[12] Thus, this kind of provision is sometimes called a "poison put."

[13] Robert J. Haft, Venture Capital and Small Business Financing 3–34 (1988 Revision).

[14] Id. at 3–42.

h) *Others*. Other provisions include those imposing limitations on optional redemptions of other debt, prohibition of sale of assets (or sale and leaseback), and the bondholder option to demand redemption in the event of a change of control of the company (the so-called bondholder "poison put").

While it should be plain from this description that lawyers have devised techniques for providing strong protection to bondholders, the fact is that in most publicly issued debt of major corporations there is not even a restriction on additional debt or on dividend payments; bondholders are "essentially unprotected."[15] Non-investment-grade, high-yield bonds, on the other hand, generally do contain substantial restrictive covenants.

**6.  Subordination.** Debt is often issued in layers of priority, with some debt subordinated to other debt, which may in turn be subordinated to a higher level of debt. Subordination is an important feature of corporate debt and raises some complex issues.

To illustrate, suppose a corporation has issued senior debt (SD) and junior debt (JD), with the JD subordinated to the SD, and both the SD and the JD unsecured. Suppose the corporation has also incurred trade debt (TD), that the corporation files for bankruptcy, and that there is no other debt outstanding. The holders of the SD, JD, and TD are all entitled to share ratably (according to the amount of their respective claims) in the assets of the corporation, but the subordination agreement survives the bankruptcy, so the SD becomes entitled not only to its share but also to the share allocated to the JD (up to an amount necessary to fully satisfy the SD claim). The right of the SD to the JD entitlement is sometimes called the "double dip" or "double dividend" benefit.[16]

A number of important issues must be addressed in drafting a subordination agreement. Among these are, first, what claims of the SD qualify for the subordination benefit? Does the claim extend to accrued interest? What happens if the SD is refinanced? Second, if there is a default on the SD, must the SD accelerate its claim and seek to enforce its rights and, if so, within what period of time? The provision covering this issue is sometimes referred to as the "fish or cut bait" provision.

---

[15] Morey W. McDaniel, *Bondholders and Corporate Governance,* 41 Bus. Lawyer 413, 426 (1986).

[16] One interesting way to achieve subordination is through the use of a chain of holding companies. The lower in the chain the greater the seniority. For example, Holding Company Top (HCT) issues debt and equity to the public. Its sole asset is the entire equity in Holding Company Bottom (HCB), which also issues debt to the public. HCB holds all the equity in Operating Company (OC), which has no debt but has all the operating assets. If OC is liquidated, the proceeds go first to HCB, with anything left over going to HCT. Thus, the debt holders of HCB must be paid off before the debt holders of HCT receive anything. This method of subordination may have the advantage of reducing bankruptcy costs. See Merrill Lynch High Yield Research Department, Analysts' Forum, *A Case of Capital Market Structure?* in Extra Credit (Merrill Lynch) 16 (March/April 1992) and Mailbox, Extra Credit 36 (May/June 1992).

Third, what happens if there is a default on the JD? Does the JD have the right to force the debtor corporation into bankruptcy, even if there is no default on the SD and the holders of the SD would prefer to allow the debtor to work its way out of the default? Fourth, is the SD required to share the benefit of subordination with other lenders? Fifth, is the SD entitled to the benefit of any subordination that the JD may enjoy with respect to lower layers of debt? Sixth, what are the "trigger events" that prevent further payments from the corporation to the JD?

**7.  Amendments and Exchange Offers.** Generally the indenture will provide for amendments. Some minor amendments may require the approval only of the indenture trustee, while others may require approval of the majority in interest (or possibly some higher percentage) of the debtholders.

Under the Trust Indenture Act of 1939, in the case of publicly issued debt, no alteration of the core terms of the debt (including duration, interest rate, and amount payable) can be made without the consent of each holder affected by the alteration; in other words, any change affects only those holders who agree to it. This rule, though intended to protect bondholders, can have significant adverse effects because of the possibility that a compromise that reduces the amount of the debt claim but is nonetheless beneficial to the debtholders (for example, because it saves the often considerable costs of a bankruptcy proceeding) may fail when some other holders refuse to consent. There may be a perverse incentive at work, a form of the so-called "prisoner's dilemma." [17] For example, suppose you hold a small amount of publicly issued bonds and the issuer is on the verge of insolvency. The bonds are trading at $700. An "exchange offer" has been made under which new bonds would be issued to the holders of the existing bonds in exchange for the existing bonds.[18] The new bonds in effect require the bondholders to accept a lower principal amount and a lower interest rate and to defer the payment of interest. In the metaphor of the financial world, they require the bondholders to "take a haircut." The offer is contingent on acceptance by 95 percent of the existing bondholders, as it must be in order to accomplish its objective. If the offer is not successful, the issuer will file for bankruptcy and the existing bonds will fall in value to $600. If the exchange offer is successful a group of new investors will contribute new equity capital, the corporation will have a new lease on life, and the new bonds will be worth $750. In other words, if the exchange offer is successful, and you exchange your old bonds for new ones, you will have bonds worth $750 each. If the exchange offer is not successful, your bonds will be worth $600 each. How do you react to the exchange offer?

[17] See Mark J. Roe, *The Voting Prohibition in Bond Workouts,* 97 Yale L.J. 232 (1987).

[18] An exchange offer, rather than a proposal to amend, will be used because of the rule that prohibits amendment of the core provisions without unanimous consent. The difference between an exchange offer and a proposal to amend (which would not bind dissenters) is essentially formal.

While it might seem at first blush that you should accept the exchange offer, you may believe that even if you do not accept, enough of the other bondholders will do so and the exchange offer will succeed; the corporation will avoid bankruptcy; and your old bonds will either be paid off at par ($1,000) or will, at the very least, be worth more than $750. Thus, you may decide to turn down the exchange offer. The problem is, of course, that if too many bondholders refuse to accept the exchange offer—that is, if there are too many holdouts—bankruptcy will ensue and all will lose. Yet there is no way in which a majority, or even some higher proportion, of the bondholders can force other bondholders to accept the exchange offer. Thus, there is a serious "holdout" problem. It is ironic, and disturbing, that (as Professor Roe points out [19]) once the corporation is in bankruptcy, under the *bankruptcy* law (as opposed to the Trust Indenture Act), a vote of a majority in number and two-thirds majority in interest of the bondholders can settle for a reduced claim and that majority's decision binds all holders. This rule, among others, encourages negotiation and compromise, which may be in the best interests of all those with an interest in the corporation. But resort to bankruptcy may result in large legal and other fees and possibly in loss of business good will or opportunities. One potential advantage of privately placed over publicly issued debt is that the former is not subject to the restraint on renegotiation of core provisions imposed by the Trust Indenture Act. But in order for a super-majority (e.g., 80 percent) of bondholders to have the legal power to force all the bondholders to "take the haircut" the indenture must grant that power. And the fact is that generally bond indentures for private placements do not do so. Perhaps the reason is that where the number of investors is small, no one investor is willing to give up a veto power over core changes and informal pressures to achieve what is plainly best for all may be considered adequate to solve the holdout problem.

A clever solution to the holdout problem is a technique known as a "consent solicitation." Under this approach, the company makes its offer to exchange the new bonds for the old bonds conditional on the bondholder consenting to amendments to the indenture eliminating important protective covenants. (While core provisions cannot be altered without the consent of each bondholder, protective covenants generally can be eliminated by a vote of a majority in interest of the bondholders.) With the protective covenants gone, the old bonds may be worth less than the new bonds. Thus, each bondholder may, in effect, be coerced into accepting the new bonds and the holdout problem disappears.[20]

---

[19] See note 21, supra.

[20] See Katz v. Oak Industries Inc., 508 A.2d 873 (Del.Ch.1986). There is some risk, however, that the coercion may be used unfairly to force the bondholders to accept bonds worth less than the value of their legitimate claim, though that risk may be small. See John C. Coffee, Jr. and William A. Klein, Bondholder Coercion: The Problem of Constrained Choice in Debt Tender Offers and Recapitalizations, 58 U. Chi. L. Rev. 1207 (1991); Marcel Kahan and Bruce Tuckman, Do Bondholders Lose from Junk Bond Covenant Changes? 66 J. of Business 499 (1993).

Another version of this problem is discussed below. Sec. III(A)(15).

**8. Consequences of Default; Bankruptcy.** The indenture is likely to contain provisions specifying the procedures to be followed in the event of violation of any of the covenants. Suppose, for example, that the debtor defaults on its obligation to pay interest. This will generally lead to an acceleration of the obligation to repay the principal amount. If the debt is secured by property, the trustee may then proceed to enforce the security interest—that is, to enforce the lien. This would involve a procedure leading to the sale of the property, with the proceeds of the sale used to satisfy the claims of the bondholders.

As a practical matter, however, the contractual or quasi-contractual procedures and rights are limited, and superseded, by the rules and procedures embodied in the federal bankruptcy law. That law is complex, but for present purposes an abbreviated (and correspondingly somewhat inaccurate) description is sufficient. Generally speaking, the bankruptcy law is invoked when the debtor is in serious financial difficulty. Two basic approaches are available—"straight" bankruptcy (sometimes called "liquidation") and reorganization (sometimes called "rehabilitation"). In a straight bankruptcy, a bankruptcy trustee sells the assets of the debtor and produces a cash fund for distribution among the various claimants. The business of the debtor can be sold as a going concern if a buyer can be found, but almost invariably operations will be terminated and the assets will be sold piecemeal.

The cash fund produced by the straight-bankruptcy liquidation is distributed in accordance with a priority among claimants: first, secured creditors, then priority creditors, then unsecured creditors, then equity claimants. The secured creditors include bondholders and others with mortgages on specific property. They are secured creditors as to that property. The amount of their claim is the face value of their bonds plus accrued interest. If this claim exceeds the value of the security (that is, the property subject to their mortgage or other lien) then the excess is treated as the claim of an unsecured creditor. For example, suppose that a company has issued first mortgage bonds with a face value of $1,000,000 and that at the time of bankruptcy it owes interest on these bonds of $100,000. The claim of the bondholders is $1,100,000. If the property can be sold (or otherwise disposed of) for more than $1,100,000, then the bondholders will receive their $1,100,000 and the excess will be available for other claimants. If the property subject to the mortgage is sold for, say $800,000, then that amount goes to the bondholders. As to their remaining claim of $300,000 they are treated as unsecured creditors. On the other hand, if the bondholders are oversecured they may continue to accrue interest up to the point that their claim for principal and interest exceeds the value of their collateral.

　　Next, consider assets not subject to mortgages or other such liens. First in line for the proceeds of the sale of these assets are the priority creditors. These are the Internal Revenue Service, people with certain kinds of wage claims, and people who have supplied services (including legal services) to the company in administering the proceeding after bankruptcy. Anything left after satisfaction of the priority claims goes to the unsecured creditors, pro rata according to the amount owed to each. Debenture holders usually are unsecured creditors; their claim is for the face value of the debentures plus accrued interest. Among the other unsecured creditors will be people who have supplied goods and services and have not been paid; these are often called trade creditors. If, at this point, it turns out that there is still something left, it goes to the preferred shareholders, if any; at the end of the line will be the common shareholders.

　　The rules become a good deal more complex when the proceeding is not a straight bankruptcy but rather a reorganization under Chapter 11 of the Bankruptcy Code.[21] A reorganization is a device for keeping the debtor "alive" despite its inability to meet its obligations to creditors. Even though the debtor may have defaulted on its obligations, secured creditors are legally restrained from enforcing their liens (that is, from seizing or forcing the sale of the property securing the debtor's obligations). There is no sale of assets for cash to satisfy the claims of creditors. If the corporation has been managed fraudulently or with gross incompetence, the bankruptcy court may order a trustee to take control of the business—but that is rare. Often, even if a trustee is not appointed, new managers will take over. Sometimes, however, particularly if management has a large equity stake in the business, the incumbent management will remain in control. The objective of the reorganization proceeding will be to "reorganize" the business—that is, restructure its operations and liabilities so as to keep the firm operating and use its future earnings to repay its claimholders and perhaps leave something for the equity holders. The secured creditors are legally entitled to receive new debt obligations with a present value equal to the amount of their claims, though possibly with different payment dates and interest rates. Before the equity receives anything, the unsecured creditors are legally entitled to receive new securities with a reorganization value that fully satisfies their claims, unless by class vote they consent to take less. As a practical matter, however, in many situations the equity-holders may have the power to force the senior or junior creditors, or both, to accept something less than their legal entitlements. This power would arise from the legal right of the equity (perhaps acting through the incumbent managers) to control the process of reorganization and thereby to (a) cause costly delays, (b) influence who gets what, and/or (c)

---

[21] For a good description, see Lynn M. LoPucki and William C. Whitford, *Bargaining Over Equity's Share in the Bankruptcy* *Reorganization of Large, Publicly Held Companies,* 139 U.Pa.L.Rev. 125 (1990).

compel a judicial valuation (which may vary from a market valuation or the creditors' subjective valuation). Thus, even if the equity has no legal right to receive anything of value in the reorganization, it may, as a practical matter, have some bargaining power. In some cases, the equity holders may be managers whose skills are essential to the prospects of successful operation of the business during or following reorganization and the equity may thereby have some additional leverage. On the other hand, in some situations, professional managers may align themselves with the debtholders rather than with the equityholders.

Given the potential leverage of the equity, an aspect of the reorganization process that becomes important is the ability of each class of creditors to agree, by a supermajority vote, to accept less than their legal entitlement. The practical result is that often the senior claimants will wind up with securities worth less than the amount of their claims even though claimants junior to them wind up with securities having some value. For example, suppose the claim of the secured creditors is $1,000,000, the claim of the unsecured creditors is $500,000, and the total value of the reorganized firm as a going concern is $1,200,000. Legally, the secured creditors are entitled to debt obligations worth $1,000,000, the junior creditors are entitled to securities worth $200,000, and the equity should receive nothing. In fact, the secured creditors might accept securities worth, say, $900,000, the unsecured creditors might accept securities worth $250,000, and the equity might receive securities (most likely common stock) worth the residual $50,000.

Judicial proceedings under Chapter 11 result in relatively small direct costs (e.g., legal and accounting fees) and often in substantial indirect costs (e.g., the loss of the time of executives and the loss of customer goodwill). Because of these costs, firms and their creditors often enter into various arrangements to "restructure" (that is, reduce or delay, or both) debt claims so as to avoid the need for a bankruptcy filing. Another alternative is the "prepackaged" bankruptcy, under which the firm and its creditors reach an agreement before the bankruptcy filing. That agreement is intended to be the basis for a final judicial decree that can be entered quickly and at low cost and that effectively binds dissenting creditors to the reorganization and gives the firm a fresh start.

Experienced lenders should be aware of what may happen to them under the bankruptcy laws in the event of insolvency. The prospect of costs to themselves and to the firms to which they lend, and the prospect of less-than-full satisfaction of the claims of senior lenders, despite the participation of junior lenders and equity claimants, should have some impact on initial credit negotiations. Among other effects, the senior lenders may demand a higher interest rate than if strict priority were rigorously enforced. The total value of the firm's securities should not be affected by the allocation of returns at the time of reorganization. The total value of securities will be reduced, however, by the expected direct and indirect costs—the deadweight costs—of insolvency proceedings.

**9. Callability.** The company may have the right to redeem the bonds before the maturity date—that is, the right to wipe out the debt by paying to the bondholders the face value of the bonds, plus any accrued interest, plus (usually) a small premium. This right is referred to as a *call feature,* since the bond can be called for redemption, or as an optional redemption right. The premium paid on redemption is referred to as a *call premium.*

The goals of a corporate borrower in insisting on a call feature can usefully be analogized to those of an individual borrower financing the purchase of a home. The home buyer may look forward to a decline in the market rate of interest and is likely to want to be free to borrow at the new rate and pay off the original loan. That is, the borrower is likely to want to be able to refinance at the new, lower rate. The banker, on the other hand, will object to this kind of heads-I-win-tails-you-lose option in the borrower and will be concerned about recovering the paperwork and other costs of setting up the loan initially. The borrower who insists on the privilege of prepayment (the equivalent of a call feature) will pay for that privilege in two ways. First, there will likely be a prepayment penalty (equivalent to a call premium). Second, the interest rate on the loan will likely be higher than it would be in the absence of the prepayment privilege.

Until recently almost all corporate bonds were callable.[22] In earlier times, the call feature was seen primarily as a device to serve the financial convenience of the issuer—for example, "if it becomes necessary at a future time to create a large new issue to be secured by the same property as that covered by the outstanding issue."[23] Interest rates then were lower and relatively more stable than they are now. As interest rates rose and became more volatile, the call feature took on increasing importance. For issuers in the current era, the call feature creates the attractive prospect, if interest rates decline, of refinancing (that is, borrowing new money and using it to repay, or "retire," existing debt) at a reduced interest rate. For debtholders, the call feature presents the correspondingly unattractive prospect of early repayment of a bond bearing a currently favorable interest rate.

During the early 1980s, interest rates rose and many bonds were issued at high rates. As interest rates fell in the later 1980s, many of these bonds were called and the bondholders lost the benefit of those high rates. In a reaction—perhaps an overreaction—to this unpleasant experience, bondholders began to insist on noncallable obligations. In the first quarter of 1992, only 9 percent of new publicly issued obligations

---

[22] See Janet S. Thatcher, *The Choice of Call Provision Terms: Evidence of the Existence of Agency Costs of Debt,* 40 J. Finance 549, 553 (1985).

[23] Arthur S. Dewing, The Financial Policy of Corporations 100 (Rev. ed. 1926). At the time Dewing wrote, most bonds were secured by liens on corporate property.

were callable and the percentage of outstanding obligations that were callable had fallen to less than 50 percent.[24]

A typical callable bond will have a schedule of call premiums, declining in amount to zero at maturity, and these premiums are now higher than they were in earlier eras. New provisions have been added to protect debtholders. For example, a provision now commonly found in publicly issued bonds provides that the bond cannot be redeemed (called) during some initial time period (e.g., five years) if the redemption is financed by borrowing at a lower interest rate.[25] This type of provision seems both ambiguous and potentially perverse in its incentives.[26] As to the ambiguity, what is the effect, for example, when a corporation sells one asset and redeems the debt and simultaneously, or after a short (or not-so-short) time, borrows new funds, at a rate lower than that of the debt that was redeemed and invests in a new asset? Should the new debt be tied to the new asset or to the redemption of the old debt? Should the outcome turn on the issuer's use of clever timing?[27] As for perverse effects, suppose that a corporation has on hand, from its operations, cash sufficient to redeem certain bonds that bear an interest rate that is substantially above the market rate. At the same time it has available to it a project which is a good one at the current interest rate but not at the interest rate paid on the outstanding bonds. The corporation, seeking to maximize its value, should redeem the bonds. But if it does so, any money it borrows to finance the project might be tied to the redemption of the existing debt. If that tie-in is made, the new project might become a loser (if either the corporation elects not to redeem the bonds or it does redeem them and must pay damages). Thus, the corporation might be induced to reject a profitable project.

[24] See Salomon Brothers, Corporate Bond Market: Performance Perspective, page 6, in the series United States Fixed Income Research, Portfolio Strategies, April 10, 1992.

[25] With this type of call provision, a bond is said to be "nonrefundable," as opposed to "noncallable."

[26] This is not to deny that the "two-tiered" call provision can serve a useful function. In fact, it can be used to allow the firm to deny bondholders a windfall gain from reduction in risk of default. See J. Thatcher, supra note 26, and discussion of this idea below, Sec. III(A)(12)–(15).

[27] In the few decided cases the rule does seem to reward clever timing and observation of formalities by interpreting the kind of provision referred to in text narrowly, by application of a "source" or tracing rule, which follows actual flows of funds. For example, in Morgan Stanley & Co. v. Archer Daniels Midland Co., 570 F.Supp. 1529 (S.D.N.Y.1983), $125 mil. of bonds were issued in May 1981 at 16.08 percent, with a provision prohibiting redemption for ten years "as part of a refunding or anticipated refunding operation by the application, directly or indirectly, of the proceeds of indebtedness for money borrowed which shall have an interest cost of less than 16.08% per annum." Id. at 1531, note 1. A year later (May 1982), the company issued $50 mil. of bonds at less than 16.08 percent. Ten months thereafter, the company issued another $86 mil. of bonds at less than 16.08 percent and "the proceeds ... were applied directly to reducing ... short-term debt." Id. at 1542, note 4. Sales of common stock raised $131 mil. in January 1983 and $15 in June 1983. The May 1981 bond issue was redeemed on August 1, 1983. The court found that the "source" of the funds for the redemption was the common stock offering and held that the bondholders had no cause of action.

Part of the problem with call provisions seems to arise from what may be thought of as a failure to separate two possible origins of any differential between the interest rate on a particular bond and the market rate. One possible origin of such a differential is a drop (since issuance of the bond) in the market interest rate. The other is that the issuer's default risk has been reduced. Consider the position of a firm that is about to issue fixed-interest bonds [28] and focuses, first, on the possibility of a drop in the market rate of interest. This is a possibility over which the issuer has no control. If the drop occurs, and the issuer can call the bonds, it will be able to obtain a replacement loan at a lower interest charge. But the potential gain to the issuer is a potential loss to the holders. If the issuer wants a call feature (a right of redemption), it will presumably be required to pay for it. The payment will take the form of a call premium or a higher interest rate, or both. In other words, when considered at the time of issuance, the inclusion of a call feature does not offer an expected gain, since the price paid (call premium plus higher interest rate) should equal (or exceed [29]) the expected value of the interest saving that can be achieved by redemption (and refinancing) if the market rate of interest falls. Still, the issuer may want a call feature because repayment of the loan may at some time be the best use of its cash flow. [30]

The analysis is different where the prospect under consideration is that the interest rate paid on the bond may exceed the market rate because of a decline in the riskiness of the debt. Here the change is associated with circumstances that are within the control of the issuer's management. For example, risk may be reduced by a decision to invest cash flow in the firm rather than to pay dividends, a decision that increases the equity cushion. Or risk may be reduced by a decision to invest in safer projects or in projects that contribute to diversification and thereby reduce the issuer's overall risk. Here, the call provision allows the issuer to make sound business decisions for the firm without concern about shifting wealth from equityholders to debtholders by

[28] The problem discussed here does not arise where the interest payable on the bonds varies according to a market-rate index. But relatively few corporate bonds pay variable-rate interest, even at a time when variable-rate home loans to individuals have become common.

[29] The holders' compensation for the call feature may exceed its expected value if the call feature introduces an element of uncertainty, a risk, that holders in the aggregate find unattractive.

[30] An interesting possibility for allowing redemption without permitting the issuer to deprive the holders of the benefit of a higher-than-market rate attributable to a change in the market rate is a bond whose call feature specifies a redemption price that is geared to an index of the market rate of return, with appropriate account taken of the remaining duration of the debt. This is called a "yield maintenance" call premium or "make-whole" provision, and has been used in some privately placed bonds. Such provisions are now commonly used in obligations privately placed with institutions such as pension funds and insurance companies, but are rarely (and only recently) encountered in publicly issued corporate bonds. See William A. Klein, C. David Anderson and Kathleen G. McGuinness, The Call Provision of Corporate Bonds: A Standard Form in Need of Change, 18 J. Corp. L. 653 (1993).

reducing default risk. (For a demonstration of the wealth-shifting proposition, see below Sec. III(A)(13) to (15)). On the other hand, some bondholders may reasonably believe that a rise in the value of their bonds resulting from a decline in default risk is a proper reward for their own good judgment about the prospects of the borrower and that they should not be deprived of the benefit of that judgment by redemption at a modest premium.

It is worth noting that where bonds are publicly traded a company can, without reliance on a call privilege, pay off its debt to some degree by buying its bonds in market transactions, provided it is willing to pay whatever premium the bonds might command in the market by virtue of the attractiveness of the interest rate or other features. Where there is no public market there is the possibility of repurchase in a negotiated private transaction. If a company has spare cash that it is intent on using to repurchase its bonds and repurchase is for some reason not possible, a good alternative might be to use the cash to buy bonds of another issuer with terms identical to those of its own bonds, so that it has an asset that offsets its liability [31] and, at least for planning purposes, can thereafter ignore the debt owed to its bondholders.

**10.  Sinking Fund.** The final feature of bonds that we examine is the *sinking fund* (or mandatory redemption) provision, which is now uncommon. The analogy to the home buyer will again be helpful. A bank that lends to a person buying a home wants not only interest but ultimate repayment of the principal and may have doubts about the capacity of the borrower to pay the full amount in a lump sum at the end of the term of the loan. (Bear in mind, however, that if the value of the home does not decline, the borrower ought to be able to borrow anew to pay off the original loan at the end of its term.) Most home loans therefore require gradual repayment (often referred to as amortization) of the principal amount of the loan regularly during their term. People who lend to corporations often insist on similar protection, which protection is referred to in the world of bonds as a sinking fund provision.

Sinking fund provisions may follow a wide variety of approaches. One is to require the borrowing firm to set aside a fixed amount of money each year toward the ultimate redemption of the entire issue of bonds. Under a modification of this approach, the firm may be allowed to use part of the required funds to repair or replace the property that is the security for the loan. Still another approach is to require the firm to redeem a specified amount of bonds each year. For example, if the term of the loan is 20 years, the firm may be required to redeem 5 percent of the original value each year. Often the firm will be allowed to meet its obligation by buying bonds in the open market. If the market price turns out to be par or less, this will, of course, be an attractive option for the firm. But there is also the possibility that the market price will be

---

[31] The offset is not perfect, of course, because of differences in firm-specific risks.

significantly higher than par (because of a decline in the market rate of interest or because of a decline in the risk of default). The bond is likely to provide for sinking fund (mandatory) redemption at par or at a modest premium. The question then arises, which bondholders will be required to accept the lower-than-market price? Pro rata redemption may seem most consistent with what bondholders are likely to want (no surprises and equal treatment), but it may be impractical. The other major possibility is selection by lottery of the bonds to be redeemed. A common provision currently in use leaves the choice among these two and other possible alternatives to the indenture trustee.

**11. Inflation, Default Risk, and Duration.** The nominal maturity date of a bond may be deceiving because the periodic interest payment includes compensation for inflation and for default risk, which means that each interest payment includes a partial recovery of investment. To illustrate, imagine three different $1,000 bonds, each with a duration of five years. Bond A is issued by the U. S. Treasury in an era in which the expected rate of inflation is zero. The interest rate is 2 percent, or $20 per year. Bond B is issued by the Treasury at a time when the expected rate of inflation is 10 percent. The interest rate is 12 percent, or $120 per year. Bond C is issued by a corporation at the same time that Bond B is issued by the Treasury. The interest rate on Bond C is 15 percent, or $150 per year. The extra 3 percent above the rate paid on Bond B is compensation for default risk.

Suppose you invested in Bond A (in an era of no expected inflation). You could spend the $20 interest payment you received each year without impairing the constant-dollar value of your investment. At the end of the five-year term of the bond, you would receive $1,000, which would have the same constant-dollar value as the $1,000 initially invested.

Suppose you invested in Bond B (when expected inflation was 10 percent). If you wanted to preserve the real value of your investment, you could not expect to spend the entire $120 interest payment received each year. You would have to figure on setting aside part of it to take account of the effects of inflation. (We will not examine the question of how much you would need to set aside each year.) More generally, if you take account of inflation and its effect on the interest rate, you must be aware that each interest payment received is in part, on a constant-dollar basis, a payment of principal, so your bond is in effect being repaid gradually over its life. If you thought that interest rates were likely to decline, you would be unhappy with this fact. You would want to pin down the current interest rate not only for your nominal principal but also for the fund you would want to set aside to cope with inflation, and possibly for the true interest element as well. In the late 1970's the financial world saw the development of a bond, called a *zero-coupon bond,* that was designed to appeal to this kind of instinct. Zero-coupon bonds are simply bonds that provide for no current interest payment and are sold at a discount. For example, if the appropriate interest rate for a borrowing were 15 percent and the only obligation of the issuer were to pay $1,000 at the end of five years, the issue price would be $497 (the present value of $1,000 discounted at 15 percent for a five-year period). In many cases, however, zero-coupon bonds were issued with call features that allowed redemption at prices calculated to allow for little more than accrued interest, thus depriving the investor of the right to continue to earn interest at the rate that was being paid at the time of issuance. Thus, the terms of the call feature took on critical importance.

Returning to our hypothetical, if you invested in Bond C and wanted to preserve the value of your investment, you would have to set aside a fund to take account not only of inflation but also of default. For example, if you invested in 100 bonds like Bond C, with an estimated default risk of 3 percent, you would expect complete default on three of them (or partial default on a larger number) and would need to set aside enough to make up for that expected loss.

## 12.  Control.

a.  *Control follows risk.* Bondholders, unlike shareholders, do not normally vote for directors, or on other issues on which shareholders vote.  Traditional bond covenants to some degree limit the freedom of action of the corporate managers, but usually such covenants leave to the shareholders, acting through directors and managers, wide latitude in determining the goals and strategies of the firm. This observation is consistent with the fact that the investment represented by bonds is far less risky than that represented by common stock. By the same token, when the firm suffers misfortune and is in, or on the verge of, default—when it cannot meet all its obligations to the bondholders—one would expect, and one finds, that bondholder representatives do tend to insist on some degree of control. Moreover, where the debt is risky, as in the case of high-yield ("junk") bonds, substantial constraints on the firm's freedom of action are likely to be imposed by the terms of the loan agreement or by the covenants (see Sec. III(A)(5) above).

b.  *"Strip" financing.* In some recent leveraged buyouts (for a description of these see Ch. 3, Sec. V(B)(2)(c)), the investors have taken equity and various levels of debt (first mortgage, second mortgage, subordinated, short term and long term) in roughly the same proportions. This technique may seem peculiar, since the equityholders may be thought of as borrowing from themselves and as creating a complex structure of debt while they are at it. There may be a number of good reasons for use of the technique, but the one of interest here has to do with control. The risky debt will come with covenants that have considerable bite to them. The investors, as shareholders, acting through their elected directors, presumably would have the power to replace management if performance is not up to expectations, but the covenants to some degree can be used to set the goals, and the minimum standards of performance, of the firm. Moreover, if the number of shareholders is large enough, they may encounter problems of collective action as shareholders. If a bond covenant is violated, any single investor, as bondholder, has the power to enforce the rule that prescribes the consequences of that default (most likely, bankruptcy). Thus, strip financing, combined with strict covenants, not only solves the problem of collective action but also, for better or worse, shifts considerable power from the majority of investors to the minority.

**13. Control, the Debt/Equity Conflict, and the Value of the Firm.** There are at least three important corporate policy issues as to which control may be exercised to favor common shareholders over bondholders. These are (i) the choice of the riskiness of investments, and (ii) the decision to invest additional capital, and (iii) the decision whether to pay dividends.[32] As to each of these issues, an unavoidable potential conflict of interest between the holders of debt and the holders of equity may result in decisions that fail to maximize total firm value. If it were feasible to draft and enforce a provision in the bond indenture requiring managers always to make that decision that maximized firm value, the problem would be solved. But it seems plain that that is not feasible; the process of making investment decisions is too complex and too subjective.

**14. The Riskiness of Investments.** One way in which control can be exercised to shift firm value to the common shareholders at the expense of the bondholders is to increase the riskiness of the firm's investments.[33] Assume, initially, that the total value of the firm is to be held constant.

Consider a firm that has total assets of $1,000 for investment and is confronted with two possible investment strategies, A and B, with the characteristics and consequences indicated below, the claim of the bondholders being $500.

## INVESTMENT A

| | Outcome* | | | Value** | | |
|---|---|---|---|---|---|---|
| Probability | Firm | Bonds | Common | Firm | Bonds | Common |
| .1 | $ 400 | $400 | $ 0 | $ 40 | $ 40 | $ 0 |
| .8 | 1,000 | 500 | 500 | 800 | 400 | 400 |
| .1 | 1,600 | 500 | 1,100 | 160 | 50 | 110 |
| 1.0 | | | | $1,000 | $490 | $510 |

* Monetary Return
** Expected Monetary Value

[32] See Ileen Malitz, *On Financial Contracting: The Determinants of Bond Covenants,* 15 Financial Management 18 (1986).

[33] See Dan Galai and Ronald W. Masulis, *The Option Pricing Model and the Risk Factor of Stock,* 3 J. Financial Economics 53 (1976).

## INVESTMENT B

| Probability | Outcome* | | | Value** | | |
| --- | --- | --- | --- | --- | --- | --- |
| | Firm | Bonds | Common | Firm | Bonds | Common |
| .3 | $ 0 | $ 0 | $ 0 | $ 0 | $ 0 | $ 0 |
| .4 | 1,000 | 500 | 500 | 400 | 200 | 200 |
| .3 | 2,000 | 500 | 1,500 | 600 | 150 | 450 |
| 1.0 | | | | $1,000 | $350 | $650 |

\* Monetary Return
\*\* Expected Monetary Value

Investment A has a probability of .1 of a value for the firm of $400, in which outcome the bonds are worth $400 and the common shares are worth nothing; a probability of .8 of a value for the firm of $1,000, with a derived value of $500 for the bonds and $500 for the common; and so forth. The expected monetary return of Investment A is $1,000; that of Investment B is precisely the same. Let us assume that the market value of the two investments is the same, despite B's greater volatility risk, because that risk can be avoided by diversification by investors. (See Sec. II(F) above.) The value of the firm, then, and the combined value of all of its securities will be the same regardless which investment is undertaken. From the perspective of the investors, however, there is a significant difference. For the bondholders, Investment B produces a higher probability of a greater default and, consequently, a lower expected return. For the common shareholders, on the other hand, Investment B has no outcome that is worse than that of Investment A and one that is much better; it is decidedly superior. From the perspective of the common shareholders, Investment B trades a risk to the bondholders for a gain to themselves. (This phenomenon may be thought of as a function of the limited liability of shareholders.)

More generally, one can imagine a set of investment opportunities producing different degrees of risk of partial or complete default on the bonds. From any starting point, holding the total market value of the firm and of all securities constant, a decision that shifts investments in such a way as to increase such risk will result in an increase in the value of the common and a decrease in the value of the bonds. Shifts can occur in either direction, but to the extent that common shareholders exercise control one would not expect to find shifts that operate to the benefit of the bondholders. In situations in which the common shareholders want to shift to a more conservative investment strategy, they may be able to deprive the bondholders of the benefit of that move by exercise of the call privilege (assuming that the bonds are callable).

It should be easy to see that the common shareholders might be better off with the riskier investment (Investment B) even if its expected value is less than that of the alternative (Investment A). For example, suppose that the 0.4 probability is changed from $1,000 to $900. The expected firm value for this outcome becomes $360, the expected value of the bonds remains $200, and that of the common $160. Even though the total expected value of the firm is $960, compared with $1,000 for Investment A, the value of the common is $610, compared with $510 for Investment A. If the goal of the managers is to maximize shareholder, as opposed to firm, wealth, they will select Investment B, even though it is inferior to Investment A from a neutral economic perspective.[34]

The opportunity suggested by this hypothetical may help explain why some firms can borrow more readily (or on better terms) than others. The potential for exploitation of the bondholders declines to the extent that the bonds are secured by property that is used in a particular kind of business and cannot be adapted to other uses. Or it may be clear that a particular firm has no opportunity to engage in new kinds of activities. Such firms should be more attractive to bondholders than, for example, firms that can rapidly shift assets from a diversified set of investments to a single investment. It also helps explain certain covenants, such as one that prohibits the sale of substantially all of the firm's assets or one that requires that the firm not enter new lines of business.

There are other ways in which bondholders can protect themselves, at least to some limited extent. One obvious possibility is to limit the duration of the loan, though that has its costs. Another possibility may be to give the bondholders an equity stake (e.g., warrants or a conversion privilege).

**15. The Decision to Invest Additional Capital.** In an article published in 1977, Professor Stewart C. Myers (Sloan School of Management, MIT) identified another circumstance in which a bondholder/shareholder conflict might lead to a failure of a firm's managers to maximize its total value.[35] That circumstance can, again, best be described by use of a hypothetical. Suppose X Corp. begins its existence in Year 1 with assets of $2,000, debt of $1,000, and equity (common stock) of $1,000. The debt bears a market rate of interest and is due at the end of Year 20.

a. *The Problem.* The firm's initial balance sheet is as shown on Balance Sheet A. Although accounting statements generally show only book value, for our purposes it is important to show market value as well.

---

[34] At a fanciful extreme, one can imagine the manager of a business, with heavy debt and insolvency imminent, converting its assets to cash, taking the cash to Las Vegas, and betting it all on one spin of the roulette wheel. That would be an example of taking a risk with what is mostly someone else's money, which is the phenomenon at work in our hypothetical. A more realistic example is the behavior, in the early 1980's, of federally insured savings and loan institutions, many of which invested insured borrowings in high-risk real estate, oil and gas, and other ventures. The potential gain would go to the owners of the savings and loan institution, while the loss would be, and has been, borne by the federal insurance agency (and ultimately by other savings and loan institutions or by the taxpayers).

[35] *Determinants of Corporate Borrowing,* 5 J. Financial Economics 147.

**Balance Sheet A**

| Assets | | | Liability and Equity | | |
|---|---|---|---|---|---|
| | Book | Mkt | | Book | Mkt |
| Investments | $2,000 | $2,000 | Debt | $1,000 | $1,000 |
| | | | Equity | 1,000 | 1,000 |

Over the next ten years the firm does poorly. At the end of the 10th year its assets carry a book value of $1,200 but have a market value of only $800.[36] This means that the firm has shown losses of $800 on its books (the decline from $2,000 to $1,200), but in fact has sustained an additional, unrealized, loss of $400. The balance sheet is shown in Balance Sheet B.

**Balance Sheet B**

| Assets | | | Liability and Equity | | |
|---|---|---|---|---|---|
| | Book | Mkt | | Book | Mkt |
| Investments | $1,200 | $800 | Debt | $1,000 | $700 |
| | | | Equity | 200 | 100 |

Assume further that the interest payments on the debt have been made and that debt is not in default [37] and therefore is not due and payable. Assume that the sole reason why the debt is worth less than the amount of its claim (that is, its face amount) is default risk; the market rate of interest has not changed.[38] While the claim of the debt exceeds the value of the firm, the equity captures some of the firm's value. Here perhaps the best way to think about the value of the equity is to observe that the equity is like an option to buy the firm from the bondholders for $1,000 any time within the next 10 years, subject to an obligation to make interest payments to keep the option in effect. See Chapter 1, Sec. XIII and Chapter 4, Sec. IV.

Suppose X Corp.'s managers become aware of an opportunity to invest in a project with a cost of $550 and a present value of $800. The project is one that can only be developed by this firm; it cannot be sold.[39] Suppose that the project has a zero variance of expected returns (in

---

[36] The relevant analysis is not dependent on the bonds selling for less than face value, though it is dependent on them having some significant risk of default. If the bonds do have a market value equal to or greater than par, however, the problem discussed in text may be avoidable by redeeming them under an optional redemption right (a call provision).

[37] If the indenture contained a covenant requiring the firm to maintain an equity cushion of, say, at least half the amount of the debt, then the firm would be in default, and, most likely, the full amount of the debt would become due and payable. The firm presumably could not pay and could be forced into bankruptcy.

[38] As an illustration of how the relative values of the debt and equity might arise, here is a set of assumptions that produces the assumed figures of $700 for debt and $100 for equity:

| Proba- | | —Outcome— | | | —Value— | |
|---|---|---|---|---|---|---|
| bility | Firm | Debt | Equity | Firm | Debt | Equity |
| 0.1 | 0 | 0 | 0 | 0 | 0 | 0 |
| 0.8 | $ 750 | $ 750 | 0 | $600 | $600 | 0 |
| 0.1 | 2,000 | 1,000 | 1,000 | 200 | 100 | 100 |
| | | | | Total | 800 | 700 | 100 |

[39] The project might, for example, be to repair or improve the firm's existing plant.

other words, it's a sure thing [40]) and must be financed with new equity. Assume that the X Corp. managers seek to maximize shareholder wealth. One financing possibility is a rights offering (see below, Sec. III(C)(1)), under which existing shareholders are in effect forced to contribute the new equity because the price is set low enough so that if they fail to do so they wind up losing wealth. Assuming this is done, the book value of the firm's assets increases by the $550 contribution, to $1,750 and the market value increases by the $800 value of the project, to $1,600, but the market value of the debt increases by $300 because, with the value added by the new project, there is no longer any risk of default. Thus, the equity increases in value by only $500. The post-offering results are as shown in Balance Sheet C.

### Balance Sheet C

| Assets | | | Liability and Equity | | |
|---|---|---|---|---|---|
| | Book | Mkt | | Book | Mkt |
| Investments | $1,750 | $1,600 | Debt | $1,000 | $1,000 |
| | | | Equity | 750 | 600 |

Were it not for the conflict between the interests of the debtholders and the interests of the equityholders, the project would be accepted and total wealth would be increased by $250—the difference between the increased value of the firm and its securities ($800), and the cost of producing that increase (that is, the amount of the additional investment, $550). If we assume, however, that the managers seek to maximize shareholder wealth, they will in fact reject the project because accepting it would lead to a decrease in shareholder wealth of $50—the post-investment value of the common, $600, reduced by the additional equity cost, $550, and by the pre-investment value of the common, $100.[41] To

[40] This assumption simplifies the explanation but its rejection would not affect the basic analysis. Implicit in the numbers used in the example in text is the assumption that the existing investment has some variance in expected outcomes. See footnote 42. If the new project does have some variance in expected outcomes, that variance may be either positively or negatively correlated with the variance of the existing investment. If the correlation is negative, the combined variance is reduced, which will tend to benefit the debt at the expense of the equity and the conflict discussed in the text is magnified. If the correlation is positive, the combined variance is magnified, which will benefit the equity. In fact, if the variance of the new project is the same as, and perfectly correlated with, the variance of the existing project hypothesized in footnote 42, it turns out that the value of the bonds, after adding the new project is $900 and the value of the equity is $700. With

these numbers, the problem presented in text disappears. It is certainly possible, however, to hypothesize numbers with which the problem does not disappear, even with a positive correlation.

[41] The same result obtains if the new equity is raised by issuing new shares to outsiders. For their $550 contribution, the outsiders would, of course, demand shares worth $550. Since the total equity would be worth $600, that would leave the original shareholders with shares worth only $50, which would be $50 less than what they started with. This observation leads to the further observation that the bondholders would be protected by a covenant requiring the firm to maintain an equity cushion of, say, $750, and explicitly requiring that the firm raise new equity capital if necessary to comply with that requirement. Merely treating the failure to maintain the specified equity cushion as an act of default may have much the same effect.

look at this another way, the project increases firm value by $250, but the additional contribution of equity results in a shift of $300 of firm wealth to the bondholders.[42] The phenomenon at work here has been referred to in an analogous situation as a "buoying-up" of the debt.[43]

Now let's look at year 10 and ask how we came to this sad state of affairs. The firm started out with a substantial amount of debt and did not do well over the preceding ten years. The likelihood of that happening is positively correlated with the variance of the firm's expected projects. So we can conclude that as the variance of a firm's projects increases and as the level of debt rises, the likelihood increases that the firm ultimately will pass up profitable projects.[44] Thus, firms with high expected variance should use low amounts of debt.

b. *Duration, Value, and Insolvency Reorganization.* The conflict between the equity and the debt is dependent on the duration of the debt. If the debt were due soon, the common shareholders could not pay it. There would be a default. If the bankruptcy procedure operated quickly, without cost, and with a rule of absolute priority, the bondholders would take over the assets of the firm, including the prospect. The financing deadlock for the new project would be ended, the new project would be undertaken, and the firm would be worth $1,050.[45]

[42] As indicated in footnote 44 if the new project has a variance identical to that hypothesized in footnote 42 for the initial investment, and positively correlated with that of the initial investment, the value of the bonds will be $900 and the value of the equity will be $700. In this situation, the contribution of an additional $550 in equity results in an increase in the value of the equity of $600 (to $700 from $100), so the investment presumably will be made.

[43] See Roe, supra note 21. Roe focuses in part on situations in which the potential gain at issue is from avoidance of bankruptcy costs, rather than from a positive-net-present-value investment, and the conflict is among bondholders rather than between bondholders and common stockholders. He provides a number of interesting real-world examples, one based loosely on the MGF Oil Corporation. Id. at n. 28. In his example, five bondholders each hold a bond with a face value of $40M and a market value of $20M. The issuer company is insolvent and faces bankruptcy. The costs of a bankruptcy proceeding can be avoided only if all the bondholders agree to a plan, or if any dissenting bondholder is paid the full amount of his or her claim. The problem posed in the hypothetical lies in the fact that each bondholder has an incentive to hold out, hoping that the others will proceed with the plan and will be forced to pay off the dissenter.

Roe also discusses situations in which a firm threatened with insolvency, or already insolvent, needs to attract new capital. One of the examples he uses is that of the Chrysler Corporation in the years 1978 to 1980. "The existing debt was so risky that providers of fresh money would have found themselves buoying up preexisting creditors (including the bondholders), unless the preexisting creditors agreed to alter the terms of their repayment." Id. at 244.

Roe argues persuasively that the buoying-up problem can be solved by permitting bondholders to be bound by a majority vote. He observes that in the case of publicly issued bonds this would require repeal of Section 316(b) of the Trust Indenture Act of 1939, 15 U.S.C. § 77ppp (1982), while a two-thirds vote is binding on the entire class of securityholders once the issuer has filed for bankruptcy. See discussion of these rules above, Sec. III(A)(6).

[44] Among finance scholars these are called "positive net present value" projects. See Chapter 5, Sec. I(A)(3)(b).

[45] Note that with the firm worth $1,050, since the claim of the bondholders is $1,000, the common shareholders would be entitled to securities worth $50. This observation helps explain why a firm may be worth more after insolvency reorganization than before and why, as a result, the com-

In fact, even if the debt were due and in default, the managers probably would file for protection under the bankruptcy law rules relating to insolvency reorganization (Chapter 11 of the Bankruptcy Code) and would have on their side the possibility of delay (with the corresponding possibility of losing the value of the prospect). What would follow then is a non-zero-sum bargaining opportunity—that is, a situation in which, if the bondholders and shareholders can agree on how to split the $250 they can preserve it, otherwise they lose it.

In any event, we see again a good reason why lenders should prefer to lend short term.

c. *Bargaining Possibilities.* In the situations contemplated by our hypothetical, additional capital can be raised and the project can be exploited if the bondholders agree to reduce their claim to, say, $800, so that the buoying up of their claim by virtue of the addition of the new capital is only $100. The result would be that the equity would be worth $800. That would be an increase of $700 from the addition of the new $550 and the equityholders would have a strong incentive to contribute the additional capital. This is another illustration of the advantage of being able to negotiate a reduction in the claim of the debtholders. As we have seen (Sec. III(A)(7)), in the case of publicly issued debt, short of bankruptcy (which imposes additional costs), the prospects for such a negotiated reduction are substantially impeded by a rule, imposed by the Trust Indenture Act, prohibiting any change in core provisions of the debt obligation without the consent of each affected debtholder. In an insolvency reorganization, the vote of a majority in number and two-thirds majority in interest is controlling even as to changes in core provisions. A similar voting rule is, of course, permissible in the case of privately placed debt.

d. *Additional Capital.* The problem presented here can be seen, from another perspective, as part of the broader problem of raising additional capital, where, by virtue of division of ownership, there may be perverse incentives that result in the failure to exploit profitable opportunities. See Chapter 2, Sec. VII(D).

e. *Covenants and the Equity Cushion.* The possibility of a firm passing up profitable projects depends on a thin equity cushion and is reduced by covenants designed to require maintenance of a specified cushion, such as covenants providing that debt cannot exceed a specified percentage of net tangible assets. Such covenants may increase the initial (ex ante) value of the firm and, for that reason, may be desirable for the equityholders as well as for the debtholders.

f. *Manipulation of Corporate Entities.* Suppose the sole asset of $X$ Corp. is a dilapidated hotel on a valuable piece of property. $X$ Corp.'s balance sheet is the same as Balance Sheet B, with the debt worth $700

mon shareholders may be entitled to some of the shares of the reorganized firm even though, before the reorganization, its liabilities exceeded its assets.

and the equity worth $100. The profitable project consists of rehabilitation of the hotel; the expected cost is $550 and the expected addition to the value of the asset is $800. Suppose that the shareholders of X Corp. form a new corporation, N Corp., and transfer all their shares to N Corp., so that X Corp. becomes a wholly owned subsidiary of N Corp. and suppose that there is nothing in the X Corp. covenants that makes N Corp. liable for the X Corp. debt. Next, N Corp. leases the hotel from X Corp. under a long-term lease with rental payments that reflect the hotel's current, dilapidated state. These rental payments should be unobjectionable to the X Corp. bondholders since they fully reflect the current value of the hotel.[46] With these rental payments, the value of X Corp. should remain the same. N Corp. then raises the needed $550 from its shareholders (formerly the X Corp. shareholders), accomplishes the rehabilitation, and reaps the profit. N Corp. will have taken advantage of the profitable opportunity without buoying up the X Corp. bonds.[47] It is true that N Corp. will have taken advantage of what had been a corporate opportunity of X Corp., but X Corp. was not in a position to exploit that opportunity and the X Corp. shareholders were under no obligation to contribute money to permit it to do so. See Chapter 3, Sec. IV(C)(2). Even if the opportunity did belong to X Corp., the taking of the opportunity by N Corp. would only violate an obligation to the shareholders of X Corp. and they can hardly complain since they are not the shareholders of N Corp. It is doubtful that the X Corp. bondholders can complain unless they can cite some covenant that has been violated.[48] If the approval of the X Corp. bondholders were required for the merger, it might be possible to offer them some benefit to induce them to grant that approval. There is, after all, a total $250 gain to be had if only a deal can be struck.

**16.  The Dividend Decision.** Perhaps the most important conflict between debt and equity relates to dividends. The less the amount a corporation pays in dividends the greater its assets, the greater the equity cushion, the less the risk of default on the debt, and the greater

---

[46] In fact, the bondholders might turn out to be better off. The rental payments will be assured. Depending on the amount of the rent, since there will be no risk, the entire $800 of value of the firm might be captured by the debt.

[47] But see note 49, supra. The amount of any buoying up will presumably not exceed $100. The equity will still gain from the transaction, which generates a total gain of $250.

[48] See Simons v. Cogan, 549 A.2d 300 (Del.1988); Wolfensohn v. Madison Fund, Inc., 253 A.2d 72 (Del.1969). See also Revlon, Inc. v. MacAndrews & Forbes Holdings, Inc., 506 A.2d 173, 182 (Del.1986)("Good

faith" obligations "are limited to the principle that one may not interfere with contractual relations by improper actions. Here, the rights of the shareholders were fixed by agreement ...." In other words, you made your bed and you must lie in it.) But see Morey W. McDaniel, *Bondholders and Stockholders,* 13 J. Corporation Law 205 (1988)(arguing for fiduciary obligation to bondholders). To reduce the risk of a successful bondholder attack, the rental payment can be set so as to increase by some modest amount the value of the X Corp. bonds and thereby cast any complaining bondholder in the role of an ingrate. See note 50, supra.

the value of the bonds.[49] For some debt the only limitation on dividends may be that no dividend can be paid that will render the corporation insolvent. As we have seen (Sec. III(A)(5)(a) above), a commonly used covenant allows dividends only to the extent of some fixed amount plus earnings (or some portion of earnings) after the date of issuance of the debt. A firm that fails to pay the full amount of the permissible dividend may bestow on bondholders a benefit for which they did not bargain. Yet often that is just what happens with many firms.[50]

Where the corporation is in a position in which it is free to pay a substantial dividend (a common situation), by doing so it may reduce the current value of the outstanding bonds.[51] In the process, however, it may forgo a profitable investment. The dividend decision is the other side of the additional-capital decision that we have just examined. If corporate managers are dedicated to maximizing shareholder wealth (a big "if"), assets that can be transferred to the shareholders, without legal restriction, are (disregarding tax considerations that may affect some shareholders) the same as assets in the hands of those shareholders. Thus, the effects are the same as we have just examined.

To illustrate the point, we can return to the previous hypothetical. At the end of 10 years, the condition of the firm was as shown in Balance Sheet B, which is repeated below.

### Balance Sheet B

| Assets | | | Liability and Equity | | |
|---|---|---|---|---|---|
| | Book | Mkt | | Book | Mkt |
| Investments | $1,200 | $800 | Debt | $1,000 | $700 |
| | | | Equity | 200 | 100 |

Change the facts reflected in Balance Sheet B by adding to the investments cash of $550 and by making corresponding changes in the debt and equity. The result is as shown in Balance Sheet D.

---

[49] Presumably there is some point at which increase in the equity cushion adds no meaningful reduction in default risk. In the case of a firm that is at this point, dividend policy may become unimportant to debtholders.

[50] Even if the dividend-limitation covenant does not operate as a restraint, a covenant requiring the maintenance of a specified equity cushion or equity-debt ratio may protect the bondholders.

[51] Note, however, that the effect may simply be to put the bondholders in the position in which they would have been if the corporation had paid out the maximum permissible dividend in earlier years. In other words, the effect may be to deprive the bondholders of a benefit for which they had not bargained—a windfall, if you will. That may be small comfort to people who had recently acquired the bonds, but perhaps they were aware of the risk and accepted it because of a higher yield than otherwise would have been available. People are, after all, free to buy U.S. Treasury bonds.

### Balance Sheet D

| Assets | | | Liability and Equity | | |
|---|---|---|---|---|---|
| | Book | Mkt | | Book | Mkt |
| Investments | $1,750 | $1,350 | Debt | $1,000 | $1,000 |
| | | | Equity | 750 | 350 |

If the cash of $550 is paid out as a dividend, the shareholders wind up with wealth of $650, consisting of the cash of $550 plus the remaining value of their equity (as shown in Balance Sheet B).[52] In other words, their wealth increases by $300, which is the amount by which the value of debt declines.

That is nothing but a wealth transfer, but there may be wealth destruction as well. Assume, as before, that the firm has a project in which it can invest the $550, that the project will have a value of $800, and that the situation is that shown in Balance Sheet D, with $550 of cash on hand. If the cash is invested in the project, the result will be as shown in Balance Sheet E.

### Balance Sheet E

| Assets | | | Liability and Equity | | |
|---|---|---|---|---|---|
| | Book | Mkt | | Book | Mkt |
| Investments | $1,750 | $1,600 | Debt | $1,000 | $1,000 |
| | | | Equity | 750 | 600 |

Assume again, however, that the managers of the firm are free to pay a dividend of $550 and that their goal is to maximize shareholder, as opposed to firm, wealth. If they pay the dividend, we return to Balance Sheet B. The wealth of the equityholders is the $100 value of the equity plus the $550 cash from the dividend, a total of $650. This is $50 more than their wealth if the cash is retained by the firm and invested in the profitable project. Thus, the firm will pay the dividend even though the effect will be to force it to forgo the profitable project.

There is, however, another side to dividend policy and the debt/equity conflict. If a corporation is not allowed to pay dividends and it has no sound investments available for its net cash flow (after all sound investments have been made), it will be forced to invest in unsound (negative net present value) projects. Thus, there is a risk that a dividend limitation imposed to ensure that a firm will not forgo sound projects will go too far and force it to invest in sound projects.

**17. Managers and Risk.** It has been assumed in the foregoing discussion that the investment strategies of the firm are determined collectively by, or in the interest of, the common shareholders. It is now

---

[52] The payment of the $550 dividend might violate state corporate law restricting dividend payments or it might violate the Uniform Fraudulent Conveyance Act. It would not be difficult, however, to construct a more complex and less dramatic hypothetical in which those restrictions would not come into play yet the same economic principles would apply.

a commonplace, however, that in many publicly held firms shareholder control is at best highly attenuated; effective control is held by managers and to some considerable extent is exercised in their interests. This phenomenon may help to explain the apparent apathy of bondholders toward the danger that the firm will increase the overall riskiness of its investments. Most shareholders invest only a small proportion of their total wealth in the shares of a single corporation; they diversify their investment portfolios. Shareholders may be risk averse with respect to their entire portfolios of investments but not with respect to the individual components of those portfolios. Consequently, shareholders may be willing to accept a high level of risk, for their investment in a particular firm, if the acceptance of that risk results in a modest increase in the firm's expected return. For managers, on the other hand, compensation from their jobs is likely to be a large proportion of total financial resources. They cannot diversify the investment of their human capital the way shareholders can diversify the investment of their financial capital. Suppose a manager, acting in the best interests of the shareholders, undertakes a large project with a big risk—a risk that is well worth taking (from the perspective of the relatively risk-neutral shareholders) in light of a high return if the project is successful. If the project is unsuccessful, the firm may become insolvent. The manager may then lose his or her job and may find it difficult to find a new one (partly because other employers may focus on the failure of the project, not on the sound decision to take a calculated risk). The result may be financial ruin for the manager. Generally, managers, because of concern for their jobs, will tend to have an interest in avoiding the kinds of outcomes that lead to default on debt. They will tend to be more risk averse than shareholders. Their interest in protecting their jobs may put them in conflict with the wealth-maximizing objectives of the shareholders. At the same time, risk aversion may align the interests of managers with those of lenders. A compensation device such as a stock option can then be seen in part as an effort to align the interests of managers with those of the common shareholders on the issue of risk. By the same token, one might expect a preference on the part of bondholders for firms in which managerial compensation is not significantly affected by extraordinary successes of the company. A reputation for financial conservatism may allow a manager to reduce the borrowing costs for the firm for which he or she works, with the fortunate consequence that the manager's risk aversion can work to the benefit, not to the detriment, of the shareholders. Bondholders should be particularly concerned about management when the prospects of the firm become so dismal as to create a strong possibility that it will go out of business. In such a situation, managers may have an incentive to take very large risks (even with low expected returns) in the hope of salvaging a going concern that will preserve their jobs.

    In the same vein, one must recognize the possibility of tacit understandings and the value of reputation. A firm with a customary dividend policy or investment strategy may be able to surprise one set of bondholders, but the next time it seeks funds it must expect to pay the price for having done so. Lenders might be expected to look with some disfavor on firms that will have no need to borrow in the foreseeable future.

Still, there are likely to remain situations in which lenders will be fearful of the kinds of risks discussed here. In those situations, lenders will demand compensation for that risk. If the price that they demand is too high, the bargain will not be made. The situation is analogous to that of the investor in Chapter 1 who hires a manager. It may be impossible to devise rules and processes that are effective to preclude self-serving conduct by the manager in derogation of the interests of the investor. That is a fact of life that the parties must then take as given. It may mean that they will not be able to make a deal. Or it may be something that they simply must learn to live with.

**18. Duration, Risk, and Control.** We have seen how a short loan duration can be used to limit the danger to debtholders of wealth transfers to equityholders resulting from investment and dividend decisions. Section III(A)(15)(b). A shift to a risky investment may not be feasible in a short time and, even if it is, may not harm the debtholders if the debt is due before the risks unfold. Where the issue is that of additional capital for a profitable project, a short duration may create a default (or an immediate prospect thereof), putting the firm under the control of the bondholders, who can then raise the capital or force the equityholders to do so. And a short duration may limit the freedom to pay dividends or the harmful effect to debtholders from any dividend that is paid.

A short loan duration may also allow the debtholder to exercise control more directly. When a firm is in trouble and its managers must go to the debtholder and seek a renewal or extension, they are likely to listen respectfully to suggestions about how the firm should be run. See Sec. III(A)(12).[53] The other side of this coin, however, is that a short duration may not mean what it seems to mean. It is one thing to set a date for repayment and another to collect from a borrower that is in financial trouble. Sometimes the lender will have little choice but to extend the due date of the loan, where the alternative is to put the borrower into bankruptcy and thereby reduce or eliminate the chance that the loan will be repaid. In fact, the lender may even be forced to lend more money in order to preserve any chance of collecting the amount of the original loan. And there may be no practical alternative to the existing management and its mode of operation.

---

[53] Debtholders must be careful, however, to guard against gaining so much control that they are treated as principals of the business, thereby becoming liable to the other creditors. See Ch. 1, Sec. VII(C)(3).

There is, of course, a negative side to short duration. It is costly for a lender to investigate the creditworthiness of a prospective borrower and to do the paper work required for any loan. Presumably these costs must be passed on to the borrower. The shorter the duration of the loan, the more often the costs will be incurred, though the costs can be reduced by renewing loans as long as there is no change in conditions, and the cost of determining whether there has been a change in conditions may be less than the cost of starting fresh.

Finally, there is another way in which duration affects the terms of the loan. Where the firm's investment is risky, the required interest payment may depend on the duration of the loan for reasons specific to the firm.[54] To illustrate this point, imagine a firm with an original investment of $1,000, financed by equity of $200 and debt of $800. Suppose we separate the future of the firm into two periods and expect that at the end of each period we will find that the investment earned interest at the rate of 10 percent but turned out to be worth either 50 percent more or 50 percent less than the amount at the beginning of that period. Thus, at the end of Period 1, the investment will be worth either $1,650 [55] or $550.[56] If the value at the end of Period 1 was $1,650, the value at the end of Period 2 will be either $2,722.50 or $907.50. If the value at the end of Period 1 was $550, the value at the end of Period 2 will be either $907.50 or $302.50. These numbers are presented in Figure 4–1.

**Figure 4—1**

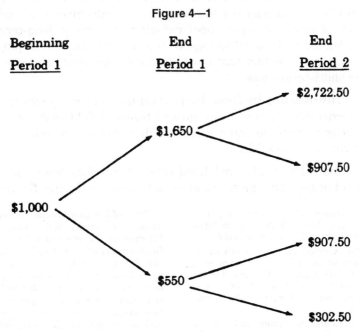

| Beginning | End | End |
| Period 1 | Period 1 | Period 2 |

$2,722.50

$1,650

$907.50

$1,000

$907.50

$550

$302.50

[54] We are not concerned here with the fact that interest rates in general tend to vary with the duration of the loan. We are not concerned, that is, with the perplexing and complex topic of the "term structure of interest rates."

[55] $1,000(1 + .5)(1 + .1).

[56] $1,000(1 − .5)(1 + .1).

For debt issued by firms with risky investment, the interest rate must compensate for the expected value of the default, plus the market risk-free rate. To put this another way, in a set of risky investments, at the outset it must be expected that the winners will pay for the losers. But with expected outcomes such as those shown in our example, the mix of winners and losers (from the debtholders' perspective) changes as we move through time. Thus, it turns out that in our example, assuming that investors are risk neutral,[57] the required interest payment for a one-period loan is at a rate of 51.25 percent, while the required rate for a two-period loan is 48.09 percent.[58]

**19. Further Observations on Duration.** We have just seen some good reasons for making loans of short duration. What are some of the reasons for longer duration? First, there may be increased negotiation and paperwork costs in periodic renewal of short-term debt, especially when lenders and borrowers find insufficient advantage to establishing long-term informal relationships with one another. Second, when a borrower invests in long-term projects it may wish to be relieved of uncertainties associated with short-term loans—mostly the uncertainty over future interest rates. Third, lenders may also wish to avoid uncertainty over future interest rates. For example, an insurance company that has sold long-term annuities may wish to match the duration of its investments to the duration of its obligations. Fourth, long-term debt (with an effective provision protecting against call) gives the lender the benefit of its good judgment about default risk. Finally, long-term debt allows a lender to take advantage of the normal, upward-sloping yield curve—that is, of the fact that most often the long-term rates are higher than the short-term rates.

**20. Innovation in Debt Instruments.** In recent years there has been considerable innovation in various terms of debt instruments.[59] A few of the more popular innovations are described below, but the degree of creativity is remarkable.

*a. Rates.* The traditional fixed interest rate has been varied in a number of ways. The most widely used variation is the floating-rate

---

[57] This assumption does not seem unrealistic since the debt will be held in large, well diversified portfolios of risky debt.

[58] If the expected rate of growth or decline in the value of the investment is 30 percent, rather than 50 percent, the required interest rate is 16.89 for a two-period loan and 23.75 percent for a one-period loan.

[59] See Kenneth A. Carow and John J. McConnell, A Survey of U.S. Corporate Financing Innovations: 1970–1997, 12 Journal of Applied Corporate Finance 55 (Spring 1999).

Three of the most common objectives of innovative security design have been to (1) manage the interest rate (and other financial price) risk faced by investors and issuers; (2) to reduce information costs faced by investors when buying securities from issuers with better information about their own prospects (a condition known as information asymmetry); and to (3) increase the tradability of financial assets.

Id. at 68.

note, in which the interest rate is periodically adjusted to reflect changes in some well-established market interest-rate index such as LIBOR (London InterBank Offered Rate). Interest payments (and other payments as well) may also be linked to a particular stock, a set of stocks, a stock index, or a commodity such as gold or oil. The effect is to shift the risk of change in the market rate of interest (or some other economic indicator) from the lender to the borrower. Another innovation is a rate that changes to reflect changes in the risk of default, as measured, for example, by some accounting ratio. This type of provision shifts the risk of a decline in creditworthiness to the borrower and thereby not only protects the lender but also provides an appropriate incentive to the borrower. Still another innovation is to denominate the interest payment in a foreign currency.

Another innovation is the increasing rate note. For example, a note might provide for a basic interest rate plus a rate increase of half a percent each quarter for the first year and a quarter of a percent per quarter thereafter. The basic rate might be tied to a market index. Such notes are generally callable at par within six months of issuance. They are used for short-term financing, but the borrower has the option to extend them by, in effect, paying a penalty.

  *b.  Duration.* A debt obligation may be made "puttable" or "extendible" by the holder. For example, a debenture with a six year maturity can be made puttable by the holder at the end of three years, which means simply that at the end of three years the holder may demand repayment, but is not required to do so. Alternatively, essentially the same result can be achieved by issuing a three-year debenture that is extendible by the holder for an additional three years.[60]

  *c.  Combinations.* The innovations as to rate and duration can, of course, be combined. Consider, for example, the "extendible reset" obligation. The initial duration is relatively short, but the issuer has the option to extend the due date, at periodic intervals, subject to a limit. If the issuer extends, the holder must be allowed to demand redemption unless the interest rate is reset. The reset rate may be either (i) a new rate based on changes in a market index or (ii) a new rate set (by an investment banker) to cause the obligation to trade at a specified price (usually 101 or 102). Under the latter formula the reset rate will vary with changes in default risk as well as market rate and the similarity to short-term debt is strong.

  **21.  A Basic Theme Revisited.** One of the basic themes of this book has been that it is important to keep in mind the interdependence of the fundamental elements of business organization—risk, return, control, and duration. See especially Chapter 1, Sec. 12. A "bond" is the sum of the rules or agreements defining the relationship of certain participants in business to the other participants (and among them-

----

[60] See id. at 66.

selves) and, as such, is a reflection of the trade-offs among the elements. Success in helping people achieve their business goals will depend in part on an awareness of how changing one element will affect the others.

## B.  SHARES OF COMMON STOCK

**1.  Introduction.**  When a corporation is formed, its articles of incorporation, or charter, will authorize the issuance, for cash or other consideration, of a fixed number of *shares of common stock*.  The number can be changed by amendment of the articles.  Not all of the authorized shares will necessarily be issued; some may be held by the corporation as *authorized but unissued* shares.  There may also be shares that were at one time issued but were reacquired by the corporation; these have traditionally been called *treasury shares*.  There seems to be no good reason for distinguishing between treasury shares and authorized but unissued shares.  Shares of common stock are usually manifested by the issuance of a piece of paper called a stock certificate, which is simply a bit of tangible evidence of the holder's pro rata share of the total stock of the corporation.  Holders of shares of common stock may be called either shareholders or stockholders, as you prefer.

Each share of common stock reflects an initial contribution to the firm and a set of rights stemming from that contribution.  Common shareholders are often thought of as the owners of the firm or as the holders of the *equity* interest in the firm.  (See Chapter 1, Sec. II(E).) The equity interest is sometimes usefully thought of as the *residual* interest—the claim to what is left after all senior claimants have been satisfied.  The claims, rights, obligations, and other attributes of common shares are determined by provisions of the corporation's articles (or charter) and its bylaws, as well as by the corporation law of the state in which the corporation is incorporated, the state and federal laws regulating issuance of and dealings in securities, and various other statutes and judicial doctrines.  Lawyers have argued at length over the fact that some state corporation laws impose fewer restrictions than others— primarily with respect to relationships between majority and minority shareholders and between management and shareholders.  (See Chapter 3, Sec. III(E).)  The differences among the state laws have been sufficient to make some states far more popular sites for incorporation than others, but at least for the purposes of the basic discussion that is offered in this Chapter, those differences seem trivial.

Long ago, there was a close relationship between the amount initially paid for common stock (that is, the amount contributed to the corporation per share, by the initial owners of the common shares) and its so-called *par value*.  In that bygone era, then, the par value of a share of common stock was somewhat akin to the face value of a bond.  Since par value serves as a floor on the price at which stock can initially be sold and imposes some limitations on dividend payment, and for a variety of other reasons, meaningful par value is a nuisance. Lawyers have found that they can avoid the nuisance by issuing common stock with no par value or with very low par value (in relationship to initial selling price) and that is now virtually the universal practice. (See Chapter 3, Sec. VI(A).)

**2. Reification and Language.** Lawyers say that a corporation is a separate entity. It is something separate, that is, from its shareholders. Even more broadly, all of us tend to reify corporations, especially the larger ones. The reality is that a corporation is an abstraction. One cannot feel, see, touch, or smell it. Yet we often talk as if that were not so. That is all well and good; reification is a convenient device for communication—in this case about a complex socio-economic organization. It is helpful, however, occasionally to remind ourselves of the reality. (See Chapter 3, Sec. I(B)(4).)

Consider one manifestation of this process of reification and its effects on our style of communication. When a large, publicly held corporation raises new equity capital, we speak of it "selling" common stock to the public. It is the "corporation" that is "selling" stock—"its" stock—to people. In the case of a small, closely held corporation, the style of communication tends to change. We speak of people contributing money or property to the firm (or, at a somewhat higher level of abstraction, to "the corporation") in return for shares in the enterprise, with pieces of paper called shares of common stock serving as tangible evidence of the arrangement. Both styles of communication can be useful and appropriate. One should be alert, however, to the possibility that reification can be misleading; it can hide the fact that the processes and arrangements referred to involve and affect people, not things.

**3. Duration.** Corporations are almost always created with no specified termination date. Similarly, the interest represented by the common stock is generally of unlimited duration. There is usually no initially agreed-upon point in time when a common shareholder becomes entitled to demand the return of his or her initial contribution or some other amount. Termination may occur involuntarily, as in the case of insolvency, or voluntarily by shareholder vote, or by virtue of certain other circumstances, but the point is that in the absence of special agreement or circumstance, there is no point at which a common shareholder is entitled to withdraw his or her investment from the enterprise (unless, of course, that shareholder has sufficient voting control to bring about a liquidation.) But see Chapter 3, Sec. III(C), on the importance of buy-out, or buy-sell, agreements for closely held corporations.

**4. Risk.** The volatility risk of common stock will depend on the nature of the business and on the nature of the corporation's financial structure. It is plain that for any corporation, the volatility risk of the common stock is greater than that of other securities. It is also plain that the "default" risk of common stock (that is, the chance of recovering less than one's investment) is greater than for bonds or other securities with fixed claims and with preferred status on liquidation. In short, among the securities issued by corporations, common stock is the most risky.

**5. Control.** We saw in Chapter 3 (Sec. II(B)(1)) that common shareholders exercise control over the corporation through the directors whom they elect. Despite all the serious problems associated with this proposition, it still has enough vitality to be thought of as a basic characteristic of common stock.

**6. Specificity.** The common shareholders are free under state law to specify precisely the nature of the business in which they intend to engage. Often, however, the relevant documents will authorize the corporation to engage in any lawful business. This allows great flexibility, which can, of course, be a good thing. The shareholders share an interest in making a profit and presumably a decision made by the majority will be in the interest of all. Those who disagree with the firm's investment strategies may sell their shares. Where a market for shares is not available, one would expect to find greater specificity as to type of business, identity of managers, and other such matters. Alternatively, one might expect devices for creating a substitute for a market, by requiring, for example, that in certain circumstances the majority must buy the shares of dissenters at a price determined under some agreed-upon formula. Impressionistic evidence supports this theory.

**7. Return.**

a. *Dividends.* Most publicly held corporations pay cash dividends to shareholders. Dividends are often said to be paid "out of" current earnings (see Chapter 3, Sec. VI(B)). In light of the fact that money is fungible, and that the word "earnings" refers to the outcome of a complex process, not to a fund, it is more accurate to say that the amount of the dividend (usually) will depend on or be limited to the amount of the corporation's current earnings. Sometimes corporations will pay dividends in amounts larger than current earnings; the excess will then usually be thought of as coming out of the previously undistributed earnings of earlier years. Typically, corporations over the long haul will pay out less than all their earnings as dividends. A portion of earnings will be retained and reinvested in the business. But all that the shareholders see is the dividend. That is their return. It is now widely accepted in the sophisticated academic financial literature that the value of shares of common stock is best thought of as a function of the dividends (including any final, liquidating dividend paid when the corporation's existence ends) that the corporation can be expected to pay out over its life. Many people consider this to be a peculiar proposition because they think instinctively about capital gain (sale price less cost) as part of the return on common stock.

The fact is, nonetheless, that capital gain must be a function of expectations about future dividends. Imagine a series of shareholders. The first shareholder pays a given amount for the shares, based on an estimate of the amount of cash dividends plus a gain (or loss) at some time in the future. The next shareholder makes the same kind of calculation. That is, the gain, if any, will depend on the next shareholder's expectation as to cash dividends plus capital gain (or loss). And so on. If we think of the entire series of shareholders, some may have greater capital gains or losses than others, depending on the timing of their purchases and sales and on collective expectations, reflected in market prices, at the time of those purchases and sales. But the gains and losses are transfers among all the shareholders who hold the shares over the entire time that they are outstanding. Those gains or losses do not increase or decrease the total return on the shares over that time. The only return that shareholders collectively can expect over the life of the shares in which they invest is the dividends (including, as indicated above, any final or liquidating dividend) paid on those shares. It can be seen, then, that if people are rational the value of the shares at any point in time must be derived solely from the series of expectations about dividends. Any gain in the value of shares must be based on expectations concerning dividends to be paid at some point in the future.

To see the same point from a different perspective, suppose that someone offered to sell you some shares of stock and that you were certain that the corporation would never, ever pay any dividends (including disguised dividends in the form of an excessive salary or the like) or any proceeds from liquidation or other distributions. You would be foolish to pay anything at all for those shares. And if you did buy them, you would have to find an equal fool to buy them from you at your cost and a greater fool to buy them from you at a gain to you. The only thing that makes shares valuable is the expectation of payments of some sort at some time in the future.

This does not mean that the shares of a corporation that pays no dividends *currently* are worthless. Many companies have operated for years without paying dividends. Many of these have been successful, growing companies that were retaining all of their earnings in order to take advantage of attractive investment opportunities. People do, rationally, pay money for shares of such companies. They do so because they expect that at some point in the future dividends will be paid.

One qualification must be added to this discussion of dividends— namely, that amounts paid out by a corporation when it purchases its own common stock must be thought of as equivalent to dividends (without regard to the tax treatment of such payments). It will be seen in Chapter 5 (Sec. IV(D)) that there are compelling reasons why a corporation might prefer a policy of paying no dividends at all and using any funds that might otherwise be paid out as dividends to buy its own common shares. For purposes of the present analysis, what is important about such a policy is that the corporation does distribute cash and that shareholders who do not sell their shares to the corporation gain as much as those who do.

b. *Earnings.* If, as we have just seen, dividends alone determine value, what is the relevance of earnings (as they are defined by traditional accounting principles)? If earnings are not paid out as dividends, and assuming that earnings have not been misstated, the amount retained will be "invested" by the corporation.[61] To the extent that earnings are retained, and invested, the value of the firm's assets should increase and its earnings and capacity to pay dividends in the future should increase correspondingly. Thus, the earnings figure is relevant in determining the value of the firm's shares because it provides information about future capacity to pay dividends. Concern with earnings is therefore entirely consistent with the proposition that the value of the shares is solely a function of dividends.

What if the retention of earnings does not produce any improvement in future earnings and dividend-paying capacity? Suppose, for example, that over a period of many years a firm reports yearly earnings of $3 per share and pays yearly dividends of $1 per share. If the earnings remain constant at $3, what is the firm doing with the $2 that it is purportedly retaining and investing each year? One possibility is that it is figuratively pouring the retained earnings down a rathole—making utterly worthless investments. More likely there is something wrong with the $3 figure. If $2 must be reinvested each year just to keep the firm at a steady level then that $2 should be regarded as part of the cost of doing business. The true earnings figure is $1 per share. Thus, by examining a firm's dividends over time, one can often gain insight into the reliability of its reported earnings figures.

c. *Dividends, Earnings, and Share Prices.* Suppose that at the beginning of the year a share of common stock of X Corporation sells for $100 and that during the year X Corp. earns $10 per share. All other variables being held constant, and assuming that the earnings figure is accurate and realistic, the price of the share at the end of the year should be $110. The wealth of shareholders will be $100 per share at the beginning of the year and $110 at the end. If, at year's end, X Corp.

---

[61] In the present context the term "invested" is used in a financial sense. It is used, that is, simply to describe a process in which the increased value of the investment that stems from earnings is retained in the corporation, as a consequence of the decision not to pay a dividend equal to those earnings. When "invested" is used in this sense, the statement that retained earnings are invested in the corporation is a pure tautology. Any amount that is not paid out by a firm is obviously "invested"—if only in the firm's checking account. Later, in Chap-ter 5, we will be required to use a more fundamental concept of investment, referring to the nonfinancial process of consciously adopting a business strategy (e.g., buying a machine) and will see the importance of distinguishing between the investment decision and the financing decision. If this seems somewhat confusing, there may be consolation in the thought that a person who has seen the problem is well ahead of the large number of people, including many experts, who have not.

retains the $10 per share of earnings, the price of the shares should remain at $110. If, on the other hand, the $10 is paid out as a dividend, the price should fall to $100. The shareholder will now have a share worth $100 plus $10 in cash. His or her wealth will be the same as if the earnings had been retained—a total of $110 consisting of the share worth $100 plus the $10 in cash. If earnings are retained to finance an unwise investment, the value of the share will be less than $110, but that outcome is a result of the unwise investment decision, not of the decision to retain.

These ideas are developed more fully later. (Chapter 5, Sec. IV.) They are introduced here as a background for the discussion of stock dividends and stock splits, which follows next.

d. *Stock Dividends and Stock Splits. Stock dividends* and *stock splits* result in the issuance of additional shares of a corporation's own stock to existing shareholders without charge to them. The characteristics of the new shares will be essentially identical to those of the old ones. There are some technical accounting differences between stock dividends and stock splits, but we can ignore them. As a practical matter, the significant difference is that the term "stock dividend" ordinarily is used to describe situations in which the number of new shares issued is small in relation to the number of shares held. For example, a corporation may issue a 5 percent stock dividend. This means that a person owning 100 shares will receive 5 new shares. The term "stock split" is used when the number of new shares is high in relation to the number of old ones. If, for example, the corporation issues one new share for each old one (so that an owner of 100 shares would receive 100 new shares, with essentially identical characteristics), the transaction will be referred to as a stock split.

Stock dividends and stock splits do not change the value of the corporation's underlying assets (disregarding trivial paperwork costs). They do not increase any shareholder's percentage interest in those underlying assets. The shareholder receives nothing but some new pieces of paper. For example, suppose that a shareholder has 100 shares worth $50 per share or a total of $5,000 and that the corporation issues 100 additional shares in a one-for-one stock split. The shareholder will now have 200 shares that should be worth $25 each or a total of $5,000, no more or less. Experience in the stock markets is substantially consistent with this expectation, though there appears to be a small, difficult-to-explain increase in the total value of the shares of firms following stock splits.[62]

What, then, is the point of issuing the new shares? Several answers have been offered.

---

[62] See Maureen McNicholls and Ajay Dravid, *Stock Dividends, Stock Splits, and Signaling,* 45 J. Finance 857 (1990)(attributing the results to signaling effects).

First, suppose that a corporation has been extremely successful and that its shares have risen dramatically in price. It is often suggested that this can interfere with efficient trading in the shares. A stock split may be thought to solve the problem by reducing the price per share. For example, suppose that shares of X Corp. sell for $500 each. The customary trading unit, called a "round lot," may be 100 shares (though a round lot of 10 shares of a particular stock with a high per-share price is possible). Brokers may charge a premium for trades in other than round lots and investors may prefer holding round lots, for inexplicable or trivial reasons. There may be some people who cannot invest $50,000 in a round lot of X Corp. shares. Existing owners may wish to sell less than $50,000 worth of their shares. A stock split may permit these people to deal in round lots. Or at least this is the street lore. Since it suggests the existence of a hide-bound, inflexible marketplace—one that is incapable of distinguishing between 100 shares of $10 stock and 100 shares of $100 stock—or nonrational investors, or both, skepticism seems justified. If the theory is valid then one would expect that a stock split would slightly enhance the total value of the equity interests.  No systematic study has confirmed this expectation.

Second, a corporation may assert that the issuance of a stock dividend or split is "tangible evidence" of the corporation's prosperity, despite its failure to pay substantial (or any) cash dividends. Upon careful scrutiny this kind of claim is hard to understand. The success or failure of the firm is reflected in its periodic reports to shareholders. It is difficult to see what additional information is conveyed by the issuance of new shares of stock. It may be, however, that management views shareholders (or at least some significant number of them) as childlike creatures to whom information must be conveyed symbolically, by the issuance of some fancy pieces of paper.  If so, one should not be surprised by disingenuous explanations.

Finally, a stock dividend or split may offer a convenient device for allowing shareholders to cash in on capital gain. Suppose, for example, that you buy 100 shares of X Corp. stock at $100 per share; that the corporation earns $10 per share and retains the entire $10, paying no dividend; and that the price of the shares rises to $110 each. The value of your investment has increased from $10,000 to $11,000—a gain of $1,000. But that doesn't pay your bills.  You could sell 9 of your shares and realize $990, but that could be inconvenient. You might also be able to borrow $1,000 against the security of your shares (that is, using your 100 shares as collateral, or security, for the loan), but again that could be inconvenient. If the corporation sends you 10 new shares as a stock dividend, you can sell those new shares (presumably for $100 each or a total of $1,000) with perhaps less inconvenience. Indeed, the corporation can make an advance arrangement with a broker to sell your new shares for you upon issuance, if you so elect (on a convenient form supplied by the corporation), in which case all you ever see is a check for, presumably, about $1,000. This is as close as one can come to a sensible reason for issuing stock dividends, but the example significantly distorts reality by focusing on an individual owning a small number of the shares of a single company. The vast majority of shares are held by individuals and institutions with much larger holdings of the shares of many companies. Imagine, for example, an individual owning a diversified portfolio of shares of the common stock of twenty different companies, with a total value of $500,000. Such an individual is likely to be buying and selling shares at least several times during each year and these transactions can easily be arranged so as to generate as much spare cash as the person wants to spend (based in part on life style and in part on the performance of the investment portfolio). All it takes to sell shares of stock (even for a small investor) is a telephone call to the owner's broker (whose firm will hold the actual shares, probably in the form of bookkeeping entries). Most reasonably well-to-do people will have some sort of interest-bearing cash fund on which they can draw for short-term needs, and if they don't they can probably borrow quite easily, short-term, from a bank or from their broker. For people like these, and for institutional investors (e.g., pension funds and university trust funds), it is difficult to view a stock dividend as anything other than a minor bookkeeping nuisance. One would suppose that it is such people and institutions whose tastes and needs should dictate the policies of most public corporations. Moreover, there is a negative aspect of stock dividends for people who attach importance to round lots. Stock dividends and splits (other than one-for-one) will destroy the round-lot character of the holdings of many existing shareholders. Beyond that, stock dividends and splits will impede trading during the period in which the paperwork associated with issuing and recording the revised holdings is completed.

**8. Classes of Stock.** Common stock may be separated into separate classes, generally for the purpose of distributing voting power separately from the basic economic claim. For example, a corporation might issue 1000 shares of Class A shares and 1000 shares of Class B shares with both classes having the same per share economic interest (in dividends and in the amount to be received on liquidation), but with the Class A shares entitled to two votes per share and the Class B shares entitled to one vote per share. Alternatively, the Class A shares might be entitled to elect 3 directors and the Class B shares only 2 directors. Still another possibility would be to make the Class B shares nonvoting. More recently, and more rarely, the separate classes might carry different economic claims, as described immediately below.

**9. "Anti-dilution" Provisions.** A venture capital investor with sufficient bargaining power, bargaining with an entrepreneur, may be able to extract a so-called "anti-dilution" provision.[63] The general idea is that the venture capital investor's investment should not be diluted on

---

[63] See Michael A. Woronoff and Jonathon A. Rosen, Understanding Anti–Dilution Provisions in Convertible Securities, 74 Fordham L. Rev. 129 (2005).

subsequent rounds of investments, but the provision has a harsher effect on the entrepreneur than that general idea might suggest. The operation of these types of provisions can most easily be illustrated with an example of a "full ratchet" provision (as opposed to variations such as a "weighted average" provision, which is not as unfavorable to the entrepreneur).

Suppose Entrepreneur (E) founded X Corp., which is initially worth $2,000; E has 1,000 shares of common. VC-1 buys 1,000 shares of "preferred" for $2/sh. for a total of $2,000. The preferred is convertible into 1,000 shares of common. So the value of X Corp., with the new money, is now $4,000. VC-1 gets a full-ratchet provision.

A year passes and X Corp. proves to be a disappointment (perhaps due to unanticipated market conditions beyond the control of E). It is now worth $3,000 total. Assuming that VC-1 converts into 1,000 shares of common, but ignoring the full ratchet, E's 1,000 shares would be worth $1,500 and VC-1's shares would be worth $1,500. Thus,

| Shareholder | Number of Shares | Value of Shares |
| --- | --- | --- |
| E | 1,000 | $1,500 |
| VC-1 | 1,000 | $1,500 |

But now assume that X Corp. desperately needs an additional $1,000. With the new money, X Corp. will be worth $4,000. VC-2 buys 1,000 shares for $1/share (a price that reflects VC-2's recognition of the effect of VC-1's full ratchet rights). Under the full ratchet provision, VC-1's conversion "price" (for his original $2,000 investment) is now $1 per share (the price paid by VC-2), or 2,000 shares. Assuming conversion by VC-1, and the application of the full ratchet, the outcome is as follows:

| Shareholder | Number of Shares | Value of Shares |
| --- | --- | --- |
| E | 1,000 | $1,000 |
| VC-1 | 2,000 | $2,000 |
| VC-2 | 1,000 | $1,000 |

You can see that what has happened is that VC-1 maintains his or her initial value at the expense of E. If the value of X Corp. is less than $3,000 the loss to E is greater. In other words, the entire decline in value comes out of E's pocket. E is in effect a guarantor of VC-1's value. But only if new money is needed, and even if the new money comes from VC-1.

Why would E agree to this? Consider a dialogue between E and VC-1 at the time E is seeking VC-1's money. VC-1 asks E if he thinks that there is any serious risk that the company will not succeed. E, of course, says no—partly because, like all entrepreneurs, he is an indefatigable optimist and partly, perhaps, because he doesn't want to send a bad signal to VC–1. VC–1 then says to himself, "Gotcha," and says to E, "In that case you should not object to a full ratchet." But now start thinking about the incentive effects on E.

**10.  Tracking Stock.** Tracking stock is a separate class of common stock of a corporation, designed to track the performance of a part of the business of the corporation.[64] For example, when General Motors acquired Electronic Data Systems Corp. (EDS), it issued Class E shares, designed to track the performance of EDS.[65] More recently, AT&T issued tracking shares in its wireless unit.

The dividends payable on tracking shares are based on the performance of the identified separate business unit, but the tracking shares do not have any special claim to the assets of that business and there is only one board of directors for the entire corporation. The rights of the holders of tracking shares are specified in the corporate charter, which, for the most part, is quite vague, at best, about the obligations of the board in resolving any conflicts between the holders of the tracking shares and the holders of the basic common shares (for example, as to allocation of funds for investment).

## C.  INTERESTS DERIVED FROM COMMON STOCK

**1.  Stock Rights.** One alternative available to a corporation that seeks to raise additional equity capital is the issuance of *stock rights* to existing shareholders. (In fact, issuance of stock rights is in effect the only permissible method of raising new equity capital if the corporation's shareholders have preemptive rights. See Ch. 3, Sec. VI(G).) A stock right is simply the right to buy additional shares of common stock, at a price below the current market price, within some prescribed, relatively short, period of time. Suppose, for example, that a share of common stock of a corporation is currently selling for $50. The corporation might issue to each shareholder the right to buy, at $30 per share, one new share for each existing share, any time within, say, the next 30 days. Once the rights are issued, the value of each existing share, shorn of the right to buy the additional share, ought to decline, on these facts, to $40 (as demonstrated immediately below). The value of the right to buy one share should be worth $10. Obviously, such a stock right is an offer that the shareholder cannot afford to refuse. Sensible shareholders who do not want to invest additional funds in the corporation will sell their rights to someone else who will exercise them or will exercise the rights and immediately sell the newly acquired shares.

To see how the issuance of the stock rights in the above example affects the value of existing shares, imagine that initially there are 1,000

---

[64] See Jeffrey J. Hass, Directorial Fiduciary Duties in a Tracking Stock Equity Structure: The Need for a Duty of Fairness, 94 Michigan L. Rev. 2089 (1996).

[65] See Solomon v. Armstrong, 746 A.2d 277 (Del.Supr.2000).

shares of common stock outstanding. The total value of all shares is therefore $50,000 (1,000 shares multiplied by the market value, $50 per share). If the market is rational, the net value of the firm (that is, the total value reduced by the amount of all claims other than that of the common stock) should similarly be $50,000. If all stock rights are exercised, the firm will receive an additional $30,000 (1,000 rights multiplied by the $30 per share exercise price). The net value of the firm will then be $80,000 (the initial $50,000 plus the additional $30,000). The total number of shares will be 2,000, so the value of each share will be $40 ($80,000 divided by 2,000 shares).

If buyers and sellers of shares and rights are rational and know what is happening, the value of the existing shares ought to fall to $40 as soon as the rights are issued. Since the holder of each right will lose $10 by failing to exercise it, rational investors will assume that all rights will in fact be exercised and that consequently the ultimate price for shares at the end of the exercise period will be $40. If rational people know that the price of a share of stock in the very near future will be $40, that is the price at which they will buy and sell it today. (This is a rudimentary aspect of the broader principle that information about known future events affecting the value of assets is fully reflected in the present price.)

Now let's examine briefly the position of the initial shareholder. Imagine a person owning one share. Its initial value is $50. When the right is issued, the value of the share falls to $40, but the right is worth $10 so the total wealth position ($50) is unchanged. If the right is exercised the total value of the new and the old share will be $80, but the shareholder will have invested an additional $30, so, again, there is no change in wealth. If the right is sold, the shareholder will have the initial share, now worth $40, plus $10 in cash (the proceeds of the sale of the right). Again, no change in total wealth. It should be apparent, then, that from the perspective of the shareholder, there is no enrichment associated with the issuance of the right.  The receipt of the right presents the stockholder with a choice either to invest additional funds in the corporation (without paying brokerage fees) or to liquidate part of his or her investment (with convenience comparable to that associated with sale of a stock dividend). Some shareholders may object to being confronted with such a choice.  Moreover, if a shareholder has an unrealized gain in the shares (that is, if the shareholder bought the shares for a price less than current market value), and elects to sell the rights, the shareholder will be required to pay tax on some of the gain. In other words, for the shareholder who elects not to increase her or his investment, the use of stock rights may trigger income-tax liability.[66]

[66] The cost, or "basis," of the original shares is allocated between those shares and the stock rights according to their relative market values.  The gain recognized for tax purposes is the difference between the proceeds of the sale of the stock rights and the amount of basis allocated to them. Int.Rev.Code § 307.

In the example used here, the exercise price is set low ($30), with the effect of forcing exercise. Thus, the corporation is assured of receiving the money it seeks to raise and it is not necessary to use the services of an underwriter to guarantee the result. The costs are therefore likely to be low compared with the cost of a direct sale of new shares to the public. Often, however, corporations set the price at a figure near the current market price and hire underwriters, as they would with a direct sale to the public. This practice is puzzling. Moreover, rights offerings are seldom used in this country,[67] and a leading textbook states, "the arguments that firms make for avoiding rights issues don't make sense."[68]

Apart from the potential tax liability mentioned above, a possible explanation is that when new shares are sold in a public offering, the investment bankers who effectuate the transaction perform, on behalf of shareholders, a "monitoring" function—that is, they examine carefully the past performance and future plans of the firm. The investment bankers guarantee (or "bond," to use a word popular among economists) their representations by putting their reputations on the line and reputation is, of course, important to any investment banking firm that expects to be called upon to perform similar services in the future. The added cost of the public offering is the price firms must pay for the "seal of approval" of the investment banker.[69] The willingness of the managers to subject themselves to outside scrutiny may be their way of proving to the investing public that they are performing effectively. This kind of conduct may tend to enhance share values and managers may have enough fidelity to the interests of shareholders, or enough concern for their own jobs, to want to try to do so.[70]

One other explanation for the avoidance of stock rights as a means of raising new equity is that if the bargain-price approach is used, the

---

[67] See Clifford W. Smith, Jr. *Alternative Methods for Raising Capital: Rights Versus Underwritten Offers,* 5 J. Financial Economics 273 (1977), reporting that over 80 percent of equity offerings examined were accomplished by sales of new securities by investment bankers. By contrast, "in the UK, as in most other European countries, quoted companies raise virtually all their new equity capital via the rights issue method." Paul Marsh, Equity Rights Issues and the Efficiency of the UK Stock Market, 34 J. Finance 839 (1979).

[68] Richard A. Brealey and Stewart C. Myers, Principles of Corporate Finance 360 (4th ed. 1991).

[69] See Clifford W. Smith, Jr., Investment Banking and the Capital Acquisition Process, 15 J. Financial Economics 3, 15–16 (1985).

[70] This explanation seems to have some force, but it raises the questions of just what it is that induces managers to want to maximize share values, why there are not better ways of proving one's competence, and why some firms seem to need the seal of approval and others do not. Bear in mind, investment bankers reflect their view of management primarily by the price they set for a new offering. Weak management performance generally will mean only that the offering price will be lower than it would be with stronger management, but presumably the new offering price will be in line with the price of existing shares (whose price will already reflect management's competence or lack of it). So it's by no means clear just what signal investment bankers are able to send to investors and how this affects management behavior and shareholder welfare.

price of the shares will fall. If the managers' stock option agreements do not contain a provision adjusting the number of option shares, or the exercise price, to take account of the decline in share price, the value of the stock options will decline. Thus, the managers will have a disincentive to using a cost-effective method of raising equity capital—namely, the issuance of stock rights.

Finally, the issuance of stock rights at a bargain price will reduce the price of existing shares and may therefore have a disruptive effect on publicly traded options.

### 2.   Options and Warrants.

a.   *Preface.* In most of the traditional literature on the financial structure of firms, options and warrants receive relatively little attention.   In part this may be attributable to the fact that warrants are relatively little used in the financing of modern public corporations. The same has been true of options until quite recently. Moreover, options are extraneous to the firm (a point explained immediately below). Nonetheless, options and warrants deserve substantial attention here, for several reasons. First, options are now widely traded and their existence is likely to have considerable impact on thinking about the financing of economic activity. Warrants are interesting in this connection because one's understanding of options can be sharpened by comparing options and warrants. Second, an examination of options and warrants provides insights into the nature of other economic relationships in firms and provides or sharpens tools for the analysis of those relationships.   Thus, for example, financial theorists have recently found it useful to think of common stock as an option to buy the firm from the bondholders. (See Sec. IV, below.) Finally, while there are dominant styles of financing public corporations, an understanding of other possibilities is important for anyone who wants to be able to understand the nature and consequences of financial arrangements in some public firms, in many closely held firms, and in other types of business organization. Warrants and options are a significant feature of privately negotiated financing, where there is ample room for creativity.

b.   *Options.* An *option* is just what the word implies. We will examine options to purchase common stock. (In Chapter 6, we will return to discuss options in greater detail.) One kind of common stock option is issued by a corporation to its employees (usually high-level executives) as a compensation and incentive device. These are generally referred to as compensatory stock options. Their popularity is attributable largely to the tax benefits they provide to the employees (usually at the cost of greater tax detriments to the employers). We will not examine these options. (Their financial characteristics are similar to those of warrants, discussed in the following subsection. Their tax treatment is complex and well beyond the scope of this book.) Compensatory stock options are mentioned only to avoid confusion with the kind of option that has more relevance to financial, or organizational, structure.

The kind of option that we will be concerned with is a contract between two individuals, in which one individual agrees to sell to the other a specified asset, such as a certain number of shares of stock, for a specified price at a specified date in the future (or, with most such options in this country, at any time before that future "expiration" date). This is an option to buy, or "call" option, as opposed to an option to sell, or "put" option. To illustrate a call option, suppose that shares of stock of *X* Corporation are selling for $50 and that an investor, Ida, owns 100 of these *X* shares. Suppose there is a speculator, Sam, who anticipates a short-term rise in the price of the stock and wants to take maximum advantage of this expectation. Sam might offer to pay Ida $100 for the right to buy her 100 shares for, say, $55 per share, any time within the next 9 months. He would be under no obligation to buy. If the deal were consummated, Ida would be the seller and Sam the buyer of a call option. This kind of option is also sometimes referred to as a *"call."* If Ida were to pay Sam for the right to sell her stock to him for, say, $45 at any time within the next 9 months, the transaction would be called a "put." The call option gives Sam an opportunity to gamble on the possibility that the price of the shares will rise, without actually buying those shares and without exposing himself to the risk of loss of more than his $100. Ida continues to bear the risk of a decline in the price of the shares. She retains legal title to the shares and the right to vote them. (The right to vote could be transferred to Sam, but this would be unusual and is not done with publicly traded options.) With the put option, by contrast, Sam is gambling that the price of the shares will not fall below $45, while Ida buys protection against the possibility that it will do so. In either case, Ida reduces the riskiness of her investment position; to that extent she shifts risk to Sam. (Where the word "option" is used without specification of put or call, generally what is meant is a call.)

An option can be thought of as a *side-bet*. It is a contract that affects the two parties to it without affecting the corporation or the other shareholders.

Suppose that Sam has paid Ida $100 for the option to buy Ida's 100 shares at $55 per share. If the price of the stock remains below $55 until the expiration date, the option will not be exercised. Ida will have won the bet with Sam. She may, however, have lost her bet—implicit in the decision not to sell her 100 shares outright—that the price of the shares would not decline. Sam will be out the entire $100. He will have lost his entire investment. Ida will still have her stock, plus the $100. (Ida will also have any dividends paid during the option period.)

If the price of the stock is above $55 just before the expiration date of the option, then, disregarding transaction costs, that option will have some value. If, for example, the price were to rise to $56, the option would be worth $100, since it would give the holder the right to buy for $5,500 stock that could be sold for $5,600. In that situation, Sam could exercise the option, sell it to someone else who would exercise it, or demand $100 from Ida for relinquishing his right. Sam would then have come out even (disregarding the forgone interest on the $100). If the price of the stock turned out to be $60 per share, the value of the option would be $500. Sam would have a gain of $400 on his investment of $100. Thus, there is a strong probability that Sam can lose everything or gain a high return. His position is much more risky than it would have been if, for example, he had invested his $100 in two shares of the common stock. He has high leverage. (See Chapter 1, Sec. II(F).)

Note that at the time the option is bought by Sam it has a value (here, $100) even though the exercise price ($55) is above the market price ($50). (When that relationship between exercise and option price obtains, the option is said to be "out of the money.") The option held by Sam, plus the remaining interest held by Ida constitute together the entire ownership interest in the stock. Ida has, in effect, carved out a part of her total bundle of ownership rights and sold that carved-out interest to Sam. At the outset, then, the value of her remaining interest ought to be $4,900—which is the value of the entire bundle of rights in the 100 shares ($5,000) less the value of the carved-out interest ($100)— unless the process of carving up the bundle increases its total value. That kind of possibility, of some increase in total value, is discussed (though not with specific references to this example) in the next chapter. For present purposes it is sufficient to note that any such increase would be relatively small. Ida will have altered the nature of her holdings (she will have reduced the volatility of her total investment, as long as the $100 is held as cash), but she will not have significantly increased her wealth. If the option is not exercised, she will be better off than she would have been had she not sold it, but the initial value of the transaction should not be judged by how things turn out. The $100 is not some sort of windfall to Ida. It can best be thought of as the proceeds of the sale of part of the bundle of rights represented by her investment in and ownership of the 100 X Corporation shares.

One other possibility deserves brief mention. Suppose that Ida does not own any shares of X stock but nonetheless enters into a contract giving Sam the right to buy 100 shares from her at $55 per share any time within the next 9 months. That is sometimes called a "*naked option.*" It has economic attributes similar to those of a "*short sale,*" which is a transaction in which a person sells stock that he or she does not own, for delivery at some specified time in the future. A person who sells short, like one who sells a naked option, is taking a risky position, gambling that the price of the stock will not rise. The seller of the naked option is content if the price of the stock does not rise above the option price. The short seller hopes for the greatest possible decline in price.

One final observation. Suppose Ida buys an option to purchase 100 shares of X Corp. common stock one year from now at $5 per share and puts aside in a savings account the $500 needed to exercise the option.

At the same time, Sam buys 100 shares of X Corp. common and simultaneously buys a put that gives him the right to sell the shares for $500 one year from now. Ida and Sam have essentially identical investments in X Corp.[71] If there is any disparity in the cost of acquiring the investment one way rather than the other, there is an opportunity to make some money on what is called "arbitrage." For the lawyer what is more important is the simple observation that there are two different ways to reach the same result. A knowledge of such realities is often valuable in helping clients structure their deals.

    c.  *Warrants.* A warrant is a form of option that is like a stock right or a compensatory option in that it is issued by the corporation. Typically, the option price of a warrant is above the market price at the time of issuance and the option or exercise period is some substantial number of years. Warrant holders, despite their relatively long-term, equity-type interest in the corporation, do not share in control; they do not vote for directors.

    Warrants are most commonly issued as part of a "package" with some other security (usually a bond or debenture). While this kind of financing device is not widely used by publicly held corporations and may not be of great aggregate economic significance, it deserves attention for the insights it offers into broader financing issues. By way of illustration, suppose that a corporation intends to raise $1,000,000 by selling its bonds and that if it wanted to sell straight bonds at par it would be required to pay 12 percent interest. This interest rate might be objectionable for two reasons. First, in the short run the required interest payments might create a cash flow problem. That is, the corporation might find it difficult to generate sufficient cash with which to meet the high interest obligation, perhaps because of an extended period of time needed to gear up for production of some new product. Second, the high interest rate might make the firm look bad, in that for some people high interest rates are thought to be synonymous with "bad risk."

    Consider three possible approaches to these problems. First, the corporation might sell $1,100,000 face value 12 percent bonds at par. The extra $100,000 could be used to help meet the cash flow problem stemming from the higher interest rate. That would not solve the "bad risk" problem. Second, the corporation might issue $1,200,000 face value 9 percent bonds and sell them, at a discount to take account of the unrealistic interest rate, for $1,000,000. That would help solve the cash flow problem, but the discount, plus the fact that the yield to maturity would presumably be 12 percent, would still probably spell "bad risk." Finally, the corporation could issue $1,000,000 face value 9 percent

---

[71] Ida will earn interest on the $500 in her savings account while Sam will receive dividends on the stock. The amount of the interest and the dividends should be predictable with reasonable accuracy and should be reflected in the option and put prices.

bonds with warrants attached. The warrants, sometimes described as a "sweetener," provide an extra item of value to the buyer that might make it possible to sell the bonds at par. The cash flow problem might be solved. If the public really thought that these were 9 percent bonds (rather than 12 percent bonds with part of the return in the form of the warrants), then the "bad risk" stigma might be avoided. When the matter is stated this baldly, it may seem unlikely that anyone would be fooled. There is, however, some evidence that people are fooled (though the ones who are fooled may be those who suppose, wrongly, that others are).

d. *The Options Markets.* Options on corporate securities are today widely traded on five options exchanges,[72] but the options traded on these exchanges represent neither ownership claims against the corporations that have issued the underlying securities nor rights against their shareholders. To facilitate trading, the terms of traded options needed to be standardized. To achieve this, the options exchanges created the Options Clearing Corporation ("OCC"), which is jointly owned by them. An OCC call option conveys the right to buy, and a put option conveys the right to sell, a specified quantity of securities within a fixed period at a specified price. The OCC is the issuer of all options (both put options and call options), and is thus the buyer to every seller and the seller to every buyer of traded options. To close out a position, the buyer of an option simply makes an offsetting sale of an identical option to the OCC, and a seller of an option simply makes an offsetting purchase.

For the last decade, the options markets have also traded options on stock indexes. Such an option may be written either on a broad-based index that is a proxy for the market as a whole or on a narrower index keyed to a particular industry or a particular country or geographic region. The best known and most heavily traded index option has been the option on the Standard & Poor's (S & P) 100, which is based on the value of the one hundred stocks in that index and trades on the Chicago Board Options Exchange (CBOE). Options on stock indexes (and futures on stock indexes) permit investors to buy and sell entire diversified portfolios very quickly and have given rise to complicated trading strategies (including practices known as "program trading" and "portfolio insurance," which are discussed below in Chapter 6). For present purposes, all that is important to keep in mind is that investors (including corporations) resort to these strategies for "hedging" purposes—that is, to quickly reduce their exposure to risk. For example, an investor with substantial stock investments could quickly buy a put option if it feels that the stock market is about to decline (or if it simply feels uncomfortable about the current level of its exposure). Hedging is an important

---

[72] These are: The American Stock Exchange, the Pacific Coast Stock Exchange, the Philadelphia Stock Exchange, the Chicago Board Options Exchange (CBOE), and the New York Stock Exchange. For an overview, see Joel Seligman, *The Structure of the Options Markets,* 10 J.Corp.L. 141 (1984).

aspect of corporate finance, but it is a means of limiting liabilities, not of raising capital. It is further considered in Section F below.

　　e.　*Further Observations on Options and Warrants.* Several miscellaneous observations on options and warrants deserve brief mention.

　　First, we have seen that an option is a side bet pursuant to which the buyer in effect acquires the opportunity to deprive the seller of all of the gain above a certain level for each share covered by the option. An option affects only the shareholder who sells it. A warrant, on the other hand, affects all the corporation's shares but deprives each share of only a part of the prospective gain above a certain level. Suppose, for example, that a corporation has a total value of $50,000 and that it has 1,000 shares of common stock, and no other securities outstanding. Imagine that we are living in a nice, simple, clean-cut world and that we can assume that the value of each share of common stock is $50 ($50,000 total value divided by 1,000 shares). If the value of the corporation were to rise to $70,000, the value of each share would be $70. Suppose, however, that when the value of the corporation is $50,000 and the value of each share is $50, the corporation sells a warrant giving the holder the right to buy 100 shares of common for $60 at any time within the next 5 years and that the corporation receives $1,000 for this warrant. Just after the sale of the warrant the corporation will be worth $51,000. It does not follow that each share of existing common will be worth $51. There is now another equity claim, the warrant, to be accounted for. Each existing shareholder has in effect exchanged, for his or her pro rata interest in the $1,000 proceeds of the sale of the warrant, a carved-out partial interest in his or her equity interest in the corporation. If, for example, the total value of the corporation at the expiration of the option period would have risen by 80 percent, to $90,000 without the sale of the warrant, then each existing share would have been worth $90. Given the sale of the warrant for $1,000, and assuming that the value of $1,000 contributed by the warrant holder rises by 80 percent, to $1,800, the value of the corporation should turn out to be $91,800. But the existing shares will not be worth $91.80—or $90. The warrant will, of course, be exercised. The corporation will issue 100 new shares and receive $6,000 ($60 per share). The new value of the corporation will be $97,800 and the new number of shares 1100, and the value of each share will be $88.[73] All during the exercise period, the value of each existing share will be affected by the prospect that part of the gains of the corporation above a certain level will be captured by the warrant holder. Just before the expiration of the five-year exercise period, it should be obvious to everyone that the warrant will be exercised. That fact should be fully reflected in the price of each existing share, so there should be no change in price when the warrant is in fact exercised. This is not to deny that there is "dilution" of the existing equity interest incident to the exercise

---

[73] $97,800 ÷ 1100 = $88.

of the warrant. It is merely to argue that the prospect of that dilution is likely to be fully reflected in the current price of existing shares.

With an option, by contrast, the holder of the option captures all of the gains on each share above a certain level. We must be careful, however, to avoid overstating the significance, from the perspective of the individual investor, of this distinction between an option and a warrant. It should be kept in mind that the owner of shares of stock can sell an option on part, rather than all, of those shares, achieving individually and voluntarily results similar to those achieved collectively by the sale of warrants by the corporation.

Second, it should be clear that the sale of an option on one's shares reveals a somewhat negative appraisal of the prospects of the corporation. A person who sells an option is betting that the price of the stock will not rise above the option price. Similarly, when a corporation sells warrants, it is betting that it will not be as successful as the purchaser of the warrants expects it will be. An optimistic management would not sell warrants (or common stock). It would wait and sell common stock after the price had risen, in the meantime relying on other sources of funds. (See Chapter 5, Sec. III(N), discussing the negative message implicit in the sale of new common stock.)

Third, we have seen that warrants are often issued as part of a bond and warrant package. Usually the warrant can be traded separately, so the purchaser can adjust the package to his or her tastes. The package, consisting of a very safe security (the bond) and a very risky security (the warrant) may have investment attributes similar to those of common stock. Other combinations can, of course, be achieved. One can combine common with warrants and bonds with common, in varying relative amounts. Obviously, the same kinds of possibilities are available with the use of options, and the addition of puts expands the possibilities even further. For our purposes, what is important is the observation that the nature of an individual's investment in a firm is not limited to the simple forms established by its financial structure. This point is elaborated below. (See Sec. IV.)

Fourth, the public has a taste for options. In recent years an active, high-volume market in options has developed. This market is based on short-term (9 months or less) options with uniform terms. Warrants, after falling out of favor, experienced renewed popularity in the 1980's. They are issued, typically, either as part of a package with a bond or as compensation to underwriters.

Finally, there are potential conflicts between option and warrant holders, on the one hand, and common shareholders, on the other. These conflicts are similar to those between common shareholders and bondholders, discussed earlier in this chapter. (Sec. III(A)(9).) One conflict has to do with investment strategy. In certain circumstances (by no means uncommon), a shift to a more risky investment strategy will increase the value of an option or warrant at the expense of the common. This outcome is a function of the fact that a firm that increases the volatility risk of its investments increases the chances of big gains and big losses. The option or warrant holder benefits from the big gains without being exposed to the big losses. Another conflict relates to dividend policy. An option or warrant holder will prefer to see the corporation pay no dividends. Money that is retained by the corporation increases the value of the option or warrant; money that is paid out as dividends benefits only the common shareholders. These potential conflicts may be insignificant in the case of options of short duration covering shares of large corporations (which ordinarily cannot quickly change the risk characteristics of their investments and do not make drastic changes in dividend policy). Perhaps this helps explain the phenomenon of a huge market in short-term options and a relative dearth of warrants. It may also help explain why warrants are a significant phenomenon in privately negotiated deals. There, it may be feasible to impose restrictions on the payment of dividends and on changes in investment strategy or the circumstances may be such as to leave management with no freedom of choice about these matters.

## D. PREFERRED STOCK

**1. Introduction.** In prevailing thought and practice, common stock (equity) and bonds (debt) are the bulwarks of the financial structure of corporations. They are the classic or pure modes. Everything else tends to be explained by comparison with common stock or bonds, or both. Preferred stock is described as a *hybrid* of the two basic securities. What this seems to mean is that as to some functional attributes it is like debt, as to others like equity, and as to still others, somewhere between the two. These attributes, which will be described below, are prescribed mostly in state corporation codes and in the corporate articles and by-laws. In this respect, preferred stock is like common.

In recent years many variations of preferred stock have appeared. Some of the most important features that are used are convertibility (into common stock) and variable rates, leading to instruments such as a convertible, adjustable rate preferred, or CAP. Another recent, and highly popular innovation is the MIPS (Monthly Income Preferred Stock), which claims the advantage for the issuer of a tax deduction of the periodic dividend. A security called "preferred" stock is often used in venture capital deals, but it can best be thought of as common stock with a liquidation preference; typically, it carries voting rights, is not entitled to dividends, and must be converted into ordinary common stock when the firm goes public.

The description that follows focuses on traditional publicly issued preferred stock, now for the most part issued only by corporations in regulated industries. As with debt obligations, in recent years there has been considerable innovation in preferred stock. (See supra Section III(A)(20).) These innovations, including mandatory conversion, adjustable conversion price, and optional exchange for debt obligations,[74] will not be discussed.

**2. Control.** Preferred shareholders do not participate in the election of directors except, as explained below, where dividends have not been paid for some specified period of time.

**3. Return.** The return to preferred stock is in the form of dividends declared by the Board of Directors. The amount of the dividend is fixed. It is often expressed as a percentage of the par value of the shares, but can be expressed simply as a dollar amount per share per year. The decision whether to pay a preferred stock dividend is within the discretion of the board. Failure to pay is not an act of default like the failure to pay interest on a debt. From the perspective of the corporation (or, perhaps more accurately, its managers and common shareholders) this is one of the attractions of preferred stock, as compared with bonds and other debt.

These days, publicly issued preferred stock is almost always cumulative, which means that if dividends are not paid in any year, the obligation accumulates. No common stock dividend can be paid unless the preferred's past unpaid (cumulative) dividends, or arrearages, and current dividends have been paid. Moreover, if preferred stock dividends are not paid, the preferred shareholders may become entitled to representation on the Board of Directors. Typically this control provision is triggered by the failure to pay anywhere from four to eight quarterly dividends. The number of directors that the preferred can then elect depends on state law and private agreement; it may or may not be a majority. In the case of so-called "preferred" stock issued privately, in venture capital situations, the preferred dividend may not be cumulative, but no dividend can be paid on common unless a dividend is paid on the preferred. In such situations, the preferred is almost certain to be convertible into common and is likely to carry a vote, so it resembles a second class of common, with a liquidation preference.

If the preferred stock dividend is not cumulative, then in the absence of a provision shifting control to the preferred, the position of the preferred may become virtually untenable. The common shareholders can exercise their control to retain all earnings, forgoing dividends themselves and paying nothing to the preferred shareholders for, say, five years. In the sixth year they can then have the corporation pay the annual preferred stock dividend and pay all the retained earnings from earlier years as dividends to themselves. It is somewhat surprising, but

---

[74] See Kenneth A. Carow and John J. McConnell, A Survey of U.S. Corporate Financing Innovations: 1970–1997, 12 Journal of Applied Corporate Finance 55 (Spring 1999).

nonetheless a fact, that cumulative preferred shareholders ordinarily are not entitled to interest on arrearages.

If the corporation is liquidated voluntarily, the preferred shareholders are entitled to a fixed sum (usually par value) plus any cumulative dividends, to the extent that funds are available, before any distribution can be made to common shareholders.

**4. Risk.** Implicit in the preceding discussion is the proposition that the expected volatility of current returns on preferred stock at any time is less than that on common and greater than that on bonds. The same kind of relationship obtains with respect to default risk. In the event of insolvency, the claim of preferred shareholders is subordinate (junior) to the claims of bondholders and other creditors but prior (senior) to the claims of common shareholders. It should be recalled, however, that the failure to pay preferred stock dividends does not trigger any right on the part of preferred shareholders to demand repayment of their investment. And even if the failure to pay dividends results in the preferred shareholders gaining control of the Board of Directors, ordinarily they cannot force liquidation over the objection of the common shareholders.

Sometimes preferred shareholders are protected by special provisions, such as a limitation on the amount of dividends that can be paid on the common. Sinking fund retirement requirements are also sometimes used to reduce the risks to the preferred. (The description of bond sinking funds, Sec. III(A)(6), is applicable to preferred stock sinking funds.)

**5. Duration and Its Consequences.** Ordinarily, the duration of the preferred stock investment is indefinite. Often the preferred stock is callable (redeemable) by the corporation, usually at a modest premium over the amount of the initial investment plus any cumulative dividends. The preferred shareholders have no right, however, to a return of their investment at some definite time in the future. This fact, together with the fact that the failure to pay dividends does not lead to a winding up of the firm, has produced some rather dramatic illustrations of the kind of conflict between junior and senior claimants that we have previously observed. (See Sec. III(A)(12) and Sec. III(C)(2)(e), above.)

Suppose that upon its formation, X Corporation raises $200,000 by selling 100,000 shares of common stock for $1 per share and 1,000 shares of cumulative preferred stock for $100 per share. Suppose that the promised dividend on the preferred is $8 per share annually and that upon liquidation the preferred is entitled to $100 plus arrearages. Suppose finally that the $200,000 of initial capital is invested in a business that has not turned out well; that the expected annual earnings of the firm are $5,000; that the liquidation value of the firm (based on these earnings) is $50,000; and that the corporation is not in arrears on preferred stock dividends but in the future will be able to pay such dividends only to the extent of current earnings.  Consider the position of the common shareholders.

If the corporation were liquidated, the entire proceeds ($50,000) would go to the preferred; the common would be wiped out. As we have seen, however, the common shareholders are under no obligation to consent to liquidation. They have nothing to lose by insisting that the corporation stay in business.  Present liquidation value is not controlling. The present value of the common will depend on the prospects for future returns to the corporation above the amount needed to satisfy the claims of the preferred. This will depend, in turn, on the dispersion of possible outcomes for the corporation.  Suppose that the present investment strategy of the corporation yields the following set of probabilities, outcomes, and values:

### STRATEGY I

| Probability | Outcome Outcome (Earnings) | Value |
|---|---|---|
| 0.2 | $4,000 | $  800 |
| 0.6 | 5,000 | 3,000 |
| 0.2 | 6,000 | 1,200 |
| 1.0 | | $5,000 |

As long as the corporation adheres to this strategy, the most it will earn is $6,000 per year. Nothing will ever be available for the common. The common might have some obstructionist or nuisance value, depending on what portion of the Board of Directors it elects, but that value presumably would be small.

Now suppose that the corporation has available to it another investment strategy, to which it can easily shift, with the following characteristics:

### STRATEGY II

| Probability | Outcome Outcome (Earnings) | Value |
|---|---|---|
| 0.4 | $    0 | $    0 |
| 0.2 | 5,000 | 1,000 |
| 0.4 | 10,000 | 4,000 |
| 1.0 | | $5,000 |

A shift to Strategy II would produce a 40 percent chance of a total return of $10,000, which would leave $2,000 for the common, after meeting the $8,000 obligation to the preferred. The prospective gain to the common from such a shift obviously would be at the expense of the preferred. In Strategy I, the entire expected return of $5,000 is allocable to the preferred; in all three possible outcomes, all the earnings in effect belong to the preferred; to the extent that any earnings are retained, the claim of the preferred rises correspondingly. In Strategy II, the expected return to the preferred is only $4,200.[75] The expected return to the common is $800.

Suppose that the common shareholders elect a majority of the directors. They are then in a position to have the corporation shift to Strategy II. While this might seem unfair to the preferred, remember that the preferred shareholders could have bargained for more control; they could have bargained for the right to compel liquidation in the event of a failure to pay their dividend; they could have made a short-term loan rather than investing as preferred shareholders. And if they had insisted on those protections, the promised rate of return would no doubt have been lower.

The most obvious protection for the preferred in situations of the sort contemplated here would be a provision giving the preferred the right to elect a majority of the board upon failure to pay the full promised dividend. But even that would not constitute complete protection: the common might be able to foresee the decline in the fortunes of the firm and shift strategy before it became necessary to miss paying any preferred stock dividends. Moreover, if there is a provision that shifts control to the preferred, we may wind up with the shoe on the other foot. If the corporation were initially embarked on Strategy II and the preferred gained control it would then be in a position to cause a shift to Strategy I, thereby depriving the common of the prospect of any return.

There appears to be no fully satisfactory solution to the problem that may be created by this kind of prospective conflict. The problem is by no means a wholly imaginary construct, and it extends beyond the preferred-common relationship. (See Sec. III(A)(9) and Sec. III(C)(2)(d), above.) Yet it appears to have received little analytic attention.

**6. Participating Preferred.** Participating preferred stock is a relatively recent innovation, used mostly for venture capital investments. It can be thought of as common stock with a liquidation preference. That is, it participates in the upside, like common stock, but on liquidation has a prior claim to a stated sum. For example, suppose that the venture capital investor, after several rounds of financing, owns all of the participating preferred stock, with 80% of the equity and a $40 liquidation preference, while the founder/entrepreneur owns all the common stock with 20% of the equity. Suppose that the firm is liquidated and the amount realized is $100. The participating preferred would receive $40 as its liquidation preference plus 80% of the remaining $60, or $48, for a total of $88, with the remaining $12 going to the common. This may be

---

[75] The expected return to the preferred consists of 0.4(0) plus 0.2($5,000) plus 0.4($8,000), or 0 plus $1,000 plus $3,200.

contrasted with convertible preferred with 80% of the equity (upon conversion) and a $40 liquidation preference. The holder of the convertible preferred would convert in anticipation of liquidation at $100, would thereby relinquish the right to a liquidation preference, and would receive $80, with the common receiving $20.

## E.  OTHER FORMS OF INVESTMENT

What follows is a brief description of several other arrangements pursuant to which firms acquire resources needed for their operations. They are of considerable economic significance. The decision to severely truncate their treatment here is arbitrary, based on the thought that more thorough discussion would add relatively little to an understanding of basic functional elements of enterprise organization and its concepts and essential terminology.

**1.  Short–Term Bank Loans.**  Many firms—particularly smaller ones, for which there is no feasible access to public investors—rely heavily on loans from commercial banks. Often these loans will be payable on demand or will be of short duration (a year or less)—though commercial banks also make business loans for longer periods (up to 8 or 10 years). Short-term loans may be renewed, but bankers do not like to see short-term financing misused, through repeated renewals, as a substitute for long-term financing. Bank policy may therefore require short-term borrowers to "clean up" their loans periodically.

With a demand loan, a bank will minimize risk, in comparison with loans of longer duration. It will at the same time gain some degree of de facto control over the borrower. If the bank dislikes the way the borrower is operating, it can threaten to demand repayment of the loan unless changes are made. Thus, in this instance, the lender does in fact have a power to control—which seems inconsistent with earlier speculations. (See Chapter 1, Sec. III(B) and (C).) A partial reconciliation of the inconsistency may lie in the fact that these kinds of loans often are made to new, growing firms and involve significant risks despite their nominally short-term nature. The right to require repayment of a demand note may, after all, be of little effect if both parties know that insistence on repayment would bankrupt the firm and leave the lender with only the most dismal prospects for recovering its investment. Thus, the bank may in fact see its position as relatively risky—which would account for some participation in control. Moreover, bankers will often be able to offer much-needed experience and advice, which will be welcomed by the borrower in a spirit of genuine cooperation. It is not uncommon, by the way, for loan agreements with banks to prohibit changes in the membership on the debtor's board of directors without bank approval.

Ordinarily banks will lend only to reasonably good credit risks. Bankers tend to be most interested in the business borrower's capacity to pay interest and repay principal—as evidenced by its cash-flow history. While many bank loans to businesses are secured by property, or guaranteed by third parties, bankers mostly do not like to lend to firms with doubtful capacity to meet their payment obligations in the normal course of business, even if they have good security. The shaky credit risks must go to *factors* and other *commercial financing institutions* that are willing to lend, at rates higher than those customary for bank loans, on the security of accounts receivable or inventory or other assets.

**2. Commercial Paper.** A firm with a short-term need for cash can borrow through the issuance of large-denomination, short-term promissory notes (for example, a promise to pay $100,000 90 days from issuance). These notes generally are issued by big, established corporations, often are traded in the securities market, and are called *commercial paper*. Purchasers may include other corporations with short-term cash surpluses. Commercial paper is generally considered to be a low-risk security, though occasional disasters (such as that of the Penn Central railroad) occasionally remind us that default on such obligations can occur. That is why the rate, though usually lower than that on other fixed obligations, is higher than that on otherwise comparable Treasury obligations.

**3. Convertible Securities.** A bond or a share of preferred stock may contain a *conversion feature*—that is, a right of the holder to convert it into common stock. For example, a corporation whose common stock is currently selling for $30 per share might sell at par a $1,000 face value (or denomination) 7 percent bond convertible at the option of the holder into 25 shares of common stock until the bond is redeemed (at maturity or earlier upon exercise of a call feature). The conversion feature is a form of option. It will have some value even though the present market price of the common is below the option price. (See discussion of options, Sec. III(C)(2) above.) Here the option price can be thought of as $40 per share since the $1,000 face value bond buys 25 shares, though that may be a bit misleading since a bond with a face value of $1,000 may have a market, or cash, value higher or lower than $1,000, depending on the current market rate of interest, the financial soundness of the issuing company, and other factors. The conversion feature, like a warrant, is a "sweetener" that allows the bond to sell at a lower apparent yield than would otherwise be required. The yield is only apparently lower because calculation of the true yield would require inclusion of the value of the conversion feature as part of the cost to the borrower and return to the lender. One of the leading financial services (Moody's) reports the estimated value of convertible bonds shorn of their conversion features.

A convertible bond is similar to a bond with warrant attached except that with the convertible bond the option cannot be separated from the pure debt aspect of the obligation. Exercise of the conversion privilege takes the form of surrendering the bond. Also, the duration of the conversion (option) period is uncertain since it expires if the bond is called for redemption. Ordinarily, convertible bonds are called when the price of the common has risen sufficiently so that the effect of the call is to force conversion. For example, starting with the hypothetical bond described above, suppose that the price of the common rises to $50. The bond will now be worth at least $1,250 since that is the value of the shares into which it can be converted (25 shares at $50 a share). The bond is likely to be worth more than $1,250 because of the right to receive interest and because of the priority in the event of insolvency. It will not be worth much more, however, because of the prospect that these two advantages (interest and priority) will be eliminated by a forced conversion. The corporation can force conversion by exercising the call feature. There may be a call premium, but it is likely to be small. Suppose that the call price is $1,050 and that the corporation issues a notice of redemption (that is, calls the bonds in for redemption). At this point holders of the bond are forced to convert; if they fail to do so they wind up with a cash payment of $1,050 from the corporation instead of common stock that can be sold for $1,250.

Holders of convertible securities do not vote for directors. Their interests are at odds with those of common shareholders with respect to dividend policy, since earnings that are retained by the corporation will increase the value of the conversion feature by increasing the value of the common stock while earnings that are paid out as dividends benefit only the existing common shareholders. Yet normal dividend policy is subject to the discretion of the board of directors, elected by the common shareholders. (Compare Sec. III(A)(9).)

**4. Leases.** Suppose that a corporation wants to build a factory. It can finance that purchase by selling new common stock or bonds or other securities. Alternatively, it can find an existing factory, or arrange for someone else to build a new one, and lease it from the owner. If the lease is for a long period of time (approaching or equal to the expected life of the factory), the lease is functionally similar economically to a purchase subject to a debt secured by a mortgage or other such lien. At one time it appeared that some companies were using long-term leases in lieu of purchases in order to avoid increasing the amount of debt shown on their books. Recent changes in accounting rules have largely put an end to this kind of slippery conduct. Currently, tax considerations play a major role in the choice between purchase and long-term lease. Where the user of equipment has suffered losses and cannot take full advantage of the deduction for accelerated depreciation, it may gain some benefit from the deduction by leasing from another firm that is in a position to take full advantage of it. Another possible advantage of leasing is that a lessor may be thought to be in a stronger position than a lender in the event of insolvency, though for this purpose the courts may carefully scrutinize transactions to determine whether a purported lease is in substance a sale subject to debt. The important point to bear in mind about long-term leases with fixed rental payments is that they create fixed obligations that in turn create the same kind of leverage and risk that is associated with other fixed obligations, such as ordinary debt or long-term fixed-salary employment contracts.

**5. Trade Credit.** A firm that buys goods and services from other firms will often be allowed some period of time (usually short) in which to pay its bills. In a continuing relationship between a firm and its suppliers some amount will, in these circumstances, always be owed by the firm to its suppliers on such *"open account"* credit. The suppliers are referred to as *trade creditors*. Trade credit in some businesses may be a significant part of the firm's source of funds. The return on the investment of the trade creditors is, of course, in some portion of the profit they make on dealing with the firm. In certain circumstances, a trade creditor may be able to exercise some degree of control over the operations of its customers, by threatening to withhold further credit that is essential to the customer. Ordinarily, however, this will occur only where there appears to be some serious prospect of insolvency. Since trade credit is of short duration, it need not be, and is not, accompanied by the kinds of elaborate agreements (like bond indentures) that ordinarily are a feature of long-term financing. A trade creditor is not locked in for a long term and need not be concerned with rules covering a wide variety of possible changes in circumstances; changes can be adjusted to, by bargain, as they arise, with protection of the creditor taking the form of the right to demand payment.

**6. Asset-backed Securities.** A financial institution's relatively illiquid assets such as credit card receivables, automobile loans, or home-mortgage loans may transferred to a trustee (or other entity). This set of assets is then used as backing for the sale of debt obligations to investors. Thus, the bundling together of the individual assets provides liquidity to the initial holder of those assets.

## F.   MISCELLANEOUS DEVICES AND HEDGING

In privately negotiated transactions one encounters a wide variety of financial devices. Chapter 6 covers these devices, including various types of financial derivatives, in greater detail. For now, three of these appear with sufficient frequency to merit brief attention.

First is the equity interest with a put. (See Chapter 2, Sec. II(E), where the same device is discussed in the partnership context.) Suppose that X Corp. seeks to raise $1,000,000 from Victor, a venture capitalist. Victor thinks well of the prospects of the firm and wants an equity participation (for tax reasons, among others). Suppose that X Corp. offers 40 percent of its common stock in return for the $1,000,000. Victor may, in addition, demand the right to "put" (that is, sell) the common stock back to the corporation for $1,000,000 at the end of, say, 5 years. In this kind of situation, the put is often said to provide "downside protection." That is, it protects Victor in the event that the firm does not prosper. In addition, it gives Victor a way to withdraw his capital; it gives him an "exit vehicle." The existing owners and managers of X Corp. may be so optimistic about the future that they are willing to give Victor the put without demanding much, if anything, in return. That is, the put may at the outset seem valuable to Victor but not to those in control of X Corp. A convertible bond provides the same basic elements: equity participation, downside protection, and an exit vehicle.

A second miscellaneous device is the equity participation with a right of repurchase on the part of the issuer. Here, the corporation might sell to Victor, for $1,000,000, a 40 percent equity interest subject to a right on its part, at its option, to repurchase that interest, for, say, $2,000,000 at the end of five years. Victor might be content to accept such a limitation on his potential profit simply because he thinks there is no real prospect of greater gain. Those in control of the corporation may be far more optimistic and may see the right of repurchase as a way of limiting Victor's participation in future gains and, by the same token, as a device for providing them with the opportunity to raise additional equity capital for a further expansion that they contemplate at the end of the five-year period.

A third and rapidly growing device is the "swap." [76] It is essentially an instrument for hedging various kinds of financial risks. For example, suppose you are a U.S. corporation that has just borrowed $100,000,000 under a ten year loan at a floating interest rate. If interest rates rise sufficiently, you face the prospect of insolvency. But because current rates were historically low, you did not want to turn down this attractive financing. Alternatively, you may have borrowed $100,000,000 in a foreign currency (for example, the Japanese yen or the German mark). If the dollar falls against the foreign currency on the date of any scheduled repayment, you are in trouble. In either of these two cases, there are several devices available to you for limiting your exposure. First, you can buy options (or "futures") on foreign currency, so that if the yen or mark rise against the dollar, your gain on the derivative security will offset your loss on the loan transaction. Similarly, one can hedge interest rate risks by buying derivative securities (options or futures) keyed to interest rates; this is the chief reason why corporate investors engage in such "side bets."

[76] For an overview of "swaps," see Henry T.C. Hu, Swaps, *The Modern Process of Financial Innovation and the Vulnerability of a Regulatory Paradigm*, 138 U.Pa.L.Rev. 333 (1989); The size of the swaps market now dwarfs many other financial markets. See Merton H. Miller, Merton Miller on Derivatives (1997); Kimberly D. Krawiec, Derivatives, Corporate Hedging, and Shareholder Wealth: Modigliani–Miller Forty Years Later, 1998 U. Ill. L. Rev. 1039. While there is some debate over how to describe the size of the market for swaps and other such financial products, there is no doubt that it is huge. See Frank Partnoy, Adding Derivatives to the Corporate Law Mix, 34 Georgia L. Rev. 599 (2000). For a good general description, see Robert W. Hamilton and Richard A. Booth, Business Basics for Law Students, Ch. 16 (1998).

But publicly traded options and futures have a short duration, and it is expensive to insure against such risks by constantly replacing expiring options with new ones. Thus, a new instrument—the swap—has become popular. Under a swap agreement, you enter into the following sort of transaction with a large financial institution (usually, a commercial bank). You would agree to pay interest at a fixed rate (typically, at a small fraction above the current floating rate) to the bank, and it would correspondingly agree to pay you interest at the floating rate (whatever it was from time to time) Thus, if interest rates do rise over the duration of your ten year loan, you are protected; if they fall, you lose on the swap transaction, but profit on the original loan. Essentially, you pass the risk of rate fluctuations on to a superior risk bearer in return for a small fee. A "currency swap" works similarly: you agree to pay the risk-bearing party a stream of payments equal to the scheduled installments on the loan in dollars, and it agrees to pay you the same stream of payments (at the current exchange rate) in the foreign currency.

The process of financial innovation is fast at work in the field of hedging and new derivative securities (options, futures, or swaps) are being constantly developed to enable corporations to hedge other financial risks. (See the further description below, Chapter 5, Sec. V(C)(1).) Most recently, the futures markets have introduced new products that permit corporations and insurers to hedge their insurance risks by buying insurance futures.[77]

## IV. FINANCIAL ALTERNATIVES INSIDE AND OUTSIDE THE FIRM

We have seen (Sec. III(C)(2), above) that options and warrants are, in many respects, similar to one another, and that one formal difference is that warrants are issued by the corporation while options are "side bets." Another way of describing that distinction is to say that a warrant is a financial device within the firm while an option is outside the firm; or that the warrant is a device created by the firm while the option is a similar device created by the financial market. In this Section we will explore more broadly the notion of financing within and outside the firm and will note a few of the factors that might affect the choice of one device over its economic equivalent.

Suppose that Ellen, an entrepreneur, wants to start a business. She is willing to invest $100,000 of her own funds and wants to take the equity position, bearing the greatest risk and taking control. She needs to borrow an additional $100,000 toward a required total investment of $200,000. Dan, an investor seeking relative safety and having no interest in control, is willing to invest $100,000 in a debt position in the firm. If we ignore important factors such as taxes and bankruptcy costs,

---

[77] See Myerson, "A Little Insurance for Insurers," N.Y. Times, August 20, 1992 at  D 1 (CBOE to introduce futures contract on insurance).

and concentrate simply on organizational forms, we will see that there are a number of organizational alternatives that are economic equivalents or near-equivalents. We will also see that functionally equivalent alternatives are available for the public corporation. Five alternatives are described below; many variations would be possible.

First, Ellen could simply borrow $100,000 from Dan and acquire the business as a sole proprietorship. Let us assume that Dan would be willing to lend nonrecourse on the security of the business. That deal, with whatever details as to interest rate, repayment schedule, and so on, that one might fill in, can be taken as establishing the basic economic arrangement. The details need not be specified, since it will be evident that they can be held constant as the formal organizational characteristics change.

Second, Ellen or Dan, or both, could form a corporation. Ellen could contribute $100,000 and take all the common stock (equity) while Dan would invest $100,000 and receive the corporation's bonds or debentures (debt). (Varying the usage, the corporation could sell its common stock to Ellen for $100,000 and its bonds to Dan for $100,000.) The counterpart in a large publicly held corporation, with many equity and debt investors, is apparent; this is the classic mode for that kind of enterprise.

Third, Ellen could form a corporation, contributing $100,000 in return for half of the common stock. She could then borrow $100,000 from Dan and contribute that fund to the corporation in return for the other half of its common. She would simultaneously arrange for all of the common stock of the corporation, now held by her, to be treated as collateral for Dan's loan to her. In short, Ellen would form a corporation with initial capital of $200,000 all represented by common stock, which would in turn serve as collateral for a $100,000 loan from Dan. Again, suppose that Dan would be willing to lend nonrecourse. (If not, he should not be willing to accept the second form, unless Ellen executed a personal guarantee of the corporate debt. In any event, the element of personal liability of Ellen for the debt to Dan can be the same regardless which form is used.) The functional organizational equivalence of this arrangement and the second, more traditional (for large firms) arrangement should be clear.

The public-corporation counterpart to the third arrangement would involve a corporation with no debt, with individual owners of common stock using that stock as collateral for personal, nonrecourse loans equal to half of the amount initially invested. Loans to individuals on the security of shares of stock of public corporations are common, most frequently taking the form of routine "margin loans." A margin loan is one that is made through a stock broker, as part of the process of trading and investing in publicly traded securities. Margin loans are so widely used, and the procedures for processing them so well developed, that relatively small loans can be made with low processing costs. The collateral is considered to be good and the result is that the interest rate is likely to be only slightly above the prime rate. (The prime rate is the rate paid by large borrowers with the highest credit rating.)

Margin loans are personal obligations of the borrower; they are with recourse. The prospect of personal liability may not be of much importance, however, since the loan agreement will provide for sale of the security when its value begins to approach the amount of the loan, and there will be an active market for the security. If the value of the collateral does decline to the point where sale is threatened, the borrower can prevent the sale (liquidation of the collateral) by investing additional funds. By the same token, if the debt were that of the corporation (that is, if debt were inside the firm, as in the second mode), and the firm were on the brink of insolvency, it could seek additional equity investments to avoid default. The equivalence is, to be sure, not perfect, but it is probably closer than might, at first blush, be thought. In any event, the important point to recognize, for our purposes, is that (disregarding taxes, bankruptcy costs, etc.) an investment in a corporation with a 50–50 debt-equity ratio is quite similar economically to an investment in an otherwise identical corporation with no debt, on 50 percent margin.

Fourth, Dan could form a corporation and contribute to it $200,000 in return for all of its common stock. (By hypothesis, he has only $100,000 to invest, but he could easily borrow the additional $100,000, short term, possibly from Ellen. Alternatively, the transaction can be "telescoped," leaving out some of the purely formalistic steps.) Once the corporation is formed, Dan can sell to Ellen for $100,000 an option to buy from him all of the common stock, for $100,000. (The proceeds of the sale of the option would then be used to pay off the short term, "clearing," loan.) The net result is that Dan's investment is $100,000, as is Ellen's, and the corporation has $200,000. Ellen would be required to make an annual payment (e.g., $8,000) to keep the option in force; this would be equivalent to interest on a debt. Exercise of the option would be equivalent to repayment of the debt; lapse would be equivalent to default. This alternative, and its economic equivalence to the other alternatives described above, are examined in more detail in Chapter 1, Sec. XIII. What we wind up with is an equity interest, the option, that is outside the firm.

The option described here seems "in substance" to be a purchase subject to debt—because we are accustomed to using the latter form to achieve the kind of economic relationship at issue. Still, there is no sharp dividing line between options and traditional equity interests. The ordinary "genuine" option can be thought of as a very highly leveraged equity interest. As we have seen, there is now an active market in options relating to the common stock of large, publicly traded corporations. These options are equity interests created outside the firm, by the market, presumably satisfying some financial objective of individuals that is not satisfied by securities issued by the firm.

Finally, Dan could form a corporation and have it issue warrants to be sold to Ellen—equity from within the firm. An exercise of the warrant by Ellen would be equivalent to only partial repayment of the debt, since it would leave Dan with an equity interest. Complete repayment, and termination of Dan's interest, could be achieved by requiring a purchase of Dan's common stock, either by the corporation or by Ellen, whenever the warrant is exercised. That would seem to be a slightly awkward arrangement; the possibility is described only to demonstrate that warrants are equity interests created by the firm.

The following table may help to provide a grasp of the ideas just developed:

### Financial Alternatives

| Nature | Source | |
|---|---|---|
| | Firm | Market |
| Equity | Common Stock Warrants | Options |
| Debt | Bonds | Margin loans Individualized secured loans |

A thorough examination of the factors that influence the choice of financial device is well beyond the scope of this book, although some of those factors will be discussed in the next chapter. Some feeling for the more important influences might, however, be conveyed by the few brief statements that follow.

If a corporation is organized with debt and equity in the classic mode (second alternative above), then in the event of default on the obligation to pay interest or principal, the equity interest is wiped out, but often only after extended and expensive judicial proceedings. Where an equity interest takes the form of an option or warrant, on the other hand, the financial equivalent to default is simply the failure to exercise the option or warrant. The equity interest is eliminated with no fuss or muss (assuming that the courts do not treat the arrangement as a debt-equity arrangement in disguise). In fact, huge amounts of equity investment (perhaps a better phrase is "super-equity" investment) in the form of options become worthless every year without being touched by the complex laws and procedures dealing with insolvency.

Options and purchases on margin are similar in many respects. Options are equivalent to purchases subject to nonrecourse loans. Margin loans are with recourse, but the economic significance of personal recourse may be small. The Federal Reserve Board determines the maximum leverage that can be achieved with margin loans. No such limitation is placed on the leverage available in the options market and the leverage in that market is extremely high compared with almost anything else, including margin loans.

While the effects on choice of financial device of the laws relating to insolvency and the regulation of leverage are not widely discussed, the effects of income taxes certainly are, especially with respect to small, closely held firms. To illustrate, if the second mode (debt and equity within the firm) is used and the corporation repays the debt to Dan, there are no income tax consequences to Ellen. If the third mode (equity within, debt outside the firm) is used and the corporation distributes $100,000 to Ellen, which she uses to repay the loan from Dan, the $100,000 may be treated as a taxable dividend to her. There are many other significant differences in the tax effects of the choice of organizational form. A knowledge of these differences is one of the basic tools of trade of a lawyer advising people on the organization of small businesses.

# Chapter 5

# VALUATION, FINANCIAL STRATEGIES, AND CAPITAL MARKETS

## I. VALUATION

### A. THE INTEREST RATE

We are about to examine methods of valuing assets and enterprises, beginning with so-called money-market instruments like bonds and notes. These methods of valuation require the application of an appropriate rate of interest. That rate could be treated as a given, determined by processes that need not concern us. It may be helpful, however, to inquire briefly into some of the underlying attributes of the rate of interest. The inquiry can best be framed by posing the question, for what does the interest paid on a bond compensate the holder of that bond?

Perhaps the most fundamental component of the interest rate is compensation for the time value of money; this component is sometimes called "pure" interest. It can best be described as what is left after taking out the other elements to be described below; or as the amount that would be paid on a risk-free bond in an era in which value of money were expected to remain constant (that is, in an era of no inflation or deflation). A recent economic study concludes that in the period 1926 to 2004, after properly accounting for inflation, the average (technically, the geometric mean) annual yield on short-term U.S. Treasury obligations was 0.7 percent and on a diversified portfolio of large company common stocks was 7.2 percent.[1]

A second important element in the interest rate for a particular obligation is compensation for the risk of default.

Another element in the interest rate has to do with the "term structure of interest rates" (reflected graphically in the "yield curve"). These phrases refer to the fact that interest rates vary with the duration of the debt. Generally (but not always), long-term obligations bear higher interest rates than shorter-term obligations. The longer the duration, the greater the effect on value of any change in market interest rates and expected rates of inflation. Thus, part of the explanation for higher interest rates on longer-term obligations may lie in their greater volatility risk.

---

[1] R. Ibbotson Associates, Stocks, Bonds, Bills and Inflation: 2005 Yearbook at 83, 91 (2005). The return on small-company stocks was 9.1 percent and on intermediate-term government bonds was 2.2 percent.

320

In recent years economists have come to accept the fact that the interest rate includes compensation for expected inflation. If the expected rate of inflation is zero, the pure interest must be at least slightly more than zero; otherwise people would hold their savings in the form of cash. If the rate of inflation is high enough, however, the pure interest element could be negative, at least in the short run. This is so because people who are committed to a plan of saving (for example, people who are saving for retirement) will be better off to invest at any positive nominal interest rate, even though it is less than sufficient to compensate for inflation, than to hold their savings in cash.

Another component referred to in the economic literature is the "liquidity" or "illiquidity" premium, described and discussed in Chapter 4 (Sec. II(D)). This may be thought of as part of compensation for volatility risk.

## B.  MARKET PRICE

One way to determine the value of an asset is simply to look to the price recently paid for identical or comparable assets in arm's length transactions. For example, if we want to know the value of shares of common stock of General Motors Corporation, we can simply look in the financial section of the daily newspaper and find the price at which such shares traded the previous day on the New York Stock Exchange and can equate this market price with value.

Valuation by reference to market transactions is also customary for other assets, such as parcels of real estate, but with many such assets comparability becomes a problem. Moreover, valuation by reference to the market prices of comparable assets involves an obvious problem of circularity; it is a method that tells us that similar assets have similar values without telling us anything about how that value is determined. The solution to the initial problem of circularity and to the problem of determining what it is that makes assets comparable lies in the basic economic tenet that the value of any asset is determined by the amount and character of the returns that one can expect to derive from it. The value of an asset is a function of its expected net returns and the estimated volatility of those returns. Two assets are comparable if they have the same expected return and the same (volatility) risk. (See Chapter 4, Sec. II(A) and (B).)

Unfortunately, even this formulation leaves a problem of circularity. If we know the volatility, we can determine an appropriate rate of return, but only by looking to comparable assets or investments; it is a market-determined rate. That leaves the question of how that rate is itself determined. Some of the determinants of the market rate of interest are suggested by the discussion, in Section A above, of the compensatory elements included in the interest rate. Those determinants in turn reflect the inclination of some people to borrow in order to be able to consume now rather than later; the inclination of other people to save now in order to be able to consume later (for example, on retirement); the inclination of others to borrow in order to finance productive processes, which is in turn a function, in part, of the productivity of capital; and the supply of money.  The economic literature on the determinants of the level of the interest rate is, at best, difficult.  We do know, however, that people lending money or investing in common stocks or other assets have definable (though often only roughly so) ideas about the rate of return that they expect from given kinds of assets.  A person investing in corporate bonds may expect a rate of return of, say, 9 percent.  A person investing in a new business venture may insist on an expected net rate of return of 20 percent.  For our purposes this is enough; it is not necessary to know how these figures are ultimately determined—though we will return to some aspects of that problem later in this Chapter (Sec. I(D)).  All we need to know is that for a given type of asset there will be an appropriate market-determined rate of return.

## C.  DISCOUNTED PRESENT VALUE

**1.  Single Amounts.**  Given the fact of a positive rate of interest, a specified amount of money available to you today is worth more than a claim to the same amount of money in the future.  This is true regardless of your inclination to save or consume.  Suppose, for example, that if you were to receive $1,000 today you would not spend it but would instead save it for a trip to Europe a year from today.  Even though you don't plan to spend the money until next year, you are still better off to receive it today—for the obvious reason that you can earn interest on it in the meantime.  Suppose that you can make a risk-free investment (for example, in an insured savings account) at 8 percent.  On that assumption, the $1,000 received today will be worth $1,080 a year hence.  Turning that around, $1,080 to be received one year hence has a *present value*—often referred to somewhat redundantly as a *discounted present value*—of $1,000.  If the $1,000 were to be received not today but, instead, one year from now, its present value would be $926 (determined by the process to be described immediately below).  The $926 is the amount which, if invested at 8 percent, would grow to $1,000 at the end of one year.

More generally, the present value of a future sum is simply the amount that one must invest today at the appropriate interest rate in order to have the future sum at the future date.  Algebraically, then, for an amount to be received one year hence,

$$P(1 + r) = A,$$

where P means the present amount, r means the annual interest rate, and A means the future amount.  To solve for P, we write the formula,

$$P = \frac{A}{1 + r.}$$

Thus, if the future amount is $1,000 and the interest rate is 8 percent, the formula yields,

$$P = \frac{\$1,000}{1 + .08} = \frac{\$1,000}{1.08} = \$926.$$

If the payment is to be received two years, rather than one year, from today, then, assuming annual compounding, the formula is:

$$P = \frac{A}{(1 + r)(1 + r)} = \frac{A}{(1 + r)^2}$$

More generally,

$$P_n = \frac{A}{(1 + r)^n,}$$

where n is the number of years to maturity.

Table 5–1 shows the present value of $1 at various years in the future at various interest rates. (The individual values can be computed easily and quickly with an inexpensive hand-held financial calculator. The entire table can be generated readily by a computer with a spread-sheet program.)

**TABLE 5–1**

**Present Value of $1: What a Dollar at End of Specified Future Year Is Worth Today**

| Year | 3% | 4% | 5% | 6% | 7% | 8% | 10% | 12% | 15% | 20% | Year |
|------|------|------|------|------|------|------|------|------|------|-------|------|
| 1 | .971 | .962 | .952 | .943 | .935 | .926 | .909 | .893 | .870 | .833 | 1 |
| 2 | .943 | .925 | .907 | .890 | .873 | .857 | .826 | .797 | .756 | .694 | 2 |
| 3 | .915 | .889 | .864 | .840 | .816 | .794 | .751 | .712 | .658 | .579 | 3 |
| 4 | .889 | .855 | .823 | .792 | .763 | .735 | .683 | .636 | .572 | .482 | 4 |
| 5 | .863 | .822 | .784 | .747 | .713 | .681 | .620 | .567 | .497 | .402 | 5 |
| 6 | .837 | .790 | .746 | .705 | .666 | .630 | .564 | .507 | .432 | .335 | 6 |
| 7 | .813 | .760 | .711 | .665 | .623 | .583 | .513 | .452 | .376 | .279 | 7 |
| 8 | .789 | .731 | .677 | .627 | .582 | .540 | .467 | .404 | .327 | .233 | 8 |
| 9 | .766 | .703 | .645 | .592 | .544 | .500 | .424 | .361 | .284 | .194 | 9 |
| 10 | .744 | .676 | .614 | .558 | .508 | .463 | .386 | .322 | .247 | .162 | 10 |
| 11 | .722 | .650 | .585 | .527 | .475 | .429 | .350 | .287 | .215 | .135 | 11 |
| 12 | .701 | .625 | .557 | .497 | .444 | .397 | .319 | .257 | .187 | .112 | 12 |
| 13 | .681 | .601 | .530 | .469 | .415 | .368 | .290 | .229 | .163 | .0935 | 13 |
| 14 | .661 | .577 | .505 | .442 | .388 | .340 | .263 | .205 | .141 | .0779 | 14 |
| 15 | .642 | .555 | .481 | .417 | .362 | .315 | .239 | .183 | .123 | .0649 | 15 |
| 16 | .623 | .534 | .458 | .394 | .339 | .292 | .218 | .163 | .107 | .0541 | 16 |
| 17 | .605 | .513 | .436 | .371 | .317 | .270 | .198 | .146 | .093 | .0451 | 17 |
| 18 | .587 | .494 | .416 | .350 | .296 | .250 | .180 | .130 | .0808 | .0376 | 18 |
| 19 | .570 | .475 | .396 | .331 | .277 | .232 | .164 | .116 | .0703 | .0313 | 19 |

| Year | 3% | 4% | 5% | 6% | 7% | 8% | 10% | 12% | 15% | 20% | Year |
|------|------|------|------|------|------|------|-------|-------|--------|---------|------|
| 20 | .554 | .456 | .377 | .312 | .258 | .215 | .149 | .104 | .0611 | .0261 | 20 |
| 25 | .478 | .375 | .295 | .233 | .184 | .146 | .0923 | .0588 | .0304 | .0105 | 25 |
| 30 | .412 | .308 | .231 | .174 | .131 | .0994 | .0573 | .0334 | .0151 | .00421 | 30 |
| 40 | .307 | .208 | .142 | .0972 | .067 | .0460 | .0221 | .0107 | .00373 | .000680 | 40 |
| 50 | .228 | .141 | .087 | .0543 | .034 | .0213 | .00852 | .00346 | .000922 | .000109 | 50 |

To determine the value of an amount greater than $1, one simply multiplies by the number of dollars. For example, the present value of $1, to be received one year from today, assuming an interest rate of 8 percent, is $.926. Correspondingly, the present value of $1,000 to be received one year from today at 8 percent is $926. The present value of the same amount two years from today, same interest rate, is $857. The present value of $1,000 to be received nine years from today, at 8 percent, is $500; another way of expressing that relationship is to say that $500 today is worth $1,000 nine years from now (at 8 percent compounded annually) or that in nine years the value of one's investment doubles, at 8 percent. For readers not familiar with numbers such as those shown in the table, a few minutes spent reviewing them will be a worthwhile experience.

**2. Annuities.** An *annuity*, as traditionally defined, is a finite series of annual payments of a specified amount for a specified number of years.[2] Suppose that you have the right to receive $1,000 one year from today plus $1,000 two years from today—a two-year annuity. The present value is obviously the combined value of each of the two payments. As we saw above, the present value of the first payment is $926, of the second payment $857. The total is $1783. Table 5–2 shows present values for a series of year-end payments for various lengths of time at various assumed interest rates. (We can ignore the algebraic formula used in computing the present values.) Using this table we could compute that the present value of $1,000 at the end of each year for two years would be $1780 ($1,000 × 1.78). (This is slightly inaccurate because of rounding off of the numbers in the table.) The present value of the same payment for 5 years would be $3,990. Again, it will be a good experience to spend a few minutes examining the information in the table.

---

[2] In recent years, the term "annuity" has been widely used to describe certain tax-favored investments with insurance companies. Essentially, they are investments with no current return, but rather a future payoff. The tax advantage is that these financial instruments (for peculiar, largely historical and political reasons) allow income and gain to be accumulated tax free until withdrawn. The traditional annuity is still sometimes encountered (and may be a sound investment apart from tax considerations), and, in any event, remains important for its value in describing financial concepts.

**TABLE 5–2**

Present Value of Annuity of $1, Received at End of Each Year

| Year | 3% | 4% | 5% | 6% | 7% | 8% | 10% | 12% | 15% | 20% | Year |
|------|------|------|------|------|------|------|------|------|------|------|------|
| 1 | 0.971 | 0.960 | 0.952 | 0.943 | 0.935 | 0.926 | 0.909 | 0.890 | 0.870 | 0.833 | 1 |
| 2 | 1.91 | 1.89 | 1.86 | 1.83 | 1.81 | 1.78 | 1.73 | 1.69 | 1.63 | 1.53 | 2 |
| 3 | 2.83 | 2.78 | 2.72 | 2.67 | 2.62 | 2.58 | 2.48 | 2.40 | 2.28 | 2.11 | 3 |
| 4 | 3.72 | 3.63 | 3.55 | 3.46 | 3.39 | 3.31 | 3.16 | 3.04 | 2.86 | 2.59 | 4 |
| 5 | 4.58 | 4.45 | 4.33 | 4.21 | 4.10 | 3.99 | 3.79 | 3.60 | 3.35 | 2.99 | 5 |
| 6 | 5.42 | 5.24 | 5.08 | 4.91 | 4.77 | 4.62 | 4.35 | 4.11 | 3.78 | 3.33 | 6 |
| 7 | 6.23 | 6.00 | 5.79 | 5.58 | 5.39 | 5.21 | 4.86 | 4.56 | 4.16 | 3.60 | 7 |
| 8 | 7.02 | 6.73 | 6.46 | 6.20 | 5.97 | 5.75 | 5.33 | 4.97 | 4.49 | 3.84 | 8 |
| 9 | 7.79 | 7.44 | 7.11 | 6.80 | 6.52 | 6.25 | 5.75 | 5.33 | 4.78 | 4.03 | 9 |
| 10 | 8.53 | 8.11 | 7.72 | 7.36 | 7.02 | 6.71 | 6.14 | 5.65 | 5.02 | 4.19 | 10 |
| 11 | 9.25 | 8.76 | 8.31 | 7.88 | 7.50 | 7.14 | 6.49 | 5.94 | 5.23 | 4.33 | 11 |
| 12 | 9.95 | 9.39 | 8.86 | 8.38 | 7.94 | 7.54 | 6.81 | 6.19 | 5.41 | 4.44 | 12 |
| 13 | 10.6 | 9.99 | 9.39 | 8.85 | 8.36 | 7.90 | 7.10 | 6.42 | 5.65 | 4.53 | 13 |
| 14 | 11.3 | 10.6 | 9.90 | 9.29 | 8.75 | 8.24 | 7.36 | 6.63 | 5.76 | 4.61 | 14 |
| 15 | 11.9 | 11.1 | 10.4 | 9.71 | 9.11 | 8.56 | 7.60 | 6.81 | 5.87 | 4.68 | 15 |
| 16 | 12.6 | 11.6 | 10.8 | 10.1 | 9.45 | 8.85 | 7.82 | 6.97 | 5.96 | 4.73 | 16 |
| 17 | 13.2 | 12.2 | 11.3 | 10.4 | 9.76 | 9.12 | 8.02 | 7.12 | 6.03 | 4.77 | 17 |
| 18 | 13.8 | 12.7 | 11.7 | 10.8 | 10.1 | 9.37 | 8.20 | 7.25 | 6.10 | 4.81 | 18 |
| 19 | 14.3 | 13.1 | 12.1 | 11.1 | 10.3 | 9.60 | 8.36 | 7.37 | 6.17 | 4.84 | 19 |
| 20 | 14.9 | 13.6 | 12.5 | 11.4 | 10.6 | 9.82 | 8.51 | 7.47 | 6.23 | 4.87 | 20 |
| 25 | 17.4 | 15.6 | 14.1 | 12.8 | 11.7 | 10.7 | 9.08 | 7.84 | 6.46 | 4.95 | 25 |
| 30 | 19.6 | 17.3 | 15.4 | 13.8 | 12.4 | 11.3 | 9.43 | 8.06 | 6.57 | 4.98 | 30 |
| 40 | 23.1 | 19.8 | 17.2 | 15.0 | 13.3 | 11.9 | 9.78 | 8.24 | 6.64 | 5.00 | 40 |
| 50 | 25.7 | 21.5 | 18.3 | 15.8 | 13.8 | 12.2 | 9.91 | 8.30 | 6.66 | 5.00 | 50 |

The present value is the financial equivalent of the series of future payments. Thus, if you have the right to $1,000 per year for 5 years, in the absence of transaction costs you should be able to sell that claim for $3,990. If you have $3,990 you should be able to trade it for the right to annual payments of $1,000 for five years. And if you want to borrow $3,990, you should be able to do so if you are willing to pay $1,000 per year for five years. (Always assuming that the appropriate interest rate is 8 percent, which assumes in turn that the person obligated to make the payment in each instance is equally creditworthy.)

### 3. Illustrations.

a. *Bonds.* Suppose that there is a corporate bond with a face value or denomination (that is, the principal sum that must be paid at the end of the term of the loan (the maturity date)) of $1,000, paying interest at the rate of 10 percent of the face value annually, and maturing in 5 years. Suppose that the market rate of interest on comparable-quality bonds is 12 percent. The most convenient way to compute the value of the bond is to divide it into two elements—an annuity and a lump-sum terminal payment. The annuity consists of the annual payments of interest of $100 for 5 years. To determine its value we simply find the entry in Table 5–2 for 5 years and 12 percent (3.60) and multiply this by $100, giving us $360. The lump-sum terminal payment is the $1,000 to be paid by the debtor when the bond matures. To determine its value we find the entry in Table 5–1 for 5 years and 12 percent (.567) and multiply this by $1,000, giving us $567. The value of the bond is the combined value of the two elements, $360 plus $567, or $927. If one were to buy the bond for $927 and hold it to maturity, the yield would be 12 percent. (See Chapter 4, Section II(C).)

b.  *Projects or Ventures; Net Present Value Method.*  Suppose that a firm contemplates entering into a new venture that will require an initial capital outlay or investment of $1,000,000; an additional capital outlay of $200,000 at the end of the first year; and another capital outlay of $300,000 at the end of the second year.  Suppose that during the first year the total revenue generated by the project will just equal the operating costs associated with that revenue;  at the end of the second year, revenue will exceed current costs by $200,000;  and that for every year thereafter revenue will exceed current costs by $300,000, until the end of the twentieth year, when the useful life of the physical assets will end, the project will be terminated, and the assets will be sold for their scrap value, estimated to be $100,000.  Finally, suppose that the appropriate discount rate is 15 percent.  We can determine the value of the project by first discounting all capital outlays (other than the initial outlay of $1,000,000) to present value, as follows:

## OUTLAYS

| Amount | End of Year | Present Value |
|---|---|---|
| $200,000 | 1 | $174,000 |
| 300,000 | 2 | 226,800 |
| | | $400,800 |

To compute the present value of the receipts, first note that the project will yield $300,000 per year for 18 years beginning at the end of the third year.  To find the present value of this element, first compute the value of an 18-year annuity of $300,000 at 15 percent.  The entry in Table 5–2 for 18 years and 15 percent is 6.10;  this is multiplied by $300,000, giving us a present value of $1,830,000.  This amount is the value as of the *beginning* of the third year, which is the same as the end of the second year.  In other words, the table gives the value at the beginning of any year for an annuity whose first payment is to be received at the end of the year.  This being so, the $1,830,000 must be treated as an amount to be received two years hence.  We discount it to present value by using the entry in Table 5–1 for 2 years and 15 percent (.756).  The result is $1,383,480.  In addition, there is the $200,000 to be realized at the end of the second year and the $100,000 to be realized at the end of the 20th year.  The total present value of the combined receipts is as follows:

## RECEIPTS

| Amount | End of Year | Present Value |
|---|---|---|
| $  200,000 | 2 | $  151,200 |
| 1,830,000 | 2 | 1,383,480 |
| 100,000 | 20 | 6,110 |
| | | $1,540,790 |

The present value of revenues or receipts ($1,540,790) exceeds the present value of outlays ($400,800) by $1,139,990. This is the present value of the project or venture. It is the figure that corresponds to the value of the bond—the $927—in the above illustration. If we subtract the $1,000,000 initial cost from the present value of the project, we arrive at the net present value. Here there is a positive *net present value*. The project is a good one, producing a present-value gain of $139,990 on an investment of $1,000,000. At a cost of $1,000,000 the project is a bargain; it's as if the bond in the preceding illustration, worth $927, could be bought for $813.

The net present value (NPV) method of valuation has become a basic technique for investment analysis by firms. It can also be used for valuation of the firm itself. It takes account of the cost of money (or the required return) and produces an answer to the question whether a project is worthwhile or not. It will also indicate which of two or more projects of equal size is the most profitable. There is another technique, called the *internal rate of return* (IRR) method, that permits a firm or other investor to rank projects of different size so that a choice can be made among profitable projects where there are not enough funds to invest in all of them.

The internal rate of return is the discount rate (determined by trial and error) at which the net present value turns out to be zero. In the preceding example, that rate is 16.7 percent, which can be thought of as the rate of return earned by the project. (Remember, at a rate of 15 percent, the net present value was $139,990.) Internal rate of return is a valuable concept or technique and is widely used. There are, however, two problems with it of which one should be aware. The first problem is technical and easily remediable. Where an investment or project is expected to produce a positive cash flow for some period of time and then a negative cash flow, with the IRR method it is mathematically possible to arrive at two different "correct" positive rates. This problem can be solved (a) by discounting any negative cash flows to present value (using the external rate of return) and treating them as initial investments or (b) by assuming that positive cash flows from the immediately preceding year or years are set aside in amounts sufficient, with interest (at the external rate of return), to fund the subsequent negative cash flow and then calculating the IRR based on the net (after the set-aside) positive cash flows and the amount of the initial investment.

The second problem with the IRR method is that the rate calculation is based on an implicit assumption that disinvested funds (that is, positive cash flow that is generated by the project or investment and must be invested elsewhere) is invested at the same rate earned by the project or investment under scrutiny. In some circumstances (for example, in many tax shelter investments), this assumption will seem unrealistic. If one finds this to be a problem, one can use some other form of cash-flow analysis. There are many possibilities. One good one begins by focusing on the positive cash flow—that is, on the cash that the investor expects to receive from the project or investment. The investor makes his or her own assumption about the rate of return at which this positive cash flow can be invested and calculates the total sum that will be available if all the positive cash flow, plus the earnings on that cash flow, is retained until the termination of the project or investment. Then one calculates (again, by trial and error) the rate that one would have been required to earn on the initial investment in order to produce the same terminal fund. The investor then decides, subjectively, whether that rate is high enough to make the project or investment seem acceptable. This technique, like NPV and IRR, is not difficult to understand and apply if one begins with a good grasp of the basic principles of present value calculation.

There is, by the way, one important advantage in the use of NPV, IRR, and related valuation methods based on analysis of cash flows: there is no need for the concept of depreciation. Anyone with the slightest familiarity with accounting will appreciate that this is a significant advantage.

**4. Fixed Perpetuities.** The traditional and probably still the most common method of valuing an investment in real estate or in a business or other asset is to compute a level amount of net income that the investment is expected to generate each year after allowance for replacement of any components with limited useful lives. Since full allowance is made for replacement, it can be assumed that the level amount can be sustained forever. The present or capital value of that investment can then be computed by a very simple formula. In this formula, the level, or fixed, sum is often called a perpetuity (which is simply an amount to be received in perpetuity). The process of determining the capital value is referred to as capitalizing or capitalization. The formula is,

$$P = \frac{A}{r,}$$

where P is the present or capital value, A is the level annual amount, and r is the interest rate or rate of return.

To illustrate, suppose that an apartment building produces a net income of $8,000 after all expenses and after making proper allowance for replacement. (Determination of the proper amount of the replacement allowance is obviously a difficult matter—one that is beyond the scope of this book). Suppose further that the $8,000 is expected to remain constant; or, perhaps more realistically, that the probability of increase is the same as the probability of decline, so that the expected net return remains $8,000. Finally, suppose that the appropriate rate of return on such investments is 10 percent. Since this rate is used to determine the capital value of the investment it is referred to as the capitalization rate. The capital value would be $80,000, determined as follows:

$$P = \frac{A}{r} = \frac{\$8,000}{.10} = \$80,000.$$

If the expected net income were $5,000, the capital value would be $50,000 ($5,000/.10). If the appropriate interest rate were 8 percent and the expected income were $8,000, the capital value would be $100,000 ($8,000/.08).

Probably the best way to gain an intuitive grasp of the substance of the formula is to think of the amount that must be invested in order to produce the known income at the assumed interest rate. Thus, if you know that you have an investment that will yield $8,000 per year and you also know that the appropriate interest rate on such investments is 10 percent, you can ask yourself, what amount would I be required to invest in order to produce that income at that interest rate? The answer, obviously, is $80,000, since at 10 percent, $80,000 will yield $8,000 per year. Algebraically, your thinking would be as follows (where P, the capital value, is the unknown):

$$P \ (.10) = \$8,000$$
$$P = \frac{8,000}{.10} = \$80,000.$$

More generally,

$$P(r) = A,$$

which takes us right back to

$$P = \frac{A}{r}.$$

The interest rate can be, and often is, transformed into a fraction, which in turn becomes a multiplier. For example, if the interest rate is 10 percent, the capital value is ten times the income, which can be seen algebraically as follows:

$$P = \frac{\$8,000}{.10} = \frac{\$8,000}{\frac{1}{10}} = \$8,000 \times 10 = \$80,000.$$

If the interest rate is 8 percent, the fraction is $\frac{1}{12.5}$ and the multiplier is 12.5; thus, if the income is \$8,000, the capital value is \$8,000 × 12.5 = \$100,000. If the interest rate is 5 percent the multiplier is 20. And so forth. There is an inverse relationship between the interest rate and the multiplier; as the interest rate rises, the multiplier declines.

**5. Perpetuities With Growth.** For valuation of a perpetual stream of income that increases at a fixed rate each year, the formula is,

$$P = \frac{A}{r\text{-}g}$$

where P is the capital value, A the amount to be received at the end of the first year, r the interest rate (discount rate), and g the expected growth in A. (A necessary condition of the formula is that r is greater than g.)

To illustrate, suppose that a real estate investment will yield a net rental income of \$4,000 at the end of the first year; that this net rental income is expected to increase each year at the rate of 6 percent; and that the appropriate discount rate is 10 percent. What is the capital or present value? Applying the formula,

$$P = \frac{\$4,000}{.10\text{-}.06} = \frac{\$4,000}{.04} = \$100,000.$$

The present or capital value is \$100,000.

To gain an intuitive grasp of this valuation technique, begin with the proposition that, barring changes in circumstances (ceteris paribus), any change in anticipated rental income will produce a corresponding change in capital value. Thus, a 6 percent change in rental income will produce a 6 percent change in capital value. The 6 percent growth in capital value can then be thought of as part of the total annual return on the property. Thus, the total return for the first year is \$10,000, which consists of the \$4,000 net rental income plus the \$6,000 (6 percent of \$100,000) increase in capital value. Since the \$10,000 fully takes account of growth, it is capitalized at the rate that would be used for a fixed perpetuity, 10 percent. Ignoring transaction costs, a person buying the property for \$100,000 and expecting to sell it at the end of one year would have a total expected net return of \$10,000 or 10 percent.

To drive the point home, consider what happens if the property is held for two years. At the beginning of the second year, by hypothesis the expected rent (at the end of the year) will have risen by 6 percent to $4,240 and the value of the property will have risen to $106,000. The increase in the value of the property at the end of the second year will be $6,360 ($106,000 × .06). The total return will be $10,600 ($4,240 + $6,360), which again is 10 percent of the initial capital value ($106,000).

This illustration has been consistent with common experience in real estate investments in an era of chronic inflation and limited supply of land. Investors recognize in such circumstances that a large part of their total return will be in the form of growth in capital value (capital gain, to use the term taken from tax law). Few investors would expect a nice, neat pattern of increases in rental income and capital value of the sort required by the formula. But they can fairly easily, and without significant loss of accuracy, translate their actual expectations into steady-growth equivalents. The formula presented here then allows a determination of capital value and a comparison of investments with different expected patterns of growth.

### 6. Common Stock: Dividend Valuation Method.

a. *The Importance of Dividends.* A share of common stock of a corporation entitles its owner to a stream of income in the form of dividends (including any final, liquidating dividend). For a person who derives no salary or fringe benefits from the ownership of the share of stock, its value is determined *solely* by the amount of the expected stream of dividend payments (see Chapter 4, Sec. III(B)(4)(a).) Earnings of the corporation are relevant only to the extent that they affect dividends. If a corporation reports earnings in excess of dividends while its dividends remain constant, one or more of three things may be happening. One possibility is that the corporation is using the excess earnings to finance worthwhile improvements or new investments or to pay off debts. If that is the case, earnings should increase, and at some time in the future (when the corporation has run out of worthwhile uses for the retained earnings) those increased earnings will necessarily be reflected as increased dividends. The second possibility is that the corporation's accounting system overstates its earnings. In this situation, dividends may never rise. The third possibility is that the earnings that are not being paid out as dividends are being invested in worthless projects—that they are being poured down a rathole.

Most people with any exposure to the stock market know that there are some corporations that pay no current dividends at all; yet their common stock is valuable. Indeed, these are often the glamour stocks. Such corporations are using their earnings to finance expansion; they tend to have ample opportunity for investing at high rates of return. Ultimately, however, they will run out of attractive investment opportunities, and at that point will begin to pay dividends. It is this prospect of dividends that determines present value. If it were clear that a corporation would never pay any dividends, that the shareholder could never expect any return, then the shares would be worthless.

What about capital gain (that is, growth in the capital value of the stock)? From the perspective of individual investors, the value of an investment in common stock (or any other property) may be determined by a combination of the expected dividend (or other current cash return) plus any expected growth in value. But (as was pointed out in Chapter 4, Sec. III(B)(7)(a)) the growth in value expected by any one investor must depend on the next owner's expectations for dividends plus growth. And so on down the line of ownership. In the absence of an expectation of growth in dividends there would be no reason for succeeding purchasers to bid up the price of the stock (barring operation of the "greater fool" phenomenon—which always has a time limit).

This is not to say that people who analyze a corporation's earnings are wasting their time. But information about earnings is relevant only so far as it bears on dividend expectations over the life of the corporation.

b. *Valuation Techniques.* The value of a share of common stock, based on expected dividends, can be calculated by the techniques that we have already developed. If dividends are expected to remain steady, the valuation formula is the same as that used for perpetuities:

$$V = \frac{D}{r,}$$

where V is the value, D is the dividend, and r is the appropriate capitalization rate. Where dividends are expected to increase at a fixed rate the formula is,

$$V = \frac{D}{r-g,}$$

where g is the rate of growth of dividends. (Remember that the rate of growth in the value of the shares of stock will be the same, all else equal, as the rate of growth of the dividend. But since it is the dividend that is the fundamental source of value, the g in the formula should be thought of as the growth in the dividend, not the growth in the capital value of the shares.)

To illustrate, if a share of stock pays a dividend of $3 per year, if this dividend is expected to remain constant for the foreseeable future, and if the appropriate capitalization rate is 20 percent, the value is,

$$V = \frac{\$3}{.2} = \$15.$$

The same result can be obtained by expressing the capitalization rate as a multiplier of 5.

If we change the facts to include expected growth at the rate of 10 percent, the value is,

$$V = \frac{\$3}{.2-.1} = \frac{\$3}{.1} = \$30.$$

The same formula can be used to derive value from earnings, simply by substituting earnings for dividends and making appropriate adjustments in the capitalization rate. If the earnings figure is an accurate economic indicator and if retained earnings are reinvested at a rate equal to the firm's capitalization rate for those earnings, the earnings-valuation formula should yield the same result as the dividend-valuation formula. (See Sec. IV of this Chapter.) Many market analysts pay more attention to earnings than to dividends—thus leading to the popularity of the price-earnings ratio as an indicator of the value of a firm's shares. In recent years, skepticism over the reliability of earnings figures has led to increased attention to dividends (see Chapter 4, Sec. III(B)(7)(b)) and to cash flow (which, roughly speaking, is earnings before the allowance for depreciation and other such noncash reductions, the appropriate size of which is so difficult to estimate).

The dividend valuation method described here applies and illustrates a fundamental valuation technique. A more recent and more sophisticated method, relying of the so-called Capital Asset Pricing Method (CAPM), is described in Section D(3), below.

## D.  THE DISCOUNT RATE

The question to be considered here is how an individual or firm determines the required rate of return, interest rate, or discount rate to be used in finding the present value of a future set of receipts and outlays.  Some of the concepts that are relied upon in responding to this question may seem to many readers to be exceedingly dry and abstruse. The presentation is relatively terse and it sometimes sidesteps difficulties that may be bothersome to particularly perceptive readers.  A more complete and deeper discussion seemed out of place in this book.  Parts 1 and 3 of this section can be skimmed, with the objective of merely becoming acquainted with some of the more obvious ideas, or skipped.

**1.  Individuals and Firms: Opportunity Cost.**  For an individual, the concept used in selecting a discount rate is that of *opportunity cost*.  The opportunity cost of making any particular investment is the lost return on the next best alternative whose rate of return is known. Fortunately, there are many obvious benchmarks—assets whose prices are established in active markets and whose rates of return can be calculated fairly readily.  There are large, active markets in Treasury obligations, corporate bonds, and common stocks of many large corporations. One can easily determine the interest rates available from savings institutions of various kinds. And so forth. Individuals can take this kind of information as given, and can select from among a variety of such investment possibilities to find the most suitable opportunity-cost benchmarks.

Suppose, for example, that you have just inherited some money and are considering investing it in a small business—one whose value cannot be determined by looking in the financial pages of the newspaper or even from data on sales of comparable businesses (because you cannot find any sufficiently comparable businesses). You contemplate buying some specified share of the business and what you want to know is how much that share is worth. How much should you be willing to pay for it? Suppose that you have a pretty good idea of the expected cash flows from the business and you want to discount these to present value. You might know from the financial pages that the expected return on risky corporate bonds is 10 percent and you might consider this to be your most likely alternative investment. Assuming that the volatility risk of such corporate bonds is lower than that associated with the business in which you are thinking of investing, 10 percent would then certainly be the minimum return that you would demand from the contemplated business investment. It would be the minimum rate that you would use in determining the value of that investment. You would tell yourself that you would be foolish to use a lower figure in valuing the business investment.  Your mental process would be the one contemplated by the notion of opportunity cost.

In this kind of thought process, the "cost" of the business investment is the forgone opportunity to invest in the corporate bonds. The rate of return on the corporate bond is the discount rate that you would use in valuing the interest in the business—as a first approximation. Undoubtedly you would want to get a bit more sophisticated about the process. You might want to adjust the 10 percent corporate-bond rate upward to take account of the greater volatility risk of the business investment and of the possible difficulty you might encounter in trying to sell it. Or you might seek a comparison of the business investment to some other kind of investment that seems more closely comparable to it and whose return you can determine with some reasonable accuracy. But the process would simply be one of comparison and that process is captured nicely by the notion of opportunity cost.  Opportunity cost can be expressed as a rate of return; and that rate of return is the discount rate used in the valuation process described earlier in this chapter.

For a firm, the idea of opportunity cost can be much the same as that for an individual.  The opportunity cost of a particular project is the forgone return on the next best alternative investment. If we avoid reifying the firm, the opportunity cost of any project is defined by the alternative uses to which each of the equity owners might put his or her pro rata share of the required outlay for that project. Again, it is the rate of return on the alternative investment that determines the discount rate by which a project is valued. In using the notion of opportunity cost to determine the appropriate discount rate for a project, it is important to take account of the project's riskiness—its "beta" (see Sec. I(A) of this chapter). A currently popular concept used in adjusting the discount rate to take account of risk is called the "Capital Asset Pricing Model" (CAPM). Description of that concept is beyond the scope of this book.

Another, more traditional, method of determining a firm's discount rate, where the firm's securities are publicly traded, is to use a "weighted average cost of capital." Before explaining that concept, however, it will be helpful to digress and introduce the distinction between managerial and investor perspective.

**2. Digression: Managerial Versus Investor Perspective.**[3] The *managerial perspective* is associated with the large publicly held corporation and is the perspective almost universally adopted in the scholarly and professional literature in the area known as "corporate finance." From this perspective, the managers of an enterprise raise capital (money) by selling securities (stocks and bonds, among others) to the investing public. The investing public is viewed as a group of consumers whose individual tastes and circumstances are fully reflected in the price they are willing to pay for particular securities. This is not to say that investors have nothing to say about the way in which the business is operated; it is not to deny, that is, that shareholders or lenders may have significant control over the basic policies of the firm. It is rather to suggest that these investors are seen (both by corporate managers and by outside observers) as strangers to the enterprise who have entered into (or will enter into) a bargain with it relating to the use of their money. This perspective is consistent with an extreme form of the separate entity theory of corporate existence. From this perspective, for example, in making decisions concerning types of securities to be issued, corporate tax effects are considered, but the individual tax effects for investors are not. (See Sec. III(L) of this Chapter.)

The perspective that will be referred to as the *investor perspective* is usually associated with the small, closely held firm and with the early stages in the development of an enterprise. The investor perspective treats the holders of securities as members of the enterprise, as integral parts of it, rather than as strangers. It is a perspective that is consistent with a bargain-type approach to the study of the organization of joint economic activity. (See Chapter 1, Sec. III(A).) On this perspective, for example, one would take full account of tax effects of a given financial structure not only for the corporation but also for the investors.

---

[3] The distinction drawn here is not found in the financial or legal literature or prac-   tice. It is an invention of the authors of this book, for better or worse.

The distinction between the two perspectives may seem purely metaphysical. We will see, however, as we reach specific issues, that perspective can have extremely important consequences for financial decisions. The fact remains that in most discussions of problems of finance the perspective is implicit. Usually it is not recognized that another perspective is possible and that a change in perspective might lead to different conclusions. This in turn can result in confusion or error or both.

**3.  The Large Corporation: Cost of Capital.** The concept of cost of capital is a product of the managerial perspective. The basic idea is that in valuing a project, for purposes of deciding whether or not it is an acceptable investment, the proper discount rate is the weighted average of the market-determined return or yield on the corporation's target mix of securities, assuming that the project to be valued is of the same level of risk as the average risk of all of the corporation's existing projects. What follows is a step-by-step explanation and elaboration of that statement.

*First.* There is some ideal, or expected, target mix of securities for each firm. We need not be concerned here with how that mix is determined. For simplicity, let's limit our attention to debt (bonds) and equity (common stock). The initial proposition, then, is that there is some predetermined target ratio of debt to equity. It may not be feasible to maintain precisely that ratio at all times, but an effort is made to do so and for purposes of analysis it is assumed that the target is achieved (at least on average).

*Second.* The cost of debt is expressed as a percentage rate of return and is derived from the terms of currently outstanding debt obligations and current securities-market prices. The coupon rate is ignored. The current market price is found; from this, the yield can be calculated. (See Chapter 4, Sec. III(A)(2) and II(C).) It is this yield that is the figure used for cost of debt. For example, if the firm has bonds outstanding that mature in one year, pay interest at the rate of 4 percent, and are currently selling for $950 (for a $1,000 face value bond), the total return to maturity will be $90 (the $40 interest payment plus the $50 difference between the purchase price and the amount payable on maturity), which is about 9½ percent of the purchase price of $950. This is the yield and the corporation's cost of debt. Note that this is a promised rate, not an expected return.[4] (See Chapter 4, Sec. II(A) and (B).)

---

[4] The authors of this book believe that the use of the promised rate rather than the expected return is wrong—that it overstates the cost of debt. Think of it this way: if you borrow money to finance an investment, it is certainly important to know whether the debt is with or without recourse, assuming that there is some chance of default. In effect, use of the prom-ised rate in the cost of debt calculation ignores the nonrecourse nature of corporate debt. It ignores the fact that lenders (holders of the debt securities) bear a portion of the risk of loss. The question then arises, why do corporate managers make this mistake? The authors surmise that the answer to this question has to do with the fact that their perspective is that of managers rather

Some account must be taken of the *flotation costs* of debt. Flotation costs include payments for the services of investment bankers, lawyers, printers, and others who must be hired in order to sell new securities to the public. These costs can be quite significant. A good way to take account of them would seem to be to treat them as a reduction in the proceeds of the issuance of the debt, the effect of which, of course, is to increase the yield. Another method is to treat them as lump-sum investment costs, to be taken into account in valuing projects. There seems to be no universally agreed-upon approach among financial experts.

It is worth noting that inclusion of the cost of debt in the cost-of-capital calculation seems to reflect a managerial perspective. If one were to take an investor perspective, one might think of capital as consisting solely of equity, with debt treated as a cost entering into the valuation process. For example, suppose that the investment consists of an apartment building. Taking an investor perspective, one might treat the payments to lenders the same as payments of property taxes, utility bills, maintenance expenses, and so forth. All of these outlays would then be discounted to present value at the cost of equity (or, if you prefer, the required rate of return on equity). This approach is alien and unacceptable, however, in the managerial-dominated intellectual world of "corporate finance," where debt and equity are both looked upon as inputs hired from outsiders.

*Third.* The cost of equity is determined under either of two formulas. In the traditional, now relatively little used, formula the cost of equity is the ratio of dividends to the current market price of common shares, expressed as a percentage. The formula is derived very simply from the valuation formula described in Section I(C)(6) above. In that formula,

$$V = \frac{D}{r,}$$

where V is value, D is expected dividend (including liquidating distributions), and r is rate of return. To determine the cost of equity, r, we simply rewrite the formula,

$$r = \frac{D}{V,}$$

with V becoming market price. With growth, the formula becomes,

---

than investors. In any event, in the literature of corporate finance the prevailing convention is clear: it is the promised rate, not the expected rate, that is used in determining cost of debt.

$$r = \frac{D}{V} + g.$$

For example, if the dividend is expected to be a level $3 per year and the current market price is $30, the cost of equity is,

$$r = \frac{D}{V} = \frac{\$3}{\$30} = 10 \text{ percent.}$$

If we were to assume that the dividend is expected to increase at the rate of 5 percent per year, the cost of capital would be,

$$r = \frac{D}{V} + g = \frac{\$3}{\$30} + .05 = 15 \text{ percent,}$$

which would, of course, imply a far more risky venture than the one whose dividends are capitalized at only 10 percent.

The more recent, and now more widely used, method of determining the cost of equity combines the risk-free interest rate with a measure of the risk premium of a firm's equity. The firm's risk premium is the market risk premium multiplied by the firm's "beta." The market risk premium is the difference between the expected return on a portfolio of all risky assets and the expected return on a risk-free investment. Historically, that difference has been around 8 percent. For example, if the return on the market portfolio is 10 percent and the return on risk-free, short term Treasury obligations is 2 percent, the market risk premium is 8 percent. The risk premium for an individual firm's equity may be higher or lower than the market risk premium, depending on the volatility of its expected performance, measured by its past performance; this firm-specific volatility is the firm's beta. Beta measures the degree to which the firm's stock price varies as the price of the market portfolio varies. The beta of the market portfolio is taken as 1.0. A stock that increases the volatility of the market portfolio will have a beta above 1.0, while a stock that decreases volatility will have a beta below 1.0. Thus, if the risk premium of the market portfolio is 8 percent and the beta of a firm's equity is .8, the risk premium for the firm's equity will be 6.4 percent. If the risk-free rate is 2 percent, the firm's cost of equity will then be 8.4 percent. This approach to determining the cost (and the value) of equity is called the Capital Asset Pricing Model (CAPM). To complete the picture, one additional thought is required. The risk premium described here is compensation for so-called "systematic risk"—that is, risk arising from events that affect the market as a whole. It is assumed that risk associated with events that affect only an individual firm (referred to as "alpha") can be neutralized by holding a diversified portfolio and that therefore there will be no compensation (no increase in the risk premium) for taking such a risk. (Compare Chapter 4(II)(F).) Finally, it must be noted that among financial economists there is considerable controversy over the validity or accuracy of the CAPM model.

One must bear in mind, however, that there may be situations in which the addition of equity capital will buoy up the firm's debt, resulting in a transfer of wealth from equityholders to debtholders. See Chapter 4, Sec. II(A)(15). From the perspective of the common shareholders, the amount of this wealth transfer is presumably part of the cost of equity (including equity created by retention of earnings), though perhaps it could be thought of simply as part of the cost of debt.

*Fourth.* Retained earnings are part of equity and are taken account of in the cost-of-equity formula described immediately above. If new equity capital is acquired (that is, if new common stock is sold), there will be flotation costs, which can be quite significant and must somehow be taken into account. There are no flotation costs for retained earnings.

*Fifth.* The weighted average cost of capital is determined by reference to the target ratio of debt to equity. For example, if the target ratio is 1:1 (50 percent debt and 50 percent equity), and if the cost of debt is 8 percent and the cost of equity is 20 percent, then, ignoring taxes, the cost of capital would be 14 percent, determined as follows:

|  | **Cost (%)** | **Weight** | **Value (%)** |
|---|---|---|---|
| Debt | 8 | .5 | 4 |
| Equity | 20 | .5 | 10 |
|  | Weighted Average |  | 14% |

*Sixth.* Under federal and state income tax laws, interest payments are deductible and dividend payments are not. To take account of this difference, the standard approach is to reduce the cost of debt, thereby producing an after-tax cost of capital. It follows that when the resulting figure is used in the valuation process, it must be applied to after-tax returns (that is, that the expected income-tax payment must be treated as an outlay like any other in the valuation process). True to the managerial perspective, tax effects at the individual level (that is, to bondholders and shareholders) are ignored. To illustrate, if the cost of debt is 8 percent before tax effects and the combined federal and state income tax rate is 50 percent, then in the formula for cost of capital with tax effects, the cost of debt would be reduced to 4 percent. The cost of equity would continue to be determined as explained immediately above.

*Seventh.* The cost of capital figure used to determine the value of projects must be adjusted to take account of any difference between the riskiness of the project under consideration and the overall level of risk of the corporation's existing activities. For projects riskier than existing activities, the rate must be increased; for less risky projects, the rate must be decreased.

*Eighth.* Investment decisions must be based on cost of capital, without regard to short-run decisions affecting capital structure. A new project may be financed by retained earnings or by the sale of new debt or equity. In determining whether the project is a good investment, the corresponding decision on the best source of financing is irrelevant—the investment decision must be based on the weighted average cost of capital. To prove this point, suppose that a project under consideration is expected to produce a return of 12 percent and that new money must be raised to finance it; that the cost of debt is 10 percent and the cost of equity is 20 percent with a 1:1 ratio. Suppose that a decision has been made to sell bonds, whose cost is 10 percent. Does that mean that the project, yielding 12 percent, is a worthwhile investment? Of course not. Imagine that the next project that comes along will produce a return of 14 percent but that at the time, the sound financing decision would be to raise the needed new funds by selling common stock. If the short-run financing decision were to determine the investment decision, the second project would be rejected despite the fact that it is superior to the first. In fact, both projects should be rejected since the cost of capital is 15 percent.

The idea can be expressed more broadly, and the broader expression may render the narrower idea easier to comprehend. Firms have a variety of sources and uses of funds. Funds are received from the sale of goods and services or, less regularly, from the sale of securities or capital assets. Funds are used to buy raw materials, to pay wages, to expand a building, to embark on a new project, and so forth. In other words, the issuance of new securities is simply one of many sources of funds and a large initial investment in a new project is one of many uses of funds. Obviously, if funds are needed for a new project, one must know whether those funds are in fact available in order to make a decision on whether to embark on the project. But the wisdom of the investment must be determined by reference to the firm's overall experience in generating funds, not on coincidental or transitory phenomena.

There is, however, a significant qualification to this notion of separating the investment decision from the financing decision. Some projects are better suited than others to supporting debt. A bank, for example, is likely to want collateral for its loans and an office building may be better collateral than the goodwill generated by an advertising campaign.

*Ninth.* A highly sophisticated analyst might use different discount rates for cash flows to be generated at different times, to take account of the "yield curve." The yield curve is a depiction of the relationship between short-term rates and long-term rates. At most times (but not always) the short-term rate is lower than the long-term rate (so the yield curve slopes upward). Thus, one might want to use a lower discount rate for near-term than for more distant expected cash flows. But this level of sophistication is not often employed.

*Tenth.* The above analysis ignores substitutes for traditional capital (debt and equity). Suppose a company is in a risky, cyclical business and keeps a healthy cash (or near-cash) balance to tide it over in bad years. This cash buffer will show up on its balance sheet as an asset, which will enhance equity. But suppose that instead it buys insurance against the risk. The insurer is now providing the cash buffer, for a fee. It is supplying what may be called "contingent" capital. Similar results can be achieved with letters of credit and other financial derivatives, again for a fee. The fees will be reflected in operating costs and will not be reflected in the "cost of capital." The distinction seems arbitrary and may be misleading.

**4. Taxation and Market Valuation.** When taxes enter the picture, to determine the market value of an asset or portfolio of assets, the before-tax rate must be applied to the before-tax return and the after-tax rate to the after-tax return. To illustrate, suppose the market rate of return on a diversified portfolio of securities with a given risk level, $x$, is 10 percent before taxes; that $I$, an individual, is taxable at a rate of 40 percent; that $F$, a charitable foundation, is not taxed; and that $I$ and $F$ each hold a portfolio of securities with $x$ level of risk and an annual yield of $10,000. $F$'s net yield after tax will be the full $10,000; $I$'s net yield after tax will be $6,000. Despite the difference in after-tax rate of return, the market value will be the same for each, $100,000. For $F$, this value is calculated by dividing the $10,000 net annual return by the after-tax discount rate, which is the same as the before-tax rate, 10 percent. For $I$, the same market value can be calculated by dividing the $6,000 after-tax return by the 6 percent after-tax rate. The same result can be reached for $I$, in this simple example, by ignoring taxes and applying the before-tax rate to the before-tax return. The use of the after-tax rate and return is needed, however, when tax effects become more complex and the tax must be calculated as an amount rather than asa percentage. What is critical, of course, is that an after-tax rate should not be applied to a before-tax return or a before-tax rate to an after-tax return.

## E. ALLOWING FOR RISK: TWO METHODS

To compare two or more investments, one must be able to control for differences in volatility risk (defined in Chapter 4, Sec. II(B)). Two widely known methods for doing this are (a) the risk-adjusted interest rate and (b) the certainty equivalent.

The concept of a certainty equivalent was described in Chapter 4, Sec. II(E). Let us use the hypothetical facts presented there. You have a certificate entitling you to either $1,000,000 or nothing, depending on the outcome of a coin flip. The expected return is $500,000. Assume again that you have decided that your certainty equivalent is $400,000.

Now assume, however, that the payoff will be deferred for one year. You want to know the present value. What interest rate do you use? If you decide to focus on the $400,000 certainty equivalent, you have already fully accounted for volatility risk, as well as default risk, and you should use the risk-free rate. Assume that that rate is 10 percent. The present value of the certificate, then, is $363,636 ($400,000/1.1).

The other approach is to focus on the $500,000 expected return and to adjust the discount rate to take account of the volatility risk. If we start with the $500,000 and want to arrive at the same present value reached by the certainty equivalent method, we would use a discount rate of 37.5 percent. The present value of $500,000 discounted at 37.5 percent for one year is $363,636. This discount rate, adjusted for risk, can be thought of as including compensation for two financial elements, (a) volatility risk and (b) time value of money. (The "default" risk is taken into account in arriving at the expected return of $500,000.)

This example suggests the advantage of the certainty-equivalent method over the risk-adjusted interest rate method: in the former there is a single adjustment for risk while in the latter the adjustment will vary with the duration of the investment. For example, look at what happens in our example with each of the two methods as we change the number of years of deferral from one to five.

| | Present Value in Dollars | |
| Number of Years of Deferral | Risk–Adjusted Interest Rate | Certainty Equivalent |
|---|---|---|
| 1 | $363,636 | $363,636 |
| 2 | 264,462 | 330,579 |
| 3 | 192,337 | 300,526 |
| 4 | 139,881 | 273,205 |
| 5 | 101,171 | 248,369 |

The problem with the risk-adjusted interest rate method is that it applies the adjustment for risk once in the case of a one-year deferral and five times in the case a five-year deferral, but the risk itself does not vary with time. Thus, in our example, we wind up under that method with a present value of $101,171 in the case of five-year deferral, and that seems plainly too low (given our assumptions).

Despite the relative advantage of the certainty-equivalent method, it is not used much. In the financial world, people rely overwhelmingly on risk-adjusted interest rates. They seem to have difficulty in arriving at certainty equivalents; certainty equivalence is an unfamiliar concept. The results in using risk-adjusted interest rates are not as bad as our example might suggest, since in most instances the rate chosen is used to compare investments of comparable duration and is adjusted to produce sensible results for that kind of investment. But the certainty equivalent method is a relatively new idea that is widely taught in business schools. In time it may become more widely used in practice and, in the meantime, it can be a useful concept for communicating with some people in some circumstances.

## II.　LEVERAGE AND CHOICE OF CAPITAL STRUCTURE

### A.　INTRODUCTION

Thus far we have assumed, at least implicitly, that the total market value of a firm's securities is equal to the value of the firm determined independently of its capital structure—independently, that is, of the relative amounts of common stock (equity), bonds (debt), and other securities. In other words, it has been assumed that the total value of all securities is the same regardless of the proportions of each. We now turn to an examination of the validity of that assumption. From a managerial perspective (see Sec. I(D)(2) above), the issue can be framed in terms of whether the cost of capital is affected by the firm's capital structure. From an investor perspective the same issue would more likely be framed in terms of whether the value of the equity interest can be increased by a judicious use of debt. Regardless how the issue is framed, the possibility that capital structure does affect the total market value of securities has a number of obviously important ramifications. To emphasize that observation, consider one of the more dramatic of these ramifications. Suppose that a corporation is financed entirely with common stock, consisting of 1,000,000 shares with a market price of $100 per share, or a total market value of $100,000,000. Now suppose that the corporation could sell $60,000,000 worth of bonds and use this money to redeem half of its common stock (500,000 shares) at $120 per share,[5] on the assumption that it would wind up with 500,000 shares of common stock worth $60,000,000 and debt worth $60,000,000 (with no other change in the nature of the corporation or its investments or prospects). In other words, suppose that by a readjustment of the capital structure alone, the total value of the securities of the corporation could be increased by 20 percent. This corporation, among other possibilities, would be a prime candidate for a take-over by speculators. A speculator could buy enough common stock to gain control of the corporation; cause the corporation to change its capital structure in the manner suggested; and then sell the common stock for a fast 20 percent profit.

Many people, over the years, have thought, and some continue to think, that the kind of scenario suggested above is entirely plausible; that a corporation that fails to finance in part with debt fails to maximize the total value of its securities (and to minimize the cost of capital) and is, among other things, a good take-over target. To understand why people might think this way and to test the validity of their

[5] 500,000 x $120 = $60,000,000.

conclusions, one must begin by mastering the concept of leverage. (See Chapter 1, Sec. II(F).) Leverage is achieved when an investor finances an investment with debt or with some other similar financial device through which another investor becomes entitled to a fixed return. The effect of leverage is to increase the volatility of the equity investment; the goal in using leverage is, correspondingly, to increase the expected return on the equity investment. (Volatility and expected return are defined and discussed in Chapter 4, Section II.)

## B.  PURE LEVERAGE EFFECT

Suppose that you know of two (moderately) risky investment opportunities with identical characteristics. The cost of each is $100,000 and the expected annual return (net) on each is $12,000 (including expected annual appreciation, if any). You have just inherited $100,000 and have no other assets and no debts. You can borrow $50,000 (with recourse) to finance the purchase of either investment, at an interest rate of 8 percent. Disregard taxes and transaction costs.

One possibility is that you simply use your $100,000 to acquire one of the risky investments. Your expected return is $12,000 or 12 percent.

A second possibility is to borrow $50,000 on each of two investments, using your own $100,000 to pay for the remaining $50,000 cost of each. Your expected net return from the two investments is now $24,000 before the payment of interest. The interest obligation is $8,000 per year (8 percent on the total borrowings of $100,000). Your expected net return after the interest payment is $16,000 ($24,000 less $8,000) or 16 percent. You have increased your expected rate of return by 4 percent. You have borrowed money at 8 percent to finance an investment that is expected to yield 12 percent—which seems to be an easy road to riches.

To take the illustration one step further, suppose that you could borrow $75,000 on each $100,000 investment and that four investment opportunities were available. You might buy all four, using, for the purchase of each one, $25,000 of your own money and $75,000 of borrowed funds. Your expected return would be $48,000 before interest; the interest payment would be $24,000 (8 percent of $300,000); and the net expected return after interest would be $24,000. The expected rate of return on your $100,000 equity would now be 24 percent.

Obviously this kind of progression cannot continue indefinitely—for example, to a point where you could borrow $95,000 at 8 percent on each of 100 investments and have an expected return of 88 percent.[6]  One reason why this possibility seems too good to be true should be easy to see—no one would lend you money at 8 percent with only a 5 percent

---

[6] On each investment, the expected return before interest is $12,000. The interest is $7,600 (8 percent of $95,000). The expected return after interest is $4,400, which is 88 percent on the equity investment of $5,000.

equity cushion, unless the investment were virtually free of risk. If such a risk-free investment were available, the lender would invest in it directly; the lender could earn the 12 percent itself and would not be willing to lend to you at 8 percent no matter how much equity you put up. In other words, an 8 percent borrowing rate is inconsistent with the availability of risk-free investments yielding 12 percent. All of which suggests that, up to now, the discussion has avoided a crucial element—risk.

## C.   LEVERAGE AND RISK

We will now take all the hypothetical facts used in the immediately preceding discussion and add the critical omitted element—namely, the variance of the expected return. (See Chapter 4, Sec. II(A) and Sec. II(B)(1).) Suppose that the expected return of $12,000 is the product of the following set of outcomes and probabilities:

| Probability | Amount | Value |
|:---:|:---:|:---:|
| ⅓ | $ 3,000 | $ 1,000 |
| ⅓ | 12,000 | 4,000 |
| ⅓ | 21,000 | 7,000 |
| 1.0 | | $12,000 |

Consider the possible outcomes with various investment strategies. If you simply acquire one investment, with no debt (no leverage), the range of possible outcomes is, of course, $3,000 to $21,000 (by hypothesis) and the expected return is $12,000.

Now suppose that you borrow $100,000 and acquire two investments (each with the expected return and variance set forth above). Assume further that each of the investments is identically affected by all risk factors, so that the outcome will always be the same for each; if one earns $3,000, the other earns $3,000; if one earns $12,000, the other earns $12,000; and so on. The expected return before interest charges is now simply doubled, as is the return for each possible outcome. The effects, after taking account of interest (at 8 percent on the $100,000 debt), are:

| Probability | Total Return | Interest | Net | Value |
|:---:|:---:|:---:|:---:|:---:|
| ⅓ | $ 6,000 | $8,000 | ($ 2,000) | ($ 667) |
| ⅓ | 24,000 | 8,000 | 16,000 | 5,333 |
| ⅓ | 42,000 | 8,000 | 34,000 | 11,333 |
| 1.0 | | | | 16,000 |

The expected return has now increased from $12,000 (12 percent) to $16,000 (16 percent), but only at the price of an increase in the range of possible outcomes (that is, at the price of an increase in volatility risk or variance) from $3,000—$21,000 to ($2,000)—$34,000.

If the total investment were increased to $400,000, with $300,000 debt (75 percent) and $100,000 equity (25 percent), then, assuming no increase in the interest rate, the effect would be as follows:

| Probability | Total Return | Interest | Net | Value |
|---|---|---|---|---|
| ⅓ | $12,000 | $24,000 | ($12,000) | ($ 4,000) |
| ⅓ | 48,000 | 24,000 | 24,000 | 8,000 |
| ⅓ | 84,000 | 24,000 | 60,000 | 20,000 |
| 1.0 | | | | $24,000 |

The expected return is now $24,000 (24 percent on equity), but the range of possible outcomes has increased to ($12,000)—$60,000. That should show how, with leverage, people can get very rich, or very poor.

The principles should be clear. Assuming an expected return higher than the interest rate, the use of debt (leverage) to increase the total investment will increase the expected return. But since there will be variance in the expected return, leverage will increase risk; it will magnify the variance. At the same time that it increases the expected return, leverage magnifies the range of possible outcomes (that is, it magnifies the risk or variance). Another way to describe leverage is to note that debt is a fixed obligation; equity has the residual claim after the fixed obligation is met. The greater the relative amount of the fixed obligation, the greater will be the changes in the return on (and value of) the residual associated with any change in the total return on (and value of) the investment.

## D.  SOME VARIATIONS

**1.  Options.**  In Chapter 4, Sec. III(C)(2), we saw that the holder of an option on common stock has a highly leveraged interest in the underlying investment (the common stock). The seller of the option has a fixed claim and the purchaser the residual. The relationship between options and leveraged equity is developed more fully in Section IV of Chapter 4. Here it is appropriate to add the probably self-evident thought that options can be and are in fact used in connection with investments other than common stock and an equity interest in any leveraged investment can be seen as an option to purchase the investment from the holder of the debt obligation (assuming that the debt is effectively nonrecourse). Options are covered in detail in Chapter 6.

**2.  Pyramiding.**  Debt can be and often is issued at more than one level of priority. There can be debt with a first claim to any assets in the event of default, debt with a second claim to the same property, and so forth. An interesting device for achieving this effect is pyramiding through the use of a chain of parent-subsidiary corporations. This device can be used to achieve high leverage.

To illustrate, suppose that there is an operating corporation, called C Corp., with a total value of $8,000,000, the claims in which consist solely of $4,000,000 of long-term debt paying 8 percent plus $4,000,000 worth of common stock. Rita, an investor with a taste for risk, buys all the C Corp. common stock, using $1,000,000 of her own money plus $3,000,000 borrowed short term on the security of the $4,000,000 worth of that common stock. She immediately forms B Corp., to which she contributes the $4,000,000 worth of C Corp. common stock, receiving in return B Corp. securities consisting of $2,000,000 worth of long-term debt paying 10 percent plus $2,000,000 worth of common stock. She then turns around and sells the B Corp. debt to public investors, for $2,000,000, and uses the proceeds to reduce her own short-term debt from $3,000,000 to $1,000,000. Finally, she forms A Corp., to which she contributes all the common stock of B Corp., in return for $1,000,000 worth of long-term A Corp. debt paying 12 percent, plus $1,000,000 worth of common stock. Again, she sells the debt to the public for $1,000,000; this sum is used to pay off the remaining $1,000,000 of her short-term debt. She now has $1,000,000 of her own money invested and owns all of the common stock of A Corp., which owns all the common stock of B Corp., which owns all the common stock of C Corp., which owns the operating assets. The combined debt consists of $1,000,000 owed by A Corp., plus $2,000,000 owed by B Corp., plus $4,000,000 owed by C Corp.—a total of $7,000,000, with a total annual interest obligation of $640,000 (9.14 percent).

The outcome can be displayed as follows:

|  | **Assets** | **Debt** | **Equity** | **Annual Interest Obligation** |
|---|---|---|---|---|
| A Corp. | B's Common Stock | $1 mil. | $1 mil. | $120,000 |
| B Corp. | C's Common Stock | $2 mil. | $2 mil. | $200,000 |
| C Corp. | Firm's Operating Assets | $4 mil. | $4 mil. | $320,000 $640,000 |

The total equity might at first blush appear to be $7,000,000, but $6,000,000 of that cannot be counted for purposes of a realistic economic analysis of the amount of the residual claim. Remember, Rita has invested only $1,000,000; all the rest of the money came from holders or purchasers of debt obligations. It is true that from the perspective of a holder of a C Corp. bond, there is an equity cushion of $4,000,000. Of this, $2,000,000 comes from B Corp. debt holders and $1,000,000 from A Corp. debt holders. Similarly, the B Corp. debt holders do have an equity cushion of $2,000,000, of which $1,000,000 is supplied by the A Corp. debt holders.

It should be apparent that the true equity is leveraged 7:1 and that the C Corp. debt holders have first claim to any income (or, in the event of liquidation, assets); the B Corp. debt holders have second claim; and the A Corp. debt holders have a third priority fixed claim. This explains the differences in interest rate. Rita, the A Corp. common shareholder, takes what is left; she has the residual. To illustrate, suppose that the operations of the firm produce net revenues of $800,000 before interest payments. This is 10 percent on total assets, which is higher than the weighted average cost of debt, so that leverage should work to the benefit of the equity interest. The easiest way to trace the economic effects is to imagine that all earnings after interest payments are paid out as dividends. C Corp. pays interest of $320,000 from its profits of $800,000. The remaining $480,000 is paid as a dividend to B Corp. B Corp. pays interest of $200,000 and pays the remaining $280,000 to A Corp. as a dividend. A Corp. pays interest of $120,000 and pays the remaining $160,000 to its shareholder as a dividend. The dividend represents a 16 percent return on the investment of $1,000,000.

Suppose, however, that the operating revenues ($800,000) are reduced by 10 percent or $80,000. Since the interest payments are a fixed obligation, the dividend to the A shareholder would be reduced by the same dollar amount; the dividend would be reduced from $160,000 to $80,000, which is 8 percent on the $1,000,000 equity investment. In other words, a 10 percent change in revenue before interest would produce a 50 percent change in return on equity. That is leverage.

Suppose that operating revenue falls to $560,000 or 7 percent on total assets. This is not enough to meet the total interest obligation of $640,000. There will be enough to pay the interest on the C and B obligations (a total of $520,000), but that leaves only $40,000 for A Corp.—$80,000 short of the amount of the fixed obligation.

To see the principles from a different perspective, suppose that the firm is liquidated. If the total proceeds were $9,000,000, $4,000,000 would go to the C Corp. bondholders. The remaining $5,000,000 would be paid as a liquidating dividend to B Corp., of which $2,000,000 would be paid to the B Corp. debenture holders. The remaining $3,000,000 would be paid as a liquidating dividend to A Corp., and from this sum, $1,000,000 would go to the debenture holders and $2,000,000 to the common shareholder. If, on the other hand, the total proceeds of the sale of operating assets were $7,000,000, nothing would be available for the A Corp. common shareholder. And if only $6,000,000 were available, then the A Corp. debenture holders would be wiped out along with the common shareholder.

The scenario presented here is an abstraction, but it is a fair reflection of the essence of real-world situations. In reality, B Corp. might have some independent business; A Corp.'s common shares might be publicly held; and so forth. But the essence of the total leverage and the different layers of debt with different effective priorities with respect to the operating revenues and wealth would be present.

Pyramiding and extreme leverage were a common feature of investments in public utilities in the '20's and early '30's. When some of the empires collapsed, there was much sympathy for people, comparable to the holders of A Corp. debentures, who lost their "hard-earned savings." After all, a debenture is supposed to be a safe investment and it is easy to ignore the element of greediness, and risk, that is suggested by high interest rates. In any case, Congress, motivated in part by a perceived need for protection of investors, adopted legislation (the Public Utilities Holding Company Act of 1935) that, among other things, limits the permissible degree of pyramiding and seeks to strengthen financial structures of public utilities.

### E.  SPURIOUS LEVERAGE

Spurious leverage is the product of myopia. It occurs when one focuses on investments rather than investors, when one fails to take account of the investor's entire financial and investment picture.

Again, suppose that you have just inherited $100,000; that you have no other assets and no debts; that there are two risky investment opportunities, each with a cost of $100,000 and an expected annual return of $12,000; and that each of these investments can be used as security for a loan of $50,000 at 8 percent, with recourse. Suppose further that at the moment your $100,000 is deposited in a savings and loan account that pays 6 percent. (It may be worth emphasizing that we depart here from the approach of most financial theory, in which borrowing and lending rates are assumed to be identical.)

Now suppose that you have decided that you want to acquire only one investment. Does it make sense to use only $50,000 of your own money and borrow the other $50,000 to finance that investment? The answer is plainly, "no." If you did so, you would be borrowing at 8 percent while you were lending at 6 percent. You would have the apparent advantage of leverage but the leverage would be spurious because your position as a debtor would be offset by your position as a creditor. Your expected return on the risky investment would be $8,000 ($12,000 less interest of $4,000 on the $50,000 loan). That would be a 16 percent rate of return on your $50,000 equity in that investment. At the same time, however, your return on your savings and loan account would be only $3,000 (6 percent of the $50,000). Your total net expected return would be $11,000 ($8,000 plus $3,000) or 11 percent. You would obviously be better off to take your entire $100,000 out of the bank and use it to acquire the risky investment. Your expected return would then be $12,000 or 12 percent. Your risks would be the same—those associated with potential variations in the returns on or value of the investment. To put it another way, you can increase your expected earnings by

$1,000 by borrowing the $50,000 from yourself at 6 percent rather than from someone else at 8 percent.

The analysis remains essentially the same if we take account of personal income taxes. True, the interest paid is deductible for tax purposes. But the interest received is taxable. The tax is based on the total income. As long as the rate is less than 100 percent, more income is always better than less. If, for example, your marginal rate is 50 percent, you are left with 50 percent after taxes and 50 percent of $12,000 is better than 50 percent of $11,000. It's as simple as that.

All this may seem so clear as to be unworthy of mention. Rest assured, however, that the phenomenon of spurious leverage is widely ignored in the real world. Time and again you will hear, if you have not already heard, supposedly astute advisors (accountants, lawyers, and others) telling people to borrow as much as they can to finance the purchase of a house—without any inquiry into the possibility of cashing in investments with returns lower than the interest rate on the proposed loan, and, often, despite an awareness of such opportunities. The same kind of mistake is made in more sophisticated transactions.

There is a related error resulting from the same tendency to look myopically at particular investment decisions and to tie together the financing decisions and the investment decision. (See Section I(D)(3) (final two paragraphs) above.) Suppose, for example, that you own $300,000 worth of common stocks of publicly traded companies, that these stocks generate dividends of $15,000 per year, and that you could, if you wished, borrow $150,000 against the security of this set of assets at a rate of 9 percent ($13,500 per year). Now suppose that you want to buy a house for $200,000; that you have $50,000 cash for the required down payment; that you can borrow $150,000 at 10 percent ($15,000) per year on a first mortgage loan on the house; and that you have decided, for good reasons, that you should not sell any of your common stock portfolio. How should you finance the purchase of the house? Obviously, by borrowing the $150,000 at 9 percent against the security of the stock portfolio rather than by borrowing the same amount at 10 percent against the security of the house. That conclusion may, in fact, be obvious to you, but it is ignored with a high degree of frequency in the real world.

## F.   LEVERAGE AND WEALTH

Again, assume that you have just inherited $100,000, which sum has just been deposited in your checking account. The $100,000 is your total wealth, or net worth. Your expected return, for the moment, is zero. Next, you use the $100,000 to by a U.S. Treasury obligation with a yield of 8 percent; that 8 percent is now your expected return. Your wealth is still $100,000. The ratio of your wealth, which might also be referred to as the price of your asset, to your expected return, which might be called your earnings on that asset, is 12.5 to 1. That is, the wealth/return or price/earnings ratio is 12.5 to 1.

Next, you sell the Treasury obligation for $100,000 and buy the risky investment with its expected return of $12,000 or 12 percent. The ratio of price to earnings is now 8.33 to 1. Your wealth is still $100,000. You may feel that you are better off now than you were when you held the Treasury obligation; your personal assessment may be that, for you, the risky investment is more valuable than the Treasury obligation. But that does not affect your wealth (as measured by the price at which you could sell).

Finally, you acquire two risky $100,000 investments, borrowing $50,000 at 8 percent against the security of each. Your net expected return is now $16,000 ($24,000 expected return less the interest of $8,000) or 16 percent. Your net worth is still $100,000. The ratio of wealth to expected return (or, if you will, of the price of your equity to your expected earnings) is now 6.25 to 1. Again, you may be happier with the expected return of $16,000 than with the expected return of $12,000, despite the greater risk. But the market value of your wealth remains constant.

The moral of this little story is that the introduction of leverage does not increase the market value of your wealth. Why not? Suppose that you are convinced that the increase in risk resulting from the leveraging does not justify an increase in required rate of return to 16 percent; that instead an increase to 14 percent is sufficient compensation for the risk. You go to a stranger and convince her of this fact. Then you offer to sell her your equity position in the two risky investments for $114,286, which you have arrived at by capitalizing the $16,000 expected return at the 14 percent rate that you both agree is the proper rate to use. The stranger should turn you down cold. In fact, she should refuse to pay you more than $100,000, not because she challenges your private assessment of value, but rather for the simple reason that by hypothesis she can acquire the same leveraged investment herself for $100,000. Assuming that there is nothing unique about your risky investment and that, consequently, she can buy the same kind of investment for $100,000, and assuming that she can create her own leverage on the same terms that were available to you, she would be foolish to pay more than $100,000 for the investment that you offer her. In other words, there is no reason why she should pay you a profit of $14,286 for creating leverage when she can easily create her own leverage.

Again, the point made here may seem clear and obvious. As we shall see, however (Section III below), the principle has by no means been obvious in the corporate context.

## III.  CAPITAL STRUCTURE

### A.  INTRODUCTION

The phrase "capital structure" refers to the relative amounts of the various types of permanent and long-term financial claims in an enterprise.[7]  In the present discussion, we can simplify, without any significant sacrifice of understanding, by focusing exclusively on the relative amounts of equity (common stock) and long-term debt (bonds and debentures).  The question with which we will be concerned is, what are the principles by which a firm determines the proper ratio of debt to equity? [8]

In the dominant traditional thinking of experts in corporate finance, an ideal capital structure would almost invariably be one that included some debt.  The thought is that there is a clear advantage that can be achieved by the use of debt and that the total value of all the securities (equity and debt) issued by a firm will be greater with debt than it will be if the same firm is financed exclusively with equity.  The other side of that coin is that the firm's cost of capital is minimized by the judicious use of debt.  Correspondingly, managers who fail to use debt in the capital structure of the firm are derelict in their duty to serve the best interests of the shareholders.  Moreover, the failure on the part of managers to exploit the advantages of debt will leave the firm vulnerable to take-over by people who will notice the unexploited opportunity.

Another, more recent view, stemming from an article published in 1958 by Franco Modigliani and Merton Miller,[9] rejects the reasoning on which the traditional approach is based and questions its conclusions.  Modigliani and Miller demonstrated that, given certain assumptions, capital structure is irrelevant to the total value of a firm's securities and,

---

[7] The word "capital" is used here to refer to what may be thought of as a financial concept.  The same word is used, in other contexts, to refer to productive capacity, as, for example, in discussions of the amount of capital per worker in a firm or industry.

"Capital structure" can be distinguished from "financial structure," the latter referring to all of the claims in an enterprise, including such items as accounts payable and short-term interest-bearing debt.

[8] The discussion here is rudimentary.  There is a rich, complex, mostly recent, body of economic and financial literature on what is generally referred to as "the determinants of capital structure." For valuable reviews, see Stewart C. Myers, Financing of Corporations, Chapter 4 in Handbook of the Economics of Finance, Vol. 1A (George M. Constantinides, Milton Harris, and René M. Stulz editors, 2003); Milton Harris and Ar-

thur Raviv, *The Theory of Capital Structure*, 46 J. Finance 297 (1991). See also Michael J. Barclay and Clifford W. Smith, Jr., *The Priority Structure of Corporate Liabilities*, 50 J. Finance 899 (1995)(data on relative amounts of "capitalized" leases (roughly speaking, leases for most of the life of the asset), secured debt, ordinary debt, subordinated debt, and preferred stock in capital structures of large sample of corporations).  A sophisticated analysis of capital structure would also include consideration of the particularized terms, or forms, of financial instruments such as common stock and bonds—that is, it would relax the useful simplifying assumption that all debt claims, and all equity claims, are alike.

[9] *The Cost of Capital, Corporation Finance and the Theory of Investment*, 48 Amer.Econ.Rev. 261–297 (1958).

correspondingly, to its cost of capital. The significance of the assumptions remains a subject of inquiry and debate.

The discussion that follows will first present the traditional position; will then offer a challenge to that position related to the Modigliani-Miller (M–M) argument; then present the M–M version of the challenge; will consider the most serious of the M–M qualifications; and finally, will consider the effects of monitoring costs and taxes.

## B.   A HYPOTHETICAL CORPORATION IN A SIMPLIFIED WORLD

Assume, for now, that there are no taxes. Corporation A has a capital structure consisting solely of 1,000 shares of common stock. Its expected net earnings are $12,000 or $12 per share. All earnings are paid out as dividends. (This last assumption is made only for the sake of ease of exposition; disregarding taxes, it is not one of the assumptions that might affect the principles to be developed.) The market value of each share, let us assume, is $100, which means that the market-determined required rate of return or capitalization rate is 12 percent, which in turn means that the multiplier for determining capital value (from either dividends or earnings) is 8.33. The market value of all shares is then $100,000. (The numbers are the same as those used in various places in Section II of this Chapter.)

The basic facts can be displayed as follows:

### CORPORATION A

| | |
|---|---:|
| Common shares | 1,000 |
| Debt | 0 |
| Total earnings (expected) | $ 12,000 |
| Earnings per share | $      12 |
| Market value per share | $    100 |
| Market value, all shares | $100,000 |

Suppose that the corporation could borrow $50,000 at 8 percent and that it could use this money to buy, at the present market price, and retire, 500 of the common shares. In other words, suppose that the firm could substitute debt for half the equity as measured by present market value. If it did this, could we expect any increase in the market value of the remaining 500 common shares, with the consequence that the total value of all of the corporation's securities would be greater than the initial $100,000? Why might it be realistic to suppose that there might be such an increase in value?

## C.   THE ADVANTAGE OF UNBUNDLING

By substituting $50,000 worth of debt for the same amount of equity, the firm creates two separate types of claim against its income where formerly there was only one. The claim of the debt holders to a

$4,000 yearly interest payment is less risky than the claim of the former (before substitution of debt for part of the equity) common shareholders; the claim of the remaining common shareholders after substitution is more risky than before. The firm now offers a wider variety of securities and is in a position to take advantage of a wider variety of tastes for risk. People who prefer intermediate risk-return relationships can satisfy their preferences by buying combinations of debt and equity. (See Sec. III(I) below.)

To illustrate the unbundling principle, consider an apples-oranges analogy. Suppose that there is a fruit stand called Stand I, where apples and oranges are sold in packages consisting of 5 apples and 5 oranges, for a total price of $1.00. There may be people who are quite content with such a combination. But suppose that there are some people who are apple lovers, who would pay $.60 for 5 apples; and other people who are orange lovers, who would pay $.60 for 5 oranges. By unbundling the apples and oranges the owner of the fruit stand could increase the total price received for them.

The same principle could be at work with respect to securities. People who are highly risk averse might be willing to pay $50,000 for a claim to $4,000 per year, with a low level of risk. They would be content, that is, with a (promised) rate of return of 8 percent. At the same time, there might be people who are not so risk averse and who would be happy with an expected rate of return of, say, 14 percent on their claim to the expected residual of $8,000.[10] Such people would, collectively, be willing to pay $57,143 ($114.29 per share) for the equity interest represented by the remaining 500 shares. In that case, the total value of all securities would have risen from $100,000 to $107,143, just as the traditional view would predict. With this ultimate outcome in sight, possibly the 500 shares that were bought and retired would have fetched a price higher than $100 per share, but that is a problematic complication that does not alter the analysis; the amount of the increase in the value of the equity interest associated with the substitution of debt for equity would be the same, though the beneficiaries of that increase might, to varying degrees, change.

## D.   THE NET INCOME PERSPECTIVE

The customary way of explaining or describing the advantage of debt focuses on net income after interest expense. Suppose that there is a firm, Corporation B, that is identical in all respects to the initial version of Corporation A, except that it was financed at the outset with $50,000 debt (at 8 percent) and 500 shares of common. The expected net

---

[10] If the variance of the $12,000 expected earnings were great enough to create some chance of default on the $4,000 annual debt claim, the expected return on the debt would be less than $4,000 and the expected return on the equity would be correspondingly greater. Compare the idea expressed in footnote 4 of this Chapter.

earnings before the payment of interest would again be $12,000; the net income after the payment of interest would be $8,000 ($16 per share). We know that the shareholders of Corporation A capitalized its income at 12 percent. If it were assumed that the increased risk associated with the introduction of leverage would be of no concern to shareholders, the $8,000 income of Corporation B would also be capitalized at 12 percent and the value of the equity interest would be $66,667 ($133 per share). (Recall that shareholders should be concerned only with risk that cannot be avoided by intelligent diversification of their investments. See Chapter 4, Sec. II(F).) It might be supposed, however, that the added risk associated with the creation of leverage would cause the shareholders to demand a higher rate of return—say, 14 percent—in which case, as we have just seen, the total value of the equity would be $57,143 ($114 per share). Using this assumption, we can show the advantage of debt by the following comparison of Corporation A and Corporation B.

| | Corporation A | Corporation B |
|---|---|---|
| Common shares | 1,000 | 500 |
| Debt (at 8%) | $ 0 | $50,000 |
| Total earnings | 12,000 | 12,000 |
| Interest | 0 | 4,000 |
| Earnings after interest | 12,000 | 8,000 |
| Earnings and dividends per share | 12 | 16 |
| Market value per share | 100 | 114 |
| Market value, all shares | 100,000 | 57,143 |
| Market value, debt | 0 | 50,000 |
| Market value, all securities | 100,000 | 107,143 |

It is clear that the total value of the B securities exceeds the total value of the A securities by $7,143 (7.14 percent). A cost-of-capital comparison shows a similar advantage of the B Corporation capital structure. Corporation A's cost of capital is simply the cost of its equity, 12 percent. Corporation B's cost of capital is the weighted average of its debt and its equity (see Sec. I(D)(3) above), which turns out to be 11.2 percent, calculated as follows:

| | Cost | Weight | Value |
|---|---|---|---|
| Debt | .08 | .47 [11] | .0376 |
| Equity | .14 | .53 | .0742 |
| Average | | 1.0 | .1118 |

## E. HOW MUCH LEVERAGE?

If the use of some leverage increases the total value of a firm's securities, does it follow that the use of even greater leverage will

[11] $50,000/$107,143 = .466.

produce further increases? In other words, are there limits to the debt-equity ratio such that at some ratio the total value of all securities begins to decline (and the cost of capital begins to rise)? Under the traditional view, the answer is that there are such limits, though we are not given rigorous formulas for finding those limits. The limiting ratio will depend on the variance of a firm's expected returns, which will in turn depend on such factors as the nature of the firm's product, the degree of competition in the industry, and the relative amount of fixed and variable costs. While the issue of optimal debt-equity ratio remains a topic of considerable debate and study among and by experts in finance, the ideas developed earlier in this book suggest one perspective that may offer a useful intuitive insight into the issue—namely, that as the relative amount of debt increases, the claim that purports to be debt can be expected to take on more and more of the characteristics of equity until at some point the purported debt amounts to equity and the purported equity amounts to a "mere" option (or super-equity interest). See Chapter 4, Sections III(C)(2) and V.

## F.  ANOTHER VIEW: HOMEMADE LEVERAGE

A different view, rejecting the foregoing analysis, rests on the observation that leverage can be created by individuals as well as by corporations and on the assumption that investors, being rational, will not pay a premium for corporate leverage when they can create their own leverage—that is, when homemade leverage is available (as, in fact, it is). We begin with an illustration of one form of this argument.

Suppose that you are an astute investor; that you have just noticed that the shares of Corporation A are selling for $100 each; and that you can borrow, for the purpose of buying those shares, up to $50 per share at 8 percent (the same rate paid by the Corporation). Suppose that you can readily buy 100 A shares (10 percent of the total) at the present market price of $100 per share. You do so, using $5,000 of your own funds and $5,000 borrowed, nonrecourse, on the security of the 100 shares (that is, using the 100 shares as collateral for the loan). You now have a claim to 10 percent of the expected earnings of A Corporation, or $1,200 per year, subject to an interest obligation of $400 per year (8 percent of $5,000). Your expected net return is $800 per year. This is precisely the same expected net return that you would have if you owned 10 percent of the equity of B Corporation. With a 10 percent equity interest in B, your pro rata share of the debt of B would be $5,000. Under the traditional view, however, a 10 percent interest in the equity of B Corporation should be worth more than $5,000. By hypothesis, above, it is worth $5,714.

The two prices are inconsistent; a state of disequilibrium exists. A 10 percent interest in B Corporation represents a claim to expected earnings of $800, subject to indebtedness within the firm of $5,000 (10 percent of the total debt of $50,000). A 10 percent interest in the earnings of A Corporation creates a claim to earnings of $800 if financed in part by debt of $5,000. Since the interest rate is the same with either investment, since there is no personal liability with respect to either investment, and since each investment produces an identical claim, it is unreasonable to assume that the difference in prices can persist. Either the price of B shares is too high or the price of A shares is too low, or there is some combination of both errors. In other words, if we assume that individuals can borrow on the same terms as can corporations, it is simply logically inconsistent to assume a set of prices for leveraged and unleveraged firms, like B Corporation and A Corporation, that is consistent with the traditional view. The total value of the claims to the identical streams of income of the two firms must be the same.

## G. EXTENDING THE ARGUMENT: ARBITRAGE

The inconsistency may become even clearer if, following the mode of analysis of Modigliani and Miller, we consider the role of "arbitrage." Arbitrage is a process in which the efforts of perceptive investors and speculators, seeking their own advantage, tends to eliminate inconsistent prices of similar or identical assets and to thereby bring about equilibrium.

To see how arbitrage might work, return to our apples-oranges example. (Sec. III(C) above.) Suppose, as before, that there is a fruit stand, called Stand I, where packages consisting of a combination of 5 apples and 5 oranges are selling for $1.00, but that there is another stand, called Stand II, where packages of 5 apples sell for $.60 and packages of 5 oranges sell for $.60. Abby, a shrewd 10-year-old, sees the opportunity to make some money. She buys a package of 5 apples and 5 oranges at Stand I for $1.00, repackages them at a trivial cost, and sells the separate elements at Stand II for $1.20. She has made a fast profit of 20 percent on her $1.00 investment. She repeats the process four more times and shortly has doubled her money. She is now prepared to buy two packages at Stand I, but, lo and behold, she finds that the price has risen. What has happened is that other children have caught on to the opportunity and their frenzied buying activity at Stand I has driven the price up to $1.09. At the same time, the new selling activity at Stand II has driven the price for 5 apples or 5 oranges down to $.55. The profit opportunity that remains is barely enough to justify the effort involved. Equilibrium has been achieved.

In this example, arbitrage eliminates inconsistent prices in two markets. The process would be even easier to accomplish, and the disequilibrium more difficult to imagine, if the inconsistency occurred within a single market. Yet the inconsistency between the price of the equity in Corporation A and the equity in Corporation B that is hypothesized under the traditional view does occur in what is likely to be a

single market.  Corporation A and Corporation B are intended to sym-
bolize companies whose common stock is actively traded on major stock
exchanges.  Those are the kinds of companies with which the exponents
of the traditional view are concerned.  People who hold and trade the
shares of such companies are likely to think of many different corporations as being essentially interchangeable investment opportunities.
Moreover, information about these common stocks is readily available
and is rapidly devoured by a host of shrewd analysts.  With these
thoughts in mind, consider how Abby, now a mature woman who spends
all her time managing her own investments, might engage in a form of
the arbitrage process with the common stock of Corporation A and
Corporation B.  The process will not be nearly as neat and tidy as it was
with the apples and the oranges.  It is still a form of arbitrage, however,
because Abby will view the two corporations as identical except for the
price differential.  She will, as we shall see, sell B stock and buy A stock
not because she thinks that A is in any significant respect different from
B but rather because she thinks of A as being identical to B but lower in
price.

Suppose that Abby happens to own 50 shares of the common stock
of Corporation B; since the total number of B shares is 500, Abby owns
10 percent.  Her pro rata interest in the earnings of the corporation is as
follows:

### CORPORATION B

| Item | Corporate Total | Abby's Share |
|---|---|---|
| Earnings before interest | $12,000 | $1,200 |
| Debt | 50,000 | 5,000 |
| Interest (8 percent) | 4,000 | 400 |
| Earnings after interest | 8,000 | 800 |
| Dividends | 8,000 | 800 |
| Market value of shares | 57,143 | 5,714 |

With this information in mind, she examines the financial data of
Corporation A and quickly recognizes that she can increase her prospective income stream with no additional risk. She sells her B shares for
$5,714 and arranges for a loan of $5,000, at 8 percent, to finance the
purchase of A shares. Since she now has a total of $10,714, she can buy
107.14 shares of A (10.7 percent of the total number of shares). This
entitles her to dividends of $1,285.68, from which she must pay interest
of $400, leaving $885.68, which is $85.68 (or 10.7 percent) more than she
was previously receiving. In tabular form:

## CORPORATION A

|  | Corporate Total | Abby's Share |
|---|---|---|
| Earnings | $12,000 | $1,285.68 |
| Dividends | 12,000 | 1,285.68 |
| Debt | 0 | 5,000.00 |
| Interest (8 percent) | 0 | 400.00 |
| Dividends after interest |  | 885.68 |

Abby is clearly better off by virtue of the change in investments. She has invested the same amount of her own funds, subject to the same leverage, and has increased her expected return. It's almost too good to be true. Remembering her childhood experience she realizes that other investors will learn of the opportunity and that, by their actions, they will drive up the price of A shares and drive down the price of B shares until equilibrium is reached. With this thought in mind she might sell B shares "short" (that is, sell borrowed shares) or borrow on the security of other assets to buy more A shares, or both. These actions would, of course, add to the forces of supply and demand that push the prices of the A and B shares into equilibrium. Ultimately the total value of the equity in each corporation, as well as the value of the debt claims against their earnings, would be the same. Capital structure is irrelevant. Q.E.D.

## H. ANOTHER PERSPECTIVE: THE ONE–OWNER CORPORATION

The proposition that capital structure is irrelevant to the total value of a firm's securities becomes virtually self-evident in the case of a corporation with only one shareholder. Imagine that there is an unincorporated business with characteristics identical to those of Corporation A except that it is unincorporated; that it is for sale for $100,000; that you want to acquire this firm and incorporate it; and that you are able to invest only $50,000 of your own money. Suppose further that you have found a bank that is willing to lend you $50,000 at 8 percent either of two ways. It will lend to the corporation if you add your personal guarantee to the corporation's promise; or it will lend to you personally, with recourse, using the shares of stock of the corporation as collateral. Disregarding tax considerations, it seems quite clear that you should be indifferent as between the two alternatives—you should be indifferent, that is, as between debt inside or outside the firm, or, if you prefer, as between corporate leverage and individual leverage. It would seem silly to suggest that you should feel richer if you use corporate rather than individual debt.

It follows that if you owned two corporations that were identical except that one was financed with corporate debt and the other with individual debt, there should be no difference in value. But if that is true for a corporation with a value of $100,000, it should also be true for a corporation worth $100,000,000. And if it is true for a corporation with only one shareholder it should be true as well for a corporation with

10,000 shareholders. What this leads to is the proposition that while there may be advantages to the use of debt, a firm with debt in its capital structure cannot be more valuable than an otherwise identical firm with no debt in its capital structure as long as the individual owners of the shares of the unleveraged corporation can borrow on the same terms as those available to the corporation. In other words, where personal debt is a perfect substitute for corporate debt, the value of a firm is not affected by its capital structure.

## I.  UNLEVERAGING

There remains the question whether corporate leverage can result in a diminution in the total value of a firm's securities. The answer is that, disregarding bankruptcy costs (that is, the legal, administrative, and other costs associated with enforcement of the debt obligations in a proceeding under the Bankruptcy Act) and taxes, leverage cannot do any harm, for the simple reason that individuals can unleverage by buying appropriate amounts of a firm's debt along with its equity. To demonstrate this point, let's return to our hypothetical corporations, A and B. Suppose that the arbitrage process has worked to reduce the value of the B equity to $50,000. Thus, we have:

|  | Corporation A | Corporation B |
|---|---|---|
| Common shares | 1,000 | 500 |
| Market value of equity | $100,000 | $50,000 |
| Market value per share | 100 | 100 |
| Debt (at 8 percent) | 0 | 50,000 |
| Total earnings | 12,000 | 12,000 |
| Interest | 0 | 4,000 |
| Earnings after interest | 12,000 | 8,000 |
| Earnings per share | 12 | 16 |

Assuming (as usual) that the two firms are identical except for capital structure, an investor can achieve the same results by investing in either. We have already seen how the investor who wants leverage can buy A shares financed in part by personal debt. At the same time, an investor who seeks to avoid the risk associated with corporate leverage can buy a combination of debt and equity. Imagine, for example, that you have $10,000 to invest. You can buy 100 shares of Corporation A's common, in which case you will have an expected return of $1,200 per year, with no leverage. Alternatively, you can buy 50 shares of B's common for $5,000 plus $5,000 worth of B's debt. The expected return on your B common would be $800 and the expected return on the B debt would be $400, a combined expected return of $1,200, which, of course, is the same as that on the pure equity investment in A. A few moments' reflection should reveal that your exposure to risk is also identical, disregarding bankruptcy costs. Bankruptcy costs are a factor for B and not for A, but in many instances their expected value is likely to be small.

Given the possibility of unleveraging, the total value of B's securities cannot fall below that of A's securities. Arbitrage would eliminate any such differential. Imagine, for example, that the price of B common shares falls to $80 per share and that you happen to own 100 shares of A common. You would sell your A shares for $10,000. You could then buy $5,000 worth of B debt plus 62.5 shares of B common. Your expected return would be $1,400—$400 interest on the debt plus $1,000 earnings (dividends) on the common. This compares with an expected return of $1,200 on the A common. The prices are in a state of disequilibrium that cannot persist.

## J. THE REAL WORLD

We now turn to an examination of some assumptions on which the irrelevance of capital structure argument depends.

**1. Rational Investors.** The objection might be made that the modern view rests on the assumption of investor rationality and that that assumption is unfounded, or at least unproved. In fact, there is ample evidence that even if some investors do behave irrationally, market prices are determined by the actions of rational investors or, in any event, are consistent with rational behavior. But let's assume that market prices are determined irrationally. In that case, the traditional view fails along with the modern view. If investors are irrational, leverage within the firm might just as easily diminish as increase the total value of a firm's securities. In an irrational world, no prediction would be possible. Corporate managers would be best advised to make the capital-structure decision by flipping a coin.

**2. Borrowing Costs.** The modern view rests on the further assumption that individuals can borrow on the same terms and with the same ease as can corporations—that is, that homemade leverage is a perfect substitute for corporate leverage. If in fact corporations can borrow more cheaply or more easily than can individuals, then individual investors who want leverage should be willing to pay a premium for the common stock of corporations that have created leverage for them— corporations, that is, with debt in their capital structures. Superficially it might seem that corporations would have some borrowing advantage over individuals for the simple reason that they would be dealing in larger amounts—they have the advantage of borrowing wholesale rather than retail. The fact is, however, that financial institutions have created a mechanism that allows individuals to borrow small amounts, on the security of common stock, with very little bother and at rates comparable to those paid by the most creditworthy corporations. The mechanism is called borrowing "on margin." What happens, in essence, is that brokerage firms (which earn commissions on the purchase and sale of securities and which, consequently, benefit from efforts that increase the volume of such transactions) borrow wholesale from banks and lend to their customers, the individual investors, for the purpose of buying or holding securities. The brokerage firm holds the securities as collateral for the loan; enforcement of the terms of the loan is much easier than is enforcement of the terms of corporate debt. The process of providing margin credit has been routinized to the point that paper work is minimal. All the customer must do is fill out a few lines on a standard-form agreement and sign it. The margin loan is not a perfect substitute for corporate debt, to be sure. The loan is with recourse and the customer-investor must maintain a minimum equity (that is, a spread between the value of the securities and the amount of the loan) during the entire period of the loan. But in many circumstances these requirements are of little, if any, significance.

Margin loans are perhaps the most obvious device for creating leverage outside the firm. There is, however, another such device by which even more extreme leverage can be created—the purchase of options on common stock. See Chapter 4, Sec. IV. Moreover, arbitrage could be performed on behalf of individuals by potentially large-scale borrowers such as mutual funds. Thus, the proposition that homemade leverage (leverage outside the firm) is a perfect substitute for corporate debt is by no means implausible.

**3.  Transaction and Information Costs.**  In order for the arbitrage process to work, and, more generally, in order for markets to reach the kind of rational equilibrium implied by the irrelevance-of-capital-structure argument, people must gather information and buy and sell securities. That is a process that involves costs. To the extent of those costs, the market prices of functionally identical securities may differ. This observation tells us nothing, however, about the direction of the "error" that will persist because of the costs of detection and correction. The error might just as easily preserve a premium for the shares of unleveraged firms as it could preserve a premium for the securities of leveraged firms. All that we know from the fact of transaction and information costs is that such errors may persist. From the knowledge of the existence of such costs we learn nothing about the direction in which the error is likely to occur. In any event, in the markets with which we are concerned, the costs referred to are small in relation to the values at stake.

**4.  Institutional Considerations.**  A large proportion of publicly traded corporate securities is held in pension funds, in private trusts, and in other such forms. The fiduciaries who manage these funds are likely to be constrained by the "prudent investor rule." That rule in effect prohibits borrowing on margin and other such use of homemade leverage. Thus, a fiduciary subject to the rule can buy the shares of a corporation that is leveraged but presumably cannot use margin loans to buy the shares of an unleveraged firm. If such fiduciaries have a taste for leverage, they might be willing to pay a premium for the shares of a corporation that provides it. It is not clear, however, that they would be required to pay such a premium. To the extent that they bid up the price of the shares of leveraged firms, unconstrained investors would sell such shares and buy the shares of unleveraged firms on margin. In other words, as long as the relative number of unconstrained investors is large, their action alone may be sufficient to eliminate any premium for corporate leverage, despite the presence of a substantial number of constrained investors.

**5. Bankruptcy Costs.** The arbitrage theory ignores the fact that as leverage increases, the possibility of bankruptcy increases and that bankruptcy is costly (because of the fees going to lawyers and accountants[12] and the loss of business as suppliers and customers become reluctant to deal with the firm except on a cash-on-delivery basis). Thus, at least when debt becomes high enough, the leveraged firm will be worth less than an otherwise comparable unleveraged firm and the force of the arbitrage proof is diminished.

**6. Leverage, Control, and Incentives.** Lenders often protect their interests with various covenants or conditions that affect control, and the greater the leverage the greater the likely shift of control from equityholders to debtholders; moreover, the incentives of managers change. See Ch. 4(A)(5, 12–15). Thus, it is simply not possible to imagine any two real-world firms that remain identical as the debt/equity ratio changes, except possibly where the amount of debt is low or the volatility of the firm's expected outcomes are low.[13]

## K. TAX EFFECTS

**1. The Relevant Rules.** Some of the tax analysis that follows is relevant to closely held firms. For the most part, however, because such firms can avoid the corporate-level tax, the focus will be (as it is in the finance literature) on publicly held corporations. The federal income tax rules that bear on the debt-versus-equity decision are as follows.

(a) Corporations are taxable at the corporate rate, which, except at very low levels of income, is a flat rate. Some corporations, however, pay no tax because they have no income—either because they operate at an economic loss or because of various tax deductions (e.g., for accelerated depreciation) or exclusions.

(b) In calculating their income subject to taxation, corporations are allowed to deduct interest payments, but not dividends.

---

[12] See Stephen J. Lubben, The Direct Costs of Corporate Reorganization: An Empirical Examination of Professional Fees in Large Chapter 11 Cases, 74 Am.Bankr.L.J. 509 (2000) (average direct expenses are 2.5 percent of assets in large Chapter 11 cases).

[13] See G. Mitu Gulati, William A. Klein and Eric M. Zolt, Connected Contracts, 47 UCLA L. Rev. 887, 911–918 (2000).

(c) Those individual investors who are subject to taxation are taxable on dividends and interest received but dividends are, since 2003, taxed at a rate lower than the rate on other sources of income such as salaries and interest.

(d) Shareholders are not currently taxable on any increase in the value of their shares—that is, unrealized capital gain—that may be attributable to corporate retained earnings. Capital gain is taxed only when realized. Thus, any tax on the gain attributable to corporate retained earnings can be deferred.

(e) The rate of taxation of realized capital gain is lower than the rate on other income.

(f) If shares are held by a taxable individual until death, they receive a date-of-death tax basis, so the prior gain escapes taxation.

(g) A substantial portion of corporate securities are held by investors such as tax-exempt organizations and pension funds that pay no tax on their income.

These rules support a number of important general observations. First, a corporation's taxable earnings that are distributed to taxable shareholders as dividends bear two taxes—one at the corporate level and one at the individual level. This is the so-called "double tax" on corporate earnings, but, since 2003, this double tax is mitigated by the reduced rate of tax on dividends (as compared with interest and other sources of income). Second, undistributed corporate earnings bear only the corporate-level tax, plus any tax that may be paid by shareholders on realized gain associated with those earnings. Third, corporate earnings that are used to pay interest on debt bear only the individual-level tax, if any.

With these rules and principles in mind we turn to a tax analysis that will, of necessity, be rudimentary but should suggest the direction of more complex analysis.

**2. Individual Rate Lower Than Corporate Rate.** The easy situation to analyze is that in which the corporate rate is higher than the individual rate. To take the extreme version of this case, suppose the corporation is taxable at a rate of 35 percent and the investors (bond-holders or shareholders) are nontaxable. Here, the value of the investments in the corporation are maximized by the greatest possible substitution of debt for equity. In other words, there is a strong tax incentive in favor of the greatest possible financial leverage. To illustrate, imagine that all the securities of the corporation are owned by a charitable organization. That organization will pay no tax on dividends, on interest, or on capital gain. Thus, for purposes of the tax analysis, the tax effects at the shareholder level can be ignored. All we need do is examine the tax effects at the corporate level, and this is simple. Suppose the corporation has net earnings of $100,000. If it has an all-equity capital structure, it will pay a tax of $35,000 on the earnings, leaving $65,000 to be held as retained earnings or to be distributed a dividend. Suppose the corporation can substitute debt for equity up to the point where the interest (payable to the charitable organization) is $100,000. The corporation will pay no tax. The charitable organization can keep the $100,000, in which case it is $35,000 ahead of where it would have been with an all-equity structure and a dividend distribution of the after-tax earnings. Or it can reinvest the $100,000 in the corporation, in which case the value of its investment will be $35,000 greater than with the all-equity structure and corporate retention of the after-tax earnings. What is true for a corporation with a single nontaxable shareholder is true pro rata for a corporation with many nontaxable shareholders.

The same analysis applies, though less dramatically, for corporations with shareholders who are taxable but at a rate lower than that of the corporation. Assume again corporate earnings of $100,000, but assume an individual rate of 20 percent. Under an all-equity structure, even if the after-tax amount could be withdrawn with no further tax (which it could not), the investor would wind up with only $65,000, because that is all that is left after the corporate tax. Under a high-debt structure, assuming the entire $100,000 is paid out as interest, the corporation pays no tax, while the investor pays a tax of $20,000 and winds up with $80,000 (which, again, can be reinvested in the corporation if that is what the investor wants).

The advantage of the high-debt structure holds even if the individual rate on dividends is lower than the rate on interest. Suppose that the individual rate on interest is 20 percent and the rate on dividends is 10 percent. If the $100,000 is paid as interest, the only tax is the individual tax of $20,000, leaving $80,000. If the $100,000 is paid as a dividend, the corporate tax is $35,000, leaving $65,000. The $65,000 paid as a dividend incurs an individual tax of $6,500, leaving only $58,500.

End of story, part one. It is this story that financial economists seem to have in mind when they refer to the "capital structure puzzle"—a phrase that captures their perplexity over why corporate America is not leveraged to the hilt.

**3. Corporate Rate Lower Than Individual Rate.** For most periods in American tax history, the top individual rates on dividends and interest have been higher—at times substantially higher—than the corporate rate.

For example, in 1980 the maximum corporate rate was 46 percent and the maximum individual rate was 70 percent (on investment income). With that relationship between the two rates, investors could find it advantageous to operate a business in corporate form despite the fact that doing so could result in a double tax, corporate and individual, on the income from that business. By using the corporate form for the business activity, investors could take advantage of the lower corporate rate, while avoiding the double tax by retaining earnings (that is, by not paying dividends). If they did wish to have the corporation pay out spare cash there were two strategies available to reduce taxes. One, as we have just seen, was to use debt in the capital structure, rather than equity, because interest paid on debt is deductible by the corporation (so that the corporate-level tax is eliminated). The other strategy was to use the spare cash to redeem common shares (non-pro-rata). Such redemptions leave nonselling shareholders with a nontaxable increase in share values (see infra Sec. IV(D)). Those shareholders who did sell generally were taxed at the lower capital-gain rate and, in any event, presumably had decided, for one reason or another, that the tax effect was acceptable. And even if earnings were ultimately paid out as fully taxed dividends, the investors had had the advantage of deferral of part of the tax they would otherwise have paid (that is, of the tax on the excess of the individual tax over the corporate tax).

a. *Focus on the corporation.* To set the stage for a more complete examination of the somewhat complex situation where the corporate rate is lower that the individual rate, we begin with a traditional form of analysis that focuses solely on the corporation (wrongly so) and supports the conclusion that tax effects favor debt over equity. Suppose that there are two corporations, A and B, in a no-tax world. Both earn $12,000, but Corporation A's capital structure consists solely of equity while B's consists of half debt and half equity. Assume that arbitrage has worked to ensure that the total value of the securities of both firms is the same, and that the total is $100,000. (See Sec. III(I) above.) The resulting financial picture can be summarized as follows:

|  | Corporation A | Corporation B |
|---|---|---|
| Market value of equity | $100,000 | $50,000 |
| Debt (at 8 percent) | 0 | 50,000 |
| Total earnings | 12,000 | 12,000 |
| Interest | 0 | 4,000 |
| Earnings after interest | 12,000 | 8,000 |

The earnings on A's equity are capitalized at 12 percent. The total value of B's securities (debt and equity) also reflects a capitalization of its total earnings (before interest) at the same 12 percent rate—which is, of course, consistent with the irrelevance-of-capital-structure principle. In other words, the total value of B's securities is determined by capitalizing its total earnings at the average-cost-of-capital rate, which is 12 percent, which is in turn the same as the cost of capital for A. Note carefully, however, that B's debt is capitalized at 8 percent while its equity is capitalized at 16 percent.

Now let's suppose that we introduce a 50 percent tax on the net income of all corporations, after the allowance of a deduction for interest. Assume further that security holders now value total securities by capitalizing (after-tax) earnings at the same rate at which they formerly valued nontaxed earnings—12 percent.[14] Corporation A pays a tax of $6,000, leaving $6,000 for security holders. Capitalized at 12 percent, this after-tax return produces a value of $50,000. For B, however, $4,000 worth of earnings goes to bondholders free of corporate tax burden. The net income of B after deduction of the interest is $8,000, resulting in a tax of $4,000, leaving $4,000 for equity holders on top of the $4,000 available for the debt holders. The $4,000 return to equity is capitalized at 16 percent, which produces a value of $25,000. This $25,000, combined with the $50,000 value of the debt, gives us a total value of $75,000 for all the securities of B—$25,000 more than the value of the securities of A. Looking at the figures from another perspective, we can say that the effect of the corporation income tax is to make the government a 50 percent partner in the equity claims, but not in the debt claims, in the corporation. Thus, the government's claim in Corporation A is to half of $100,000, or $50,000, while its claim in B is to half of only $50,000, or $25,000. The true complexities of the corporation income tax (especially regarding the treatment of losses) would require some modifications and qualifications if one sought complete precision in this analysis, but those would be minor quibbles. They would not affect the basic point of this analysis, which is that the securities of the corporation using debt are significantly more valuable than those of the corporation using (less or) no debt and the difference is attributable solely to the apparent tax advantages of debt. This is the essence of the view—reflected in the "capital structure puzzle" phrase—that American corporations should be more highly leveraged than they are. The picture changes, however, when we consider the possibility that earnings will not be paid out as dividends, but instead will be held and reinvested by the corporation in a manner that results in an increase in the value of the shares equal to the amount of those earnings.

b. *The Complete Picture.* If individual taxes are ignored, then as long as the corporation can invest earnings at its present rate of return on existing investments, any retained earnings will show up in the form of increased share value and the shareholders will be equally well off if earnings are retained as they will be if those earnings are paid out as dividends. (This point is demonstrated and the tax effects examined in Section IV of this Chapter.) One must bear in mind, however, that corporate earnings used to pay interest on debt are distributed and taxed to the debtholders currently, while corporate earnings available to holders of equity interests can be retained and reinvested. Consequently, when one takes account of individual income taxes, there may be a substantial advantage to retaining earnings in the corporation, as opposed to paying them out as dividends, and even, in some circumstances,

---

[14] This assumption of an unchanging capitalization rate (which is the rate that new investors can earn after the tax is imposed) requires an extreme position on the ability of new investors to shift the corporate tax, but it is not a critical assumption. The same kinds of results are obtained if the capitalization rate changes, as long as the rate is the same for the total value of all securities for both A and B.

as opposed to paying them out as interest. The potential advantage of retention lies in the tax saving at the individual level from (i) deferral of the individual tax on those earnings until they are ultimately realized, (ii) the possibility of a favorable rate on capital gain, and (iii) the possibility that the shares will be held until death and the gain will escape taxation entirely, and (iv) the possibility that the shares will be given to a low-bracket person or to a charitable organization.

If $100 of corporate earnings is paid out as interest, it will attract no corporate tax but will be subject to individual taxation. If the recipient is in a 70 percent marginal tax bracket the tax will be $70 and the amount left after tax will be $30. Suppose the corporate rate is 50 percent. If the $100 is a return to equity that is retained by the corporation, it will bear a corporate tax of $50, leaving $50 allocable to the equity. Even if it is contemplated that the retained $50 will ultimately be realized by equity owners who are taxable at marginal tax rates of 70 percent, the present value of the ultimate tax burden might be as low as, say, 10 percent, after taking account of the individual tax advantage of retention. A 10 percent tax on $50 is only $5, which means that the value of the retained earnings would be $45, as compared to the $30 paid out as interest.

Obviously, then, as long as the maximum individual rate exceeds the maximum corporate rate, the tax system may favor equity over debt. The significance of the individual tax rate suggests in turn a point that has long been obvious to investors—that debt appeals to some investors and equity appeals to others, that there will be a demand for a substantial amount of each, and that there will be a separate clientele for each. Starting with this kind of thought, Merton Miller demonstrated that in the aggregate there will be some (unspecified) optimal ratio of debt to equity, but that there is no such optimal ratio for all firms. His conclusions are summarized, in part, in the following passage: [15]

> There will be an equilibrium level of aggregate corporate debt, . . . and hence an equilibrium debt-equity ratio for the corporate sector as a whole. *But there would be no optimum debt ratio for any individual firm.* Companies following a no-leverage or low leverage strategy (like I.B.M. or Kodak) would find a market among investors in the high tax brackets; those opting for a high leverage strategy (like the electric utilities) would find the natural clientele for their securities at the other end of the scale. But one clientele is as good as the other. And in this important sense it would still be true that the value of any firm, in equilibrium, would be independent of its capital structure, despite the deductibility of interest payments in computing corporate income taxes. [16]

[15] Merton H. Miller, Debt and Taxes, 32 Journal of Finance 261, 269 (May 1977). See also, Joseph E. Stiglitz, Taxation, Corporate Financial Policy, and the Cost of Capital, 2 Journal of Public Economics 1 (1973).

[16] The details of corporate strategy and investor valuation at the micro level implied by this model are interesting in their own

One might add the thought that corporate managers of publicly held corporations probably are entitled to take the market prices of securities as given and as fully reflecting the effects of market forces in determining the aggregate equilibrium amounts of debt and equity.[17] Tax considerations would be reflected in those prices. Managers could then simply seek to minimize the cost of capital and in doing so properly take into account the tax saving associated with corporate debt. In other words, it was not inappropriate for managers to disregard individual tax effects, since they are reflected in the market prices of the securities of their firm. It is inappropriate, however, for scholars and other observers attempting to understand and explain the system as a whole to ignore those individual tax effects. And a lawyer or other person hired to advise people on an appropriate capital structure for a corporate investment would be chargeable with gross incompetence if he or she ignored individual tax effects.

One final point may deserve brief consideration, at least by those readers whose interest has been especially aroused by the issues discussed in this subsection. In the passage quoted above, Professor Miller said that there was no preferred capital-structure strategy "for any individual firm"—though he seemed to retreat a bit from this position in the footnote at the end of the passage. While the issue of optimal capital structure is no doubt extremely complex, our analysis here does seem to suggest, contrary to the Miller statement, that there is at least one factor that should have a significant impact on the capital-structure decisions of individual firms. That factor consists of the opportunities of such firms for profitable investment of retained earnings. Firms searching for funds and individuals searching for investments (note the managerial perspective here) interact so as to produce an equilibrium set of market prices of, and corresponding returns on, debt and equity. The process producing this equilibrium presumably takes tax effects fully into account. But the equilibrium analysis assumes that some firms would retain and reinvest earnings in order thereby to produce a tax advantage for high-bracket investors. It is by no means unreasonable to assume that some firms would be better situated than others to retain and reinvest earnings. A small firm manufacturing computers, for example, may have better (that is, more profitable) opportunities for investing its profits in expanded output than a large firm in the same industry (because of antitrust constraints, among other possibilities) or a firm of similar size in an industry with less growth potential. Firms lacking opportunities for expansion in their traditional activity may lack expertise in making investments in other activities. Firms with superior opportunities for expansion thus will have a comparative advantage in

right, but further analysis is best deferred to another occasion. [Footnote from quoted work.]

[17] See Dan S. Dhaliwal, Merle Erickson, and Robert Trezevant, A Test of the Theory of Tax Clienteles for Dividend Policies, 52 Nat'l Tax J. 179 (1999) (data supports theory that prices reflect tax clienteles).

issuing equity and retaining earnings and ought to exploit that advantage.

The same point can perhaps be made with even greater force and simplicity if we take an investor perspective, by imagining a corporation with a single investor whose tax rate is significantly higher than that of the corporation. If the corporation has opportunities for expansion, then, depending on the rate differential and the period of retention (and corresponding deferral of the individual tax), it may be advantageous to finance with equity rather than debt in order to take advantage of the immunity of retained earnings from individual taxation; the investor may prefer retained earnings taxed at the corporate rate to interest taxed at the individual rate. If, on the other hand, the firm has no attractive investment opportunities and therefore contemplates distribution of its earnings, it should be financed heavily with debt in order to minimize the corporate tax. The more general point is that capital-structure strategy will obviously depend in large part on the investment opportunities of the firm. It may be worth noting once more, by the way, that this observation will seem elementary to lawyers and accountants experienced in advising on the incorporation of small businesses.

c. *Another Perspective.* The perspective of the discussion in the preceding subsection remained (until the final paragraph) essentially managerial in the sense that it viewed securities holders as consumers rather than owners. The concern was in large part with aggregate phenomena. If we adopt an investor and single-firm perspective, we can demonstrate much the same general principle (namely, that when the maximum individual rate exceeds the maximum corporate rate the tax system does not clearly favor corporate debt over equity) in a manner that may be even more convincing and, in any event, may yield additional insights. Here we will assume the need for use of borrowed funds and will demonstrate that the tax system does not necessarily favor corporate as opposed to individual borrowing.[18]

Imagine the following facts: An individual has the opportunity to invest in a project that will cost $100,000 and has an expected annual return of $12,000, before tax. The individual will invest $50,000 of his own funds and will borrow $50,000 at 8 percent. The project will be held in corporate form and the lender is willing to lend either to the corporation or to the individual, nonrecourse, with the shares of the corporation as security for the loan. Thus, there are two financing possibilities. The corporation can be financed, formally, only with equity supplied by its sole shareholder partly with his own funds and partly with borrowed funds. Or the corporation can issue 50–50 debt and equity, with the individual investor owning the equity and the corporation incurring the debt. Assume that the corporate tax rate is 50 percent, and that the individual tax rate on interest and dividends is 70

---

[18] This approach was taken in Donald E. Farrar and Lee L. Selwyn, Taxes, Corporate     Financial Policy and Return to Investors, 20 Nat'l Tax J. 444 (Dec. 1967).

percent and on capital gain is 30 percent. All earnings of the corporation, after payment of the corporate tax, will be retained by the corporation until the distant future and will be reinvested at the same 12 percent rate of return. In the distant future, the shareholder will sell his entire interest in the corporation, including, of course, his interest in the retained earnings, and at that future time the gain will be treated as capital gain. The present value of the future capital-gain tax on the individual is 10 percent.

First, look at what happens if the debt is issued by the corporation.

## CORPORATE–LEVEL DEBT

### Corporation

| | |
|---|---|
| Income | $12,000 |
| Interest paid | – 4,000 |
| Taxable income | 8,000 |
| Tax (corporate) | – 4,000 |
| Retained earnings | $ 4,000 |

### Investor (shareholder)

| | |
|---|---|
| Share-value gain from retained earnings | $ 4,000 |
| Tax on share-value gain (present value, 10%) | – 400 |
| Net gain | $ 3,600 |

### Total Taxes

| | |
|---|---|
| Corporation | $ 4,000 |
| Individual | + 400 |
| Total | $ 4,400 |

Given the assumptions, the outcome is straightforward and should be easy to understand. The corporation earns $12,000, pays $4,000 in interest and $4,000 in taxes (50 percent of the taxable income of $8,000), leaving after-tax earnings of $4,000, which are retained by the corporation. The $4,000 retained by the corporation is treated as a gain (unrealized in a tax sense) of $4,000 to the investor/shareholder—which requires only the entirely plausible assumption that a dollar held in the corporate pocket is worth just as much as a dollar held in the individual pocket (disregarding, for the moment, the individual tax). The present value of the ultimate individual tax burden on the retained earnings is $400, leaving a net present-value gain of $3,600. The total present-value taxes are $4,400.

Now consider what happens if the debt is incurred by the individual/shareholder.

## INDIVIDUAL–LEVEL DEBT

**Corporation**

| | | |
|---|---|---|
| Income | $12,000 | |
| Tax (corporate) | – 6,000 | |
| Retained earnings | $6,000 | |

**Investor (shareholder)**

**Gain**

| | | |
|---|---|---|
| Share-value gain<br>from retained earnings | $ 6,000 | |
| Tax saving from<br>interest deduction | +2,800 | |
| Total gain | $ 8,800 | $8,800 |

**Tax and interest**

| | | |
|---|---|---|
| Tax on share-value gain<br>(present value, 10%) | $   600 | |
| Interest payment | +4,000 | |
| Total investor cost | $ 4,600 | –$4,600 |
| Net gain | | $4,200 |

**Total taxes**

| | | |
|---|---|---|
| Corporation | $ 6,000 | |
| Individual | +600 | |
| Subtotal | 6,600 | |
| Less individual saving | –2,800 | |
| Net | $ 3,800 | |

Here, at the corporate level the outcome is again straightforward and easy to understand. Earnings of $12,000 are taxed at 50 percent, leaving after-tax earnings of $6,000, which are retained. The retained amount is again treated as a gain to the investor/shareholder subject to a present-value tax of $600 (10 percent). The debt, now held at the individual level, produces two numbers. First, there is simply the $4,000 interest payment that must be made by the individual. This payment in turn produces a tax deduction on the individual's personal income tax return. (Since it is hypothesized that the individual pays income tax at the rate of 70 percent, the individual must have income from other sources such as dividends and interest from other investments,[19] against which the interest can be deducted.) The tax saving from the deduction is $2,800. To put that in slightly different perspective, the net interest cost to the individual is $1,200 ($4,000 minus $2,800) after taking account of individual-level tax effects. The net gain is $4,200. This is $600 more than when the debt was held by the corporation and, of course, the total taxes of $3,800 are $600 less than before. The reduction in total taxes and the increase in gain is a result of offsetting the $4,000 in interest against individual income taxed at 70 percent rather than against corporate income taxed at 50 percent. The 20 percent rate differential applied to the $4,000 deduction produces a saving of $800 in taxes, which is reduced to $600 by the increase in the tax on retained earnings. There is one minor problem. The individual

[19] Sec. 163(d) of the Internal Revenue Code might bar deductions against income from other sources, such as compensation for services.

must somehow make the $4,000 interest payment without withdrawing money from the corporation in a manner that would result in additional tax. $2,800 of the needed $4,000 can be thought of as coming from the tax saving generated by that interest payment. The remaining $1,200 must come from some other personal source—without taking money out of the corporation. To keep things simple, it can be assumed that this comes from an additional loan on the security of the now-more-valuable equity interest in the corporation. That makes the analysis for the subsequent years a bit more complex, but in no way does this complexity undercut the basic tax benefit principle.

The moral of the story is that debt should be held by individuals, rather than by corporations, where the individual rate is sufficiently higher than the corporate rate and earnings can be retained and reinvested at a reasonable rate of return for a sufficiently long period of time.[20] What is true for the one-shareholder case is equally true for the many-shareholder case. It is simply not true, therefore, that the tax system unqualifiedly favors corporate debt financing.[21]

## L. MONITORING PROBLEMS

One intriguing recently developed approach to the explanation of capital structure is based on the difficulty (or, to use the language of economists, the "costs") of "monitoring" management—that is, the difficulty of detecting and controlling opportunism (shirking, cheating, stealing, and other self-serving behavior).[22] Consider, for example, a restaurant owned and managed by two individuals. Suppose that the two owner-managers have decided to seek funds from investors to build another restaurant and that the new investors will not take part in the management of the business. Potential equity investors may, quite understandably, be concerned about the problem of opportunistic behavior by the owner-managers. The restaurant business is notoriously one in which opportunistic behavior by managers is difficult to detect or control. Cash paid for a dinner may wind up in a manager's pocket, suppliers may pay kick-backs to a manager, a manager's friends and relatives may be treated to free dinners, and so forth. An outsider asked

---

[20] A more precise statement can be found in the Farrar and Selwyn article cited in footnote 18.

[21] Under rates in effect in 2002 for high-income individuals and high-income corporations, the hypothetical case results in a slight edge to corporate debt. If the corporate rate is 35 percent, the individual rate is 38 percent, and the individual effective rate on capital gain attributable to retained corporate earnings is 10 percent, the use of corporate debt results in total taxes of $3,200, while individual debt results in total taxes of $3,270. On the other hand, if the

individual contemplates holding the equity until death, so the capital gain rate is zero, total taxes using corporate debt are $2,800 (the corporate tax alone), while total taxes using individual debt are $2,680 (corporate tax of $4,200 less individual tax saving of $1,520).

[22] The discussion that follows is derived from Michael Jensen and William H. Meckling, *Theory of the Firm: Managerial Behavior, Agency Costs, and Ownership Structure*, 3 J. Fin. Econ. 305 (1976).

to make an equity investment in such a business might exact a high price for the investment, by demanding a larger portion of the total equity than would be appropriate in the absence of the possibility of opportunistic behavior by the owner-managers. From the owner-managers' perspective, the cost of raising equity capital would seem high (unless they were in fact willing, and expected to be able, to shirk, cheat, and steal enough to compensate them for this added cost). If the owner-managers raise the additional capital by borrowing, the problem of opportunism largely disappears, for the simple reason that a lender (a holder of debt, as opposed to equity) is entitled to a fixed return and need not be concerned with the profitability of a firm as long as it does not become insolvent (an outcome that the owner-managers in most circumstances have ample incentive to avoid). Thus, lenders (debt holders) would not demand the premium for the risk of opportunism that equity investors might demand and the cost of debt to that extent would become relatively cheaper than the cost of equity.

There is, however, another type of opportunism that can adversely affect debt holders—namely, an unanticipated increase in the variance (volatility risk) of the firm's investments. This form of opportunism is likely to become a significant problem for debt holders only when the ratio of debt to equity is high. We have seen the effects of this phenomenon before. See Chapter 2, Sec. II(B) and Chapter 4, Sec. III(A)(9). To illustrate, suppose Susan forms a corporation in which she invests $10,000 in return for the entire equity and suppose the corporation is able to raise $90,000 by issuing debt to unsuspecting investors at an interest rate of 10 percent. Suppose further that Susan is free to invest as she wishes and that two projects are presented to her. Each project requires an investment of $100,000. Project A (the type of investment the debt holders had in mind but failed to insist upon) has a virtually certain expectation of returning $110,000 at the end of a year; its expected return is $110,000. Project B has a 50 percent chance of returning $180,000 at the end of a year and a 50 percent chance of returning nothing. Its expected return is $90,000. Assuming that Susan is not strongly risk averse and is unconcerned about the possibility of gaining a bad reputation, she has a strong incentive to invest in Project B. If that project proves successful, she can repay the debt, with interest (a total of $99,000) and keep the remaining $81,000 as her return on equity. There is a 50 percent probability of that happening, so her expected return is $40,500, on an investment of $10,000, for an expected rate of return of 305 percent. Her expected rate of return on Project A is only 10 percent ($110,000 less $99,000 to the debt holders, leaving $11,000 for Susan, on an investment of $10,000). Project B is a good one for Susan because it is a bad one for the lenders. If Susan selects that project, the lenders bear most of the risk of loss even though they are entitled to only a fixed, modest portion of the gain. Their expected return is $49,500 (a 50 percent probability that the project will be successful and they will receive their promised return of $99,000 and a 50 percent probability that they will receive nothing).[23]

The possibility of managerial opportunism of the sort suggested above depends on the level of debt, the nature of the business, the protections included in the debt agreement, and the duration of the debt. We have previously examined possibilities for limiting opportunism by imposing on the borrower various obligations (reflected in "covenants"). See Chapter 4, Sec. III(A)(5). For example, the problem of changing the risk characteristics of the firm might be controlled by a simple agreement that no such change in the business can be made without the permission of the lender. Moreover, if the debt is of short duration, the possibilities for opportunism are greatly reduced. Let us assume, however, that the debt is to be of moderate or long duration and that it is not feasible to impose limitations on the borrower's investments or business strategies. We are left, then, with the question, what are the constraints on the use of debt associated with the level of debt and the nature of the business? (Another way to look at the same question might be to ask why some firms issue debt with covenants requiring the maintenance of a minimum equity cushion and others do not.) It should be clear that the higher the level of debt the greater the risk to the debtholders that a change in investment risk will increase the default risk of the debt and shift wealth from debtholders to equityholders, which helps explain why corporations reach a limit in the use of debt where the interest rate or the controls on investment become intolerable. (This idea is pursued more fully below. See Sec. III(O).) By the same token, corporations whose investment behavior is regulated (for example, public utilities) tend to pose a relatively low possibility of opportunism, which may help explain why such corporations typically have higher-than-average ratios of debt to equity. Similarly, the possibility of opportunism may help us understand why those corporations that have the greatest ability to vary the risk of their investments (such as conglomerates, which can sell a low-risk division and buy a high-risk one) tend to rely more heavily on equity as the source of their capital. Moreover, the possibility of changes in the level of risk of a firm's investments may explain the appeal of convertible bonds. As the risk rises, the value of the pure debt element falls, but the value of the conversion privilege rises (since increased variance of outcomes increases the value of an option). Thus, the convertible bond reduces the effect on

[23] To summarize:

| | Project A Investment $100,000 Outcomes | | | | Project B Investment $100,000 Outcomes | | | |
|---|---|---|---|---|---|---|---|---|
| | Probability | Expected Return | | | Probability | | Expected Return | |
| | 1.0 | | | | 0.5 | 0.5 | | |
| Total Return | $110,000 | $110,000 | Total Return | | $180,000 | –0– | $90,000 | |
| Debt | 99,000 | 99,000 | Debt | | 99,000 | –0– | 49,500 | |
| Equity | 11,000 | 11,000 | Equity | | 81,000 | –0– | 40,500 | |

the borrower of changes in risk level (due to opportunism or to accident), which reduces the uncertainty faced by the borrower and should, therefore, reduce the return demanded and paid. This explanation is consistent with the fact that convertible bonds are issued more by small, unstable firms, for which there is relatively great uncertainty about risk level, than by firms that are large and stable.

More generally, the implications of this discussion are that corporations choose between issuing debt and equity based in part on the relative monitoring costs that the investors holding these securities would experience. The less the monitoring problems faced by investors, the more they will pay for their securities, and hence the lower the corporation's cost of capital. Of course, the possibility of opportunism cannot supply a general explanation of corporate financial structures. In a simple example, such as the initial hypothetical involving the restaurant, where the potential opportunism consisted of shirking, cheating, and stealing, the solution was to have a capital structure in which management owned all the equity and outsiders invested as lenders. Here the opportunism theory seems to explain why one capital structure might be preferred over another. This is fine as far as it goes, but it does not address the question of the optimal capital structure of the large corporation, where it is not financially feasible for managers to hold a significant portion of the equity. What the opportunism theory does suggest is that from time to time as the nature of a corporation's business changes, it may find it cheaper to use one form of security (debt or equity) than another. For example, a corporation that starts out having a potential for managerial shirking that is high in relation to its total value may find that its capital needs can be met most cheaply by issuing debt securities; then it may grow into a conglomerate, at which point the holders of its debt securities are subject to new risks and it may find that its financial needs can be met more cheaply through equity issuances.

The second form of opportunism, involving the manipulation of investment risk, helps explain limits on debt ratios, but fails to explain why debt is issued by the firm rather than by individuals. Assuming, for example, that a public utility is a better candidate for loans than is a conglomerate, we must ask why public utilities do not rely entirely on equity capital, with the expectation that their shareholders will, if they wish, create their own leverage and that the advantage they can achieve by being able to offer low-risk shares as security for their debt will be reflected in a reduced cost of equity for the firm. There may be good answers to this inquiry (for example, the ability of the firm to provide guarantees that the shareholders cannot provide or economies that arise when the firm's creditworthiness is tested in a single transaction undertaken by the firm rather than in a series of transactions undertaken by individual shareholders), but further exploration is beyond the scope of this book.

## M. MANAGERIALISM

In firms characterized by separation of ownership and control, managers seem to exhibit a preference for retaining enough of the cash generated by the operations of the firm to meet most of the firm's financial needs, including the financing of expansion.[24] In other words, managers prefer to rely on internally generated funds (often referred to loosely as "retained earnings") as opposed to outside funds (from bank borrowing or issuance of new debt or equity securities). To the extent that managers act in accordance with a preference for internally generated funds they may, simply by retaining funds, increase the value of the firm's equity. But that increase may not occur or it may be in an amount less than the amount retained. If a policy of retaining earnings does increase the value of the equity, the effect will be to reduce leverage, which may reduce the total value of all securities. These observations lead to the question of why the preference exists and how it can be expected to affect shareholder wealth.

One explanation for a preference for internally generated funds is simply that managers should be able to plan the operations of the firm well enough that they can avoid the expense of seeking outside funds. On this view, it is wasteful, for example, to pay dividends and then raise money by issuing new securities; such behavior shows bad planning.

Managers may also retain earnings as a way of accumulating spare cash for financing new investments. Suppose that a corporation has no reasonable prospect of borrowing on favorable terms for new investments, so that in the absence of spare cash it would be required to issue new common stock to finance any attractive new investment. At the time the new investment opportunity arose, the managers might have unique information leading them to believe that the common is underpriced. Selling underpriced shares transfers wealth from existing shareholders to new shareholders. The managers might be unwilling to do this and might, therefore, pass up an attractive project.[25] In the same vein, the managers might be reluctant to issue new common because they think that such action will (unreasonably, in their view) be taken as a signal that they lack confidence in the future of the corporation and will result in a decline in the value of the common shares. (See Sec. III(N) below.) Again, a good investment opportunity might be lost for want of spare cash.

Another view of the preference for internally generated funds, less favorable to management, is based on the notion of "managerialism."

[24] See, e.g., Stewart C. Myers, *The Capital Structure Puzzle*, 39 J. Finance 575 (1984).

[25] See Stewart C. Myers and Nicholas S. Majluf, *Corporate Financing and Invest-* *ment Decisions When Firms Have Information That Investors Do Not Have*, 13 J. Financial Economics 187 (1984).

Under this theory, described in Chapter 3, Sec. V(A)(2), managers seek not to maximize profits but rather to produce an acceptable level of profits while taking life easy, building an empire, or engaging in other such self-serving behavior. Part of the mind-set envisioned by this theory is a strong inclination to hoard cash and to avoid going to the marketplace for funds. One explanation that has been offered for this preference is that scrutiny of management increases when outside funds are sought and managerialist managers abhor close scrutiny.[26] In other words, if managers know that there are skeletons in the corporate closet (that is, nonpublic unfavorable information), they will be reluctant to go to investment bankers seeking to raise new funds, because the investment bankers are likely to find the skeletons and require, as a condition of raising the new funds, that they be exposed to public view. This theory of managerial preference for retained earnings as a source of investment funds is consistent with evidence that firms that do not raise new equity funds show a low rate of return on reinvested earnings.[27]

Another explanation of the managerialist preference for internally generated capital and reluctance to go to the market for new money may be suggested by the following hypothetical. Suppose a corporation is run by empire-building managers. The initial capital was $1 million, all of which was contributed in return for common stock. The market rate of return is 10 percent. The initial investment has earned 10 percent, or $100,000 per year. Each year management has paid $60,000 in dividends and has invested $40,000 in new projects. Each new project has had a rate of return of 5 percent, so that in effect $20,000 of shareholder wealth is wasted each year and, because investors in the marketplace have caught on to the managerial reality, the value of the shares held by the investors is 20 percent less than what it would be with competent managers.[28] The value of the original $1 million investment is now $800,000. Now suppose management wants to raise $500,000 by selling new common stock, to finance a new project. Suppose that for some reason, while the expected return on the project is 10 percent, or $50,000, per year, everyone expects that, as before, management will waste 20 percent of this annual return.[29] Thus, if the new $500,000 is

---

[26] See Frank H. Easterbrook, *Two Agency–Cost Explanations of Dividends,* 74 Amer. Econ. Rev. 650 (1984); Michael S. Rozeff, *Growth, Beta and Agency Costs as Determinants of Dividend Payout Ratios,* 5 J. Financial Research 249 (1982).

[27] See Merritt B. Fox, Finance and Industrial Performance in a Dynamic Economy 234–235 (1987), citing William J. Baumol, Peggy Heim, Burton G. Malkiel, and Richard E. Quandt, *Earnings Retention, New Capital and the Growth of the Firm,* 52 Rev. of Economics and Statistics 345 (1970); and William J. Baumol, Peggy Heim, Burton G. Malkiel, and Richard E. Quandt *Earnings*

*Retention, New Capital and the Growth of the Firm: A Comment,* 55 Rev. of Economics and Statistics 128 (1973).

[28] To be more precise, the value of the original investment is reduced initially to $800,000. If the dividends are invested outside the firm, at the market rate, to produce a return of 10 percent, the initial $800,000 investment grows at an annual rate of 8 percent.

[29] This might happen if management is competent in selecting and managing major projects but has a propensity for wasting 20 percent of the return on such projects by

raised, and invested in the new project, the net earnings after wastage will be $40,000. In order to raise the $500,000, the corporation will be required to issue new common shares in sufficient number to allocate to the new investors $50,000 per year of earnings, which means that it will be necessary to divert to them $10,000 per year of existing earnings. This will mean that existing investors will suffer a decline in the value of their investment of $100,000, to $700,000.[30]  In effect the $100,000 loss results from the subsidy that the existing investors would be required to pay to the new investors to induce them to invest with the present, inefficient management team. The greater the amount of the new investment, the worse off are the existing shareholders.  The original investors are losers to the extent that earnings are reinvested.  They are double losers when new equity money is raised. It may be that the incumbent managers can keep their jobs if the worst they do is invest earnings (internally generated funds) unwisely. Causing shareholders a noticeable capital loss by raising new money may be too much. If the managers are aware of this prospect, but nonetheless want to be able to make the additional $500,000 investment, they may decide to retain more than $40,000 in earnings from the original project. If they do this and if investors are savvy enough, the price of the existing common should immediately fall. In fact, the mere possibility of such action by the managers may adversely affect current share prices.[31]

In a situation such as this, if management is somehow able to commit, or "bond," itself to paying all earnings out as dividends, the shareholders will be better off and maybe, in the long run, the managers will as well. If management is able to convince investors that it will not offer itself the opportunity to invest unwisely, it should be able to raise new money, for its empire-building purposes, without loss to the existing shareholders, if (and only if) it can convince new investors that the new money will be invested at an appropriate rate of return. Thus, we have an explanation, consistent with a preference for reliance on internally generated funds, for paying dividends while at the same time raising new money in the marketplace.

The theories suggested here find empirical support in evidence that "most leverage-increasing transactions, including stock repurchases and exchange of debt or preferred for common, debt for preferred, and income bonds for preferred, result in significantly positive increases in common stock prices." [32]  This evidence is consistent with the view that

---

making bad investments in other projects. Alternatively, it could be assumed that the $500,000 project would produce a return of 10 percent if managed by someone else but only 8 percent if managed by our hypothetical managers.

[30] This assumes that the sale of the new common to raise the $500,000 was unanticipated. If the sale was anticipated, the market value of the old common would reflect the sale and would have fallen to $700,000 in anticipation of the event. The essential point is the same: the retention of earnings to finance bad projects is bad enough for shareholders and the sale of new equity for similar projects makes things even worse.

[31] Compare Myers and Majluf, supra note 25.

[32] Michael C. Jensen, *Agency Costs of Free Cash Flow, Corporate Finance, and*

investors reward managers who commit, or bond, themselves to reduce the scope of their discretion over the funds generated by the firm's operations. Managers can retain earnings on equity (by not paying dividends), but are obligated to pay the interest on debt. The more debt, the less discretion and, other things equal, the greater the total value of all securities.

However, another theory, next discussed, can also explain this data.

## N.  ASYMMETRIC INFORMATION AND SIGNALING

The evidence that the market price of common stock falls when leverage is reduced (e.g., by the sale of new common stock) and rises when leverage is increased (e.g., by redemption of common stock) can also be interpreted as a rational market response to the signal management implicitly gives when it chooses between debt and equity. Briefly, if managers are more optimistic about the future of the firm than is the stock market (that is, if they believe the stock price undervalues the firm), they may be inclined to raise new money by borrowing (incurring debt), while if they are pessimistic, they will be inclined to sell new equity interests. Similarly, optimistic managers may be inclined to borrow money simply for the purpose of redeeming common stock, while pessimistic managers may be inclined to sell new common stock to pay off debt.[33]

An assumption underlying this theory about behavior affecting capital structure is that managers have better information about the prospects of the firm than do investors. That is, there is "asymmetric information," as opposed to equal information for all ("perfect information"). The theory then is simple common sense. Suppose you are a manager who owns common stock, or options to buy common stock, in the firm, or that you act as if you own common or options because you

*Takeovers,* 76 Amer. Econ. Rev. 323, 325 (1986). For a useful compilation and analysis of the data, see Clifford Smith, *Investment Banking and the Capital Acquisition Process,* 15 J. Financial Economics 3 (1986). Consistent with this evidence is a finding that public utilities tend to be highly leveraged, which is consistent with the fact that "regulators face political incentives to transfer wealth from investors to customers." M. Barclay and C. Smith, supra note 8, at 908.

It is worth noting here that in many corporations management will have opportunities to invest in new projects with higher-than-market rates of return and may use internally generated funds for those projects. But shareholder wealth does not depend on the use of internally generated funds. If the favorable opportunities are available, their value will be reflected in the price of the existing shares even if management elects to pay dividends and go to the marketplace for money to finance them. See infra Sec. IV(C).

[33] See Wayne H. Mikkelson and Megan Patrick, *Valuation Effects of Security Offerings and the Issuance Process,* 15 J. Financial Economics 31 (1986), reporting empirical support for the proposition that "market participants respond to insiders' incentive to issue shares that are priced too high and to retire shares that are priced too low." But see M. Barclay and C. Smith, supra note 8, at 909: "[W]hile signaling models may help explain the choice of security at issuance, our evidence suggests that they have little power in explaining the variation in priority structure across firms."

seek to benefit continuing common shareholders. Suppose you have information that leads you to believe that the firm will prosper and you believe that this information is not yet fully reflected in the price of the common shares. If you cause the firm to borrow money and redeem the common shares of some shareholders at the current market price, the expected increase in the value of the firm will be shared by a fewer number of claimants; the remaining, or continuing, shareholders will be better off than they would otherwise have been.[34] If the firm needs new funds, it should borrow rather than sell common shares to new investors, in order to avoid selling the new common too cheaply or, if you prefer, sharing the future increase in firm value with newcomers. If the firm needs funds and cannot borrow, it should raise the money pro rata from present shareholders by a rights offering. On the other hand, if you have information suggesting that bad times are coming and the price of the common is likely to decline, you should cause the firm to sell as much common stock as it can and use the money to retire debt or pay dividends. (Or it may keep the cash and buy common shares when the price falls.)

So far so good, but what about the market effects of announcement of a financing decision? It may be that investors cannot know as much as managers about a firm's prospects, but it seems reasonable to expect that they will be aware of the implications of a financing strategy. If a firm announces that it intends to redeem common stock (with or without borrowing), or borrow money for a new project, investors may interpret that announcement as good evidence (a signal) of favorable prospects for the firm. If they do, the price of the common should rise almost immediately. Empirical studies suggest that this is in fact what happens.[35] Investors might have some reason to be concerned, however,

---

[34] The conduct suggested here seems consistent with a loyalty to nonselling, or continuing, shareholders, but not to selling shareholders. One can question whether the selling shareholders are entitled to feel aggrieved and, more broadly, how the hypothesized managerial conduct prospectively affects the pricing of common stocks. The management conduct can be thought of as a form of insider trading, but based on general information the use of which would presumably not be proscribed by rules prohibiting certain insider trading or rules requiring the divulgence of material information. Maybe it is a sufficient answer to the concern expressed here to observe, as explained in the next paragraph of text, that the *announcement* of a leverage-increasing transaction will drive up the price of the common almost immediately to a new equilibrium point, so the selling shareholders do not lose much, and they are not, after all, required to sell. In any event, it is not difficult to imagine why managers would be concerned with the good will of continuing shareholders, not of those who sell.

[35] See C. Smith, supra note 32. Most of the ideas in this section of text are suggested by or derived from the Smith article. W. Mikkelson and M. Patrick, supra note 33, suggest that not all the information content of the capital-structure-change announcement is quickly incorporated in the price. It is interesting, and consistent with our speculations on signaling, that the price effect is increased when the announcement is that common stock is to be sold not only by the firm but by management as well. See Ronald W. Masulis and Ashok N. Korwar, *Seasoned Equity Offerings, An Empirical Investigation,* 15 J. Financial Economics 91 (1986).

The evidence relating to the issuance or redemption of common is also consistent with an older theory to the effect that price

about trickery—that is, about pessimistic managers redeeming common in the hope of creating a false impression of favorable prospects so they can make a quick profit. This possibility, implying an endless chain of each side trying to outguess the other, suggests indeterminacy.

Suppose that managers are pessimistic and announce a decision to issue new common shares. Investors should take that as a signal of unfavorable prospects.[36] The price of the common should fall almost immediately (before the new shares can be sold) and the potential advantage of selling the common should evaporate. Thus, one would not expect firms to sell new common unless they are in a position to convince investors that there is a good reason for doing so other than taking advantage of asymmetric information.

This discussion of the role of asymmetric information and signalling obviously could be extended and cries out for more empirical testing. The ideas are new in the financial literature and their implications are far from fully developed. It does seem clear, however, that a complete theory of capital structure must take account of those ideas. The static models described at the beginning of this section (III) and, at least until recently, widely accepted in academic circles seem to ignore an important dynamic aspect of the real world of financial markets.

## O.  ANOTHER PERSPECTIVE:  EXTREME LEVERAGE

Another perspective, under which an equityholder is viewed as holding an option to buy the corporation from the debtholder, may help in providing at least an intuitive sense of the limits on the use of debt. (See Chapter 1, Sec. XIII(B) and Chapter 4, Sec. IV.)  Recall the example in Chapter 2, Sec. II(D), in which Pamela wants to borrow $199,000 from Abe and Bill for one year and invest $1,000 of her own money, to buy a grocery store for $200,000.  Assume that there is no potential gain from management change and no undervaluation.  The debt/equity ratio contemplated is truly 199:1.[37]  As suggested in Chapter 2, the $1,000 payment seems unrealistically low, even with a high "interest" rate.

changes are a simple response to supply and demand. The theory has been rejected by most current scholars on the ground that common stocks of different firms are almost perfect substitutes for one another and that consequently one would expect the supply and demand curves confronting a particular firm to be almost perfectly elastic. See Paul Asquith and David W. Mullins, Jr., *Equity Issues and Offering Dilution*, 15 J. Financial Economics 61 (1986).

[36] Consistent with this idea is the finding that firms that finance acquisitions by issuing their own common stock experience negative stock market returns while those that finance acquisition by paying cash ex-

perience positive returns. Andrade, Gregor, Mark Mitchell, and Erik Stafford, *New Evidence and Perspectives on Mergers*, 15 J. of Econ. Perspectives 103, 111 (2001). The authors of this study note that the announcement of "a stock-financed merger represents a combination of a merger announcement and an equity issue announcement." Id.

[37] The issue is perhaps easiest to grasp if one imagines a person seeking to borrow $199,000, nonrecourse, to buy $200,000 worth of common stock of a publicly traded corporation.

Suppose that the interest rate that is contemplated is 20.6 percent, so that at the end of the year Pamela will owe $240,000 (120.6% of $199,000). If we think of the transaction as the purchase of an option, the duration of the option would be one year and the exercise price would be $240,000. What would be the price of the option? That is, what would Pamela be required to pay for it? The answer to that question tells us the minimum amount that Pamela would be required to invest in order to buy a residual, or equity, interest in the firm subject to a "debt" that requires a payment of $240,000 at the end of one year.

The amount that Pamela must pay for the option depends on the variance of the expected outcomes for the value of the firm and on the market interest rate. Assume a risk-free market interest rate of 10 percent and assume that everyone is risk neutral (that is, no one is risk averse). Suppose there is a 50 percent chance that at the end of the year the firm will be worth $275,000 and a 50 percent chance that it will be worth $165,000. The expected value is $220,000; this is equal to the original $200,000 plus 10 percent, so the investment would be acceptable for a risk-neutral investor. These facts are displayed in Table 1.

**Table 1**

Start: $200,000
End of Year
    .5 Probability    $275,000
    .5 Probability     165,000
Expected Value    $220,000

What would Pamela pay, and Abe and Bill demand, for the option?[38] If the firm turns out to be worth $275,000 at the end of the year, Pamela will exercise the option and pay the $240,000 option price. Abe and Bill will receive $240,000 and Pamela will have a gain of $35,000. For her, the expected value of that outcome is $17,500 (50% probability of $35,000). If the firm is worth $165,000, Pamela will not exercise the option, so her expected value for that outcome is zero. Abe and Bill will have the firm, worth $165,000. Thus, the combined expected return on Pamela's option is the average of $35,000 and zero, or $17,500. The present value, at the beginning of the year, at a discount rate of 10 percent, is $15,909. That is the price that Pamela should be willing to pay for the option (assuming no risk aversion). Her position is shown in Table 2.

[38] There is a complex algebraic formula for determining the option price, given the duration of the option, the expected variance of the price of the asset, the market interest rate, and the exercise price. The formula is called the Black/Scholes option pricing formula, after the two economists who figured it out. The rudimentary numerical examples in text should provide the intuition behind the formula.

## Table 2

| Probability | Outcome | Amount to Pamela | Expected Value to Pamela |
|---|---|---|---|
| .5 | $275,000 | $35,000 | $17,500 |
| .5 | -0- | -0- | -0- |
| Expected Value (end of year) | | | $17,500 |
| Present Value (beginning of year) | | | $15,909 |

The $15,909 that Pamela should expect to invest is also the amount that Abe and Bill should be willing to accept. At the end of the year they would receive either $240,000 (if the firm turns out to be worth $275,000 and Pamela exercises the option) or $165,000 (if the firm turns out to be worth that much and Pamela does not exercise the option), with a 50 percent chance of each outcome. The expected return is $202,500 ($120,000 plus $82,500). If Pamela invests $15,909, their investment is $184,091. At 10 percent, for one year, that grows to $202,500. So if they invest $184,091, their expected return is 10 percent, which is the assumed market interest rate. So the numbers work out just right. These numbers are shown in Table 3.

## Table 3

| Probability | Outcome | Amount to Abe & Bill | Expected Value to Abe & Bill |
|---|---|---|---|
| .5 | $275,000 | $240,000 | $120,000 |
| .5 | 165,000 | 165,000 | 82,500 |
| Expected Value (end of year) | | | $202,500 |
| Present Value (beginning of year) | | | $184,091 |
| Investment by Abe and Bill | | | $184,091 |
| Expected return required (10%) | | | 18,409 |
| Expected value required | | | $202,500 |

What this shows is that on the assumed facts, with a modest variance in expected outcomes and a high "interest" rate, the minimum option price, or "equity," is $15,909.[39] In other words, there are logically derived limits to the use of leverage. There is, of course, an

[39] To return to the problem as originally posed, what interest rate would Abe and Bill charge if they were to invest $199,000 and Pamela were to invest $1,000? At the end of the year, Abe and Bill must be entitled to $199,000 plus some amount of interest. Their expected return at the end of the year, assuming an interest rate of 10 percent, must be $199,000 plus 10 percent of $199,000 (1.1 times $199,000), which is $218,900. If it turns out that the firm is worth $165,000, they will own it. There is a 50 percent prospect of that outcome, so the expected future value of that outcome is $82,500. For Abe and Bill to be satisfied, the expected value of the other outcome must therefore be the required $218,900 less $82,500, or $136,400. There is a 50 percent probability of an outcome of $275,000, so they must get $272,800 on that outcome to yield the expected $136,400 (50 percent times $272,800 equals $136,400). So, the contract with Pamela must require that at the end of the year she must either pay Abe and Bill $272,800 (which she will do if it is worth $275,000) or turn the firm over to them (which she will do if it is worth $165,000). The $272,800 required payment implies a nominal "interest payment" of $73,800 on the original $199,000 ($272,800 less $199,000 equals $73,800), or 37 percent. Pamela would invest $1,000 in return for a 50 percent chance of receiving $2,200 ($275,000 less $272,800), so her expected return at the end of the year would be $1,100 and her expected rate of return would be 10 percent.

additional set of considerations that in fact will increase the required equity if the transaction is a true loan and Pamela has a true equity claim. With a true equity claim, Pamela will have control, which raises problems of moral hazard and asymmetric information, as well as the enforcement barrier and the costs associated with the bankruptcy law, all of which would increase the amount she would be required to invest. These observations may provide some insight into why leverage is not more extreme than it is and why options are so popular despite the fact that they provide leverage without the tax benefits of debt. The fact remains, however, that many profit-making corporations fail to use even a comfortable amount of leverage and in the current tax regime that reality is difficult to reconcile with the notion that managers ought to be maximizing shareholder wealth by reducing corporate taxes.

## IV. DIVIDEND POLICY

### A. CONSTRAINTS

State statutes, elaborated in judicial decisions, impose limitations on the freedom of corporations to pay dividends on their common shares. (See Chapter 3, Sec. VI(B)). Very roughly, a corporation may legally pay dividends to the extent that it has either current earnings or past earnings that have not already supported earlier dividends. In some circumstances dividends may legally be paid even in the absence of such current or past earnings. In no event, however, can a corporation legally make a dividend payment if that payment would result in its insolvency. For most corporations these rules are of no practical significance. Most corporations that have been in business for more than a few years and have had even the most modest success will have enough accumulated earnings (that is, past earnings not offset by past dividends) to permit the payment of any dividend that might reasonably be contemplated.

Constraints on the freedom to pay dividends may also be imposed by the terms of lending agreements, but again, for most corporations these constraints ordinarily will come into play only in unusual situations where the corporation has suffered substantial losses.

There may, of course, be practical constraints. The corporation may be committed to a large-scale expansion and at the same time may have decided (wisely or not) that it will not raise new capital externally to finance that expansion. Or the corporation may be confronted with the need to repay a large loan—one that, for some reason, its managers consider it cannot replace with other debt or with new equity. In such cases, the corporation is unlikely to have any spare cash for dividends.

In most cases, however, the people who make the corporation's dividend decisions will have considerable leeway. The question then becomes, what kind of dividend policy should be adopted?

## B.  THE CONVENTIONAL VIEW

**1.  General Description.**  The conventional view, still widely held, begins with the notion that dividends should be as stable as possible and should constitute a generous fraction of earnings.  Failure to maintain a stable and generous dividend, it is claimed, will mean a failure to maximize share values.  Generally, this set of views is neither precisely stated nor rigorously analyzed.

**2.  Unwarranted Assumptions.**

a.  *Earnings and Idle Cash.*  In much of the "street talk" about dividend policy, earnings seem to be treated as a source of dividends. This is technically erroneous. A firm with substantial earnings does not necessarily have the cash needed to pay dividends; a firm without earnings may have ample cash for such distributions. "Earnings" is a bookkeeping concept and dividends must be paid in cash. True, a firm that has healthy earnings is more likely to have spare cash with which to pay dividends than is one that is not doing so well. To that extent, there is a correlation between the level of a firm's earnings and its dividend-paying capacity; there is, then, some common sense behind the notion that earnings are a source of dividends. But that notion is still, at best, imprecise. It is better to think of dividends as a use of cash along with other uses—ranging from the payment of wages to the purchase of new plant and equipment—and to recognize that cash can be generated not only by the operation of the firm (the net effects of which are reflected in the firm's earnings) but also by selling new securities to the public. The last part of this observation leads directly to the next point to be discussed.

b.  *The Dividend Decision and the Investment Decision.*  A far more serious and fundamental defect in the conventional view is its implicit, often unwarranted, assumption that the dividend decision and the investment decision are linked to one another. In its clearest man-ifestation, the defect lies in the assumption that a choice must always be made between generous dividends, on the one hand, and expansion, on the other. The key to this assumption, in turn, is the further, underlying assumption—one that may or may not be justified for a particular corporation—that no change in the firm's capital is possible. In other words, the critical underlying assumption is that the firm cannot sell new debt or equity and that it cannot redeem existing equity or pay off existing debt. Only if this underlying fixed-capital assumption is made is it true that any funds not paid out as dividends will be invested in expansion of existing business operations of the firm or in development or acquisition of new lines of business and that a firm's opportunities to expand its existing operations or enter into new ventures will be limited by the availability of internally generated funds.

**3. Elaboration.** Even though the earnings-equals-cash and fixed-capital assumptions may be unwarranted for many corporations, it will be useful to grant those assumptions and proceed to examine the logic and the common sense of the conventional view. It will be seen that, with the assumptions granted, dividend policy should depend on whether the investments available to the firm are more or less attractive than those available to the shareholders. For purposes of illustration we can use the hypothetical facts relied upon previously in this chapter, here assuming no debt. The financial picture of the corporation at the beginning of the year is as follows:

| | |
|---|---|
| Number of shares | 1,000 |
| Earnings (expected) | $ 12,000 |
| Dividend (expected) | $ 12,000 |
| Earnings and dividend per share | $ 12 |
| Market value per share | $ 100 |
| Market value, all shares | $100,000 |
| Capitalization rate | 12% |

Suppose that at the end of the year the corporation has earned the $12,000; that it has this amount of cash in hand; and that it is confronted with a choice between paying the $12,000 out as a dividend or investing it in a project that has an expected return of 12 percent. Disregarding taxes, the shareholders will be equally well off, financially, with either choice. If the $12,000 is retained and invested, the expected earnings of the firm will increase by 12 percent by virtue of the new investment. The market value of each share will increase by the same percentage, to $112.[40] If, on the other hand, the firm pays the $12,000 out as dividends, each share will again be worth $100 but the owner of each share will have received a $12 dividend payment and will have total assets of $112, which, of course, is precisely the same as if the earnings had been retained. Only the form of the shareholders' wealth is different, which may or may not be significant. (The significance of the difference in form is discussed in succeeding subsections.) To make the same point in somewhat different terms, at the end of the year the owner of a share has a $100 interest in the basic assets of the firm and a $12 interest in the year's earnings. Since, by hypothesis, the shareholder demands and expects a 12 percent return on his or her investment, it must be assumed that the shareholder has alternative investment opportunities that will yield 12 percent. A shareholder who contemplates investing the $12 should be indifferent between investment in the

[40] The outcome is a tautology, as the following arithmetic exercise will demonstrate. The total investment after the investment of the $12,000 is $112,000. The expected earnings figure, given the assumption of a 12 percent rate of return on the new, as well as on the old, investment, is therefore .12($112,000) = $13,440. Taking those earnings we can turn right around and recompute capital value: $13,440/.12 = $112,000. The value of each share is $112,000/1,000 = $112.

corporation and investment in some alternative: indifferent, that is, between any given amount of dividends and the same amount of capital appreciation. (Remember, we are disregarding taxes for now.) A shareholder who wants cash for current consumption purposes will likewise be indifferent as long as the $12 gain in the value of his or her shares can be converted into cash costlessly, either by borrowing or by selling a part of the total investment.

If we change our assumptions about the investment opportunities of the firm, the conclusion changes. Suppose that any funds retained by the firm will be invested in a project that yields only 6 percent. In that case, if the $12,000 is retained and invested by the firm, the value of each share will rise to only $106 [41] and the shareholder will prefer that the corporation pay the amount out as dividend. If, on the other hand, the corporation (but not the shareholder) can invest the $12,000 at 18 percent, then if the $12,000 is retained and invested the value of each share will rise to $118 and the shareholder should prefer that the corporation retain the amount rather than pay it out.

An intriguing and difficult issue raised by this analysis is whether it is reasonable to suppose that the investment opportunities of shareholders and corporations are likely to be different. If, for example, the shareholders of General Motors can invest in IBM, why isn't General Motors itself free to make the same investment? Part of the answer is that the managers of General Motors may not be expert in selecting investments outside its basic industry. Shareholders of General Motors might object to having its managers making stock market investments for them, or even to their making direct investments in the computer industry. And a General Motors program of investment outside its traditional lines of business, particularly in the form of market purchases of the common stock of firms in other industries, might be looked upon as a sign of the failure of the managers of General Motors in those traditional lines.[42]

**4. A Revisionist Restatement.** A modern, rigorous analyst with an aversion to the customary statement of the conventional view should be far more receptive to a revised restatement of the conventional view that reflects the underlying common sense of that position without being prey to its errors. That statement might read more or less as follows:

A firm with substantial earnings is likely to generate spare cash— that is, cash that is not needed to maintain the existing level of

---

[41] The total earnings of the corporation will be $12,000 on the initial $100,000 worth of assets plus $720 on the retained $12,000, a total of $12,720, or $12.72 per share. Since the capitalization rate will remain 12 percent, the value of each share will be $12.72/.12 = $106.

[42] See Jeremy Stein, Agency, Information, and Corporate Investment, Chapter 2, pages 136–155, in Handbook of the Economics of Finance, Vol. 1A (George M. Constantinides, Milton Harris, and René M. Stulz editors, 2003).

investment. Most mature firms have limited opportunities to earn acceptable returns by expansion of their existing business or by entering new businesses and are reluctant to invest in the securities of other firms. When such mature firms retain their spare cash rather than paying it out as dividends, they will therefore be likely to invest that cash in projects with low rates of return. Accordingly, the shareholders will gain from a policy of generous dividend payments. Shareholders are inconvenienced by irregular cash flows and corporate managers can without great difficulty adjust their cash resources so as to pay steady dividends. Thus, if share values are to be maximized, dividends should be not only generous but stable.[43] It will be demonstrated below, however, that in most instances what can be accomplished with a policy of generous and stable dividends can probably be accomplished better with a policy of periodic redemption of shares. See Sec. IV(D).

**5. Tax Effects and Clientele Effects.** The tax effects of dividend policy depend on the relative tax rates of, and rate of return available to, the corporation and the shareholders.[44] (The analysis here ignores an alternative to payment of dividends—namely, the use of a firm's spare cash to redeem or repurchase its own shares, which is discussed in IV(D) below.)

(a) Assume that shareholders can invest dividends outside the corporate form and earn the same rate of return that the corporation can earn on its projects and that transaction costs are small enough to be ignored. In this situation, the following propositions describe wealth-optimizing corporate dividend policy.

First, if the corporate rate and the shareholder rate are the same, then the tax consequences of dividend policy do not affect shareholder wealth. To illustrate, assume that the rate of return on investments is 10 percent, that the corporate and individual tax rates are both 50 percent, and that after-tax corporate earnings[45] of $1,000 are to be invested for one year, either by the corporation or by the shareholders. If the corporation retains the $1,000, at the end of the year it will have earned a return of $100 and will pay a tax of $50, leaving an additional $50 for

---

[43] This view is consistent with recent theorizing, and empirical studies, discussed earlier in this chapter, at Sec. III(M) and (N). The problem with a stable and generous dividend policy as a means of protecting shareholders from wasteful use of funds is that dividend policy often can be changed without serious adverse consequences to management. It is for that reason that the use of debt, with its firm obligation to make cash payments to investors (in the form of interest payments and ultimate repayment of principal), is a preferred method of "bonding" a management commitment to refrain from making wasteful investments. see M. Jensen, supra note 29, at 324.

[44] See William D. Andrews, Reporter's Study of the Taxation of Corporate Distributions, in A.L.I., Federal Income Tax Project, Subchapter C, at 327, 349–52 (1982); Alvin C. Warren, Jr., *The Timing of Taxes*, 39 Nat'l Tax J. 499, 501 (1986); Eric M. Zolt, *Corporate Taxation After the Tax Reform Act of 1986: A State of Disequilibrium*, 66, N.C.L.Rev. 839 (1988).

[45] Assuming that an investment has been made in corporate form, the tax on earnings of the corporation cannot be avoided. It is only the tax on the earnings on those after-tax earnings that is relevant.

distribution to shareholders. If the corporation then distributes the total of $1,050 (the original $1,000 plus the additional $50), the shareholders will pay a tax of $525 and will be left with $525. If, on the other hand, the $1,000 is paid out at the beginning of the year as a dividend to the shareholders, they will pay a tax of $500 on the dividend and will be left with $500. If they invest that sum at an after-tax rate of 5 percent, they will have, at the end of the year, $525. The outcomes reflect a trade-off between (i) a tax at the beginning of the year on $1,000 plus a tax at the end of the year on $50 and (ii) a tax at the end of the year on $1,050. The outcome is the same either way. The deferral of the tax on the $1,000 is an advantage that is offset by the taxation of a larger sum at the end of the year.

Second, if the shareholder rate is lower than the corporate rate,[46] shareholder wealth is maximized if all earnings are distributed.[47] Returning to the hypothetical used in the preceding paragraph, assume that everything remains the same except for the shareholder tax rate, which is now 30 percent. If earnings are retained, the corporation at the end of the year will, as before, distribute $1,050. The shareholders will pay a tax of $315 and will be left with $735 after tax. If, on the other hand, the corporation distributes the $1,000 at the beginning of the year, the shareholders will pay a tax of $300 and will be left with $700. The return on the $700 at the shareholder after-tax rate of return, 7 percent, will be $49, and at the end of the year the shareholders will have $749. This is $14 more than they will have if the earnings are retained by the corporation. That $14 is 2 percent of $700 and 2 percent is the difference between the after-tax corporate rate of return (50 percent of 10 percent, or 5 percent) and the after-tax individual rate of return (70 percent of 10 percent, or 7 percent). In other words, distributions are advantageous because the shareholders can invest at a higher after-tax rate of return than can the corporation. The wealth effect is magnified as the duration of the period of retention is extended, for the obvious reason that the longer one pays an additional tax, the worse off one is.

Third, if the shareholder rate is higher than the corporate rate, shareholder wealth is maximized if earnings are retained. The longer the period of retention (or, if you will, the period of deferral of the higher shareholder tax) the better. To illustrate, return to our hypothetical and

[46] There have always been special categories of individual taxpayers with low rates—most notably charitable foundations and pension funds. Corporate shareholders have also long paid a low rate on dividends, as have some foreigners.

[47] The point is more general: wealth maximization is achieved by distributing not just earnings but all assets. This is another way of observing that if the corporate rate is higher than the individual rate, there is a tax disadvantage to equity investment in corporations. In other words, tax considerations argue for avoiding the corporate form and, if the corporate form is used, for maximum use of debt in the capital structure. Thus, where the corporate rate exceeds the individual rate, if possible, the partnership form (see Chapter 2, Sec. X(A)) should be used or an S election should be made (see Chapter 3, Sec. VII(E)) or high leverage should be used (see Chapter 5, Sec. III(K)(6)).

assume that the individual rate is 70 percent. If earnings of $1,000 are retained, at the end of the year the corporation distributes $1,050 and the shareholders are left with $315. If the corporation distributes the $1,000 at the beginning of the year, the shareholders are left with $300. They earn at the after-tax rate of 3 percent and at the end of the year have $309. The $309 represents a reduction of $6, which is 2 percent of $300. That two percent is the difference between the corporation's and the shareholders' after-tax rate of return. Again, as the period of retention is extended, the wealth effect is magnified.

(b) Assume that any dividends received by the shareholders will be invested in corporate form, so that the corporate tax on the reinvested earnings cannot be avoided. On this assumption, shareholder wealth is maximized if earnings are retained. To illustrate, return to the original version of our hypothetical, with the corporate and shareholder rates both set at 50 percent. We have seen that if the corporation retains the earnings, the shareholders are left with $525. Suppose that at the beginning of the year the corporation distributes the earnings, $1,000, and the shareholders reinvest the after-tax amount, $500, in the corporation. The corporation will earn, on the $500, after tax, $25. If it distributes this amount, and assuming that the distribution is treated as a $500 recovery of investment and a dividend of $25, the shareholders will wind up, after tax, with only $512.50. In the original hypothetical, the shareholders could either pay a tax on $1,000 at the beginning of the year and a tax on $50 at the end of the year or a tax at the end of the year on $1,050. On the assumption of reinvestment in the corporate form, there is a tax at the beginning of the year on the $1,000, plus a corporate tax at the end of the year on the $50, plus a shareholder tax at the end of the year on $25. The advantage of retention holds regardless of the shareholder rate of taxation (as long as the rate is above zero).[48]

The numbers are summarized in Table 5–3.

[48] Assume that the shareholder rate is 70 percent. We have seen that if earnings are retained, the shareholders are left with $315. If the earnings are paid out and reinvested, the amount reinvested is $300; at the end of the year this will have grown at the corporate after-tax rate to $315. When this $315 is distributed to the shareholders they will pay an additional tax of $10.50 and will be left with $304.50.

Assuming a shareholder rate of 30 percent, if earnings are retained the net to shareholders at the end of the year is $735. If the earnings are distributed at the beginning of the year and reinvested, the $700 reinvestment results in a distribution of $735, which results in an additional shareholder tax of $10.50, leaving $724.50.

**Table 5–3**
Shareholder Wealth: Effects of Dividend Policy
Corporate Tax Rate 50%

| | **Shareholder Tax Rate** | | |
| | 50% | 70% | 30% |
|---|---|---|---|
| **Dividend Policy** | | | |
| Earnings retained | $525.00 | $315.00 | $735.00 |
| Earnings distributed | | | |
| Noncorporate reinvestment | 525.00 | 309.00 | 749.00 |
| Corporate reinvestment | 512.50 | 304.50 | 724.50 |

(c) If the shareholder tax rate is higher than the corporate tax rate, there is, as we have seen, a tax advantage to retention. If, however, the corporate rate of return is lower than the shareholder rate of return, then the corporate investment disadvantage must be weighed against the tax advantage of retention. Putting that another way, the tax advantage will make it desirable for a corporation to retain and invest funds at rates lower than those available to shareholders, but only up to some limit. It may be worth noting, however, that a corporation always has available to it one investment opportunity with a rate of return equivalent to that available to its shareholders—namely, the purchase of its own shares. To put the point another way, it was assumed in the discussion above that corporations must either retain earnings or pay dividends. In fact, there is a third alternative, redemption of shares (most importantly, non-pro-rata redemption). The effect of the redemption possibility is explored further below (Sec. IV(D)).

(d) The ideas presented here suggest a clientele effect. These effects are complex and one should be cautious in generalizing. The following thoughts are presented tentatively and diffidently. Where a corporation has good investment opportunities that must be exploited in corporate form, it should retain earnings and appeal to shareholders with a preference for such investments.[49] Where it is thought that dividend policy will depend on shareholder tax rates, the corporation should adopt a dividend policy and stick with it; investors can then sort themselves out. Presumably the corporations that adopt a retention policy (and seek to appeal to high-rate shareholders) should be those with good investment opportunities. Moreover, corporations should not invest spare cash in projects that could be operated without the corporate form, unless the corporate tax rate is lower than the shareholder tax rate.[50]

(e) There are peculiar tax rules for corporate shareholders, rules that favor dividends over retention. Under federal income tax law, generally, 70 percent of dividends received by a corporation from another corporation are excluded from income subject to tax. Thus, the effective rate on dividends received by corporations is around 10.5 percent. The rate of tax on realized capital gain is 35 percent. To the extent that realization of the capital gain is pushed into the future, the present value

---

[49] It must be assumed that the market for investments is sufficiently efficient that after-tax rates of return on unincorporated and on incorporated investments will be comparable. The question of why investors might prefer one type of investment to another is beyond the scope of this book.

[50] In the post-1987 era, the corporate rate will normally be higher than the shareholder rate, but a corporation with a net operating loss carryforward may be thought to have a zero tax rate, for as long as the carryforward can be expected to last.

of the tax is reduced, but if the deferral is for a relatively short period of time it is plain that the effective (present value) rate on capital gain may be higher than the rate on dividends. It is worth noting, however, that corporations hold only a small portion of the total shares of publicly traded corporations.

(f) To some degree taxable individuals, by borrowing, can avoid the adverse tax effects of dividends, where the corporation pays part of its earnings out as dividends and retains part to generate capital appreciation. To illustrate suppose that a corporation's shares sell for $100 each, that it earns $12 per year per share, pays a dividend of $5, and retains $7 (which results in a corresponding $7 increase in the value of the share). Suppose further that the individual borrowing rate is 10 percent. An individual could borrow $50 and invest $50 of his own money, purchasing one share. The dividend of $5 would be offset by the interest of $5, leaving the individual with capital appreciation of $7. The debt would, of course, create leverage and thereby increase the risk (and expected return) as compared with an outright purchase of the share. But if the added risk is unacceptable, the individual might be able to offset it with other investments. The point is that corporate dividend policy can to some extent be neutralized by the use of individual (home-made) leverage.

**6. Transaction and Information Costs.** A corporation that does not pay dividends imposes burdens on those of its shareholders who want a cash return for purposes of consumption. Shareholders can convert share-value increases into cash by selling part of their holdings, or by borrowing against them, but not without some inconvenience and the payment of brokerage fees. These transaction costs are likely to be small. People with any substantial amount of investment in the securities of public corporations will have diversified portfolios and will be engaged in a continuing process of buying and selling. In this process it is by no means burdensome to withdraw cash for consumption purposes. One simply needs to be sufficiently realistic and perceptive to understand the economic realities. It appears, however, that understanding of economic reality is in short supply and that many corporations, responding wholly or in part to the demands of shareholders, persist in pursuing policies that may fail to maximize share values by failing to minimize taxes. A significant number of corporations pay dividends at the same time that they are raising capital by selling new securities. And relatively few corporations actively pursue the redemption strategy, though the number doing so has increased significantly in recent years. (Again, see Sec. IV(D), below.) An economist might explain this phenomenon by saying that the information costs of the retention strategy are high— that it is too costly to try to educate corporate managers or shareholders, or both, about the possible advantages of avoiding dividend payments.

For shareholders with small holdings, the process of converting share-value increases into cash is likely to be a bit more costly in relation to the total value of their holdings than for those with larger holdings. But the small-potatoes investors don't amount to much in the aggregate and even for them the tax advantages of retention no doubt substantially outweigh the transaction costs imposed by such a policy.

So far we have considered only the transaction costs imposed on those shareholders who want cash for current consumption purposes. There will always be many other shareholders who want to reinvest the returns on their current investments. For them, a policy of retention reduces transaction costs.

A retention policy also reduces corporate transaction costs. For one thing, the payment of dividends imposes paperwork and mailing costs, albeit minor ones. More significant are *flotation costs*—the legal, accounting, brokerage, printing, and other costs associated with the sale of securities to the public—costs that, in some circumstances, are avoided by a retention policy.

**7. Wealth Transfers Between Equityholders and Debtholders.** Where a firm has issued debt and the debt is subject to a risk of default, the retention of assets (as opposed to the payment of dividends or the use of funds for repurchase of shares) will increase the equity cushion and decrease the risk of default. See Chapter 4, Sec. III(A)(16). Thus, retention of assets will benefit debtholders at the expense of equityholders. Payment of dividends, and repurchase of shares, will have the opposite effect. Potential wealth transfer will therefore be an important determinant of dividend policy for corporations with equity cushions thin enough to create a significant risk of default on their debt. One would expect, however, that, at least in the long run, most debtholders would protect themselves with appropriate limitations on distributions.

To illustrate this point, recall the situation described in Chapter 4, Sec. II(A)(15), Balance Sheet B, which is set forth below.

### Balance Sheet B

| | Assets | | | Liability and Equity | |
|---|---|---|---|---|---|
| | Book | Mkt | | Book | Mkt |
| Investments | $1,200 | $800 | Debt | $1,000 | $700 |
| | | | Equity | 200 | 100 |

The debt is not in default and is not due for another ten years and the firm's investment has some risk. Thus, even though the debt claim is $1,000 and the firm value is $800, the debt has a market value of only $700. Now suppose we add $500 cash to the balance sheet. The result is reflected in Balance Sheet B–B.

**Balance Sheet B–B**

| Assets | | | Liability and Equity | | |
|---|---|---|---|---|---|
| | Book | Mkt | | Book | Mkt |
| Investments | $1,700 | $1,300 | Debt | $1,000 | $1,000 |
| | | | Equity | 700 | 300 |

The addition of the cash buoys up the debt by $300 and adds only $200 to the value of the equity. Suppose the corporation finds itself in the situation reflected in Balance Sheet B–B and is free to pay a dividend of $500. If the dividend is not paid, the wealth of the debtholders is $1,000 and the wealth of the equityholders is $300. If $500 is paid as a dividend, the value of the claims in the corporations is reflected in Balance Sheet B, with the debt having a value of $700 and equity a value of $100, but the equityholders also have the $500 cash, so their total wealth is $600. Thus, starting with Balance Sheet B–B, the payment of the dividend results in a wealth shift from debt to equity of $300; the wealth of the equityholders is doubled while that of the debtholders is decreased by 30 percent.

**8. Management's Incentive Compensation.** If a corporation pays dividends, the value of the common stock should fall to reflect the payment, but the shareholders' wealth is not reduced because they have the money formerly held by the corporation. The payment of dividends does, however, result in a decline in the value of any option on the common stock. From the perspective of an option holder, dividend payments are distributions of corporate assets to shareholders, with the option holders not participating in the distribution. Many corporate managers hold stock options (granted to them as part of their compensation). Ordinarily the exercise price of these options is not affected by dividend policy. Thus, managers who hold options have an incentive to discourage the payment of dividends. (See Chapter 4, Sec. III(C)(2)(d) (final paragraph).) The same incentive can arise from bonus and other incentive compensation plans based on profits, since dividends reduce total corporate assets and the profits of a corporation will tend to rise as the total assets of the corporation rise. That is one reason why most corporate bonuses are based on some measure of return on investment (ROI), such as rate of return on equity, rather than on profits.

## C. SEPARATION OF THE INVESTMENT DECISION AND THE DIVIDEND DECISION

**1. Introduction: The Irrelevance of Dividends.** As has already been suggested, if we permit changes in the corporation's capital, there is no necessary connection between the dividend decision and the investment decision. If a corporation lacks spare cash, because it has paid dividends or for any other reason, it can still take advantage of investment opportunities as long as it is able to finance those investments by selling new securities. At the same time, a corporation that finds itself with spare cash and no attractive investments need not pay a dividend; it can instead use that cash to purchase its own securities. Given these possibilities, and assuming no taxes or transaction costs, it can be demonstrated that the total value of a firm is determined by its investment decisions and not by its dividend policy.

**2. Demonstration.** As before, imagine a corporation with 1,000 shares of common stock and no other securities. Beginning-of-the-year expected earnings are $12,000 and are capitalized at 12 percent. The total value of all shares, consequently, is $100,000 and the value of each share is $100. Now assume that we are at the end of the year; that the $12,000 of earnings is available in the form of cash; and that this amount can be invested to yield 12 percent. We have seen (Sec. IV(B)(3)) that if the earnings are retained and invested, at a 12 percent rate of return, the value of each share will be $112. Suppose that we take the investment decision as given but assume that the corporation pays out the $12,000 cash, as a dividend. That means that the corporation will need to raise $12,000 by selling new equity. One can think of the newly raised $12,000 as earning the same 12 percent rate of return as the original $100,000 and, thus, as having no effect on the value of that initial amount. Alternatively, one can think of the newly raised $12,000 being used to pay the dividend and the $12,000 of year-end earnings being used to finance the new investment. On either perspective, it might be intuitively evident that each share will still be worth $100, after the payment of the $12 dividend and the sale of the new shares, and that consequently no shareholder will be better or worse off by virtue of the decision to pay the dividend (assuming that $12 in cash is just as good as $12 in the form of increased share value, a proposition that follows logically from the assumption of no transaction costs). For those who are unable or unwilling to rely on intuition, a bit of algebra is required.

We know that the corporation must sell enough shares to raise $12,000. We need to know the number of shares that will be sold and the price of all the shares after the sale of the new shares, assuming that the price of the new shares and of the old must be the same. Let n represent the number of new shares to be sold and p the price of those shares and of the old shares after those new shares are sold. The number of new shares multiplied by their price must equal $12,000. Thus,

$$n(p) = \$12{,}000,$$

$$p = \frac{\$12{,}000}{n}.$$

We also know that with the new investment the total value of the firm will be $112,000. The price of each share after the new shares are sold will be $112,000 divided by the total number of the new shares (n) plus the old shares (1,000). Thus,

$$p = \frac{\$112,000}{1,000 + n.}$$

We can now solve for p and n. It turns out that n is 120 and p is $100.[51]

Thus, the price of each old share will be $100. Each holder of an old share will also have a $12 cash dividend, which makes the total $112, which is the same as the value of each share if no dividend had been paid and the amount that was in fact paid out in dividends had instead been retained and used to finance the investment.[52]

To complete the demonstration, suppose that the corporate investment opportunity has an expected return of 18 percent. Here, if the $12,000 is retained and invested, the value of each share will be $118. (See Sec. IV(B)(3) above.) If, on the other hand, the $12,000 is paid out and the corporation must raise $12,000 by selling new equity, it turns out that the number of new shares to be sold is 113.2 and that the price of each share, new and old, is $106.[53] The $106 share value combined with the $12 dividend provides a total value of $118, which again is the same as the total value to the shareholder of each old share if no dividend is paid. What happens in this situation is that the corporation has an exceptionally attractive investment opportunity. It can invest at 18 percent when the prevailing market rate is 12 percent. Once this good news is known to the investing public it should be reflected in share prices. The beginning-of-the-year value of the corporation should rise to $106. It is the investment opportunity (and anticipated decision to invest) that drives up the price of the shares, not the dividend decision.

---

[51]

$$p = \frac{\$12,000}{n} \quad \text{and} \quad p = \frac{\$112,000}{1,000 + n.}$$

So,

$$\frac{\$12,000}{n} = \frac{\$112,000}{1,000 + n,}$$

$$\$112,000\, n = \$12,000,000 + 12,000\, n$$
$$100,000\, n = 12,000,000$$
$$n = 120$$
$$p = \frac{\$12,000}{n} = \frac{12,000}{120} = \$100$$

[52] If you are troubled by the fact that in this discussion one source of funds has been tied to one use of funds, you have learned well the lesson of Sec. I(D)(3) and are on your way to true financial sophistication, if not already there. The error of tying together a source and a use was made consciously for ease of exposition.

[53] Expected value of the firm is:

$$\frac{12,000 + .18\,(12,000)}{.12} = \$118,000$$

Then,

$$p = \frac{12,000}{n} = \frac{118,000}{1,000 + n,}$$

$$118,000\, n = 12,000,000 + 12,000\, n,$$
$$106,000\, n = 12,000,000,$$
$$n = 113.2, \text{ and}$$
$$p = \frac{\$12,000}{113.2} = \$106.$$

Similarly, if the corporation decides to invest $12,000 at a rate of return of 6 percent, this decision will depress the price of the stock, independently of the dividend decision. If $12,000 is retained and invested in the 6 percent project, the value of each share will be $106. If the $12,000 is paid out as dividends and $12,000 is raised by selling new shares, the number of new shares sold will be 127.65 and the price of each new and old share will be $94, which, together with the $12 dividend, produces the total of $106.

**3. Taxes and Transaction Costs.** Taxes and transaction costs alter the analysis in essentially the same ways described above (Sec. IV(B)(5) and (6)), except that flotation costs may deserve greater emphasis.

## D.  REDEMPTION

Suppose, again, that our hypothetical corporation has reached the end of the year with earnings and spare cash of $12,000 and a total value of $112,000 (including the spare cash) or $112 per share. Suppose further that it has decided not to invest the $12,000. Instead of paying a dividend, it can use the cash to buy (redeem) its shares from those shareholders willing to sell. It might do this simply by buying shares on the market. With its $12,000 it should be able to buy 107 shares at the existing price of $112 per share. The total value of the corporation will then be $100,000 and the value of each of the remaining 893 shares will be $112. The corporation will be rid of the spare cash and each of the original shareholders will have either cash of $112 per share or shares each of which is worth that amount. What is important is that the $12 gain is made available to the shareholders who hold on to their shares in the form of unrealized (and therefore untaxed) capital appreciation. For taxable shareholders other than taxable corporations this is clearly preferable to the same amount of gain in the form of dividends. These shareholders will enjoy the substantial tax advantage of deferral of tax—equivalent to an interest-free loan from the government of the amount of the tax—until they decide to sell. Even if they decide to sell some of their shares in order to draw down their gain, they will have the advantage of paying tax only on the pro rata gain on the shares that they sell, rather than on the entire proceeds of the sale. For example, imagine a shareholder who bought 100 shares at $100 per share at the beginning of the year, for a total of $10,000. At the end of the year the shares are worth $112 each, for a total of $11,200, and the shareholder sells 18 shares for $112, a total of $2,016. The amount subject to tax is only the $216 difference between the proceeds of the sale ($2,016) and the cost of the shares sold ($1,800). This obviously beats paying tax on the entire amount of any dividend that might be received. Moreover, in recent years, though not currently, the individual federal income tax rate on long-term capital gains has been substantially lower than the rate on dividends. (If the shares sold in our example had been held for at least one year, the $216 would be long-term capital gain.) Finally, capital gain can be offset by capital losses, if any; net capital losses offset ordinary income, such as dividends, only to a maximum amount of $3,000.

Nontaxable shareholders should be indifferent as to whether their gain is in the form of dividends or capital gain.

What this analysis leads to is the proposition that for corporations with spare cash that they want to disburse rather than invest, as well as for corporations that have investment uses for all their spare cash, tax considerations militate against the payment of dividends. The transaction costs previously discussed (Sec. IV(B)(6)) may or may not on balance point in the opposite direction, but even if they do it seems clear that they are overwhelmed by the tax effects. There is, however, another kind of transaction cost that must be considered in connection with the redemption strategy.

Redemptions can be accomplished in several ways. One possibility is simply a privately negotiated transaction with one or more individual shareholders. This approach raises serious problems of fairness to those shareholders who are not given the opportunity to sell their shares to the corporation. Even if considerations of fairness do not rule out redemptions from selected shareholders, coping with the problem of fairness may mean substantial legal fees. A second possibility for redemption is stock-market purchases by the corporation. This approach raises complex and troublesome securities-law problems, especially where the transactions are substantial in relation to the total value of firm's equity. One concern reflected in the law is that purchases of its shares by a corporation may distort market prices by creating false impressions of demand for the shares. (One aspect of the feared phenomenon is called "painting the tape," a process that depends on the questionable notion that share prices respond to patterns of previous prices that are charted by speculators.) Another concern of the law is that the corporation may be buying shares when it has unrevealed ("inside") information that would affect the price. Again, coping with the legal issues associated with these concerns may be costly.

A third alternative is the purchase of shares pursuant to a so-called "tender offer." What this means is a formal, public offer by the corporation to buy shares directly from any shareholder who wants to sell. This approach also raises some difficult legal issues, which in turn, again, may mean significant fees to lawyers.

When all is said and done, however, the costs associated with these legal problems ordinarily seem likely to be small in relation to the potential tax advantages of the redemption strategy.[54] The compelling case for avoidance of dividend payments has had a substantial effect. "While 402 of the 500 stocks in the [Standard and Poor's] index did pay dividends [in 1999, compared with 98 percent 20 years earlier], only one of the top 15 performers, and 14 of the top 50 did so."[55] Correspondingly, redemptions have increased dramatically. "In 1999 alone, 1,253 companies on the New York Stock Exchange repurchased their own shares, spending an estimated $181 billion—nearly as much as the $216 billion that NYSE companies distributed as dividends during that year."[56] Still, most major corporations continue to pay dividends and there is no satisfactory explanation. There are, to be sure, certain irrationalities— for example, in trust law—that are offered as explanations. But such explanations merely shift the inquiry, there being no satisfactory answer to the question of why those irrationalities persist.[57]

There is one troubling aspect of redemptions as compared with dividends. As previously demonstrated, when cash is used to pay dividends the effect is to reduce the value of the corporation and, thus, the price of the common stock. If the same cash is used to redeem stock, the value of the remaining stock is not reduced. Holders of call options, who are not entitled to dividends, thus fare better with redemptions than with dividends. In recent years call options have been a substantial part of the compensation package of corporate executives. One can question whether the financial benefit of redemption (or, for that matter, of retained earnings) is an appropriate element of executive compensation. This is only part of the broader questions raised by executive stock options—questions that are beyond the scope of this book.

---

[54] Redemptions in small amounts may also be objectionable because they force shareholders to decide whether to increase their share holdings and the need to make that choice may favor well-informed shareholders (generally, those with large holdings) over the less-informed. See Michael J. Brennan and Anjan V. Thakor, Shareholder Preferences and Dividend Policy, 45 J. Finance 993 (1990). This consideration seems trivial.

[55] Floyd Norris, Growing Number of Companies Choose Not to Offer Dividends, N.Y. Times (National ed.), January 4, 2000, page 1, col. 1. The five largest companies not paying dividends were Microsoft, Cisco, America Online, Oracle, and MCI World-Com, none of which ever paid a dividend.

[56] Justin Pettit, Is a Share Buyback Right for Your Company? 79 Harvard Bus. Rev. 141 (April 2001). Gustavo Grullon and Roni Michaely, The Information Content of Share Repurchase Programs, 59 Journal of Finance 651 (2004), reports (using a different data base) that "in 1999 and 2000, for

the first time in history, industrial corporations spent more money on share repurchases than they did on dividends." For a thorough and insightful discussion of redemption and repurchase strategies and the arguments in favor of those strategies, with the suggestion that tax considerations have not in fact played a substantial role, see William W. Bratton, The New Dividend Puzzle, 93 Georgetown L.J. 845 (2005).

[57] Under trust law, in the absence of an express provision to the contrary in the trust instrument, all gain in share value is allocated to principal. In the absence of dividends, therefore, there is no "income" to be paid to income (current) beneficiaries. This rule seriously limits the freedom of trustees to invest in the shares of companies that pay no dividends. But why does the rule persist? And why do lawyers persist in failing to "draft around" it? Why is a lawyer who fails to do so not guilty of malpractice?

One other observation about redemptions deserves brief discussion. The analysis here (and in the better financial literature) suggests that the reason for a redemption strategy is simply that the corporation has no attractive investment opportunities. (The same point can be made about the payment of dividends, though perhaps with less force because of the longstanding tradition of dividend payment, at least for mature companies.) Corporate managers may be reluctant to acknowledge that they have run out of good investment opportunities. Often they will express the same thought somewhat obliquely by saying that the corporation's own shares represent the best investment available to it. That may be a bit disingenuous if it implies that a comparison was made between the value of the corporation's own shares and the value of shares of other corporations. Moreover, the purchase by a corporation of its own shares is not an "investment" in the normal sense of that word, since cash is paid out to shareholders. Corporate managers also sometimes assert that purchases of common shares must be made in order to have shares available for employee options or for acquisitions. But new common stock can be issued for such purposes. There may be some minor convenience associated with acquisition on the market as opposed to issuance of new shares, but the plainly dominant difference in the two alternatives is that in the former the corporation disburses cash and in the latter it does not. In other words, redemption generally means spare cash—period. There is, however, a significant exception—namely, redemptions that are incident to a struggle for control. Where outsiders are trying to acquire enough shares to take control of a corporation, insiders (those currently in control) may use corporate assets to acquire shares in an effort to ward off the take-over attempt. In this situation, the purchase of shares does not necessarily imply the availability of spare cash and may, in fact, require corporate borrowing.

Finally, there is a possibility that share repurchases by a public company will result in an increase in its share price. This possibility arises from the recently popular but still somewhat controversial theory that there is a downward sloping demand curve for the shares of individual companies (based on the notion of "heterogeneous expectations" among shareholders). "Downward sloping demand curve" means that some of a company's shareholders value the shares less than others and the shareholders with the lowest valuation (the pessimists) will be the marginal shareholders who determine the market price. A share repurchase will tend to cash out these pessimists, leaving in place those shareholders with a higher valuation (the optimists), who will become the marginal holders and thus set the market price at a higher amount. This idea, though supported by substantial evidence, is at odds with traditional financial theory, which posits that markets are "efficient"; that the shares of all companies are perfect substitutes for one another; that arbitragers will buy up any temporarily undervalued shares; and that the pessimists will sell their shares to the arbitragers until the demand curve becomes flat. The "efficient capital market hypothesis" (ECMH) and its limitations (including heterogeneous expectations) are discussed in Chapter 6 below.

# Chapter 6

# FINANCIAL MARKETS

## I. INTRODUCTION

We began this book by focusing on the relationships among the human actors involved in business organizations or entities. To this point, we have covered many aspects of these relationships, as well as the corporate finance tools that participants in business enterprises use to arrange and order their affairs. Now, we want to place these basic concepts in the context of modern financial markets. As with Chapters 4 and 5, there is a break of sorts from our previous coverage, but there is continuity as well. At their heart, financial markets are devices for allocating control, risk, and return, and for resolving, or attempting to resolve, some of the tensions and conflicts that arise in business relationships. But the financial markets also present enormous complexity and new problems, which we will cover here.

During 2008, the markets experienced a crisis that reshaped the way regulators and market participants think about finance and financial market regulation. This Chapter will examine the financial instruments that were at the center of this crisis, particularly *derivatives*. It also will look at the evolving structure of financial markets and the relevant efficiency and behavioral theories that attempt to describe market behavior. We close with a Section on new regulatory approaches. The financial and regulatory complexity described in this Chapter will help illuminate many of the core concepts we have covered throughout this book.

Given the complexity of modern financial markets, important questions arise about the tradeoffs between efficiency and transparency. This tradeoff is important to many of the topics in this Chapter. On one hand, financial market participants benefit from innovations that reduce the costs of trading, that "complete markets" by allowing access to new financial instruments, and that enable parties to avoid the costs associated with antiquated regulation or market structures. On the other hand, improvements in these efficiency-related areas do not come without costs, and there is a dark side to financial innovation. As the costs of individual trades has declined and investors and institutions have accessed new markets and instruments, the information gaps between buyers and sellers of financial instruments frequently have increased. Likewise, as exposure to financial risks has increased, disclosure of that exposure has declined. Overall, as markets have become increasingly deregulated, information asymmetry has increased, at least in some market segments. Although deregulation may have produced some efficiency gains, there also appear to be costs associated with decreased transparency. A continuing policy question will be where the tradeoff should be struck between the reduced costs of deregulation and the reduced transparency that seems to follow from it.

Before we can address the policy questions associated with the challenges of modern financial markets, we will need to develop some vocabulary and tools. That examination begins with derivatives. We want to take a step back now, and use the language and characteristics of derivatives to help us rethink the nature of business organizations.

## II.  RETHINKING BUSINESS ORGANIZATIONS USING DERIVATIVES

### A.  CATEGORIES AND USES OF DERIVATIVES

Derivatives are financial instruments whose value is "derived" from some underlying instrument or index. The market for derivatives is the largest market in the world. As of 2009, the "notional value" of derivatives outstanding, as measured by the size of the instruments and indices underlying the derivatives, was more than half a quadrillion dollars, larger than all of the world's other markets—stocks, bonds, commodities, and real estate—combined.

There are two basic categories of derivatives: *options* and *forwards*. An option represents the *right* to buy or sell something at a specified time and exercise price. A forward represents the *obligation* to buy or sell something at a specified time and price. Some of the vocabulary of derivatives varies depending on where they are traded, on regulated exchanges or in private "over-the-counter" markets. For example, forwards traded on exchanges are called futures, while options traded on exchanges are still called options. Over-the-counter derivatives, those not traded on exchanges, often are abbreviated as "OTC" derivatives.

It is useful to recognize upfront that derivatives are used primarily for three purposes: *hedging, speculation,* and *arbitrage*. Hedging refers to a reducing risk. For example, a farmer could use futures or forwards to lock in the price at which he will sell wheat he expects to harvest in three months. The forward contract would obligate him to sell, and his counterparty to buy, the wheat on a specified future date. Alternatively, he might purchase a put option on wheat, to insure against price declines. Such options have been traded on exchanges in the United States since 1984. A wheat put option would give him the right to sell wheat at a specified price, and would protect him against a decline below that price. We can think of a future or forward as a symmetric hedge (the farmer would both give up the potential for gain if prices rose and eliminate the risk of loss if prices fell), whereas an option would be an asymmetric hedge (the farmer would pay a premium to insurance against the risk of loss if prices fell, but would keep the potential for gain if prices rose).

Speculation refers to taking on increased risk, with the expectation, or at least the hope, of increased return. Speculators trade both options and forwards, betting that assets are mispriced, in the same way speculate by trading shares and bonds. Speculators frequently use derivatives as a more efficient or less costly means of getting financial exposure to the underlying asset. For example, if a speculator were to believe that a particular stock was likely to rise in price, it might prefer to buy a *security future*, a contract for the future delivery of that stock, because the rules governing securities futures permit traders to borrow more money than the rules governing stocks. Alternatively, the speculator might use options to calibrate a bet so that it would pay money only if the stock rose above a particular price. A speculator who believed a $20 stock would increase substantially could buy a call option with an exercise price of $30. Such a highly speculative option would be cheap—say, $1—just like car insurance with a high deductible, or a bet to win $100 on a long shot at the horse track. If the stock price increased to $50, the call option buyer would make $20—the difference between $50 and the $30 exercise price—on a position that cost just $1 upfront. In both cases, the future and the option would enable the speculator to pay less money upfront for a bet, relative to the upfront cost of buying the underlying stock.

Derivatives have been criticized because they frequently are used as a means of obtaining more leverage than would be available in the market for the underlying assets. On futures exchanges, margin requirements are set by the exchange to restrict leverage, and they are recalculated on a daily basis. But in the OTC markets, margin is a matter for private negotiation, and more leverage may be possible. Others have criticized derivatives speculation as inherently unproductive activity than diverts resources and human capital away from other pursuits. Defenders of derivatives argue that speculation provides liquidity and helps makes markets more efficient by reducing transaction costs. Although there is little possibility at present that derivatives will be abolished or curtailed by governmental action, the leverage available for their purchase is receiving Congressional attention, and increased margin requirements are likely.

Arbitrage refers to capturing riskless profits based on pricing anomalies among financial markets and products. In the purest sense, one might use derivatives to synthetically replicate the payoffs of an asset for a cheaper price. For example, if call options on a stock are cheap, and put options on the same stock are expensive, a trader might create "synthetic stock," replicating the economic profile of stock by buying cheap call options and selling expensive put options. The options would mimic the upside and downside profile of the stock, but at lower cost.

Many arbitrage opportunities are fleeting, and are quickly eliminating as parties use derivatives to replicate other assets. Other arbitrage opportunities persist, which has puzzled economists.

One especially controversial and important form of arbitrage is *regulatory arbitrage*. Regulatory arbitrage refers to derivatives transactions designed specifically to reduce costs or capture profit opportunities created by differential laws or regulations.[1] Derivatives have proven an efficient mechanism for avoiding the costs associated with regulation, including tax and accounting rules, capital charges, and investment restrictions. For example, if the capital gains from the above option trade were taxed at a lower rate than the capital gains from trading stock, parties would have an incentive to trade the options instead. As another example, if a pension fund is not permitted to trade risky financial assets such as foreign currency, it might nevertheless obtain economic exposure to those assets by using a derivative instead of a direct investment in the prohibited trade. Derivatives frequently are used to avoid accounting disclosures by moving liabilities *off-balance sheet*. Although regulatory arbitrage is costly, some economists defend the practice, claiming it enables parties to avoid overly-costly rules.[2]

We already have discussed some of the complexities of options, and we will address many more of them shortly. But at the outset, we want to return to the basic relationships among owners and creditors from Chapter 1, and explain how those relationships can be recharacterized using options and forwards. We also want to expand on some of the valuation concepts from Chapter 5. Then, we will turn to the use of derivatives in hybrid instruments and structured finance.

## B.  OPTIONS

Options are increasingly important to the understanding of business organizations, for two reasons. First, options, particularly call options, are a major component of employee compensation and corporate disclosure, and raise valuation questions that cannot be addressed through the valuation methods described in Chapter 5. Second, options illuminate certain key aspects of the relationship among the participants in a firm, particularly the relationship among different slices of the firm's capital structure, principally equity and debt.

**1.  Options Valuation.** The valuation of options is more complicated than the valuation of bonds or stocks, because of the asymmetric nature of the option payoff. For example, call options have limited downside, but unlimited upside. The basic formula used to value call options on stock is known as the Black–Scholes model, although there are more recently developed, more computationally intensive methods as well (known generally as binomial pricing models). We will focus on the

---

[1] See Frank Partnoy, Financial Derivatives and the Costs of Regulatory Arbitrage, 22 Iowa J. Corp. L. 211 (1997).

[2] See Merton Miller, Merton Miller on Derivatives 3 (1997).

Black–Scholes model, as it is commonly used, simpler, and more easily illustrates the intuition of option valuation.

The Black–Scholes model states that the value of a call option on stock depends on six factors: (1) the price of the stock, (2) the exercise or strike price of the option, (3) the time to maturity of the option, (4) the risk-free interest rate, (5) the dividends paid on the stock, and (6) the volatility of the stock's annual rate of return. Companies that grant stock options to employees are required to make disclosures about these variables. For example, in 2008 Google disclosed the following assumptions:

| | |
|---|---|
| Risk-free rate: | 3.2% |
| Expected time to maturity: | 5.3 years |
| Dividend yield: | 0 (Google did not pay dividends) |
| Expected volatility: | 35% |

Note that two of these variables, the risk-free rate and dividend yield, are easily observable. The risk-free rate is based on the rate for U.S. government bonds. The dividend yield is simple, because Google did not pay dividends (for companies that do pay dividends, it also is easy to calculate based on the size of the dividends). The two other reported variables listed above have the modifier "expected." The reason time to maturity is reported as "expected" is that one cannot be certain about when employees will exercise their options. Companies typically estimate when options will be exercised by examining the actual behavior of employees of companies that have similar demographics and geographical locations to see when they have exercised recently granted options. The notion of "expected" volatility is even more difficult. The volatility of annual returns typically is estimated based on other options that are traded based on the company's shares. Alternatively, one could estimate volatility based on the stock's historical returns.

Once we have these four variables, it is straightforward to value an option simply by plugging these numbers, along with the first two variables—the stock price and exercise price—into the model. (Versions of the Black–Scholes model are available for free on the Internet, or can be reconstructed relatively easily using spreadsheet software.) For example, if Google had granted call options with an exercise price of $500 during 2008, when the stock price also was $500, those options would have a value of $185.81 each.

As a practical matter, the key variable in assessing the value of stock options is volatility. Most stock options have roughly similar characteristics, and changes in risk-free rates and dividend yields do not matter dramatically to the value of options. As a rough rule-of-thumb, many people assume that stock option grants are worth roughly one-third of the underlying stock price at the time of grant. However, call options based on stocks that are much more volatile would be much more valuable, relative to the stock. For example, if we assumed that Google's expected volatility were 75%, instead of 35%, the options would be worth $321.95 each, nearly twice as much.

Although companies typically grant stock options *at-the-money*, so that the exercise price is equal to the stock price when the option is granted, they need not do so. Indeed, a stock option that is *in-the-money*, with the exercise price below the stock price, is more valuable than an at-the-money option. (For example, you would rather have a Google call option with an exercise price of $100 to one with an exercise price of $500). Until recently, accounting rules penalized companies that granted in-the-money options by requiring that in-the-money grants, but not at-the-money grants, be recorded as an expense. That rule has changed, so that even at-the-money option grants now must be recorded as an expense.

One final point: there is a difference between the theoretical value of an option and its actual value. The Black–Scholes model assumes that there are no transaction costs, margin requirements, or taxes. It also does not take into account the fact that options awarded as compensation can be subject to trading restrictions and vesting limitations. Moreover, the value of stock options to employees, from their undiversified perspective, typically will be significantly less than the value of comparable options traded in the market, where people can and do diversify their holdings. Simply put, a CEO would rather own options on other companies than her own, and she will value her own stock options less. Indeed, this non-diversification discount can be as much as fifty percent. Because of these complications, option valuation, like the valuation of stocks, can be more art than science. Nevertheless, the Black–Scholes model is a baseline for option valuation, and Black–Scholes valuations frequently are used by market participants and disclosed in public filings.

**2. Options and the Theory of the Firm.** Options also can help us understand the relationships among participants in a firm. Recall Pamela and Shirley, our business participants from the early Chapters. Pamela owned a grocery store, and Shirley was her creditor. Pamela had the residual claim on profits, whereas Shirley had a fixed claim. To simplify, we can think of Pamela was the holder of equity, whereas Shirley was the holder of debt.

We can reframe the relationship between Pamela and Shirley using options, from two very different perspectives, both of which illuminate the tensions among these two people and, more generally, between equity and debt. The two perspectives vary depending on which slice of the firm's capital structure, equity or debt, we think of as owning the underlying assets of the business.

First, we can assume, as we normally would, that Pamela, the holder of equity, owns the underlying assets of her business. We call this the *equity ownership perspective.*[3] We know that Pamela, as the holder of equity, does not bear unlimited downside risk in this business. If the value of the assets declines dramatically, she can walk away from the business and file for bankruptcy protection. If she holds her business in a corporation, she is generally protected by limited liability. Thus, under normal circumstances, she cannot lose more than the amount of her equity investment.

How can we use options to characterize Pamela's limited liability? One way of thinking about the relationship between these two people is that Pamela has bought a put option from Shirley. In other words, Pamela has the right to sell the assets of the business to Shirley. The exercise price of this put option is set at the point where the value of the assets is equal to the value of the debt. Shirley bears the downside business risk once the value of Pamela's equity has been wiped out. Shirley's position is equivalent to selling a put option.

For example, suppose Pamela invested $100 in her business and owned all of the stock, and Shirley loaned $100 to the business and is its the sole creditor. Also, assume that Pamela has not personally guaranteed the loan made by Shirley to her company (as most banks would probably require if they were the lender). The value of Pamela's firm's assets would be $200. We can, and normally would, think of Pamela as owning all of these assets. However, we also know that Pamela's downside is limited to her $100 investment. If the value of the assets declines to $50, so that the firm is insolvent, Pamela does not lose any additional money. Instead, conceptually, she has the right to sell the assets to Shirley for $100, the amount of the debt. Alternatively, we might imagine that Pamela loses $150, the full decline in the value of the assets, but makes $50 on the put option she has purchased from Shirley, for a net loss of $100. Either way, the put option limits Pamela's downside to $100, the amount of her initial investment.

Effectively, the put option is an insurance policy that protects shareholders from losing more than their initial investment. Creditors bear any additional declines in value. This insurance protection is another way of thinking about limited liability, one of the central concepts of business law. The interest payments received by creditors are a kind of insurance premium they receive in exchange for bearing the downside risk of declines in asset value below the value of equity. Again, Pamela has bought a put option, whereas Shirley has sold a put option.

As a second perspective, we can assume that Shirley, the creditor, owns the underlying assets of the business. We call this the *debt ownership perspective.* This alternative conception might see odd at first, because we normally think of the equity holder as owning a business's

---

[3] In their pathbreaking options pricing article, Fisher Black and Myron Scholes pointed out that equity can be characterized as having call option-like characteris-tics. See Fisher Black & Myron S. Scholes, The Pricing of Options and Corporate Lia-bilities, 81 J. Pol. Econ. 637 (1973).

assets. However, this perspective makes sense if you think of the power creditors wield in a business, particularly when the business is not doing well.

If we think of Shirley as owning the assets of the business, then we must keep in mind that Shirley has transferred the upside associated with those assets to Pamela. As long as the assets are worth more than the debt, Pamela has the right to any additional gains in value. Conceptually, Pamela can be thought of as buying a call option from Shirley. As with the put option, the exercise price of this call option is set at the point where the value of the assets is equal to the value of the debt. In other words, Shirley gives up the upside business risk once the value of the assets is sufficiently high to cover the debt. Again, Pamela has bought a call option, whereas Shirley has sold a call option.

Notice that from either the equity or debt ownership perspective, the equity has bought an option, whereas the debt has sold an option. The equity is *long* an option, whereas the debt is *short* an option. Viewing the firm participants through the lens of options thus illuminates some important characteristics about how these parties are shifting risk and return. The equity holder has upside and limited downside. The debt holder has limited upside and bears any additional downside risk once the equity holder is wiped out. Equity benefits more than debt if the business takes on riskier or more volatile projects.

Corporate law generally assigns control to equity, and the debt then bargains for specific contractual protections to protect its interests. Managers generally owe fiduciary duties to shareholders, not bondholders. But these two option perspectives suggest that this assignment of fiduciary duties is not the only possibility. Both equity and debt have contingent, derivative payoffs based on the value of a business's underlying assets. Indeed, when the value of a firm's assets declines to the point of insolvency, corporate law's fiduciary duties, and the standing to enforce those duties, typically shift so that they are owed, not to the equity, but to the debt holders.

Recharacterizing the firm using options also highlights some important lessons about distinctions among the slices of a firm's capital structure. For example, one firm might decide to raise capital by issuing primarily equity, along with a smaller amount of call options, but no debt, whereas another firm might decide to raise capital by issuing primarily debt, along with a smaller amount of equity, but no call options. (Options issued by a firm typically are known as *warrants*.) Consider this example of an "Equity Firm" and a "Debt Firm," each of which has raised $1,100 of capital in total, using two different financial instruments:

|  | Equity Firm | Debt Firm |
| --- | --- | --- |
| Warrants | 100 | 0 |
| equity | 1,000 | 100 |
| Debt | 0 | 1,000 |

Note a rule requiring managers of these two firm to maximize the value of equity would lead to different results for the two firms. The "Equity Firm" would take on more conservative projects than the "Debt Firm." Arguably, a fixed rule that tells all business managers to focus on maximizing the equity value ignores the fact that at some firms equity is at the bottom of the capital structure, whereas at other firms it is at the top. This is a puzzling result, especially if one assumes that these two firms are economically equivalent in every other way, except for their capital structure decisions. Possibly, the assignment of fiduciary duties to the equity reflects the fact that equity holders typically buy in secondary markets and do not have the same opportunity to negotiate the terms of the business relationship (as debt holders typically do). In this sense, fiduciary duties are default rules, because individual contracting is not feasible. In any event, the message from option theory is one that most business participants are well aware of: pay attention to a firm's capital structure.

## C.  FORWARDS

It also can be illuminating to think about how participant in a business can use forwards, the other type of derivative. Suppose, as before, that Pamela owns all of the equity of her firm (estimated to be worth $1,000 today), but has agreed to sell all of her shares to Shirley in one year for $1,100. In other words, Pamela and Shirley have entered into a derivative forward contract, obligating each of them: Pamela is obligated to transfer the shares to Shirley in one year; Shirley is obligated to pay Pamela $1,100 at that time.

Is Pamela still a shareholder? In other words, what happens to a share position when we add a forward contract? The result of the forward agreement is that Pamela no longer bears the risks associated with the firm's residual gains and losses. Assuming Shirley is financial solvent in one year and honors their forward agreement, Pamela will receive $1,100, no more and no less.

In contrast, Shirley, by virtue of the forward contract, has became a kind of virtual shareholder. Although she will not have any of the formal control rights associated with Pamela's shares—Pamela will still have the right to vote and receive dividends, for example—Shirley will bear the risks associated with firm's residual gains and losses. In one year, Shirley will pay $1,100 for the shares, at which point she formally will become a shareholder.

This example might seem strange at first, but in fact shareholders commonly use a variety of forward contracts to transfer the risks associated with equity investments. The most common kind of forward transaction is known as a *swap*. Swaps are private contracts between two parties, and can be thought of as a series of forward contracts. Each of the parties is obligated to make a series of payments on specified future dates. When the two parties enter into a swap, they typically set the terms so that neither party makes any payment to the other upfront. Instead, the parties simply sign a contract, and agree to exchange payments over time. Then, the value of the swap to a particular party can become positive or negative as the underlying financial variables change.

Some of the earliest swaps were based on interest rates, and *interest rate swaps* remain the most common form of swap today. An interest rate swap is just a package of forward contracts, each set for a different date, so that the parties are obligated to exchange payments periodically in the future, typically a fixed rate of interest in exchange for a floating rate of interest. For example, suppose a homeowner has a mortgage with a floating rate of interest, and would prefer to pay a fixed rate. Renegotiating the mortgage might be complicated or costly, so instead of doing that the homeowner agrees to an interest rate swap in which he will make a fixed payment to the swap counterparty every month in exchange for a floating monthly payment based on some interest rate, such as LIBOR, the London Inter–Bank Offered Rate. This swap will act as a hedge of the floating interest rate risk on his home mortgage. If interest rates increase, he will pay more on his home loan, but he also will receive a higher payment from the counterparty on the swap. The swap payment will offset the higher loan interest cost. Conversely, if interest rates decline, he will pay less on his home loan, but also will receive less from the counterparty on the swap. If the swap is structured to match the floating rate loan payments, the swap payments and loan payments will exactly cancel each other out, leaving only the fixed rate obligation on the swap. Thus, an interest rate swap can transform a floating rate obligation into a fixed rate obligation.

Swaps can be based on just about any financial instrument or index, including equity. For example, the above arrangement between Pamela and Shirley typically would be called an "equity swap" or "equity total return swap." The idea is that the two parties privately agree to swap payments at some specified future date. They have entered into a forward agreement, or a series of forward agreements. Such a swap can be transformative. From an economic perspective, it can turn a shareholder into a non-shareholder, or vice versa. And like derivatives generally, these kinds of swaps have become quite common. As of mid–2009, the International Swaps and Derivatives Association estimated that the total notional amount outstanding of equity derivatives was almost $9 trillion,[4] roughly a quarter of the value of all U.S. stocks.

Equity swaps have been especially controversial because they can be used change the nature of share ownership. In one recent example, a hedge fund called Perry Corp., purchased shares of Mylan Pharmaceuti-

---

[4] ISDA 2009 Mid–Year Market Survey,
http://www.isda.org/statistics/recent.
html#2009mid.

cals, which had announced a takeover of King Pharmaceuticals. Perry owned shares of King, which had appreciated substantially after the takeover was announced, and Perry wanted to ensure that the deal would go through, so that the King shares would appreciate even more. However, the takeover required approval by Mylan shareholders, some of whom opposed the deal. To help push the deal through, Perry bought roughly 10% of Mylan's shares, and planned to vote those shares in favor of the takeover.

The complication arose because Perry also entered into an equity swap. In a private contract with Goldman Sachs, Perry agreed to pass through any change in the value of Mylan's shares to Goldman. If Mylan shares increased in value, Perry would pay Goldman the increase, and vice versa. Effectively, Perry used the swap to transfer the economic risk associated with its investment in Mylan, but it kept the voting rights because it still retained the shares. As a result, even if it believed that Mylan was overpaying for King, it had an economic interest in voting its Mylan shares for the merger, contrary to the interests of all other Mylan shareholders. Conceptually, Perry split apart its interest in Mylan into two pieces: an economic interest in the value of the shares (which it passed along to Goldman through the swap) and a legal interest in voting the shares (which it held by retaining the shares). Economically, Perry's interest in Mylan was zero, but it still got to vote.

Litigation ensued, as did a debate about when and whether parties such as Perry should be permitted to split the economic and legal interests of shares by using derivatives. Some argued that Perry's shares should not be entitled to vote, because they were burdened, or *encumbered*, by the swap. The argument was that such *encumbered shares* did not satisfy the typical rationale for allocating votes to shareholders, namely that shareholders bear the residual gains and losses associated with corporate decisions. Others argued that encumbered shares should still be entitled to vote, but should be publicly disclosed. Most disputes have settled without judicial decision, and the few courts to address related issues have ranged widely, from criticizing shareholders who use swaps to giving swaps the same rights as actual shareholders. Whatever the arguments, though, no court has yet invalidated an economic re-allocation of share rights.

Another form of swap that has been controversial, in part for similar reasons, is the *credit default swap*. A credit default swap is a private contract between two parties, known as the buyer of protection and the seller of protection, who agree that (1) the buyer will make a series of insurance-like payments to the seller, and (2) the seller will make a payment to the buyer if a specified credit obligation defaults, or fails to pay. For example, a CDS buyer might pay a premium for a 5–year swap based on specified General Electric bonds. If those bonds experience an event of default, known as a "credit event," during the following five years, the buyer will receive a payment. If not, the buyer will have lost the premium. Thus, CDS are like options on defaults—except that the term "credit event" can sometimes be defined more broadly so that a payment is due simply because the bond is downgraded by a credit rating agency.

CDS have been compared to insurance, but they differ in several important ways. First, insurance is a regulated industry, whereas the CDS market is not. Instead, CDS fit within a regulatory exemption for swaps, which was part of the Commodity Futures Modernization Act of 2000, a law that generally removed swaps from the regulatory framework applicable to other financial instruments, including securities and exchange-traded options and futures. The rationale for this sweeping exemption was both that the participants in this market were highly sophisticated and that OTC derivatives (including swaps) spread risk throughout the market, rather than concentrating it in a few institutions. Although this diffusion of risk was thought desirable, the insolvency and bailout of American International Group (or "AIG") in 2008 as a result of its inability to meet its CDS obligations suggest that deregulation may not spread risk and can concentrate it in non-transparent ways. By issuing over $80 billion in CDS obligations, AIG so concentrated risk that the federal government concluded that a failure to bail it out might create a contagion of financial failures among other financial institutions. In any event, Congress appears likely in 2010 to end this exemption and tighten the controls on OTC derivatives, either by requiring the use of exchanges or clearinghouses or by specifying margin requirements (thereby in effect reducing leverage).

A second distinction between CDS and insurance is that a party buying insurance is expected to have an insurable interest in the underlying obligation in order for the contract to be enforceable, but the buyer of a CDS is not. Indeed, the parties to CDS contracts frequently will have no interest in the underlying bonds they are effectively insuring against default. Nor is the seller of CDS required to be a regulated entity or to maintain reserves in order to be able to repay the buyers of protection, although in practice major CDS dealers, such as banks, are subject to capital requirements more generally.

Like all derivatives, CDS are used for hedging, speculation, and arbitrage. CDS were first created in 1997, and their use increased dramatically during the following decade. By 2008, there were approximately $60 trillion of CDS outstanding in terms of the notional value of the underlying credit obligations. By 2009, though, that amount had been sliced in half, in part because the financial crisis deterred CDS activity and in part because the collapse of Lehman Brothers led many CDS counterparties to cut their positions. American International Group, or AIG, required substantial government assistance after it sold half a trillion dollars of CDS protection without hedging the risk of defaults or setting aside sufficient capital to cover expected defaults.

CDS present some of the same challenges as encumbered shares. For example, before and during the 2008 financial crisis, leaders of major financial institutions claimed that parties had bought protection against their institutions defaulting by purchasing CDS, and then simultaneously shorted the shares of those institutions, driving stock prices down. They claimed that declining share prices triggered a liquidity crisis, which prevented them from being able to borrow, and accordingly blamed CDS counterparties for the banking collapse in 2008. The counterparties responded that the financial institutions were near default because of bad decisions, and losses on complex financial instruments, not because of any short-term squeeze. Others have argued that, whatever happened during the financial crisis, CDS buyers continue to face perverse incentives to force companies into bankruptcy, or other events of default. They have argued that CDS market participants who also own bonds should not be permitted to exercise any bondholder rights, including votes on exchange offers, for the same reason that someone who, like Perry Corporation, owned shares together with a swap should not be permitted to vote.

## D.  HYBRIDS

We now know that traditional financial instruments such as equity and debt can be described using the language of options and forwards. But the complexity of the story does not end there. The characteristics of the financial claims on firms can be even more varied, so that they are *hybrids* of other financial instruments.

This idea of a hybrid financial claim is not new. Recall that preferred stock is a hybrid of equity and debt. It has an infinite life, like equity, but is paid a fixed rate, like debt. Some preferred stocks can be converted into common stock at a future date, at the option of the preferred stockholder. Other preferred stocks have a cumulative dividend, an obligation that accumulates when it isn't paid (unlike a common stock dividend, which does not accumulate). Thus, preferred stock sits in the middle of a company's capital structure, above debt but below equity. It is a type of hybrid.

There is no limit to the kind of hybrid instruments that market participants can create, and modern hybrids can have fantastic and varied characteristics. Some companies still label their hybrid instruments as preferred stock. Other companies use more exotic-sounding names, including clever acronyms based on the characteristics of a particular security.

The key questions about hybrid instruments involve legal rules. When the rules for debt and equity are different, how are hybrid instruments to be treated? For example, interest on debt is tax deductible, but dividends on equity are not. Can a company deduct payments to its preferred shareholders for tax purposes? What about the credit rating agencies, which issue ratings of corporate debt and are critical to a company's ability to raise money in the financial markets? When the agencies rate a company's debt, they look at the ratio of debt to equity to assess the risk of a company defaulting. How should they assess preferred stock? And what about the all-important accounting rules? Analysts compare companies by looking at the relative amounts of equity and debt on their balance sheets. Where do preferred stock and other hybrids fit?

Over time, financial engineers and lawyers have been very good at answering these questions. They have designed novel types of hybrid instruments to take advantage of tax deductions, favorable credit ratings, and to minimize the amount of debt disclosed in financial statements. These hybrid instruments have become quite common today, and they continue present novel issues for lawyers and business people. In several prominent securities lawsuits, the plaintiffs have included these hybrid financial instruments.

Hybrid instruments can be very intricate, but it is worth briefly exploring one early and relatively straightforward hybrid transaction in some detail, to give you a sense of how and why the basic characteristics of financial instruments might be altered. Hybrid transactions can be innovative and very profitable. This transaction was labeled the "Deal of the Year" in 1993 and generated $26 million in fees for the bankers at Salomon Brothers, then a prominent investment bank, who created it. Since then, hybrids have become much more common and complex, but they remain directed at many of the same objectives as this one, and are still just as profitable for the lawyers and bankers who create them.

This particular hybrid instrument was called "Decs" (for Dividend Enhanced Convertible Stock), and was issued by First Data Corp., the data processing subsidiary of American Express. The payouts on Decs were divided into two classes: one set of payments received during the first three years, and another set of payments received after that. The first set of payouts was simple. If you bought 100 Decs, American Express (not its subsidiary, First Data) would pay you a high dividend for three years, much like a typical preferred stock. The second set of payouts was more complex. At the end of three years, your Decs would automatically be converted into common stock of First Data (not its parent, American Express), according to a specified schedule. Essentially, an investor buying Decs was committing to buy First Data stock in the future in a forward contract.

For American Express and First Data, Decs were a financial chameleon that could appear to be equity or debt, depending on who was looking at them. As a result, the regulatory benefits of Decs were substantial. First, Salomon Brothers obtained an opinion that the three years of dividend payments would be treated as "interest" so that First Data could deduct them for income tax purposes. In other words, tax lawyers were willing to call Decs "debt" for tax purposes. Second, because American Express had agreed to pay the first three years of dividends, the credit rating agencies gave the Decs a high rating based on the financial statements of American Express, not those of First Data. The rating agencies also gave the Decs themselves a high rating and treated them as equity in their analyses of First Data, which made First Data appear to have less debt. In other words, the agencies were willing to call Decs "equity" for purposes of determining their ratings. Third, accountants did not include Decs among either American Express's or First Data's other debts and obligations, even though they were being treated as debt for other purposes.

Which parties were right about Decs? Did the Decs have a fixed claim or a residual claim? Should the Decs have been treated as equity or debt? Would your answer depend on whether the question relates to taxes, credit ratings, or accounting? How can regulation possibly keep up with this type of financial innovation? There are no easy answers, and these questions have become only more complicated since the creation of Decs. For example, parties more recently have created new instruments, with elaborate acronyms such as FELINE PRIDES (Flexible Equity–Linked Exchangeable Security Preferred Redeemable Increased Dividend Equity Securities), that are designed to be tax deductible, treated as equity for credit rating purposes, not to be included as a liability on the balance sheet, and not to dilute the common shares.

The dizzying array of hybrids can make it difficult to understand a firm's capital structure. For example, in its 2009 annual Form 10–K filing, JPMorgan Chase & Co. included among its registered issued securities, not only common stock, but 26 other financial instruments, ranging from "Capped Quarterly Observation Notes Linked to the S & P 500" to "KEYnotes Exchange Traded Notes Linked to the First Trust Enhanced 130/30 Large Cap Index." Hybrids can make corporate finance look like Alice in Wonderland.

## E.  STRUCTURED FINANCE

**1.  Structured Finance and Securitization.** Hybrid financial instruments are related to a broader category of financial transactions known generally as *structured finance*. Structured finance has dramatically affected thinking about firms and markets. The term generally refers to methods of transferring risk among various legal entities, often using or more of the derivatives described above. Like hybrids, the types of structured finance transactions are limited only by the imagination of the financial market participants that create, buy, and sell them.

The most common form of structured finance transaction is known as *securitization*. Securitization is a method financial market participants use to separate the risks and expected returns associated with various assets. The simplest forms of securitizations are known as *asset-backed securities*. Asset-backed securities represent claims on a pool of assets, such as home mortgage loans, credit card receivables, or corporate bonds and loans. The range of assets that can be "securitized" is infinite, and includes not only traditional financial instruments, but derivatives as well.

Historically, securitizations began with attempts in the late 1970s to package real estate mortgages into portfolios so that they could be sold to the broader capital markets. For example, if 1,000 home mortgages were pooled into a single portfolio, investors could assume that the portfolio would perform predictably according to standard assumptions about normal default rates. This first generation of pooled instruments involved simply "pass through" certificates; that is, if you bought 1% of the portfolio, you received 1% of all payments on the mortgages. But this still involved more volatility than investors wanted (as the cash flows might vary significantly when mortgages were prepaid, etc.). The next step was to pool the mortgages and then issue bonds against them. Now, the payments were precisely defined.

But what if the mortgages did not produce a sufficient cash flow to pay principal and interest on the bonds? To guard against default, underwriters developed a variety of techniques. One was overcollateralization: that is, to support a $100 million in bonds, $120 million in mortgages might be deposited in the pool. Another was the use of credit enhancements, such as insurance from a "monoline" insurance company (the term "monoline" reflected that the only form of insurance that they issued was on bonds against their default). Finally, "tranching" was developed, which involves subordinating lower classes of debt securities to a senior class. Suppose $1 billion in home mortgages are now placed in our pool, and three classes of debt are issued. At the top of this ladder might be $500 million in senior secured bonds; next, a "mezzanine" layer of $300 million in subordinated bonds would be issued, followed by a bottom or "equity" layer of $200 million. Payments on the two junior layers would be subordinated to the senior debt layer, so that all payments would first go to the senior debt before the other classes received anything. This structure allowed credit rating agencies to award investment grade status (typically, AAA) to the senior debt, which made these investments attractive to those financial institutions (most notably, pension funds) that had a low taste for risk. Originally, the underwriters would retain much of the junior layer as a bonding device to signal their confidence in the quality of the collateral, but later hedge funds, which have a greater taste for risk, came to buy the junior level. In this light, the key stages of a securitization transaction are (1) pooling and (2) tranching. Once this methodology had been developed, securitizations could be applied to any form of financial asset or account receivable: car loans, credit card receivables, even, doctors' and hospital receivables.

But still another problem had to be addressed: bankruptcy risks. If, hypothetically, Ford Motor Company wanted to securitize its auto loans, transferring them to a pool and issuing bonds against them on the basis just discussed, the investors still had to worry about what would happen

if Ford became bankrupt. Could other creditors—tort creditors, employees or pensioners, or tax authorities—seek to claim that the Ford auto
loans should be shared with all creditors in bankruptcy on the theory
that these loans still belonged to Ford? To guard against this possibility,
elaborate procedures are employed to assure, and lawyers must opine,
that there has been a "true sale." This typically requires the creation of
a new entity–a corporation, or trust, or LLC–that buys the loans from
Ford with the proceeds from the bonds that it simultaneously issues.
This new entity—usually called a "Special Purpose Entity" (or
"SPE")—will have no other activity or business so that it cannot
generate any other liabilities. Only then is the transaction considered
"bankruptcy remote" such that Ford's creditors cannot reach the assets
in the pool. But the result is that the SPE can issue its bonds at a lower
interest rate than could Ford (if it retained the loans and simply issued
its own bonds), because the SPE has been cordoned off from the
liabilities overhanging Ford.

The important idea to remember here is that by pooling and
tranching in this fashion, the securities issued by the SPE can be sold for
more collectively than the sum of the separate prices of the individual
assets in the market. Ultimately, the SPE device enables a company that
owns or acquires assets to transfer some or all of the financial risk
associated with those assets to investors.

Another advantage of the SPE technique involves accounting. The
company may be able to retain some of the assets' economic potential
while nevertheless removing those assets from its balance sheet. This
characteristic motivated early structured finance transactions, and continues to be an important factor in some transactions (but not most
asset-backed securitizations). The motivation began during the 1980s,
when the Emerging Issues Task Force of the Financial Accounting
Standards Board issued an opinion called EITF 90–15, which essentially
said that companies could move assets off their books if outsiders bore at
least three percent of the residual risk of the assets. This accounting
opinion came to be known as the "three percent rule."

SPEs became infamous in the aftermath of the collapse of Enron
Corporation, which used derivatives to take on billions of dollars of risk,
and then moved those risks off-balance sheet by using SPEs, based on
the three percent rule. Ultimately, Enron's list of SPEs and related
entities stretched to sixty single-spaced pages. Enron also used offshore
SPEs to do various OTC derivatives deals, including swaps that enabled
Enron to borrow money without recording the debt.[5] For example,
Enron and Chase Manhattan Bank did swaps using an SPE called
Mahonia, which was incorporated in the island of Jersey, a regulatory
haven in Europe. Chase effectively controlled Mahonia, so in reality

[5] Frank Partnoy, Infectious Greed: How
Deceit and Risk Corrupted the Financial
Markets 301 (2003).

Enron was doing the swap with Chase. Enron effectively borrowed billions of dollars from Chase by structuring the swaps so that Chase paid Mahonia (and therefore Enron) money early on, and then Enron promised to pay Mahonia (and therefore Chase) money in the future.

After the collapse of Enron, the interest in SPEs and structured finance shifted to an instrument known as a Collateralized Debt Obligation, or CDO. CDOs were originally developed by Drexel Burnham Lambert during the 1980s as a way of repackaging low-rated "junk bonds" to avoid regulatory requirements. More recently, CDOs have used as the preferred means for marketing portfolios of real estate mortgages, as earlier described. Again, the idea behind a CDO was to split the risk associated with assets into slices with varying degrees of credit risk. For example, a CDO backed by $100 of assets might issue $70 of AAA-rated bonds, $20 of BBB-rated bonds, and $10 of unrated bonds. The idea was that the value of the sum of the CDO pieces would be greater than the value of the original assets whole, because different clienteles of investors valued these slices differently.

Parties also began creating *synthetic* CDOs, SPEs whose "assets" consisted, not of actual loans or bonds, but of derivatives based on those assets. The mechanics of synthetic CDOs were similar to those of previous CDOs, but the underlying assets of synthetic CDOs were derivative contracts, particularly swaps, with counterparties based on one or more financial instruments or indices. These CDOs were called "synthetic" because they were entirely manufactured; they did not consist of any real assets. Nevertheless, the synthetic CDO tranches paid real returns, based on the SPE's right to receive cash from the derivatives and swaps.

Why might the CDO pieces, synthetic or otherwise, be worth more than the underlying assets? One reason is that the credit ratings added value to the assets by enabling institutional investors to buy exposure to them, which they otherwise could not have done. The CDO can be thought of as a kind of high-finance nuclear fission, splitting apart the atomic components of the assets, and thereby unlocking the additional value embedded in those assets simply by dividing them. But is the value added real? Or are investors paying more for individual pieces than they should, either because they misvalue the assets or misperceive their risks? The recent financial crisis delivered a partial answer to this difficult question.

**2. Structured Finance and the Financial Crisis.** At the center of the crisis were roughly a trillion dollars of CDOs backed by "subprime" mortgage loans. The credit rating agencies gave high ratings to the tranches of these CDOs, based on their mathematical financial models that suggested the likelihood of widespread defaults on these mortgage loans was remote.

Some have argued that a primary cause of the recent credit market turmoil was overdependence on credit ratings and credit rating agencies. Without such overdependence, the argument goes, the complex financial instruments, particularly CDOs, that were at the center of the crisis could not, and would not, have been created or sold. Indeed, the failure of the credit rating agencies can be seen as an example of the failure more generally of financial market gatekeepers, including investment bankers, accountants, and lawyers.[6]

It is apparent that the rating agencies were an important factor driving the creation of CDOs based on mortgage loans. Historically, the rationale was based on the investment grade "cliff" noted by W. Braddock Hickman,[7] and later Michael Milken, who saw that portfolios of sub-investment grade rated bonds outperformed more highly-rated bonds on a risk adjusted basis. Market participants adapted this insight to mortgages of various types, which were pooled into new highly-rated fixed income instruments. Surprisingly, this "cliff" persisted over time, in both corporate bond and mortgage markets; the large yield discontinuity between investment grade and below-investment grade (with BBB- being the lowest investment grade rating) ratings did not disappear even after large amounts of securities were issued. To the contrary, in the early 2000s, rating agency models, and assumptions about historical default, expected recoveries and the correlation of defaults suggested that mortgage-backed securities could be repackaged and resold in ways that would outperform, not only the mortgage-backed securities themselves, but other comparably rated securities.

As the credit derivatives market was experiencing record growth, fixed income structurers and investors, with the assistance of credit rating agencies, searched for new mortgage loans that could be securitized to create highly-rated fixed income instruments with attractive yields relative to comparable investments. To meet this demand, arrangers began to create synthetic CDOs, based on credit default swaps. These were essentially derivative side bets based on the underlying mortgage-backed securities, so that investors could obtain exposure to the performance of a pool of mortgages without any need for an SPE to actually buy the mortgage-backed securities. Synthetic CDOs obtained exposure to hundreds of billions of dollars of mortgage loans through credit default swap transactions.

The linchpin of a CDO backed by credit default swaps was the credit rating. Investors typically did not examine the underlying assets of a

---

[6] The core idea underlying such gatekeepers is that they possess a reputational capital that they have acquired over many years and many clients, which they can pledge to assure investors so that they will rely on representations that they would not accept if made only by the issuer. This certification function has, however, a dark side: sometimes gatekeepers cannot be trusted, as the 2008 financial meltdown reveals. See John C. Coffee, Jr., Gatekeepers: The Role of the Professions and Corporate Governance (2006).

[7] See W. Braddock Hickman, *Corporate Bond Quality and Investor Experience*, National Bureau of Economic Research (1958).

synthetic CDO or SIV in any detail or at all. One might criticize them for not doing so, except that structured finance is inherently opaque and requires specialists to evaluate these transactions. Often, the underlying assets were not even specified when the deals were sold. Instead, investors relied on parameters set by the arrangers, bankers, and rating agencies to constrain the assets that could be purchased originally, and held over time.

If the credit rating agencies, and their clients, had used reasonable and accurate models and assumptions, then in principle these transactions might not have been problematic. However, the rating agencies faced financial incentives to use unreasonable and inaccurate assumptions and models to complete deals and thereby earn greater fees.[8] Even when their models were sound, a second basic problem was that the rating agencies did not engage in any factual verification (or "due diligence" in lawyers' vernacular) of the factual information provided to them by the promoters and underwriters of these transactions. [9]Had they done responsible due diligence, they would have likely discovered that, after 2000, the quality of the collateral was deteriorating rapidly. In retrospect, it is now clear that loan originators (smaller savings and loan institutions and mortgage brokers) were increasingly making loans to non-creditworthy borrowers. These loans were known as "liar's loans," because there was no documentation in the loan file that the borrower had a job or assets or an acceptable credit history. Why would loan originators make such non-creditworthy loans? The simple answer is that they found they could package them and sell them to underwriters who would in turn securitize them to the capital markets based on inflated credit ratings. This is only a variation on the familiar moral hazard problem: if you are not exposed to a risk because you can transfer the financial asset after only a brief holding period to others, then you have little incentive to monitor or take precautions. Quickly, this produce a record bubble, as money flooded into the mortgage market (and virtually anyone could get a mortgage).

These problems were aggravated by a system of executive compensation within many financial institutions that misaligned the interest of the executive and the firm. If executives could expect bonuses in the millions (or sometimes tens of millions) from closing a deal, they had less

---

[8] Mason, Joseph R. and Joshua Rosner, "Where Did the Risk Go? How Misapplied Bond Ratings Cause Mortgage Backed Securities and Collateralized Debt Obligation Market Disruptions," SSRN Working Paper: http://ssrn.com/abstract=1027475 May 3, 2007.

[9] The SEC investigation of the credit rating agencies found that the struggled to adapt to the complexity of mortgage-backed structured finance deals. See Securities and Exchange Commission, "Summary Report of Issues Identified in the Commission Staff's Examinations of Select Credit Rating Agencies," July 2008, at 12 ("One analyst expressed concern that her firm's model did not capture 'half' of the deal's risk, but that 'it could be structured by cows and we would rate it.' "). The SEC also found that "Rating agencies made 'out of model' adjustments and did not document the rationale for the adjustment." Id. at 14.

reason to fear the long-term consequences to their firm. Essentially, these executives were subjecting their firms to liabilities that could arise over the long-term, while pocketing shorter-term bonuses for themselves. As a consequence, executive compensation has become an extremely controversial political issue, which the federal government now regulates in the case of firms that received bailout funds.

The 2008 financial meltdown was partly driven by the risk that the failure of one financial institution could cause the failure of other financial institutions, much like the proverbial chain of falling dominoes. In its wake, much attention has focused on "systemic risk"—i.e., the rise of interlinked financial failures. AIG supplied the paradigm of this problem, because if it could not pay on the roughly $80 billion in CDS that it issued, other financial firms might also become insolvent. In part, this problem was exacerbated by a lack of transparency. Major financial institutions had taken on exposure to over-rated CDOs that declined sharply in value, along with housing prices. They avoided recognizing losses on the tranches of these vehicles, particularly the most senior AAA tranches, because they did not, and were not required to, mark their investments to market. The crisis of late 2008 may have been triggered by the public's realization that many of these financial institutions were insolvent, based on the declines in the value of their mortgage investments. Only government support prevented the collapse of many of these institutions. The principal issue in considering financial reform legislation is how to address systemic risk. The options include closer prudential financial of "systemically significant" financial institutions and some separation of higher risk activities from such firms.

## III.  THE EVOLVING NATURE OF FINANCIAL MARKETS

### A.  EXCHANGE AND OVER-THE-COUNTER MARKETS

Now that we have a thorough understanding of derivatives, and the modes of financial product innovation, we are going to shift to a different kind of financial innovation, based on where and how these instruments are traded. Financial markets play important roles in the economy and for businesses, but—perhaps surprisingly—not because they are a source of equity capital. Instead, the main importance of financial markets is two-fold. First, financial markets can provide *liquidity* to investors, thus enabling investors to be confident that they can quickly dispose of their investments without having to search for purchasers. Second, financial markets can function as a *disciplinary* mechanism, by allocating capital to more efficient users, penalizing managers who fail to pursue shareholder interests, and reducing the need for legal intervention.

Although many people think of the financial markets as a way for corporations to raise money, in fact, since World War II, net annual equity issuance by U.S. corporations has consistently been flat or negative (except for two brief periods during the early 1990s and early

2000s). To the extent corporations have issued net equity more recently, those issues has been limited to the financial sector, particularly in the aftermath of the financial crisis as financial institutions raised large amounts of equity capital. In general, public corporations have largely financed their expansion through retained cash flow and debt borrowings. Corporations have also used derivatives and other new financial instruments to raise limited amounts of capital, but these markets serve purposes other than raising capital—most notably, risk shifting.

Accordingly, it is important to distinguish between the *primary* market, where issuers sell shares to investors, and the *secondary* market, where investors and institutions trade with each other. The value of equity securities traded in secondary markets is a significant multiple of the value of equities sold in primary markets. And the value of non-equity financial markets—bonds, commodities, and derivatives, which are almost entirely secondary in nature—is significantly larger than the value of equity markets.

Traditionally, a company seeking to raise new capital from the public could not sell its securities directly into the stock market, but rather approached an investment banking firm that specialized in "underwriting" such issuances. This "underwriter" would either agree to buy the securities from the issuer at a fixed price for resale, at a slightly higher price, to the public (thereby permitting the issuer to shift most of the risk of market fluctuations to the underwriter) or the underwriter would serve as the issuer's agent in seeking to sell the securities on its behalf (but would not buy the offered securities itself). This latter arrangement was called a "best efforts" underwriting and tended to be used mainly in the case of higher risk offerings where the underwriter is unwilling to commit its own capital.

In either case, the investment banking firm that agreed to represent an issuer would typically assemble an underwriting syndicate of other such firms, which then directly would market the stock to their individual clients and institutional investors. Although these purchasers might eventually resell the stock on the stock market, the primary offering— that is, the process by which the corporation raised equity capital— occurred off the exchange through direct marketing of the securities by the members of the underwriting syndicate. Of course, if the corporation's stock was already traded (i.e., if it was not an initial public offering), the price of the new offering would be chiefly determined by the trading price of the stock in the secondary market (since shares of the same class are fungible), but the offering would still be sold directly by the underwriters to purchasers that they solicited.

Although there is thus today some overlap between the primary and secondary markets, offerings by corporations directly into the secondary market are very much the exception, rather than the rule. Basically, the stock and derivatives exchanges remain secondary markets in which stockholders and investors trade anonymously, while the primary market operates through the institutional structure of the underwriting group or syndicate.

**1. The New York Stock Exchange.** By far the best known, oldest, and most prestigious U.S. exchange is the New York Stock Exchange. A listing on the NYSE has signified that a corporation achieved front-rank status in its industry and had sustained earnings and shareholder acceptance. Less mature companies, or ones with a smaller shareholder base, listed on smaller, regional exchanges.

After a series of mergers, the NYSE became part of a global holding company known as NYSE Euronext, which includes six stock exchanges in seven countries as well as eight derivatives exchanges. Over 8,500 stocks are listed and actively traded on the NYSE Euronext exchanges. The NYSE continues to include most of the major blue chip corporations in the U.S., though not some major computer and software firms, such as Microsoft, Apple, or Intel.

The NYSE still has a physical location with an actual trading floor. While once standard, this is becoming rare, as most exchanges now trade electronically and do not use a trading floor. On the NYSE's trading floor, there are posts at which specific securities are traded by specialists, who in a sense possess a monopoly over the trading of that stock. But, by law, the specialist cannot buy or sell a stock if any other broker wishes to trade at that price for a customer, and the specialist must also buy or sell at its posted price if no other broker is willing to trade at that price. The specialist is thus subject to both a negative obligation not to trade when others are willing and an affirmative obligation to trade when others are not. Its role is more that of an auctioneer, matching buy and sell orders at a price that balances supply and demand, but with a statutory obligation to serve as the buyer or seller of last resort. The statutory goal in requiring the specialist to intervene in this fashion is to reduce volatility and mitigate rapid price movements. The specialist's own trading has recently accounted for about one-eighth of total volume.

Only stocks listed on the NYSE may be traded there. To be listed, a company must meet size and share ownership requirements that are more rigorous than those of other exchanges. Listed companies also must comply with NYSE listing standards. For example, NYSE listed companies must have a majority of independent directors, and must give shareholders more extensive voting rights than specified in state law. NYSE listing rules require that board committees—including the audit, nominating, and compensation committees—be staffed entirely by independent directors and that the independent directors undertake an annual review of the performance of the chief executive officer.

Although the NYSE historically was a not-for-profit organization, it "demutualized" in 2005 and is now a publicly held corporation owned by basically the same shareholders as own other public corporations. This transition to for-profit status has raised issues about the NYSE's role as a self-regulator, in particular because it had considerable regulatory oversight over its competitive rivals. Possibly, as a result, the SEC encouraged a merger of the regulatory and enforcement arms of the NYSE and Nasdaq, and approved the consolidation of the various exchange regulatory functions in 2007. Today, the Financial Industry Regulatory Authority, known as FINRA, oversees nearly every aspect of the securities markets and the U.S. exchanges, including the NYSE and Nasdaq. FINRA is a private corporation, not a government agency. FINRA acts as a self-regulatory organization under contract with brokerage firms, trading markets, and exchanges.

**2.  Nasdaq and the OTC Market.** Nasdaq (which originally was an acronym for National Association of Securities Dealers Automated Quotation) is a computerized, electronic dealer market. Over-the-counter dealer markets long predated Nasdaq, which only began operations in 1971, but Nasdaq immediately upgraded the technology underlying dealer markets from telephone contacts to an electronic screen on which all dealers' quotations were listed. Trading became computerized, so that orders could be entered and securities purchased simply by hitting a computer button. For many years, Nasdaq's status was anomalous; it was not technically a national securities exchange (exchanges must be approved by the SEC under § 6 of the Securities Exchange Act), but simply a electronic market owned by a "registered securities association" (i.e., the National Association of Securities Dealers ("NASD")). This anomaly ended in 2006 when the SEC finally approved Nasdaq's application to become a national securities exchange. It is now the "Nasdaq Stock Market LLC."

Nasdaq was founded by the NASD, a self-regulatory organization that Congress created by virtue of the Maloney Act, which in 1938 added Section 15A to the Securities Exchange Act. As a reform measure following stock exchange scandals, Section 15A provided for a "registered securities association" that would be created to supervise broker-dealers. The NASD was founded the next year, and remains the only such "association" formed (although in theory others could be). Every broker-dealer that dealt with public customers had to belong to the NASD, and that requirement continued after FINRA took over the consolidated regulatory role in 2007. Although the NASD originally owned Nasdaq, the NASD sold off most of its ownership, believing that there was a conflict between its regulatory role and the ownership of a market. Today, a majority of Nasdaq is owned by public and institutional shareholders.

As a *dealer* market, Nasdaq operates in a very different fashion than *auction* market of the NYSE. First, every customer's purchase or sale on Nasdaq is with a dealer; buyers do not directly interact with sellers as they do on an exchange, but must trade with an intermediary. Thus, when 100 shares of XYZ Corp. are bought and sold in this market, there are two transactions: a buyer buys 100 shares from a dealer, and the dealer turns around and buys 100 shares from a seller. The dealer's profit is the spread between the "bid" and "asked" prices on these two transactions.

A more significant difference is that, in contrast to an auction market, which has a single specialist for each stock, dealer markets have multiple dealers trading each stock. There are more than 500 market makers on Nasdaq, and its most actively traded stocks can have dozens of market makers. Dealers compete to offer the best "bid" and "asked" prices. All these quotations appear on the Nasdaq's electronic screen. Thus, when a customer gives an order to a broker to buy or sell a stock, the broker looks at the Nasdaq screen to find the highest "bid" (or buy) price or the lowest "offer" (or sell) price. This difference is known as the "inside spread" or "NBBO" (for "National Best Bid and Offer"). The broker is under a legal duty (known as the "duty of best execution") to take the customer's transaction to a dealer offering the best bid or offered price for that security at the desired volume. From a public policy perspective, the premise is that competition among the dealers will narrow the NBBO spread and thus minimize the cost that the customer must pay for the dealer's services as a financial intermediary.

Nasdaq lists about 3,200 companies, and trades more shares than any other exchange, even the NYSE. Like the NYSE, it imposes listed criteria, though these criteria vary based on the market segment category of Nasdaq listing. The top level of listing is the Nasdaq Global Select Market, which has the most rigorous listing criteria, including many of the same independence requirements as the NYSE. Just below that level is Nasdaq's Global Market and then the Capital Market, which has more lenient listing requirements in terms of minimum shareholder equity, pre-tax profits, and market value.

If a company does not qualify for the NYSE or for any of these Nasdaq levels of listing, it can apply to be traded as an *over-the-counter* equity security listed on the OTC Bulletin Board, or OTCBB. The OTCBB is a regulated electronic quotation service that displays real-time quotes, last sale prices, and volume information through market data vendor terminals and websites. The OTCBB provides access to more than 3,300 securities, but it is simply a quotation medium for subscribing members, and should not be confused with the Nasdaq stock market. The OTCBB does not impose listing standards, though it does require the filing of a Form 211, which requires the disclosure of certain material information and a certification of accuracy signed by a principal corporate official.

The OTCBB is distinct from the *pink sheets*, which provide an Internet-based electronic quotation service for OTC securities. If a company is not a reporting company, or otherwise cannot qualify for the OTC Bulletin Board, it can still have its securities traded, but only in an unregulated over-the-counter market. Since 1904, an organization formerly known as the National Quotation Bureau, but now called Pink

Sheets LLC, has published daily quotations for thinly-traded OTC stocks.[61] These quotations are not firm "bids" or "asked" prices, because there is no assurance that anyone will actually buy or sell at these prices. Historically, these quotations were once published on long pink sheets, and the name "pink sheets" has stuck, even though the quotations are now electronically disseminated. Most of these companies are inactive "shell" companies; almost none file reports with the SEC; many border on insolvency; few have ever registered their stock with the SEC, but some prominent corporations once started out at this level. It is a totally free market, but a thin one–meaning that a substantial shareholder cannot expect to liquidate its holdings without causing the market price to collapse.

**3. The History of Auction Markets Versus Dealer Markets.** As the previous discussion has shown, there have long been two basic kinds of secondary markets for equity securities: (1) exchange markets; and (2) dealer markets. The first are "auction" markets in which a "specialist" matches incoming buy and sell orders and intervenes itself only as a buyer or seller of last resort; in contrast, in dealer markets, dealers compete for customers' buy and sell orders and, until recently, every transaction was between a public customer and a dealer (without public buy orders crossing with public sell orders, as they do in auction markets). Economists sometimes describe auction markets as "order driven," and dealer markets as "quote driven"; that is, in the latter, prices change when a dealer changes its quote, but in the former the specialist is principally serving as an auctioneer to match orders to buy and sell from customers.

Which is better? Proponents of the auction market argue (with some empirical support) that the fact that public orders cannot meet public orders in a dealer market implies that dealer markets involve unnecessary costs that are paid to a financial intermediary whose services are not always necessary. Proponents of a dealer market reply that the specialist is a de facto monopolist, who will not narrow the bid/asked spread as efficiently as the competition among multiple dealers.

This debate will continue but both markets have converged, largely as the result of scandals that compelled the SEC to change the rules. Two major scandals forced changes in Nasdaq's operating rules. First, during the market collapse in October 1987, many Nasdaq dealers simply refused to respond to phone calls from customers and simply shut down operations rather than buy stocks for which they were market makers in a rapidly declining market. No similar problems surfaced on the NYSE, although some of its specialists did become insolvent during the crash because of their obligation to serve as the buyer of last resort. This behavior undercut Nasdaq's reputation as a high liquidity market and forced SEC-imposed changes. In response, the SEC compelled Nasdaq to develop a computerized order system now known as the Small Order Execution System (SOES), which requires that a market maker who receives a SOES order by computerized assignment must execute that order at its quoted price (up to a specified maximum quantity). With the advent of SOES, Nasdaq became more like the NYSE in that its market makers were subject to an automatic execution system and could not cease to trade at their discretion.

The second major scandal that cast a major shadow over Nasdaq broke in 1994 when evidence surfaced that Nasdaq dealers were collusively maintaining artificially wide bid/asked spreads on Nasdaq stocks. Specifically, two finance professors published an academic study that concluded that Nasdaq market-makers were purposefully avoiding odd-eighth quotes (that is, they would only quote prices in quarter point intervals) in order to (widen the spread).[10] In effect, by declining to trade on the odd eighths of a point, dealers were collectively conspiring to maintain the spread at a minimum of a quarter of a point. Tape recordings subpoenaed by the SEC and the Department of Justice suggested that such a pricing convention had developed and that broker dealers who violated it were subject to threats and intimidation. All told, the practice resembled a massive price-fixing conspiracy to maintain artificially wide bid/asked spreads on Nasdaq. Although this issue was never resolved in court, the major market makers settled a private class action by paying a then record $1.1 billion settlement in 1997. In 1996, the SEC censured the NASD and forced a formal reorganization under which the latter's regulatory functions were placed in a separate subsidiary, NASD Regulation, Inc., in order to maintain their independence.

Assume for the moment that 20 dealers trade a Nasdaq stock, each quoting a bid and asked price. Assume next that the highest "bid" price is $20 and the lowest "asked" price is $20.25. If this spread of 25 cents between the highest bid and the lowest asked price (which is known in the market's jargon as the "NBBO" for national best bid and offer) is still artificially wide (as it seems here, where the spread is 25 cents), how can it be feasibly narrowed? Under the SEC's Order Handling Rules, customers can today place a "limit order" to buy or sell a stock at a price between the bid/asked spread. Incoming orders on the other side would then trade with this order as the inside best bid or asked price. For example, if the spread were a very wide $20 bid and $20.25 asked, a customer could place a buy limit order at $20.10. The result would be that $20.10 would become the NBBO bid price, and the next incoming

---

[10] See Paul Christie & William Schultz, Why Do Nasdaq Market Makers Avoid Odd–Eighth Quotes, 49 J. Fin. 1813 (1994). A voluminous literature followed providing alternative interpretations and theories.

This episode also led the SEC to seek to develop a new source of competition to narrow the bid/asked spread. If dealers might collude, the SEC decided that it needed to find an additional source of competition. Recognizing that institutional and public customers could to a degree provide that competitive pressure and thereby narrow bid/asked spreads, the SEC developed an ingenious order handling procedure for introducing greater competition into the Nasdaq market through the means of *limit orders*. (A "limit order" is an order to buy or sell a stock at a *specific* price. An order to buy 100 shares at $20 is a limit order; it will not be executed at a higher price. Limit orders are contrasted with "market orders," which are simply orders to buy or sell at the *best available* price in the market.)

sell order would cross with that $20.10 bid price (rather than the lower dealers' best bid of $20.00). In essence, this procedure uses customers to supplement the seemingly limited competition among dealers. In fact, these new rules quickly narrowed the bid/asked spread by roughly 30% by introducing a new source of competition (i.e. customers willing to enter limit orders).

Another major development narrowing spreads occurred in 1998 when Congress mandated that securities prices be quoted in decimals, not the traditional eights of a point in which securities prices had been quoted for centuries. As securities came to be traded in pennies, the average spread on Nasdaq fell to just a few cents, thereby reducing the real costs of trading for the retail investor. Some evidence suggests that Nasdaq spreads have fallen to below the cost of trading on the NYSE, particularly for large and liquid stocks.

Although Congress envisioned some degree of competition in 1975 when it passed comprehensive legislation to implement a National Market System, the NYSE and Nasdaq have not competed to offer superior price quotations in the same stocks. Instead, the NYSE and Nasdaq competed for listings. Companies listed on either Nasdaq or the NYSE, but seldom both. More recently, the growth of alternative trading platforms has created price competition in the same stocks. We return to that issue, along with the broad question about how technology has changed financial markets, after we consider the parallel development of derivative markets.

**4. Derivatives Markets.** Historically, derivatives trading, like stock trading, was split between exchanges and over-the-counter markets. Unlike stock trading, which was centered in New York, options and futures trading developed in Chicago. The Chicago Board of Trade was formed in 1848 as a centralized place to trade forward contracts based on agricultural products. Standardized futures were introduced because of concerns about the enforcement of individual private forward contracts. Trading standardized futures was seen as more reliable, and these markets quickly became more liquid than private markets for forward trades. Over time, new futures exchanges developed to trade a wide range of products, including commodities and foreign exchange, again primarily in Chicago. More recently, these exchanges also began trading futures based financial variables such as interest rates.

To ensure liquidity, futures exchanges offer only a relatively small number of contract types, with clearly specified standardized parameters. The terms are precisely specified, including the specific underlying instrument, when the contract can be traded and in what size, and the maturity date. Contracts either require physical delivery of the underlying product, or can be settled in cash at maturity.

The first options exchange, the Chicago Board Options Exchange, began operating in 1973, just as the Black–Scholes option pricing model was being published. Options exchanges began trading options based on many of the same variables as futures, including commodities and foreign exchange. Stock options became increasingly popular, and, as with futures, the options traded on exchanges were highly standardized.

Today, options and futures are traded on dozens of derivatives exchanges. Because derivatives often are more volatile than the underlying instruments, one of the major concerns of these exchanges is how to provide for the *margin* and *settlement* of trades. Margin refers to the amount of money than a party must deposit to cover any potential future loss on the positions. For stocks, the amount of margin is limited to 50% of the underlying positions, but the same is not true for derivatives, most of which can be traded with much lower levels of margin. In addition, derivatives exchanges typically require parties to deposit additional "mark-to-market" margin if changes in prices increase the party's expected potential future loss on the position. Clients typically hold a margin account with the exchange or its *clearing house*, and adjust the amount of margin they have on deposit on a daily basis. Either the exchange or its clearing house, a related entity that takes care of processing payments and trades, also will arrange for the settlement of trades at maturity. One of the objectives of a derivatives exchange and clearing house is to ensure a smooth settlement process, and to avoid serious adverse consequences from the default of one of its clients.

Unlike the derivatives exchanges, the over-the-counter, or OTC, derivatives markets are an informal connection of dealers and market makers who privately trade bilateral contracts, sometimes through private electronic trading platforms. Whereas the derivatives exchanges guarantee payment through their system of margin and settlement, the OTC derivatives market participants take on the risk of their counterparties defaulting. This risk is known as *credit risk*.

The bulk of OTC derivatives are structured as swaps, and are documented using standardized agreements created by a trade association known as the International Swaps and Derivatives Association, or ISDA. ISDA was created in 1985, after the Financial Accounting Standards Board suggested that banks might need to report swaps on their balance sheets. The ten largest swaps dealers saw a need to respond in concert and to "organize before any problems arise."[11] They argued that swaps were not really assets or liabilities, and that including swaps in their financial statements would lead investors to falsely believe the banks were riskier than they really were. ISDA won this argument, and swaps have remained an *off-balance sheet* item, disclosed only in footnotes to the financial statements. Over time, ISDA has become a powerful lobbying force for the continued deregulation of derivatives,

[11] Frank Partnoy, Infectious Greed: How Deceit and Risk Corrupted the Financial Markets 47 (2003).

and ISDA continues to publish standard form contracts used by derivatives counterparties.

OTC derivatives have grown from a relatively small business during the late 1980s, to one of the leading profit centers of most major banks. The OTC derivatives market was $605 trillion in June 2009, as measured by the "notional" value of the financial instruments underlying the OTC derivatives contracts. By another measure, known as "market value," based on the amount of money owed by parties to OTC derivatives, the size of the market was $25 trillion.[12] By comparison to these two measures, the total notional value of the U.S. stock market is in the range of $30 trillion, or roughly five percent of the size of the OTC derivatives market. A "market value" measure for equity markets, based on the amount of money owed by parties to positions in stock, also would be just a fraction of the comparable derivatives market measure. By any measure, the OTC derivatives market is significantly larger than the U.S. stock market.

Commentators have been concerned about the potential effects of a default by a major OTC derivatives dealer since the collapse of a hedge fund known as Long–Term Capital Management in 1998. The Federal Reserve organized a private rescue effort of that fund, which had OTC derivatives of roughly $1.25 trillion with several banks. Still, neither Congress nor regulators implemented any regulatory framework for OTC derivatives. Instead, in 2000, Congress passed the Commodity Futures Modernization Act, which cemented the largely deregulated status of derivatives. A year later, the collapse of Enron, a major OTC derivatives trader, also triggered concerns about the potential contagion effects of a default, although again derivatives were left largely unregulated. The concerns about the effects of a default by a major derivatives counterparty were the primary reason cited by regulators in their rescues of various financial institutions and American International Group during 2008.

The original rationale for permitting OTC derivatives to be traded in private, largely unregulated markets was that these contracts were highly customized and therefore were not susceptible to being traded on exchanges, where options and futures were highly standardized. However, many OTC derivatives, such as interest rate swaps, have become highly standardized, and the documentation developed by ISDA is essentially boilerplate that is only rarely modified in individual transactions. Moreover, many OTC derivatives have become traded on private electronic exchanges that closely resembled the Nasdaq dealer market for stocks. As of late 2009, there were proposals in Congress to move some OTC derivatives onto exchange-like platforms, where parties would be subject to the kinds of margin and settlement requirements that apply to exchange-traded options and futures.

---

[12] Bank for International Settlements, Regular OTC Derivatives Market Statistics, Nov. 12, 2009, http://www.bis.org/publ/otc_hy0911.htm.

## B.  THE IMPACT OF TECHNOLOGY AND NEW TRADING PLATFORMS

Both the exchanges and over-the-counter markets described above have evolved in dramatic ways as new technologies and trading platforms have developed. Some of these changes have been due to the increase in computing power, as well as the speed and advances associated with the Internet. Other changes have been due to regulatory arbitrage, as market participants have sought to avoid the regulatory costs associated with particular trading venues. There also have been numerous changes, both in the structure of financial markets, and in how and which financial instruments are traded on these markets. This section traces the history of these developments.

**1.  The Rise of ECNs and Alternative Trading Systems.** As noted above, for years, a stable equilibrium persisted under which the NYSE and Nasdaq, and some smaller exchanges, competed for U.S. stock listings, but did not trade stocks listed on the other. This equilibrium was disrupted in the mid–1990s when a new entrant in this competition appeared on the scene: the electronic communications network (or "ECN"). ECNs grew quickly—by 2000, they were trading 50% or more of the shares listed on Nasdaq (and a much smaller 5% of the shares listed on the NYSE). More recently, ECNs have virtually taken over many markets, particularly the markets for certain derivatives.

What caused the sudden growth of this new competitor? There are multiple answers. Historically, the original reason was a desire for anonymity on the part of institutional investors. The most common type of alternative trading system is essentially a bulletin board on which customers can display bids and offers anonymously, hoping to attract a counterpart without disclosing to the world their willingness to trade at that price. The first such system (and, by far, the largest still) was Instinet, which was founded in 1969 as a registered broker-dealer. Instinet developed a closed subscriber system which permitted its subscribers (chiefly, institutional investors) to trade large blocks of stock chiefly among themselves. Because this trading could occur on an anonymous basis, an institution holding a 5% stake in a company that did not want to disclose the potentially embarrassing fact that it was willing to sell a significant piece of that stock below the current market price found this forum attractive. If it sold instead on Nasdaq, traders might quickly reduce the price of the stock based on the institution's identity and known ownership of a large block. Institutions also feared that their buying activity on a public market would cause other traders to rush to buy the same security in anticipation that the institution would make large volume purchases that would raise the security's price (this practice is known as "front-running"). By trading anonymously on Instinet, they solved that problem.

Although alternative trading systems started out as matching systems by which institutions could trade privately without alerting the market as to their intentions, retail investors soon found their own use for them. Their desire was to avoid costly brokerage commissions and to obtain executions inside the dealer's spread. Most ECNs charged their customers a subscription fee to use their system that was only a fraction of the typical retail brokerage fee. To understand how ECNs enabled the investor to obtain executions inside the bid/asked spread, the dealer's spread, imagine that a stock is trading at $18.00 bid and $18.25 asked (or a 25 cent spread). An institution that wished to buy must pay $18.25 and one that wished to sell must do so at $18.00, with the dealer who handles both transactions pocketing the 25 cent spread. However, if the two investors could transact the same purchase and sale directly on Instinet, they could cross their orders at the midpoint of the spread and each save 12½ cents by eliminating the dealer as an unnecessary intermediary. Actively trading investors saw enormous savings from use of this forum.

Instinet's success at creating a dealer-less market caused other systems to emulate it by developing alternative approaches. Another electronic alternative trading system that developed in the 1990's was the Portfolio System for Institutional Trading ("POSIT"), which introduced a crossing system for batches of orders. Unlike Instinet's system (which permitted subscribers to electronically "hit" anonymous offers posted in an electronic order book), a crossing system automatically matches buyers and sellers who indicate a willingness to trade at a specified price.

A considerable range of alternative trading systems developed during the 1990s. Some were bulletin board systems on which institutions indicated (often anonymously) a desire to trade a stock at a specific price. Another institution could then contact the first (by telephone or computer) and negotiate a price for a transaction between them. Other systems were crossing systems that executed at the midpoint of the bid/asked spread set on another exchange. Others used proprietary algorithms to match buy and sell orders, or they ran daily auctions, matching buyers and sellers willing to trade at prices that overlap. An important distinction exists between passive systems that execute at the midpoint of another exchange's prices and those (such as the largest alternative trading system, Instinet) on which actual price discovery occurs.

The factor that most accelerated the growth of these new trading systems was the adoption by the SEC in 1986 of new Order Handling Rules, which were introduced in response to the earlier noted scandal involving collusion among dealers to maintain an artificially wide bid/asked spread on Nasdaq. In response, the Order Handling Rules essentially permitted customers to introduce limit orders inside the dealer's bid/asked spread. But they also made "electronic communication networks" the preferred vehicle for introducing limit orders and they mandated that superior prices displayed on an ECN had to be both shown on the Nasdaq screen and accessible to public customers (and not just to the ECN's subscribers).[13] As a result, public customers could not only seek better prices and lower brokerage commissions on an ECN, but they could post limit orders on them inside the bid/asked spreads of Nasdaq dealers. Virtually overnight, their popularity soared.

The growth of alternative trading systems challenged not only the traditional markets, but also the SEC. Because these alternative systems had long been registered as broker-dealers, and not as formal exchanges, they were less pervasively regulated than were the traditional exchanges. Beyond this disparity, the SEC was concerned that these systems were not integrated with the National Market System, which is composed of the stock exchanges, Nasdaq, and certain over-the-counter dealers. Potentially, the self-segregation of alternative trading systems raised the danger of a two-tier market in which institutions received superior prices to those available to individuals in the public market. The failure to integrate markets also interfered with price discovery and overall market efficiency.

In late 1998, the SEC responded to these developments by adopting Regulation ATS.[14] It basically permits alternative trading systems to choose to be regulated either as broker-dealers or as exchanges. However, alternative systems that account for 5% or more of trading volume (and thus have a potentially "significant" impact on the market) are required to link up with a registered exchange or Nasdaq and to publicly display their best priced orders. To further the integration of the equity market, these systems must allow dealers on Nasdaq or members of the exchanges to execute against these publicly displayed orders. The basic target of these rules at the time was Instinet, and the SEC's goal was to take its order flow out of a "private club" and force it into the public quotation stream.

**2. The "New" National Market System.** The 1975 Securities Act Amendments, which ended fixed brokerage commissions, envisioned a national market system that would ensure effective price competition among exchanges. Such price competition never arose, at least not before the appearance of the ECNs and the use of limit orders to narrow the bid/asked spread. By 2000, however, the marketplace was changing and many investors were voicing displeasure with the traditional exchanges. Spreads had narrowed as the result of the Order Handling Rules, but liquidity in consequence had decreased. As spreads became razor thin, specialists and Nasdaq market-makers became less eager to handle large orders and insisted on breaking them into smaller units, thereby delaying their execution and exposing the customer to potentially adverse market movements during the interim.

At this point, a basic truth becomes apparent: different customers want different things from securities markets. Typically, retail custom-

---

[13] See Securities Exchange Act Release No. 37619A (Sept. 12, 1996).

[14] See Securities Exchange Act Release No. 34–39884 (Apr. 17, 1998).

ers (who usually trade in small quantities) want the narrowest spread possible, but large institutions may prefer high liquidity, fast execution, and anonymity. These different preferences complicated the SEC's efforts to achieve a truly integrated national market system. Of course, one solution might be that different investors with different preferences could trade in different markets. But this answer raised a deeper fear for the SEC: namely, market fragmentation, which might result in securities trading at different prices in different markets, with an overall loss in market efficiency.

For the SEC, the greatest challenge in the design of a national market system has been the tension between its desire to foster price competition and its fear of market fragmentation. This issue came to a head as the NYSE and Nasdaq began to trade the same securities, based on different trading systems and rules. In general, Nasdaq is a more automated market and can execute orders more rapidly, whereas the NYSE specialist conducts a slower auction. But the NYSE's auction system permits public orders to trade with each other without the intervention of a dealer and at prices that often are superior to the dealers' bid/asked spread. A particularly controversial difference between the two markets was their treatment of "trade-throughs"—trades at prices inferior to the inside bid and asked spread (or "NBBO" for "National Best Bid and Offer"). "Trade-throughs" were forbidden in the auction system, but were not uncommon in a dealer system. Both sides lobbied intensively. Finally, in 2005, after years of debate, the Commission took a strong position and prohibited "trade-throughs"—but only by a 3–2 vote of the SEC's five commissioners.[15]

Regulation NMS (which stands for "National Market System") was the culmination of a decade long effort to design a truly integrated national market system. Why then did it divide the Commission? The political answer is that different interest groups wanted different things– all of which are inherently desirable. Regulation NMS's most controversial provision is its "trade-through rule" (Rule 611), which requires securities markets to establish, maintain and enforce written policies and procedures reasonably designed to prevent the execution of trades in NMS securities at prices inferior to "protected quotations" displayed by other trading centers. On the practical level, this implied that Nasdaq had to seek to prevent trades on it that were inferior to the NBBO. Historically, the New York Stock Exchange ("NYSE") and the regional exchanges that belonged to the Intermarket Trading System had long been subject to such a "trade-through" rule, but Nasdaq was not. Thus, trades on Nasdaq in stocks listed elsewhere could occur at inferior prices to the quotations on other markets. Brokers who traded at such prices still had to justify how trading at an inferior price satisfied their duty of "best execution" to their client. But frequently their justification would be that their client wanted more volume than the NYSE specialist would

[15] Securities Exchange Act Release No. 51809 (Jun. 9, 2005).

supply at the superior price. Or, the client wanted an instantaneous transaction (before prices changed in a volatile market), and it could trade more quickly (and in higher volume) on Nasdaq's automated market than on the slower NYSE. Ultimately, the SEC's adoption of a rule prohibiting trade-throughs was intended to encourage and reward the display of public limit orders (which would be disfavored if brokers and dealers could ignore them and trade at an inferior price). But by supporting limit orders, the SEC favored the NYSE over Nasdaq. However, as its price for extending the trade-through rule to Nasdaq, the SEC insisted that the NYSE become a faster, more automated exchange. The trade-through prohibition also threatened the ECNs because they were now restricted in their ability to match orders at prices inferior to the best price (or NBBO) in the national market system, even if some of their customers wanted precisely that. Revealingly, in 2005, both Archipelago and Instinet, the two largest ECNs, merged with the NYSE and Nasdaq, respectively, as it was becoming evident that the SEC would adopt Regulation NMS.

One lesson of Regulation NMS is that the interests of institutional investors and retail investors may necessarily be in some conflict. Large mutual funds prefer high liquidity (i.e., the ability to buy and sell in large volume without affecting the market price) to the narrowest spread, while retail investors (who trade in smaller quantities) prefer a narrow spread and protection against trade-throughs. Critics of the "trade-through" rule accused the SEC of paternalistically deciding that "best price" was more important than speed or anonymity, when sophisticated investors believed otherwise. But retail investors may be unable to monitor whether their brokers are truly complying with their duty of best execution. The SEC justified its position by announcing that it was giving priority to the interests of "long-term investors."

Regulation NMS has also hastened the convergence of dealer and auction markets. Because the SEC conditioned its approval of the trade-through rule on a provision requiring that it apply only to quotations that can be automatically executed on an immediate basis, this condition forced the NYSE to move toward significantly greater use of electronic trading. The traditional trading floor dominated by the specialist (whose manual execution of trades was inevitably slower) may gradually be coming to an end. From the SEC staff's perspective, this compromise of a universal trade-through rule with the precondition that all trading centers offer immediate electronic trading avoided the danger of market fragmentation (i.e., the risk that the national market could divide into multiple pools that traded the same security at different prices), while also protecting institutional customers from the risk that slow markets would expose them to adverse price changes.

**3. Dark Pools.** More recently, *dark pools* have emerged as another form of alternative trading platform. Dark pools, sometimes called dark pools of liquidity, are crossing networks that provide liquidity to parties who want to trade large numbers of shares anonymously, without revealing themselves to the open market. Dark pools consist of non-public trading in NMS stocks. The trading is "dark" because it is not included in the consolidated quotation data for NMS stocks that is widely disseminated to the public. Although many market participants favor dark pools, regulators have expressed concerns about the increase in the number and size of actively trading dark pools, from about 10 in 2002 to about 29 in 2009. For the second quarter of 2009, the trading volume of dark pools was approximately 7.2% of the total share volume in NMS stocks. Given this size, dark pools are a significant source of liquidity for NMS stocks.

The largest dark pools are sponsored by securities firms, primarily to execute the orders of the customers as well as proprietary trades on behalf of the firms. The regulatory concerns are focused on the limited two-tiered transparency that has arisen as a result of dark pools, where a first tier of dark pool members has access to information about stock prices and liquidity, but the second tier of investors more broadly does not have access.

In late 2009, the SEC proposed new rules to make dark pool trading more transparent. The proposals generally would require that information about an investor's interest in buying or selling a stock be made available to the public instead of just to a select group operating within a particular dark pool. They also would require that dark pools publicly identify that it was their pool that executed particular trades. The overall thrust of the proposals was to make dark pools more transparent. Market participants argued that new regulations would increase the cost of trading in dark pools. Again, these arguments demonstrate some of the tradeoffs between transparency and efficiency.

**4. The Impact of New Technology.** The most obvious impact of the Internet on the securities market has been the already discussed rapid growth of alternative trading systems. But other impacts may be at least as important. For optimists, the major impact is the prospect of a "democratization of financial markets," propelled by the potentially universal access to information that the Internet offers investors. For pessimists, the Internet raises enormous and possibly insurmountable regulatory and jurisdictional problems.

On the positive side, the Internet and related technology facilitate the instant delivery of information. Not only are real time securities prices widely available on the Web, but Web sites and search engines now provide investors with sophisticated research tools. For example, one service (Quicken) has personal finance programs that permit investors to search through some twelve thousand stocks, based on some thirty-three different variables. Investors can simply ask such services to identify or rank all equity securities in terms of their chosen variable or ratio. As a result, the line between the professional securities analyst and the amateur trader is far less clear-cut than it used to be. Reinforcing this development is, of course, the rapid growth of on-line brokerage firms, which has radically reduced the costs of trading.

The corresponding downside is that the Internet has also brought about a significant increase in "noisy" and unreliable information. Some of this information consists simply of rumors and gossip, but the Internet also invites predatory individuals or groups seeking to manipulate the prices of thinly traded stocks to introduce false information on an anonymous basis onto electronic bulletin boards and chat rooms. Where once the crooked "boiler room" operation could reach no more than a few dozen investors by phone calls in a day, now the same fraudulent promoters can post chat room predictions that may be seen or heard by a million investors.

Issuers have also responded to the opportunities offered by the Internet. Most have their own Web sites, and a few have effected direct stock offerings over the Internet. Just as the rise of alternative trading systems has reduced the role for the financial intermediary and permitted more direct investor-to-investor transactions, so too is there a prospect that issuers can dispense with (or at least rely less heavily upon) underwriters. For the present, however, this is more a prospect than a reality, because for the small issuer underwriters supply a critical element that technology does not render obsolete: namely, reputational capital. That is, investors may rely on the underwriter's reputation in evaluating an initial public offering, as much as, or more than, they rely upon the issuer's disclosures.

The SEC has taken major steps over the last several years to facilitate the electronic delivery of prospectuses and other securities-related disclosures. Since 2005, electronic delivery of information is permitted, and sales may be confirmed electronically. Electronic proxies are also coming into use for shareholder meetings. Gradually, the SEC came to allow the often sensitive information provided at "roadshows" (which are meetings held by an issuer with institutional investor and securities analysts during the period immediately prior to a public offering of its securities) to be broadcast on the Internet (or other public means) to public investors.

For the SEC and for state securities regulators, the Internet poses major jurisdictional challenges. U.S. law—both federal law and common law—has long held that a person outside the jurisdiction subjects itself to the law of the jurisdiction if it directs an offer from outside the jurisdiction to persons within the jurisdiction. Under this rule, an e-mail from an offerer in France or California to recipients in the U.S. or New York, respectively, would seemingly subject the offerer to the jurisdiction of the U.S. courts or New York courts, as the case may be. But the Internet is different from e-mail. Inherently, it is a passive medium which the user accesses. Thus the offerer does not "direct" any communication into the jurisdiction. Given the resulting legal uncertainty, the majority of U.S. states have adopted a uniform exemption: so long as the

Web site contains a disclaimer that no offers or sales can be made to its residents and in fact no such offers or sales are made, then the Web site will be viewed as outside the state's jurisdictional reach.

The SEC has taken a similar position with regard to the posting of offering or soliciting materials on Web sites by foreign persons. In a recent interpretive release on the application of the federal securities laws to offshore Internet advertising and offers, the SEC stated that it would not view offering materials placed on a Web site by issuers, broker-dealers, exchanges, or investment advisers to trigger registration requirements under the federal securities law if they were not "targeted" at the United States. In considering whether an offer was targeted at U.S. residents, the SEC considers whether (1) the Web site included a prominent disclaimer that the offer was not directed to U.S. residents, and (2) the offerer implemented procedures "reasonably designed to guard against sales to U.S. persons in the offshore offerings."[16] The practical result of this position is that a U.S. citizen who wishes to buy foreign securities from a foreign broker-dealer must go through a U.S. broker-dealer. Although this position may be legally defensible, it requires multiple layers of financial intermediation before a cross-border securities transaction can be executed. In an era of on-line trading and Web sites accessible on a world-wide basis, it remains uncertain whether the SEC can hold to its position.

**5.  A Transitional Evaluation.** U.S. securities markets have undergone major shocks in recent years. Over the course of less than a decade, they have experienced (1) privatization, moving from "clubby" not-for-profit organizations to private corporations owned by shareholders eager to see their share value maximized; (2) the transition to electronic trading and the appearance of the ECNs; (3) decimalization and the disappearance of trading based on the traditional eight of a point convention; (4) the use of limit orders as a new source of price competition, and (5) globalization and the new challenge of foreign competition in London, Europe, and Asia. Today, securities exchanges have entered a period of rapid, worldwide consolidation. The major U.S. exchanges are today actively pursuing major foreign acquisitions as they seek to become globally integrated. How many exchanges will remain at the end of this process remains an open question. But here, another new development has surfaced: foreign issuers appear to be resisting the more strongly regulatory style of the SEC (and the greater risk of securities litigation and enforcement actions in the U.S.).

During 2009, the U.S. Congress debated legislation that would require the migration of many OTC derivatives to centralized exchange and clearing platforms. Meanwhile, many OTC derivatives trading platforms independently began to centralize, particularly with respect to the clearing function. Given the widespread concerns during the financial

[16] See Securities Act Release No. 33–7516 (Mar. 23, 1998).

crisis about defaults, many market participants favored a move to a centralized clearing system that would resolve the transparency challenges that arise when multiple parties are trading bilateral contracts. With centralized clearing, concerns about whether a default by one party would lead numerous counterparties to become insolvent would be minimized.

Centralized exchanges for OTC derivatives have proved more controversial. Many parties argued that the trading of many derivatives would be impossible, or at least unprofitable, on exchanges, because of the customized nature of such trades. Others argued that so-called "end users" (industrial corporations that use derivatives) should be treated differently from derivatives dealers (the banks that make markets in swaps and other OTC derivatives). Again, the perceived tradeoff is between efficiency and transparency. In late 2009, the OTC derivatives markets remained large and liquid, yet still relatively opaque.

## IV.  MARKET EFFICIENCY AND BEHAVIORAL FINANCE

Questions about market efficiency and transparency are central to our understanding of financial markets. Emerging research in behavioral finance is suggesting that markets might not be as efficient, and market participants might not be as economically rational, as many people have thought. In this Section, we cover the evolution of the debate about market efficiency.

Securities trade in the secondary market in large part because the trading parties believe that the securities are either undervalued or overvalued. Yet, perhaps surprisingly, a financial theory—supported by many empirical studies but challenged by more recent such studies— holds that these belief are largely misguided. According to this theory— known as the Efficient Capital Market Hypothesis ("ECMH")—while there may be perfectly rational reasons to trade securities (for example, to achieve better portfolio diversification), pursuit of undervalued stocks in a deep, liquid securities market is likely to be fruitless, because securities prices reflect all publicly available information. That is, new information is absorbed into the market price so immediately that it is impossible for any trader to earn profits by trading on such information. Put differently, a market is efficient with respect to specific information if prices act *as if* everyone knows the information. The implication of this hypothesis is that no amount of diligent research or hard work by sophisticated security analysts will enable them to identify undervalued stocks. In short, there are no undervalued stocks; nor are there market trends that can be observed and exploited. Price movements are by definition unpredictable, because they are triggered by the release of previously unknown information. Under the ECMH, any change in a security's price must be the result of new and unforeseen information (either about the security or the state of the world generally). Moreover, the market price of a security is the best estimate of its true or fundamental value.

While most economists agree that the principal securities markets are at least to some degree "efficient," there has long been considerable disagreement among them about the degree of efficiency. It has been customary to subdivide efficient market theory into three levels: First, there is the "weak version," which says simply that past *price* information about a security does not enable one to predict the security's future price movements. For example, knowledge that a security has closed higher on the last five trading days or that its last five transactions in the past hour have been dramatically upward, does not enable one to predict the next price movement. At one time it was thought that the empirical evidence for this proposition was overwhelming. That thought was comforting to economists, since it is consistent with the broader notion that markets behave consistently with economic rationality (even though individual actions may respond to considerations other than economic rationality). Some studies, however, suggest that securities prices do indeed follow patterns that cannot be reconciled with any discernible rational economic theory or model. Perhaps most telling are studies supporting a pattern of reversion to mean—that is, a tendency for prices to decline when the market has recently done well and rise when the market has recently done poorly. It may be that some of these studies to some degree reflect only chance correlations found by a process of "dredging" a large data base. Or there may be rational economic explanations that have not been discovered. Moreover, there is a serious problem with all tests of the ECMH: any test of efficiency must rely on, and simultaneously test, an economic theory or model that specifies "correct" securities prices, and there is in fact no general agreement on that fundamental economic model. For the present, this part of the ECMH remains a matter of active study and debate.

Next, there is the "semi-strong version" of the ECMH. It holds that the market price quickly reflects all publicly available information. This version of the ECMH means, for example, that one cannot profit (at least systematically) by buying the publicly traded common stock of a corporation shortly after the announcement of an unexpected earnings increase or a tender offer for the stock at a large premium, because the market will have incorporated the new information into the stock's price before the stock can be bought. It is relatively easy to test this hypothesis. Computerized records of securities prices, going back many years, are readily available. Economists have used these data bases to test various theories or "filters." For example, one might hypothesize that abnormal profits (that is, profits in excess of those that are earned simply by buying and holding a diversified portfolio of securities) can be made by buying common stock shortly after the announcement of an earnings increase and then test this theory against market data. Early "event" studies, which focused on highly publicized events such as mergers or dividends, provided support for the semi-strong version of the ECMH. More recent studies, focusing on more technical and complex information, have found that such information is incorporated in prices far more slowly than the ECMH would predict. The most famous of these more recent studies find "post-earnings-announcement drift"—that is, the information conveyed by news of changes in expected earnings (good or bad) is fully reflected in prices only over a period of several months.

Under the "strong-form" version of the ECMH, even non-public information is reflected in securities prices. To some extent, casual observation reveals this to be true, as stock prices of takeover and merger targets often run up in the days prior to the public announcement of the transaction; presumably insider trading supplies the mechanism underlying this recurrent pattern. Still, because the market does not fully absorb such inside information (that is, the market adjusts upward further on the public announcement), one obviously can profit on inside information. Hence few observers accept this "strong form" version of the ECMH, even though it is recognized that undisclosed information can be partially (and sometimes completely) reflected in the stock price.

The policy implications of the ECMH seem devastatingly blunt for the securities research industry. If prices cannot be predicted because they move randomly, securities research arguably is worthless (except to the extent it helps investors either to identify the risk level of securities or to diversify their portfolios). At first blush, then, mutual funds seemingly waste millions in paying for such research. Further, active trading strategies also seem wasteful, as investors cannot outperform the market and therefore should just buy and hold. Thus, the rapid, in-and-out trading style of many institutional investors seems a hopeless pursuit of unobtainable trading profits. Yet, as the debate over the ECMH has deepened in recent years, these implications, which initially seemed obvious, no longer appear so.

On one level, the market has responded to the ECMH by developing new securities products. The best example is the index fund, which is a mutual fund that does not attempt to outperform the market, but rather invests in a representative sample or index of the market. This investment approach is now widely followed as well by pension funds and other institutional investors. Similarly, new portfolio trading strategies—such as program trading and portfolio insurance (discussed below)—are an indication that ECMH's implications have caused at least some investors to shift their focus from trading individual stocks to trading portfolios.

Still, the debate has been most intense over the question of whether securities research is valueless. Here, economists have increasingly focused on the question: what makes the market efficient? This simple question highlights a seeming paradox about the ECMH. The conventional answer is that market efficiency—i.e. the market's ability to absorb new information into price almost instantaneously—is the product of the near perfect competition among securities analysts, professional traders, and insiders to search out new information about corporate issuers in order to trade on it profitably. Sometimes, an analyst will find such an item of new or unrecognized information and profit thereby, but, as in any other market that approaches perfect competition, the profits are thin. Yet, if this is so, why do security analysts continue to invest time and money in what appear to be unprofitable search activities? Put differently, if the return on investment in information is low, one cannot reasonably expect the search activities to continue that keep the market efficient. This problem has troubled some financial economists, who have answered that therefore the market can never be perfectly efficient; rather there must be some "equilibrium level of disequilibrium" at which those professionally involved in information search activities earn a normal profit. Similarly, others who take this relative efficiency perspective argue that the extent of market efficiency is a function of the cost of acquiring information, and thus capital market efficiency depends on the structure of the market for information. Many familiar market institutions, such as the investment banking firm, can be understood as market mechanisms for reducing information costs.

A critical factor from this perspective is the manner in which new information reaches the market. Some new information—such as a Federal Reserve Board announcement of a change in interest rates—will be assimilated by virtually all traders almost costlessly and instantaneously; other kinds of information, however, will reach only the professional analyst community; and still other forms of information will require a process of decoding—that is, the market learns about the new information derivatively by observing the trading behavior of those who are aware of it. In such cases, the market's response to this new information will be slower as it gradually permeates the market from its initial narrow starting point. To generalize, those who take this "relative" efficiency perspective argue that the speed of the market's response will depend upon the initial distribution of the information. Because the initial distribution of information is, in turn, largely a function of its cost, it follows that the cheaper the information is to acquire, the more efficient will be the market. From this perspective, one may think of the federal securities laws and the SEC as a strategy for the collectivization and broad dissemination of securities information, in order thereby both to reduce the cost of information acquisition and to increase the speed of its dissemination.

Although the idea that market price accurately reflects all publicly available firm-specific information is widely held among economists, not all accept the proposition that the stock market is therefore *allocatively* efficient. Increasingly, some draw a distinction between "speculative efficiency" and "allocative efficiency." Speculative efficiency refers to the earlier noted finding that one cannot beat the market by trading immediately after the release of new information (in the hope that the market will respond only gradually). Allocative efficiency asserts more broadly that stock prices represent the present value of forecasted future dividends.

Faith in the "efficiency" of the market as a whole was badly shaken in 1987, when the value of publicly traded stocks, as measured by the Dow Jones Industrial Average, fell by 36 percent over a two-week period. It is difficult (though not impossible) to suppose that such a radical change was attributable to a rational reaction to new information. Instead, the more logical inference seemed to be that in some fundamental sense the market as a whole must have been overpriced before the decline or underpriced afterwards. This inference also seemed to make sense based on the even greater decline in the NASDAQ market from September 2000 to March 2001, or in the sharp decline in financial services stocks during late 2008 and early 2009 (and the subsequent and nearly as sharp rise during the last nine months of 2009).

Recent research supports such skepticism. In the wake of the 1987 stock market crash, economists began to reexamine stock market volatility and the relationship between stock price movements and changes in real economic outputs. In a series of papers, Professor Shiller compared actual stock prices with "perfect forecast" stock prices, which were the prices that should have been obtained if the subsequent dividend performance of these companies had been known. His findings, which are controversial, suggest that actual stock price movements are too great in relation to actual subsequent events to be explained as a reaction to new information. One implication of this work is that this excessive market volatility is the result of social and psychological forces (i.e., fads and panics), and thus the stock market should not be assumed to be allocatively efficient.

Correspondingly, financial theorists, impressed by the persistence of high stock market volatility, have begun to develop a number of modifications of the ECMH. One of the most promising approaches is a new branch of finance theory commonly called "behavioral finance." Behavioral finance makes use of the extensive empirical evidence that has been developed by experimental psychologists demonstrating that people, far from being fully rational, suffer a number of common cognitive defects and biases that distort their decisionmaking. Behavioral finance theorists posit that these biases and defects distort investors' decisions just as they distort other decisions, and that as a result stock prices deviate in systematic and predictable ways from the prices that would be set in a market of purely rational investors. For example, the human tendency to give too much weight to recent events ("representativeness bias") may explain why stock prices often "overreact" to earnings announcements and other market events.

A central question raised by the behavioral finance approach is how "irrational" traders can distort market prices if there also are rational traders in the market. After all, rational investors would presumably recognize mispriced stocks, buy those that are undervalued while selling those that are overvalued, and by doing so bring stocks back to their correct values. One answer to this question has been offered by a behavioral finance model commonly known as the "noise trading" model. This model assumes that there is a significant population of irrational traders in the securities market at any given moment, each striving to anticipate the often arbitrary trading behavior of other traders, rather than analyzing fundamental business prospects. Their aggregate influence is so pronounced that rational arbitrageurs are unwilling to bet against noise traders at sufficient levels to maintain securities prices that reflect only fundamental information. Classical economic theory rejected this possibility, instead adopting the view that in competitive markets irrational traders would soon be systematically separated from their money. The noise theorists argue that the "survival of the fittest" is assured only if rational traders can afford to arbitrage the disparities between current "irrational" prices and the intrinsic values that fundamental information suggests should govern. But because such arbitrage is very costly and long-term, they argue, rational arbitrageurs begin seeking to anticipate the noise traders' next move. To put it differently, optimistic investors, especially in a thin market, may drive prices up to unrealistically high levels, and arbitrageurs may not be willing to bet on when reality will take hold. In fact, some arbitrageurs may add to the distortion by betting that the irrational exuberance will continue.

Why has "noise trading" and stock volatility increased? Some economists argue that excessive trading may be a consequence of reduced transaction costs (including lower brokerage commissions) as the result of financial deregulation and increased competition in the securities industry. Some thus recommend that securities trading be subjected to a transaction tax to reduce "excessive trading."

Research in behavioral economics also suggests that investors are prone to make systemic cognitive errors in their decisions. Examples include overconfidence and loss aversion. Just as 80% of people believe they are of above average skill in driving a car, most people are overconfident as investors. People tend to trade more often than they should and believe they are more financially successful than they really are. And just as gamblers bet more when they are losing, investors are more willing to take risks to avoid losses than to make gains. Once investors have lost money, they tend to trade more and take on greater risks, in an effort to dig out of the hope. Finally, as with other areas of consumer behavior, investors are influenced by emotion, marketing, and advertising.

Another modification of standard efficient market theory that may explain many market anomalies is the "heterogeneous expectations" model. The heterogeneous expectations model recognizes that different investors hold differing beliefs about the likely risks and returns associated with particular securities. In other words, people disagree. When investors disagree about stock values and short selling is restricted, securities tend to end up in the hands of the individuals who subjectively value them most highly. Indeed, if people were not risk averse, all the shares issued by any particular firm should end up in the hands of the single individual who values that firm most highly. But most people are risk averse. Even an investor who is extremely optimistic about a particular firm's prospects (that is, who perceives the stock to be seriously "underpriced") will stop buying shares at some point to avoid putting too many eggs in one basket.

An important implication of the heterogeneous expectations model of stock prices is that at a very high price, a firm can only sell a few shares of stock to the "superoptimists" who value the company most highly. To sell more shares the firm must lower the price. This increases demand for the firm's shares both because less-optimistic individuals who do not already own shares may decide they are worth buying, and because the superoptimists who already hold shares perceive the lowered price as a "bargain" that compensates them for the additional risk they accept if they increase their holdings. The result is a classic downward-sloping demand function for any particular company's stock. A downward-sloping demand curve in turn explains a variety of anomalous market phenomena, from the "high beta" effect, to the observation that corporate stock repurchases raise share prices, to the puzzle of large takeover premiums.

A second implication of heterogeneous expectations models is that stock markets can be informationally efficient (prices respond quickly to new information) without being allocatively efficient (price reflects the best possible estimate of the economic value of the firm's future earnings.) This is because the market price of a company's stock does not reflect the *best* opinion of its value, or even the *average* opinion; rather, it reflects the opinion of the *marginal* investor (that is, the least-optimistic of the relatively optimistic set of investors who choose to hold the limited supply of outstanding shares).

Nevertheless, while the classical ECMH cannot be reconciled with evidence of a variety of anomalies and discontinuities that can be explained by behavioral finance or heterogeneous expectations models, it remains a simple and useful tool for understanding many market phenomena. ECMH may be compared with Newtonian physics. One can treat ECMH as an effective, practical, and useful view of the world despite an awareness of its departure from complete scientific accuracy.

Although the debate between those who see the market as only "relatively" or "speculatively" efficient and those who see it as "allocatively" efficient may seem a tempest in an academic teapot, it is relevant to a number of regulatory and policy issues that are examined next.

## V. NEW REGULATORY APPROACHES

Finally, we turn to some of the approaches to regulating financial markets. Legal and political forces have rapidly transformed the structure of the securities markets. Chief among these forces are: (1) the steady movement towards globalization of the securities markets, and (2) a continuing effort within the U.S. to deregulate and purge the federal securities laws of those provisions that have become obsolete.

### A. GLOBALIZATION AND FOREIGN COMPETITION

The United States has long enjoyed a worldwide economic dominance in the financial services industry. Foreign issuers have flocked to the deeper U.S. equity markets, both to conduct initial public offerings and seasoned equity offerings. The attractions were multiple. The U.S. has a lower cost of capital, and, probably as a result, cross-listing issuers could expect a positive stock market reaction on the announcement of their decision to cross-list in the United States. Also, they would gain enhanced visibility and a listed stock that they could use as a currency for future acquisitions.

But more recently, this migration of foreign issuers to the U.S. equity markets slowed, and some foreign firms even began to delist. Why? To some degree, deregulation and improved technology had broken down informational barriers and market segmentation and as a result made it less necessary for foreign issuers to come to the U.S. to access U.S. institutional investors. Nonetheless, foreign corporations have continued to shift their initial public offerings to other markets (most notably London and Hong Kong). Some have blamed this development on the Sarbanes–Oxley Act of 2002 and the more litigious legal environment in the United States. In truth, the shift to other listing venues clearly began in the late 1990s, well before the passage of Sarbanes–Oxley. Although it remains the case that the U.S. equity markets offer a lower cost of capital and a significant valuation premium to foreign firms that list on it, this is not decisive for all issuers. Thus, several reports by "blue ribbon" committees have warned that the U.S. faces a crisis over maintaining its international competitiveness.

From the perspective of foreign issuers, many seem to prefer the lighter regulation, lower disclosure standards, and lesser litigation risk of foreign markets. In part, this may be because controlling shareholders prefer to extract private benefits of control from their companies than to lower the firm's cost of capital by listing in the U.S. Or, it may be because the more restrictive regulatory philosophy of the United States is perceived by some foreign issuers as imposing wasteful costs on them. Little consensus exists today.

For U.S. regulators, the dilemma is that if they relax disclosure or enforcement standards to attract foreign listings, they may endanger the lower cost of capital that has long characterized U.S. markets and benefited the U.S. economy. That lower cost appears directly related to the greater transparency in the U.S. market and the higher investor confidence in firms trading there. For U.S. exchanges, now privatized and intent on maximizing share value, the practical message has also become clear. Less able to attract foreign listings, they have begun to acquire foreign exchanges, possibly in part because the foreign exchange will not be subject to SEC jurisdiction. We discussed some of these transactions above; others seem likely.

## B. DISCLOSURE AND ACCOUNTING HARMONIZATION

At the same time as European firms are migrating to the U.S. to list, a major effort is continuing to harmonize international disclosure and accounting standards. The International Accounting Standards Board, a private international organization, and the International Organization of Securities Commissions ("IOSCO") have reached agreement on a core set of international accounting standards. The intent of the effort is to develop a set of international standards that would permit corporations complying with them to trade on any securities exchange in the world and to solicit sales, based on such financial disclosure, without having to comply with the special accounting standards of any individual country.

At present, non-U.S. companies that comply with their home country's accounting standards must "reconcile" their financial statements to U.S. "generally accepted accounting standards" ("US GAAP") in order to file with the SEC or list their securities in the United States. Resentment at this requirement has become a factor in some foreign issuers' reluctance to list on U.S. exchanges. For years, the SEC and the Financial Accounting Standards Board ("FASB"), an independent body to which the SEC has delegated its authority over accounting principles, resisted efforts to compromise US GAAP with international accounting standards ("IAS"), believing the U.S.'s standards were superior. However, in the wake of Enron, WorldCom and related scandals, this position became less tenable. Concomitantly, the European Union mandated that all issuers listed on European exchanges comply with IAS or a functional equivalent as of 2006. This hastened the pace of efforts to achieve convergence between US GAAP and IAS, and the FASB in 2002 entered into a formal accord (known as the "Norwalk Agreement") with the International Accounting Standards Board to collaborate on achieving convergence in accounting practices. Although progress is being made, there remain gaps between US GAAP and IAS. Efforts at harmonization continue in the aftermath of the financial crisis.

Contemporaneously, the Sarbanes–Oxley Act in 2002 accelerated worldwide efforts to harmonize auditing rules, both because it mandated that foreign firms listed in the U.S. must comply with its internal control requirements and because it required audit firms to be subject to public regulation. Although that statute's allegedly extraterritorial application of U.S. standards produced considerable international friction, convergence is occurring, and currently the International Auditing and Assurance Standards Board ("IAASB") is promulgating international auditing standards that over 70 countries have adopted.

## C.　DEREGULATION

Over the past twenty years, many of the basic assumptions of the federal securities laws have been critically re-examined, and a new system of securities regulations has gradually emerged through SEC exemptions and administrative simplification. Still, a broad consensus remains that some provisions of the federal securities laws have become obsolete (which is not surprising given that these statutes are nearly seventy years old) and need to be superseded by a more modern regulatory approach that is sensitive to developments in modern technology.

**1.　Integrated Disclosure and Shelf Registration.** At bottom, the federal securities laws consist of antifraud rules and a mandatory disclosure system. The Securities Act of 1933 (the " '33 Act") essentially requires that before securities are sold to the public, a disclosure document, known as a "registration statement", must be filed with the SEC and declared "effective" by it; then, a portion of that document—the prospectus—must be circulated to potential investors. Supplementing this "truth in securities" policy of the '33 Act, the Securities Exchange Act of 1934 (the " '34 Act") requires publicly held companies (i.e., basically those trading on a securities exchange or having 500 or more shareholders) to file regular reports with the SEC on a continuous basis. Specifically, such issuers must file an Annual Report on Form 10–K and quarterly reports on Form 10–Q after the first three quarters of their fiscal year. Thus, the '33 Act focuses on the primary securities market, while the '34 Act's intent is to inform the secondary market. Absent the '34 Act's periodic reporting requirements, investors would only be entitled to receive new information about securities trading in the market in the infrequent event that the issuer undertook a new public offering.

Sensible as the policy of both Acts are, the result of these two overlapping disclosure systems was often duplication and sometimes inconsistent presentations of the same information. Beginning in the late 1970's, the SEC began to shift the focus of its mandatory disclosure system to the '34 Act. It did so in a series of steps, first by standardizing the disclosure requirements for both '33 and '34 Act filings,[17] and then by upgrading the annual report to shareholders, so that it contained a "Basic Information Package," consisting of specified financial and business information. Finally, the SEC permitted issuers to incorporate by

---

[17] Regulation S–K, adopted in 1977, essentially began this process of harmonizing the two disclosure systems. Previously, a separate body of lore and learning had developed under each of the two statutes. Accounting standards were similarly standardized in a revised Regulation S–X.

reference, in one filing, material contained in a different document filed under the other Act. Essentially, incorporation by reference greatly reduced the duplication and overlap between these two disclosure systems. Today, many publicly held issuers can prepare a registration statement under the '33 Act by simply incorporating by reference the material it earlier filed with the SEC in its principal '34 Act disclosure document. The process can be completed in two or three days, where once it took several months.

Not all corporate issuers, however, are permitted to use incorporation by reference. Rather, the SEC developed a three-level hierarchy of corporations. At the bottom are companies making their initial public offering or that have not been subject to the '34 Act's periodic reporting system for a sufficient period to acquaint the market with them. These companies must file a full-scale, lengthy registration statement on Form S–1. Next, there are companies that (i) have been subject to the '34 Act's requirements for at least twelve calendar months (and are not in default on any debt obligation), and (ii) have an aggregate equity market value of at least $75 million (excluding stock held by affiliates). These companies may use a procedure, described below, called "shelf registration" and may register securities on Form S–3. This Form S–3 consists of only one or two pages of text and then a list of '34 Act filings that are incorporated by reference. (However, the special liabilities for material misstatements and omissions contained in the '33 Act apply to the documents so listed). The assumption here is that in such cases the ECMH correctly predicts that such an issuer's public filings with the SEC under the '34 Act will have been quickly absorbed by the market and will already have been accurately reflected in price. Accordingly, the '33 Act registration process is expedited on the assumption that the market already has assimilated all material background information about the company and only new information about the proposed offering need be disclosed in detail. Finally, "Well–Known Seasoned Issuers" (or "WKSIs" in the popular parlance) are companies that are eligible for Form S–3 and also have either (i) a "public float" (i.e., the stock held by non-affiliates) of $700 million or more in the case of equity offerings, or (ii) $1 billion or more outstanding in aggregate principal amount of debt securities in the case of debt offerings. They qualify for a procedure, discussed below, known as "automatic shelf registration."

Traditionally, the registration of securities under the '33 Act was a slow process involving lengthy SEC prior review before the securities could be sold to the public. The major step in the SEC's liberalization of '33 Act procedures was its decision in the early 1980s to permit "shelf registration"—that is, the registration for future issuance of securities that are not to be presently offered. Previously, such delayed offerings had been forbidden because of a concern that the information in them would become stale. However, under the integrated disclosure system, a registration statement can today incorporate by reference subsequently filed '34 Act reports, and thus the registration statement never in theory becomes stale. More importantly, the basic precept guiding the SEC was that so long as '34 Act filings were kept current, the market would be adequately informed, and registration under the '33 Act was no longer an important event that needed to be carefully regulated. As a result, companies can now register shares for up to three years in advance and sell them virtually on a day or two's notice. This quicker access to the market has enabled corporate issuers to solicit competitive bids from underwriters, where previously the registration process was sufficiently slow and cumbersome that competitive bidding for equity securities was not feasible.

Initially, shelf registration was little used in the case of equity securities. Underwriters resisted it because the accelerated pace of shelf registration gave them little time to sell the securities. Even more important, the filing of a shelf registration statement covering equity securities tended to produce a decline in the issuer's stock price. In general, the announcement of an equity offering typically has this impact because the market takes the announcement as a signal that management believes the stock to be fully valued (i.e., it does not expect the stock price to rise much more). Even the filing of a shelf registration statement (which only implied that stock was likely to be issued in the near future) seemed to elicit a similar negative price reaction.

In response, in the early 1990's, the SEC adopted a system known as "universal shelf registration," under which the issuer does not allocate the securities it expects to sell between various classes of debt and equity securities, but simply announces that it may sell up to a specified level, reserving the right to determine the class of the actual securities to be sold until the time of issuance. This solution alleviated the discount problem (although it blinded the market as to the issuer's intentions).

The traditional restrictions surrounding a registered public offering greatly limited the information that could be made available to the market and prospective investors. First, Section 5(c) of the '33 Act mandated a "quiet period" prior to the filing of the registration statement with the SEC during which the prospective issuer could make no statement that conditioned the market. Second, Section 5(b) precluded any form of written communication (with some modest exceptions) that might be used to solicit investor interest, other than the prospectus filed with the SEC. Particularly in the case of seasoned issuers, this attempt to protect investors from overreaching resulted in a loss of information to the market. Corporate officials could only engage in limited communications with securities analysts or the media in the period preceding a securities offering.

In 2005, the SEC cut back sharply on these prophylactic rules. While the "quiet period" remains in place for smaller companies and new issuers, the SEC basically cut it back to a 30 day period prior to the filing of the registration statement and completely eliminated it for "Well

Known Seasoned Issuers" (or "WKSIs"). In addition, the restrictions on written communications were relaxed, by permitting the use of a document known as the "Free Writing Prospectus," provided that it was filed with the SEC and certain standard disclaimers were included. Although the issuer and the underwriters will still have antifraud liability for this document, its use does not invalidate the offering; as a result, it vastly increased the range of marketing activities, including through T.V., websites and other electronic media, in which the issuer and the underwriters can engage. Next, the 2005 offering reforms eliminated the need to deliver the prospectus by mailing, permitting electronic delivery across the board (whether or not the investor consented). This represented a major cost saving for the securities industry. Finally, the Well–Known Seasoned Issuer (or "WKSI") was permitted to use "automatic shelf registration," which effectively guaranteed it immediate access to the market without any delay while the SEC reviewed its registration statement. Instead, the registration statement is effective when filed and securities may be sold immediately. WKSIs were also given the right to register unlimited amounts of securities. Thus, from a registration system in which delays of several months were the norm, securities regulation has evolved to the point where the largest issuers can immediately file and sell unlimited quantities of securities without prior SEC approval. The SEC estimated in 2004 that roughly 30% of all issuers would qualify as "WKSIs" and that WKSI issuers historically represented 95% of U.S. equity market capitalization and 96% of the total debt raised in registered offerings.

**2. Private Placements and Rule 144A.** The general requirement of the '33 Act that sales of securities be registered with the SEC is subject to several important exceptions. Section 4(2) of the '33 Act exempts transactions "not involving any public offering." Section 4(1) exempts "transactions by any person other than an issuer, underwriter or dealer." The interplay of these two provisions is complicated. For most of the history of the '33 Act, the § 4(2) "private offering" exemption was narrowly read to be available only when the offering was made exclusively to persons "able to fend for themselves."[18] This language was read by the SEC to imply that only private sales (i.e., not involving public solicitation) to sophisticated professionals and institutional investors could safely be made in reliance upon this exemption. Even then, any resale by such a sophisticated person to a member of the "public" (i.e. to persons who needed the '33 Act's protections and therefore were not able to "fend for themselves") could result in the loss of this exemption, because such a resale could make the seller into an "underwriter" under the '33 Act's highly technical definition of that term.[19]

---

[18] See SEC v. Ralston Purina Co., 346 U.S. 119 (1953).

[19] Under Section 2(11) of the 1933 Act, an underwriter is defined to include a person who acquires securities "with a view to ... the distribution" of the securities. Resales within a brief period were generally viewed by the SEC as demonstrating such an original intent to distribute.

As a result, investors who purchased securities in a private placement held illiquid securities which could not be readily resold and which
therefore were valued at a substantial discount off registered shares of
the same class. If they did resell and their purchasers were not qualified
sophisticated investors, then the issuer also lost the § 4(2) exemption,
and all investors in the offering acquired a right to rescind. Beginning in
the 1970s, these restrictions on private resales were gradually eased by
the SEC. First, Rule 144 was adopted, which established a safe harbor
standard for when "restricted securities" (i.e., securities purchased in a
private placement) might be resold by the purchaser into the market
without registration under the '33 Act. Essentially, a one year holding
period is now required, and the volume of securities that could be so
resold has been progressively relaxed, until today the greater of 1
percent of the class or the average weekly trading volume of the stock
may be sold in any three month period. Essentially, this means that after
a one year holding period, a purchaser in a private placement may sell at
least 1 percent of the class every three months thereafter, or 4 percent
during the second year alone. After the second year of holding, any
purchaser who does not "control" the issuer is free to resell all its
"restricted securities," provided certain other conditions are satisfied.
Thus, relatively few investors will face volume restrictions on resale
after the first year of holding, and almost none after the second.

Rule 144 eased the investor's problems about when resale was
permitted, but not the issuer's uncertainty about who qualified as a
sophisticated purchaser for purposes of a private placement. As late as
the early 1970s, the SEC seemed to be restricting this category to
persons having an insider relationship with the issuer. Eventually, after
much criticism, the SEC relaxed this standard to recognize that economic bargaining power was an adequate substitute for insider access because it also enabled one "to fend for oneself." A series of rules, now
known as Regulation D, which were adopted beginning in the late 1970s,
established a safe harbor standard for issuers seeking to use the private
placement exemption. In particular, the SEC adopted and gradually
expanded a definition of "accredited investors" in these rules that
allowed issuers to rely simply on objective criteria about a purchaser's
status as an institutional investor or as a sufficiently wealthy individual
in determining such investor's ability to fend for itself. As a result, most
of the uncertainty and risk that once surrounded private placements has
today been largely eliminated, and the use of this exemption has been
encouraged.

One troublesome area, however, still remained. Suppose one institutional investor (Bank A) buys restricted securities in a private placement
and, before the two year holding period under Rule 144 has run, sells
them to another institutional investor (Bank B) in what securities
lawyers called a "private sale." While it is clear that such a resale of

stock purchased in a private placement to another sophisticated purchaser was permissible in theory, the standards applicable to it were uncertain. How long did the second purchaser have to hold before it could resell? Did it have to be furnished information similar to that provided the initial purchaser? Could it resell into the market or only to other sophisticated purchasers? In the late 1980's the SEC adopted Rule 144A to resolve these questions. Essentially, it established a safe harbor under which persons purchasing securities in a private placement may resell in private sales, without any requisite holding period, to other sophisticated purchasers—in effect, making their own private placement. Some controversy surrounded the initial proposal of this rule because it contemplated a private resale market in restricted securities from which ordinary investors would be excluded. The major securities exchanges were concerned that its adoption might fragment the securities markets into private and public trading markets, thereby reducing liquidity from the public market. In the face of this criticism, the SEC retreated and revised Rule 144A so that it would apply only to securities of a class not publicly traded on an exchange or NASDAQ. Still, the prospect remains for the future that private and public markets may yet arise in which the same class of securities may be traded, but at a price differential that reflects the limitations on resale of the securities traded in the private market.

**3. Banking Reform.** Since 1933, the Glass–Steagall Act has mandated a tripartite division of financial services into commercial banking, investment banking, and insurance. As a result, commercial banks could not underwrite securities (at least until the 1990s, when a partial exemption was created by the Federal Reserve), and investment banks could not engage in many traditional banking activities (such as accepting demand deposits). Originally, the rationale for the separation of these financial activities was a fear of conflicts of interest. If banks could underwrite securities, it was feared that banks might take excessive risks or might dump their weak loans on the public by causing their financially strained corporate debtors to issue bonds to the public to pay off the bank's loans. Whatever the rationale for this wall of separation, the wall began to crumble in the late 1980s. In 1987, the Federal Reserve Board permitted the securities affiliates of banks to underwrite a limited range of securities (commercial paper, mortgage-backed securities, securitized accounts receivable and municipal revenue bonds). Then, in 1989, the Federal Reserve Board opened the door considerably farther by permitting some of these affiliates to underwrite corporate debt securities. Beginning in 1990, it allowed bank affiliates to underwrite equity securities on a limited basis.

Throughout the 1990s, Congress repeatedly attempted to repeal Glass–Steagall, and several bills passed either the Senate or the House (or both), but a compromise was recurrently blocked by some interest group. Finally in 1999, legislation was enacted.

Financial industry consolidation has followed, and the largest commercial banks have now moved up in the rankings of underwriters to be at or near the top. Their ability to make bank loans may give them an advantage in the competition to be lead underwriter for the largest issuers. The Glass–Steagall Act, along with the federal structure of the United States, served to keep the scale of U.S. banks considerably smaller than that of the largest banks in Germany, Japan or the U.K. With its repeal, the growth of American financial institutions to the same scale as that of the "universal banks" that characterize Europe and Japan seems probable. Indeed, the 1998 merger of Citicorp and Travelers Insurance may have already foreshadowed this trend, which should continue.

Following the financial crisis of 2008, there was further bank consolidation, and the few remaining investment banks converted into bank holding companies. Legislators and regulators expressed concerns about the "too big to fail" problem of very large banks, and the moral hazard that resulted from the expectation of government assistance in the event of crisis. As of late 2009, Congress was debating financial reform legislation that would impose some new restrictions on banks and create a new consumer protection agency in financial services.

**4. Derivatives.** Derivatives remain a controversial topic among regulators. The primary focus has been to force some "plain vanilla" derivatives to be traded on exchanges or through a centralized clearing house, instead of in private OTC markets. The regulatory turf over derivatives is split into three parts: (1) commodity-related derivatives, which are regulated by the Commodity Futures Trading Commission, (2) security-related derivatives, which are regulated by the Securities Exchange Commission, and (3) other privately traded derivatives, which are not regulated by any government agency.

Another regulatory issue related to derivatives is regulation related to credit rating agencies, which played a prominent role in the creation and sale of complex financial instruments. Both legislators and regulators have proposed eliminating "regulatory licenses," legal rules that depend on credit ratings in ways that unlock access to the capital markets. For example, some regulated investors can only buy highly rated financial instruments. Others experience lower capital charges for highly rated instruments. The SEC has proposed rules to eliminate certain aspects of regulatory dependence on ratings.[20]

[20] See Securities and Exchange Commission, References to Ratings of Nationally Recognized Statistical Rating Organizations, Release Nos. IC–28327, IA–2751, File No. S7–19–08, 2008.

# TABLE OF CASES

References are to Pages.

---

457

# INDEX

References are to pages.

464    *INDEX*

**References are to pages.**

†